GLOBAL
ENVIRONMENTAL CHANGE

GLOBAL ENVIRONMENTAL CHANGE

A NATURAL AND CULTURAL ENVIRONMENTAL HISTORY

A. M. MANNION

Department of Geography University of Reading

Longman
Scientific &
Technical

Copublished in the United States with
John Wiley & Sons, Inc., New York

Longman Scientific and Technical
Longman Group UK Ltd, Longman House
Burnt Mill, Harlow, Essex CM20 2JE, England
and Associated Companies throughout the world

Copublished in the United States with
John Wiley & Sons Inc., 605 Third Avenue, New York, NY 10158

© Longman Group UK Limited 1991

First published 1991

British Library Cataloguing in Publication Data
Mannion, A. M.
    Global environmental change: a natural and cultural environmental history.
    1. Environmental change, history
    I. Title
    333.709

ISBN 0-582-00351-2

Library of Congress Cataloguing-in-Publication Data
Mannion, Antoinette M.
    Global environmental change: a natural and cultural environmental history/
    A.M. Mannion.
    p. cm.
    Includes bibliographical references.
    ISBN 0-470-21678-6
    1. Man–Influence on nature–History. 2. Paleoecology. 3. Climatic changes.
    I Title.
    GF75.M34 1991
    304.2–dc20
    90-335 29
    CIP

Set in Times

Produced by Longman Group (FE) Limited
Printed in Hong Kong

For MDT, and in memory of JCM and ANC.

CONTENTS

PREFACE

Global environmental change is intended, as the subtitle suggests, to provide
a synopsis of natural and cultural environmental history during the last 3
Myr. The underpinning *raison d'être* for this text derives from a variety of
factors which originate from my research interests and teaching commit-
ments. The former are primarily concerned with Quaternary research, the
aim of which is to elucidate past environments using an amalgam of approaches; this diversity is precisely what attracted me to it initially. The
latter, on the other hand, have perforce focused under the title of biogeography on an equally broad spectrum of topics, ranging from the poles to the
tropics, which are more concerned with the present than with the past. Juxta-
posing and integrating the two has never been problematic since interpreting
the past is based, as far as possible, on observable present-day interrelationships between earth surface processes and biota and because these interrelationships are themselves a manifestation of their past history. Nevertheless
there are, as far as I am aware, no textbooks which attempt such integration
and it is this niche that I anticipate this book will fill. It is also particularly
apposite, at a time when there is growing concern about the likely impact of
the enhanced greenhouse effect, to draw attention to the significance of elucidating past environmental changes in order to plan for the future.

The first four chapters of this book are thus concerned with temporal
aspects of environmental change, dealing initially with the oscillations that
have occurred between ice ages and interglacials in the last 3 Myr and then
with the development of human communities as agents of environmental
change throughout prehistory and history. The next four chapters examine
the changes that have manifested in the last two centuries as a result of
industrial development and agricultural innovations in both the developed
and the developing world. These chapters also refer to the impetus of social,
economic and political factors on environment since these are just as important as agents of change as the physical processes that can transform landscapes. In addition, consideration is given in Chapter 8 to the potential
environmental impact of new developments, notably tourism, biotechnology
and genetic engineering. At a time when the enhanced greenhouse effect is
achieving pre-eminence in the media as a major force on the global landscape it is important to remember that there are other forces at work.
Genetic engineering, for example, has the potential to provide an equally
potent means of transforming the environment, a fact which has largely been

overlooked in most textbooks which deal with the biosphere. Finally a perspective is presented, summarising past environmental changes and their relationships with the present, and which is a precursor to the presentation of some tentative prospects for the future of planet earth and civilisation.

Fulfilling these broadly based objectives in a limited space has been a difficult task that has led me to adopt two eclectic policies. Firstly, to achieve as wide as possible a spatial coverage I have used a broad spectrum of examples to illustrate specific types of environmental change, though the lack of available information on Eastern Bloc nations in particular has thwarted this aim to a certain extent. Secondly I have as far as possible confined the literature researched to 1984 and post-1984 publications in order to present data that are as up to date as possible. These policies are reflected in an extensive list of references which should render the book useful as a work of reference as well as a course textbook. In relation to dates quoted in the text, all are given in years AD unless otherwise stated; Myr BP refers to million years before present kyr BP refers to thousands of years before present.

This book is intended for undergraduate courses in geography and environmental science, especially those taught in years two and three after students have accrued a basic understanding of earth surface processes. As the title suggests, it is not aimed specifically at a British audience and it should appeal to a broad spectrum of students wherever they are based. This an exciting time to be writing about environmental change; the emergence of environmental problems as major issues in local, national and international politics is a very significant turning-point in the history of the people/ environment relationship. Hopefully it heralds a much needed and overdue move towards environmental protection and away from environmental confrontation that has for so long created environmental degradation. If this book goes some way towards increasing environmental awareness it will have fulfilled my objectives.

Antoinette M Mannion
Reading
October 1989

ACKNOWLEDGEMENTS

The compilation of this book owes much to many people. Dr M D Turnbull has word processed most of the text and helped with information for sections 6.4 and 8.4, as well as assisting with all the other chores associated with the production of a book. Sheila Dance, assisted by Joy Liddell, of the Drawing Office, Department of Geography, University of Reading, compiled the diagrams and tables. The efforts of these collaborators have been unstinting and have made this book possible; for this I am most grateful. I also wish to record my thanks to Maurice Parry, a former colleague at Reading, who has kindly vetted the manuscript chapter by chapter as I have written it over the last 18 months. Discussions with numerous colleagues at Reading, notably Dr S R Bowlby, Dr E A Cater and Dr J G Soussan, have also been extremely useful and I am most grateful for their time. In addition, I am indebted to the members of the inter-library loans section of Reading University library for their patience and proficiency at finding innumerable references. However, all the views and any inaccuracies in the text are entirely my personal responsibility.

We are grateful to the following for permission to reproduce copyright material:

Academic Press and the authors for fig. 3.3 from fig. 14.1 (Lanpo & Weiwen, 1985); Blackie & Son Ltd. for table 5.1 from a table in *Land Use and Landscape Planning* ed. by Lovejoy (1973) published by Leonard Hill (Blunden, 1985); Butterworth Scientific Ltd. for fig. 7.3 from fig. 1, p. 89, fig. 2 & inset, p. 92 (Whitlow, 1988); the editor, *Current Research in the Pleistocene* for fig. 2.5 from fig. 1, p. 88 (Davis & Sellers, 1987); Dahlem Konferenzen for table 7.1 from tables 2 & 3 pp. 699 & 701 (Dregne, 1987); Elsevier Science Publishers (Physical Sciences & Engineering Div.) and the author, Prof. N. Shackleton for fig. 1.7 from part of fig. 2, p. 239 (Shackleton et al., 1983); Gebrüder Borntraeger for fig. 1.6 from fig. 15, pp. 80-81 (Hooghiemstra, 1984); the Controller of Her Majesty's Stationery Office for fig. 6.4 from figs. 4 & 9 (Nitrate Co-ordination Group 1986); International Council for Research in Agroforestry (Nairobi) for fig. 8.2 from fig. 4, p. 235 (Kanf & Wilson, 1987); Longman Group UK Ltd. for figs. 3.1 & 3.2 from figures, pp. 264-265 (Foley, 1987), 6.1 from a figure, p. 2 (Morgan, 1986a) and table 1.2 from a table, p. 260 in *Processes in Physical Geography* by Thompson et al., 1986 (Odum 1975 & Simmons, 1979); Kluwer

Academic Publishers for fig. 1.4 from part of figs. 2, 3 & 4, pp. 335-337 (Pfister, 1984) and table 8.4 from table 1, p. 103 (Nair, 1985); Macmillan Magazines Ltd.. and the respective authors for figs. 1.2 from part of fig. 4, p. 132 (Brassell et al., 1986), 1.3 from 5 figures: fig. 1, p. 592 (Lorius *et al.*, 1985), fig. 1, p. 408 (Barnola *et al.*, 1987), fig. 1, p. 403 (Jouzel *et al.*, 1987), figs. 3 & 4, p. 320 (De Angelis *et al.*, 1987) & figs. 1.7 from fig. 1c, p. 137 (Chappell & Shackleton, 1986), 2.2 from fig. 2, p. 590 (Atkinson *et al.*, 1987), 5.1 from part of fig. 1, p. 237 (Friedli *et al.*, 1986) Copyright © 1985, 1986, 1987 Macmillan Magazines Ltd.; New Scientist for figs. 5.1 from a diagram, p. 3 (Gribbin, 1988a), 5.2 from diagrams, pp 2 & 3 (Woodward, 1989); Oxford University Press for fig. 1.5 from fig. 5.1, p. 142 (Goudie, 1983); Pergamon Press PLC for fig. 5.1 from part of fig. 2, p 2447 (Khalil & Rasmussen, 1987) Copyright 1987 Pergamon Press PLC; Pergamon Press PLC and the author, Prof. D. Bowen for tables 1.3 & 1.5 from part of chart 1 (Bowen *et al.*, 1986 a & b & Šibrava, 1986) Copyright 1986 Pergamon Press PLC; The University of Minnesota Press for table 2.7 from table 11-2, p. 173 (Davis, 1984) Copyright © by the University of Minnesota; John Wiley & Sons Ltd. for fig. 2.1 from fig. 1.2, p. 11 (Birks, 1986) Copyright © 1986 John Wiley & Sons Ltd.

Whilst every effort has been made to trace the owners of copyright material, in a few cases this has proved impossible and we take this opportunity to offer our apologies to any copyright holders whose rights we may have unwittingly infringed.

1

ENVIROMENTAL CHANGE: AGENTS, PROCESSES AND THE QUATERNARY PERIOD

1.1 THE NATURE AND AGENTS OF ENVIRONMENTAL CHANGE

Environmental change is a continual process that has been in operation since the earth first came into existence some 5 Myr BP. Since then, dynamic systems of energy and material transfers have operated on a global scale to bring about gradual and sometimes catastrophic transformations of the atmosphere, hydrosphere, lithosphere and biosphere. For most of earth history the agents of change have been the natural elements of wind, ice, water, plants and animals; all of these have interacted to produce dynamic ecosystems that both control and are controlled by each other. Some 2 or 3 Myr BP, however, a new agent of change emerged in the form of hominids, culminating in the evolution of *Homo sapiens sapiens* or modern humans, that are considered by many to be the most powerful present generators of environmental change. As knowledge has progressed and science and technology have developed, human beings have achieved a greater insight into environmental change and the processes responsible, and at the same time have developed the ability to alter the environment drastically. This is frequently inadvertent modification through agencies such as agricultural and industrial pollutants. Just as frequently, environmental change is brought about by direct and deliberate human activity such as deforestation and urban development.

1.1.1 THE DEVELOPMENT OF IDEAS IN RELATION TO ENVIRONMENTAL CHANGE

Human beings must always have been concerned with their environment since it was their immediate surroundings that provided the resources necessary for survival. For pre-literate times the only testimony to this lies in prehistoric cave paintings which are evident in many parts of the world. Well-known examples include the Lascaux caves of the Dordogne and the Altamira caves of the east Pyrenees, France, wherein there are cave paintings of animals such as aurochs, horse, deer and wolf. These are attributed to the work of upper palaeolithic hunter-gatherer groups who lived in the region *c.* 17 kyr BP.

With the rise of the ancient Mediterranean civilisations of Greece and Rome came the first written accounts of places, trade routes, crops etc. Herodotus (*c.* 485–425 BC), a Greek scholar often described as the father of history, recorded a variety of environmental features such as the regime of the River Nile, and later another Greek scholar, Aristotle (384–322 BC) advanced the idea of a spherical rather than a flat earth. He also introduced mathematical concepts for the measurement of global features such as latitude and longitude. This tradition was continued by Eratosthenes (276–194 BC) who constructed the first reasonably accurate maps, and by Ptolemy (AD 90–168) who produced a massive eight-volume work entitled *Geography* containing details of map projections and methods for the calculation of the earth's dimensions. Similarly Strabo (64 BC–AD 20), a Roman scholar, produced a seventeen-volume work entitled *Geographica* which examined much of the then known world and involved a recognition of dualism in geography: that of people (human geography) and places (physical geography).

Ideas changed little during the Middle Ages when European scholars returned to the concept of a flat earth to conform with ecclesiastical teaching. Once again civilisations of the Mediterranean, principally the Arab world, augmented the information of the Greeks, while in China geographical knowledge was well advanced, although inaccessible to European scholars until Marco Polo's (1255–1325) expeditions. The Renaissance, however, brought a scientific revival to Europe including renewed interest in Ptolemy's *Geography* which provided explorers such as Columbus with a basic mathematical approach to location. Travellers provided a pot-pourri of descriptive information on people and places which, in addition to the publication of Mercator's map projections in 1569, led to the production of the first globes and new maps.

The bipartite nature of geography, first intimated in Strabo's work, involving human and physical divisions, was formalised by a Dutch scholar Varenius (1622–50) who originated the ideas of regional or 'special' geography and systematic or 'general' geography. The latter, he advocated, could be studied using natural laws and was thus a more exact science. This approach was continued by Immanuel Kant (1724–1804) who strongly argued for a scientific base to the study of geographical or environmental phenomena which he considered to be just as essential as the exact sciences. This stance was continued by von Humboldt (1769–1859) and Ritter (1779–1859) who developed an inductive approach to explaining natural phenomena. The former, a renowned explorer, published a five-volume work entitled *Kosmos* (1845–62) in which he attempted not only to describe natural phenomena, such as rocks, plants and animals, but to explain their occurrence and to undertake comparative studies.

However, the deductive and mechanistic philosophy earlier advocated by Newton (1642–1727) was continued in the work of Charles Darwin (1809–82). In 1859 he published his classic work the *Origin of Species* in which he charted the development of life, and advanced theories on evolution. For the student of environmental changes this is a most significant publication since it suggests a relationship between environment and organisms and, moreover, charts a developmental sequence. If organisms changed due to environ-

mental parameters, then environment itself must have changed. It is, therefore, perhaps no coincidence that many other notable scientists began to advance theories relating to environmental change at much the same time and,
perhaps more pertinently, though not explicitly, introduced the idea of dynamism into environmental studies.

By the end of the eighteenth century the diluvial theory, the proposal of
the biblical Flood as a major agent in shaping the face of the earth, was
being questioned. Scientists such as James Hutton and John Playfair were
among the first to advance the theory of glaciation. The former's observations of erratic boulders in the Jura Mountains, noted earlier by a Swiss
minister, Bernard Friederich Kuhn, led him to invoke glacier ice as the agent
of transportation (Hutton 1795). Nevertheless, it was not until the 1820s that
the glacial theory became more widely proposed and although Agassiz
presented the theory to the Swiss Society of Natural Sciences in 1837,
numerous earlier workers had already published evidence for glacial processes. These included Jean-Pierre Perraudin, a Swiss mountaineer, Jean de
Charpentier, a naturalist, and Ignace Venetz, a highway engineer, all of
whom proposed that Swiss glaciers had extended beyond their present positions. Despite this wider acclaim the glacial theory was still rejected by
many in favour of Charles Lyell's (1833) explanation for erratics, drift, etc.
as being the products of floating icebergs. This idea was also given credence
by reports of boulder-containing icebergs from contemporary explorers like
Darwin himself.

However, William Buckland, who was appointed professor of geology at
Oxford in 1820, was the first to acknowledge that neither the diluvial nor
iceberg drift theories could provide satisfactory explanations for all the evidence and eventually, in 1840, he and Charles Lyell accepted Agassiz's
views. Despite residual resistance in the scientific community, the glacial
theory became widely accepted by the mid–1860s. By this time further developments were in hand. Evidence for changing sea-levels was compiled by
Jamieson (1865) based on evidence from Scotland, North America and Scandinavia; von Richtofen (1882) advanced a wind-borne origin for loess deposits; Gilbert (1890) presented evidence to show that the Great Salt Lake of
Utah is only a remnant of a much larger lake, and in Britain Archibald
Geikie (1863) suggested the idea of multiple glaciation. This latter involved
several cold stages or glacials, separated by warm stages or interglacials and
was further substantiated by James Geikie (1874). Moreover, Penck and
Brückner in 1909 interpreted Alpine terrace sequences in terms of oscillating
warm and cold stages.

Inevitably, as evidence on environmental change accrued, attention also
focused on the underlying cause of climatic change. Adhémar, a French
mathematician, was the first to involve the astronomical theory in studies of
the ice ages. He proposed in 1842 that changes in the orbit of the earth
round the sun may be responsible for climatic change of such great magnitude. A similar approach was advanced by a Scottish geologist, James Croll,
who in 1864 suggested that changes in the earth's orbital eccentricity might
cause ice ages. This theory he explained in full in his book *Climate and
Time*, published in 1875, which was accepted by both Archibald and James
Geikie, giving it much credence in the geological community. Owing to the
inability of geologists to substantiate Croll's predictions in the absence of
reliable dating techniques, his theories fell into disuse until their revival in
the 1920–40 period by Milutin Milankovitch, a Yugoslavian astronomer

(section 1.2.4). Although numerous other theories for causes of climatic change have been proposed, Milankovitch's ideas have become more widely accepted since the 1950s when evidence from deep-sea core stratigraphy first came to light.

The late eighteenth and early nineteenth centuries also witnessed the establishment of new methods based principally on biological remains for examining the nature of environmental change, and thus establishing the general field of palaeoecology. Plant macrofossils were among the first biological indicators to be used to interpret Quaternary palaeoenvironments (reviewed in Mannion 1986a). Blytt (1876) and Sernander (1908), both Scandinavian geologists, used macrofossils in peat deposits to explain the forest history of northwest Europe and associated climatic changes. Similarly, von Post (1916) developed pollen analysis as a means of examining environmental change. The two are complementary techniques and have played a major role in examining vegetation change during interglacial stages and the post-glacial period, as will be shown in Chapter 2. Numerous other fossil groups of plants and animals have also been used as indicators of past environments in the last 50 years (see review in Berglund 1986).

Apart from the inception of the glacial theory and its development during the nineteenth century, there were other notable developments in the early twentieth century which also significantly altered scientific thought. For example, Davis in 1909 advanced a theory which he called 'the geographical cycle'. This encapsulates an idealised landscape originating with mountain uplift and culminating in lowland plains. While this is no longer an accepted theory, it is historically significant in so far as it invokes the idea of continual processes and the idea of continual change. This theoretical treatment of landscape development has a counterpart in ecological studies. In 1916 Clements wrote: 'As an organism the climax formation arises, grows, matures and dies. Its response to the habitat is shown in processes or functions and in structures which are the record as well as the result of these functions.' Thus Clements expressed the nature of vegetation communities as ever-changing entities, and while there is much debate about the acceptability of his ideas (Mannion 1986b) he was responsible for injecting the idea of dynamism into ecological systems.

Ideas relating to environmental change have been in turmoil in the last 200 years. The acceptance of the glacial theory not only led to the development of Quaternary geology but also initiated related studies into climatic and ecological change. Similarly, the recognition that change is often gradual and continuous has prompted investigation of environmental processes and the development of techniques to determine the nature, direction and rate of environmental change.

1.1.2 MODERN CONCEPTS: ENVIRONMENTAL SYSTEMS

Since the 1930s the concept of general systems has been imbued in environmental studies. Tansley in 1935 first introduced the ecosystem concept into ecology stating:

> The more fundamental conception is . . . the whole system including not only the organism complex, but also the whole complex of physical

factors forming what we call the environment. . . . We cannot separate [the organisms] from their special environment in which they form one physical system. . . . It is the system so formed which provides the basic units of nature on the face of the earth. . . . These ecosystems as we may call them, are of the most various kinds and sizes.

Ecosystems thus represent one particular type of system in which living organisms play a fundamental role. In addition, the ecosystem concept promotes a holistic approach, linking both biotic and abiotic components which interact to create an identifiable whole.

Geographers have also adopted this approach and as Chorley and Kennedy (1971) point out, it has many advantages for the study of physical geography. On the one hand it provides a means of subdividing a complex entity, the environment, into identifiable parts while maintaining a holistic approach by emphasising interrelationships. On the other hand, the approach lends itself to quantification which ultimately may be used for prediction and so may provide a significant contribution to environmental management programmes. Different types of system have been recognised and these are described in Table 1.1. Almost all environmental systems are functionally open systems characterised by import and export of both energy and matter, although occasionally some may be closed systems, allowing only the exchange of energy.

All natural systems are in a state of dynamic equilibrium: a balance between inputs, outputs, elements and processes is achieved. To maintain this state all systems have controls known as negative feedback loops wherein output influences input. Negative feedback has a stabilising influence, and in ecosystems it is often effected via population changes. For example, the depletion of a particular food source by an expanding animal population may cause an increase in mortality and thus force a return to the status quo. In some cases, catastrophic events can be part of the negative feedback loops in ecosystems. These have been called eustresses by Rapport *et al.* (1985) and have been discussed more fully by Vogal (1980). An example of such a stress is the dependence of many boreal forest species on periodic fires to release seeds from cones and thus ensure reproductive success. Conversely, positive feedback will result in a new system. For example, the removal of vegetation from a catchment may create changes in the local hydrological cycle and lead to accelerated soil erosion. The remaining soil system may thus become so degraded that it is incapable of supporting a vegetation

Table 1.1. Types of environmental systems and their characteristics.

Type of system	Characteristics	Example
1. Morphologic:	Observable physical properties such as height, slope angle, sediment type	A desert dune system
2. Cascading:	Has a flux or cascade of energy and/or matter	The solar energy cascade
3. Process - response:	Combines morphologic and cascading systems; morphological variables may control and be controlled by the flux of energy and/or matter	Erosion of a river bed as more energy is made available through increased discharge
4. Control:	Combines a process-response system with the controlling presence of an intelligence (usually humans)	Urban development or deforestation causing changes in local hydrological cycles
5. Ecosystem:	Involves interactions between biotic factors (including humans) and abiotic factors such as landforms, soils etc.	A small pond at the local scale to the global biosphere/lithosphere at the large scale

cover similar to the original. Positive feedback is a major agent of environmental change.

Most environmental systems, however, have both resilience and resistance to change and it may be that positive feedback occurs over such a long time period, especially in relation to the human life span, that change is gradual and almost imperceptible. This occurs because environmental systems are complex and the response to positive feedback is slow: an effect called lag time. In most environmental systems a lagged response is usually more common than immediate change. For example, the elimination of grazing or firing in moorland ecosystems may result ultimately in woodland establishment, but it will take some 20–50 years. Similarly, it is only in the last decade that the ravages of 'acid rain' on Scandinavian lakes have been recognised, although the actual process of acidification began several decades ago with increased use of fossil fuels (Ch. 5). It may be some considerable time before a threshold between one ecosystem and its replacement is crossed.

Some lithological changes in the geological record may well represent the operation of positive feedback over very long periods. Conversely, catastrophic changes such as volcanic eruption may occur to create completely new landscapes. The creation of the island of Surtsey off the coast of Iceland between 1963 and 1966 (Fridriksson 1987), and the alarmingly rapid demise of tropical forests in Amazonia due to human agencies, are examples in which external factors, and not just positive feedback, have overwhelmed internal ecosystem mechanisms. In these cases thresholds were rapidly crossed and a lagged response was replaced by an immediate one.

1.1.3 THE AGENTS AND PROCESSES INVOLVED IN ENVIRONMENTAL CHANGE

Positive feedback, whether it is gradual or catastrophic, is necessary for environmental change to occur. Since all environmental components are part of feedback loops, each may be involved in exerting stress and may be recipients of the resulting strain. The role of any one, or group, of environmental components in initiating stress and ultimate change will vary in magnitude spatially and temporally. The outcome will depend on the internal resilience of the given environmental system and if thresholds are passed there will be changes in the energy and matter networks within and between systems. The former may involve changes in solar energy input (i.e. climatic change) and its subsequent transmission via food webs in ecosystems while the latter will involve changes in biogeochemical cycles.

During the past 2 or 3 Myr, the major agents of environmental change have been climate and humans, both of which directly affect the processes operative in environmental systems, as described in Thompson *et al.* (1986). This is brought about by controlling energy transfers, the hydrological cycle, sediment transport systems, soil processes and ecosystem function. Changes in solar energy receipt are the key to climatic change since they directly influence the hydrological cycle, wind systems and the amount of energy available for ecosystem function, on a global basis. These in turn affect the global cycles of the major nutrients, especially the carbon cycle. Human agencies of environmental change have only become significant in the last 15 kyr or so, but as technology has developed their impact has greatly increased. Environmental change has occurred as humans have exploited the environment for resources. Their impact has been direct as natural ecosystems have been cleared to provide land for agriculture and urbanisation, and as land-based resources, such as minerals, have been extracted. Human communities have also brought about indirect and often inadvertent environmental change as a by-product of resource use and agricultural and technological innovations. Much of this is in the form of pollution. These themes will be developed in Chapters 5–8.

The human impact on environment is chiefly due to the need to manipulate energy. Table 1.2 charts a classification of ecosystem types based on energy characteristics devised by Odum (1975). Here a distinction is drawn between solar-powered ecosystems, human-subsidised solar-powered ecosystems and fuel-powered urban–industrialised systems. Only green plants can manufacture food energy, a process operating in all ecosystems which people can manipulate by transposing ecosystems into agro-ecosystems and channelling energy flow into a specific plant or animal harvest for human consumption. This can be achieved relatively simply by hunter-gathering activities or in a more sophisticated way by enhancing nutrient availability, and by introducing plant and animal breeding and mechanisation. This latter has become increasingly necessary in order to sustain population growth and the urban industrial systems, and involves a considerable addition of fossil-fuel energy. Moreover, the continued exploitation of fossil fuels for industrial purposes and the development of new energy sources such as nuclear power have themselves a considerable environmental impact (Ch. 5). Thus one of the major reasons for human-induced environmental change is the necessity to manipulate energy transfers. It could also be argued that recre-

	Annual energy flow (kJ m^{-2})	
	Range	Estimated average
1. Unsubsidised natural solar-powered ecosystems, e.g. open oceans, upland forests. Anthropogenic factor: hunter-gatherer shifting cultivation	4 130 - 41 800	8 360
2. Naturally subsidised solar-powered ecosystems e.g. tidal estuary, coral reef, some rainforests. In these ecosystems natural processes augment solar energy input. Tides, waves, for example, cause an import of organic matter and/or recycling of nutrients, while energy from the sun is used in the production of organic matter. Anthropogenic factor: fishing, hunter-gatherer	41 800 - 167 200	83 600
3. Human-subsidised solar-powered ecosystems, e.g. agriculture, aquaculture, silviculture. These are food- and fibre-producing ecosystems which are subsidised by fuel or energy provided by human communities, e.g. mechanised farming, use of pesticides, fertilisers, etc.	41 800 - 167 200	83 600
4. Fuel-powered urban-industrial systems, e.g. cities, suburbs, industrial estates. These are the wealth-generating systems (as well as pollution-generating) in which the sun has been replaced as the chief energy source by fuel. These ecosystems (including socio-economic systems) are totally dependent upon types 1, 2 and 3 for life support, including fuel and food	418 000 - 12 540 000	8 360 000

Table 1.2. The classification of ecosystems based on energy characteristics. (Based on Odum 1975 and Simmons 1979.)

ation needs are a by-product of energy use which has facilitated mechanisation that, in the developed world at least, has resulted in increased leisure time.

1.1.4 THE EMERGENCE OF *HOMO SAPIENS SAPIENS* AS AN AGENT OF CHANGE

Since humans are considered to be one of the most significant perpetrators of environmental change, it is appropriate to examine briefly the development of the species, their communities and their technology.

Palaeoanthropology is the study of the evolution of humans, and until the 1970s was primarily based on interpreting the fossil record. Biomolecular evidence is, however, now contributing to the examination of hominid evolution. A technique called DNA annealing (deoxyribonucleic acid or DNA is inherited material passed to subsequent generations in the genes) has revealed how closely related humans are to the great apes. It is possible to separate the two strands of the double helix that make up DNA. Single strands from different animals can then be mixed to form a hybrid double helix, and where there are matching (complementary) units the two strands coalesce. If heat is then applied, the strands will separate again: higher temperatures are required to separate strands with the greatest degree of complementarity, i.e. those which are most closely related. According to Lambert (1987) chimpanzee and human DNA consist of nucleotide sequences that are

Fig. 1.1. Human evolution in relation to technological and food-procurement strategies. (Dates in parentheses are in years BP.)

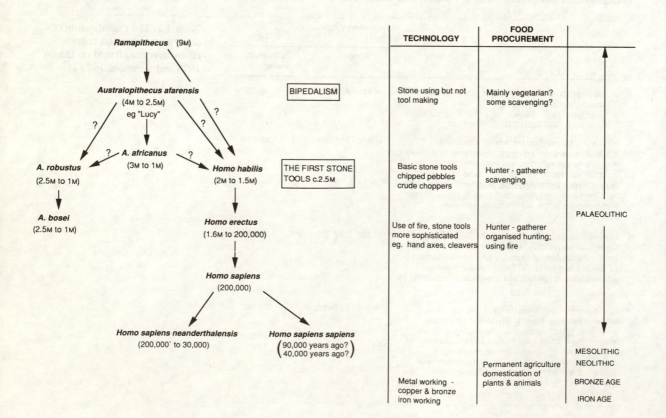

99 per cent identical and this is confirmed if the amino acids in the proteins for which the genetic material codes are compared. In addition, molecular biologists believe that changes to the constituents of these fundamental molecules of life have occurred on a regular basis and thus behave as a molecular clock. By comparing information from securely dated fossils, the present evidence suggests that the first hominids diverged from an ape-like ancestor some 5 Myr BP. Although this was a controversial theory in the late 1970s, it has since been confirmed by further work on new fossil discoveries.

A schema for human evolution is given in Fig. 1.1. By approximately 3.75 Myr BP, bipedal hominids had developed, probably from ramapithecine apes. The first evidence for bipedalism was found at Laetoli in East Africa by Leakey (1979), in the form of footprints in ash layers. It is unclear exactly what advantages bipedalism conferred on these early hominids, but presumably it facilitated more efficient resource use. Lambert (1987), for example, suggests that hands were freed for using and making tools; this in turn may have stimulated brain development enabling better survival strategies to be devised. These early hominids are the australopithecines which flourished between 4 Myr and 2 Myr BP. Perhaps the best-known fossil of *Australopithecus afarensis* is that of 'Lucy', which was discovered in the Hadar region of Ethiopia in 1974, and which is approximately 3 Myr old. According to S J M Davis (1987) hominids of this species were mainly fruit eaters and may themselves have been preyed upon by large carnivores such as hyenas and leopards. As Fig. 1.1 shows, *A. afarensis* may have been the ancestor to the genus *Homo* and was almost certainly the ancestor of other australopithecines.

The evolution of *Homo habilis* occurred some 2 Myr BP, by which time the ability to make crude stone tools had also developed and diet may have included more meat as scavenging became part of the food-procuring strategy. *Homo habilis* was the ancestor of *H. erectus* which had evolved by *c*. 1.6 Myr BP. Evidence from East Africa (Leakey 1982), for example, indicates that hunting, possibly in organised groups and using fire, had superseded scavenging at a time when stone tool kits were becoming more sophisticated. Thus human groups were beginning to emerge as dominants within ecosystems rather than being simply integral components. The next stage in the development of modern humans (*H. sapiens sapiens*) is also controversial since the fossil record is difficult to interpret and there is apparently conflicting biomolecular evidence (Lewin 1987).

In Europe, for example, there is evidence from artefacts indicating that *H. erectus* had spread there from Africa by 1.5 Myr BP. However, fossil hominid remains, such as the Tautavel skull from southwest France, are dated to between 500 kyr and 20 kyr BP, and exhibit most of the features that are found in *H. sapiens*. The fossil record can be interpreted in two ways. One hypothesis is that ancestral populations of *H. erectus* independently evolved to archaic *H. sapiens* and then to *H. sapiens sapiens* which therefore originated in several different places. Another hypothesis is that *H. sapiens* had a single origin, in Africa, and then migrated into Europe, Asia, etc. Lewin (1987) also suggests that a combination of these could also have occurred, i.e. a single geographic origin might have been followed by migrations with interbreeding between the migrants and established populations of archaic *sapiens*. The European fossil evidence favours the first hypothesis. Molecular evidence based on mitochondrial DNA, however, indicates that modern humans originated from a population that existed 200 kyr BP in Africa and then spread to other parts of the world without interbreeding with local groups. Stringer and Andrews (1988) have also suggested that the genetic similarities between European and Australian populations indicate a closer evolutionary relationship than would be likely if the multiregional hypothesis is correct. The current debate lies in the calculation of the rate of change and therefore the reliability of the molecular clock as an accurate dating tool.

Conventionally, Neanderthals are also considered to be a form of modern humans or *H. sapiens* and probably evolved some 200 kyr BP from the same ancestor as *H. sapiens sapiens*. Most Neanderthal fossils are dated to *c.* 70–30 kyr BP, the first part of the last glaciation (Würm or Weichselian in Europe, Devensian in Britain), and the species died out about 30 kyr BP. New evidence from Israel (Valladas *et al.* 1988), however, indicates that modern humans were present there 90 kyr BP, while European dates extend only as far back as 40 kyr. Modern humans may therefore have actually predated Neanderthals and thus the relationship between the two and their ancestry remains controversial. By 10 kyr BP, modern humans had colonised all the continents except Antarctica. Evidence from many parts of the world indicates that their life-style was much more sophisticated than their australopithecine ancestors, with more elaborate stone tools showing regional variation, more innovative hunting gear and the development of artistic techniques.

By the end of the last glaciation, upper palaeolithic groups were adapting to a warmer climate and what may be described as a transitional mesolithic culture developed that lasted for only approximately 5 kyr. Hunter-gathering food-procurement strategies were still important, but Wymer (1982) describes the approach as barbarism in contrast to earlier palaeolithic savagery. The former involves directed hunter-gathering with deliberate manipulation of animal herds (and possibly vegetation) rather than indiscriminate exploitation of resources. Further innovations in relation to resource use led to the neolithic cultural stage, or new stone age. By approximately 12 kyr BP agricultural practices were beginning to develop, the earliest being in the Fertile Crescent of the Middle East where wheat and barley were domesticated. By 7 kyr BP millet, rice and soybeans were being cultivated in China; and in Central America, cotton, maize and squash had been domesticated by 5 kyr BP. In addition, sheep, goats, cattle and pigs had become domesticated and pottery was being produced. Thus, *H. sapiens sapiens* was learning to control the environment and to harness its resources, bringing about changes that were independent of natural processes such as climatic change. These themes will be explored further in Chapter 3.

1.2 QUATERNARY GEOLOGY AND CLIMATIC CHANGE

As stated in section 1.1.1 above, many of the eighteenth-century geologists who inaugurated the glacial theory recognised the significance of climatic change in shaping the earth's surface during the last 2–3 Myr. Many of the stratigraphic changes and superficial deposits that these and later workers recognised have been related to periods of different climatic regimes, particularly cold stages (glacials and stadials) and warm stages (interglacials and interstadials). Although it is now accepted that in most parts of the world the terrestrial record is fragmentary rendering it liable to misinterpretation, it has played a major role in unravelling the record of environmental change.

That the terrestrial record is often incomplete is reinforced by evidence from ocean-core stratigraphy which provides the opportunity to examine uninterrupted Quaternary sequences, and should ultimately provide the basis for global correlations. This palaeo-oceanographic work has contributed a great deal to studies of environmental change and in particular has led to the reinstatement of the astronomical theory (section 1.1.1) as a means of establishing causes of climatic change. Studies of climatic change have also been advanced by evidence from historical and meteorological records as well as from cryogenic studies based on polar ice cores. Although this text is primarily concerned with environmental change during the last 15 kyr, events of the last 2–3 Myr will be briefly discussed below since the most recent period cannot be considered entirely in isolation from the rest of the Quaternary.

1.2.1 QUATERNARY SUBDIVISIONS BASED ON THE TERRESTRIAL RECORD

Before examining the problems involved in delimiting the various stages of the Quaternary, the stratigraphic position of its commencement, the Pliocene–Pleistocene (Tertiary–Quaternary) boundary must be considered. This has been, and is still, the subject of much debate. Age estimates, based on floral and faunal elements that indicate a sharp change from warm to cold conditions, range from c. 1.6 to 2.5 Myr. In 1985 the International Commission on Stratigraphy (Bassett 1985) formally adopted a stratigraphic horizon where claystone overlies a sapropel bed (sapropel = black mud rich in organic calcium carbonate) in a geological section at Vrica in Calabria, Italy, as the official marker immediately below the initial appearance of *Cytheropteron testudo*, a thermophobic (cold-loving) foraminifera. This horizon is dated to c. 1.8 Myr. However, this demarcation has recently been questioned by Jenkins (1987) who disputes the identification of *C. testudo*, believing it to be an unknown species related to *C. wellmani*, which is not a cold-water indicator. Moreover, estimates for the onset of glaciation have been placed as far back as 3.5 Myr, based on the presence of ice-rafted debris in ocean cores (e.g. Opdyke *et al.* 1966), glacial deposits (e.g. Kvasov and Blazhchiskin 1978) and potassium–argon dated tillites (eg. Clapperton 1979). If a date of 1.8 Myr is accepted as the base of the Quaternary, these data place the onset of glaciation in the Pliocene. There is also general agreement from widespread evidence in the North Atlantic region for the onset of glaciation at c. 2.45 Myr. Shackleton *et al.* (1984) for example, suggest that ice-sheet initiation began at c. 2.40 Myr and this is supported by numerous other studies such as that of Loubere (1988). His analysis of foraminiferal assemblages and oxygen isotope ratios from Deep Sea Drilling Project Site 584 in the northeastern Atlantic indicate that the advent of glaciation was the result of progressively deteriorating climatic cycles prior to 2.5 Myr BP (see also section 1.2.4). Similarly, Zagwijn (1985) has dated an early glaciation in the Netherlands (the Praetiglian) at c. 2.3 Myr.

There are also numerous problems associated with the delimitation and correlation of Quaternary deposits intra- and intercontinentally. This is again a consequence of the fragmentary nature of the record, the inadequacy of dating techniques and reliance, at least until the 1950s, on the fourfold glaciation model proposed in 1909 by Penk and Brückner. This classic model, based on glacial moraines and the terraces of the Rhine, named the four glacial stages, each separated by a warm interglacial interval, as the Günz (oldest), Mindel, Riss and Würm. This was a quite remarkable achievement in its day, but its universal acceptance resulted in almost all European Quaternary deposits being categorised into one or other of its stages, despite growing evidence for considerable regional variation. Since the 1950s, however, the trend has been towards the development of regional sequences, each with their own terminology and some intercontinental correlations have been made which can be validated by radiocarbon and other types of dating techniques. It is now clear, for example, that the Weichselian, Devensian, Würm, Wisconsin and Valdai stadials, which represent the last glaciation in northwest Europe, Britain, the Alpine Foreland, North America and European Russia respectively, were contemporaneous. Similarly, the succeeding warm stage, known as the Holocene in Europe and North America, is contemporaneous with the Flandrian in Britain.

The difficulties of correlating deposits are also accentuated with older material: as research proceeds there is often need for re-evaluation. Problems of this kind are well illustrated by two examples. Firstly, Zagwijn (1975) has compared the Quaternary sequence of the Netherlands with that of East Anglia in Britain, and has demonstrated that the latter sequence has two hiatuses in the early and middle Quaternary, representing more than a 1 Myr. Secondly, Green et al. (1984) have presented evidence from Marsworth in Buckinghamshire, UK, to show that there is an interglacial deposit, hitherto unrecorded in Britain, which underlies Coombe rock and deposits of Ipswichian age. An age of 140–170 kyr BP has been obtained for this 'new interglacial', which places it (see Table 1.3) in what has traditionally been the penultimate glaciation in Britain, the Wolstonian (Mitchell et al. 1973). This is now considered to be an extremely complex period in terms of environmental change, with a cold period, evidenced by the Coombe rock of Marsworth, separating the Ipswichian from the 'new' interglacial.

A recent project by the International Geological Correlation Programme (Šibrava et al. 1986) has focused on the correlation of Quaternary stages across the northern hemisphere. Some of their results are summarised in Table 1.3 which also shows the regional terminologies that are currently in use, approximate dates and the relationship between the terrestrial and the marine stages. The latter will be discussed in more detail in section 1.2.2 below. In Europe, for example, this work has provided evidence for nine glacial stages and nine interglacials. As Bowen et al. (1986a) state: 'A large degree of hemispheric correlation of glaciation events is evident. . . . But many problems remain . . . A provisional correlation . . . of this kind. . . is also a working hypothesis or series of hypotheses for further verification, discussion and certainly for further work which it must inevitably occasion.' This generally broad correlation must imply a hemispheric, or more likely global, control of environmental change with climatic change being the most obvious mechanism. This will be further discussed in section 1.2.4.

Table 1.3. Correlations between various Quaternary sequences in the northern hemisphere. (Based on Bowen *et al.* 1986a and Šibrava, 1986.)

	NORTH EUROPEAN STAGES	U.K.	NETHERLANDS	NORTH GERMANY	POLAND	U.S.S.R.	ALPINE REGION (AUSTRIA & GERMANY)	NORTH AMERICA	MARINE STAGES	DATES IN 10^3 YEARS
IG	HOLOCENE	FLANDRIAN						HOLOCENE	1	
									2	13
G1	WEICHSEL	LATE DEVENSIAN	WEICHSELIAN	WEICHSEL GLACIATION	MAIN STADIAL	LATE VALDAI G.	MAX WURM G. STILLFRIED B.	LATE WISCONSIN MIDDLE WISCONSIN EARLY WISCONSIN	3	32-35
									4	64-65 / 75-79
		MIDDLE DEVENSIAN		LOW TERRACE	PREGRUNDZIAD STADIAL	LOESS FLUVIAL DEPOSITS	FIRST WURM G. STILLFRIED A	EOWISCONSIN	5 a / b / c / d / e	
		EARLY DEVENSIAN			KASZUWSTADIAL KASZULY STADIAL					122
IG1	EEM	IPSWICHIAN	EEMIAN	EEMIAN	EEMIAN	MIKULINO	MONDSEE & SOMBERG	SANGAMOAN		128-132
G2	WARTHE	Lower organic deposits at Marsworth?		SAALE 3 G. RUGEN I.G. SAALE 2 G.	WARTA GLACIATION	MOSCOW	LATE RISS LATE RISS RISS? LATE RISS TERRACE	LATE ILLINOIAN	6	195-198
IG2	SAALE / DRENTHE (TREENE?)	Lower organic deposits at Marsworth?		TREENE WENNINGSTEDTER & KITTMITZER PALAEOSOLS	LUBLIN I.G. POLICHNA I.S.	ODINTSOVU I.S.	PARABRAUN-EARTH	ILLINOIAN	7	251-262
G3	DRENTHE		DRENTHE GLACIATION	DRENTHE G. MAIN TERRACE	ODRA G. PODWINEK I.S. PRE-MAXIMUM STADIAL	DNEIPER GLACIATION	ANTEPENULTIMATE G EARLY RISS MINDEL HIGH TERRACE	EARLY ILLINOIAN	8	297-302
IG3	DOMNITZ (WACKEN)		HOOGEVEEN I.S.	FREYBURGER BODEN	MAZOVIAN	ROMNY	REDDISH PARABRAUN-EARTH		9	338-347
G4	FUHNE (MEHLECK)			ELDERITZER TERRACE ERKNER ORGANIC SEDIMENTS	PRE-MAXIMUM STADIAL? WILGA G.?	ORCHIK STAGE (PRONYA GLACIATION)	GL4 TERRACE (PRE-RISS TERRACE)		10	367-352
IG4	HOLSTEIN (MULDSBERG)		HOLSTEIN	HOLSTEIN	FERDYNANDOW	LICHVIN	REDDISH PARABRAUN-EARTH		11	440-428
G5	ELSTER 2	LOWESTOFT TILL		ELSTER 2 G. FLUVIAL GRAVELS	SAN G. KOCK STADIAL?	OKA GLACIATION	GL5 GLACIATION OF ALPS LATE MINDEL GUNZ MINDEL GL5 TERRACE		12	472-480
IG5	ELSTER 1/2			VOIGSTEDT	LUSZAVA I.G.?		RIESENBADEN PALAEOSOL		13	502-?
G6	ELSTER 1	CORTON SAND CROMER TILL		ELSTER 1 G. FLUVIAL GRAVELS	NALECZOIRG SERNIKI STADIAL?		LOWER INTERTERRACE GRAVEL EARLY MINDEL DONAU	PRE-ILLINOIAN	14	542-562
IG6	CROWER (INTERGLACIAL 4)	CROMERIAN	INTERGLACIAL 4	VOIGSTEDT	PODLASIE I.G.		RIESENBODEN PALAEOSOL		15	592-630
G7	GLACIAL C	BEESTONIAN	GLACIAL C		PRE-CROMERIAN GLACIATIONS		MIDDLE INTERTERRACE GRAVEL		16	627-687
1G7	INTERGLACIAL 3	PASTONIAN	INTERGLACIAL 3				RIESENBODEN PALAEOSOL		17	647-718
G8	GLACIAL B		GLACIAL B				UPPER TERRACE GRAVEL GL8 GLACIATION		18	688-782
IG8	INTERGLACIAL 2		INTERGLACIAL 2				RIESENBODEN PALAEOSOL		19	706-790
G9	GLACIAL A		GLACIAL A	HELME FLUVIAL GRAVELS			EARLY GUNZ?		20	729-812
IG9	ARTEN (INTERGLACIAL 1)		INTERGLACIAL 1	UPPER MUSCHELTONE				INTERGLACIAL	21	782-?

Additional column labels within table (vertical text):
- U.K. column: WOLSTONIAN COMPLEX / HOXNIAN / ANGLIAN / PRE CROMERIAN GLACIATION PLATEAU DRIFT
- NETHERLANDS column: SAALIAN COMPLEX / PEELO FORMATION / ELSTERIAN
- NORTH GERMANY column: FLUVIAL GRAVELS
- POLAND column: VISTULIAN / CENTRAL POLISH GLACIATION / SOUTH-POLISH GLACIATION
- U.S.S.R. column: DNEIPER STAGE / OKA GLACIATION

1.2.2 THE RECORD OF CLIMATIC CHANGE FROM THE OCEANS AND ICE CORES

In the last three decades palaeoenvironmental studies have been revolutionised by evidence from deep oceanic sediment cores. The ocean basins receive some 6–11 billion (10^9) tonnes (t) of sediment annually, the terrigenous component of which is derived from adjacent continental land masses. As this material settles, biogenic material, consisting of the remains of marine organisms, is incorporated into the mineral matrix. These generally uninterrupted sequences of sediment have been widely investigated.

Much of the research has focused on calcareous foraminiferal tests, the shells of protozoan organisms that are important components of the marine zooplankton, and in particular on the oxygen isotope ($^{18}O/^{16}O$) composition of the calcium carbonate. Although the interpretation of oxygen isotope ratios is complicated (see Bradley 1985) the basic premiss is that during cold periods ocean waters become enriched in ^{18}O (the heavier isotope) and that this enrichment is reflected in the ^{18}O content of the foraminiferal tests. Conversely, in warmer periods the ^{18}O content is relatively depleted. The mechanism for the observed fractionation is that the lighter $H_2^{16}O$ water evaporates in preference to the heavier ^{18}O form, and that this inherent thermodynamic tendency leads to a more marked isotope imbalance in atmospheric water vapour the lower the ambient temperature. During cold periods the relatively $H_2^{16}O$-laden air deposits the water in glaciers and ice sheets, whence it returns to the oceans during warm periods.

Oxygen isotope analyses have now been undertaken on a number of marine sediment cores from various parts of the world and all reveal similar changes, implying that the ^{18}O signal is a reflection of changes in continental ice volume. Moreover, it is generally accepted that these changes are synchronous, and this is why oxygen isotope stages, such as those given in Table 1.3, provide a means of correlating widely distributed sediments and a stratigraphic framework for the Quaternary to which terrestrial deposits can be related. An independently dated time-scale has been derived for the various oxygen isotope stages based on palaeomagnetic measurements and radiometric dating techniques such as radiocarbon and uranium-series dating. Figure 1.2 illustrates the oxygen isotope marine stages and the dates attributed to them. Of particular interest is the nature of the transition from glacial to interglacial periods which in all oceanic cores appears to be extremely rapid. Such changes have been described by Broecker and van Donk (1970) as terminations, the most recent being termination I which occurs at the end of the last glacial (Weichselian, Devensian, Würm, Valdai, Wisconsin) stage. Age estimates for terminations are also given in Fig. 1.2.

More recent work by Jones and Keigwin (1988) on the oxygen isotope stratigraphy of a core from Fram Strait in the Norwegian–Greenland Sea indicates that at approximately 15 kyr BP an early deglacial event occurred which resulted in the disintegration of the Barents Shelf ice sheet. This may, according to Jones and Keigwin, have caused a eustatic rise in sea-level of some 15 m which in turn may have triggered further deglacial events.

It is also clear from Table 1.3 that the interglacials are relatively short lived compared with glacial episodes. For example, both Fig. 1.2 and Table 1.3 indicate that the last interglacial lasted for only *c.* 20 kyr while the last glacial stage was *c.* 100 kyr long. Moreover, it is also clear that the glacial stages were not characterised simply by one long uninterrupted ice advance. There is also terrestrial evidence for relatively short-lived warmer periods, the interstadials, during these cold stages. In Britain, for example, there is evidence for two such stages (named after specific localities): one is the Chelfordian interstadial dated at *c.* 60 kyr, and the other is the Upton Warren interstadial dated at *c.* 42–43 kyr. (These are not marked in Table 1.2 in order to simplify the main correlations.) There are also numerous examples of interstadial deposits in Europe (see Šibrava *et al.* 1986) in Europe. These indicate the complexity of environmental change and the non-uniformity of cold stages wherein two or more glacial expansions may have taken place. These changes are also reflected in the oxygen isotope record of marine sediment cores which show minor as well as major peaks and troughs of global ice volume.

More recently, attention has focused on the stratigraphic variation in un-

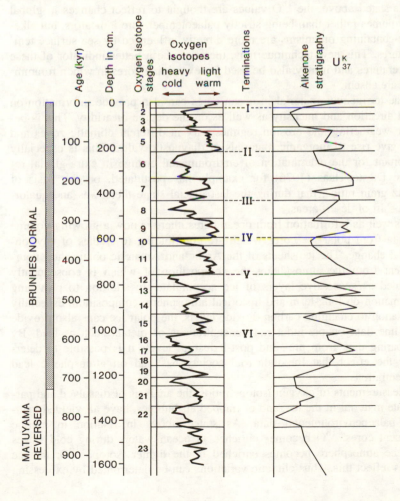

Fig. 1.2. Oxygen isotope stages, terminations and alkenone stratigraphy. (Based on Shackleton and Opdyke 1973; Broecker and van Donk 1970; Brassell *et al.* 1986.)

saturated long-chain alkenones (lipid components of cell membranes) as palaeoclimatic indicators, especially for the reconstruction of sea surface temperatures (Brassell *et al.* 1986). Alkenones, with a large number of carbon atoms (C_{37} to C_{39}), have been identified from the marine coccolithophore *Emiliani huxleyi* and it was discovered that the degree of unsaturation (i.e. where there are multiple rather than single bonds between adjacent carbon atoms) is temperature dependent. Under laboratory conditions, the molecules are more unsaturated at higher temperatures than they are at lower temperatures. In addition, Brassell *et al.* report that variations in alkenone saturation occur in different climatic regions of the oceans, again reflecting temperature dependence. Variations in the alkenone unsaturation index (U^K_{37}) were also determined for an ocean-sediment core extracted from the Kane Gap in the eastern equatorial Atlantic and compared with the oxygen isotope ratios of foraminiferal tests. These down-core variations exhibit similar trends and in glacial stages, with higher ^{18}O values, the U^K_{37} index is low. The converse occurs in interglacial periods, as is shown in Fig. 1.2. The reason why these changes in alkenone structure should occur is not clear, but Brassell *et al.* suggest that it is a response of aquatic organisms to environmental stress. By changing the molecular composition of their lipid (fat) bilayers, of which alkenones are an important component, the organisms can maintain fluidity of their membranes.

As stated above, the ^{18}O values are thought to reflect changes in global ice volumes rather than being strictly palaeotemperature indicators, but alkenone-containing organisms are more directly influenced by sea surface temperatures. This new technique may, therefore, be a better indicator of these temperatures and it may also be used for examining cores in which foraminifera are absent.

The terrigenous material in ocean cores can also provide information on wind direction and intensity as well as on the degree of aridity. This is because weathering and erosion regimes vary in different climatic zones and may give rise to inorganic materials of diagnostic value. This is especially important for the examination of environmental change in extra-glacial regions. Diester-Haas (1976) for example has postulated, on the basis of quartz grain ratios, that during the last glacial stage there was an equatorward shift of desert areas.

As well as information from ocean cores, there is now a growing volume of data from polar ice cores which are contributing to studies of environmental change. The ice sheets of the Arctic and Antarctic obtain their nourishment from the atmosphere, the composition of which is consequently recorded as successive layers of ice accumulate. In addition to providing information on long-term and historical atmospheric composition, especially in relation to changing carbon dioxide levels, the polar ice caps also provide base-line data on pre-industrial concentrations of metals such as lead. By comparing data from pre- and post-industrial levels it is possible to determine the effect that the industrial society has had on atmospheric lead concentrations.

Measurements of oxygen isotope ratios, the analysis of dissolved and particulate material in the ice, and of trapped air bubbles, have all yielded valuable palaeoenvironmental data. As stated above in relation to marine sediment cores, ^{18}O becomes enriched in ocean waters during cold stages and the atmosphere becomes enriched in the lighter isotope ^{16}O: the ice sheets reflect this. Thus climatic variations can be determined by expressing observed $^{18}O/^{16}O$ ratios relative to the isotopic composition of a water standard (Standard Mean Ocean Water). Such data are now available for a number of ice cores from Antarctica and the Arctic. Figure 1.3 illustrates the ^{18}O record from the Vostok core (Lorius *et al.* 1985) which has been divided into eight stages, representing the last climatic cycle from the end of the last glacial period. Stage A corresponds to the present Holocene, while stage G represents the last interglacial and stage H is the terminal part of the penultimate glaciation. Stages B–F represent the last glacial period in which stages E and C are interstadials. Although Lorius *et al.* point out the difficulties of translating the isotope record into a palaeotemperature curve, they estimate that the change from stages H to G involved a 10 °C temperature difference with an 8 °C difference between stages A and B; while the interstadials C and E involved changes of 2 and 4 °C respectively (see Coleopteran evidence in section 2.1.2).

Similar trends are reflected in the Vostok deuterium profile from this core (Jouzel *et al.* 1987b), which is also illustrated in Fig. 1.3. Deuterium is a heavy isotope of hydrogen and its distribution in ice cores mirrors that of the oxygen isotopes because it is similarly affected by temperature variations. Analysis of the deuterium profile confirms the earlier work of Lorius *et al.* (1985), notably that there was an 11 °C temperature amplitude in the last climatic cycle and that the last interglacial was some 2 °C warmer than the present Holocene. In addition, Barnola *et al.* (1987) have examined the

Fig. 1.3. Palaeoenvironmental data from the Vostok ice core. (Based on Lorius *et al.* 1985; Barnola *et al.* 1987; De Angelis *et al.* 1987.)

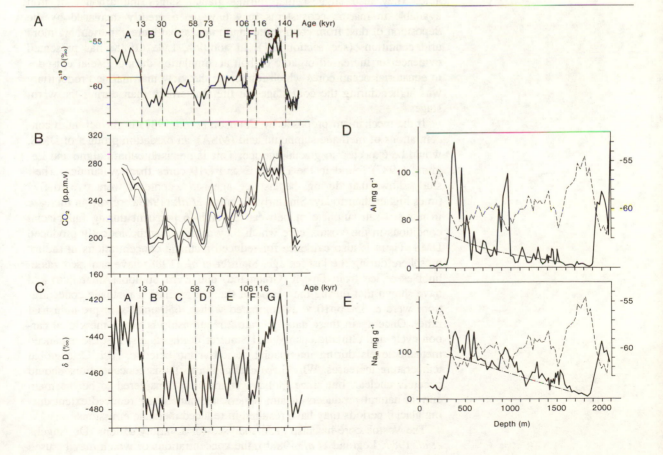

carbon dioxide content of air enclosed in the pores of the Vostok core. As Fig. 1.3 shows, atmospheric carbon dioxide concentrations have also varied considerably over the last climatic cycle, especially between glacial and interglacial periods, and such changes are also apparent in several other ice cores (Paterson and Hammer 1987). The transition between the last glacial period and the Holocene, for example, is characterised by a rise in carbon dioxide concentrations from c. 190 ppm to c. 270 ppm and a slightly steeper rise occurred at the transition from the penultimate glaciation to the last interglacial. These results are particularly interesting because they suggest a link between climatic change and the global carbon cycle. How the two interact, however, is the subject of much debate but almost certainly involves biological systems. Charlson *et al.* (1987) have suggested that oceanic phytoplankton populations can contribute to the regulation of climate because they produce dimethylsulphide (DMS). This is an important source of cloud condensation nuclei and so if phytoplankton productivity increases, as it might during glacial periods, the higher concentrations of DMS would enhance cloud cover, causing more heat to be reradiated back to the upper atmosphere and thus helping to maintain the colder temperatures. Enhanced marine productivity would also lead to the depletion of the atmospheric carbon dioxide pool. Further evidence for this has been presented by Martin and Fitzwater (1988) who have shown that the productivity of marine phytoplankton is enhanced if more dissolved iron is available. They also suggest that during glacial stages the amount of iron available in marine ecosystems may have been greatly increased by the deposition of dust from continental land masses that were experiencing more arid conditions (see section 2.1). In addition, Lyle (1988) has presented evidence for increased organic carbon accumulation during glacial episodes in equatorial ocean cores which reinforces the view that marine productivity was higher during the cold stages of the Quaternary than during the warm stages.

If the mechanism proposed by Charlson *et al.* (1987) is correct, high concentrations of methane sulphonic acid (MSA), an oxidation product of DMS, would be expected in glacial-age ice. This is precisely what Saigne and Legrand (1987) found in the Dome C and D10 cores from Antarctica. Their study shows that during the last ice age MSA contents were two to five times higher than today. Similarly, Legrand *et al.* (1988a) report an increase in non-sea salt sulphate of between 20 and 46 per cent during full glacial conditions in the Vostok core which they associate with biotically produced DMS. There is also evidence for reduced methane concentrations in the atmosphere during the last ice age. Stauffer *et al.* (1988) have analysed gas in bubbles of ice from Dye 3 (Greenland) and Byrd Station (Antarctica) and have shown that during the period of the last glaciation methane concentrations were c. 350 $pp10^9 v$, as compared with c. 650 $pp10^9 v$ in pre-industrial times. Once again these data indicate a relationship between the global carbon cycle and climatic change and Stauffer *et al.* suggest that the enhanced methane levels during interglacial periods contributed c. 0.1 °C to global temperature increases. Why these changes in methane concentrations should occur is unclear, but since global wetlands are considered to be the main current natural producers of atmospheric methane, their reduced extent during glacial periods may have resulted in reduced methane emissions.

The Vostok core has also been analysed for a variety of ions (De Angelis *et al.* 1987; Legrand *et al.* 1988b), the concentrations of which may be used to identify marine salts such as sodium chloride and sodium sulphate, terrestrial salts such as calcium and magnesium nitrates and sulphates, terrestrial dust for which aluminium concentrations are used as a surrogate measure, and strong mineral acids such as nitric, sulphuric and hydrochloric acids. Over the 160 kyr represented by this core (Fig. 1.3), indicators of both marine and terrestrial inputs achieved higher concentrations during periods of cold climatic conditions, especially between 110 kyr and 15 kyr BP (the last glacial period) and were considerably reduced during the last and present (Holocene) interglacials. These data indicate that the Antarctic ice sheet was receiving greater inputs of aeolian and marine deposits during cold periods when arid conditions prevailed in neighbouring continental regions such as Australia and, as sea-levels were lower (section 1.3.4), continental shelf areas were exposed. The concentrations of acids, however, show no such variation and since these compounds are associated with volcanic activity there appears to be no long-term relationship between volcanism and climate (section 1.2.4).

Data such as these can also be used to facilitate climatic modelling. For example, Harvey (1988) has used aerosol data from Arctic and Antarctic cores in an energy balance climatic model to show that enhanced concentrations of these substances in the atmosphere could have depressed global temperatures by a further 2–3 °C during the last glacial maximum. Since aerosol concentrations in the ice cores increase only after significant cooling, Harvey suggests that they constituted a positive feedback mechanism by magnifying the original temperature decrease brought about by other forcing agents such as changing orbital parameters and changes in carbon dioxide concentrations. While the palaeoenvironmental data suggest a relationship between climatic change and aerosol sulphate in accord with Charlson *et al.*'s (1987) hypothesis, Schwartz (1988) has called for a more cautionary approach. He argues that there is no evidence to show that anthropogenically produced sulphur dioxide emissions, the precursors of aerosol sulphate (a major cause of acid rain–see section 5.3.2), has had an appreciable effect on global temperature during the last 200 years. The possibility that a cooling trend caused by this mechanism is being counteracted by enhanced greenhouse warming (section 5.3.1) is also discounted by Schwartz (1988) on the basis that the rate of global warming is the same in both hemispheres. If such a cooling trend existed it would be greater in the northern hemisphere because it is there that the most significant producers of sulphur pollutants are located.

Although the above is only a brief review of some of the literature, it is clear that palaeo-oceanography and ice-core data have a major role to play in determining the nature and direction of environmental change. Moreover, the fact that that there is a generally high degree of correspondence between the two reflects a common causality. This is generally considered to be climatic change brought about by changes in the earth's orbit, as suggested by the Milankovitch theory which is discussed in section 1.2.4.

1.2.3 EVIDENCE FOR CLIMATIC CHANGE FROM HISTORICAL AND METEOROLOGICAL RECORDS

Historical data as a source of information on climatic change are spatially and temporally fragmentary. This is a vast subject and although it has been reviewed at length elsewhere (eg. Wigley *et al.* 1981, Lamb 1982) it is an essential component of any text on environmental change because it reveals a great deal about historic changes prior to the establishment of instrumental observations. As Bradley (1985) states, there are three major categories of historical data that can be useful in building up a picture of climatic change. The first category involves observations on weather events, such as the frequency of spring frosts, and the second category involves the recording of events, such as droughts or floods, which are the response to meteorological conditions. Thirdly, there are records based on phenological rhythms such as the dates when specific plants first flower. While it is impossible to fully evaluate all these sources of proxy climatic information, some examples should serve to illustrate their significance for the examination of environmental change.

Pfister (1978), on the basis of data relating to the number of days with snow cover for sites in the upper and lower plateaux of Switzerland, has shown that during the eighteenth century snow cover was much more continuous than in the 1962–63 period, the most severe winter so far of the twentieth century. The period 1691–1700 experienced more than 65 snow days per year in contrast to recent recordings of less than 35 days. Manley (1974) has also shown, from temperature records, that this period in central England was one of severe winters. Parry (1978) used meteorological data in conjunction with historical farm records of crop production to show how summer warmth affected the oat harvest of farms in the Lammermuir Hills, southeast Scotland. His data reveal that during the thirteenth century crop failures occurred approximately once in 20 years. Numerous other records (Lamb 1984) also indicate that this generally was a warmer period than at present. However, Parry (1978) also shows that by the close of the seventeenth century the crop failure rate was almost one year in every two, reflecting much shorter growing seasons and colder conditions than at present.

Historical records of floods and droughts may also be used as proxy climatic data. Hassan (1981), for example, has examined records of Nile floods for the period 640–1921. On the basis of centennial averages, his research shows that episodes of low Nile discharge dominated the period 930–1070 and 1180–1350, while high discharge was characteristic of the period 1070–1180 and again between 1350 and 1470. These variations relate to increased or decreased discharge from the White Nile that is supplied with moisture from the equatorial rains of East Africa which also affect East African lake levels. High levels of Lake Chad between 1855 and 1890, for example, also correspond to periods of high Nile discharge. Hassan and Stucki (1987) have suggested that such increases in discharge are the result of enhanced winter and early spring precipitation over eastern Africa and Ethiopia. The reasons for these fluctuations in moisture availability are far from clear and may relate to shifts in the monsoons or the effects of the jet stream on the westerlies. However, Hassan (1981) has also pointed out that there are other relationships, such as the coincidence of low Nile discharge between 1470–1500 and 1640–70 with the 'Little Ice Age' of Europe, which implies more general, possibly global, climatic fluctuations.

In terms of phenological data as proxy climatic records, the longest and perhaps best-known series concerns the dates of flowering of cherry trees in Japan. The date of blooming correlates with spring warmth. From Arakawa's (1956) compilation of the admittedly rather sparse records from Kyoto, the eleventh to fourteenth centuries were relatively cool, with average flowering dates of 15–17 April, while the fifteenth, seventeenth, nineteenth and twentieth centuries were warmer, with average flowering dates of 12–14 April. Other phenological records relate to crop production, as exemplified by the work of Parry (1978) quoted above. Phenological rhythms are also reflected in the annual growth rings of trees, which are the focus of studies on dendrochronology (Fritts 1976). The basis of this type of work involves establishing a link between biological output, such as ring width, and measured climatic variables to establish a calibration scale. This can then be applied to tree-rings of earlier periods for which there are no instrumental measurements. Aniol and Eckstein (1984) have used this approach to reconstruct July temperatures near the timber line in Swedish Lapland back to 1680. Their results show that mean July temperatures were below average between 1680 and 1690, 1715 and 1738, 1740 and 1754 and 1768 and 1774.

A combination of these approaches may be used to obtain proxy climatic records, as Pfister (1984) has demonstrated in a study of sixteenth to nineteenth century climate in Switzerland. Measured variables were compared with descriptive information that was standardised by using a numerical code and 10-year means were derived for temperature and precipitation values. Pfister's results are summarised in Fig. 1.4, which shows the summer temperature and precipitation characteristics of the 'Little Ice Age' when springs and winters were colder and drier and there were periods when glacier advances occurred.

The most reliable records of climatic change are, however, derived from instrumental records. Unfortunately, such systematic records do not generally extend very far back in time, and vary in extent from region to region. Figure 1.5, for example, illustrates the temperature variations that have occurred in Britain during the last 400 years. Since the nineteenth century there has been a gradual warming trend, which Lamb (1986) states has been approximately 1 °C on a global basis. In Britain, 1826 saw the warmest summer of the entire 300-year period of continuous temperature observations, and 1846 saw another warm summer with humid conditions that facilitated the spread of the potato blight fungus (*Phytophthera infestans*) which caused widespread famine in Ireland. The 1920s and 1930s were also periods of global warming, most noticeable in high latitudes where ice margins retreated. Lamb (1982), for example, states that in Spitsbergen the open season for shipping extended from 3 months of the year, as was the case prior to

Fig. 1.4. Temperature, precipitation and glacier fluctuations in Switzerland from the early sixteenth to the nineteenth centuries. (After Pfister, 1984.)

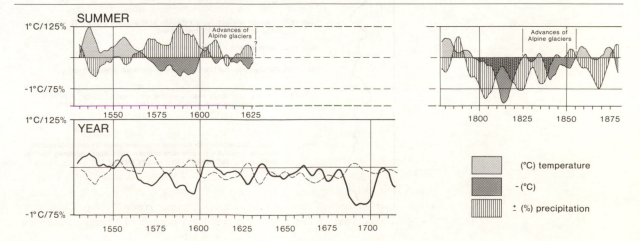

1920, to over 7 months by the late 1930s.

In more recent years, however, some data reflect a cooling tendency. Goudie (1983) cites temperature measurements from Oxford which show that the onset of spring has gradually become later since 1961–70, with a mean date of 19 March; while between 1922 and 1960 the 10-year mean dates were on or before 13 March. The length of the growing season in the corn belt of the USA has also declined over the last 30 years, from an average of just over 200 days to 165 days; and in Europe glaciers have readvanced. Kristjansson (1986), for example, notes the absence of Arctic drift ice from Icelandic harbours in the period 1920–64, and its unwelcome return in 1965 and 1968 when it hampered fishing activities. Currently, there is considerable debate about the increasing concentration of carbon dioxide in the atmosphere and its potential warming effect. This will be discussed in Chapter 5.

Fig. 1.5. Climatic tendencies in Britain since AD1690. (From Goudie 1983.)

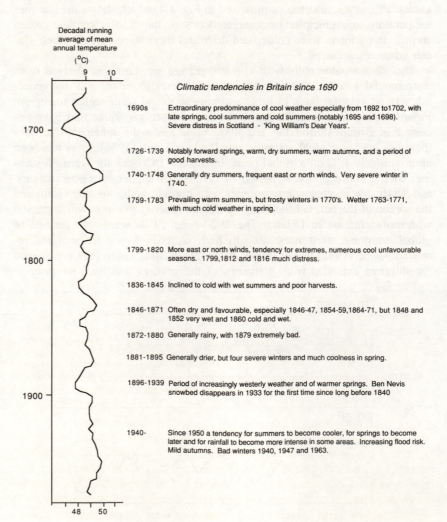

Climatic tendencies in Britain since 1690

1690s — Extraordinary predominance of cool weather especially from 1692 to1702, with late springs, cool summers and cold summers (notably 1695 and 1698). Severe distress in Scotland - 'King William's Dear Years'.

1726-1739 — Notably forward springs, warm, dry summers, warm autumns, and a period of good harvests.

1740-1748 — Generally dry summers, frequent east or north winds. Very severe winter in 1740.

1759-1783 — Prevailing warm summers, but frosty winters in 1770's. Wetter 1763-1771, with much cold weather in spring.

1799-1820 — More east or north winds, tendency for extremes, numerous cool unfavourable seasons. 1799,1812 and 1816 much distress.

1836-1845 — Inclined to cold with wet summers and poor harvests.

1846-1871 — Often dry and favourable, especially 1846-47, 1854-59,1864-71, but 1848 and 1852 very wet and 1860 cold and wet.

1872-1880 — Generally rainy, with 1879 extremely bad.

1881-1895 — Generally drier, but four severe winters and much coolness in spring.

1896-1939 — Period of increasingly westerly weather and of warmer springs. Ben Nevis snowbed disappears in 1933 for the first time since long before 1840

1940- — Since 1950 a tendency for summers to become cooler, for springs to become later and for rainfall to become more intense in some areas. Increasing flood risk. Mild autumns. Bad winters 1940, 1947 and 1963.

1.2.4 CAUSES OF CLIMATIC CHANGE

Fluctuations and changes in climate occur both spatially and temporally, the causes of which are a source of considerable speculation and controversy. External factors, such as changes in solar radiation, and internal factors, such as adjustments within the earth's atmospheric circulation, may either singly or in combination, be responsible. Moreover, human activity may contribute to climatic change by inadvertently affecting the global carbon cycle. The earth's climatic system is extremely complex, with elaborate feedback mechanisms that both influence and are influenced by earth surface processes, the hydrological cycle, ecosystem function and human activity. Thus it is perhaps not surprising that the mechanisms of climatic processes are not yet completely understood. This makes it all the more difficult to ascertain the nature and causes of climatic change, which, apart from information from the short period of instrumental records, can only be examined via a proxy record contained within the earth itself, such as marine sediments and ice cores discussed in section 1.2.2 above.

During the last century, numerous theories relating to climatic change have been advanced. Several have emphasised changes in the quantity and quality of solar radiation. Sunspot cycles, for example, have often been cited as one possible cause of changes in the amount of radiation emanating from the sun. Sunspots vary in an approximately 11-year cycle as high-energy particles drift equatorwards from the sun's middle latitudes. There are numerous historical accounts attributing the occurrence of natural disasters, such as floods and droughts, to sunspot maxima and minima. Currie and Fairbridge (1985) review the evidence for this solar cycle signal in drought/flood proxy records from North America, Argentina and the Nile catchment, and also suggest that the cycle can be seen in world-wide air-temperature and air-pressure data. Their analysis of a drought/flood index for Beijing, northeastern China, since 1470 also suggests that 11-year cycles are apparent, but that the 18.6-year lunar tidal-forcing cycle is also significant. Moreover, there are historic data (Eddy 1976) to show that there have been times when the general course of the 11-year sunspot cycle has been interrupted. Two periods are of especial note and are termed the Spörer Minimum, which occurred between 1400 and 1510, and the Maunder Minimum of 1645–1715. Both of these periods coincided with periods when global temperatures were noticeably cooler, especially during the Little Ice Age in Europe (see Fig. 1.4).

Much scepticism has been expressed regarding the significance of sunspots in climatic perturbations, not least because clear relationships do not always exist between sunspot numbers and observed weather and because correlations are frequently possible only with parts of records of historic meteorological and/or hazard phenomena. New evidence has, however, recently been presented by Labitzke (1987) and van Loon and Labitzke (1988) to clarify the relationship between the 11-year sunspot cycle and surface weather. This involves the quasi-biennial oscillation (QBO), the reversal between the easterly and westerly direction of winds in the stratosphere over the equator which occurs every 26 months, and winter stratospheric temperatures at 30 mb pressure over the North Pole. Using such data for the past 36 years, van Loon and Labitzke have shown that there are positive correlations between warmer winters during the sun's more active periods and between colder winters when the sun is least active and when the QBO is in a westerly direction. Conversely, the reverse of these trends occurs when the QBO is in its easterly phase. The implications of these trends in relation to surface weather involves their effects on pressure systems. For example, the higher temperatures of the westerly QBO phase when the sun is most active help to create higher pressures over North America and lower pressures over the adjacent oceans. Since pressure differentials control air movements which in turn control surface temperatures, the resulting northerly airflows over the Atlantic seaboard of the USA bring colder and more frosty weather than usual. This trend is confirmed by van Loon and Labitzke's examination of winter temperatures for Charleston. Thus it seems likely that sunspot frequency may indeed play a significant role in determining climatic characteristics, and it will be interesting to see if historic data have greater statistical significance when this new QBO factor is taken into account.

The quality and quantity of solar radiation reaching the earth's surface are also affected by other variables. Volcanic eruptions, for example, result in the emission of dust into the atmosphere which may scatter and partially reflect incoming solar radiation, leading to reduced temperatures. In general these are probably fairly short-lived events except for extremely large eruptions. The emission of particulate material from Krakatoa in the 1880s, in combination with those from Katmai in 1912, caused a global decrease in solar radiation of between 10 and 20 per cent (Goudie 1983). It is of note, as Lamb (1982) has shown, that many of the coldest and wettest summers in Britain in the eighteenth and nineteenth centuries occurred when there was a high incidence of volcanic dust in the atmosphere, while warmer episodes as in the 1920s–1940s were relatively dust-free. It is also interesting to speculate whether enhanced amounts of volcanic dust in the atmosphere affected the productivity of marine phytoplankton (as discussed in section 1.2.2) which in turn may have depleted the atmospheric pool of carbon dioxide that resulted in periods of short-term cooling.

It has also been suggested that adjustments and readjustments may take place within the internal components of the climatic system itself. Feedbacks (section 1.1.2) may occur to stabilise or destabilise the system. For example, whatever the primary cause of ice-sheet initiation may be, the presence of extensive ice may act as a positive feedback since its higher albedo would cause more insolation to be reflected back into the atmosphere. Consequent lower temperatures may lead to continued ice accumulation. Ultimately a point may be reached where other variables, such as moisture availability, lead to a halt in the process. Other components of the atmosphere may also create positive feedback. The significance of carbon dioxide levels, for example, has already been discussed in section 1.2.2. The carbon dioxide data from polar ice clearly show that the colder periods of the Quaternary were characterised by reduced concentrations of atmospheric carbon dioxide, but the mechanism necessary to bring about this relationship remains enigmatic.

The astronomical theory of climatic change that involves changes in the earth's orbital characteristics have been reviewed by Imbrie and Imbrie (1979). It involves shifts in the angle of the ecliptic (the tilt of the earth's axis of rotation from the plane in which the earth orbits the sun), changes in the eccentricity of the earth's orbit and the precession of the equinoxes. Each of these factors varies in a cyclical manner. The first exhibits a periodicity of *c.* 40 kyr, the second of *c.* 96 kyr and the third, which is due to a slight conical movement of the earth's axis that causes a slow shifting of the spring and autumn equinoxes and summer and winter solstices (all these delimit the seasons), has a periodicity of *c.* 21 kyr. Milankovitch (section 1.1.1) in 1941 was among the first to calculate the combined climatic effects of these three variables, but until the 1970s his ideas were viewed with considerable scepticism.

Hays *et al.* (1976) analysed the temperature records of ocean cores (see Fig. 1.2) and identified three main cycles which correspond to the Milankovitch cycles. For example, the longest cycle, related to the earth's elliptical orbit, is *c.* 100 kyr, which is approximately equivalent to each major glaciation. Although these data indicate a causal relationship between the earth's orbital variations and climatic change, the mechanism whereby this is effected remains unknown. Milankovitch considered that the radiation anomalies created by orbital variations were most crucial in high northern latitudes where continental ice sheets accumulated. If summer radiation receipts are low, winter snow cover will persist into the summer months, and will eventually persist all year round. Milankovitch calculated that when minimum obliquity coincided with high eccentricity and when the northern hemisphere summer coincided with the aphelion (i.e. when the earth is furthest from the sun) insolation conditions would most favour glaciation. He also calculated that such conditions would have occurred at *c.* 185 kyr, 115 kyr and 70 kyr BP, when winters were warmer and enhanced evaporation occurred from subtropical oceans to provide adequate precipitation for the growing ice sheets. The ocean-core evidence also suggests that these were indeed periods of continental ice accumulation.

A recent synthesis of North Atlantic ocean-core evidence by Ruddiman and Raymo (1988) has confirmed these earlier results and has shown that the last 3.5 Myr were affected by three distinct climatic regimes. During the earliest period between 2.47 and 3.4 Myr BP, when ice sheets in the northern hemisphere were small or non-existent, there were only small-scale quasi-periodic oscillations. Between 2.47 and 0.734 Myr BP the rhythmic climatic changes were controlled mainly by the 41 kyr cycle of orbital obliquity, and during the most recent period (0.734 Myr to date) larger-amplitude climatic changes resulted from 100 kyr cycles controlled by orbital eccentricity. These changes resulted in firstly, the initiation of glaciation in the northern hemisphere at *c.* 2.47 Myr BP and secondly an intensification of glaciation at 0.734 Myr BP. What is not clear, however, is why changes in these regimes should have occurred.

It is improbable that volcanic activity was a primary cause and this is endorsed by Ruddiman and Raymo who state that 'vulcanism does not appear to provide persistent enough forcing (i.e. decadal repetition) to maintain the climatic system in one regime for intervals lasting a million years'. They also believe that changes within the atmosphere–ocean–ice system itself were unlikely and propose that tectonic changes may have altered the earth's surface which in turn affected atmospheric circulation patterns. Of particular interest are the large-scale uplifts of mountain ranges that have occurred in Tibet and western North America during the last 3 Myr. Liu and Menglin (1984) have presented evidence to show that 2–3 km of net uplift have occurred in Tibet and the High Himalayan Mountains, which means that 75 per cent of the net elevation of the region was attained during the period of instigation and intensification of Northern Hemisphere glaciation. There is

Weertman (1983) have proposed that zonal mean albedo would have been significantly increased so that more heat would be reradiated back into the atmosphere, ultimately causing global cooling. The precise nature of this relationship is uncertain but it remains a potential link between uplift and glaciation. On the other hand, Ruddiman *et al.* (1986) have suggested that tectonic uplift in middle latitudes may have altered the planetary wave structure which cooled the northern hemisphere land masses and thus enhanced their sensitivity to changes in insolation brought about by orbital changes. Ruddiman and Raymo (1988) have expanded this theory and hypothesise that the effect of mountain building allows more rapid growth of ice sheets, especially during periods when ice sheets are relatively small. What is needed to test these hypotheses is more precise geological evidence about the timing and rates of uplift. Was uplift gradual during the last 2 Myr, and if so were critical elevations reached at which control of the planetary waves became effective at the same time as the major climatic regimes developed, i.e. 3.15–2.4 and 0.45–0.3 Myr BP? Alternatively, was uplift accelerated at these particular times?

Moreover, in regard to recent climatic changes, it is difficult to determine precisely which changes are due to natural climatic variation and which are due to human activity. These latter will be more fully discussed in Chapter 5 and relate to fossil-fuel burning, deforestation and atmospheric pollutants.

1.3 Environmental Change During the Quaternary Period

While the foregoing sections broadly consider the evidence for climatic change and in particular the cyclical variations of the last 2–3 Myr, the terrestrial and oceanic records reveal that the nature and direction of environmental change has varied considerably on a global basis. Much more information is available for the northern hemisphere, largely because it is here that such studies first began and because there is more extensive terrestrial evidence. Moreover, although not directly glaciated as is the case for the higher latitudes, lower latitudes also experienced environmental change as global climatic shifts occurred. For example, desert regions expanded and contracted and there is evidence to show that vegetation belts of the subtropics and tropics were substantially altered. In addition, the growth and demise of polar ice caps caused massive changes in the hydrological cycle. In relation to the present day, ice ages were periods when much more water was incarcerated in the ice caps, and as a result sea-levels were much lower. Thus large proportions of what are now continental shelf areas were dry land.

1.3.1 Environmental Change in High latitudes

Areas of high latitude are those which have been most directly affected by the advance and retreat of glaciers and ice caps. Indeed, Arctic and Antarctic zones are currently experiencing glaciation, and it is from these areas that much can be learnt about glacial processes. However, in latitudes adjacent to the polar ice masses, the terrestrial record of glaciations that occurred prior to the last major ice advance is frequently blurred or non-existent because the erosive power of ice is such that it will destroy earlier stratigraphic evidence.

For example, Lundquist (1986) states that there is evidence for four major glacial stages in southern Denmark, an area marginal to the main Scandinavian ice sheets. These glacial stages correspond to the north European stages given in Table 1.3: namely the pre-Crower glaciation, the Elsterian complex, the Saalian complex and the Weichselian. Both the Elsterian and Saalian stages were characterised by two major ice advances and several interstadials, which again broadly correspond to the north European sequence of Table 1.3 except for the absence of evidence for the Futune (G4) glacial stage. In the central areas of Scandinavia, however, only one glacial stage corresponding to the Weichselian can be clearly distinguished, although there are a few sites of Eemian interglacial age such as Leveäniemi in Swedish Lapland and at Fjösanger near Bergen, Norway.

In Siberia, Arkhipov *et al.* (1986a) have recognised three periods of ice advance, namely the Shaitan, Bakhta and Zyrianka. These are given in Table 1.4 and are each characterised by two glacial advances separated by interstadial periods. The Tobol and Kazantsevo interglacial periods are represented by marine facies in northern Siberia that have been correlated with Holsteinian and Eemian facies in northwest Europe on the basis of foraminiferal fossil assemblages. According to Arkhipov *et al.*, these correlations are also justified by a comparison of mammal-bearing deposits in Siberia with those in western Europe. However, not all of Siberia experienced ice cover during the glacial stages. In those areas peripheral to the ice sheets, periglacial conditions prevailed, characterised by sparse vegetation leaving skeletal soils vulnerable to wind erosion. As a consequence, loess, an aeolian deposit consisting mainly of silt, accumulated in extraglacial regions during cold stages while in the intervening warm stages soil complexes developed. Arkhipov *et*

Glacial complex (Gc) or Interglacial (IG)	Northern Europe	Siberia		Deposits in the extraglacial zone
Gc	Weichselian	Zyrianka	Sartan glacial advance	Yel'tsovka loess
			Karginsky interstadial complex	Iskitim soil complex
				Tula soil complex
			Early Sartan glacial advance	Loess
IG	Eemian	Kazantsevo		Berd soil
Gc	Saale complex	Bakhta	Taz glacial advance	
			Shirta interstadial	Suzun loess
			Samarovo glacial advance	
IG	Holstein	Tobol		Lacustrine and fluvial deposits
Gc	Elster complex	Shaitan	Late Shaitan glacial advance	Loess
			Unnamed interstadial	Loess deposition on Ob Plateau
			Early Shaitan glacial advance	
IG	Cromer	Talagaikino		Loess deposition on the Ob Plateau

Table 1.4. The correlation of Quaternary deposits in Siberia with the Quaternary stages of northern Europe. (Based on Arkhipov *et al.* 1986a, b.)

al. (1986b) have related such deposits to the various glacial and interglacial stages, as shown in Table 1.4. Loess deposits are also widespread in the temperate zone, and their significance as indicators of environmental change will be discussed more fully in section 1.3.2.

1.3.2 ENVIRONMENTAL CHANGE IN MIDDLE LATITUDES

As implied in Table 1.3, large areas of the temperate zone of the northern hemisphere have been affected by glacial advances and retreats during the Quaternary period. The same is probably true of the equivalent latitudinal zones in the southern hemisphere, although the absence of extensive land masses in this region means that there is a paucity of terrestrial deposits and thus a limited source of information on environmental change. Conversely, there is a wealth of information from the northern hemisphere, and examples from Britain, China and the western USA will be presented to illustrate the magnitude of environmental change in glaciated and extra-glacial areas.

Bowen *et al.* (1986) have recently summarised the Quaternary history of the British Isles (Table 1.5) for which there is evidence of five glacial events in the early Pleistocene. The first is the Baventian, evidence for which occurs in East Anglia and consists of far-travelled heavy minerals and chert in

Table 1.5. The stages of the British Quaternary in relation to oxygen isotope stages and approximate dates. (Based on Bowen *et al.* 1986a, b and Šibrava 1986.)

	STAGE NAMES	GLACIAL EPISODES	INTER GLACIALS INTER STADIALS	0^{18} STAGES	APPROXIMATE DATES 10^3 YRS BP
LATE QUATERNARY	FLANDRIAN			1	10
	LATE	LOCH LOMOND GLAC.			
			WINDERMERE I.S.		14
	DEVENSIAN	DIMLINGTON GLAC.		2, 3, 4,	
	MIDDLE			5a, b, c, d.	
			UPTON WARREN I.S.		
	EARLY		CHELFORD I.S.		
	IPSWICHIAN		IPSWICHIAN I.G.	5e	122
MIDDLE QUATERNARY	WOLSTONIAN COMPLEX		MARSWORTH I.G.?	7? 6, 7, 8	128-132
	HOXNIAN		HOXNIAN I.G.	9, 10, 11	297-302
	ANGLIAN	LOWESTOFT GLAC.	CORTON I.S.?	12, 13, 14	440-428
		NORTH SEA DRIFT GLAC.			
	CROMERIAN		CROMERIAN I.G.	15	542-562
EARLY QUATERNARY	BEESTONIAN	GLACIATION IN WEST MIDLANDS & N. WALES		16	592-630
	PASTONIAN		PASTONIAN	17	627-687
	PRE-PASTONIAN	GLACIATION "			647-718
		GLACIATION "	?		
		GLACIATION "	?		
			?		
	BAVENTIAN	GLACIATION IN NORTH SEA REGION			
	BRAMERTONIAN				
	ANTIAN				I.G. = Interglacial
	THURNIAN				I.S. = Interstadial
	LUDHAMIAN				
	PRE-LUDHAMIAN				

marine clays which may have been derived from a North Sea ice sheet. The next four glacial stages, three occurring in the pre-Pastonian stage and separated from the final early Quaternary glacial period of the Beestonian by the Pastonian interglacial, are represented by erratic materials in North Wales and the West Midlands and, in the extraglacial region of the Thames Valley, by the Middle Thames Gravel Formation. Bowen *et al.* consider that it is not yet possible to ascertain the limits of the glacial advances during these periods, or to correlate them with oxygen isotope stages.

The post-Beestonian stage is known as the Cromerian, named after the Cromer Forest-bed Formation of East Anglia, plant fossil evidence for which is reviewed in Mannion (1986b). During the optimum of this interglacial, deciduous woodland, consisting mainly of oak, elm and lime, prevailed: Etruscan rhinoceros, giant beaver and Derringer's bear dominated the fauna. In the succeeding cold stage, the Anglian, Britain experienced the most extensive ice cover of the Quaternary, with ice extending to a position approximately equivalent to a line between Bristol and north London. Two glacial episodes occurred during this period, which were both cold and arid, and witnessed the diversion of the River Thames from the Vale of St Albans and Essex to its present course through London.

Numerous lacustrine sequences in East Anglia, particularly those at Hoxne and Marks Tey, also provide evidence of the subsequent interglacial period, the Hoxnian. Once again the optimum of this temperate stage was dominated by mixed-oak deciduous forest. Temperatures were warmer by 1–2 °C than they are today, and conditions were more oceanic than in earlier or later temperate periods. The predominant mammal fauna consisted of lemming, horse and red deer.

The penultimate cold stage of the British Isles, the Wolstonian, is currently the subject of much debate, instigated by the discovery in 1984 of deposits at Marsworth, Buckinghamshire (section 1.2.1), which contain mammal-bearing sediments indicative of a post-Hoxnian and pre-Ipswichian temperate period (Green *et al.* 1984). Although there is no direct evidence for a truly glacial episode between the two, there is evidence for an intervening cold period. Thus, while the term Wolstonian may be retained for this stage (geologically, a stage may represent a series of deposits reflecting a variety of palaeoenvironments), this new evidence indicates that the Wolstonian was an extremely complex period of environmental change, consisting of at least a cool–temperate–cool–temperate sequence, with only one of the cool stages experiencing actual glaciation. The older temperate period, so far unnamed, contains fossils of brown bear, mammoth and an extinct horse. The Ipswichian assemblages contain remains of hippopotamus, narrow-nosed rhinoceros, elephant, giant deer and water vole. The latter assemblage, as well as being present in the younger Marsworth organic horizons, is also typical of Ipswichian interglacial deposits elsewhere, which are further characterised by plant remains indicative of mixed deciduous woodland during the optimum.

The final cold stage experienced in Britain is that of the Devensian which, in common with the Anglian, was arid and witnessed two interstadials. Whether the early Devensian period was one of glacial advance is debatable, but there is clear evidence for extensive late Devensian glaciation, known as the Dimlington stadial, which occurred approximately 18 kyr BP. By approximately 14 000 kyr BP, Britain was ice free, and only a relatively minor recrudescence (Loch Lomond glaciation) of glacial ice occurred in upland regions *c.* 12–11 kyr BP, before Britain entered the present interglacial–the Flandrian. These events will be discussed in Chapters 2 and 3.

As stated in section 1.3.1, many extraglacial areas were subject to the deposition of loess during cold stages, and during intervening warm stages soil development occurred which is often preserved as palaeosols or fossil soils. Loess is a widespread deposit in Eurasia, North and South America and New Zealand, and the stratigraphic sequence preserved in such deposits provides the key to Quaternary environmental change in these areas. Among the most extensive loess deposits are those in China, especially in the loess plateau of the middle Yellow River, where it has been extensively investigated at Luochuan in the province of Shaanxi (Tungsheng *et al.* 1986; Kukla 1987). Here, loess derived from more arid northern periglacial and western desert regions has been investigated using palaeomagnetic, palaeoecological and geochemical methods. Four major units have been distinguished, which are given in Table 1.6, along with various subdivisions, oxygen isotope stages and approximate dates (compare Table 1.2). There is overall agree-

Table 1.6. The loess sequence from Luochuan, Shaanxi Province, China. (Based on Tungsheng *et al.* 1986 and Kukla 1987.) (Dates based on Bowen *et al.* 1986a.)

PERIOD	LOESS UNIT	LOESS-PALAEOSOL SEQUENCE	OXYGEN ISOTOPE STAGE		Approx Age 10^3 yrs
HOLOCENE	LOESS	S0	1	W	
UPPER PLEISTOCENE	MALAN LOESS	L1	2	C	13
			3	W	32-35
			4	C	64-65
			5	W	75-79
MIDDLE PLEISTOCENE	UPPER LISHI LOESS	S1			128-132
		L2	6	C	195-198
		S2	7	W	251-252
		L3	8	C	297-302
		S3	9	W	347-338
		L4	10	C	367-352
		S4	11	W	440-428
		L5	12	C	472-480
		S5	13	W	502
			14	C	542-562
			15	W	592-630
		L6	16	C	627-687
		S6	17	W	647-718
		L7	18	C	688-782
		S7	19	W	706-790
		L8	20	C	792-812
		S8	21	W	792
		L9	22-25	CWCW	800
LOWER MIDDLE PLEISTOCENE	LOWER LISHI LOESS	S9	26-27	CW	
		L10	28	C	
		S10	29	W	
		L11	30	C	970
		S11	31	W	
		L12	32	C	
		S12	33	W	
		L13	34	C	
		S13	35	W	
		L14	36	C	
		S14	37	W	
		L15	38	C	1150
LOWER PLEISTOCENE	WUCHENG LOESS	WS1			
		WL1			
		WS2			
		WL2			
		WS3			
		WL3			
		WS4			
		WL4			
PLIO-PLEISTOCENE BOUNDARY					
PLIOCENE	RED CLAY				

C = cold   W = warm

ment between the loess stratigraphy and the oxygen isotope stages, once again implying global rather than local climatic change. Loess layers relate to colder periods, while palaeosol horizons relate to warm periods. For the Lishi loess, for example, Tungsheng *et al.* (1986) suggest that the warmer stages were characterised by forest steppe, with a higher average precipitation and temperature than the intervening cold stages when the aeolian material was deposited in a drier environment of desert steppe.

There is a considerable body of evidence for lake-level change especially during the late Quaternary. Smith and Street-Perrott (1983), for example, have examined the evidence for lake-level changes in the so-called pluvial lakes of the western USA. The geomorphological and stratigraphic evidence from these closed lake basins indicates that between 24 kyr and 14 kyr BP most lake levels were higher than at present. Between 14 kyr and 10 kyr BP considerable changes in lake levels occurred, especially between 14 kyr and 13 kyr BP, when many lakes experienced declining water levels. During the period 12–10 kyr BP, there was a great deal of regional variation in lake level, with some lakes, such as Mojave, Searles, Mono and Tulare, experiencing high levels. Conversely, between 10 kyr and 5 kyr BP, lake levels declined: between 6 kyr and 5 kyr BP all lakes in this region were experiencing low levels. These data also broadly, in terms of timing, concur with lake-level reconstruction in Africa (Street-Perrott and Harrison 1985), except that by 6 kyr BP African lake levels were once again high. All of these changes are considered to be the result of changing patterns of atmospheric circulation, with implications for changing precipitation and evaporation rates. It is also highly likely that the earlier periods of the Quaternary experienced similar fluctuations in lake levels as climatic cycles developed, although there is little evidence to substantiate this (see Funza example in section 1.3.3).

1.3.3 Environmental Change in Low Latitudes

As stated in section 1.2.1, correlations of terrestrial stratigraphic sequences are often difficult because of the fragmentary nature of the record. This also means that it is difficult to unravel the history of environmental change. It may be, however, that the low latitudes contain sites where there is a continuous unfragmented history of environmental change, as has been demonstrated by Hooghiemstra's (1984) analysis of a 3.5 Myr sequence of lacustrine sediments from Funza on the High Plain of Bogotá, Colombia, South America.

Hooghiemstra has analysed the fossil pollen assemblages in a 357 m core from this site and has used the information as proxy-climatic data. Fifty-five pollen assemblage zones have been identified, and various sections of the core have been dated using potassium–argon and fission-track dating on volcanic ash layers. The results are given in Fig. 1.6. Some twenty-seven climatic cycles have been identified, each consisting of two pollen zones reflecting the altitudinal position of the forest line.

Hooghiemstra (1984, 1988) has also related the pollen sequences of Funza to ocean-core stratigraphy (section 1.2.2) and, especially for the upper part of the core, there are close relationships between the two, as shown in Fig. 1.6. In general, peaks in arboreal (tree) pollen relate to periods when the oceans were warmer, i.e. during interglacials or interstadials. Many of these changes occurred with a periodicity of *c*. 100 kyr, and thus support the orbital forcing theory of Milankovitch. However, there are difficulties in correlating these two sets of data, since they relate to very different parameters. The oxygen isotope stratigraphy relates to ice volume (section 1.2.2), while the pollen record reflects changes in the altitudinal position of forest, which in turn relates to temperature and humidity. While temperature changes will affect both ice volume and forest cover, the latter two may react in different ways. Nevertheless, Fig. 1.6 illustrates that there have been considerable environmental changes in the High Plain of Bogotá during the last 3.5 Myr, and the presence of such a long, apparently unbroken, terrestrial record is quite remarkable.

The distribution and variety of indicator species such as those indicative of deep water and marsh environments, have also been analysed to provide information on lake-level changes. During cooler periods, the lake level was high relative to warmer times. This is also shown on Fig. 1.6, but it does not necessarily imply higher precipitation in cooler periods, since the lake level will also have been controlled by different evaporation regimes.

There is a considerable body of evidence to suggest that in other parts of the intertropical zone the cold stages of the Quaternary were characterised by much cooler and drier climates. Williams (1985) summarises much of the evidence from this region, and in Africa, for example, geomorphological and

Fig. 1.6. The palaeoenvironmental record from Funza, High Plain of Bogotá, Columbia. (Based on Hooghiemstra 1984 with oxygen isotope stages from Shackleton and Oplyke 1973.)

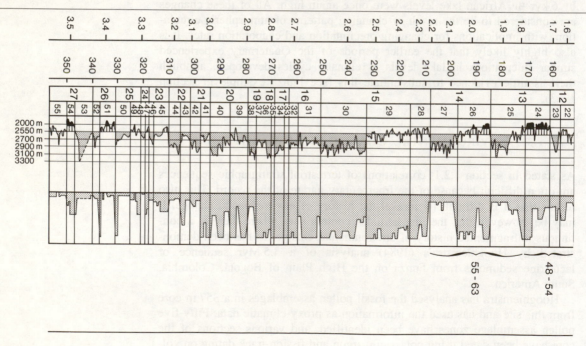

palaeoecological evidence suggest that between 25 kyr and 17 kyr BP, which equates approximately with the last glacial maximum, conditions were colder and drier. Evidence from ocean cores also indicates that more aeolian material was deposited during this period, confirming the terrestrial evidence for drier conditions, and implying that wind erosion was a significant agent of environmental change. Similarly, there is evidence from Australia (Bowler 1976) to show that prior to the last glacial maximum the southern Australian landscape was lake-covered, but that by approximately 17–15 kyr BP, most of these inland lakes had become dry. This decline in rainfall is also suggested by pollen assemblages from Lynch's Crater in northeastern Queensland (Kershaw 1978), which reflect an annual decline in rainfall from *c.* 2500 mm to 500 mm during the period 80–20 kyr BP. At this time sea-levels were also lower, creating land bridges with New Guinea.

Further work from an equatorial Atlantic ocean core (Pokras and Mix, 1987) also provides evidence for periods of enhanced aridity in tropical Africa during the late Quaternary. High concentrations of the freshwater diatom species *Melosira* occur at regular intervals in this core and are thought to derive from lake beds in tropical Africa that underwent deflation and wind erosion during drier periods. Pokras and Mix suggest that the accumulation of this species relates to the 23 kyr precessional period suggested in the Milankovitch theory (section 1.2.4). This implies that the

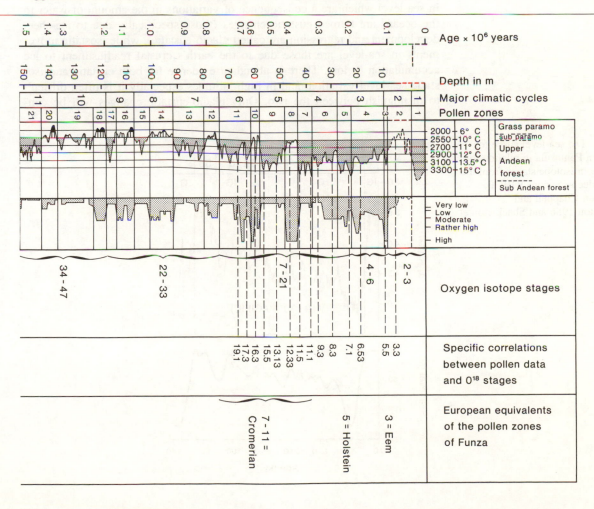

tropical, monsoonal climates of Africa are more directly influenced by
variations in low-latitude solar radiation than by the orbital forcing that
instigates the glacial–interglacial climatic cycle, or by changes in the obliquity of the earth's axis.

1.3.4 SEA-LEVEL CHANGES

The foregoing sections illustrate both the general nature (section 1.2) and,
via examples (sections 1.3.1–1.3.3), the more specific nature of environmental change during the Quaternary period. All of the evidence suggests that
climate provided the overall control of earth surface and biotic processes,
especially via the 100 kyr climatic cycle predicted by Milankovitch (1941,
section 1.2.4). Climatic processes affect not only the distribution and transport of heat energy, but also the global hydrological cycle. Alternating cold
and warm stages and/or glacials and interglacials caused changes in that
cycle, affecting the distribution of the main global reservoirs of water. As
local and polar ice sheets waxed and waned, so too did the volume of water
contained within the oceans, bringing about changes in sea-level. In addition, as ice sheets accumulated in high latitudes, land masses became depressed beneath their weight and subsequently rose as ice melted. Changes
in sea-level which are a consequence of variations in the amount of water in
the oceans are termed eustatic changes (those specifically due to ice-sheet
development and regression are called glacio-eustatic), while isostatic movements in sea-level are those due to the earth's crustal readjustment to ice
accumulation or loss. There is abundant evidence for both eustatic and isostatic sea-level variation, and in high latitudes especially it is often difficult
to distinguish between the two. Only glacio-eustatic changes will be con-

Fig. 1.7. The sea-level curve for
the Huon Peninsula in relation to
the oxygen isotope stages from the
Pacific deep-sea core V19-30.
(Based on Chappell and
Shackleton 1986 and Shackleton *et
al.* 1983.)

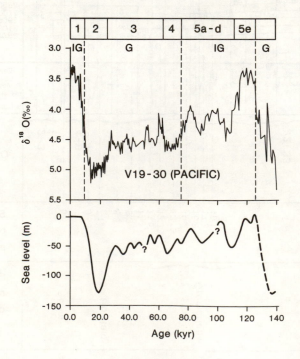

sidered here in order to provide a general framework of Quaternary sea-level changes, especially in relation to ocean-core data (section 1.2.2).

The most reliable information on glacio-eustatic sea-level changes derives from lower and middle latitudes which are tectonically stable. Harmon *et al.* (1983), for example, using uranium-series dating on corals and speleothems (= secondary mineral deposits) from fossil coral reefs and beach deposits in Bermuda, have shown that during the last 250 kyr sea-level has been higher than present on only two occasions. The first was *c.* 200 kyr BP, when sea-level was 1 m higher, and the second was *c.* 125 kyr BP, when it was 5±1 m higher. In addition, the Bahamanian data reveal that these periods of higher sea-level were relatively short lived, lasting only *c.* 10 kyr, and that in the succeeding 5 kyr sea-levels dropped by 12–14 m. Chappell and Shackleton (1986) have suggested that the sea-level curve derived from studies on the coral reefs of the Huon Peninsula, New Guinea, may be representative of global late Quaternary sea-level changes, since there is generally good agreement between data from this and other widely dispersed sites in the Caribbean, the Pacific and Timor. The results from the Huon Peninsula are given in Fig. 1.7, which shows that high sea-levels occurred during oxygen isotope stage 5e, which is equivalent to the last interglacial. During this period, sea-level was approximately 6 m above the present level, while during the last glacial maximum 18 kyr BP, sea-levels were approximately 130 m lower.

As an example of sea-level changes at a more local scale, Zubakov (1988) has identified eight saline-water events in the Black–Azov Sea region during the last 1.1 Myr. These events relate to the transgression of Mediterranean waters, as ice sheets melted and interglacial conditions ensued. A number of incursions from the Caspian Sea are also recorded which relate to pluvial phases that occurred as ice sheets were accumulating. For example, the Eltigenian beds contain a stenohaline fauna and are dated at approximately 120 kyr BP, indicating that these deposits accumulated during the interglacial period. The subsequent cold phase is represented by marine sediments with Caspian molluscs, dated to *c.* 100 kyr BP.

1.4 Conclusion

Since the early nineteenth century, ideas relating to environmental processes and environmental change have undergone considerable refinement. The inception of the glacial theory along with the development of ecological principles injected the notion of dynamism as an important component of earth-surface phenomena, and instigated earth-surface process studies. The advent of the systems philosophy inaugurated what may be termed the jigsaw approach to environmental studies, whereby the components of earth-surface systems may be isolated, examined and the results used to recompile the jigsaw to determine whether or not the pieces fit together. If not, the whole must be disassembled and the examining process begun again. The more evidence that is compiled, the more difficult it is to reassemble the components, but the resulting hypotheses are more robust.

The examination of environmental change involves just such an as-

sembling and disassembling approach. The development of deep ocean-
core stratigraphic studies, for example, has led to a reappraisal of the
terrestrial record for ice-sheet development and demise, lake-level and
sea-level changes. Ocean-core data are now being supplemented by information from polar ice cores, and should eventually provide a global
framework for investigating environmental change. The terrestrial record based on sedimentary and fossil evidence from high, middle and low
latitudes should provide a means of more finely resolving this global
record. The ultimate goal is one that involves the use of such data for
the prediction of future rates and directions of environmental change,
though this is made more complex by the emergence of *Homo sapiens
sapiens* as a major agent of environmental change during the last 12 kyr.

Further Reading

Bradley R S 1985 *Quaternary paleoclimatology*. George Allen and
Unwin, Boston, London & Sydney

Foley R 1987 *Another unique species: patterns in human evolutionary
ecology*. Longman, London

Goudie A 1983 *Environmental change* 2nd edn. Clarendon Press, Oxford

Holt-Jensen A 1987 *Geography: its history and concepts* 2nd edn. Harper
and Row, London

Lamb H H 1988 *Weather, climate and human affairs*. Routledge, London

Ruddiman W F, Wright H E Jr (eds) 1987 *North America and adjacent
oceans during the last deglaciation*. The Geological Society of America

Šibrava V, Bowen D Q, Richmond G M (eds) 1986 Quaternary glaciations in the northern hemisphere. *Quat. Science Rev.*, **5**

Thompson R D, Mannion A M, Mitchell C W, Parry M, Townshend
J R G 1986 *Processes in physical geography*. Longman, London

2

ENVIRONMENTAL CHANGE IN THE LATE- AND POST-GLACIAL PERIODS

2.1 INTRODUCTION

As the last ice-sheets waned some 14–15 kyr BP, environmental change occurred relatively rapidly and varied considerably on a global basis. Overall, climatic amelioration ensued as ice-sheets retreated in high and higher-middle latitudes to approximately their present positions. As a result, ecosystems became re-established in regions that had been previously covered in ice. Simultaneously, the ecosystems of lower-middle and low latitudes underwent adjustment as new climatic regimes became established. Some areas such as Britain were not destined to become completely ice-free until 10 kyr BP, and the period 14–10 kyr BP was one of rapid climatic and ecological change. The adjustment to more congenial climatic regimes involved considerable changes in floral and faunal elements as well as changes in soil genesis. The fossil record indicates that biotic and pedogenic development did not always occur in tandem, and it is the fossil record that provides the most comprehensive evidence for the nature and direction of environmental change during the last 15 kyr. This period also witnessed tremendous changes in the development and activities of human communities as *Homo sapiens sapiens* began to emerge as a dominant force in environmental systems. Innovations in resource use, especially the domestication of plants and animals and the establishment of agricultural systems also brought about environmental change, and it is not always possible to distinguish from the available evidence which changes relate to climatic change and which to human activity.

2.2 THE INTERGLACIAL CYCLE

Although this chapter deals with the specific environmental changes that have occurred in the last 15 kyr, it is important to realise that this is probably part of another interglacial period. While it is by no means certain that another ice age will develop, there is every reason to suppose that the repeated cycle of cold and warm stages or glacials and interglacials, as reflected in the deep-sea core, ice core and terrestrial stratigraphy (sections 1.2 and 1.3) will continue. Moreover, if the fossil evidence, particularly pollen assemblages, for the last 15 kyr is compared with that from previous interglacials, a number of similarities are obvious which also imply that the climatic cycles so far experienced will continue. First recognised by Jessen and Milthers (1928) Iversen (1958), on the basis of Danish evidence, proposed a simple model of the ecological processes operative during interglacials. A modified version of this scheme is given in Fig. 2.1, along with similar schemes for other areas of western Europe, the eastern Mediterranean and Florida. Each cycle comprises four stages which provide a framework not only for the investigation of earlier interglacial deposits but also for the environmental changes of the last 15 kyr.

The first phase is termed the cryocratic phase and is characterised by cold, arid continental conditions with skeletal, cryoturbated, base-rich soils supporting hardy herbs that today have an Arctic–Alpine distribution and are shade intolerant. As temperature ameliorates, the unleached base-rich soils are colonised by shade-intolerant herbaceous species, shrubs and pioneer tree species to create grasslands, scrub and open woodlands during the protocratic phase. This is followed by the mesocratic phase during the climatic optimum of the interglacial, when brown-earth mull soils support temperate deciduous woodland as shade-intolerant species decline. The tree species characteristic of this period may invade as a direct response to climatic amelioration or because

Fig. 2.1. The ecological changes occurring in various regions during the interglacial cycle. (From Birks 1986.)

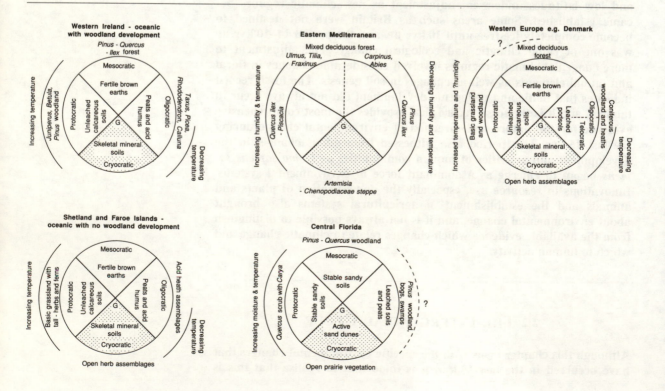

skeletal soils have been modified by vegetation communities of the protocratic phase. The final phase in the interglacial cycle is the telocratic phase and is retrogressive. It is characterised by podzolised soils and peats which have become nutrient depleted and which carry acidic woodland dominated by conifers and ericaceous heaths. The latter part of the mesocratic phase and the early part of the telocratic phase have been termed the oligocratic phase by Andersen (1966), who has suggested that the soil deterioration characteristic of this period may occur prior to climatic deterioration, as a result of natural soil processes such as leaching. Ultimately the cryocratic phase is re-established and the glacial–interglacial cycle begins again.

Taking the evidence for the interglacials of the British Isles (see Godwin 1975) as an example, it is clear that the actual plant species which become established vary between interglacials, which is why it is possible to distinguish between interglacial sites of different ages. Nevertheless, if the plants are categorised as protocratic, mesocratic etc., each of the interglacial periods recognised in Britain follows Iversen's (1958) general model. This illustrates parallelism of development and reflects the overriding control of climate on environmental change during an interglacial cycle, while in any specific phase pedogenic characteristics, competition, migration rates and source areas of propagules will influence the floristic composition.

While Iversen's (1958) model was designed to provide a framework for the examination of interglacial sequences in northwest Europe, where the optimum stage of the interglacials was characterised by mixed deciduous forest, Birks (1986) has reviewed the evidence for the applicability of this model to other regions (Fig. 2.1) and the species

Table 2.1. Characteristic plant assemblages of the interglacial cycle. (Based on Birks 1986.)

PHASE OF INTERGLACIAL CYCLE	FAROE AND SHETLAND ISLANDS	WESTERN IRELAND	EASTERN MEDITERRANEAN REGION	FLORIDA
CRYOCRATIC PHASE	SPARCE COVER OF ARCTIC-ALPINE HERBS SOILS: SKELETAL MINERAL		*ARTEMISIA* - GOOSEFOOT STEPPE	OPEN PRAIRIE VEGETATION SOILS: ACTIVE SAND DUNES
PROTOCRATIC PHASE	GRASSLAND WITH ABUNDANT TALL HERBS AND FERNS SOILS: UNLEACHED CALCAREOUS SOILS	PINE, BIRCH, POPLAR, JUNIPER WOODLAND SOILS: UNLEACHED CALCAREOUS SOILS	HOLLY OAK - PISTACHIO WOODLAND ELM, LIME, ASH	OAK SCRUB WITH HICKORY SOILS: STABLE SANDY
MESOCRATIC PHASE	GRASSLAND WITH ABUNDANT TALL HERBS AND FERNS SOILS: FERTILE BROWN EARTHS	PINE, OAK AND HOLLY FOREST SOILS: BROWN EARTH	ELM, LIME, ASH HORNBEAM AND FIR	PINE, OAK WOODLAND SOILS: STABLE SANDY
OLIGOCRATIC PHASE	ACID HEATH AND BOG COMMUNITIES SOILS: PODSOLS PEAT	FIR, SPRUCE, HEATHS RHODODENDRON SOILS: PODSOLS, PEATS	PINE HOLLY, OAK	PINE WOODLAND, BOGS, SWAMPS SOILS: LEACHED SOILS AND PEATS
TELOCRATIC PHASE			AND PINE	
ORIGINAL SOURCE	Birks and Peglar (1979)	Watts (1967)	Van der Hammen *et al.* (1971)	Watts (1971, 1980a)

which are characteristic of each phase are given in Table 2.1. In all cases, climate is the overriding control on the developmental sequence, and the parallelism of development suggests that the glacial–interglacial cycle does indeed provide a useful framework within which to examine the environmental changes of the last 15 kyr.

2.3 THE LATE-GLACIAL PERIOD

The end of the last cryocratic phase of northwest Europe occurred as the last ice-sheets waned (see Table 1.2 for the regional terminology), leading into the last protocratic phase that began approximately 14.5 kyr BP. This protocratic phase includes the late-glacial period and the first thousand years or so of the Holocene, which began 10 kyr BP ago. The late-glacial was a period of rapid environmental change instigated by ameliorating and then fluctuating temperatures. On a continental scale, the magnitude and direction of such changes varied considerably, as is illustrated by the examples given below.

2.3.1 CLIMATIC CHANGE DURING THE LATE-GLACIAL PERIOD

The evidence from the ocean cores (section 1.2.2) indicates that ice ages ended relatively abruptly, with the change from glacial to interglacial conditions taking place within just a few thousand years. While this is true of the early glacial periods of the Quaternary just as much as it is true of the last glacial period, it is of the latter that most evidence is available. Even before the development of radiocarbon dating in the 1940s and 1950s, lithological and palaeobotanical evidence from various parts of northwest Europe indicated that the end of the last glaciation was both short-lived as well as climatically and ecologically complex. Amongst the earliest evidence for climatic oscillations during this period (c. 15 kyr–10 kyr BP) was that discovered by Hartz and Milthers (1901) in a lake basin at Allerød in Denmark. Here, there are laminated lower and upper clays, containing soliflucted pebbles, which are separated by an organic mud. The latter contains remains of birches, while the clays contain the remains of arctic–alpine species and dwarf shrubs. The sequence is interpreted as representing two tundra-like phases separated by a temperate period. Since this early work, other sites have been investigated and much has been written about the regional trends and anomalies that occur in palaeobotanical data throughout Europe. In other parts of the world there is no such overwhelming terrestrial evidence for this climatic oscillation (section 2.3.2). Thus, any consideration of climatic change during this period must be related to specific sites from which palaeoecological data are available, since despite their drawbacks these are the greatest source of information on which to make climatic inferences. It is also necessary to refer to ocean-core and ice-core data to provide evidence that is independent of the terrestrial record.

In relation to the latter, Duplessy et al. (1981) presented evidence from the northeast Atlantic to show that the last glaciation (Termination I in

Fig. 1.2) consisted of two steps which they denoted Termination IA and IB, and which were separated by a warm phase equivalent to the terrestrial Bølling/Allerød stage (section 2.3.2). The onset of termination IA occurred at *c*. 15 kyr BP and continued until *c*. 13.3 kyr BP, while Termination IB began at *c*. 10 kyr BP and lasted until 8.5 kyr BP. Similar results have also been obtained by Weaver and Pujol (1988) from cores from the Alboran Sea (western Mediterranean) and the adjacent Atlantic ocean. Remains of coccolith floras from these latter cores also reflect changing surface water temperatures. For example, *Gephyrocapsa muellerae* is abundant in colder water prior to Terminations IA and IB and is reduced in the intervening warmer period when *G. oceania* is most abundant.

Berger *et al*. (1987) have summarised much of the evidence for the glacial-Holocene transition from the ocean cores and have shown that the Younger Dryas cold period is well marked in many areas, suggesting that it was a widespread phenomenon. However, since the Milankovitch hypothesis for climatic change (section 1.2.4) cannot account for this relatively short-lived climatic excursion, Berger *et al*. have suggested that the causal mechanism must relate to positive and negative feedbacks occurring during the transitional period between glacial and interglacial. They hypothesise that such an excursion may be due to the effects of glacial meltwater, since this is unique to a glacial–interglacial transition, on the production of North Atlantic Deep Water (NADW). This is significant in the circulation of North Atlantic waters, which in turn play an important role in atmospheric circulation. On the basis of biotic and abiotic evidence from the ocean cores, Berger *et al*. suggest that the Younger Dryas regression was essentially caused by an influx of meltwater from the Arctic that temporarily suppressed the production of NADW.

New evidence from a South China Sea core (Broecker *et al*. 1988) suggests that the Younger Dryas event, even if widespread, was probably not a global event. Foraminiferal assemblages from this core show that between 14 and 13 kyr BP there was abrupt warming which continued uninterrupted into the Holocene. These data have led Broecker *et al*. to suggest that this cooling event, so well documented in the North Atlantic region, was due to the diversion of meltwater discharge from the Mississippi basin into the St Lawrence. This theory lends support to Berger *et al*.'s (1987) contention that glacial meltwater discharge affected NADW production, which in turn affected atmospheric circulation. This has also been discussed by Overpeck *et al*. (1989) who have reviewed the palaeoclimatic evidence for this period from high- and low-latitude North Atlantic regions. Recognising that there were three periods of broadly synchronous abrupt climatic change at c. 13–12.6 kyr BP, 11 kyr BP and 10 kyr BP, Overpeck *et al*. argue that while astronomical (Milankovitch) forcing instigated the change from glacial to interglacial conditions, internal reactions within the earth's atmosphere–ocean system translated the transition from a state of gradual change to one that was manifest as a series of abrupt climatic events. In common with Berger *et al*. (1987), they highlight the role of variations in meltwater discharge from the Mississippi and St Lawrence rivers, which in turn are linked to the melting history of the Laurentide Ice Sheet, as climatic determinants during this period.

There is also evidence for the Younger Dryas cold period from Arctic and Antarctic ice cores. For example, at Dye 3 and Camp Century in Greenland, the Younger Dryas/Holocene transition is dated to 10720 ± 150 years BP

(Dansgaard 1987), and is marked by an abrupt shift in [18]O concentrations (section 1.2.2) as is the earlier Allerød period, and both are characterised by higher [18]O values. Hammer *et al.* (1985) have also shown that during the Allerød and Holocene considerably less dust was deposited at Dye 3 in contrast to the Younger Dryas (and the period of the last glacial maximum) when colder and more arid conditions resulted in the deposition of dust (probably loess) derived from adjacent continental areas. Jouzel *et al.* (1987a) have also presented evidence from Antarctic ice cores for a two-stage transition between the last glacial maximum and the Holocene, although the [18]O signal is not as strong as it is in the Arctic cores. The two warming periods are dated as occurring between 15.5 and 13.2 kyr BP, and between 11.6 and 10.2 kyr BP, with an intervening colder period between *c.* 12.8 kyr and 11.6 kyr BP: thus placing the cooling phase approximately 1.5 kyr before that of the northern hemisphere. Allowing for uncertainties in the dating, this cooler interval may be equivalent to the European Younger Dryas.

Thus the evidence for a global cooling event prior to the Holocene is inconclusive, although there is sufficient evidence to show that it was a fairly widespread event and one which had its greatest expression in the North Atlantic and adjacent land masses, especially in the British Isles. Here, more precise palaeoclimatic reconstructions of the late-glacial period have been facilitated by coleopteran analysis. According to Coope (1986), climatic conditions, particularly temperature, are among the most important factors that determine the geographical range of insects. Atkinson *et al.* (1987) have defined the climatic tolerances of 350 beetle species previously identified from late-glacial deposits relating to the last 22 kyr, and on the basis of their mutual climatic range, derived from the intersection of their

Fig. 2.2. Reconstructed mean temperatures for the warmest and coldest months of the year based on coleopteran assemblages from twenty-six sites in Britain and Ireland relating to selected periods during the the lasts 22 kyr. (From Atkinson *et a*l. 1987.)

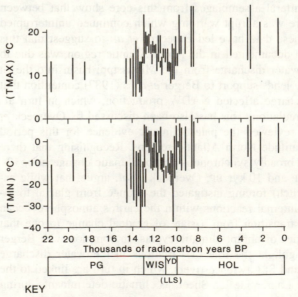

KEY

PG = Pleniglacial period (maximum advance of Devensian ice)

WIS = Windermere Interstadial

YD (LLS) = Younger Dryas (Loch Lomond Stadial)

HOL = Holocene

tolerance ranges, have reconstructed temperature changes. Their results are given in Fig. 2.2, which shows that between 22 and 18 kyr BP, when ice cover was at its maximum, average summer temperatures were less than 10 °C and the coldest winter month was *c.* –16 °C. Between 14.5 and *c.* 13 kyr BP, during which period ice retreated from England and Wales and then Scotland, climate remained cold and continental, with winter temperatures as low as –20 °C to –25 °C, giving rise to a temperature range of between 30 and 35 °C, which is considerably larger than that of today at 14 °C. Such low winter temperatures are attributed to the presence of continuous sea ice on the Atlantic, as has also been suggested by Ruddiman and McIntyre's (1981) investigation of ocean cores from the Atlantic.

Just prior to 13 kyr BP, however, the coleopteran evidence suggests that there was rapid warming and presumably this represents the terrestrial biotic expression of Termination IA as defined by Duplessy *et al.* (1981) from the northeast Atlantic (see above). Between 13.3 and 12.5 kyr BP, summer temperatures rose to 17–18 °C and winter temperatures ameliorated to 0–1 °C,

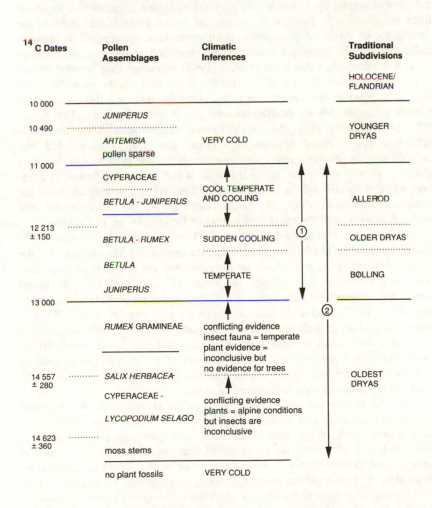

Table 2.2. The late-glacial environment as deduced from fossil plant and coleopteran assemblages from Low Wray Bay, Lake Windermere, English Lake District. (Based on Pennington 1977 and Coope 1977.)

① Length of interstadial on the basis of plant remains (Pennington, 1977)
② Length of interstadial on the basis of coleopteran assemblages (Coope, 1977)

but this warm period was short-lived. A cooling trend occurred between 12.5 and 12 kyr BP, and although summer temperatures remained constant for some 500 years, winter temperatures declined from *c.* –5 °C at 12 kyr BP to *c.* –17 °C at 10.5 kyr BP; and from 11.4 kyr BP summer temperatures once again declined to *c.* 10 °C by 10.5 kyr BP. The equivalent of Duplessy *et al.*'s (1981) Termination IB is recorded in the coleopteran data at *c.* 10.5 kyr BP, and by 9.8 kyr BP temperatures had returned to those similar to present.

Atkinson *et al.* (1987) have also used the data to calculate rates of temperature change. They estimate that during the warming periods, centred on 13 kyr BP and 10 kyr BP, changes occurred at the rate of 2.6 °C per century and 1.7 °C per century respectively. Conversely, the cooling phases of 12.5 kyr BP and 10.5 kyr BP were slower, but even so temperature changes were still occurring relatively rapidly. Thus, it is perhaps not surprising that the palaeobotanical evidence for this period is often at variance from site to site and often in apparent conflict with coleopteran evidence. This is illustrated if comparisons are made between the palaeobotanical (Pennington 1977) and palaeocoleopteran evidence (Coope 1977) from Lake Windermere (Table 2.2). For example, by 13 kyr BP, coleopteran evidence suggests that temperatures were similar to those of today, but the pollen assemblages indicate the dominance of Arctic–Alpine plant species which, if interpreted as climatic indicators, would suggest a much harsher and colder regime. Since, however, it is clear from Atkinson *et al.*'s (1987) synthesis that thermal conditions were ameliorating rapidly, it seems likely that plants were less well able to respond to the climatic stimulus, possibly because habitats remained relatively hostile due to insufficient time for soil development. This possibility becomes even more likely if the habitat requirements of the more thermophilous native British species, such as oak and elm, are considered. Not only do they require climatic conditions similar to the present day, but they also require well-developed soils. It is also possible that the period in question was too short-lived for such thermophilous species to migrate from the refuges in Europe to which they had retreated during the earlier severe cold period that witnessed the maximum extent of Devensian ice in Britain.

Conversely, a comparison between the fossil coleopteran (Coope 1977) and pollen-analytical (Pennington 1977) data from Lake Windermere for the period between *c.* 12 and 10 kyr BP suggests that the two sets of indicators were in agreement. Both suggest the onset of cold conditions. As stated above, the coleopteran data indicate a decline in average summer temperatures to *c.* 10 °C, and a decline in winter temperatures to *c.* –17 °C. The pollen assemblages indicate a return to Arctic-tundra conditions, with a vegetation dominated by open-habitat grasses and sedges. It seems highly likely that this close agreement is a function of the more gradual cooling that occurred, providing sufficient time in this instance for the vegetation to establish equilibrium with habitat and climate.

Thus, the last protocratic phase, at least in the British Isles, was a period of complex climatic and ecological changes. Lowe and Gray (1980) have summarised much of the British and northwest European pollen-analytical data for this period, and have suggested that the major climatic changes were related to oscillations of the oceanic polar front. The same conclusion, in relation to British palaeocoleopteran data, is advocated by Atkinson *et al.* (1987), who also refer to Ruddiman and McIntyre's (1981) work on Atlantic ocean cores. These latter have suggested that since the last glacial maximum the eastern edge of the oceanic polar front has shifted position several times, as shown in Fig. 2.3. As the last ice sheet waned, this front rapidly moved northeastwards from a position at the latitude of northern Spain to one north of Iceland, bringing in its wake a rapidly ameliorating temperature regime to the British Isles (and northwest Europe). It then returned *c*. 12 kyr BP, bringing cold polar waters south and instigated a climatic regime which in turn prompted the redevelopment of Arctic–Alpine vegetation communities in many parts of Britain. In addition, local ice caps became re-established in many upland areas in Britain, where this period is known as the Loch Lomond stadial. As Fig. 2.3 shows, by 10 kyr BP the polar front had retreated northeast and ameliorated temperatures ensued.

If this hypothesis is correct, the late-glacial movements of the polar front could explain many of the phenomena observed in the palaeoenvironmental record. Firstly, the steep temperature gradient across the front may have been responsible for the rapid temperature changes postulated by Atkinson *et al*. (1987) for the warming periods of 13 kyr BP and 10 kyr BP. Secondly, since such a movement of the polar front was time-transgressive, the ecological response was also probably time-transgressive and thus similar fossil assemblages between sites do not necessarily imply synchroneity. Thirdly, since the movement of the polar front was over the Atlantic Ocean, it may account for the fact that the late-glacial oscillation was recorded in maritime western Europe but is not particularly well marked in pollen assemblages in eastern and southern Europe (W A Watts 1980b). Such regional differences will be discussed in section 2.3.2.

In addition, in their synthesis of late-glacial events, Lowe and Gray (1980) state that the western edge of the oceanic polar front had remained relatively stable in comparison to the shifts of the eastern edge. This, they claim, is the reason why the late-glacial oscillation has not been convincingly demonstrated in eastern North America. Recently, however, Mott *et al*. (1986) have presented palynological evidence from fourteen sites in Atlantic Canada to show that just prior to 11 kyr BP there was a climatic warming which resulted in the formation of open spruce woodlands. At *c*. 11 kyr BP there was a reversion to less favourable conditions when soils became unstable, tree populations diminished, and local glaciers readvanced in Quebec. Mott *et al*.'s data indicate that this cooler period lasted until *c*. 10 kyr BP, when there was renewed climatic amelioration. These results and other data

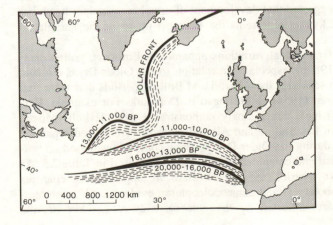

Fig. 2.3. Changes in the position of the oceanic polar front between 20 and 10 kyr BP. (Based on Ruddiman and McIntyre 1981.)

summarised by Peteet (1987a and b) would indeed suggest that a late-glacial oscillation was registered in Atlantic Canada, the implication being that the western margin of the oceanic polar front was moving in the same direction as the eastern margin.

Such results are perhaps what might be expected if this late-glacial oscillation is the result of glacial meltwater suppressing the NADW production (section 2.3.1) and they also lead to the conclusion that other palaeoenvironmental studies, especially in New England, USA, should be reappraised (section 2.3.3).

2.3.2 REGIONAL VARIATIONS IN ENVIRONMENTAL CHANGE DURING THE LATE-GLACIAL PERIOD

As discussed in section 2.3.1, the climatic changes of the late-glacial period were both rapid and variable. Thus it is not surprising that the ecological response, evidence for which is derived from fossil floral and faunal assemblages, was also spatially variable and much of the available data for Europe have been summarised by W A Watts (1980b) and Birks (1986).

In the British Isles alone there is considerable variation from site to site and Table 2.2 details the changes that occurred in the catchment of Lake Windermere (Pennington 1977) since this is generally regarded as a reference site. Although fossil coleopteran evidence indicates that temperatures had ameliorated much earlier, there is no significant palaeobotanical evidence for woodland development until 13 kyr BP. Between 13 and 11 kyr BP, two periods of woodland development occurred, separated by a short-lived cool period equivalent to the European Younger Dryas. Both were dominated by tree birches and by 11 kyr BP there was a return to Arctic assemblages as climate deteriorated prior to a further warming trend that began *c.* 10.5 kyr BP.

Elsewhere in Britain, however, the period represented by the Windermere interstadial (*sensuo* Pennington 1977) was not always characterised by two periods of woodland development. The equivalent of the European Bølling oscillation is not always registered. Similarly the nature of the vegetation communities during the interstadial varies from site to site. In southeast England, for example, pine was present along with birch (Godwin 1975), whereas in eastern Scotland park tundra persisted with only scattered birches. In Ireland there is little evidence to suggest well-developed birch woodland and Watts (1977) has suggested that development of crowberry–juniper heath between 12.4 and 12 kyr BP represents the warmest phase of the late-glacial period.

There are similar regional variations apparent in European pollen diagrams (W A Watts 1980b), especially in relation to the Older Dryas climatic deterioration which separates the Allerød and Bølling periods that were first recognised by Iversen (1954) at Böllingsö in Denmark. For example, Berglund *et al.* (1984) have convincingly demonstrated from Hvkulls Mosse, Skvne, Sweden, that the Bølling and Allerød periods were indeed separated by a cooler period during the Older Dryas. Their conclusions, based on pollen, plant macrofossil and coleopteran data, are summarised in Table 2.3. As in the English Lake District (see above), there are apparent discrepancies between the palaeobotanical and palaeocoleopteran evidence. Although temperate conditions are indicated by the coleoptera at *c.* 12.5 kyr BP, the palaelobotanical evidence suggests the presence of tundra conditions, and it is not until *c*. 11.4 kyr BP that the vegetation communities appear to be in equilibrium with average summer temperatures. The Allerød/Younger Dryas transition reflects relatively sudden climatic deterioration, while in the middle of the Younger Dryas the coleopteran evidence indicates a warming period and a time-lag of approximately 300 years before the vegetation communities respond.

However, as Watts (1980b) has demonstrated, there is no convincing evidence for similar oscillations in the Alpine region, or in southern Europe. Ammann *et al*. (1984), for example, have shown that at Lobsigensee in the southern Alpine foreland, the rise in juniper and tree birches, which began at *c*. 13 kyr BP, and the inspread of pine from *c*. 12 kyr BP, continued uninterrupted until *c*. 11 kyr BP. After this time, more open vegetation communities developed in response to the climatic deterioration which occurred during the Younger Dryas, although the palaeoecological data suggest that the

Table 2.3. The late-glacial environment at Håkulls Mosse, Southwest Sweden. (Based on Berglund *et al*. 1984.)

^{14}C Dates	Zones	Palaeoenvironment
	Preboreal (beginning of Holocene)	
10 000		VERY STABLE SOILS WOODLAND TUNDRA WITH TREE BIRCH, JUNIPER AND HEATH TEMPERATE COLEOPTERA
10 200	YOUNGER DRYAS	MORE STABLE SOILS SUBARCTIC TUNDRA, HEATH EXPANSION TEMPERATE COLEOPTERA
10 500		INTENSE SOIL EROSION SUB-ARCTIC OCEANIC TUNDRA COLD-DEMANDING COLEOPTERA
11 000		VERY STABLE SOILS WOODLAND TUNDRA WITH TREE BIRCH, JUNIPER AND CROWBERRY HEATH MIXED COLEOPTERA
11 500	ALLERØD	DECREASING SOIL EROSION OPEN TUNDRA VEGETATION WITH DWARF BIRCHES TEMPERATE AND COLD COLEOPTERA
12 000	OLDER DRYAS	INCREASED SOIL EROSION OPEN STEPPE TUNDRA VEGETATION HIGH GRASS-DRIER? TEMPERATE COLEOPTERA
12 300		OPEN STEPPE TUNDRA VEGETATION MORE STABLE SOILS TEMPERATE COLEOPTERA
12 500	BØLLING	MELTING OF DEAD ICE UNSTABLE SOILS SOLIFLUCTION EXTREMELY SPARSE VEGETATION

cooling trend was not as severe as it was in Britain or Scandinavia. This presumably reflects the greater distance from the influence of the oceanic polar front (section 2.3.1).

A more recent survey of late-glacial and early Holocene records from southwest Europe by Turner and Hannon (1988) confirms Watts's (1980b) general conclusions. Their comparison of sites from northern and north-western Spain and the Pyrenees shows that the late-glacial climatic amelior-ation was time-transgressive. For example, Turner and Hannon (1988) show that it began between 500 and 1,000 years later in the British Isles than in northwest Spain. Here amelioration began *c*. 14 kyr BP, and witnessed the onset of deciduous oak forest development which did not begin in the Pyrenees until *c*. 10 kyr BP. Similarly, the palaeoecological expression of the Younger Dryas cooling event is variable. In the Pyrenean sites it is repre-sented by only a small expansion of herbaceous plant communities with very little depression of the tree line. In the Pays Basque region, however, the early climatic amelioration was not strong and the scanty birch and pine forest was replaced by acid heathland during the Younger Dryas, with sub-sequent development of oak–hazel forest in the early Holocene. Moreover, Turner and Hannon (1988) question the evidence for separate warm periods during the late-glacial of southwest Europe, equivalent to the Bølling and Allerød. Only two sites in northwest Spain show evidence for two periods of birch/pine woodland expansion separated by a period characterised by open habitat taxa. Although there is no firm dating control, it seems unlikely that this intervening period is chronologically equivalent to the Younger Dryas, since it is clear that climatic change was time-transgressive.

According to Khotinsky (1984), who has summarised the post-glacial vegetation history of the USSR, there were considerable variations in the late-glacial flora of the European USSR, and in Siberia. Three cold periods have been delimited, approximately equivalent to the Oldest, Older and Younger Dryas of Fig. 2.2, with warmer periods equivalent to the Bølling and Allerød in between. The colder periods were characterised by cold steppe and/or tundra communities, while the intervening warmer periods witnessed woodland expansion. At Polovetsko-Kupanskoye mire, 150 km north of Moscow, for example, the Allerød period was dominated by spruce woodland, prior to the Younger Dryas period when open birch woodlands with an *Artemisia* ground flora predominated. The later change from the Younger Dryas to the Holocene is dated at 10.3 kyr BP, after which the major vegetation zones of tundra, forest and steppe developed in northern Eurasia.

In North America, apart from the work of Mott *et al*. (1986) described in section 2.3.1, there is no convincing palaeoecological expression of climatic oscillations similar to those of maritime Europe during the late glacial. Peteet (1987b), however, has suggested that the palaeoecological evidence for this period in the northeast USA should be re-examined since there is a clear possibility that the decrease in hardwoods between 10 and 11 kyr BP which were accompanied by an increase in many coniferous species, may have been a response to enhanced seasonality rather than simply the onset of colder winter temperatures. Using data on present-day boundary conditions in the North Atlantic, orbital values, ice conditions and estimated sea-surface temperatures for 11 kyr BP, Peteet has suggested that cooling effects were greater in coastal areas and that summer temperature increases of between 4 and 10 °C were experienced in more continental areas. This would explain, in agreement with Watts (1980, section 2.3.1) why the evidence for the Younger Dryas cooling event is more pronounced in maritime Europe and the Canadian maritime provinces. Peteet also suggests that the enhanced seasonality may account for the lack of modern analogues, i.e. modern plant assemblages similar to those of the late-glacial period.

In the southern hemisphere, palaeoenvironmental data are considerably scarcer than in the northern hemisphere, and consequently it is even more difficult to reach any general conclusions. As stated in section 2.3.1, there is evidence from Antarctic ice cores for a two-stage transition from the last glacial maximum to the Holocene. There is, however, very little palaeoecological evidence to suggest that such an oscillation was manifested in the plant and animal assemblages of adjacent land masses. This may be due to the reduced intensity of the oscillation (as indicated by the ice-core data, section 2.3.1) and/or a consequence of the location of terrestrial areas far distant from the polar region.

In their survey of the evidence for this period from the southern hemisphere, Rind *et al.* (1986) have shown that there is some limited evidence from glacial deposits to indicate glacial activity during this period in Brazil, Peru, New Zealand and South Georgia, but there is convincing palaeoecological data from only a few sites. In Chile, Heusser (1984) has presented evidence from Alerce and Taiquemó for a cooler and wetter period between 11 and 10 kyr BP, though even this is not confirmed by coleopteran analysis of a nearby site at Caunahue (Ashworth and Hoganson 1984). Butzer (1984) has also provided geomorphological evidence from South Africa for a late-glacial oscillation at about this time, but as with the Chilean data, it is not overwhelmingly convincing. As in most of North America, the majority of palaeobotanical evidence for the southern hemisphere suggests a gradual successional development of vegetation communities in response to a general warming trend as the last glacial period drew to a close.

2.3.3 FAUNAL CHANGES DURING THE LATE-GLACIAL PERIOD

Much of the foregoing discussion has focused on evidence from fossil pollen and fossil coleopteran assemblages which indicate that the period between *c.* 15 and 10 kyr BP was one of rapid ecological change. It was also a period that witnessed major changes in vertebrate faunas. In relation to the British Isles, for example, Sutcliffe (1985) states; 'But the faunal changes of the British Isles, especially those which occurred towards the end of the Pleistocene (by which time most familiar present-day species of mammals had already evolved), are unsurpassed in their contrast.' Although best documented in Europe and North America, similar changes were occurring in other parts of the world.

Table 2.4 provides a summary of the dominant fossil mammal species present in the British Isles during the middle and later Quaternary, taking into account the stratigraphic revisions necessitated by the recently discovered site at Marsworth (C P Green *et al.* 1984; section 1.3.2 and Table 1.5). Although Table 2.4 presents only a fraction of the available evidence (see Sutcliffe 1985 and Stuart 1982 for more detail), it shows that tremendous changes occurred in the distribution of mammals during this period of *c.* 1 Myr. During the last interglacial in Britain (Ipswichian, *sensuo stricto*), for example, hippopotamus roamed the area of what is now central London, accompanied by cave lions, straight-tusked elephant, narrow-nosed rhinoceros, as well as wild boar, bison and giant ox. Thus, the interglacial mammal faunas, as evidenced by fossils from the earlier Hoxnian and Cromerian interglacials as well as the Ipswichian, were very different to those of the current interglacial period. The optimum phase of the Ipswichian, was probably warmer than today, since many deposits of this period (reviewed in Mannion 1986b) contain fruits of water-chestnut (*Trapa natans*) which is a thermophilous aquatic that today reaches its northerly distribution in central France. These warmer, possibly more continental conditions, and the presence of extensive mixed oak forest favoured the spread of species such as hippopotamus up to an altitude of 400 m in the Yorkshire Moors (Sutcliffe 1985). Sometime during the following glacial period of the Devensian, the hippopotamus and straight-tusked elephant disappeared from the British Isles, never to return.

The advent of the Devensian ice, which reached its maximum extension approximately 18 kyr BP, brought great changes in the herbivorous mammalian fauna. Collared lemmings, reindeer and musk ox, for example, along with woolly mammoth and woolly rhinoceros occupied the tundra zone to the south of the ice sheet. The carnivorous species, however, remained relatively unaffected, predating on cold-tolerant herbivores instead of temperate

Table 2.4. Typical mammalian faunas of middle and upper Quaternary desposits in the UK. (Based on Sutcliffe 1985.)

	Stage	Typical mammal fauna	Approximate age (Years BP)
HOLOCENE	FLANDRIAN	European elk, giant ox, red deer, wild boar, wolf, beaver.	
			10,000
UPPER QUATERNARY	DEVENSIAN	Lemming, spotted hyaena, cave lion, brown bear, woolly mammoth, horse, woolly rhinoceros, red deer, reindeer, bison, musk ox.	
			120,000
	IPSWICHIAN	Hippopotamus, straight-tusked elephant, spotted hyaena, narrow-nosed rhinoceros, fallow deer.	
			130,000
MIDDLE QUATERNARY / WOLSTONIAN COMPLEX	MARSWORTH* LOWER CHANNEL	Brown bear, mammoth, horse, extinct horse (*Equus hydruntinus*) a small wolf, a large lion, northern vole.	170,000
		Vole, lemming, ground squirrel, cave lion, brown bear, mammoth, straight-tusked elephant, horse, Merck's narrow-nosed and woolly rhinoceros, red deer, giant ox, bison.	
	HOXNIAN	Lemming, horse, red deer, straight tusked elephant, Merck's and narrow-nosed rhinoceros, fallow deer.	3-400,000?

* From Green *et al.,* (1984)

species. However, the closing phase of the Devensian witnessed further considerable changes in mammalian faunas, notably the extinction of many large species. According to Saunders (1987), mammoth, horse, woolly rhinoceros and reindeer all occur in Devensian deposits between 26 and 18 kyr, when Arctic tundra was prevalent. Until recently, it was generally considered that of these species, mammoth did not survive into the late Devensian. Coope and Lister (1987) have now reported the presence of a mammoth skeleton at Condover, near Shrewsbury, which is radiocarbon dated to *c.* 12.8 kyr BP, some 5 kyr younger than previous finds. This suggests that the advent of full-glacial conditions did not instigate the final extinction of this species as had been thought. Nevertheless, by the opening of the Flandrian, 10 kyr BP, many of these large mammals, including the woolly rhinoceros, woolly mammoth, bison, cave lion and spotted hyaena had disappeared from the British landscape and even the giant deer, so prolific in deposits of late-glacial age in Ireland, is last recorded prior to the Younger Dryas cold period.

Clearly these extinctions caused a significant alteration in the mammalian faunas (especially megafaunas, whose body weight exceeded 44 kg) in the British Isles. Similar changes occurred in many other parts of the world at the same time, and some of the most notable extinctions are given in Table 2.5. Kurtén and Anderson (1980) present evidence for the extinctions of thirty-five megafaunal species by the close of the last ice age (Wisconsin) in North America *c.* 10 kyr BP. Dates from Rancho La Brea, Los Angeles (Marcus and Berger 1984), one of the most important bone-bearing sites in North America, suggest that extinction occurred *c.* 11 kyr BP over a relatively short time-span. In South America there is evidence for the extinction of forty-six genera at about this time, including *Glyptodon*, a mastodon relative of the armadillo. Extinctions also occurred in Australia in the period 26–15 kyr BP (Horton 1984). Losses in northern Eurasia and Africa were not quite so severe, but nevertheless significant.

Marshall (1984) has summarised the dates for extinctions; most fall in the

Area / Country	Species
North America	Shasta ground sloth, Jefferson's ground sloth, sabre toothed cats, scimitar cat, giant beaver, North American camel, mastodont and mammoth Total = 33 genera % extinct = 73.3
South America	*Glyptodon* (a relative of the armadillo), a giant ground sloth, a sabre tooth cat, various horses, a giant capybara Total = 46 genera % extinct = 79.6
Australia	Various Protemnodons (wallabies), Procoptodons (large kangaroos), various *Macropus spp.* (kangaroos), *Megalania* (a large lizard), *Thylacoleo* (a marsupial lion) Total = 19 genera % extinct = 86.4
Northern Eurasia	Woolly rhinoceros, woolly mammoth, straight-tusked elephant, giant deer, bison, hippopotamus, musk ox Total = 17 geneva % extinct = ? but low
Africa	*Hipparion*, a large true horse; a species of elephant, giant deer, camel and three bovids Total = 7 genera % extinct = 14.3

Table 2.5. The chief mammalian extinctions that occurred during the later part of the upper Quaternary in various parts of the world. (Based on Martin 1984.)

range 12–8 kyr BP and there is currently much speculation as to the cause (Martin and Klein 1984). Was climatic change or human activity the underlying factor, or posssibly a combination of both? There is clear evidence that humans did hunt some of these large animals. In Britain, for example, barbed bone points have been found in association with a skeleton of the elk *Alces alces* at High Furlong near Blackpool (Hallam *et al.* 1973), which is dated at 11–12 kyr BP. Martin (1973, 1984) has suggested that people were responsible for most of these extinctions, at least in North America. His view is based on the fact that such animals had survived earlier cold periods, including actual ice ages, that many of the extinctions coincide with the arrival of humans in North America (the Clovis culture); that areas such as Madagascar and New Zealand witnessed extinctions as humans arrived or some time after; that a megafauna similar to that of the late Quaternary survived in Africa. The question of when humans first arrived in the Americas is as much a focus of controversy as the extinction question. Dillehay and Collins (1988) have presented evidence for human presence at Monte Verde, Chile *c.* 33 kyr BP. Even if this is debatable, since it predates other sites by *c.* 20 kyr there is evidence for human presence at Taima-Taima in Venezuela (summarised in Gruhn and Bryan 1984) associated with a mastodon kill, at *c.* 13 kyr BP, some 1000 years before the major extinction period. Of course this need not imply the absence of a relationship between human populations and animal extinctions, but the presence of humans considerably prior to extinctions weakens the case for cause and effect.

A similar debate exists in relation to the extinction of the Australian megafauna. Horton (1984), for example, has suggested that humans, present in Australia for at least 40 kyr, did not play a major role in extinction, but rather that enhanced aridity caused the demise of woodland habitats to which most of the megafaunal species were adapted. In Europe, the Younger Dryas cold event (section 2.3.1) may have been responsible for the extinction of at least some species. The giant deer, for example, disappeared from Ireland prior to a cold stage equivalent to the Younger Dryas, and some 2 kyr before human colonisation of the island. Although this cold stage was not widely registered in North America (section 2.3.2), the relatively rapid climatic and ecological changes that occurred may well have contributed to the demise of many faunal species. Possibly, both human populations and climatic change were instrumental in affecting the faunal elements of dynamic ecological systems.

2.4 THE EARLY POST-GLACIAL PERIOD. (*c.* 10–5 KYR BP)

By 10 kyr BP temperatures were once again ameliorating in the Northern Hemisphere after the short-lived cold period of the Younger Dryas, and ushered in the mesocratic phase of the interglacial cycle (Fig. 2.1). In northwest Europe this phase, which witnessed extensive forest cover, lasted until approximately 5 kyr BP. New vegetation patterns became established in both the Northern and Southern hemispheres which experienced the immigration and expansion of various taxa from refugia.

This period marks the opening of the Holocene stage (Flandrian in Britain), which is equivalent to oxygen isotope stage 1 in the ocean-core record (Fig. 1.2). As in the preceding protocratic phase, there were considerable regional variations in the response of flora and fauna to climatic change. There is also considerable debate as to the role of humans in environmental change during this period (as will be discussed in Ch. 3).

2.4.1 CLIMATIC CHANGE DURING THE EARLY POST-GLACIAL PERIOD. (c. 10–5 KYR BP).

As Fig. 2.4 shows, the position of the oceanic polar front was once again in a more northerly location. This northward movement brought an abrupt end to the Younger Dryas cold stage (section 2.3) and is registered as Termination IB in cores from the northeast Atlantic (Duplessy *et al*. 1981; section 2.2.1). The abruptness of this event was also registered in coleopteran assemblages in Britain. Figure 2.2 shows that by *c*. 9.8 kyr BP annual temperatures similar to those at present had been attained. Atkinson *et al*. (1987) have suggested that temperatures during this period were increasing by *c*. 1.7 °C per century, not as rapidly as in the early part of the protocratic phase (section 2.3.1), but of sufficient magnitude to promote considerable environmental change.

Proxy climatic data, notably ^{18}O concentrations from polar ice cores, also reflect changing temperatures. At Camp Century in Greenland, for example, ^{18}O concentrations increase at *c*. 10.3 kyr BP, and rise rapidly thereafter until *c*. 9.8 kyr BP, remaining more or less constant for the remainder of the Holocene (Dansgaard *et al*. 1984). Antarctic ice cores, however, do not show quite the same trends (section 2.3.1) and the warming trend is considered by Jouzel *et al*. (1987) to have occurred between 11.6 and 10.2 kyr BP, approximately 1 kyr before that in the Arctic ice. Until more accurate dating is available, it is not possible to reconcile the Arctic and Antarctic ice records, if such is indeed warranted since the two events may be related and metachronous rather than unrelated and/or synchronous. In terms of overall patterns of climatic change, however, there is clearly a high degree of concurrence between North Atlantic ocean cores, Arctic ice cores and

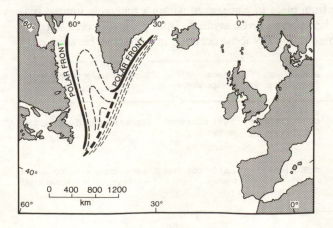

Fig. 2.4. Changes in the position of the oceanic polar front during the early Holocene. (Based on Ruddiman and McIntryre 1981.)

coleopteran evidence, which adds to their credibility as accurate records of climatic change. Further evidence is needed from the southern hemisphere before more positive conclusions can be reached concerning the nature, rate and timing of climatic change.

In general, the opening of the Holocene was characterised by climatic amelioration. But once begun, did climates stabilise, and if so, have they remained more or less consistent since *c.* 10 kyr BP to the present? The answer, based on evidence from a wide variety of palaeoenvironmental indicators, must be no. It is, however, virtually impossible to generalise about Holocene climatic trends, not least because so much of the evidence is derived from palaeobotanical investigations and there are many arguments for and against the use of plant remains as proxy climatic indicators. Suffice it to say that while plants and vegetation communities are determined to a large extent by macroclimatic parameters, and thus fossil floras can be used as some form of palaeoclimatic indicators, most plants will survive under a relatively wide range of environmental conditions. Consequently, fossil plant assemblages can only be used in a general way to reconstruct past climatic regimes in terms of temperature and precipitation, but they cannot be used to reconstruct, for example, precise palaeotemperature regimes, as Atkinson *et al.* (1987) have demonstrated for fossil coleopteran assemblages. These comments of course relate to the Holocene in general, but are just as apposite to the early Holocene which is the subject of this section.

In relation to the mesocratic phase of the present interglacial, *c.* 10–5 kyr BP, there is evidence from Arctic ice cores for maximum temperatures being obtained by *c.* 5 kyr BP. So-called 'climatic optimum' (mainly temperature) conditions were thus achieved by the end of the mesocratic phase. As Goudie (1983) has documented, the term 'climatic optimum' has historic associations with early Quaternary scientists in Europe, and is a reflection of conditions that produced what Clements in 1916 (section 1.1.1) described as the 'climatic climax' in Britain (and large areas of temperate northwest Europe). The changing climate of the early Holocene did not always, as is apparent from palaeoenvironmental studies in semi-arid and tropical areas, bring about the most advantageous conditions for ecosystem development which is implied in the term 'climatic optimum'. As a result, the term 'hypsithermal' is frequently, though not always consistently, used to denote the period *c.* 9 kyr BP to 2.55 kyr BP, which includes the 5 kyr of the early Holocene as here defined.

Precisely when optimum temperatures were reached during this period varies considerably from place to place, even within a relatively limited spatial context. At the hemisphere level, evidence from polar ice cores suggests that the warmest phase of the Holocene occurred in Antarctica between *c.* 11

Table 2.6. Estimated temperature and precipitation changes during the Holocene in the Midwest of the USA. (Based on Webb 1985.)	Approximate Date K yrs B.P.	Annual Precipitation	Annual Temperatures	Implications for vegetation
	9	ca. 10 - 20% more than at 6K yrs.	0.5° C lower than present	Prairie / forest border moves east
	6	ca. 20% less than present	1.5° C higher than present	Prairie / forest border moves west Northward retreat of Boreal forest

and 8 kyr BP, and in the Arctic between *c*. 5 and 4 kyr BP (summarised in Bradley 1985). In Europe, Birks (1986) has suggested that seasonality was more intense during the early Holocene, especially in relation to insolation, which was approximately 7 per cent greater than it is today; and Godwin (1975) has suggested that during the thermal maximum (*c*. 5 kyr BP) mean summer temperatures were approximately 2 °C warmer than today. However, more precise palaeoclimatic reconstructions are elusive and it is virtually impossible to determine which changes in the palaeobotanical record are due directly to climatic changes and which are successional responses (see Mannion 1986c for a discussion on vegetation succession) instigated initially by climatic change, and which then promote further environmental change that is not a direct result of climatic change.

It is generally believed that in Britain a more continental climate persisted prior to 7 kyr BP, with slightly less rainfall than at present and hot though short summers and slightly colder winters. After 7 kyr BP a more oceanic climate developed, possibly because of the severing of Britain from the continent as post-glacial sea-levels rose, bringing ameliorated winter temperatures, longer spring and autumn seasons and increased rainfall.

Climatic reconstructions of the early Holocene in North America have also been undertaken by Webb (1985), who has used mathematical transfer functions for reconstructing past climate from palynological data. Such an approach is based on the premiss that regional climate is the major factor in determining the nature of vegetation communities. Howe and Webb (1983) have confirmed this by establishing the relationship between modern vegetation assemblages in North America and broad-scale climatic patterns. They argue that if such an association occurs spatially, then it should also occur on a temporal basis. As Birks (1986) points out, this is a simplistic approach since there are many other factors to take into account, such as soil type and rates of migration. Nevertheless, using such an approach, Webb (1985) has estimated palaeotemperatures and palaeoprecipitation rates for the Midwest of the USA and his results are summarised in Table 2.6. In particular, he

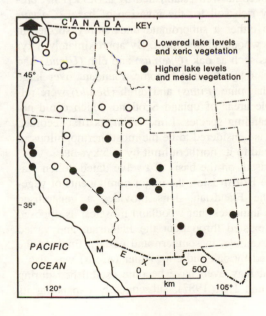

Fig. 2.5. Lake level changes as indicators of early Holocene (11.5–7 kyr BP) climatic characteristics of western North America. (Based on Davis and Sellers 1987.)

attributes changes in the position of the prairie/forest border to changing precipitation rates, and the northward extension of boreal forest in Canada as a consequence of temperature increase. Webb has also suggested that the compilation of similar data for other areas of the earth's surface should considerably enhance the understanding of Holocene climatic change, and may be valuable for producing predictive models of future climatic change.

In western North America, the early Holocene was characterised by contrasting palaeoclimates from region to region. Davis and Sellers (1987) have summarised the results of palynological and lake level studies which are given in Fig. 2.5. This shows that during the period 11.5–7 kyr BP the Pacific northwest experienced aridity as lake levels declined and xeric vegetation communities developed. In contrast, the American southwest experienced a pluvial phase with elevated lake levels and an expansion of mesic vegetation communities, except in the western Sierra Nevada, which also experienced an arid phase. Such contrasts reflect changing atmospheric circulation patterns which occurred as deglaciation proceeded and temperatures ameliorated.

2.4.2 REGIONAL VARIATIONS IN ENVIRONMENTAL CHANGE DURING THE EARLY HOLOCENE

This is a topic of immense proportions, which has been partially reviewed by Roberts (1989), and the examples given below should serve to illustrate the magnitude of environmental change that occurred during this *c.* 5 kyr period.

In Britain the opening of the Flandrian (Holocene) witnessed the invasion of tundra vegetation, dominated by grasses, sedges and dwarf shrubs, by pioneer tree species tolerant of relatively poor soils and little shade. The first of these invaders was the tree birch (*Betula pubescens* and *B. pendula*), which was rapidly followed by pine (*Pinus sylvestris*) under relatively dry continental conditions that were at least as warm as today (section 2.4.1). These species appear to have become well established by *c.* 9.5 kyr BP, presumably creating a sufficiently rich soil for the invasion of hazel (*Corylus avellana*) that may have been either a subordinate understorey species in birch and pine woodland, or a woodland dominant. By approximately 8 kyr BP, more thermophilous species such as oak (*Quercus*) and elm (*Ulmus*) had become established, and by *c.* 6 kyr BP had become abundant over large parts of the British Isles, so that pine (*Pinus*) and birch (*Betula*) were relegated to the more inhospitable areas of upland Scotland which could not support the more warmth-demanding species. Lime (*Tilia*) is first recorded in Britain by *c.* 7.5 kyr BP and is considered to be the most thermophilous of the postglacial invaders. It spread to its northern limit by *c.* 5 kyr BP.

Bennett (1988) has summarised, on the basis of twelve dated pollen diagrams from various parts of the British Isles, the major components of vegetation communities during the Flandrian. This provides a generalised representation but nevertheless indicates that woodland mosaics, as opposed to single species woodlands, existed throughout the Flandrian and varied spatially and temporally. For example, in southern and eastern England the dominant lime was accompanied by oak and elm. Alder (*Alnus*) was also a relatively common species that may even have become established during the late-glacial period (Bush and Hall 1987), subsequently expanding its population to become locally abundant by *c.* 7 kyr BP, especially in wetter environments. Ash (*Fraxinus*) was one of the later mesocratic species to expand, and populations increased between 6 and 5 kyr BP. It may have occupied sites that were too damp for oak and elm, but not wet enough for alder.

It is also apparent, by comparing pollen diagrams from various parts of the British Isles, that not everywhere became forest-covered during the early Flandrian. Godwin (1975) estimates that there was a 60 per cent forest cover by *c.* 5 kyr BP, and Rackham (1986) has implied that areas such as northern Scotland and the Outer Hebrides lay beyond the limits for continuous forest cover. It is difficult to refute or confirm either of these statements. However, in the Outer Hebrides, pollen diagrams (Mannion and Moseley 1990) show only low frequencies of arboreal pollen which may be attributed to long-distance transport from the mainland; on the other hand there are abundant remains of trees preserved beneath the peat deposits of these islands (Wilkins 1984). Thus the palaeobotanical evidence is conflicting, and as Mannion and Moseley (1990) have suggested, low arboreal pollen concentrations may be a result of exposure to Atlantic winds that could have impaired flowering capacity and hence pollen productivity, rather than due to the absence of trees.

Until recently, it has been generally considered that grasslands in Britain were the result of anthropogenic activity, having their origins in the advent of neolithic agricultural practices that developed after *c.* 5 kyr BP (see Ch. 3). Work in the Yorkshire Dales (Bush and Flenley 1987), however, has shown that grassland communities originating in the late-glacial period persisted well into the Flandrian and may have been the progenitors of modern grasslands in this area today. Grasslands probably also existed in river valleys and coastal areas that were less suitable for trees, and in some areas especially in upland regions, blanket and ombrogenous bogs developed in response to the more oceanic climate that developed after *c.* 7 kyr BP.

Faunal changes accompanied the floral changes. Following the extinctions that occurred in the late-glacial period (section 2.3.3), the development of a forest cover probably encouraged an increase in herbivores, notably aurochs, elk, red deer and roe deer. The woodmouse, bank vole and field vole also arrived in Britain in the early Flandrian, along with the hedgehog, badger, wild boar, beaver, mole, wolf and marten. Of particular interest is the record of the European pond tortoise (*Emys orbicularis*), since the northern limit of this species is controlled by temperature and cloudiness during the summer. According to Stuart (1982) a mean July temperature of 17–18 °C, with abundant sunshine and few damp, cloudy or rainy days are necessary for reproductive success. Its presence in Flandrian deposits indicates that during the hypsithermal, summer temperatures were warmer than today by 1–3 °C. It does not occur after 5 kyr BP in Britain, though is recorded much later in Denmark and southern Sweden, reflecting the more continental nature of the climate on the European mainland.

Changes of a similar magnitude to those occurring in Britain were also characteristic of the mesocratic phase elsewhere. In northwest Europe (see summary in Birks 1986), the trends were similar to those of Britain. In the USSR, Khotinsky (1984) states that the opening of the Holocene witnessed the rapid establishment of zonal vegetation types with tundra in the north, steppe in the south and forests dominated by birch, pine, spruce and larch in between. For example, in the northeast USSR birch expanded some 100–200 km north into what is now a tundra zone, and in the forest zone (central USSR) spruce was an important component of the vegetation of Siberia where larch is today the dominant. In general, the vegetation of the forest zone became more complex during the period 9–5.5 kyr BP, with spruce–larch associations being dominant in the northern taiga, spruce–fir in the south and spruce–cedar in between.

Table 2.7, compiled by Davis (1984), summarises the major vegetation changes that occurred during the Holocene in the eastern USA. As in the British Isles, forest mosaics of varying character developed in response to climatic amelioration, especially after 12 kyr BP, and as a consequence of the varying migration rates of individual species. In particular, there was an expansion northwards of boreal and temperate taxa during the early Holocene. In southern New England, for example, by 12.5 kyr BP tundra vegetation had been replaced by open spruce woodland and this in turn was replaced by mixed temperate forest which persisted, with varying composition, until *c.* 5 kyr BP. Later Holocene changes will be discussed in section 2.5.2.

There is also evidence from tropical rainforest regions for Holocene environmental change, much of which has been recently summarised by Walker and Chen (1987). Palaeoenvironmental research in these areas is of particular interest as it questions the hitherto generally accepted notion that rainforest is floristically diverse because it has been favoured by a long period of stability in so-called but as yet unidentified 'refugium' areas that facilitated speciation. In fact, most recent work suggests that quite the opposite occurred (see discussion in Colinvaux 1989). Walker and Chen (1987) adopt the date of 10 kyr BP for their discussion, but they also point out the lack of synchroneity that exists between records from various sites, and that the range lies between 16 kyr BP and 7 kyr BP. Prior to 10 kyr BP, however, there is considerable evidence to show that rainforests were much reduced in extent, despite the fact that they may have expanded onto emergent continental shelf areas when sea-levels were much lower (section 1.3.4). In New Guinea, for example, rainforests occupied only 75 per cent of their present area and only 60 per cent of their altitudinal range at the last glacial maximum (*c.* 18 kyr BP). The variations may have been much greater elsewhere, as indeed Hamilton (1982) has suggested for African lowland rainforests.

Table 2.7. The major changes in forest composition in the eastern USA as inferred from Holocene pollen stratigraphy. (From Davis 1984.)

Age Kyr BP	Northern New England	Southern New England	Central Appalachians	Coastal Plain	Central Florida
2	Expansion of boreal elements		Oak, hickory, sweetgum, pine		Sand-pine scrub
	Deciduous forest Hemlock decline		Hemlock decline	Pine, oak, hickory	
5					
	Expansion of temperate elements		Oak, hickory sweetgum, chestnut	Oak, sweetgum, hickory, pine	
	Mixed forest				
10		Mixed forest			Oak scrub
	Tundra	Open spruce Woodland	Oak, hornbeam, spruce	Mesic deciduous forest	
12.5		Tundra	Spruce forest with pine and deciduous trees		
15	Ice			Pine and spruce forest	
		Ice	Jack pine, spruce		?

There is also evidence from northeastern Australia, New Guinea, Africa and South America for considerable vegetation change at *c*. 10 kyr BP. Six sites in northeast Australia have been palynologically investigated, and Walker and Chen (1987) show that all experienced the replacement of grassy sclerophyllous woodland dominated by Eucalyptus between *c*. 10 and 7 kyr BP by rainforest, and that the replacement occurred rapidly in 1–1.5 kyr. Similarly, Livingstone (1982) has demonstrated the replacement of drier savannas by rainforest in parts of Africa, a process that was initiated after the more arid phase of the last glacial maximum. (That some parts of the tropics were more arid during glacial times is confirmed by ocean core evidence, see section 1.2.2.) Colinvaux (1987, 1989) has also discussed the evidence for Holocene environmental change in Amazonia and although few sites have been investigated, there is virtually no evidence to support the refugium hypothesis. Colinvaux has suggested that geomorphic processes, notably changes in hydrological regimes which bring about flooding, changes in river morphology and catchment dissection, along with naturally occurring fires, may have been responsible, at least in part, for promoting species diversity. This requires further substantiation, but Colinvaux's synthesis, like that of Walker and Chen (1987), illustrates the dynamic nature of these tropical regions and highlights the fact that the rainforests of today are the products, for whatever reason, of a changing Holocene, and not the manifestation of stable environmental conditions that are supposed to have persisted over long periods of 1 Myr or more.

2.5 THE LATER POST-GLACIAL PERIOD (5 KYR BP TO PRESENT)

In northwest Europe, palaeoenvironmental evidence indicates that the oligocratic phase of the interglacial cycle (Fig. 2.1) had been initiated by *c*. 5 kyr BP. In particular, Huntley and Birks' (1983) isopollen maps for northwest Europe show that the replacement of deciduous forest by such vegetation types as heathlands, moorlands and peatlands had begun by this time. The question of climatic change, however, is more vexed since there is evidence for climatic deterioration from various areas anytime between 5 and 2.5 kyr BP. Moreover, although these vegetation changes signify the occurrence of environmental change, the interglacial cycle as proposed by Iversen (1958; section 2.2) does not always need climatic change as its primary driving force. This is particularly so for the oligocratic phase, since Iversen proposed that soil deterioration, due to progressive leaching causing nutrient impoverishment, could initiate retrogressive vegetational development. Furthermore, unravelling the palaeoenvironmental record for this period is made more complex by the fact that there is unequivocal evidence for human activity. Much the same can be said of the environmental changes occurring elsewhere in the world during this period and this section will, as far as possible, consider those changes that can be attributed to natural agencies.

2.5.1 Climatic Change During the Later Post-glacial Period (5 kyr bp to Present)

Although there is abundant evidence for climatic change during this period, it is rather piecemeal and difficult to synthesise: some of the more recent trends have already been referred to in section 1.2.3.

Bradley (1985) has summarised the ^{18}O data from polar ice cores which have been used to estimate temperature changes. For example, following the hypsithermal maximum recorded in Arctic ice cores, there is evidence for a temperature decline of *c*. 1 °C per century during the period 5–3 kyr BP, with an ensuing slightly warmer period between 2.5 and 1 kyr BP. Evidence from Antarctic ice cores, however, suggests that temperatures declined after *c*. 5.5 kyr BP, with minimum temperatures occurring between 3.5 and 1.5 kyr BP. Bradley has also discussed the discrepancies that exist between ice cores from the Arctic for the last thousand years, and suggests that, since the ^{18}O record is based on snowfall events which vary seasonally in terms of duration and frequency, the climatic signal afforded by ^{18}O values is likely to be a result of these variables as well as changes in mean annual temperature. These comments reinforce the view, given in section 1.2.2, that ^{18}O records are not necessarily reliable surrogates for palaeotemperature regimes. Nevertheless, some trends are apparent from the Arctic cores which can be substantiated by independent evidence, namely warm periods centered on 1250 and the sixteenth century, and decreased snowfall during the seventeenth to nineteenth centuries.

Evidence for climatic change during the late Holocene from sources other than the polar ice caps is just as diverse. In Britain, for example, there is little palaeoenvironmental evidence to show that any climatic deterioration occurred prior to *c*. 2.8 kyr BP. After this date there was a general trend towards more oceanic conditions, with increased rainfall and decreased temperatures, though this was probably time transgressive, beginning first in western Ireland and northwest Scotland and then spreading into England and Wales. In northwest Europe, however, there is evidence for climatic deterioration beginning at *c*. 5 kyr BP, following a period when conditions were generally thought to be more xerothermic, i.e. more continental, with less rainfall and a more pronounced annual range of temperature. Berglund (1983) has synthesised much of the available palaeoecological data for Scandinavia and eastern Greenland, and concludes that climatic deterioration began between 4 and 5 kyr BP. These climatic changes caused accelerated peat formation and higher lake levels. The temperature trends suggested in this synthesis are in general agreement with Kutzbach and Guetter's (1986) atmospheric modelling prediction for declining temperatures in the northern hemisphere after *c*. 6 kyr BP, while the British evidence is not. This may possibly be due to the dampening effect of maritime influences on the British Isles which probably intensified as sea-levels rose following deglaciation and severed Britain from Europe.

Kullman (1988), however, has examined changes in the position of the forest–Alpine ecotone in the Scandes Mountains of central Sweden. He found pollen-analytical evidence for climatic deterioration at *c*. 5.3, 3.3 and 0.8–0.3 kyr BP. The first substantiates Berglund's (1983) conclusion, for which there is also widespread evidence elsewhere in Europe, including the

USSR (Khotinsky 1984); the second date is more akin to the British evidence and according to Kullman (1988) it marks a distinct thermal decline that was of sufficient magnitude to be 'the largest and/or most lasting during the entire Holocene', and which caused the displacement downslope of the closed pine forest belt in the Scandes Mountains by at least 45m. The final dates relate to the 'Little Ice Age', when the pine forest retreated a further 30m downslope.

Evidence for climatic change during the last 2 kyr in the northern hemisphere has also been compiled by Williams and Wigley (1983). Using proxy-climatic data derived from glacier, tree-line, tree-ring, pollen and ice-core variations, they have shown that three specific episodes can be distinguished in what Kutzbach and Guetter's (1986) simulation model indicates to be a general cooling period. These are (a) a cold period between the eighth and tenth centuries, (b) a medieval warm period c. twelfth century and (c) the 'Little Ice Age' c. fifteenth to nineteenth centuries (see also section 1.2.3). This summary, however, must be tempered by the fact, as Williams and Wigley (1983) point out, that the data are generally consistent intra-regionally but are not always entirely consistent inter-regionally in relation to the timing of the minima and maxima of summer temperatures on which the study is based. They conclude that 'much of the data used in this study has [sic] been published only in the last few years, so a few years ago we might have come to entirely different conclusions, as we may a few years hence'. This statement is included here since it once again reflects the 'jigsaw puzzle' nature of the subject and thus reinforces the statement made in section 1.4 which relates to the necessity for continuous reappraisal of the evidence for environmental change.

Williams and Wigley's synthesis shows that the 'Little Ice Age' was a very significant period of climatic variability during the last 2 kyr, as is also suggested by Grove's (1988) synthesis. Further evidence for it has been documented by L G Thompson et al. (1986, 1987), who have shown that it was definitively recorded in the Quelecaya ice cap of Peru between 1490 and 1880. The ^{18}O records and other palaeoenvironmental data indicate that it began abruptly, ended even more abruptly, and was a period characterised by an enhanced atmospheric dust load. Initial sharp increases in precipitation at 1490 were followed by a decline in temperature by 1520, and the 1720–1860 period was apparently very dry. Grove (1988) has summarised much of the evidence for the 'Little Ice Age' from various parts of the world and although this is most abundant in the northern hemisphere, there is sufficient evidence from the southern hemisphere to suggest that it was a global event, though not always inter-regionally synchronous. Salinger (1976), has presented corroborating data from New Zealand, and Rull et al. (1987) have presented palynological data from the Venezuelan Andes showing that there was a 200m lowering of the vegetation belts between 700 and 380 years BP. The cause of this oscillation is, however, not apparent and it may be that, like the Younger Dryas (section 2.3.2), it is not due to changes in the earth's orbit as suggested by the Milankovitch hypothesis but possibly a response to increases in atmospheric particulate matter that influenced the receipt of insolation.

As stated in section 2.4.1, pollen analytical data have been used to reconstruct Holocene climates in North America (Webb 1985). Such data show that by 6 kyr BP (Table 2.6) temperatures had increased by between 1 and 2 °C in the Midwest, for example. A further study has been undertaken by

Forester *et al.* (1987), who, on the basis of fossil ostracodes and diatoms in Holocene sediments from Elk Lake, north-central Minnesota, have suggested the climatic changes summarised in Table 2.8. This study confirms Webb's (1985) conclusion for early Holocene temperature increases and reflects their persistence until at least 4 kyr BP. Forester *et al.* (1987) conclude that climatic change occurred in small steps, effecting the change from the prairie-like climate of interval 1 to the present-day climate, and was the result of zonal flow dominance prior to 7 kyr BP and its gradual replacement by seasonal zonal and meridional flow after 4 kyr BP, which is similar to present.

Evidence for climatic change in eastern North America during the last 2 kyr has also been presented by Gajewski (1988) using a similar approach to that of Webb (1985, see section 2.4.1). Gajewski has shown that the last 2 kyr have been characterised by a long-term cooling trend with minor fluctuations. These latter occur around 1.5 kyr BP, which was a warmer interval, and between 200 and 500 years ago which was a colder interval equivalent to the 'Little Ice Age' (section 1.2.3).

In the southern hemisphere, the colder temperatures indicated by ^{18}O values in Antarctic ice cores at *c.* 5.5 kyr BP appear to be confirmed by changes in tree lines and forest composition in parts of Australia. Markgraf *et al.* (1986), for example, attribute changes in forest composition in southwestern Tasmania to a decrease in temperature and a more or less pronounced decrease in precipitation at this time. Similarly, Dodson *et al.* (1986) have demonstrated the retreat of cool temperate rainforest and wet eucalyptus forest at *c.* 5 kyr BP from Barrington Tops in New South Wales, which they sugggest is due to reduced temperatures. A subsequent expansion of these vegetation types is dated in the pollen record to *c.* 1.5 kyr BP which, interestingly, ends a period of minimum temperatures in Antarctic ice (Barkov *et al.* 1977).

There is also evidence for a decline in temperatures between 3 and 3.5 kyr BP, at least in southeast Australia, which is in agreement with the Antarctic ice-core data. Martin (1986), for example, reports evidence for vegetation instability due to drought, frost and soil erosion in the Alpine zone of the Kosciusko National Park, New South Wales; and Dodson *et al.* (1986) have shown that shrubland and grassland communities declined as peat formation began at Barrington Tops, New South Wales. Both of these changes

---

Table 2.8. Characteristics of mid-Holocene climate in Northern Minnesota, USA. (Based on Forester *et al.* 1987.)

Approximate Date (K yrs B.P.)	Temperature characteristics	Precipitation characteristics
7.8 to 6.7	Mean-annual air temperature 1.5° C colder than present; long cold winters and cool, dry summers	70% of present precipitation, less than evaporation rates
6.7 to 5.78	Average mean-annual air temperatures similar to present mean of 3.7° C, warm summers persistent at temperatures greater than 20° C	85% of present precipitation, higher than evaporation rates
5.78 to 4.0	Average mean-annual air temperatures similar to present mean of 3.7° C, warm summers in discrete episodes	90% of present precipitation

are attributed to declining temperatures. Further information on climatic change in the southern hemisphere during the later Holocene is relatively thin, although the possibility of a 'Little Ice Age' cooling period has already been discussed.

In addition to the major climatic oscillations of the later Holocene which are considered above, there are also changes which have occurred in the last 200 years. These are related to fossil-fuel use and will be discussed in Chapter 5.

2.5.2 REGIONAL VARIATIONS IN ENVIRONMENTAL CHANGE DURING THE LATER HOLOCENE (*c.* 5 KYR BP TO PRESENT)

Just as it is difficult to unravel the record of climatic change during the later Holocene, it is equally difficult to distinguish environmental changes that were a response to natural rather than cultural agencies. The impact of human communities, already apparent during the early Holocene, intensified from *c.* 5 kyr BP throughout northwest Europe as will be examined in Chapters 3 and 4. Moreover, the impact of human communities may well have combined with climatic and edaphic changes to mould the landscape so that the pattern of environmental change is discernible but cause and effect are obscured.

Birks (1986) has suggested that the progressive leaching of brown earth soils of the mesocratic stage of the interglacial cycle played a significant role in initiating the oligocratic stage. The development of relatively nutrient-poor podzolised soils with mor humus provided a much less favourable environment for the maintenance of a mixed deciduous forest cover and may, if iron-pan formation occurred, have altered local hydrological cycles. There is evidence that such changes occurred during earlier interglacials (Andersen 1966), causing the replacement of forest with poorer vegetation communities such as heaths, without the stimulus of either climatic deterioration or human activity. Andersen (1978), among others, has also demonstrated that this may have been the case during the Holocene in eastern Denmark. Here, from *c.* 6 kyr BP, more open forests of oak, holly and birch replaced dense forests of elm, hazel and lime. Where hydrological cycles were locally altered by the impedance of drainage, especially in upland areas, blanket mires may have developed. The extensive blanket peat areas of Britain, which occur in areas above 300m OD, may have developed under similar conditions although there is much dispute as to individual origins. Birks (1975), for example, on the basis of radiocarbon-dated pine stumps, has shown that in parts of upland and northern Scotland peat initiation was the result of natural soil degradation. There is, however, a considerable body of evidence from other parts of Britain for an anthropogenic cause for peat formation (e.g. Moore 1975) or for one associated with climatic change. Similarly the post-6 kyr BP expansion of spruce in Scandinavia, which is still occurring today may have been a response to climatic change or a consequence of delayed migration. Its spread may also have been facilitated by human disturbance of the mesocratic forest. Since, however, it is a significant component of the oligocratic phase of earlier interglacials in northwest Europe and prefers podzolic soils, its spread during the later Holocene may well have been a response to soil deterioration and/or climatic deterioration.

Whatever the causes of these floristic changes, the later Holocene witnessed the opening up of the forest canopy, the development of widespread moorlands and heathlands and peat accumulation. However, perhaps the most enigmatic event that occurred throughout Europe at the opening of this oligocratic phase is that of the elm decline, which is radiocarbon dated to a few centuries before and after 5 kyr BP. Despite a wealth of information relating to this event, there is still considerable dispute as to its cause(s). The classic interpretation of events at and around the elm decline is that of Iversen (1941, 1944). His pollen analysis of Danish sites shows an initial decline in elm and ivy and a contemporaneous increase in ash. These changes Iversen interpreted as climatic since ivy, as well as holly and mistletoe, is particularly sensitive to winter temperatures. He concluded that an increase in continentality, with greater seasonal extremes of temperature, was responsible and this is in general agreement with other northwest European evidence for climatic deterioration at this time (section 2.5.1). Stratigraphically above (i.e. after) these changes Iversen (1941) also demonstrated that oak, lime, ash and elm underwent a further though temporary decline as birch, alder and hazel increased in association with charcoal remains. These changes he attributed to clearance or 'Landnam' phases due to human activity. Troels-Smith (1960), however, has questioned the climatic interpretation and has suggested that the earlier elm decline was also anthropogenic since elm, ivy and mistletoe may have been used as fodder plants, for which practice there are modern analogues. Troels-Smith was also one of the first researchers to suggest that Dutch elm disease may have played some part in this neolithic elm decline.

Reviewing the evidence for the elm decline in Britain Smith (1981) emphasises that there is nothing in the palaeobotanical record which necessitates a climatic interpretation. There is, for example, no evidence for a primary elm decline such as Iversen (1941) found in Denmark. Almost all pollen diagrams from the British Isles record an elm decline only in association with other changes that can be interpreted as representing anthropogenic interference in woodland ecosystems. These include the presence of cereal pollen and pollen of ruderal species such as ribwort plantain (*Plantago lanceolata*), the presence of charcoal, increases in grass and herb pollen and occasionally the presence of neolithic artefacts. Indeed, some of these features are characteristic of the Danish sites on which Iversen (1941) initially worked, and are related to his Landnam phases which he envisaged as a three-stage process. Stage one included a decline of the dominant arboreal taxa and an increase in grass and herb pollen as clearance was effected. Stage two was characterised by the presence of pollen of cereals, ribwort plantain and other ruderals, and was a period of farming, although increasing birch, sometimes alder and then hazel pollen suggested to Iversen that woodland succession and regeneration were also in progress and which culminated in stage three. How long such clearance phases lasted is debatable, but Iversen suggested that they were probably short-lived, possibly only 50 years or so (Iversen, 1956) since forest regeneration, while initially providing new shoots for animals, would relatively quickly form a closed canopy and early agriculturalists might then find it more appropriate to move to a new area and begin the process again.

Subsequent work by Troels-Smith (1956) on the Danish bog Amosen led to some modifications of Iversen's (1941, 1956) ideas. Here, Troels-Smith found evidence for farming practices at the level of Iversen's (1941) initial elm decline and below the Landnam phase. These included the presence of

cereal and broad-leaved plantain (*P. major*) pollen as well as pollen of ram-
sons such as wild garlic (*Allium* cf. *ursinum*), but no evidence of pasture.
The presence of species such as wild garlic is particularly interesting since it
is sensitive to trampling, and this led Troels-Smith to suggest that the elm
decline was caused by the stripping of elm leaves for use as a feed for
stalled rather than grazing animals. This impaired the flowering capacity and
thus pollen productivity of the elm population. Later, Troels-Smith (1960)
also suggested that species such as ivy may have been used for the same
purpose.

There is now, however, evidence for opening of the forest canopy, minor
clearance phases and cereal cultivation in some parts of Britain and Ireland
prior to the elm decline (Edwards and Hirons 1984). These findings imply
that there may not be an association between the first agricultural practices
and the elm decline since some arable farming at least clearly pre-dates it.
Since a climatic cause for the elm decline in the British Isles has also been
rejected, there is renewed debate as to the cause, especially in relation to the
possibility of Dutch elm disease. This has been prompted by observations on
the recent outbreak of Dutch elm disease that has caused the serious demise
of elm populations in Britain and parts of Europe (Rackham 1986) and by a
number of recent palaeoecological investigations. The disease results from
infection by *Ceratocystis ulmi*, a microscopic fungus that is transmitted by
two elm bark beetles, *Scolytus scolytus* and *S. multistriatus*. Girling and
Greig (1985) recorded, for the first time in palaeoentomological studies,
beetle cases of *S. scolytus* in a horizon some 10 cm below the elm decline,
from Flandrian deposits at Hampstead Heath, London. This of course is not
conclusive that elm disease was responsible for the neolithic elm decline,
since *S. scolytus* can exist independently of *C. ulmi*, but it is the first palaeoecological evidence to suggest even a vague association between the two.
Girling and Greig have postulated that elm populations may have been
weakened by disease prior to neolithic agriculture and that the subsequent
human impact hastened their decline.

Recent work by Perry and Moore (1987) has added further, though again
not conclusive, evidence that elm disease may have played a part in the
neolithic elm decline. They have examined the pollen assemblages from
humus profiles in Scords Wood in Kent where the recent elm decline began
in 1978 and which lost all adult elms in the following 5 years. The pollen
assemblages representing this period show changes that are very similar to
the changes that characterise the neolithic elm decline. Elm pollen itself declines from levels greater than 10 per cent to nil, while other tree and shrub
proportions are unaffected. Some other non-tree taxa, however, increase
either during or after the elm decline. These include wild garlic and black-
berry (*Rubus*) which presumably, as woodland components, increase their
flowering as the canopy is opened up. Other taxa, notably ribwort plantain
(*Plantago lanceolata*), daisies (*Bidens type*) and bellflower (*Campanula*),
that are not woodland components, also increase in frequency and which,
Perry and Moore suggest, is also due to the more open nature of the canopy
that facilitates better dispersal. Thus, this study provides a rather convincing
modern analogue and the fact that elm disease has a long history of presence
in Europe (Rackham 1980) must surely rank it as a prime candidate responsible for the neolithic elm decline, a conclusion that is strongly favoured by
Rackham (1986). Molloy and O'Connell (1987) have also presented a convincing argument for elm disease as the major cause of the neolithic elm

decline in western Ireland and, from further afield, Davis (1981) has suggested that the decline of the eastern hemlock (*Tsuga canadensis*) at 4.85 kyr BP in North America was also pathogen-related. This is further substantiated by Allison *et al.* (1986) who have found many similarities between events during this decline and those during the decline of the American chestnut (*Castanea dentata*) which was almost exterminated by a fungal pathogen in the early 1900s. The evidence presented by all these studies is, however, circumstantial and in no way conclusive. Research is clearly needed to elucidate further this most significant event in European prehistory. Nevertheless, whatever the prime cause of the elm decline, the period from *c.* 5 kyr BP witnessed significant environmental change in Europe, especially in terms of vegetation communities, with the overall reduction of forest cover and its replacement by more open habitats.

In North America (Table 2.7) the post-5 kyr BP period also saw considerable environmental changes, including the decline of eastern hemlock. Davis (1984), summarising the evidence for the eastern USA, shows that there was a trend, especially from 2 kyr BP, involving an expansion of boreal elements that indicates cooling. This is also suggested by Gajewski (section 2.5.1), and it is apparent from numerous studies of lacustrine sequences (summarised in Mannion 1987a, b, 1989a, b) that the later advent of European settlement had a considerable environmental impact. This will be discussed in Chapter 4. Palynological evidence from Canada for the last 2–3 kyr (Ritchie 1988) reflects a similar pattern to that of the USA. In the west, boreal forests extended further south at the same time as there was an increase in spruce (*Picea*) in the ecotone between the boreal and temperate forests of southern Quebec in the east. In the Ungava–Quebec region, the northern limits of spruce-dominated forest and shrub tundra moved southward and in the western interior the prairie zone was pushed south.

2.6 CONCLUSION

The foregoing sections illustrate the extent and diversity of environmental changes that have occurred in the last 10–12 kyr. The evidence presented, which is most abundant from the northern hemisphere, relies heavily on palaeoenvironmental data, especially that from the oceans, ice cores and pollen analysis of limnic sediments and peats. Improvements in methods of analysis and interpretation should lead to a better and more comprehensive understanding of the causes, consequences and rates of environmental change and ultimately to predictive models.

The transition from full glacial conditions to the present interglacial was indeed complex as ecological systems adjusted to ameliorated climates. The final phase of deglaciation, *c.* 15–10 kyr BP, witnessed rapid climatic changes of which palaeocoleopteran evidence appears to be the best indicator to date. Most of this work is, however, confined to the British Isles and its wider application should lead to greater appreciation of thermal regimes, not only during the late-glacial period but also during the Holocene. Whether the late-glacial oscillation was a global event is also open to question, but recent evidence suggests that it was more widespread than hitherto suspected. Certainly, the evidence from northwest Europe indicates that it was a period of rapid climatic and associated ecological changes, most of which have no modern analogues, and which may be a reflection of disequilibrium between climatic and ecological systems.

The period 10–5 kyr BP saw the establishment of optimum interglacial conditions, characterised in temperate latitudes by the development of mixed deciduous forests. Tree-lines reached their maximum heights in many parts of the world, especially in the early part of this period. Palynological data cannot, however, be used in isolation to infer temperature and precipitation changes since the migration rates of individual species and edaphic changes must also have affected the vegetation communities and thus the pollen assemblages. Palaeoecological data from this period, and the later Holocene, have a significant role to play in elucidating such problems as the refuge hypothesis in relation to tropical rainforests, and the premiss that long periods of stability result in ecological diversity. The present state of knowledge implies that tropical forest diversity is not the result of stability but is more likely to be a consequence of instability.

The later Holocene, especially in northwest Europe also opens with another controversial datum, the elm decline. Climatic change, human interference and disease have all been implicated and it may be that all three factors contributed to this significant alteration in European temperate forests. The last 5 kyr in general have witnessed the development of the later stages of the interglacial cycle and there is abundant evidence for climatic deterioration, especially a cooling trend over the last 2 kyr. One of the most notable periods is that of the 'Little Ice Age', which was probably a global event, centred on the fourteenth to the nineteenth centuries.

Throughout much of the later Holocene there is also abundant evidence for human activity, particularly the development of prehistoric farming practices. These will be considered in Chapter 3, while more recent environmental changes related to agricultural and industrial development during the last 300 years will be examined in Chapters 5 and 6.

FURTHER READING

Berger W H, Labeyrie L D (eds) 1987 *Abrupt climatic change*. D Reidel, Dordrecht, Boston, Lancaster and Tokyo

Douglas I, Spencer T (eds) 1985 *Environmental change and tropical geomorphology*. George Allen and Unwin, Boston, London and Sydney

Hecht A D (ed) 1985 *Paleoclimate analysis and modeling*. John Wiley, New York, Chichester, Brisbane, Toronto and Singapore

Martin P S, Klein R G (eds) 1984 *Quaternary extinctions*. University of Arizona Press, Tucson

Rampino M R, Sanders J E, Newman W S, Kønigsson L K (eds) 1987 *Climate: history, periodicity and predictability*. Van Nostrand Reinhold, New York

Ruddiman W F, Wright Jr H E (eds) 1987 *North America and adjacent oceans during the last deglaciation*. Geological Society of America, Boulder, Colorado

Sutcliffe A J 1985 *On the track of ice age mammals*. British Museum (Natural History), London

Vogel J C (ed) 1984 *Late Cainozoic palaeoclimates of the southern hemisphere*. A A Balkema, Rotterdam

3

PREHISTORIC COMMUNITIES AS AGENTS OF ENVIRONMENTAL CHANGE

3.1 INTRODUCTION

The ability of hominids to use, and later modify, their environment more effectively than their predecessors probably began when they learnt to make tools *c.* 2 Myr BP. The earliest tools were made of stone and it is for this reason that the earliest cultures are known as palaeolithic (old stone age). The practice of stone tool manufacture has dominated the history of human beings since it persisted until metal-using technology was developed, only *c.* 9 kyr BP, when the first copper tools were produced. That is not to say that the palaeolithic period was one of stagnation and uniformity. Numerous innovations occurred as food-procuring strategies became more calculated and sophisticated. Deliberate herding of animals during the later palaeolithic and mesolithic (middle stone age) periods culminated in the domestication of both plants and animals that led to permanent agriculture during the neolithic (new stone age). In many ways the selection of specific plants and animals and the initiation of agricultural systems was more significant in terms of environmental change than the later innovation of metal technology. The copper, bronze and iron implements that were developed in later prehistory served only to intensify the processes begun during the neolithic by providing more effective tools.

The beginning of the domestication process, continued today in plant and animal breeding programmes, along with the use of fire and the invention of the wheel, must rank among the most important thresholds in human history and indeed in environmental history. They essentially represent the emergence of *Homo sapiens sapiens* as a controller of environment, especially of ecosystems, rather than as an integral component. They also provided the means whereby ecosystems could be transposed into agro-ecosystems which ultimately led to the agricultural systems of today. Such innovations in food procurement also led to changes in social organisation, as did the advent of metal technology which further enhanced the efficiency of agricultural practices and probably had implications for population growth.

Although the evidence for the changing nature of environment during prehistory is patchy, especially for the earlier periods, the people–environment relationship is so important that a summary, of necessity brief, is essential to a text on environmental change.

3.2 HUNTER-GATHERERS

For a large part of human history hunting and gathering have dominated food-procurement strategies, as they still do in many parts of the world today. The hominids, as indeed their ape-like ancestors, must have relied on local sources of food that they selectively chose. Since the evidence for early palaeolithic resource use is fragmentary, any reconstructions that have been attempted are generally highly conjectural. The evidence for the middle, and particularly the later palaeolithic periods is more abundant, while the mesolithic and neolithic periods are relatively well represented in the archaeological record, though interpretations are often constrained by inadequate dating controls and an imperfect understanding of palaeoenvironmental evidence.

3.2.1 THE EMERGENCE AND MIGRATIONS OF PALAEOLITHIC GROUPS

The evolution of hominids has already been referred to in section 1.1.4 (also Fig. 1.1). According to Stringer and Andrews (1988) the debate between the multiregional model for human evolution and the single origin model is swinging towards the latter as the most apposite explanation. This involves the presence, probably in Africa about 200 kyr BP, of a common ancestral

Table 3.1. Hominid colonisation during the Quaternary. (Based on Foley 1987.)

Approximate date millions of years BP	Characteristics
Pre 1.5	Hominids confined to the eastern and southern regions of sub-Saharan Africa (Evidence for hominid presence elsewhere is controversial and and unreliable)
1.5 to 1.0	Hominids (probably *H. erectus*) in sub-Saharan Africa and in S.E. Asia. Presumably they also colonised intermediate areas, although the evidence to date is equivocal.
1.0 to 0.7	Hominids migrate into warm temperate zones, including Mediterranean Europe, though there are disputed claims for an earlier occupation.
0.7 to 0.3	*H. erectus* colonises the more northerly temperate environments
0.3 to 0.04	More northerly latitudes were colonised, though probably not extreme arctic regions. (During this period *H. sapiens* evolved from *H. erectus* .)
0.04 to 0.01	Almost all the globe was colonised by this time except Antarctica. Hominids reached Australasia very early in this period. (Domestication and agricultural practices first developed c. 0.1 Ma B.P.)
Post 0.01	Continued colonisation of remote areas. (Metallurgical technologies first developed c. 0.05 Ma B.P.)

population that was already anatomically similar to *H. sapiens*. Subsequently regional differentiation occurred in Africa, then these groups migrated to other parts of the world, where modern characteristics developed. This is in contrast to the multiregional theory which requires an early and middle Quaternary migration of the ancestor of *H. sapiens*, *H. erectus*, from Africa into other parts of the world where local differentiation and evolution occurred to produce modern humans. On the basis of biomolecular evidence, however, the latter theory is not as likely as the first.

The evidence on which patterns of hominid radiation from Africa have been reconstructed is fragmentary and frequently suffers from inadequate dating control. Table 3.1, however, summarises the main conclusions that can be drawn on present data. The most secure evidence for hominid radiation from Africa is between 1.5 and 1.0 Myr BP and Larichev *et al.* (1987) have suggested that early colonisation of northern Asia may even pre-date 0.7 Myr BP. Lambert (1987) suggests that *H. habilis* may have been present in Southeast Asia, but Foley (1987) states that *H. erectus* was the first hominid to migrate from sub-Saharan Africa. After Africa and Eurasia were colonised, Australasia was next, probably about 40 kyr BP. Groube *et al.* (1986), for example, have presented evidence for occupation of the raised terraces of the Huon Peninsula of New Guinea at *c.* 40 kyr BP. The earliest date for mainland Australia is 38 kyr BP (Pearce and Barbetti 1981) at Upper Swan in southwestern Australia. The colonisation of the Americas appears to have occurred relatively late in the Quaternary period, though once again this is a subject of considerable dispute (Bray 1988). Dillehay and Collins (1988) have presented evidence for human occupation at Monte Verde, central Chile, which they suggest dates to *c.* 33 kyr BP. They acknowledge that

Fig. 3.1. The dispersal of early hominids from Africa (the lines give tentative routes and approximate dates in millions of years BP). (From Foley 1987, with minor changes.)

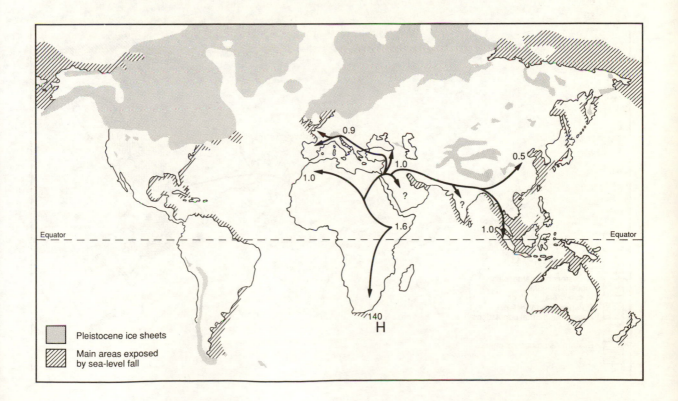

Pleistocene ice sheets

Main areas exposed by sea-level fall

the evidence is not conclusive, but if their suppositions are correct it means that humans were present in the Americas some 20 kyrs earlier than hitherto supposed. Upper levels at the Monte Verde site, however, contain artefacts that are unequivocal indicators of human presence and these are dated to *c.* 13 kyr BP (Quivira and Dillehay 1988), a date more in line with other evidence in the Americas for the earliest human occupation (see summaries in Bray 1988 and Bednarik 1989).

Figures 3.1 and 3.2 summarise the sequence of hominid radiation from the African source area. The former, to a large extent conjectural because of paucity of evidence, relates to early hominid radiation, while the latter relates to the dispersal of anatomically modern humans. Foley (1987) has examined these patterns and suggests that they were probably affected by geographical barriers. This seems to be particularly significant in view of the relatively late colonisation of Australasia and the Americas. In addition, Foley has suggested that these patterns can be related to ecological conditions. The first hominids evolved in savanna environments similar to those of East Africa today, where indeed some of the most important hominid fossil-bearing sites are located (Leakey 1981, 1982; Harris *et al.* 1988). Such environments (M M Cole 1986) are characterised by pronounced seasonality which influences the distribution of plant and animal biomass. This would have provided the resource base for early hominids and according to Foley (1987) availability and the way in which biomass was exploited influenced early hominid evolutionary trends, which culminated in the evolution of *Homo sapiens sapiens*. The use of resources will be discussed in section 3.2.2, but brief mention must be made here in order to comprehend radiative patterns of hominid migrations.

Fig. 3.2. The dispersal of anatomically modern humans from Africa (the lines give approximate dates in thousands of years BP). (From Foley 1987 with minor changes.)

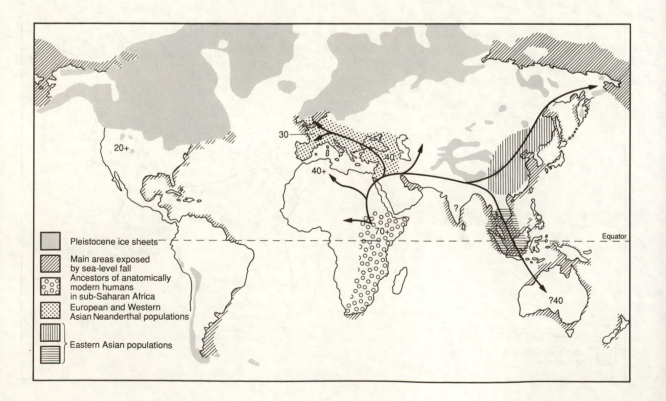

Pleistocene ice sheets

Main areas exposed by sea-level fall

Ancestors of anatomically modern humans in sub-Saharan Africa

European and Western Asian Neanderthal populations

Eastern Asian populations

Seasonality of rainfall is one of the most important constraints on savanna ecosystems and as Cole (1986) has shown for East African savannas, annual biomass or primary productivity varies considerably between the wet and dry seasons. Of equal significance is the presence of a diverse range of herbivorous ungulates, often reaching high populations that are also seasonal. Such seasonality is today manifested in the food-procuring strategies of many primates who have both a dry-season and a wet-season strategy. Foley (1987) suggests that early hominids may have developed similar strategies, especially if they were in competition with other primates, as seems likely. During the wet season, for example, abundant plant material would pose no problem for food procurement, but during the dry season competition between individuals and between different species would be more acute. Plant resources are confined to seeds, rhizomes and roots, i.e. mostly below-ground biomass. A shift to animal biomass, obtainable from herbivores concentrated around water-holes, would reduce competition and provide an acceptable supplement to the meagre plant resources. There is evidence from several East African sites (e.g. Olduvai Bed 1, Bunn and Kroll 1986) that contain stone tools in association with mammal bones (some with cut marks) which suggests that hominids had become omnivores in contrast to the earlier Australopithecines that were probably herbivores. Foley (1987) also suggests that such adaptations would have had significant evolutionary and behavioural consequences as well as providing hominids with an ecological advantage necessary for Darwin's 'survival of the fittest'. These are listed in Table 3.2, and have considerable implications for social organisation.

Returning to the question of hominid movement out of Africa, this adaptation to a seasonal savanna environment, while speculative but logically possible, may also have determined the patterns of hominid migration. Figure 3.1 shows that, overall, more temperate latitudes were favoured by early *H. erectus* migrants over tropical rainforest environments, which presumably reflects the adaptation of these early hominids to seasonal climates and their associated biomass characteristics. However, this process was mirrored by a radiation of other animal species such as hyena, wolf and lion (A Turner 1984), all of which are meat-eaters. The question that arises from this asso-

Characteristic	Rationale
1. Brain size	Animal species with diverse foraging strategies tend to have a larger brain size than species that enjoy a more consistent and reliable food source. Thus the expansion of foraging strategy and dietary requirements of early hominids may have resulted in increased brain size that is characteristic of hominid evolution.
2. Food-sharing	Carnivory provides a concentrated food source in contrast to the more diffuse nature of plant resources. One large herbivore provides more food than required by one person. Thus, opportunities for food sharing would have arisen and encouraged social groups.
3. Spatial Organisation	Carnivores and omnivores have larger foraging areas than herbivores. Territory defence is usual only where resources are reliable which is not characteristic of savannas. Thus, conditions prevailed that encouraged mobility with complex patterns of concentration and dispersion. (This relates to 2. above)
4. Tool-making	This may have been promoted by the need for butchering animals or as a means of extracting below-ground plant biomass. Early meat-eating hominids may have been scavengers rather than hunters and tools may have provided an advantage for using carcasses of thick-skinned mammals that were impenetrable to other carnivores

Table 3.2. Possible hominid evolutionary and behavioural consequences of wet- and dry-season food-procurement strategies in a savanna environment. (Based on Foley 1987.)

ciation is whether hominids were behaving as a unique species or whether they were only one component of a biogeographical event which involved the radiation of a number of species that had developed similar adaptational strategies. Clearly, the food-procuring strategies necessary for survival in the savanna environment conferred advantages to certain species, as is suggested in Table 3.2. Another pertinent question is whether a carnivorous or omnivorous diet conferred an advantage over a herbivorous one and if so, did it contribute to hominid success? Such questions provide an incentive for further research, and the current state of knowledge only presents an opportunity for speculation. Inevitably, the evolutionary history of early hominids and their subsequent migration will be reassessed in the next few decades as further evidence is compiled.

In summary, stone-using *H. erectus* populations expanded beyond the region of origin in sub-Saharan Africa into Southeast Asia between 1.5 and 1.0 Myr BP and by 300 kyr BP had colonised the north temperate zone, expanding to all but the most extreme Arctic regions by 40 kyr BP. For example, Wymer's (1988) summary of palaeolithic archaeology in Britain indicates that humans had reached Britain before the Anglian glacial stage (see Table 1.3), probably during the Cromerian interglacial *c.* 0.6 Myr BP. By *c.* 0.2 Myr BP *H. sapiens* had evolved, once again in Africa, and then radiated, as shown in Fig. 3.2, into Europe and Asia and finally into Australia and the Americas. Stone-tool making had already begun in Africa, first by *H. habilis* and developed into more sophisticated types by *H. erectus*. This knowledge was presumably taken by migrants into other parts of the world, where it developed *in situ* and from which the later mesolithic and neolithic technologies arose.

3.2.2 RESOURCE USE BY PALAEOLITHIC GROUPS AND THEIR ENVIRONMENTAL IMPACT

Any attempt at compiling a history of resource use by palaeolithic people must be very conjectural since it is heavily constrained by scanty evidence and the fact that most of it derives from stone artefacts. Clearly stone played a major role in palaeolithic subsistence strategies, but the absence of other artefacts, especially those of wood, is probably more a reflection of poor preservation than of their unimportance.

Lambert (1987) states that the earliest stone artefacts were produced by *H. habilis* about 2.5 Myr BP. Evidence for these early artefacts comes from numerous African sites, the most well known being the Olduvai Gorge where the earliest assemblages are dated to *c.* 1.9 Myr BP. These are known as Olduvai artefacts which represent the oldest known tool-making tradition. Gowlett (1988) has reviewed the evidence for this and the later traditions of the developed Oldowan and the Acheulean. Conventionally, these three traditions have been viewed as separate entities, though there is now reason to believe that there is some overlap between them. It may well be that the same human groups produced different types of stone tool for different purposes or used different raw materials. Nevertheless, these tools represent one aspect of resource use by early human groups and in the Olduvai Gorge *H. habilis* exploited basalt and quartzite pebbles that were chipped into crude choppers, scrapers, burins and hammerstones. By *c.* 1.6 Myr BP, at about the same time as *H. erectus* appeared, hand-axes were being produced which are considered typical of the Acheulean tradition which spread, as *H. erectus* populations migrated, into Europe and India, while the chopper-core Oldowan tradition spread into China, Java and Europe.

Precisely when the ancestors of modern humans began to use fire is also a matter for conjecture. While there is controversial evidence from Choukoutien in China for the incidence of fire approximately 1 Myr BP, recent work by Brain and Sillen (1988) from the Swartkrans Cave in South Africa indicates that fire may have been used much earlier. Brain and Sillen have recovered burnt bones, as well as bones bearing marks consistent with butchery, from an occupation level in the cave which they date to 1.0–1.5 Myr

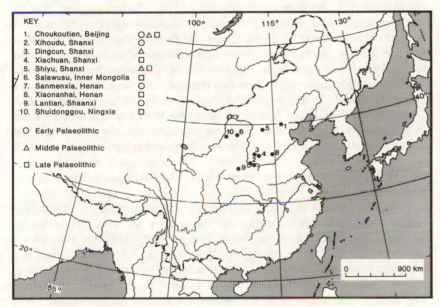

KEY

1. Choukoutien, Beijing ○△□
2. Xihoudu, Shanxi ○
3. Dingcun, Shanxi △
4. Xiachuan, Shanxi □
5. Shiyu, Shanxi △□
6. Salawusu, Inner Mongolia □
7. Sanmenxia, Henan ○
8. Xiaonanhai, Henan □
9. Lantian, Shaanxi ○○
10. Shuidonggou, Ningxia □

○ Early Palaeolithic

△ Middle Palaeolithic

□ Late Palaeolithic

Fig. 3.3. The development of palaeolithic traditions in north China (dates are in millions of years BP). (Based on Lanpo and Weiwen 1985 and map in Rukang and Olsen 1985.)

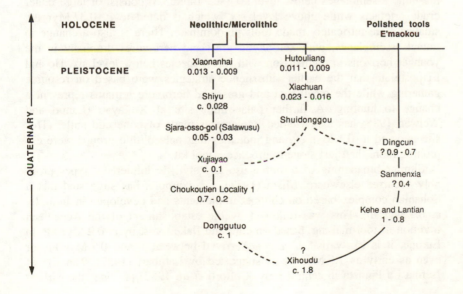

BP. These deposits also contain remains of *Australopithecus robustus*, but since remains of *Homo* spp. are found in lower horizons it is not clear which species used the fires. Nevertheless, the evidence points to a much earlier use of fire, either accidental or deliberate, than hitherto suspected.

Figure 3.3 summarises the development of palaeolithic traditions in north China, where there are a number of significant archaeological sites. Unfortunately, the dating of some of these is questionable (Xinzhi and Linghong 1985) and until further advances are made the dates given in Fig. 3.3 must remain tentative. This is particularly so in relation to Xihondu, Shaanxi Province (Lanpo 1985), which is part of a complex of palaeolithic localities near Kehe. At this site, cores, flakes, choppers and scrapers have been found in association with deer antlers that bear signs of chopping and scraping, and mammalian ribs which appear to have been burnt. Lanpo suggests that the site is at least 1 Myr old and palaeomagnetic dating suggests that it is 1.8 Myr BP. This, however, is controversial and there is also some evidence to indicate that the artefacts may have been transported in water. The oldest hominid-fossil bearing site in China is that of Yuanmou, Yunnan Province (Rukang and Xingren 1985) where two teeth of *H. erectus* have been found which are thought to date to 0.7–0.5 Myr BP, though once again this date is controversial. Remains of *H. erectus* have also been found at two localities in Lantian County in Shaanxi Province (Rukang and Xingren 1985). The oldest is a cranium, found at Gongwangling, which pre-dates a mandible discovered at Chenjiawo. The age range for these fossils is probably 0.8–0.65 Myr BP and both are associated with cores, flakes and scrapers as well as vertebrate remains.

However, perhaps the most well-known archaeological site in China is that of Choukoutien, near Beijing, the stratigraphy and fossils of which are summarised in Table 3.3. According to Senshui (1985) the lithic assemblages show a typological development and the presence of numerous ash layers and burnt bone attest to human use of fire, though whether this was manipulation of naturally occurring fire is open to question. Ho and Li (1987) have suggested that evidence from Choukoutien and other sites in north China indicates two different subsistence strategies. At Choukoutien, for example, the lithic assemblages below level six (see Table 3.3) consist of large rather crude artefacts while above level six, which is dated to *c*. 0.37 Myr BP, smaller more intricately made tools predominate. There is also a change in faunal assemblages, with xerophytic grassland herbivores dominant in the younger horizons in comparison with forest species below level six. Ho and Li postulate that the earlier subsistence strategies were based on resource gathering while the small tool and grassland herbivore remains represent a change to hunting. A further palaeolithic site at Xujiayao (Lanpo and Weiwen 1985) has also yielded implements made of bone and antler. This site is dated to 0.1 Myr BP, and indicates that palaeolithic groups were exploiting more than just stone to produce a tool kit.

Similar broadening of resource use and stylistic implement types probably occurred elsewhere. Misra (1987), for example, has suggested that a Sohanian complex based on chopper implements had developed in India by *c*. 0.3 Myr BP. This was followed by the establishment of the Acheulean tradition of tool-making, based on core and flake tools, by *c*. 0.2 Myr BP. In Europe, it is likely that *H. erectus* arrived between 1 and 0.7 Myr BP, or even as early as 1.5 Myr BP as suggested by Lambert (1987). The site of Isernia La Pinneta in central Italy (Coltorti *et al*. 1982) provides the earliest most securely dated evidence for human presence in Europe at 0.73 Myr BP. Gamble (1984) has proposed a regional model for palaeolithic Europe consisting of three major provinces which reflect the effect of increasing latitude on the growing season. These are: (a) the northern province which includes the British Isles and extends across the north European plain; (b) a southern province centred on the latitudes of the Alps; (c) a Mediterranean province. These can be further subdivided into eastern, central and western areas in relation to the east–west axis of mountain chains. Gamble (1986) has also reviewed at length the evidence for palaeolithic industries and subsistence patterns in each of these and suggests that the early palaeolithic, between 73 kyr and 35 kyr BP, was characterised by two main lithic technologies. The first involves a core/flake/chopping tool complex which is relatively simple technologically in comparison with Acheulean-type material. The latter was produced by more sophisticated reductionist techniques. Both of these earlier palaeolithic traditions are distinct from the lithic industries of the upper palaeolithic (post *c*. 35 kyr BP) in so far as these implements are

Table 3.3. The chief characteristics of the Choukoutien (Locality 1) archaeological site near Beijing, China. (Based on Senshui 1985.)

	Layers	Stratigraphy	Evidence for use of fire	Lithic industry	*H. erectus* fossils	Approx Dates (Myr BP)
Late stage of the Early Palaeolithic	1 - 2	Coarse breccia with stalagmites		Vein quartz remains dominant raw material but milky quartz nodules and flint were also used. Flake tools increase in frequency and heavy cave tools decrease. Stone awls appear for the first time.		
	3	Coarse breccia	✓		✓	0.3 to 0.2
	4	Upper ash layer	✓		✓	
	5	Black & grey clay stalagmite crust				
Middle stage of the Early Palaeolithic	6	Hard breccia	✓	Quartz is the dominant raw material but sandstone and rock crystal were also used. Flake tools predominate over core tools	✓	0.4 to 0.3
	7	Cross-bedded sands				
Early stage of the Early Palaeolithic	8 - 9	Coarse breccia with ash lenses	✓	Quartz and sandstone were used as raw materials. The lithic assemblages are typologically simple choppers & scrapers with a predominance of core tools	✓	
	10	Red clay with weakly brecciated limestone blocks	✓		✓	0.66 to 0.4
	11	Reddish breccia	✓		✓	

generally smaller, and were probably hafted precursors of mesolithic micro-liths, as well as being more varied to include projectile points and needles. These variations in lithic industries between the earlier (pre *c*. 35 kyr BP) and later palaeolithic Gamble attributes to distinct behavioural differences relating to food procurement which are akin to Wymer's (1982) distinction between savagery and barbarism (section 1.1.4). Gamble (1986) also draws attention to the dispute that exists in classifying hominid fossils from this period, a debate that has also been reviewed by Stringer (1986) in relation to the British fossil hominid record. For example, remains of a skull found at Swanscombe in southern England are thought by Stringer to be repre-sentative of Neanderthal precursors rather than *H. erectus*.

In the upper palaeolithic period (*c*. 35–10 kyr BP) there is evidence for use of more diverse materials for tool-making. In the southwest province, for example, ornamental beads, antler picks, needles and spear-throwers occur along with cave paintings, which are confined to this region. Interestingly, there is no evidence for human occupation in the northwest and north-central areas between 20 and 17 kyr BP, presumably due to the last major ice ad-vance (see section 1.2). Artefactual evidence for the upper palaeolithic also indicates that there was a trend towards smaller implements which may have been hafted and which Gamble (1986) suggests may represent the economis-ing of raw materials.

It is clear from the archaeological sites discussed above, that stone was one of the major resources used by palaeolithic groups. (It must, however, always be borne in mind that stone artefacts survive better than bone or wood implements and thus present a very biased picture of human resource use.) The main question that presents itself relates to the other resources used by palaeolithic groups. In section 3.2.1 it was suggested that *H. habilis* had developed an omnivorous diet that assisted in ensuring the survival and subsequent spread of hominid groups. There is certainly abundant evidence, including that from the sites described above, for human use of other mam-mal species. The presence of butchered animal bones in many archaeological sites, for example, illustrates this point.

Scavenging may have been one form of animal exploitation. Deliberate hunting, which involves a predetermined strategy, is yet another form of such exploitation. Did the adoption of such strategies play a role in both resource use and human evolution? Moreover, what was the role of plant resources, which apparently dominated the food-procuring strategies of the Australopithecene ancestors of modern humans, in the subsistence of homi-nids? Unfortunately, neither question can be answered with any certainty. While it is apparent, from archaeological sites throughout the world, that animals played an important role in palaeolithic subsistence, it is by no means clear how animals were exploited and what the social implications of such exploitation might have been in terms of the responsibilities that may have developed within a hominid group. Though entirely conjectural, this latter is a logical assumption if sharing of scavenged or hunted animals oc-curred. Such questions, although the remits of archaeologists and anthropo-logists, remain significant for the student of environmental change because they help to identify at which point in time human communities developed from being integrated ecosystem components to controllers of ecosystem function.

The evidence from Choukoutien in China suggests that *H. erectus* was an active hunter and may have been able to manipulate, if not make, fire. Similarly, research at Olorgesailie in Kenya (Isaac 1977; Shipman *et al.* 1981) that was probably inhabited by *H. erectus* and which has yielded Acheulean hand-axes, also indicates that hunting occurred. Here, it is an abundance of *Theropithecus oswaldi* bones, an extinct giant gelada baboon, which Shipman *et al.* suggest were dismembered by early hominids using hand-axes. This conclusion is highly conjectural and highlights the difficulties involved in interpreting the fossil record, as Potts (1984) has detailed. While there is a general consensus that early hominids included meat in their diet, it is much more problematic to ascertain the nature of meat acquisition. More pertinently, scavenging and hunting require different skills: the former is more opportunistic while the latter is a much more planned operation. Both, however, require some knowledge of prey movements and it is not unreasonable to suppose that scavenging led to an appreciation of an omnivorous diet that ultimately led to the development of hunting strategies. The fossil record sheds little light on when such a change in subsistence may have happened. Neither does it clarify the process of development from indiscriminate hunting to selective herding, a process which Wymer (1982) describes as the transition between savagery and barbarism that occurred in the upper palaeolithic.

How reliant *Australopithecus* and descendants, including *H. sapiens sapiens*, were on plant resources is equally obscure, largely because the fossil record reveals little information. In view of the dental characteristics of fossil remains, it appears that plant resources have always figured highly in hominid diets. Fossil evidence for the manipulation of plant resources is, however, confined to the Holocene (sections 2.4 and 2.5) though this is in no way suggestive that plant resources were unimportant in pre-neolithic subsistence strategies. Indeed, it is most unfortunate that there is so little evidence for human use of plant resources prior to *c.* 10 kyr BP, but fruits, nuts and seeds, etc. are generally only preserved in anaerobic environments that are not characteristic of early hominid occupation sites. What little evidence there is for plant use in Europe has been reviewed by Tyldesley and Bahn (1983). This includes evidence for the use of wood, e.g. yew spears found at Clacton-on-Sea, Essex, and at Lehringen, Saxony (Oakley *et al.* 1977). In addition, Hansen and Renfrew (1978) have reported remains of wild oats and barley in levels *c.* 12 kyr old at Franchti Cave, Greece, and Wendorf *et al.* (1979) have found evidence for cultivated wheat and barley in the Egyptian upper palaeolithic. There is also evidence for upper palaeolithic exploitation of marine resources in South Africa (Klein 1979) and northern Spain (Clark and Straus 1983).

It is also of note that there is not a great deal of evidence for human presence from European interglacial sequences. Currant (1986), for example, has discussed possible reasons for this, especially in relation to the mesocratic phase of British interglacials which was characterised by deciduous woodland (section 2.2). Since interglacials were relatively short-lived periods in comparison to the cold stages, it may be that early human groups did not adapt to such a forested environment because of greater familiarity with more open habitats and/or because of lack of pressure to do so. This is endorsed by Gamble (1986) who suggests that hominid survival strategies were more in tune with the longer cold stages of the Quaternary period (see section 1.2), when more open habitats predominated, than with the forested interglacial periods.

Overall, there is convincing evidence for palaeolithic exploitation of animals, not least from the famous cave paintings of southwest Europe which frequently depict both the hunter and the hunted. There is little evidence for plant exploitation, though undoubtedly this also played a role in palaeolithic subsistence. Numerous hypotheses have been advanced to explain resource-use strategies, but there is little in the fossil record to substantiate such claims with any degree of certainty. Neither is there any convincing evidence that palaeolithic groups had a lasting effect on their environment as later stone age peoples undoubtedly exerted in the mesolithic and neolithic periods. It would appear, despite the ingenuity reflected in the development of lithic technologies, that humans were integral rather than dominant ecosystem components throughout the palaeolithic period.

3.2.3 THE DEVELOPMENT OF MESOLITHIC GROUPS AND THEIR ENVIRONMENTAL IMPACT

In comparison with the palaeolithic period, the mesolithic period was short-lived, lasting from *c*. 10 kyr BP to 5 kyr BP. It is a transitional period between the old and new stone ages and had its widest expression in Europe, where it coincides with the protocratic and mesocratic phases of the interglacial cycle (Fig. 2.1) during which temperate forest replaced vast tracts of tundra. As Zvelbil (1986) has pointed out, the use of the term mesolithic is somewhat spurious since it is often used to delimit a particular chronological period. While this is loosely correct, it must be borne in mind that it is a term applied to early post-glacial temperate and boreal zone industries that developed in response to a forested environment and which did not occur elsewhere in the Old World where palaeolithic traditions gave way to those of the neolithic period.

As stated in section 3.2.2, there is little evidence for exploitation of forested environments in the earlier European interglacials. Why then should the forest biome of the current interglacial have been the focus of human activity? Presumably, there were unprecedented social and/or ecological pressures that instigated exploitation of these expanding forested environments. Possibly population pressures ensued as the flora and fauna, to which palaeolithic groups had adapted, began to diminish. As discussed in section 2.3.3, human pressures may have brought about the extinction of many large herbivores between 12 and 10 kyr BP.

Whatever the reason for the change in habitat preference, deposits of the mesolithic period have yielded implements that are different in character to those of the palaeolithic period. They are characterised by microliths, many of which were used as tips for arrows, as well as axes and adzes that were attached to wooden hafts and may have been used for creating small forest clearances and for making canoes and paddles.

One of the most significant mesolithic sites in Europe is that of Star Carr in Yorkshire, Britain. Here, a wide range of materials have been preserved in an anaerobic peaty environment that developed as an ancient lake silted up. The site has been excavated by Clark (1954, 1972) who has reconstructed the activities of the occupants. The habitation site consists of a platform of cut birch brushwood that was placed in the reedswamp at the edge of the lake and which may have been covered by animal skins to form tent-like dwellings. A variety of animal bones reflects the regional fauna, e.g. various deer, badger, fox and numerous birds, as well as other animals that were used as food. Of these latter, red deer were most abundant, followed by roe deer, elk, aurochs and pig. Remains of domesticated dog, the earliest domesticated animal found in Britain, were also present. Clark also examined the remains of deer antlers from the site and has suggested that the site was seasonally rather than permanently occupied. The preponderance of antlers that had been broken from the animals' skulls suggests that they were hunted during a period from March to October when stags carried their antlers. Further analysis of deer-teeth characteristics from this site by Legge and Rowley-Conwy (1989), however, indicates that Star Carr was inhabited during the summer. There is also the possibility that stag frontlets with the antlers still in place may have been used in ritual activities, and there is evidence that antlers of red-deer were used for making barbed points. The presence of stone burins, awls and scrapers indicate that animal skins may have been processed, possibly for the provision of shelter, clothing and/or containers. Wood, as attested by the birch platform, was also used in the mesolithic economy of this site. The remains of a wooden paddle indicates that the inhabitants made boats and the presence of rolls of birch-bark may relate to the extraction of resin, possibly for fixing arrowheads and spearheads.

If the site was seasonally occupied, what were the inhabitants doing during the remaining parts of the year? Clark (1972) proposes that these hunter-gatherers were exploiting nearby easily accessible upland areas during the summer when deer were enjoying upland grazing. Conversely, Legge and Rowley-Conwy (1989) suggest that sea-coast environments were exploited during the winter. Whatever the reality of these seasonal models, the remains indicate that mesolithic people were using a wide range of resources and evidence for this is widespread in Europe in general. From Oronsay, Inner Hebrides, for example, Mellars (1987) has excavated a number of shell-midden sites dated at c. 5 kyr BP. The abundant remains of molluscs, especially limpets, seals, birds and fish, especially the coalfish (*Pollachius virens*), indicate that the inhabitants relied heavily on marine resources in an environment that probably contained very limited animal resources. Similarly, research in the Netherlands, Denmark and Germany (summarised in Barker 1985) points to the exploitation of red deer, roe deer and aurochs as well as coastal resources by mesolithic groups. Indeed, Price (1987) has suggested that marine resources may have contributed up to 90 per cent of the diet of some north European mesolithic groups and that carbon isotope analysis of human bone reflects a change towards terrestrial food sources only in the neolithic period.

As for the upper palaeolithic period, the evidence from mesolithic sites in Europe provide clear evidence for animal-resource exploitation. Evidence for plant-resource exploitation is much less widespread, although it has already been suggested in section 2.4.2 that mesolithic communities may have played a significant role in environmental change during the early post-glacial period. The abundance of hazel in British early post-glacial pollen diagrams, for example, may have been a response of the species to burning and/or coppicing. Moreover, Simmons and Dimbleby (1974) have suggested that ivy (*Hedera helix*) may have been used as a fodder crop, and Simmons (1975) has drawn attention to the number of upland pollen diagrams that contain evidence of clearance, often associated with charcoal remains.

Simmons and Innes (1987) have presented further evidence for forest disturbance, especially during the later mesolithic, *c*. 8.5–5.3 kyr BP, in northern England. They suggest that fire was used as part of a deliberate management strategy at a time when sea-levels were rising and thus limiting the more easily exploited coastal zone. The development of a closed forest canopy associated with climatic climax vegetation (section 2.2) would have curtailed ecological succession, of which valuable food-yielding species such as hazel are an important part, and confined game animals to an environment that, because of its density, was not easily penetrated by mesolithic hunters. These ecological factors, possibly coupled with increasing mesolithic populations, may have provided sufficient pressure for the initiation of new management strategies. Fire is a particularly important ecosystem management technique that is still widely used today and would have been advantageous, provided that it was adequately controlled, to both hazel and game animals. Rowley-Conwy (1984) believes that resource use at this time would have become much more concentrated as more specialised foraging systems developed, leading to a more sedentary existence and a precursor to permanent agriculture. Such a process may also have led to environmental degradation including the initiation of peat formation, and Simmons and Innes (1985) have demonstrated that mesolithic resource use may have initiated the development of less productive heath and moor in parts of upland Britain.

If this is so, increased pressure on resources would have occurred, requiring more sophisticated food-producing rather than food-procurement strategies. There is also evidence, albeit limited, for declining marine resources (Rowley-Conwy 1984) that would have exacerbated the problem of limited resources. Simmons and Innes (1987) conclude '. . . Holocene economic adaptations may be viewed as a progressive intensification of food production; early mesolithic foraging followed by advanced foraging with environmental manipulation which culminated in a control of food resources tantamount to horticulture and herding of ungulates'. Thus, the basis of food procurement strategies were already present in indigenous mesolithic populations and it would not have required such a massive change in society, as is often conjectured, to incorporate the new resources that characterise neolithic agriculture. Simmons and Innes suggest that the development of neolithic economies heralded a change in the scale of food production rather than a fundamental change in community structure. What these new resources were and where they originated will be discussed in section 3.3.

3.3 EARLY AGRICULTURALISTS

When, where and how agriculture developed has been the focus of considerable research during the last century. Traditionally, the emergence of agriculture has been regarded as 'revolutionary'. Obviously, it was a very important development in human history but, in view of the concluding remarks in section 3.2.3, it in all likelihood developed and spread gradually rather than suddenly. The cultural changes that ensued, however, probably reflected the enhanced capacity of human groups to compartmentalise their activities in an environment that provided a more reliable food resource. This may have enabled permanent

settlements to develop, higher populations to be supported and monuments such as Stonehenge to be constructed. The domestication of plants and animals played a crucial role in the development of human communities and in environmental change during the postglacial period. It provided the means whereby ecosystems were transposed into agro-ecosystems and was fundamental to the emergence of *Homo sapiens sapiens* as a controller of ecosystems.

3.3.1 THE DOMESTICATION OF ANIMALS AND PLANTS

Both animal and plant domestication were preceded by hunting and gathering. Presumably, humans recognised that some animals and plants were more useful than others as sources of food and that it was preferable to ensure an adequate proximal food supply rather than have to engage in relatively haphazard foraging and hunting, even if this was already being controlled by positive management (section 3.2.3). Traditionally, the Near East has been regarded as the focus of much of the early domestication of animals and plants, and although there is much convincing archaeological evidence for this, there is also evidence to show that domestication (and cultivation) occurred in different parts of the world and at different times (Harlan 1986).

According to S J M Davis (1987), the most important domesticated animals, i.e. sheep, goats, cattle and pigs, were domesticated in the early part of the post-glacial period between 8 and 10 kyr BP (Table 3.4). It is also generally agreed that the earliest domesticated species was the dog, whose ancestor was the wolf (*Canis lupus*), and which originated *c.* 12 kyr BP in the Near East. There is little evidence from the fossil record for butchering of the species, except in South America (Fiedel 1987), and it is most likely that dogs were used, as they are today, for herding, hunting and possibly guarding.

The Near East was also the centre of domestication for sheep and goats. There is genetic evidence to suggest that domesticated sheep were derived from the southwest Asian moufflon (*Ovis orientalis*), since the two have the same number of chromosomes (Nadler *et al.* 1973). Similarly, S J M Davis (1987) cites evidence for the domestication of goats in the Near East from the bezoar goat (*Capra aegagrus*) at about the same time as sheep were domesticated. This was probably about 9 kyr BP, a date supported by Wagstaff (1985) whose summary of Near Eastern sites shows that the bones of both sheep and goats, with sufficient signs of morphological variation to be those of domesticated rather than wild species, are frequently found in archaeological horizons dated to *c.* 9 kyr BP. The ancestors of modern farmyard pigs were wild boar (*Sus scrofa*), which has a very wide distribution across Eurasia and may have been domesticated almost anywhere at any time. The earliest known domesticated pig remains have also been found in the Near East and are probably not much younger than domesticated sheep remains. The same is true for cattle, which were domesticated from wild aurochs (*Bos primigenus*).

Palaeoenvironmental and zooarchaeological studies in the Near East also provide information on the environmental changes that occurred as domestication proceeded. For example, Moore (1985) has summarised much of the data for this region and has presented evidence from a number of sites which reflect the transition from palaeolithic hunter-gatherer to neolithic farmer. This is illustrated in Table 3.5, which shows that as domestication of animals and plants occurred there were major social changes in terms of settlement patterns and artefact production. Moore (1985) has also proposed a model for agricultural development in this region which has many features in common with that proposed by Simmons and Innes (1987) for agricultural development in the British Isles (section 3.2.3). Moore (1985) argues that an infrastructure for agricultural development was already in place in the Levant during epipalaeolithic 2, by which time forest was replacing steppe and population numbers were increasing. Mobility was reduced as hunting territories were reduced, paving the way for a more sedentary existence. Continued population growth, which is more characteristic of a sedentary rather

Table 3.4. Regions of origin and approximate dates for some of the most common domesticated plants and animals. (Based on Harlan 1986 and S J M Davis 1987.)

Plants Species	Region of origin	Approximate Date K yrs. B.P.
Emmer wheat	Near East	9 - 10
Einkorn wheat	Near East	9.5 - 8.5
Barley	Near East	9.5 - 8.5
Pea	Near East	9.5 - 8.5
Lentil	Near East	9.5 - 8.5
Flax	Near East	9.5 - 8.5
Vetch	Near East	9.5 - 8.5
Naked wheat	Near East	9.0 - 8.5
Cucurbita pepo	Tropical America	10.7 - 9.8
Capsicum	Tropical America	8.5 - 7.5
Common bean	Tropical America	7.7
Lima bean	Tropical America	7.7
Maize	Tropical America	7.5

Animal Species	Region of origin	Approximate Date K yrs. B.P.
Dog	Near East	12
Sheep	Near East	9
Goat	Near East	9
Cattle	Near East	8
Pig	Near East	7
Horse	Southern Russia	6
Llama	Andean puna	6
Alpaca	Andean puna	6
Chicken	India - Burma	2? *
Turkey	Mexico	?

*   Recent work by West and Zhou, (1988) suggests a date of c. 8 K years B.P.

than a mobile life-style, and the enhanced pressure on natural resources, could well have stimulated plant and animal domestication to ensure adequate food supplies. Moreover, the interchange of ideas within groups may have led to the cultural innovations listed in Table 3.5. The archaeological evidence indicates that both domesticated and wild plant and animal species were important in human subsistence until the developed neolithic when emphasis switched almost entirely to domesticated species. Thus for some 4–5 kyr cultivation and pastoralism were practised alongside hunting and gathering. This is probably a sufficiently long period for the former to have developed, almost imperceptibly, from the latter. A similar model for agricultural development is suggested in Fig. 3.4.

Returning to the question of animal domestication, however, there is also evidence to suggest that some animals were domesticated in South America.

Table 3.5. Changes in food-procuring strategies from the palaeolithic to the neolithic in the Levant and associated cultural changes. (Based on Moore 1985.)

Approx date K yrs. B.C. [1]	Stage	Subsistence changes	Cultural changes
5.0 - 3.75	Developed Neolithic 4	More productive agricultural and herding economy that was begun in Neolithic 2 and 3	Development of Calcolithic culture (copper using). Similar building to Neolithic 2 & 3. Wider range of pottery styles. Increased population.
6.0 - 5.0	Developed Neolithic 3	Advanced strains of wheat, barley & pulses were grown. Increasing concentration on agriculture & herding as hunting diminished in importance. Cattle & pigs domesticated.	Same size sites and building traditions as Neolithic 1. Pottery manufacture began 6 K yrs. B.C. Agricultural tools more obvious.
7.6 - 6.0	Archaic Neolithic 2	Gazelle replaced by domesticated sheep & goat. Cattle & pigs were under closer control & other game still hunted. Expansion in range of cultivated crops	Increase in settlement size & development of rectangular homes. More varied artefacts than in Neolithic 1, especially bone tools, ornamental material & clay figurines of humans & animals
8.5 - 7.6	Archaic Neolithic 1	Selective & efficient exploitation of wild cattle, pigs, goats & gazelle in a Hunter/gathering economy. Peas, lentils, emmer & einkorn wheat cultivated	Village development eg Jericho, with oval houses. Small stone tools, also bowls, querns, needles. Exchange networks began. Burial of dead.
10.0 - 8.5	Epipalaeolithic 2	Hunter/gathering economy with more intense use of animals. Planting & harvesting of cereals & possibly pulses; possible use of acorns.	Larger campsites than in Epipalaeolithic 1. Chipped stone tools & plant processing equipment. Increase in population.
18.0 - 10.0	Epipalaeolithic 1	Mobile hunter/gatherers, main prey = gazelle, fallow deer. No evidence for plant use but it was probably very important.	Dispersed population with small camp sites. Chipped stone tools & plant processing equipment.

1. Dates are quoted as B.C. following Moore, 1985

Novoa and Wheeler (1984) and Wheeler (1984), for example, have proposed that the llama and alpaca originated from the guanaco (*Lama guanicoe*) by about 6 kyr BP in the Andes, and according to Fiedel (1987) hunting of such camelid species became widespread after *c.* 8 kyr BP. As well as giving meat, these animals provided fibre and the llama was probably also used as a beast of burden. Guinea-pigs (*Cavia apera*) were also domesticated in the Andean region of South America (Wing 1978) by about 3 kyr BP, while Mexico also appears to have provided a centre of domestication for the turkey, a descendant of the wild turkey (*Meleagris galloparo*), although there is, however, no precise evidence as to when this occurred (Crawford 1984). There is also speculation in relation to the domestication of the chicken (*Gallus domesticus*), the evidence for which has been reviewed by West and Zhou (1988). On the basis of archaeological and palaeoenvironmental evidence they conclude that chickens were first domesticated from the red jungle fowl (*Gallus gallus*) in Southeast Asia some time before 8 kyr BP, by which time the species had become established in China, but only spread into Europe *c.* 3 kyr BP.

Overall, there is little evidence to show that animals were domesticated in Europe, at least originally. Certainly, the Near East witnessed the earliest domestications of the most common farm animals that characterise, for example, archaeological sites of neolithic and later age in Britain. This is no reason to suppose that domestication of wild sheep, etc. did not occur *in situ* elsewhere. There is evidence, for example, from sites in Yugoslavia and Greece for local domestication of cattle and pigs. This may have occurred

Fig. 3.4. The transition from hunting and gathering food-procurement strategies to permanent agriculture and associated cultural changes.

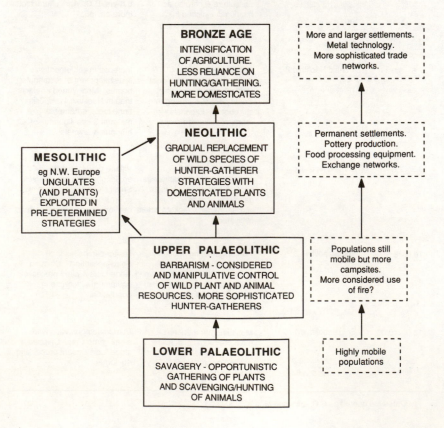

before 8 kyr BP, pre-dating the Near Eastern sites (Protsch and Berger 1973). As Table 3.4 shows, however, one species intimately associated with human history probably did originate in Europe. This, the horse, was domesticated from its wild ancestor (*Equus ferus* or *E. caballus ferus*). Sherratt (1981) has suggested that it was first domesticated by Ukrainian people about 4 kyr BP for transport rather than food.

That plant domestication preceded animal domestication is suggested by palaeobotanical evidence from the Near East. In the Levant (Table 3.5) plant domestication occurred during the epipalaeolithic two period between 10 and 8.5 kyr BP. According to Zohary (1986), excavations at a number of early neolithic villages in the Near East (e.g. Jericho, Ramad and Tell Aswad) indicate that by *c.* 9 kyr BP cereal crops were being sown and harvested. The dominant crops were emmer wheat (*Triticum turgidum* subsp. *dicoccum*), einkorn wheat (*T. monococcum*) and barley (*Hordeum vulgare*), all of which are members of the grass (*Gramineae*) family. The most common pulses which were domesticated by this time include the lentil (*Lens culinaris*) and pea (*Pisum sativum*), although the bitter vetch (*Vicia ervilia*), chickpea (*Cicer arietirium*) and possibly the broadbean (*V. faba*) were also part of the arable economy. Flax (*Linum usitatissimum*) is also present in early neolithic deposits, and although these finds may represent its wild ancestors, there is clear evidence for its domestication by *c.* 8 kyr BP. Thus, many of the crops which underpin modern agricultural systems were being genetically controlled in food-procuring regimes by 8 kyr BP (Table 3.4).

Zohary (1986) has shown that the wild ancestors of most of these early crops exhibited a relatively limited distribution. Wild emmer wheat and chickpea are endemic to the Near East while wild einkorn wheat, barley, bitter vetch, lentil and pea have a wider distribution, but all occur in the Near East. All of these species were thus focused on an area that already possessed a well-organised hunter-gatherer community in which settlement patterns were emerging. In addition, these wild plant species all possessed attributes that were of value in human nutrition, notably large food reserves. As Hopf (1986) has pointed out, the albumen-rich pulses were the ideal complement to the carbohydrate-rich cereals. This, in combination with the animal protein of hunted ungulates must have provided a very satisfactory nutritional base for the omnivorous *Homo sapiens sapiens*. Ultimately, all of these crops became incorporated into the agricultural economies of prehistoric Europe and most of Asia.

In addition to the main crops discussed above, there are numerous other plants, many of which originated as weeds of the primary crops, which underwent domestication in the later prehistoric period. The most well known of these are oat (*Avena sativa*), false flax (*Camelina sativa*) and rye (*Secale cereali*). Oat and rye, for example, only appear as domesticated species from 3 to 4 kyr BP. By 3 kyr BP a wider range of crops had become established based on wild progenitors from Asia and Africa. These include sorghum (*Sorghum bicolor*), sesame (*Sesamum indicum*), common rice (*Oryza sativa*) and the cottons (*Gossypium arboreum* and *G. herbaceum*).

According to Zohary and Hopf (1988), rice (*O. sativa*) is a south- and east-Asiatic element but because of the ease with which its wild relatives hybridise the exact centre of domestication has not yet been determined. The earliest finds of rice that can be positively identified as domesticated are from sites in India and Pakistan dated *c.* 4.5 kyr BP. Earlier finds date to *c.* 7 kyr BP, but it is not clear whether these are the remains of wild or domesticated species. Oka (1988) states that the wild progenitor of *O. sativa* is *O. rufipogon*, while that of *O. glaberrinia*, another domesticated rice which originated in Africa, is *O. breviligulata*.

Arboriculture was also a relatively late development in prehistoric times despite the fact that fruits and nuts almost certainly constituted a significant component of hominid diet, and probably also for the earliest ancestors of the Australopithecines. Traditionally, species such as the peach and apricot have been among the mainstays of Mediterranean agriculture but both were imported from eastern Asia (Zohary 1986), as was the citron (*Citrus medica*), the first of the southeast Asian citrus fruits to enter the Mediterranean region. All appeared about 3 kyr BP. Likewise, cultivation of the olive which is an endemic species and no doubt utilised for centuries, was only begun about *c*. 6 kyr BP, when cultivation of the vine (*Vitis vinifera*) and fig (*Ficus spp.*) probably also commenced (Spiegel-Roy 1986).

The domestication of plants was not, however, confined to the Old World and many of the plants that were domesticated in the New World (see Table 3.4) and subsequently introduced into the Old World have transformed many of the world's agricultural systems. According to Fiedel (1987), over 100 species of plants were originally cultivated and domesticated by indigenous Americans. The most familiar of these crops are maize and potatoes, but tomatoes, pumpkins, avocados, sunflowers, tobacco, capsicums and chilli peppers all have their origins in the Americas, particularly in South America and Mexico. According to Harlan (1986) plant husbandry was being practised by approximately 10 kyr BP in tropical America. Harlan suggests that the agricultural systems in this region were slow to develop and that the domestication of individual species occurred over a long time period in contrast to the Near East where some six or eight species rapidly provided an agricultural base. However, it should be borne in mind that the Near East has been favoured by archaeological and palaeoenvironmental research while the diffuse and sparse nature of the evidence from the Americas makes any synthesis highly tentative.

Traditionally there has been the question of whether or not the basic premisses of agriculture were transposed from the Old World into the New by migrating people. Although this may be unlikely, it is not impossible, and the debate may have some relevance to the model for agricultural development suggested in Fig. 3.4. The relatively late colonisation of the Americas at approximately 12 kyr BP, if the earlier claims are discounted (section 3.2.1), was undertaken by migrants from Asia entering the Americas via the land bridge provided by the Aleutian Islands that were probably part of a connecting isthmus between northeast Asia and Alaska at a time in the early Holocene when sea-levels were lower. Such people had presumably developed upper palaeolithic food-procuring methods in Asia, involving precise control of naturally occurring plants and animals in relatively sophisticated hunter-gatherer strategies. Assuming that early Americans practised such strategies, it is likely that they developed a similar infrastructure for resource use to that of European mesolithic and neolithic peoples, thus establishing an ecological rapport that eventually resulted in domestication and arable cultivation, just as it did in the Old World, though somewhat later.

As Table 3.4 shows, the earliest domesticated plants found in the Americas include the pumpkin (*Cucurbita pepo*) and gourds, though there is the possibility that the latter did not originate in South America (Harlan 1986)

and may have been introduced from Africa. Harlan (1986) has pointed out
that the common bean (*Phaseolus vulgaris*) and lima bean (*P. lunatus*) were
fully domesticated by *c.* 8 kyr BP, which implies that plant husbandry was in
operation for some time previously. Research by MacNeish (1978) and
Byers and MacNeish (1967–76) in the Tehuacán region of Mexico also indicates that incipient agriculture was being practised by the end of the El
Reigo phase *c.* 8 kyr BP when squash, amaranth, chilli pepper and avocado
may have been cultivated, although the evidence is controversial. There is
also evidence for cultivation of the pepper (*Capsicum*) in this area at *c.*
8.5–6.5 kyr BP, and it is here that maize first appears in the archaeological
record at *c.* 7.5 kyr BP in the Coxcatlan phase. However, it is not at all clear
how, where or when maize was domesticated. MacNeish (1985) believes
that it dates to *c.* 7 kyr BP and was initially domesticated in a small area of
Mexico located north of Chiapas and south of Mexico City. What the wild
ancestors of the species were remains controversial, although Mangelsdorf
(1986) has presented evidence, based on genetic characteristics and plant-
breeding experiments, which indicates that one of these ancestors may be a
recently discovered grass called perennial teosinte (*Zea diploperennis*). This,
Mangelsdorf suggests, may have hybridised with an as yet unknown primitive pod-popcorn to produce *Z. mays*.

There is also evidence for early agriculture in New Guinea, *c.* 9 kyr BP,
and in China, *c.* 8 kyr BP which, together with the examples quoted above,
suggest that domestication was occurring in widely dispersed areas and that
the period 10–7 kyr BP was a crucial one in the history of agriculture. From
this time, agricultural systems began to develop and to diffuse from one
region to another and from one cultural group to another.

3.3.2 THE SPREAD OF PASTORALISM AND CROP CULTIVATION

Just as the available evidence for plant and animal domestication in the archaeological and palaeoenvironmental record presents a rather hazy picture
of the origins of agriculture, so too is the evidence for the subsequent development of agricultural systems. The most complete data are available for
Europe, but there is a dearth of evidence from most of the rest of the world.
It is no more easy to answer the question of how agriculture, or ideas relating to agricultural practice, spread than it is to answer the question as to
why agriculture began in the first place. Necessity, for whatever reason, and
inventiveness probably both played a part in the origins and spread of agriculture. Unfortunately, the record of past societies and their activities cannot
reveal motives and thus hypotheses are legion in relation to these two questions, with little concrete factual evidence to favour one hypothesis over
another.

The spread of agriculture may be effected by either stimulus diffusion,
involving the transferance of ideas, or by migration in which people move
into new areas taking with them already developed practices and tools. It
seems highly likely that both processes occurred in the past. The most well-
documented example of agricultural diffusion is that which occurred as agricultural practices spread outward from the Near East. According to Zohary
(1986), various combinations of the crops that originated in the Near East
formed the basis for agricultural systems in Europe, the Nile Valley, central
Asia and the Indus basin and that their establishment was relatively rapid.

As shown in Fig. 3.5, agriculture appeared in Greece by *c.* 8 kyr BP and by 7 kyr BP it had spread to the Danube, Nile valley, the Caspian Sea area and to Pakistan. By *c.* 5.5 kyr BP the first traces of permanent agriculture appeared in Britain. Since there is little substantive evidence to support the traditional hypothesis of waves of migrants moving out from the Near East centre and since indigenous groups had already developed a suitable hunter-gatherer infrastructure (section 3.2.3), it can only be supposed that these new domesticates gradually replaced naturally occurring plant and animal species. This is the process suggested in Fig. 3.4. There is also evidence to show that the range of domesticated species was enhanced by additions, such as millet, from outside the Near East and there are numerous examples in Barker's (1985) synthesis of prehistoric farming in Europe for *in situ* domestications of both plants and animals.

Fig. 3.5. The spread of agriculture from the Near East into Europe, Asia and the Nile. (Based on Zohary and Hopf 1988.)

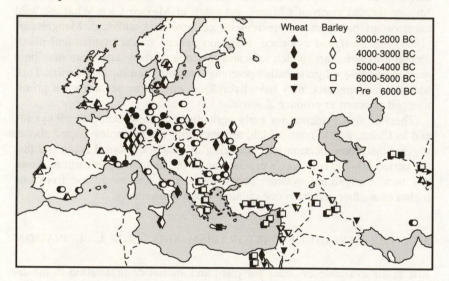

(A)   The spread of wheat and barley from the Near East into Europe, Asia and the Nile Basin

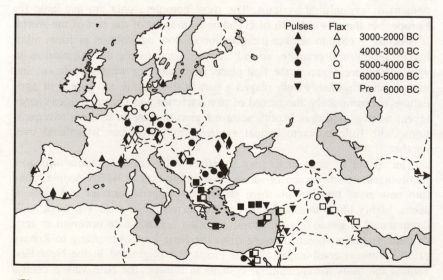

(B)   The spread of pulses and flax from the Near East into Europe, Asia and the Nile Basin

Barker (1985) has also speculated on the role of changing Holocene environments as a stimulus to agricultural development and the apparent reluctance of palaeolithic groups to exploit the interglacial forests has already been pointed out (section 3.2.2). Could the emergence of agriculture and its spread have been a response to changing climates that resulted in widespread forest development in Europe? The palaeoenvironmental record in Britain suggests several factors of relevance to this question. Firstly, the areas most densely forested were initially avoided by early agriculturalists who primarily exploited the lightly wooded chalk areas of the southeast. This perhaps implies lack of ability, in terms of technology, to clear and cultivate the more densely forested areas, but also reflects the necessity of utilising some woodland areas rather than entirely avoiding them. Secondly, the already well-developed hunter-gatherer system relied to a large extent on woodland habitats: so the infrastructure was already in place for further advancement. Thirdly, in contrast to European evidence, there are no changes in the palaeoenvironmental record which require a climatic cause for the elm decline, a horizon intricately associated with the establishment of neolithic agriculture even if its primary cause was Dutch elm disease (section 2.4.2). All of these factors imply cultural reasons, possibly population pressure, rather than climatic or ecological stimuli for the initiation of agriculture, at least in Britain and possibly elsewhere in Europe.

A further hypothesis for the development and spread of agriculture has been proposed by Bainbridge (1985), who focuses on the use of acorns, which were probably a staple food in areas like the Near East and Mexico, that were characterised in the early Holocene by oak forest development. Bainbridge has pointed out that many of the archaeological sites in these areas contain acorns and/or food processing implements that could have been used for grinding acorns into flour or oil. Using ethnographic parallels between ancient Californian Indians and the ancient societies that initiated agriculture, Bainbridge has suggested that acorns may have preceded grains as a staple food because they occurred naturally and prolifically, are nutritious and are easily stored. Grazing by goats, both wild and later domesticated species, in tandem with the use of oak branches, etc. for fuel, cooking and house construction as well as burning to herd animals and possibly climatic change may have resulted in large-scale reductions in acorn production. So, without destroying the oak woodland but simply by curtailing reproductive capacity and thus impairing acorn production, an important resource may have become so limited that innovations were essential to maintain human populations. Burning in particular may have encouraged the spread of open-habitat species like the grasses which provided the progenitors of emmer and einkorn wheat and barley. In consequence, balanoculture, as Bainbridge describes the utilisation of acorns (from the Greek word *balanos*, meaning acorn), may have led to the exploitation, and ultimately the domestication, of plants such as members of the grass and pulse families which complemented the diet of animal protein that was provided by hunting strategies. Thus, granoculture may have begun within what may be described as a traditional upper palaeolithic and/or mesolithic society that was generally reliant on naturally occurring ecosystem components.

Such a proposal has analogies with the suggestion by Hawkes (1969) who proposed that domestication occurred by what is known as the 'rubbish heap' hypothesis. This implicates both plants and humans in a symbiotic relationship. Humans sought out plants with a good food reserve, like that of acorns, and when these declined, they sought out grasses and pulses with equally good food reserves. Such plants were reciprocally encouraged by the higher nutrient levels of nitrates and phosphates that probably typified camp-sites and which could not survive in woodland shade.

Symbiosis between plants, animals and human groups may thus have led, almost imperceptibly, to the replacement of natural ecosystem components by domesticated species as suggested in Fig. 3.4. As a result, pastoral and arable agricultural systems emerged from natural ecosystems and sub-sequently intensified. What is perhaps of most significance is the developing ability of human groups to genetically control organisms. The selection of particular plants and animals by humans conferred advantages not enjoyed by any other species and led to the emergence of human groups as control-lers of environment. Through the ages this has become more sophisticated and not always to the advantage of human groups. As stated in section 3.2.1, ecological factors may well have influenced the development of early homi-nids, but by *c.* 10 kyr BP humans were beginning to turn the tables. Having already learnt to exploit ecosystem resources in well-organised hunter-gatherer strategies, humans began to manipulate the genetic resource base via plant and animal breeding that represents a primitive approach to genetic engineering which in its modern form may well provide a potent agent of future environmental change, as will be discussed in Chapter 8.

3.3.3 THE ROLES OF PASTORALISM AND CROP CULTIVATION IN ENVIRONMENTAL CHANGE

Some of the environmental changes brought about by the development of agriculture are fairly obvious. The introduction of domesticated species pro-vided a food source that supplemented natural plant and animal resources. In this sense, species diversity was increased, but as clearance of natural vege-tation was undertaken to make way for arable fields, species diversity, at least locally, decreased. When agricultural systems replace ecosystems there is a tendency to simplify the system in terms of the range of species present. This ensures less competition for light and nutrients so that these resources are channelled towards the crops. Thus the inception of agricultural systems can alter energy flows and biogeochemical cycles which are fundamental to all such systems as well as to natural ecosystems. Geomorphic, pedological and hydrological systems may also be radically altered when cultivation re-places natural vegetation growth.

As stated in sections 3.2.2 and 3.2.3, the use of fire was probably fairly commonplace in the hunter-gatherer strategies of the upper palaeolithic and mesolithic periods and may have been used by earlier palaeolithic groups. In relation to early palaeolithic resource use there is little evidence that wide-spread or long-lasting environmental change was brought about by human activity. There is, however, evidence for a period of deforestation in the mesocratic phase of the Hoxnian interglacial in Britain (see Table 1.3). This was first recognised by West (1956) in the pollen assemblages from Hoxne in East Anglia and its possible causes have been examined by Wymer (1982, 1983). The association of the horizons in which the event is recorded and the occurrence of lower palaeolithic hand-axes implies some relationship be-tween the two and it is not impossible that early hunter-gatherer groups were using fire to herd animals. The evidence is not conclusive, however, and the occurrence of similar contemporary deforestation events at other Hoxnian interglacial sites such as Mark's Tey, Essex (Turner 1970) indicate that it was not a local event, as might be expected with a controlled burn, but either a large-scale conflagration due to natural causes or a climatic fluctuation that was of sufficient intensity to be registered regionally.

In the context of the mesolithic of northwest Europe, there is abundant evidence for the role of fire in bringing about environmental changes, though it is quite possible that at least some fires occurred naturally rather than being deliberately set by humans. Indeed, the notion of the use of fire as a means of ecosystem manipulation by mesolithic hunter-gatherers in the protocratic and mesocratic periods of the post-glacial period has found much favour with palaeoecologists (e.g. Smith 1970, 1984; Simmons 1983) and prehistorians (e.g. Mellars 1976). Brief reference has already been made to this in sections 2.4.2 and 3.2.3, but a more in-depth consideration is warranted in order to highlight the environmental changes that such a powerful agent may bring about.

As Simmons and Innes (1987) point out in the context of the British Isles, most of the evidence available to date relates to the later rather than the earlier mesolithic period, i.e. 8.5–5.3 kyr BP, and is more concentrated in upland rather than in lowland regions. By this time, a distinct later mesolithic stone-using industry had developed consisting of narrow-blade artefacts in contrast to the early mesolithic broad-blade industry. Britain was severed from the European continent by this time, and deciduous forests were increasing in density and diversity (see Fig. 2.6). Pollen diagrams from the Pennines and North York Moors (summarised in Simmons and Innes 1985, 1987) exhibit changes in the pollen spectra which can be interpreted as a consequence of human activity and since many of these are associated with charcoal and/or mesolithic artefacts, it is not unreasonable to assume a cause-and-effect relationship, though this cannot be unequivocally proven.

Many of these sites, as shown schematically in Fig. 3.6, exhibit a fall in arboreal pollen, increases in hazel (*Corylus avellana*) pollen and that of shrubs such as willow (*Salix* spp.) and heather (*Calluna*), as well as increases in ruderal species such as docks (*Rumex* spp.), plantains (*Plantago* spp.), bracken (*Pteridium aquilinum*) and nettles (*Urtica* spp.). These changes all point to the opening up of the forest canopy, and the presence of

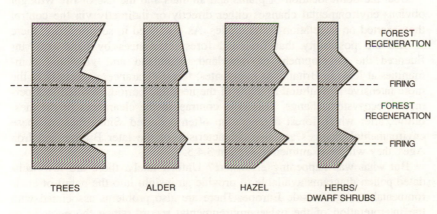

TREES   ALDER   HAZEL   HERBS/ DWARF SHRUBS

FOREST REGENERATION

FIRING

FOREST REGENERATION

FIRING

------ charcoal

Fig. 3.6. A schematic representation of mesolithic interference using fire in the mid post-glacial forests of upland Britain.

charcoal at many sites indicates that the primary cause was fire. Such clearances also appear to have been relatively short-lived and were followed by
forest regeneration, though several sites contain evidence for further burning
at a later date. In the process of regeneration, succession from a field layer
to a closed canopy would occur, thus ensuring the presence of a wide range
of habitats. Moreover, firing of vegetation is today a widespread management technique used to encourage new growth that is particularly palatable
to animals. Mesolithic groups may have used such a strategy to encourage
ungulate herds, particularly deer, that would concentrate in these more favourable clearings but which were not too far away from the cover provided
by undisturbed forest. Mellars (1976), for example, has suggested that the
carrying capacity of an area for ungulate browsers may be considerably increased if firing is practised.

Other wildlife may be similarly influenced and plant resources may also
be enhanced by occasional and/or regular firing. Attention has already been
drawn to the proliferation of hazel in postglacial pollen diagrams (see section 2.4.2) and the possibility that it was favoured by the use of fire. In view
of the large number of archaeological sites at which hazel nuts are found
(Price 1987), it is highly likely that they constituted a significant part of
mesolithic diets. Smith (1984) has also reviewed the evidence for the post-
glacial rise in alder (*Alnus*) and has suggested that it may have been indirectly favoured by mesolithic interference with the forest cover that reduced
competition. It is also possible that the controlled use of fire provided just
the tool that mesolithic groups needed for survival in a predominantly
wooded environment. Controlled use of such a powerful agent does, however, require considerable premeditation and organisation, attributes that
were essential for the acceptance and utilisation of domesticated species that
occurred during the British neolithic (section 3.2.2).

Fire may not, however, always have been the main agent of change in
early post-glacial forests. Bush (1988) has suggested that mesolithic groups
may have been responsible for arresting post-glacial forest succession in the
Yorkshire Wolds as early as *c.* 8.9 kyr BP. Such disturbance is recorded in
sediments at Willow Garth in the Great Wold Valley, and although there is
no evidence for firing, Bush has suggested that human groups may have
been manipulating the local ecosystem to promote the growth of large-
seeded grasses and influence the grazing patterns of ungulates.

Both the domestication of plants and animals and the use of fire wrought
obvious environmental changes either directly or indirectly via the control
they exerted on vegetation communities. As discussed in section 2.5.2, there
is also the possibility that fire, and forest clearances by hand-axes, influenced the development of moorland, heathland and grassland communities at least in Britain. At many sites, forest clearance, especially in the
more intensive agricultural systems of the neolithic period, resulted in a permanent ecosystem change. This is in contrast to the clearances of the mesolithic, after which forest regeneration often occurred. Since most of these
environmental changes are also characteristic of the later Bronze and Iron
Ages, they will be examined in section 3.4.3.

But what was happening elsewhere? Unfortunately, there are few well-
dated pollen diagrams available to provide an insight into the detail of environmental change outside Europe. There are also problems associated with
the interpretation of the palaeoenvironmental record, since the ecology of
many tropical species, for example, is not well documented and because it is

often difficult to distinguish the pollen of cultivated species from domesticated species. Both cereals and rice are members of the Gramineae family and all produce similar pollen grains. However, Hamilton *et al.* (1986) have presented evidence for forest clearance in southwest Uganda that attests to human intervention in the ecosystem which pre-dates 4.8 kyr BP. Both burning and soil erosion are associated with the clearances which are among the earliest so far recorded in tropical Africa. Hamilton *et al.* present no evidence for cultivated plants, but the absence of burning in modern moist African forests for game hunting would imply that clearance was for cultivation rather than animal husbandry.

Flenley (1988) has also summarised the palynological evidence for land-use changes in southeast Asia where there is evidence to suggest that vegetation disturbances may have begun as early as 10 kyr BP. In Sumatra, for example, human groups were clearing upland forests by *c*. 7 kyr BP. Clearances, possibly for shifting cultivation, were not sufficiently intense to prevent forest regeneration and only since 2 kyr BP have permanent clearings occurred. As Flenley shows, there is also the possibility that burning was practised by 10 kyr BP, with clearance of swamps as early as 9 kyr BP and forest clearance by 5 kyr BP or earlier, though there is little indication in the fossil record to suggest what was being cultivated. Archaeological evidence from Kuk Swamp in the New Guinea highlands, however, reinforces the presumption that crop cultivation occurred. Here, Golson (1977) has revealed the remains of drainage ditches in a grey clay deposited *c*. 6 kyr BP.

Overall, the examples presented above indicate that early post-glacial hunter-gatherers and agriculturalists were exerting considerable control on the environment, bringing about changes that were sometimes transitory and reversible and sometimes permanent. The ability to more finely resolve palaeoenvironmental evidence should ultimately lead to a greater awareness of the relationship between upper palaeolithic, mesolithic and neolithic groups and their environment.

3.4 THE METAL-USING CULTURES

The development of metal technology, which began with the use of copper, enhanced the ability of humans to manipulate their environment and to bring about environmental change. During the Bronze and Iron Ages, the processes involved in environmental manipulation that originated in the earlier postglacial period intensified. Animal and plant husbandry became the norm as more reliance was placed on domesticated species, and crop production systems became more sophisticated. Once again it is from Europe and the Near East that most evidence is available for Bronze and Iron Age resource use. It is also of interest to note that, while early hominid behaviour was influenced by ecological conditions in Africa (section 3.2.1), human groups in the Bronze and Iron Ages were developing technologies and strategies with which they sought to become masters of, rather than servants to, their environment.

3.4.1 THE EMERGENCE AND SPREAD OF METAL-USING
GROUPS

Precisely when and how metal-working technologies were originally developed is far from clear. According to Mellaart (1967) there is evidence for lead smelting as early as 8 kyr BP at Çatal Hüyük, a settlement that developed in central Anatolia where neolithic agricultural practices were well established. However, evidence for widespread metal-working is not apparent in the archaeological record until *c.* 7 kyr BP, when copper oxide ores were exploited to produce copper. This, as Fig. 3.7 shows, probably began in the area between the Black and Caspian Seas and the Persian Gulf where copper ores are widespread. There is also the possibility that copper working began independently elsewhere since Spencer and Thomas (1978) have reported finds of copper and bronze implements from Thailand dated to between 7 and 6 kyr BP. The advent of copper exploitation instigated a trend towards the use of metal rather than stone tools and this change in material culture is often described as the Chalcolithic. According to Moore (1985), one such Chalcolithic culture, the Halaf, originated in northern Jezireh and Assyria *c.* 7 kyr BP, and spread later into the Levant as shown in Table 3.5.

The Chalcolithic or Copper Age appears to have been relatively short-lived, possibly because copper is a soft metal and while it is malleable, copper implements are not particularly robust. Copper exploitation led to the development of bronze. Initially, arsenic bronzes were produced which Wagstaff (1985) implies may have been almost accidental, resulting from the exploitation of mixed copper and arsenic ores which are common in many areas of the Near East. In addition, Wertime (1973) reports that tin bronze replaced arsenic bronze during the period 4-5 kyr BP in this region, though it is not apparent where the tin originated from. Most archaeologists agree, however, that copper- and particularly bronze-working led to the production of durable tools and probably enhanced trade and contacts between human groups as they sought raw materials and/or finished products. Moreover, the

Fig. 3.7. Early metallurgical industries and their spread. (Based on The Times *Concise Atlas of World History* 1982.)

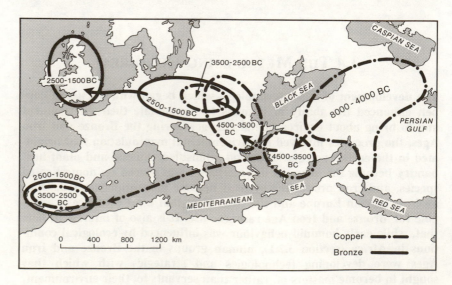

skills required for metal-working probably led to greater division of labour within human groups as craft specialists emerged, though this would only have been possible if food surplus to the needs of those engaged in agriculture was being produced.

From a centre of origin in the Near East, copper- and bronze-working spread further afield (Fig. 3.7), reaching the Balkans by 5 kyr BP, the southern Iberian Peninsula by 4.5 kyr BP and the rest of Europe, including the peripheral areas of Britain and southern Sweden, by 3.8 kyr BP. Thus, within 3 kyr from its inception, metal-working had spread to most of Europe and into northern India and China, where agricultural systems based on domesticated plants and animals were already in place. The impact of this technology on agricultural practices and on the environment will be examined in section 3.4.3.

As bronze-working commenced in Britain almost 4 kyr BP, iron-working was beginning in the Near East. According to Collis (1984), the earliest authenticated find of an iron object is from Alaça Hüyük (situated near the modern city of Ankara, Turkey) and is dated to *c.* 4.4 kyr BP. The find comprises a dagger in association with other grave-goods made of bronze. There has also been much speculation as to why iron-working was not developed earlier, especially as iron ores are much more widespread and locally available than ores of copper and tin. Waldbaum (1978) has suggested that this may be a consequence of the techniques involved in the production of the metals, since copper and bronze are easier to produce and cast and only with the addition of carbon are iron implements harder and more durable. This latter developed later in prehistory and may have been accidental, as charcoal used in smelting would have provided a source of carbon. Waldbaum also suggests that a shortage of tin, essential for bronze production, may have occurred and although it is not obvious from the archaeological record that tin became scarce, there is much evidence to suggest that there was a period of general upheaval at the end of the second millennium BC. This may have disrupted trade routes and thus the transport of raw materials. Such a shortage may have stimulated iron-working and once the technology was mastered the advantages of a cheaper and more widespread raw material would have become apparent.

The more general use of iron occurred between 3.2 and 2.8 kyr BP in the Near East, and by 3.2 kyr BP iron-working had spread to Greece, though bronze continued to be used for the majority of implements, especially weaponry and armour. The Phoenicians also introduced iron-working into North Africa 2.9 kyr BP and it spread from cities such as Carthage into what are now Nigeria and the Sudan by *c.* 2.5 kyr BP. Here, local metallurgical innovations occurred and hierarchical social groupings developed (McIntosh and McIntosh 1988). By this time, iron-working had also spread throughout Europe and into Britain. There is also the possibility that iron-working began independently elsewhere. The Times 'The World' (1986) suggests that iron-working in India, the earliest evidence for which dates to 3.3 kyr BP, may have been independent of the Near East, as was that of China. As with the development of bronze implements, the emergence of iron tools allowed further agricultural developments to take place as well as social changes which contributed to the emergence of the Greek and Roman Empires that replaced the Assyrians and Egyptians as world powers.

3.4.2 Bronze Age and Iron Age Resource Exploitation

The development of the agricultural systems initiated in the neolithic period continued during the Bronze Age. Greater reliance was placed on domesticated plants and animals, though hunting and gathering were still practised. It is likely that food surpluses were produced which facilitated the division of labour in society and allowed the development of specialist craftspeople skilled in metal-working. Copper and bronze were produced and the resource base was expanded by tapping the metal ores that provided raw materials. Thus there was a trend away from the exclusive use of stone for implements that had dominated human history for some 3 Myr. Silver and gold were also worked from which ornaments and jewellery were produced, as exemplified by grave-goods and gold hoards. The Bronze Age also witnessed additions to the megalithic monuments of Stonehenge in Wiltshire, Britain and New Grange in Ireland, both of which originated in the neolithic period. The latter is a passage grave which, according to O'Kelly (1982) was begun some 5.2 kyr BP and was used as a Bronze Age site of cremation and burial, though its impressive structure probably means that it was used for the remains of a person of some importance. By this time, and as suggested in Table 3.5, numerous large settlements had developed in areas like the basins of the rivers Tigris and Euphrates in Mesopotamia, the Nile in Egypt, the Indus in India and the Yellow River in China which were thriving agricultural regions. In some cases irrigation systems were constructed.

A complete survey of resource use during this period and the Iron Age is impossible in a text such as this, but the following examples illustrate the people/environment relationship. In Egypt, for example, cereals, especially barley, became the predominant food source by c. 4.5 kyr BP and necessitated the construction of irrigation systems to harness the Nile floods: another way in which humans exerted control over natural resources. According to Butzer (1976) the development of shadoof, a contrivance for raising water by a bucket into a series of artificial basins in which the Nile flood waters could be stored for later use, occurred at 3.35 kyr BP. These systems increased the land area that could be cultivated by 10–15 per cent and which was probably used as small garden plots. At the same time, population increased and settlements such as Memphis emerged.

In the Balkans, where local sources of copper occur in the Dinaric Alps, metallurgy developed rapidly from c. 6 kyr BP. New and larger settlements developed and arable agriculture intensified. This latter is suggested in pollen diagrams from Gromolava on the Sava River in Yugoslavia, which contain high percentages of cereal and weed pollen (Bottema 1975). There is also evidence for the exploitation of secondary animal products, such as wool, which is characteristic of many Bronze Age communities in Europe. Loom weights and spindle whorls from many archaeological sites in the Balkans indicate that weaving was commonplace. Moreover, sheep were part of a mixed farming economy that included einkorn and emmer wheats together with six-row barley, millet and flax (Barker 1985). It is possible that climatic deterioration occurred in the third millennium BC which may have led to greater reliance on pastoralism as the increased incidence of late spring frosts curtailed arable productivity. Although cereals and legumes continued to be cultivated, the shift towards pastoralism could have caused the development of smaller and more dispersed settlements, as suggested by

Bankoff *et al.* (1980). During the next thousand years, metal implements, hitherto confined to the higher levels of society for ornaments and weapons, became much more widely used and Barker (1985) suggests that the occurrence of new crops, such as rye and spelt, may be a reflection of a trend towards cooler and wetter conditions that developed all over Europe. In the second millenium BC, iron-working became established, although it was not until a few centuries BC that iron implements, including iron ploughs, became widespread.

In Britain, the prehistoric farming of which has been documented by Fowler (1983), the Bronze Age which began *c.* 4 kyr BP and witnessed the establishment of field systems, especially in lowland Britain on the chalk soils of the south. The open, predominantly non-wooded landscape that typifies much of southern Britain today owes its origins to the intensification of agricultural systems that originated in the neolithic period which were based on mixed farming. There is also archaeological and palynological evidence for forest clearance and cereal cultivation in many upland areas of the north and west and in Ireland (Mitchell 1976) as clearance became widespread and more permanent. In areas like the North York Moors there is also evidence for extensive soil deterioration (Dimbleby 1962) as will be discussed in section 3.4.3. As in other parts of Europe, there was growing reliance on domesticated plants and animals and a considerable reduction in hunting and gathering. In the Boyne Valley of Ireland, dominated by the impressive passage grave of New Grange, there is palaeobotanical evidence for a mixed-farming economy (Groenman-van Waateringe and Pals 1982). Emmer wheat, barley and vetch formed the basis of the arable economy while cattle and pigs dominated the pastoral sector and may have been used for the manuring of crops as well as for meat and secondary products.

There is evidence for climatic deterioration after *c.* 3 kyr BP in Britain, though this varied in intensity from place to place. Lamb (1981) has estimated that the growing season may have been shortened by as much as 5 weeks as temperatures in the 3–2.75 kyr BP period declined by 2 °C. Agricultural systems appear in general to have adjusted to these changes (see section 2.5.1) although there is also evidence for some abandonment in upland regions. On Dartmoor, for example, upland pastures and well-established late Bronze Age arable systems were abandoned and there was some forest regeneration as well as increased peat growth (summary in Cunliffe 1985). In southern England, which may not have been so severely affected by climatic change as the more marginal upland areas, population had increased and a number of defended hill-forts had been constructed by *c.* 2.4 kyr BP, each of which, Cunliffe (1985) suggests, controlled a specific territory within which numerous smaller settlements were established. One of the most notable of these Iron Age hill-forts is that of Danebury in Hampshire (Cunliffe 1984). The general establishment of such fortified centres may well be a reflection of more intense land-use necessitated both by increased population and the decrease in cultivable upland areas. Certainly the evidence from Danebury indicates an intense mixed-farming system in its catchment, with open pasture on the upland down, arable cultivation on gentle slopes and the edges of water-meadows where cattle were grazed in the spring and autumn. There is also evidence from elsewhere in southern Britain for similar intensification of farming systems, many of which exacerbated soil erosion begun earlier in the Bronze Age and which was one of the ways in which human communities brought about environmental change.

3.4.3 THE ROLES OF BRONZE AND IRON AGE GROUPS IN ENVIRONMENTAL CHANGE

The ways in which Bronze Age and Iron Age groups brought about environmental change were not dissimilar to those of the earlier neolithic groups, but were more intense. Clearance for agriculture continued and the resulting more open landscape became more susceptible to soil erosion. The landscape of northwest Europe witnessed the establishment of nucleated and dispersed settlements which had hitherto only been characteristic of the Near East where large cities, like Jericho and Çatal Hüyük, flourished. A range of new monuments also appeared, the most impressive of which are the megaliths such as Stonehenge in Britain and the stone alignments near Carnac in France, though many of these had their origins in the neolithic period. Barrows, cairns and dolmens which still persist in large numbers on the European landscape all attest to the practice of burial of the dead. These constructions bear witness today to the cultural impact of human groups on the landscape.

In the Near East new crops such as the olive, vine and fig were domesticated and as agricultural systems expanded the character of the landscape changed. Wagstaff (1985) states that woodland clearance continued and van Zeist *et al.* (1975) have shown, via pollen analysis, that in southwestern Turkey the natural woodlands were extensively cleared for cereal cultivation between 4 and 2 kyr BP when fruit trees were also introduced. In addition, the development of irrigation systems in Egypt (section 3.4.2), Persia, the Negev Desert and Mesopotamia created new landscape features as well as facilitating the expansion of agriculture. In all probability, the harnessing of waters from the Tigris and Euphrates which began *c.* 5 kyr BP enabled the development of the twelve city-states that comprised the Sumerian civilisation and in which the city of Ur was pre-eminent though short-lived. According to Wagstaff (1985) problems such as salinisation arose due to over-irrigation, especially in lower Mesopotamia, and may have led by *c.* 4.4 kyr BP to increasing reliance on barley, which is more tolerant of halophilous conditions than wheat. Environmental problems such as this may have contributed to the decline of Ur *c.* 4 kyr BP because of the unsuitability of the land for a more diverse range of crops. It is likely that environmental issues related to food provision were just as important in ancient civilisations as they are in the political climate of today.

In Mediterranean Europe, agricultural systems also expanded and wrought ecological and geomorphological changes that were concomitant with social and political changes. The Early Bronze Age of the Aegean region, for example, witnessed the emergence from neolithic societies of the Minoan and then the Mycenaean state societies in the second millennium BC. As in the Near East, cultivation of the olive and vine were developed as agricultural systems became more intense and spread into areas like Almeria in Spain which could only be sufficiently productive if irrigation was practised. Problems associated with an overstretched agricultural system such as poor harvests and droughts may have contributed to the collapse of the Mycenaean culture *c.* 3 kyr BP, by creating political instability. There is also evidence from the Balkan region that environmental problems associated with agriculture caused social reorganisations even earlier than that of

Sumeria and Mycenae. Dennell (1983) presents evidence from several sites, such as Nova Zagora and Ezero in Bulgaria, for extensive colluvial deposits which formed as a result of excessive upland grazing.

Environmental changes were also occurring during the Bronze Age and Iron Age in more peripheral areas of Europe. In Britain there is evidence for extensive forest clearance and areas such as Dartmoor – that today would be considered marginal for arable cultivation – were exploited (section 3.4.2). Dimbleby (1984) has summarised some of the effects of Bronze Age agriculture on the British landscape, the most significant of which relate to soil degradation. Studies on buried soils preserved beneath Bronze Age earthworks indicate that in areas where soils have a low base status, especially in upland areas, the removal of forest cover led first to acidification and then to podzolisation in drier areas and peat formation in wetter areas. Frequently, such soil changes preceded colonisation by moorland species like heather (*Calluna vulgaris*) since the reduced base status precluded regeneration of forest even after the abandonment of farming. There is also evidence for accelerated soil erosion, a process of environmental degradation that began in the neolithic, from many parts of Britain during the Bronze Age. Haworth (1985), for example, has related changes in the diatom assemblages of sediments from Barfield Tarn in the English Lake District to erosion of glacial clays caused by neolithic farming in the catchment. Similarly, Brown and Barber (1985) have shown that sediment deposition accelerated rapidly in the catchment of the Ripple Brook, a tributary of the River Severn, in the late Bronze Age and early Iron Age (c. 2.9–2.3 kyr BP). The introduction of the iron plough into early British agricultural systems also exacerbated soil erosion. Bell (1983) has shown that colluviation accelerated in the South Downs during the Iron Age, although it undoubtedly occurred earlier, removing loess-rich soils from the hilltops into the valley bottoms. Here, pockets of fertile land were created at the expense of the uplands, a process which Cunliffe (1985) suggests provided location sites for later Saxon and medieval villages and farmsteads.

The examples given above bear witness to the considerable impact of prehistoric cultures on the European landscape and it is possible to discern in Bronze Age and Iron Age Europe the vestiges of modern agricultural landscapes. Moreover, the albeit patchy evidence indicates that problems of soil erosion, leaching and salinisation were of considerable significance, as they are today.

3.5 CONCLUSION

This chapter reflects on the emergence of *Homo sapiens sapiens* as a manipulator and controller of environmental processes. It is perhaps ironic that those very forces of ecological systems which helped to stimulate hominid development should eventually come under hominid control. Stone, wild animals and plants were among the first resources to be used, and by the upper palaeolithic, if not earlier, humans were using controlled fires to manipulate flora and fauna in well-organised hunter-gatherer food-procuring strategies.

A major, though probably gradual, turning-point in human and environmental history was the domestication of plants and animals some 10 kyr BP. This process, which allowed humans to control the fundamental genetic characteristics of plants and animals, was an essential precursor to the development of agricultural systems that in turn led to major changes in social organisation and which underpinned some of the most powerful ancient civilisations. These may well have risen and fallen on the strength of their ability to manipulate food production and the new resources of copper, tin and iron on which metallurgical industries were dependent and which facilitated agricultural intensification. The development of irrigation systems in more arid regions provided a further means by which humans learnt to manipulate their natural resources and to exert more control over water supplies, an essential ingredient to efficient crop production.

The ability to manipulate the environment, however, did not develop trouble free. The archaeological record clearly attests to problems of environmental management such as over-grazing, declining soil fertility, soil erosion and salinisation. Such problems are just as important today, as will be discussed in Chapters 6 and 7.

FURTHER READING

Barker G 1985 *Prehistoric farming in Europe*. Cambridge University Press

Bogucki P 1988 *Forest farmers and stockholders*. Cambridge University Press

Gamble C 1986 *The palaeolithic settlement of Europe*. Cambridge University Press

National Geographic 1988 The peopling of the earth. *National Geographic* **174**, (4)

Rukang W, Olsen J W (eds) 1985 *Palaeoanthropology and palaeolithic archaeology in the People's Republic of China*. Academic Press, London and New York

Soffer O (ed) 1987 *The Pleistocene Old World : regional perspectives*. Plenum Press, New York and London

Wagstaff J M 1985 *The evolution of Middle Eastern landscapes: an outline to AD 1840*. Croom Helm, London and Sydney

Zohary D, Hopf M 1988 *Domestication of plants in the Old World*. Clarendon Press, Oxford

ENVIRONMENTAL CHANGE IN THE HISTORIC PERIOD

4.1 INTRODUCTION

The point in time when prehistory ended and history began is an arbitrary distinction from region to region and country to country. Since many of the technological innovations that enabled human communities to manipulate their environment were developed in Europe, history as defined here begins with the Greek and Roman Empires. These civilisations wrought considerable environmental change and the Romans especially influenced the people–environment relationship throughout Europe, as will be briefly discussed below. Since an appraisal of global environmental change throughout the historic period is beyond the scope of this text, emphasis will be placed on developments in Britain though, as referred to in section 1.1.1, many European, Islamic and Chinese scholars contributed considerably to global geographical knowledge.

Prior to the eighteenth century Britain was predominantly rural with an agriculturally based economy. Agricultural improvements in the seventeenth century, however, provided a sound base for industrial development and from the mid 1700s the Industrial Revolution occurred along with the rise of urban centres. Such innovations laid the foundations for modern society but were not without cost in terms of environmental change. The increased use of coal, and subsequently other fossil fuels, as well as the production of artificial fertilisers, were to have far-reaching environmental effects, some of which are only just coming to light today.

In addition, Britain along with other European countries has greatly influenced environmental change in many other parts of the world. This began in the fifteenth century which was a period of exploration when the New World was discovered and trade links established with the Far East. The initial impact of Europeans in these new-found lands was relatively slight, but new territories were annexed as empires were consolidated and resources exploited. The eighteenth and nineteenth centuries witnessed large-scale expansion of European interests in their colonies and the environmental impact of this will be discussed in relation to Africa, the Americas and Australia.

4.2 ENVIRONMENTAL CHANGE IN PRE-INDUSTRIAL BRITAIN AND EUROPE

After the fall of the Mycenaean civilisation *c.* 1200 BC, southeastern Europe entered what is called the 'Greek Dark Age' which lasted for some 400 years until the emergence of the city-states that characterise classical Greece. In terms of the landscape, the Greek temples of this period vie in their impressiveness with the earlier megalithic monuments of western Europe and their occurrence, together with the remains of large cities such as Troy (in modern Turkey), attest to the trading and colonising abilities of this ancient civilisation. By the third century BC, however, Rome was developing as a major Mediterranean power and the Greek Empire declined as the military power of Rome prevailed. Meanwhile the rest of Europe was experiencing the development of iron metallurgy which facilitated the widespread use of the plough and agricultural intensification (section 3.4.3).

The colonisation of Britain by Rome brought about the superimposition on the landscape of villas, towns and roads as well as the first drainage networks in the Fens. Agriculture, especially in the southeast of England, intensified and several new crops were established. The gradual decline of the Roman Empire and the departure of the Romans from Britain saw a return to rural dominance, influenced by Saxon peoples from nearby Europe. The Anglo-Saxon landscape, moulded as it was by Roman colonists for improved crop production to provide a surplus for Roman armies in Europe, remained rural, though not stagnant. The adoption of Christianity brought the Cistercian farmers who were paramount in the development of the wool trade and the later cloth industry. Medieval Britain, despite the desertion of villages and the Black Death, appears to have been reasonably affluent by the time the Tudor dynasty was established in 1465.

In the following 200 years, many local industries were established, based on mineral ores and especially on wool for the cloth industry. Coal-mining was initiated and coal gradually usurped charcoal as the major fuel source. Industry and the populace were rurally based and dispersed, though London was growing in importance as a major European trading centre. Agricultural innovations, as well as those in the metal and cloth industries, occurred from which the Industrial Revolution of the mid-1700s sprang.

4.2.1 THE ENVIRONMENTAL IMPACT OF THE GREEKS AND ROMANS

Although the abundance of archaeological remains attest to the considerable influence of classical Greece and the sophistication of its society, there is very little other evidence to bear witness to the impact of this civilisation on the landscape. Agriculture intensified as the olive was once again brought into widespread cultivation (Boardman 1976) and numerous classical authors refer to the cutting and burning of forest as populations expanded. According to Champion *et al.* (1984) there is written evidence for the intensive production of cereals and pulses while cultivation of the olive and vine provided products that could be traded.

It is also likely that population growth together with considerable metallurgical expertise provided both the motive and the means for expansion. A shortage of areas for arable cultivation necessitated expansion while metal goods, wine and olives provided surpluses that could be used for trade in exchange for raw materials and/or food. The imprint of Greek society is to be found in areas like southern France or Spain where similar polycultural agricultural systems developed. It is also of interest that society was sufficiently well organised and affluent to support scholarly work which is manifested in the abundance of Greek literature and the interest that the Greeks developed in relation to earth surface features (see section 1.1.1).

Similarly, there is much written and archaeological evidence for the Romans' military and social organisation, and Potter (1987) has documented many of the changes that occurred in Roman Italy. In relation to landscape changes, the most significant developments in Italy were centred on land tenure and the spread of villas and farms. The latter used slave labour derived from the conquered lands of Europe and were concerned with wine and cereal production. The character of land tenure also changed as small-holdings became submerged into large estates (the *latifundia*), though this process was reversed as the Roman Empire declined in the second century AD. Aerial photography has revealed vestiges of Roman field systems in many parts of Italy such as the Apulian Tavoliere where colonists divided the land into grids of square fields in a process known as centuriation and built farms, often in rectangular enclosures, each one having its own approach road. Lines of pits were also constructed in alignment with the roads and were used for storing the olive crop.

According to Rees (1987) a bipartite division of the empire's lands into Mediterranean areas, with hot dry summers, and the Northern Provinces, with a cooler wetter climate and more severe winters, was characterised by different farming techniques, notably 'dry farming' in the former and 'humid farming' in the latter. 'Dry farming' involved arable crop production in lowland, mainly coastal areas and alluvial plains with vine and olive cultivation on less productive slopes and summer pasture in higher areas. In the Northern Provinces, arable and mixed farming characteristic of Iron Age communities (sections 3.4.2 and 3.4.3) dominated lowland areas while pasture for stock rearing prevailed in the upland zone.

In view of environmental limitations, a crop–fallow system dominated Mediterranean agriculture with intensive ploughing to prepare the ground. According to Rees (1987) one crop was obtained every 2 years to take advantage of 2 years' worth of rainfall. The emphasis was on water conservation which was facilitated by the creation of a fine tilth that reduced evaporation from the lower levels of the soil and encouraged percolation of the winter rains. Frequent weeding of the crop also helped to conserve moisture by reducing transpiration, while the use of fallow and the practice of stubble burning helped to maintain soil fertility in the absence of grazing animals that were confined to the uplands. The impact of Roman farming on

Mediterranean landscapes is also witnessed by the remains of drainage networks. At the local level, open or covered drains were constructed to conserve water and were positioned to keep soil erosion to a minimum. In other areas, such as the Po Valley, large-scale drainage networks were constructed to increase the land suitable for agriculture. Elsewhere, such as southern Spain, irrigation networks provided an adequate water supply for fruit, olives and vines. Wheat and spelt were the main cereal crops with millet in the Middle East and Gaul. Legumes were also important, grown in rotation with cereals to replenish nitrogen in the soil they also provided animal fodder. Fruit, vegetables (such as beans, turnip, carrots and peas) and a variety of herbs were also significant crops and were produced in irrigated market gardens and orchards. There is also evidence (Wacher 1987) for an increased range of secondary animal products such as cheeses, glue and lard as well as the keeping of animals, like the dog and barbary ape, for pets.

In the Northern Provinces such as Britain the agricultural practices, settlements and communication networks of the Romans also changed the character of the landscape. While the indigenous agricultural systems remained largely intact, the remains of villas, ancient roads and drainage networks attest to the imposition of Roman life on an Iron Age, mainly rurally based, local population. According to Dimbleby (1984) one of the reasons that the Romans were keen to annex Britain was to enhance their supply of cereals and during the period of Roman occupation (43–410) arable cultivation intensified. This was made possible by the adoption of Roman technology including better ploughs, scythes, sickles and water mills. In addition, the Romans introduced a number of new plants into Britain such as the sweet chestnut (*Castanea sativa*), which is now widespread, and the walnut (*Juglans regia*). There is also the possibility that vines (*Vitis vinifera*) were cultivated (Crawford 1985) and there is evidence, from plant macrofossils preserved in urban sites such as London, for the importation of many exotic crops. These include cucumber, gold of pleasure, peach, olive, fig and coriander (Jones 1981).

What is not clear, however, from palaeoenvironmental or archaeological studies, is how significant woodland was in the economy of Roman Britain. While there is some evidence (summarised in Turner 1981) for woodland clearance as arable farming expanded to meet the needs of local people and the occupying military, as well as for export, it is probable that coppicing or some form of woodland management was widespread to accommodate the needs of the bath-houses that are a common feature of Roman villas (Dimbleby 1984). The technological ability of the Romans to affect the landscape, however, is not in doubt. Large-scale drainage networks in the Fens, for example, allowed this hitherto unproductive area to be used for cattle grazing (Cunliffe 1985), producing both meat and leather. There is also evidence for greater development of extractive industries and pottery manufacture. In the Weald, for example, the Romans established military ironworks based on local deposits of iron ore, and Cleere (1976) has estimated that some 550 t of iron were produced each year, requiring a considerable quantity of charcoal. This could only be derived by felling and/or managing an extensive woodland area. Thus the construction of quarries and slag-heaps as well as deforestation all contributed to environmental change in this part of Britain. Rackham (1986) states: 'Roman metallurgy influenced more woodland than medieval, and may not have been much surpassed even in the seventeenth century.' Similarly, the establishment of large pottery-producing centres, such as in the New Forest and the Nene Valley exerted a toll on native woods.

While the industriousness of the Romans caused irrevocable changes on British woodlands, the intensive arable farming systems of southern Britain also came under stress as the Roman Empire itself began to disintegrate. Many areas, including those of the productive chalklands, witnessed the abandonment of arable farming and a return to pasture as Britain (and Europe) entered the Dark Ages.

4.2.2 THE BRITISH LANDSCAPE IN THE DARK AGES AND MEDIEVAL PERIODS

Information on the early part of this period is relatively scarce, especially in relation to human impact on the environment and on environmental processes. What data there are derive from limited archaeological excavations of settlements and a very few written records which relate to social organisation rather than environmental issues. Nevertheless there appears to be, in the recent literature pertaining to the so-called 'Dark Ages', a consensus among historians and archaeologists that there was considerable continuity from the earlier Romano-British period rather than large-scale disruption of social organisation and general stagnation. Continuity, however, does not necessarily imply lack of dynamism, and undoubtedly significant changes occurred in the British landscape as they did in the pre-Roman eras of British prehistory (sections 3.2.3, 3.3.3 and 3.4.3).

The decline of Roman influence in Britain was a gradual process, as was the demise of the Roman Empire. Similarly, the advent of the Saxons from the adjacent North Sea margins of Europe into Britain, which began in Roman times, was a gradual process involving infiltration and assimilation as well as invasion. It may well be that environmental issues were at the root of these processes. The fall of Rome and its outposts, in common with a number of contemporary civilisations such as Han China and Parthia (the Persian Empire), was at least in part, brought about by continuous raiding of the empire's margins by nomadic tribesmen like the Huns. In times of food scarcity, resulting from over-grazing of herds and/or ecological change, such peoples plundered the empire's boundaries so that Rome was forced to expend much resource in the provision of vast, often mercenary, legions for combat. In Britain for example, land- and sea-based raids were regularly carried out by the Scots, Picts and Saxons. Poor trade balances and internal politics also served to diminish Rome's power and in the seventh century, some 200 years after the Romans left Britain, the rise of Islam finally ended the pre-eminence of western Europe as a major power.

In Britain, one of the major changes that occurred as Roman influence diminished was the decline of the many towns that had been established. This too was gradual: some towns like London continued to flourish, though not as opulently, and others such as Exeter appear to have been continuously occupied but not as centres of regional power (see discussion in Arnold 1988). Ultimately, the infrastructure of towns, villas and roads fell into general disrepair but nevertheless their remains provided landscape features that are still in evidence today.

In terms of the rural landscape, however, the produce of which had sustained the invading army and the Roman hierarchy as well as the indigenous population, there was little disruption. Although the evidence is sparse, the major casualty of the British countryside appears to have been the Roman villas, the majority of which were simply abandoned. Since Wacher (1987) states that these provided a home for the estate managers, that is, the Roman supervisors, rather than the workers, it is perhaps not so surprising that after their demise agricultural techniques continued more or less undisturbed. While there is evidence to suggest that some abandonment of arable farming in the more productive region of southern England occurred (section 4.2.1) this may be simply explained by a relaxation of intensive farming (akin to the extensification of agriculture that is happening today in western Europe; sections 6.2.1 and 6.2.3) as population levels declined and the need for a surplus, which was often used to support Roman armies abroad, diminished. This is purely conjectural but it may well have been a contributing factor.

There is also palaeoecological evidence for forest regeneration in some parts of Britain (Turner 1981) as the extent of pasture and arable land declined. The amount of secondary woodland that developed appears to have varied from site to site and certainly never allowed forest to recover to its pre-Iron Age extent. Higham (1987) has summarised much of the available data for the northern counties of England and concludes that, in general, the rural character of the region, created during the Iron Age and under Roman occupation, continued throughout the fifth and sixth centuries AD. Rackham (1986) has also compared the extent of woodlands mentioned in the Anglo-Saxon charters, compiled between 600 and 1080, with that recorded in the Domesday Book of 1086. The two compare well, once again reflecting continuity in the countryside during the so-called 'Dark Ages'. Furthermore, there is ample suggestion in the Anglo-Saxon charters for intensive use of woodland as part of the rural economy. Coppicing was widespread, providing rods and fuel and the woodlands were used for pannage. Rackham states: 'The Anglo-Saxons in 600 years probably increased the area of farmland, managed the woodland more intensively, and made many minor alterations. But they did not radically reorganise the woodland landscape.'

Palaeoecological evidence for land-use change during the first millenium AD has been summarised by M Jones (1986). At Hockham Mere in East Anglia, for example, the first 300 years saw arable farming increase at the expense of pasture while the reverse is true during the following 200 years. Arable farming once again increased in the seventh and eighth centuries AD and was followed by a slight reduction in agricultural activities overall. According to Jones this interplay between pasture, arable and woodland is reflected in pollen diagrams from the South Downs of Sussex, from Snelsmere on the Berkshire Downs and from various sites in County Durham, although the timing of events varied considerably from place to place and all were relatively minor in relation to the widespread forest clearance of earlier millennia (section 3.4.3). There is also evidence for localised forest clearance in the tenth and eleventh centuries. For example, Tallis (1985, 1987) has examined the historical record of peat erosion in the southern Pennines. His studies indicate that Viking settlers may have initiated gullying as they removed the woodland cover from nearby hillslopes, thus disrupting local hydrological regimes.

In terms of settlement pattern, the demise of urban centres as the Romans withdrew gave rise to a rurally based economy centred on small, scattered settlements and individual farmsteads. This is confirmed by Hall (1988) who states that areas of light soil, especially along the slopes of major river valleys such as the Nene, were favoured for settlement as they had been during the prehistoric and Roman periods. Clay-rich soils were generally avoided. This situation was to change, however, by the time the Normans invaded and Hall suggests that the dispersed settlement pattern was abandoned to be replaced by villages with strip fields. Todd (1987) has also examined the evidence for rural settlement and society in the English southwest and suggests that the population was fairly evenly scattered everywhere but in the uplands. Pasture was abundant, supporting mainly sheep, and the agricultural economy was based on mixed farming as it was in most other parts of Britain. In the northern counties in which the establishment of Christianity led to the construction of hundreds of churches and the rise to power of numerous monasteries, settlement remained dispersed. Higham (1987) suggests that the predominance of sheep herding was not conducive to nucleation and kept the populace dispersed. Remains of many of these ancient monasteries and churches, that produced the written records for the activities of the day e.g. Bede's *Historia Ecclesiastica*, provide evidence of the importance of the church during this period.

When the Normans arrived in Britain in 1066 they found a landscape that, according to Rackham (1985), was only 15 per cent wooded with widespread heathland and a scattered, predominantly rural population. The Domesday Book of 1086 presents much information regarding the character of the medieval English landscape. Woodland apart, 35 per cent of England was arable land and a further 30 per cent was pasture, the remainder consisting of non-agricultural land such as moorlands and heaths as well as settlement. In the ensuing 400 years before the first Tudor monarch many changes occurred, including the rise to power of the monasteries and their involvement in sheep farming as well as a large population increase in the twelfth and thirteenth centuries. The village became the focus of settlement, in contrast to the dispersed nature of earlier dwellings, and although towns once again became established the population was still largely rurally based. In addition, land which had hitherto remained unproductive was brought into cultivation, often under the guidance of Cistercian monks who first came to Britain in 1128. Many of their monasteries were sited in fairly remote upland moorland regions which they used for extensive cattle and, especially, sheep grazing. The latter provided the much-needed raw materials for the developing wool industry.

The need for more pasture, mainly to increase wool output for cloth manufacture and export, as well as the need for more arable land to support increasing populations, placed more pressure on the land. As a result many landscape changes occurred. The areas designated as royal forests (e.g. the New Forest) by William the Conqueror and his successors, which were protected by special laws and which had curtailed agricultural expansion even though they were not always well wooded (the original meaning of the word 'forest' was 'outside', and was used in the eleventh century to denote land that was governed by forest law rather than common law; M Jones 1986), gradually declined in extent after 1200 (Cantor 1982) as agricultural land encroached. Nevertheless, management remained intensive as both the crown and the people found a source of revenue from the wood itself, which was coppiced and pollarded to provide a regular harvest, as well as from the pannage and herbage that the forests provided for pigs and other domestic animals. The crown also derived appreciable revenue in rent from the tenants who maintained animal herds, stud farms and various metal industries.

Cantor (1982) states that by 1334 the area of the royal forests had shrunk to about two-thirds of their 1250 extent because of an inability to enforce the forest law and because taxes on other industries exceeded forest revenues. By the late fifteenth century, by which time the Tudors were installed in the monarchy, woodland cover had significantly diminished leaving only vestiges of which some, such as Epping Forest and the New Forest, have survived to the present day.

According to Greig (1988) the most significant staple crops in medieval Britain were wheat, barley, oats and rye. Barley was also used to make ale and the most commonly grown vegetables were members of the cabbage and onion families. Non-staple foods that were grown include herbs such as parsley (*Petroselinium crispum*) and mint (*Mentha* spp.) while fruit growing was confined to gardens and orchards and included apples, pears, plums and cherries. As Greig (1988) reports, much of the evidence for fruit consumption, both imported and locally grown, comes from the archaeobotanical record preserved in urban cesspits and latrines. The remains of grapes and figs are most common, the latter being entirely imported while the former may have been locally grown in southern England and/or imported. In addition, flax (*Linum usitatissimum*) and hemp (*Cannabis sativa*) were often cultivated as garden crops for fibre while there was a marked increase in the cultivation of legumes which were mostly used as fodder. Overall, the historical and archaeological record suggests that between the twelfth and fifteenth centuries the range of fruit and herbs gradually increased but that the staple foods remained the cereals.

In terms of livestock, cattle, sheep and pigs were the most important animals, providing meat, milk and fibre as well as fertiliser. As Grant (1988) states, however, wild animals were also important components of the English medieval economy. Hunting once again resumed significance in contrast to the earlier Anglo-Saxon period, though populations of the native red and roe deer and the introduced fallow deer were managed in enclosed parks. By the thirteenth century, more animals were being reared as a source of meat and as a consequence the area of pasturage increased and horses replaced cattle for farm work.

The most common, but by no means universal, method of farming was via the open-field system which was often associated with nucleated settlements (Astill 1988). Within such a system the resources of the manor were distributed between the inhabitants so that each had access to arable and pastureland, while some land was left fallow so that animals could roam and manure the fields, thus maintaining fertility. Astill states that the arable areas were subdivided into two or three parts within which each farmer worked individual long plots. An overseer such as a reeve or herdsman ensured that all farmers contributed to the collective functioning of the manor and that common grazing was available in marginal areas or 'waste'. As Astill points out, variations on this system occurred throughout England and the amount of common grazing land varied from place to place. The vestiges of these systems can still be seen in many parts of Britain today and characterise, along with villages, champion countryside such as the Midlands (Williamson and Bellamy 1987).

This organisation of land is in contrast to that of the so-called ancient woodland regions of the Welsh Borders and southeast England where settlement was more dispersed with more discrete and less communal landholdings. According to Cantor (1987) the 'run–rig' or 'infield–outfield' system was another variation on the open-field system and was particularly common in areas of poorer land such as northwest England. Essentially, one field closest to the village or farmstead, the infield, was intensively and often permanently cultivated while another field, the outfield, more distant from the settlement, was cultivated less intensively with only half of it being cultivated for a few years before being left fallow.

Other areas of the countryside also changed in character as more land for agriculture was sought. Many wetland areas came under pressure. Williams (1982) states: 'Of all the landscapes created by the reclamation of waste during the medieval period that of the marshlands was the most spectacular.' Prior to this period and apart from the efforts of the Romans in the Fens (section 4.2.1), settlement had avoided low-lying marshy areas despite the fact that their produce contributed to the local economy. Much of that, however, was to change in the 1100–1300 period, leaving a legacy which persists to the present day. The Norfolk Broads, for example, were formed as a result of medieval peat digging and subsequent flooding of the pits. The most obvious example of medieval reclamation is that of the Fens of East Anglia. Settlements established during Anglo-Saxon times expanded. According to Rackham (1986) this was facilitated by the construction (in the thirteenth century) of new banks and ditches, the most extensive of which was the remade 'Roman Bank' of about one 100 km to keep the waters of the Wash at bay. In consequence the Fens rapidly enjoyed economic preeminence. Rackham (1986), referring to the Lay Subsidy agreement of 1334, states that 31 of the 106 richest places in England were situated in the seaward Fens. The economy, based on grass, revolved around animal products including meat, butter and wool as well as reeds and sedge for thatching and fuel. Other marshland areas, such as the Somerset Levels and Romney Marsh, underwent similar reclamation schemes that afforded economic prosperity.

Prosperity, however, was to be short-lived for the British countryside, one in which an extensive road network was now in place and one which enjoyed considerable trade with its European neighbours. The large-scale abandonment of villages and hamlets (Beresford and Hirst 1971) have been attributed by Cantor (1982) to a complex set of factors including the Black Death of 1348 and the conversion of arable land to sheep pasture that resulted in evictions. It is also likely that the onset of the 'Little Ice Age' (sections 1.2.3 and 2.5.1), which brought a reduction in the growing season and increased crop failures, played a significant role in village abandonment. Whatever the cause, an economic recession ensued.

4.2.3 Tudor and Post-tudor Influences on the British Landscape

By the time that Henry VII, the first Tudor monarch, ascended to the English throne in 1485 there had been an economic recovery. Cantor (1987) suggests that this was due to the entrepreneurial activities of church and state magnates, the more well-to-do families as well as wealthier peasants who established the yeoman farmer class. These groups took the opportunity to expand and develop their estates and exploited the economic plight of landowners in need of tenants to furnish their revenue. In effect a new landowning and land-leasing élite emerged in which merchants and lawyers were just as prominent as those royally connected. One of their legacies to the present-day landscape was the impressive residential buildings that attest to the fine architecture of the time.

New centres of affluence also emerged, especially towns like Norwich, Bury St Edmunds and Exeter which were associated with cloth manufacture. This was a major growth industry which had developed from the wool production of the earlier period, when much of this raw material was exported to neighbouring Europe. As a result, the West Country, East Anglia and the West Riding of Yorkshire had developed as major cloth-producing regions for the home and European market (Ramsay 1982). London and the crown also benefited considerably from the wool trade. The former, by now a major centre in European trade, became more affluent as craftspeople and merchants became established. The crown derived considerable revenue from the cloth export tax and from import taxes on such commodities as dyestuffs. According to Ramsay (1982) the rise to pre-eminence of this industry and associated trade derives from the quality of the product, associated craft skills and political stability. Even during the Civil War of 1642–45, trade networks were not appreciably disrupted. Other aspects of the landscape were also changed, including improvements in communications and in river navigation, for example the Rivers Aire and Calder were deepened in the early 1700s to provide for the needs of the Yorkshire wool industry.

Other industrial developments were also occurring in the fifteenth and sixteenth centuries. Many were based on metallurgy and almost all were rurally based, taking advantage of water-power, the availability of charcoal from dispersed woodland and the still largely dispersed rural population which was engaged in both agriculture and manufacturing. The Weald, as it had been in Romano-British times (section 4.2.1), was the chief centre of iron production. Its natural resources of abundant ironstone, easily dammed incised rivers that provided water-power for bellows and hammers, and abundant charcoal, along with the region's proximity to London, ensured its pre-eminence. Two other areas were also developing as major centres of iron production for similar reasons. These were the Forest of Dean, where the foundations of the iron industry had been established in the Roman period, and the Cleveland Hills where, in common with the Weald, blast-furnaces were commonplace landscape features. Other metals were also being exploited on an increasingly commercial basis. Examples include lead-mining in Derbyshire which had also been initiated in the Roman period. The history of this is reflected in the geochemical record of local peat deposits (Lee and Tallis 1973; Livett et al. 1979) which show an increase in lead deposition from c. 1400 onward, with massive increases between 1600 and 1700. Similarly, the tin industry in Cornwall, glass-making in the Midlands and salt production in Cheshire became established, and although such activities were on a relatively small scale, they provided the industrial base which was the precursor to the Industrial Revolution (section 4.3).

However, the Industrial Revolution of the eighteenth century would not have been possible without the development of coal-mining. Blunden and Turner (1985) have suggested that of all the innovations during this period, coal-mining on a large scale had the greatest impact on the landscape. Deforestation over the preceding millennia and the relatively ineffectual attempts of the Norman and Tudor dynasties to establish conservation measures had resulted in a dearth of fuel resources that were so essential to the developing manufacturing base. Coal provided an acceptable alternative and by 1600 most of the fields worked today were in use, though on a localised scale. This new source of fuel allowed metallurgical industries to shift from the traditional areas like the Weald to areas such as South Wales, Shropshire and the Midlands. As a result, local landscapes became more 'industrialised' and the populace increasingly shifted from agricultural activities to industrial ones, though still on a local scale in a predominantly rural environment. Although it was slow to be accepted as a domestic fuel, the use of coal gradually rose as the price of wood rapidly increased. Much of the coal produced from the Northeast catered for the London market. According to Clay (1984b) cargoes arriving in London rose by 1500 per cent between the 1580s and the 1700s, reaching an average of 450 000 t per year. By this time, coal was also the predominant fuel used in most industrial activities and within the next 300 years it was adopted in the iron-smelting industries. Those coalfields with relatively easy access to cheap water transport underwent the most rapid development, e.g. the Northeast, Shropshire fields with access to the River Severn, Nottingham fields adjacent to the River Trent and fields in South Wales from where coal could be transported by sea. As deeper mines and more sophisticated equipment became necessary to retrieve the coal, more capital was needed. In consequence, mining activities became separated from agriculture and coal-extractive industries on a large scale were born, controlled by entrepreneurs not directly involved in the industry itself.

The nature of agricultural practices also changed between the fourteenth and seventeenth centuries, contributing towards the changing character of the British landscape. Agriculture was affected by the 'Little Ice Age' (section 2.5.1), the evidence for which has been reviewed by Grove (1988), which caused farm abandonment in southeast Scotland and Dartmoor. Grove (1988) states that by 1500, summers were c. 0.7 °C cooler than in the previous two centuries, which reduced the growing season. This would have been particularly crucial in marginal upland areas but Grove (1988) suggests that even in lowland England the growing season may have been reduced by as much as 5 weeks, which may have been responsible, in part, for rural depopulation and the desertion of villages. Moreover, other parts of Europe, especially Scandinavia, suffered declines in population and agricultural production after 1300, which also suggests that climate played a significant role in environmental change during this period.

Changes in the rural landscape have been discussed by Butlin (1982) and Clay (1984a) while Thirsk (1987) has examined agrarian history between 1500 and 1750. According to the latter, many of the innovations associated with the so-called Agricultural Revolution of 1750–1850 were already occurring in the previous 200 years. Agricultural efficiency increased, enabling the support of 3 million more people in 1700 than in 1540, though many only managed to scrape a bare living in conditions verging on famine. The changes which wrought this increased productivity included the adoption of a 3–4 year crop rotation followed by grass leys of 6–12 years; the more intensive use of a more varied range of fertilisers such as marl, lime, seaweed; the ponding of streams so that the fertility of water-meadows was replenished by silt deposition; the introduction of new crops such as rapeseed, lucerne and vegetables such as potatoes; improved breeds of animals; and reclamation of wetlands to provide more arable land (see below).

Butlin (1982) has also examined the changes that occurred in land tenure of which enclosure was particularly significant. This involved the enclosing of agricultural units by hedges or walls, replacing the more open field systems that were so characteristic of the earlier Anglo-Saxon and Norman periods. The rate and timing of enclosure varied considerably during the 1500–1800 period and much of it was enforced by Act of Parliament. Overall, enclosures reduced the amount of common land and led to a decline of the small farmer, a process that continued in the post-1800 period. According to Rackham (1986) the hedges planted between 1750 and 1850 were at least equal in extent to all those planted in the previous 500 years, adding considerably to an already common feature of the British landscape.

The need for more arable land, as population expanded, also brought about other landscape changes, including the reclamation of wetlands. Once again interest turned to the Fens as agricultural entrepreneurs recognised the potential of the area for crop production. Vermuyden, a Dutch engineer, was responsible for designing and constructing a new drainage network. This included diversion of the Great Ouse River which created the Old and New Bedford Rivers in 1637 and 1651. As Rackham (1986) recounts, the scheme was not particularly successful either in terms of drainage or local popularity since it severely limited common rights and was constructed to benefit the investors rather than the indigenous populace. It also initiated environmental degradation, especially soil and peat erosion as the land surface shrank. Nevertheless, between 1637 and 1725 some 2500 km^2 of the Fens were drained and successfully converted into agricultural land (Ratcliffe 1984). Further drain construction was also necessary to ensure efficiency, often in conjunction with windmills to pump drainage water into channels. The system is maintained today by electric pumps.

The changes in agriculture and industry that were characteristic of Britain during this period were also occurring in other European nations, trade with whom was well established. The fifteenth and sixteenth centuries were also periods of extensive exploration. Columbus, Vasco da Gama and Magellan are but a few of the notables who established the existence of hitherto unexplored lands. By 1700, several European nations had established colonies in Africa, Southeast Asia and the Americas, where they had profound effects on the indigenous people and their landscapes as will be discussed in section 4.4.

4.3 ENVIRONMENTAL CHANGE IN INDUSTRIAL BRITAIN

Between 1700 and 1800 the population of Britain increased from 5 million to more than 10 million and the gross national product rose by an average of 2 per cent per annum between 1760 and 1830 (The Times *The World* 1986). The development of industrial innovations, so apparent in the earlier 200 years, accelerated. Britain became known as 'the workshop of the world' as industry became the mainstay of the country's economy. Urban centres like Birmingham, which had hitherto been home to semi-rural industries, flourished. This was a period of rapid change both in terms of social organisation and the landscape. The growth of urban centres, wherein industry was concentrated, encroached on the rural landscape and encouraged the movement of people from the countryside into the towns and cities. For the first time in its history, Britain became an industrial rather than a rural society. Changes in agriculture, many of which like the industrial base were already developing in the previous 200 years, led to increases in productivity that were essential for the maintenance of a rapidly growing population. In consequence, the British landscape was irrevocably changed as industry, more intensive agriculture and higher populations exacted their toll.

In addition, national and international politics have come to play a significant role in landscape change since they influence trade as well as agricultural and industrial production and economic policies. Political and trade liaisons such as the European Economic Community (the EEC or 'Common Market') have greatly influenced, for example, agricultural policies. Moreover, many of the environmental problems which have arisen because of industrial and agricultural activities have become political issues of both national and international significance, a classic case being that of acidification (Ch. 5). Of prime concern in this section, however, are the more immediate changes that occurred as Britain's industrial base became pre-eminent.

4.3.1 THE ENVIRONMENTAL CONSEQUENCES OF INDUSTRIALISATION

In Chapter 1 (section 1.1.2) reference was made to Odum's (1975) classification of ecosystems based on energy characteristics. In addition, section 4.2 documents the development of Britain's agricultural and industrial base which are typical of types 3 and 4 ecosystems listed in Table 1.2. The latter, the fuel-powered urban–industrial systems, arose as a consequence of the Industrial Revolution, and while these are the wealth-generating systems they also have a major impact on neighbouring ecosystems. On the one hand, the population of such systems is not engaged in food production and is reliant on the solar-powered and human-subsidised solar-powered ecosystems. These, therefore, have to be more efficient in order to provide food in excess of the requirements of the food producers. On the other hand, such neighbouring ecosystems are frequently in receipt of urban–industrial waste products such as sewage, mineral extractive waste and chemical waste, as well as domestic refuse. These are often the major sources of pollution which occurs well beyond the urban boundary (section 5.4). All of these factors contributed to the shaping of the British landscape in the nineteenth and twentieth centuries.

The close relationship that exists between agriculture and industry is, according to Berg (1985), well illustrated by events in Britain during the 1700–1820 period. The rise of large-scale capitalist farming on a landlord–tenant basis, one outcome of the enclosure movement, allowed urban centres to develop because such agricultural systems were able to produce food surpluses as a result of the innovations described in section 4.2.3. In addition, industrial developments with their associated scientific progress had considerable repercussions for agriculture, one of the most notable being the production of artificial nitrate fertilisers which superseded the use of natural nitrates (guano) imported from Chile between 1820 and 1850 (section 6.3).

In terms of the direct impact of industry on the British landscape it is perhaps the exploitation of natural resources that wrought the most extensive changes. In 1840 there were 250 active tin-mines in Cornwall and although the industry was to decline in significance in the next 30 years, the mining and smelting activities, and associated workers' houses, have left the vestiges of an industrial landscape on what today is primarily a rural area noted for its tourist industry. In fact, Cornwall in the middle of the nineteenth century had one of the most industrialised landscapes in Britain and the mines employed about 30 000 people. In the 1860s industrial decline had set in and, as Blunden and Turner (1985) comment, many of the industrial relics of this period remain as a testimony to the heyday of the tin industry. For example, the engine houses and tall chimney flues of two mine complexes at Botallack and Levant in West Penwith, which allowed tin to be recovered from beneath the sea-bed, remain although many of the waste tips have since been overgrown. However, as the tin-mining industry declined, attention turned to Cornwall's china clay as the pottery industry, centred on Stoke-on-Trent in Staffordshire, expanded and sought raw materials. This industry continues to have a considerable impact on the landscape today, as has been discussed by Bradshaw and Chadwick (1980).

Changes in energy provision also brought about landscape changes especially during the Victorian era (1837–1901) when there was a massive change from water and wind power to coal. Between 1750 and 1850, water-power sustained the early years of industrial development. Thompson (1985) states that in 1850 water-power, facilitated by mill-races, weirs, dams and reservoirs, provided about one-third of all industrial power, declining to about 10 or 12 per cent by 1870 as coal-generated steam became the major source of energy. The demand for coal thus increased, creating a very different landscape to that which was harnessed for the provision of water-power. Thompson (1985) describes these new developments as: 'Awesome, grimy and distinctive colliery landscapes of pithead gear, coal heaps, and a maze of tramroads and colliery railways, usually accompanied by colliery villages and always by a thick layering of the surrounding country with coal dust. ...' As coal output increased from 27 to 230 million t per year, landscapes such as this proliferated as existing coalfields, such as the Northeast, expanded and new fields, such as South Yorkshire and Kent, were developed. Thompson suggests that some 60 701 ha of land were exploited for coal during the nineteenth century and thus lost to agriculture.

These coal-rich areas were also the focus of industrial development and consequently industry, along with the people (section 4.3.2), moved out of the countryside. The population of Birmingham, for example, trebled during Victoria's reign to reach half a million by the first census of 1801 (Mingay 1981). More land was annexed for urban spread and railway construction. Railways replaced canals as the major form of transport and provided an extensive communications network in all but the most inaccessible areas. Good communications and the increasing mechanisation of agriculture also led to the expansion of towns outside the coalfields. Many of these, such as Peterborough, Lincoln and Ipswich, were already important market towns and increasingly became involved with the provision of agricultural implements. Moreover, the large increases in urban populations created environmental change within the urban centres themselves where pollution, due to coal burning and mineral processing, was developing on a large scale (section 4.3.3). On the one hand, the increases in population necessitated large-scale building programmes which were not controlled as they now are by local planning authorities. Haphazard housing and industrial development meant that a high proportion of urban dwellers lived in squalor in over-crowded accommodation with little sanitation. Hare (1954) cites, for example, the situation of one street in Leeds where only three toilets were available for 368 people and the plight of 20 000 people living in Liverpool cellars to whom no sanitation was available. This was despite the fact that by the 1830s running water, baths and water-closets were available although they were only affordable by the upper middle and upper classes (Mumford 1966). As a consequence, both excreta and domestic rubbish accumulated in the streets, providing a considerable health hazard. This Boyden (1987) indicates contributed to a much higher mortality rate in urban centres than in rural areas and to the high incidence of typhus that eventually precipitated the Public Health Movement of nineteenth-century Britain, prompted also by several outbreaks of cholera between 1830 and 1862. The 1875 Public Health Act, for example, established a government Department of Health to oversee legislation relating to sanitation.

An indirect impact of industrial development on the British landscape also resulted from the move of industrialists into the countryside. Here, people such as Sir William Armstrong, a noted manufacturer of armaments, and Theodore Mander, a varnish and paint manufacturer, built impressive country houses. The countryside was thus of considerable value for sporting activities as well as agriculture and, as discussed in section 4.3.3, the Victorian era produced many noted natural scientists and environmentally conscious lobbyists.

4.3.2 ENVIRONMENTAL CHANGE IN RURAL BRITAIN IN THE POST-1750 PERIOD

As stated in section 4.3.1, the generation of fuel-powered urban–industrial ecosystems led to an increasing dependency of a large proportion of the population on less-populated food-producing systems. As a result, subsistence farming declined and agriculture became more commercialised or industrialised, thus emphasising the close link between agriculture and industry. While the urban centres relied on rural society for their food, farmers became more and more reliant on industry to produce the necessary components to make food production more efficient.

In 1851 the size of the agricultural labour force had reached a peak. In conjunction with horticulture and forestry, it employed more than 2 million people, more than 20 per cent of Britain's population (Mingay 1981). By 1896, however, only 1.5 million people were engaged in the food- and wood-producing industries, representing less than 10 per cent of the population. There was also a sustained population growth in general between these years, from 17.9 million in 1851 to 32.5 million in 1901, although this expansion in population began considerably earlier, from 6.7 million in 1761 to 15.9 million in 1841 (Grigg 1980) as industrial development occurred. Thus the development of the fuel-powered, predominantly urban ecosystems of Britain prompted considerable changes in agricultural practices. Grigg (1980) reports that during the eighteenth and early nineteenth centuries there was a marked increase of land under cultivation with a concomitant reduction in waste land, some of which was used to expand arable production and the remainder for pasture. The introduction of new crops and new rotations, etc. that began in the middle of the seventeenth century (section 4.2.3) already provided a base for agricultural intensification during the 1750–1850 period, though Grigg (1980) suggests that British agriculture was under pressure during this period especially during the Napoleonic Wars of the early nineteenth century when wheat harvests were poor. It was during this period that the potato, grown earlier in very limited amounts as a fodder crop, became a significant food crop, though it was often used as a substitute for wheat in bread- and pastry-making. Moreover, between 1780 and 1801 the price of wheat trebled, which also implies that British agriculture was unable to increase productivity in line with the rapidly increasing population. Poverty rather than affluence appears to have been prevalent in the worker classes of rural societies and industrial output, rather than agricultural output, was responsible for the increased wealth of Britain, though much of the finance originated from the landowning élite.

Nevertheless, Holderness (1981) states that British farmers were producing sufficient carbohydrate and protein to support c. 80 per cent of the population in 1860. Imports of food were, however, growing; the repeal of the Corn Laws in 1846, which had hitherto protected British agriculture from cheap imports, later resulted in free trade in foodstuffs. Despite a decline in the rate of population increase between 1850 and 1900, the absolute increase in population resulted in a considerable expansion in food imports between 1860 and 1910. By 1910, 85 per cent of grain for bread-making was imported, along with 45 per cent of meat, much of which came from North America and Australia. Moreover, during Victoria's reign the amount of wool supplied to the wool industry from abroad, especially Australia, increased to 80 per cent by c. 1900. There was also a general trend towards importing the basic raw materials which underpinned British industry, especially jute, rubber and leather. Both the needs of the population and industry itself helped to diminish the significance of British agriculture. The more affluent standard of living afforded by industrial occupations led to a demand for animal products such as butter and cheese, and although British farmers recognised this growing market, imports of dairy produce from Ireland, Europe and North America were necessary to satisfy it. Industry itself also contributed to agricultural change; for example, butter substitutes based on imported oils and fats began to replace butter in the diet of many, especially the poor.

According to Prince (1981), the 1880s witnessed a fundamental change in agriculture. Prior to this period wheat was the most important food crop and output was enhanced by increasing manuring and applying artificial fertilisers. Bad harvests in the late 1870s and the growing importation of cereals led to a change in policy. More emphasis was placed on animals and animal products and Prince indicates that grazing became predominant in western Britain, as arable lands were set to permanent grass, while eastern Britain remained reliant on cereal production. Although the increasing use of cereals for animal feed also meant that many cereal farmers focused their efforts on animal products (Grigg 1987), the quality of life diminished for cereal growers. The extensive railway network of the Victorian era also facilitated the transportation and rapid dissemination of animal products, especially milk, to the populace of towns and suburbs.

The 1750–1900 period also witnessed tremendous changes in the distribution of population. This has been discussed by Armstrong (1981) who cites various regional trends and implicates rural poverty, the demand for labour from the developing industrial base (section 4.3.1) as well as changes in mortality rates. Overall, there was a general movement of people out of the countryside into the towns. The agricultural labour force was at a peak by 1850 and while the number of actual farmers changed little in the ensuing 60 years, the number of labourers fell by 23 per cent by 1911, representing only 8.5 per cent of the total occupied labour force in comparison to 21.5 per cent in 1850. The low wages, long working hours and the increasing use of machinery all contributed to the decline in rural populations.

The latter half of the nineteenth century also witnessed a closer liaison between agriculture and science. Plant and animal breeding, for example, were well established prior to the First World War, crop protection chemicals were being produced and artificial fertilisers were being used. All of these innovations were designed to increase the output of plant and animal products as they are today. Mechanisation also became more sophisticated; according to Grigg (1987) the first tractors appeared in the USA in the 1890s and were subsequently employed in Britain during the First World War.

All of these developments have provided the base for modern British agriculture and that of the developed world in general. While agricultural systems may vary considerably from region to region and nation to nation, the common denominator is a much enhanced input of fossil fuel energy both directly and indirectly. Thus coal and oil have become the mainstay of these agricultural systems, replacing human labour and animal manuring, just as coal and oil underpin much of industry. As will be discussed in Chapter 6, the 'industrialisation' of agriculture, so effectively adopted by the Victorians, has also brought about many indirect environmental changes which are now developing into environmental problems.

Agricultural practices have also altered the character of the countryside, especially since the Second World War. This prompted more intervention by the state in order to ensure self-sufficiency in food production and was manifested in the 1947 Agriculture Act which guaranteed specific prices for certain crops, especially cereals. In consequence, the arable acreage increased. This support for agriculture is continued today under the auspices of the EEC's Common Agricultural Policy. This involves the purchase of produce by intervention agencies to maintain prices, as well as the provision of grants for the reclamation of marginal land and for mechanisation. Thus agriculture has become commercialised and innovations have become legion to increase yields. Hedgerows have been decimated in many parts of Britain, especially in eastern England, to create large fields that are more suited to highly mechanised farming that has also become more monocultural. As Mercer and Puttnam (1988) point out, approximately half of Norfolk's hedgerows disappeared between 1946 and 1970, and in East Anglia in general hedgerows disappeared more rapidly between 1969 and 1985 than in any other part of England (section 6.2.1). Virtually nowhere in Britain has escaped changes in the environment as a result of post-war agriculture. Moreover, such changes have created a considerable conflict of interest between conservationists and agribusiness interests as will be discussed in section 6.2.

4.3.3 THE ENVIRONMENT AS A POLITICAL ISSUE

In many ways the environment has always been a political issue simply because the main agencies of change, agriculture and industry, have been primarily concerned with the exploitation of natural resources. Both are intricately linked to economics and trade, which in turn are major concerns within politics. Although, as Sandbach (1980) indicates, it was during the 1965–1975 period that many of the industrialised countries became particularly concerned about environmental problems, there are examples of legislation going back to the medieval period (section 4.2.3) which were aimed at conservation, especially in relation to woodlands. Most of these early attempts were, however, ineffectual and it was not until the latter part of the nineteenth century that widespread concern for the environment arose. According to Lowe and Goyder (1983) the Commons, Open Spaces and Footpaths Preservation Society, the oldest national environmental group, was established in 1865. From then on, numerous groups developed which were capable of mustering public opinion and of influencing legislation.

Lowe and Goyder (1983) recognise three major periods in the ensuing years when environmental organisations flourished. The first is between *c.* 1885 and 1910 when groups such as the Royal Society for the Protection of Birds, The National Trust, the Metropolitan and Public Gardens Association, the Garden Cities Association (now the Town and County Planning Association) and the Coal (National) Smoke Abatement Society (now the National Society for Clean Air) were founded. Many of these were instrumental in effecting legislation for environmental (and social) improvement which Lowe and Goyder suggest may have been a response of Victorian society to the so-called 'Great Depression' of the 1880s and disenchantment with an industrialised society. As Lowe (1983) has pointed out, concern for the environment during this period was also a product of Victorian interests in natural history and this was a time when scientists were promoting new theories, such as the glacial theory, to explain environmental change (section 1.1.1). One example of such legislation includes the Ancient Monuments Act of 1882 which enabled the state, with the agreement of the owner, either to purchase monuments or to become their guardian.

The second period when environmental groups flourished was the interwar years of 1925–35, when societies such as the National Trust for Scotland, the Rambler's Association, the Ancient Monuments Society and the Council for the Preservation of Rural England were established, as well as many local groups. By this time, the growing populace was taking more interest in the countryside and various groups were active in influencing local government policies. One of the most significant legislative acts of this period was the Country Planning Act of 1932 which gave powers to local authorities to undertake rural planning schemes.

The final period when the environmental movement thrived began about 1955. Over the next 10 years, societies like the Civic Trust, the Victorian Society, the British Trust for Conservation Volunteers, the Council for Nature, and the Noise Abatement Society were founded. In common with the earlier periods when environmental groups expanded, this was a time of economic stagnation or recession and Lowe and Goyder (1983) suggest that; '. . . environmental groups arose at these times as more and more people turned to count the mounting external costs of unbridled economic growth and sought to reassert non-material values'. The fact that these groups witnessed considerable membership expansion in the 1970s, which was also a period of economic recession when many new groups, such as Friends of the Earth, the Ecology Party and the Farming and Wildlife Advisory Group be-

came established, reinforces Lowe and Goyder's view that a downturn in
economic fortune promotes environmental awareness. Increasing mobility
and leisure time must also, however, enhance environmental awareness. The
former, for example, facilitated by the expansion of canal, road and railway
networks that made industrial pre-eminence possible, have also provided
greater access to the countryside even to the most urbanised (and subur-
banised) people. In addition, a very significant consequence of industrialisation and the mechanisation of domestic chores has been to provide a
considerable amount of non-working time and a relatively high standard of
living that has allowed the population to take holidays (Ch. 8) either in Britain or abroad.

A great deal of legislation relating to the environment has also been effected during the post-1955 period. One example is the Clean Air Act of
1956 which was prompted by the Beaver Committee of Inquiry. According
to Sanderson (1974), three of the eleven members of the committee were
also members of the Coal (National) Smoke Abatement Society, reflecting
the influence of one environmental movement on government policy. This
Act of Parliament was vital to the health of urban populations, especially
that of London (Brimblecombe 1987). Here industrial development, and the
widespread use of coal as a major source of both industrial and domestic
fuel, resulted in the emission of a considerable volume of particulate matter.
This, together with sulphuric acid droplets produced from sulphur dioxide,
provides condensation nuclei and as a result London experienced some of
the worst smogs in its history. Brimblecombe (1977), for example, has
shown that the number of fog-days per year increased from $c.$ 20 to $c.$ 55
between 1850 and 1875, and the number of deaths from bronchial and related diseases also increased. No doubt the infamous London smog of De-
cember 1952, which lasted for 5 days and during which some 4000 deaths
occurred, also helped to precipitate the Clean Air Act of 1956 which required curtailment of particulate emissions and more effective dispersal via
the construction of tall chimney stacks on power stations. By 1970, emissions of smoke had been reduced to about 10 per cent of 1956 levels. This
legislation, however, did very little to curtail emissions of gaseous material
which are now considered to be among the main causes of acid rain (section
5.3.2).

One of the most significant developments in post-war Britain in relation
to the environment was the creation of the Nature Conservancy in 1949.
Several environmental groups were instrumental in the setting up of this
government agency, including the Britch Ecological Society (Sheail 1987).
The remit of this organisation was to provide advice on the conservation and
control of the British flora and fauna, to establish and manage nature reserves and to organise and develop the research and scientific services
necessary for these functions. Currently, the advisory capacity and the maintenance of nature reserves remain the prime concern of what is now the
Nature Conservancy Council (NCC), which was reconstituted as a new
statutory body in 1973 and which is responsible to the Secretary of State for
the Environment. Between 1965 and 1973 the Nature Conservancy had been
a constituent of the National Environment Reseach Council (NERC) and
when the split occurred as a result of the Nature Conservancy Council Bill,
it shed its research base which remains under the auspices of the NERC as
the Institute of Terrestrial Ecology.

The most important role of the NCC today is in the implementation of the Wildlife and Countryside Act of 1981. As Lowe (1983) suggests, this contentious Act marked the move of conservation into party politics since both Labour and Liberal parties disagreed with the Conservative view that there was no need for controls on agricultural change in order to safeguard wildlife. This remains a contentious issue today, as has been recently demonstrated by the furore surrounding the proposed afforestation of large areas of the flowlands of northern Scotland. Many of the problems associated with this bill have been discussed by Blunden and Curry (1985) and highlight the agriculture versus conservation debate (section 6.2). Inevitably, financial and economic factors constrain the NCC's efforts in conservation. For example, compensation may be paid to a farmer for maintaining a site of special scientific interest (SSSI); alternatively such a site may be purchased. Moreover, the requirement that farmers must advise the NCC of their intentions to alter SSSI's is not always complied with and many such sites have been lost as a result. The outcome may be a steep fine for the farmer but it can in no way compensate the community for the loss of an important wildlife habitat. As Blunden and Curry (1985) suggest, the lack of a consensus among conservationists as to what effective controls can be imposed on farmers make it likely that the most powerful control may be an indirect one, resulting from the reductions of EEC subsidies as Europe produces an ever increasing food surplus. The reduction in such subsidies may render it uneconomic to further intensify agriculture by reclaiming what is often marginal land. Conservation may thus occur by default!

As stated above, the 1970s also witnessed the establishment of many new groups that were concerned with environmental problems. One of the best known of these is Friends of the Earth (FoE), which is one of the few international environmental organisations which frequently reaches newspaper headlines because of its often confrontational approach to preserving and improving environmental quality. According to Lowe and Goyder (1983), FoE originated in the USA in 1969, a year before the British group was established. Financed by individual donations, FoE is a rigorously organised group with world-wide local branches and a strong technical expertise that focuses on specific problems rather than on environmental problems in general. For example, FoE have been particularly active in drawing attention to the dumping of nuclear waste.

In addition to the organisations discussed above, which represent only a few of the active environmental groups, a number of political parties have emerged since 1970 which orientate their policies to environmental issues. These are the so-called 'Green parties', the emergence of which is summarised in Earth Report (1988). The first of these was founded in New Zealand in 1972 as the Values Party and although it failed to gain any seats in national elections its programme became acknowledged as the first statement of Green politics. It espoused a steady-state population and economy, decentralised government, peacemaking and soft energy systems (i.e. renewable sources of energy rather than nuclear energy and fossil fuels). The Ecology Party of Britain was founded in 1973 and since 1987 has been known as the Green Party. Like its New Zealand counterpart it failed to win any parliamentary seats in the last general election, but according to Earth Report (1988) it secured 1.36 per cent of the vote. In contrast, the Green Party of West Germany wields considerable political influence. In 1983 it won 5 per cent of the national vote in the general election, giving it 27 seats in the Bundestag which increased to 42 seats in the 1987 general election. Apart from appealing to a wide spectrum of voters which has contributed to its success, the Green Party of West Germany is well known for its anti-nuclear stance. Other European countries which have Greens in parliamentary seats include Belgium and Italy, but it is surprising that such a party has only recently been formed in the USA and as yet carries little political influence despite the fact that Americans are among the most environmentally conscious nations.

Thus, the percolation into mainstream national policies of environmentally aware groups is increasing, both in numbers and, if West Germany is representative, such groups are also gathering in momentum. As well as this trend, and the proliferation of local and national groups concerned with practical conservation and environmental matters, several events of the last few years have highlighted the significance of environmental issues in international politics. Acid rain, for example, has been a subject of much controversy and a source of irritation between the USA and Canada and between Scandinavian countries and the rest of Europe, especially Britain. This is because pollution recognises no national or political boundaries and because the global hydrospheric and climatic systems are frequently the major routes whereby pollutants such as acid rain are transported. In addition, the nuclear reactor accident at Chernobyl in 1986 resulted in the contamination of many areas well beyond the boundaries of the USSR and provides an excellent example of the need for international cooperation in curbing radioactive emissions. There is also international concern about increasing atmospheric carbon dioxide levels and their impact on climate as well as consternation about the stratospheric ozone layer. In relation to the latter, ozone depletion may also be a contributory factor to global climatic change and the Montreal Protocol was established in 1987 under the auspices of the United Nations (United Nations Environment Programme 1987) which sought to curb emission of those substances, such as chlorofluorocarbons, which may deplete the ozone layer. These issues will be discussed in Chapter 5.

4.4 ENVIRONMENTAL CHANGE IN AFRICA AND THE NEW WORLD SINCE *C.* 1500

The period 1500–1940 was not only significant in terms of the agricultural and industrial developments that transformed the European landscape, it was also a period of tremendous cultural and environmental change in the Americas, Africa and Australia as Europeans annexed these territories, imposing European traditions and agricultural practices on indigenous peoples. The major impact was concentrated in the 1850–1920 period when large numbers of Europeans migrated to North America and Australia and when the annexation of lands in Africa reached a peak.

The most significant environmental changes that Europeans brought about were due to deforestation and the spread of agriculture. The literature abounds with examples of failures and ensuing environmental degradation rather than with success. This is especially true of Africa,

while in North America and Australia subsequent improvements in land management have arrested but not, as will be discussed in Chapter 6, obliterated them.

4.4.1 POST-EUROPEAN SETTLEMENT CHANGES IN THE ENVIRONMENT OF AFRICA

As Fage (1978) points out, the annexation by the Portuguese of the fortress town of Ceuta from the Moroccans in 1415 marked the beginning of European colonialism in Africa. Assisted by the geographical and navigational expertise developed by Islamic scholars and the production of more accurate maps (section 1.1.1), the fifteenth century became an era of exploration dominated by Europeans, particularly the Portuguese, Spanish, Venetians and Genoese. Contact was made with India and China as well as Africa and trade routes were expanded. By the end of the nineteenth century, Europeans were in control of almost the entire continent of Africa. The Portuguese were joined by the Spanish, Dutch and British whose primary interest in Africa lay in the slave trade which supplied labour to European colonies, particularly North America and the Caribbean. Despite the demise of slavery by the middle of the nineteenth century, there was still a considerable European interest in Africa, and in the latter half of that century European countries formally annexed African territories in their desire for political as well as commercial influence. Since then, the majority of these colonies have become independent but the legacy of European influence remains.

Land degradation, one of the major problems in Africa today, has often been considered to be a direct outcome of colonialism. Both Kjekshus (1977) and Vail (1977, 1983) argue that prior to the 1880s there was an overall balance between African populations and their environment which was disrupted by colonial influences such as introduced disease, warfare and especially the imposition of unfamiliar people–land relationships. The latter includes the introduction of new crops, new agricultural techniques and the direction of profits into Europe. Blaikie (1986), however, equating colonialism with capitalism, has argued against this by suggesting that it is all too easy to use colonialism as a scapegoat for all of Africa's environmental problems both old and new. In addition, he (Blaikie 1985, 1986) draws attention to the fact that such problems can be just as symptomatic of Marxist- and communist-based agricultural systems and, more importantly, he highlights the social factors which in many cases underpin land degradation problems and which must be considered in tandem with environmental measures if effective amelioration programmes are to be successful.

Such comments are by no means intended to exonerate colonialism as a significant factor in Africa's land degradation problems but to suggest that a wider perspective is needed to completely understand them. Moreover, it is important to point out that many colonial governments were instrumental in initiating conservation programmes, with varying degrees of success, whose primary aim was to safeguard the environment. The examples which follow provide a basic introduction to some of the problems involved.

As stated above, the post-1880 period was particularly significant in Africa's history because there was a major expansion of European influence. Many of the changes that ensued in the next 50 years have been examined by Blaikie and Brookfield (1987) who indicate that one of the major reasons for land degradation was the large-scale social disruption brought about primarily by the annexation of land from the indigenous farmers by European planters and ranchers. In Zimbabwe, for example, Palmer (1977) states that 6 million ha, nearly 17 per cent of the entire country, was managed by Europeans after 1890. This view is also promoted by Stocking (1985) who draws attention to the creation of Native Reserves which were designed to limit indigenous groups to specific, often poorer, areas. Other causes of social disruption include the spread of diseases such as rinderpest, a debilitating and often fatal disease of cattle which Richards (1985) states was imported in infected cattle from Europe, and the trypanosomic diseases of cattle and humans that are spread by tsetse fly.

The outcome of these disruptions was to create overpopulation in many areas. Robinson (1978) has described the impact of such processes on the Swaka people of Zambia, a farming group involved in an extensive food-producing system that necessitated the import of biomass nutrients from a wide area to supplement the soil nutrient store of a smaller area which was cultivated. As the land reserves of these people were considerably reduced in 1929 they curtailed the length of fallow to such an extent that nutrient pools became depleted and degradation ensued. In addition, Robinson reports that high population densities created by land reservation in other parts of Zambia, especially the hilly areas of the east, ultimately led to soil erosion.

Otieno and Rowntree (1987) also present evidence for degradation brought about by British colonialism on the Machakos and Baringo Districts of Kenya. Here, before the British arrived in 1890, shifting agriculture and pastoralism were the means of subsistence for the Kamba people of the Machakos Hills, while in Baringo a varied land use predominated, from cultivation near the southern shores of Lake Baringo, to pastoral subsistence in the dry bush country north of the lake and a system similar to that of the Kamba in the Tugen Hills. Between 1896 and 1902, the British were responsible for constructing the Uganda railway which benefited the Kamba so that their populations expanded as trade increased and food relief was brought in during times of drought. The agricultural innovations had far-reaching effects including a general trend towards expanding the cultivated area, facilitated by introducing the hoe and plough to replace the digging-stick, the introduction of cash crops and better seed strains to improve productivity. In 1906, reservations, or native land units, were also introduced to make way for scheduled areas which were set aside for European settlers and crown lands. As population numbers increased in the native land units, greater environmental pressure was exerted and exacerbated by the expansion of cultivated areas and the introduction of a taxation system. The outcome of all these changes was a reduction in grazing land and increased exposure of cultivated land to sheet-wash erosion.

In Machakos District the impact of erosion was obvious by 1917. In 20 years degradation had become manifest, resulting in non-vegetated land areas and exposed soils, despite the earlier introduction of soil-conservation measures which included the discouragement of shifting cultivation and an embargo on the cultivation of steep slopes. Although afforestation programmes were initiated in the 1920s, as well as land enclosure and terracing to combat the erosion problem, degradation remained a stark reality affecting between 37 and 75 percent of the land (Munro 1975). Similar problems developed in the Baringo District, especially in the Tugen Hills which Otieno and Rowntree (1987) believe contributed to the movement of people into the south Baringo plains in the 1920s. Such problems, both social and environmental, were exacerbated by drought periods as well as outbreaks of pests. Conservation measures in the 1930s, including the exclusion of cattle and goats from certain areas as well as the clearance of native bush land and grass planting, were ineffective at combating the problems and later attempts have not been overly successful either. Thus, in this instance and despite attempts to rectify the problems created by colonial superimposition, a colonial regime wreaked not only environmental change but also environmental degradation and social upheaval.

As Watts (1984) has demonstrated, the imposition of colonialism in northern Nigeria also created social problems that resulted in environmental change. Prior to colonial occupation, the savanna region of Hausaland with its erratic wet season was just as subject to drought and ensuing famine as it is now, but Watts argues that social organisation, consisting of a number of households organised into small communities with a state structure, provided a buffer against disaster. The extended household was the basic unit of production, employing intercropping of sorghums and millets which have complementary ecological requirements. Foraging and hunting were also practised to supplement cultivated crops. Village heads were responsible for storage of crops and redistribution in times of shortage, and when this was acute the district chiefs distributed food from central granaries. Such organisation by no means completely alleviated the effects of poor harvests and famine, but rendered it less acute while the intercropping practices were more ecologically suited to a relatively fragile environment. Colonialism disrupted this infrastructure via the introduction of taxation, cash crop production for export and monetisation. The former necessitated increased cash crop production, such as groundnuts and cotton, which were also subject to fluctuations in external market prices. The environmental outcome of changes in what Watts describes as the social relations of production, led to an increase in cultivated area, increasing use of marginal land, a reduction in livestock and thus a reduction in the availability of manure, all of which increased the marginality of an area that was already ecologically fragile.

Both successes and failures of colonial imposition in Africa can also be seen if reference is made to the introduction of cash crops. These are crops grown specifically for export to raise income. As Crowder (1982) points out, the introduction of such crops to many African countries may have been the responsibility of Europeans, but the expansion of such production was often via the impetus of indigenous people. The introduction of such crops to the Machakos and Baringo Districts of Kenya (see above) obviously had detrimental effects, largely by reducing the amount of land for grazing and thus promoting overgrazing that ultimately enhanced erosion. The way in which such crops were grown also, in many cases, led to environmental degradation. Blaikie and Brookfield (1987) point out the detrimental effects of monoculture and quote the example of the Cassmance area of Senegal where groundnuts were introduced and which de Wilde (1967) has shown caused considerable losses in organic matter and colloidal humus from the soil within only 2 years. In addition, the introduction of such crops often occurred at the expense of crops like cowpea (*Vigna unguiculata*), which provide a better protective cover for the soil. Not all cash crop introductions have had deleterious impacts, especially if intercropping techniques are used which involve the planting of different crops during a given season in the same field. The crops grown must be carefully selected to achieve a balance between the different nutrients required by specific crops and the degree of soil protection that each crop affords. The advantages of intercropping have been described by Richards (1985) in relation to West Africa and include increased productivity, and more effective pest and disease control.

Colonialism also had a major impact on conservation policies in Africa. As Anderson (1984) has pointed out, conservation policies have been intrinsic components of colonial attitudes since the 1890s and developed in response to a growing awareness of environmental problems, especially in relation to soil erosion and forest resources. Grove (1987), for example, has examined the importance of the colonial context in conservation policies in the Cape Colony. These related to forest protection and game reservation but failed to address the wider environmental issues of degradation. It is now considered that this and similar policies were ineffectual because they failed to acknowledge the significance and the ecological basis of traditional shifting agricultural systems. This is a theme which, in conjunction with other traditional food-producing strategies, is examined by Richards (1985) who suggests that improvements in these may well be the key to an indigenous agricultural revolution as exemplified in West Africa today. These factors went unrecognised by colonial governments, and they have remained largely unrecognised by post-colonial governments.

In relation to forest conservation in Africa, colonial regimes have also achieved a mixture of successes and failures. As in the case of soil erosion, many forest conservation programmes have at best achieved only partial success because of their inability to recognise and reconcile conflicts of interest, and their failure to take into account social factors such as native land rights. Anderson (1987) has examined the significance of these factors in the conservation history of the Lembus Forest. Here, conflicts arose because of three different sets of interests. Social indigenous groups wanted to continue their traditional exploitation, but commercial exploitation and the development of a timber industry was the prime concern of a business consortium via a concession which was granted with little restriction by the High Commissioner for East Africa in 1904, and the Forestry Department wanted to maintain both the forest and a financial return. Conflicts arose between the timber company and the Forestry Department because the former failed to supply plans for exploitation and because their policy of avoiding clear-felling hampered reafforestation plans. At the same time, the generous terms of the concession enabled the timber company to avoid paying high royalties so that income to the government also remained low. Eventually, growing public concern about the exploitation and the improved financial status of the Forestry Department, led to greater official control by 1945.

As conservation measures became more effective, other conflicts arose involving native rights. These were initially assured by the Coryndon Definition, a document drawn up by Governor Coryndon to define grazing, gathering and cultivation rights within Lembus Forest. While policies elsewhere were aimed at confining native groups in reservations, the Coryndon Definition remained an anathema. Local groups ensured that they used their rights to the full and the cultivation of Lembus Forest glades increased to such an extent that conservation activities were jeopardised. In 1956 the Forestry Department was forced to concede to the claims of the Tugen people, in a political climate that warranted conciliation between natives and colonial government. Thus it was agreed that control of the forest should revert to the Baringo African District Council when the timber company's agreement was due to be terminated in 1959.

While these examples of colonial policies are limited in number, they illustrate the conflicts of interest that existed in Africa in the late nineteenth and early twentieth centuries in relation to environmental resources. Despite the introduction of conservation programmes, land degradation appears to have been exacerbated by a disregard for traditional land-use practices and indigenous social factors. Today, much of Africa retains the legacies of these events but, as will be discussed in Chapter 7, modern resource exploitation and agricultural systems have also failed, by and large, to adequately address these problems.

4.4.2 POST-EUROPEAN SETTLEMENT CHANGES IN THE ENVIRONMENT OF THE AMERICAS

Although the continent of America had been discovered in the late fifteenth century (see De Vorsey 1987 for a review of the discovery and exploration of eastern North America) it was in the island groups of the Caribbean that European settlement was first established. Here, the Spanish led by Columbus founded the first European colony of La Isabela in 1493 in what is now the Dominican Republic. Deagan (1988) states that it was not until 1517 that colonial attention became directed to mainland Central and South America, by which time mineral resources had been depleted and the indigenous Caribbean Amerindian cultures had been subjugated to their Spanish masters via a system of forced labour. This, plus relocation and imported diseases led to a general population decline, the repercussions of which caused the disappearance of indigenous native cultures and prompted the Spanish to seek their labour force from peripheral islands and the mainland areas even before European settlement was widespread. This was the precursor to the slave trade that later extended to Africa.

The Spanish colonists increased their interests in the region by exploiting Mexican silver and bringing to an end the indigenous Aztec Empire in 1521 (Nostrand 1987). A need for further trading and strategic bases prompted the Spanish to establish colonies in other Caribbean islands and in Florida. By this time the French had begun to make inroads into Atlantic Canada, with settlements established in the Maritime Provinces that were based primarily on the fishing industry and the fur trade, but which were relatively low key in comparison with the Spanish settlements. Harris (1987) states that even by 1700 there were only *c.* 20 000 people of French origin who were widely scattered from Newfoundland to the Mississippi. Two thousand of these lived in Quebec, with a further 1200 in Montreal. According to Mitchell (1987) the British too entered the North American arena relatively late, with some 250 000 settlers established by 1700 in small settlements dispersed along the Atlantic seaboard from southern Maine to South Carolina which have been discussed by Meinig (1986). The Spanish, French and British all brought their own distinctive traditions, social organisation and agricultural systems which, as populations expanded, impinged on the native Indian traditions, displacing traditional land-use and social organisations.

Pre-Columbian cultures, as the indigenous groups of the Americas are known, practised varied food-procuring strategies and reference has already been made to the plant and animal domestications that occurred in Central and South America (section 3.3.1). Collier (1964) has suggested that by the time Europeans arrived in North America there were approximately 1 million Indians, organised into 600 different societies in regions that were as varied as the Arctic tundra of Alaska and the humid swamplands adjoining the Gulf of Mexico. These groups were experienced hunter-gatherers whose use of fire for nearly 10 000 years had enabled them to control their environment in much the same way that mesolithic and neolithic groups had achieved in Britain 8 kyr BP (sections 3.2.3 and 3.3.2). There is also palaeoecological evidence (e.g. Delcourt and Delcourt 1987) to suggest that many of these groups were becoming increasingly sedentary and involved in crop production.

It is clear from most history texts that the advent of Europeans heralded a very important stage in landscape development. As in the case of Africa (section 4.4.1) and Australia (section 4.4.3), changes in social structure wrought by the imposition and adoption of European values and traditions, especially agrarian traditions, not only occurred in tandem with environmental change but were often the major motivating force. As Assadourian (1987) has noted in relation to the Peruvian Andean region of South America, the demise of the Inca state in 1533 and the concomitant decline in indigenous populations resulted in a transformation of the agrarian landscape. Land was abandoned as food requirements declined and irrigation systems, previously constructed to enhance crop productivity, fell into disrepair. Just as the state-controlled food distribution infrastructure of pre-colonial northern Nigeria (section 4.4.1) was disrupted, so too was that of the remaining indigenous Peruvians who were subject to taxation which was required in cash, rather than in kind, by their Spanish overseers. The need for cash, plus the need for labour in the Spanish-dominated silver-mines of Potosí, led to a redistribution of population from scattered villages to a few larger towns.

By 1600, what had been a scattered population engaged in agricultural systems based on native crops had become a dual society with a much reduced indigenous territory where pre-colonial traditions persisted and a few centres of denser population engaged in mining and cash-crop production. These crops included grapes, olives, sugar-cane and cereals as well as European cattle and poultry. While the outcome of these enterprises was primarily a net export of commodities to Spain, environmental change ensued as population distributions changed in accord with the Spanish overseers' requirements for seasonal labour and as cash cropping transformed land-use patterns. According to Morse (1987) and Newson (1987) similar changes in population distribution occurred elsewhere in South America in response to colonial rule and the necessity of the colonists to establish centres of control. Morse (1987) points out that many of these centres are today the capitals of many South American countries. Examples include Mexico City, Panama City, Bogotá, Quito, Lima and Buenos Aires, all of which were established in the period 1520–1650.

Changes in social organisation and land-use, similar to those described above in Peru, also occurred elsewhere. In particular the *encomienda* system of labour distribution was widespread. This system involved the allocation of native Indians to Spanish property owners to whom taxes in kind or in silver were due and who were responsible for the introduction of Christian civilisation. As Spanish immigration increased and settlements expanded, the demand for food increased and the labour required for the growing number of *estancias*, land used for grazing, and *characas*, land used for crop production, was supplied via the *encomienda* system as well as paid Indian workers, serfs and free groups of day workers. However, Mörner's (1987) review of rural economy in South America during the colonial period indicates that the decline of indigenous populations, such as that described above for Peru, was widespread. One consequence of this was a change in land tenure as Spanish-owned estates, the *haciendas*, absorbed land abandoned by natives and the extent of land controlled by ecclesiastical groups such as the Jesuits and Augustinians increased. The labour to work these estates was increasingly provided by slaves imported from Africa, and Mörner states that by 1767 Jesuit estates in the coastal area of Peru employed 5224 slaves, 62 per cent of whom were used in sugar plantations and a further 30 per cent in vineyards.

While sugar and vines constituted the main cash crops in this region, different cash crops dominated other parts of Spanish South America. In what is now Ecuador, for example, cacao production dominated the wet tropical Guayas Province and sheep-grazing, to support a textile industry, dominated the highlands. In Venezuela, cacao cultivation was also important on the lowland coastal regions and valleys and in the uplands cattle ranches were established, both of which were largely controlled by landowners living in Caracas. According to Mörner, records of 1684 show that 172 people, approximately a quarter of the citizens of Caracas, held 167 cacao plantations and 28 cattle ranches.

In Brazil, the impact of Portuguese colonists was also considerable. Between 1500 and 1549, Johnson (1987) states that there were four stages of increasing Portuguese involvement in the development of Brazil, from early land leases to the final establishment of a royal administration via a royal governor. According to Schwartz (1985 and 1987) this short period was one of considerable change, principally witnessing the establishment of sugar-cane agriculture. As in Spanish South America, native populations declined and imported African slaves augmented local labour resources. Initially the dark red massapé soils of the northeast coastal region were favoured for sugar-cane production which was organised on an *engheno* or plantation basis. Since the produce was intended primarily for export, mills were situated either along river valleys or on the coast where most settlement was concentrated. Gradually, sugar-cane cultivation extended south along the coast to Rio de Janeiro and the industry rapidly replaced the wood-export industry in economic terms as Brazil, between 1580 and 1680, became the world's largest producer and exporter of sugar (Schwartz 1987).

Dyewood was one of the first resources of Brazil to be exploited by early Portuguese colonists, but attention soon turned to other trees which could be used for shipbuilding and furniture-making, especially brazilwood (*Caesalpina echinata*). However, despite the fact that rubber (*Hevea brasiliensis*) was utilised by native peoples, its successful cultivation was not achieved by nineteenth-century colonists. As Dean (1987) discusses, the major contribution made by Brazil to the rubber industry was the supply of seeds to Kew Gardens that ultimately led to the establishment of plantations in Southeast Asia. Cash crops other than sugar also became important, notably tobacco, and horses and cattle imported from Europe formed the basis for the development of ranching, especially outside the sugar- and tobacco-producing regions. Schwartz (1987) states that there were more than 1 million head of cattle in the northeast region by 1710 which supplied the transport needs of the sugar industry as well as beef and hides to the growing coastal settlements. Overall, the establishment of colonial rule in Spanish and Portuguese

South America brought about major changes in agrarian systems. In particular, pre-Columbian crops like manioc, potatoes, maize, squash and beans, which continued to be grown by indigenous groups on a subsistence basis, became subordinate to the cash crops introduced by the Europeans which were mainly exported to provide revenues for the colonising nation.

The exploitation of the native labour force and African slaves was not confined to agricultural systems. In fact it was the lure and discovery of precious metals that prompted both the discovery and subsequent exploitation of South America. Reference has already been made above to the silver-mines of Potosí in Peru which were first exploited in the 1540s (Tandeter 1987) and which were worked by Indian labour drafted in from as far away as 1200 km. The Spanish search for gold and silver was mainly responsible for rapid colonisation and the establishment of settlements, and subsequent agricultural development to support them. Extraction and processing created landscape changes as waste material was discarded and housing for machinery and the labour force was constructed. Bakewell (1987) has reviewed the major developments in the mining industry that occurred during the colonial period in Spanish South America and has also pointed out the repercussions that such enterprises, based mainly on silver, gold and mercury, had on the indigenous Indians and on colonial society. Apart from wealth generation, the mining industries prompted both external and internal trade and determined where the power bases of colonial South America were situated. In Brazil the discovery of precious metals on a large scale came much later than in Spanish South America. According to Russell-Wood (1987), major gold strikes occurred some two centuries after colonisation in many areas but especially in the Minas Gerais region, north of Rio de Janeiro. Townships became established, African slaves were imported to provide labour, and agriculture which by this time was experiencing a recession due to falling tobacco and sugar prices, was stimulated.

In North America the major impact of a rapidly increasing population was not felt until the mid-nineteenth century, but early settlers of the seventeenth and eighteenth centuries also left their mark on the environment. Cronon (1983) has reconstructed the early colonial history of New England from an ecological perspective. He emphasises the patchwork nature of the varied habitats of the region, including many different forest mosaics, coastal salt marshes and well-grassed valleys all of which exhibited seasonal cycles in tune with the seasonal climate. The indigenous Indian groups exploited these habitats via a mobile existence even where crop-growing was practised, and fire was extensively used to clear forest for agriculture as well as to maintain a more open parkland that was favoured by wildlife which was also exploited. A similar picture is presented by Delcourt et al. (1986) and Delcourt (1987) who have examined the impact of indigenous groups in the Little Tennessee River Valley using palaeoenvironmental techniques. Here crop cultivation and the manipulation of forest resources and forest boundaries were just as important as Cronon (1983) indicates for New England. In contrast, the British colonists of the seventeenth century created permanent settlements that infringed on the Indian idea of communal territory. Thus the landscape changed in character as boundaries were constructed around colonial farms and farming practices prevented forest regeneration. At the same time, the introduction of European diseases caused Indian populations to decline so that their land-management practices, especially firing, also declined. In consequence, the forest either became more dense in areas that remained unsettled by Europeans or became permanent fields. Cronon believes that this profoundly altered the wildlife ecology as well as the vegetation.

In addition, many of the early colonists developed a lumber industry which required a different exploitation of the forest than that practised by the Indians. White pine (*Pinus strobus*) was especially prized for the construction of ship masts, and in view of the shortage of timber in England (sections 4.2.2 and 4.2.3) an export trade based on the lumber industry had become well established by the mid-1600s. Despite attempts at conservation via unenforced laws limiting the felling of particular species, wasteful use of timber continued and white pine in particular continued to be depleted. As markets expanded, populations increased, more fuel-wood was required and more land was needed for agriculture, more forest disappeared either by felling, girdling (which involved bark stripping that prevented leafing and caused death), or burning. One outcome of this forest demise was an increase in flood frequency and runoff in general. Cronon also states that local climates were affected by these changes with wider fluctuations in temperature, more rapid snowmelts and deeper freezing of the soil in winter. Delcourt and Harris (1980) have also suggested that depletion of organic reserves in above- and below-ground biomass caused a reduction in soil fertility.

Other developments, with parallels in the pre-Industrial Revolution period of Britain (section 4.2.3), occurred in New England that also had environmental impacts. Cronon (1983) lists the technological developments that allowed dams, irrigation channels and canals to be constructed; the establishment of iron-smelting furnaces that relied even more on the forest resource; and the construction of tanneries that encouraged the exploitation of oak and hemlock for their bark.

Evidence for these environmental changes, all primarily the consequence of natural resource exploitation, is not confined to documentary records and contemporary colonial accounts such as those used by Cronon. Palaeoecological investigations of lake sediments in many parts of North America also yield data that provide an insight into the direction and timing of the colonial impact on lake catchments. Much of this information has been reviewed by Mannion (1986d, 1989a) especially in relation to the process of cultural eutrophication. This will be examined in Chapter 6, but merits mention here since the onset of cultural eutrophication in North America can be traced via the sedimentary record of lake ecosystems to the colonial period. Eutrophication involves the enrichment of lake waters by increased nutrient input from the catchment that causes changes in the micro- and macro-biota of lake waters and where this is brought about either directly or indirectly by human activity it is known as cultural eutrophication. At Harvey's Lake in Vermont, for example, Engstrom *et al.* (1985) have shown that both enhanced soil erosion and inputs of human and animal wastes caused changes in the lake biota *c.* 1780 as a consequence of European settlement and the establishment of permanent agriculture. A large-scale study by Bradbury (1975) who investigated nine lacustrine sequences in Minnesota and Dakota has also demonstrated that cultural eutrophication was a widespread event associated with European settlement in these areas in the late 1800s and early 1900s.

Two studies on Frains Lake in Michigan also illustrate the effects of European settlement in its catchment. Davis (1976) has examined the erosion rates that have occurred in relation to land-use history and has shown that just after 1826, when European settlement was established, there was a change in sediment type reflecting accelerated erosion due to deforestation. Davis also shows that prior to this disturbance sedimentation was occurring at a low rate, increasing markedly after 1830, the implication being that before disturbance $c.$ 9 t km^{-2} of mineral matter per year were lost from the watershed and after a short interval when erosion rates were between thirty and eighty times greater than in pre-settlement times, erosion was removing $c.$ 90 t km^{-2} of mineral material per year by 1900 which is about average for the interval examined. In a related study, Carney (1982) has shown that biotic changes also occurred as lake biota reacted to changing inputs. Increases in the accumulation rates of two groups of algae, diatoms and chrysophytes, immediately after the 1830 horizon, and variations in the range of species present indicate a change from oligotrophic or nutrient-poor waters to eutrophic or nutrient-rich ones. This Carney attributes to clear-felling of the forest and the establishment of intensive agriculture.

There is also a great deal of palaeoecological evidence for the impact of European settlement on the Great Lakes. In Lake Ontario, Stoermer *et al.* (1985b) have shown that there was a major disturbance in the period 1831–47 when eutrophication occurred due to nutrient loading caused by deforestation for agriculture. As in the case of Frains Lake, the subsequent period, to $c.$ 1900, was one of apparent stabilisation when there was a reduction in nutrient loading as land-use patterns in the catchment stabilised after the initial ploughing-up period. A period of enrichment is recorded in the sediments of Lake Superior which dates to $c.$ 1850–1900 and which is attributed by Stoermer *et al.* (1985a) to similar catchment perturbations.

While palaeoecological data provide evidence for lake catchment disturbance they also, via pollen analysis, provide evidence for changes in forest composition and extent which resulted from early colonial exploitation. Gajewski *et al.* (1985) have presented such data from three lakes in northwest Wisconsin which show that after 1850 the proportions of non-tree pollen increased markedly, representing deforestation. At the same time, disturbance indicators and grass (Gramineae) pollen increased, reflecting the spread of agriculture. Further data for forest disturbance caused by European settlement in the eastern USA have been summarised by Davis (1984). Data from Linsley Pond in Connecticut, for example, show that in 1700 there was a decrease in hemlock (*Tsuga canadensis*) and an increase in herbs such as grasses (Gramineae), ragweed (*Ambrosia*) and docks (*Rumex* spp.) as a farm was established in the vicinity of the lake (Brugam 1978). Several sites in the western USA also contain evidence for deforestation and logging which caused a decrease in conifer pollen and an increase in grasses (Baker 1984).

However, the North American environment was subject to increased deforestation, logging and urbanisation in the period 1840–1920 when there was a major increase in the population. According to Ward (1987) the population of the USA in this period increased from 17 million to more than 105 million and Wynn (1987) states that the population of Canada increased from $c.$ 3.5 million in 1871 to $c.$ 8.8 million in 1921. These increases were due to mass migration from Europe and high birth-rates in colonial settlements that were already well established. By this time, the Industrial Revolution was well under way (sections 4.3.1 and 4.3.2) and the technological innovations that resulted provided further means to modify the environment. Even allowing for the vast territories being opened up, the environmental implications of such large population increases and technological changes

were significant and there is considerable documentary and palaeoenvironmental evidence to substantiate this.

Many of the palaeoenvironmental studies referred to above also show the
effects of increased human activity. For example, in Frains Lake (Carney
1982) there is evidence for increased cultural eutrophication caused by enhanced nutrient inputs as pig farming and road networks were constructed in
the 1930s. Similarly, enhanced cultural eutrophication brought about by increased phosphate loading occurred in Lake Ontario after 1900 (Stoermer *et
al.* 1985a) and at Linsley Pond, Brugam (1978) records a period of extensive
deforestation in the early nineteenth century as more land was used for agriculture. There is also geochemical evidence from Great Lake sediments for
industrial expansion. Edgington and Robbins (1976) have shown that lead
levels in cores from southern Lake Michigan increased markedly between
1900 and 1920 due to coal combustion. In the post-1853 period there were
increases in organic pigments due to enhanced eutrophication in Lake Min-
netonka, Minnesota (Engstrom and Swain 1986). Even as far afield as the
Rocky Mountains, chemical analysis of lake sediments by Baron *et al.*
(1986) indicates that lead enrichment occurred between 1855 and 1905 due
to small-scale lead-mining activities in Colorado. There have been numerous
geochemical investigations of lake sediments in Canada (e.g. Dickman and
Thode 1985, Nriagu and Coker 1983) which reflect high sulphur and pyrite
concentrations resulting from iron-ore and copper smelting that began in the
late 1800s. Much of this information is reviewed in Mannion (1989b) and
will be examined in Chapter 5 along with evidence for acidification in North
America which also began during this period when large-scale industrialisation occurred.

Documentary evidence relating to environmental change during this
major expansionary period is also available. Burgess and Sharpe (1981), for
example, have examined changes in the wooded area of Cadiz Township in
Wisconsin. They show that the major period of deforestation between 1831
and 1882 involved the fragmentation of an almost continuous forest cover
due to an expansion in agricultural land. Such fragmentation is also referred
to in the classic work of Weaver and Clements in 1929 which documents the
character of the forests surrounding the Great Lakes. Whitney (1987) also
points out that logging, in conjunction with an increased incidence of firing,
has greatly altered the character of the Great Lakes forest. Both logging and
settlement spread during the 1870s and 1880s, with the lumber industry concentrating on white pine (*Pinus strobus*) and to a lesser extent red pine (*P.
resinosa*) which became exhausted in the 1890s. In consequence, attention
turned to hemlock (*Tsuga canadensis*) which provided not only a lumber
substitute for pine but was also a major source of tannin for the leather
industry. By 1912, sugar maple (*Acer saccharum*) was also being heavily
exploited, facilitated by the advent of efficient saws, drying kilns and railway development. This, and other hardwoods, supplied both lumber and tannin as well as supporting a wood-chemical industry.

Whitney states that: 'By 1920, forty years of lumbering and cordwood
cutting had removed most of the merchantable pine, hemlock and even the
smaller hardwoods.' The overall result was a replacement of these old-
growth forests by second-growth forests dominated by sugar maple (*A. saccharum*). In addition, the increased incidence of deliberate and accidental
fires created major changes in the mixed-pine forest, encouraging oak
(*Quercus alba* and *Q. rubra*) and aspen (*Populus tremuloides* and *P. gran-*

didentata) which had hitherto been minor constituents of the forest. Between 1920 and 1940 firing was limited by better fire-fighting policies and, eventually, reafforestation programmes were established in the 1930s. These measures allowed the oak, aspen and jack pine (*Pinus banksiana*) populations to mature and since the 1950s these have formed the basis of the pulpwood industry in the region.

Another example of environmental change during the colonial period in the Great Lakes region is that of the Simcoe–Couchiching basin in Ontario. Using population data and an erosive land-use (ELU) index derived from information on crop areas in combination with the distribution of erosive rainfall and the degree of soil protection afforded by different land-use practices, Wilson and Ryan (1988) have reconstructed landscape change in the region since 1800. They recognise three periods which reflect the expansion and contraction of agriculture. Before 1891, the ELU increased as agriculture expanded, signifying accelerated erosion; between 1911 and 1961 the ELU declined as yields in the area under grass increased providing soil protection; while the ELU for 1981 reflects disturbance almost as great as that in the initial expansionary phase due to increased grain-growing.

Although agricultural development and the establishment of logging industries fundamentally altered large parts of North America, there were also efforts to preserve the landscape as concern about environmental damage mounted. One direct outcome of this was the establishment of national parks. Six national parks were set up by 1900, the first being Yellowstone National Park which was designated as such in 1872 (Moran *et al.* 1986). Forest policy will be discussed in section 8.2.1 and problems associated with agricultural practices, which began in the colonial period, will be examined in Chapter 6.

4.4.3 Post-european Settlement Changes in the Environment of Australia

As stated by Powell in 1976 and reiterated by Conacher in 1986, environmental problems, especially environmental degradation, have been associated with Australia's development since Europeans first colonised the continent in 1788. Overall, the distribution of natural vegetation communities in Australia, which have been described by Carnahan (1986), relate to gradients of effective precipitation which decline markedly towards the arid interior of the continent. These vegetation communities, dominated by eucalypts, acacias and spinifex grasses, underpin the indigenous ecosystems which were more or less intact prior to European colonisation. There is, however, evidence from palaeoecological studies on lake sediments in many parts of Australia for frequent firing, some of which was undoubtedly due to burning by Aboriginal groups. Kershaw (1986), for example, has suggested that the replacement of rainforest by sclerophyll woodland in the vicinity of Lynch's Crater, Queensland, during the last glacial period (*c.* 20 kyr BP) may have been a response to increased burning by Aboriginals. Nevertheless, such influence on Australian vegetation has been relatively insignificant in comparison to the changes wrought by European colonists. Rickard (1988), for example, has drawn attention to the way in which early settlers perceived their new homeland, scotching the myth that they saw Australia as an aesthetically hostile environment.

The most significant impact of European settlement on the Australian environment has been the introduction of extensive livestock grazing to some 60 per cent of the total land area. In addition, mining activities, urban settlement and the introduction of a wide range of exotic plants and animals have all contributed to environmental change during Australia's 200 years of European occupation. While the Aboriginals used burning as a technique for manipulating natural resources, the Europeans instituted new patterns of burning that had far more severe environmental effects.

In section 4.3.2 reference was made to the growing volumes of both meat and wool imported into Britain from Australia during the nineteenth and early twentieth centuries. This was made possible by the expansion of ranching into the more arid rangelands of Australia which lay beyond the humid woodlands fringing the coast of south and southeast Australia where the original colonists of 1788–1800 settled. Heathcote (1983) has described the period between the 1830s and 1920s as the golden age of ranching, stimulated by the growing European market as well as the developing home market as the numbers of migrants from Europe increased. By 1888, there were 80 million sheep, mainly confined to the semi-arid grasslands south of the Tropic of Capricorn and especially in New South Wales, as well as 8 million cattle and 1 million horses (Heathcote 1987). At this stage in Australia's history the cattlemen were the most adventurous, pushing their ranches into the arid centre of Australia, the Northern Territory and even into the Kimberley region of the northwest. By this time pigs, donkeys, goats and camels had been introduced, all contributing to environmental degradation. Meanwhile, only 2.8 million ha, or about 0.5 per cent of the continent, had been converted to arable land, concentrated in the coastal areas and the red soil plains of South Australia and Victoria (Heathcote 1987).

Thus within the first century of European settlement considerable environmental change had occurred and even in the early nineteenth century there was growing concern about environmental degradation. Messer (1987), for example, has drawn attention to government intervention in 1803 to reduce indiscriminate clearance of vegetation. Nevertheless, sheep and cattle herds continued to increase and expand into unoccupied areas of the vast continent, increasing the extent of damaged land and ousting the Aboriginal populations from their homelands. The environmental problems relating to such large-scale ranching are also much the same now as they were in 1888, due to the mismanagement of that most valuable natural resource, the land and its soil, and an incomplete understanding of environmental processes and interactions. No doubt the lure of big profits motivated resource exploitation to a greater or lesser degree as the demand for animal products increased and as ranchers based their exploitation strategies on unsuitable European farming practices.

The most widespread environmental problem consequent on large-scale cattle and sheep ranching is erosion. This relates to the imperfectly understood characteristics and processes of the indigenous ecosystems and the way in which the Australian landscape developed prior to European colonisation. Ranching also contributes considerably to the process of desertification. Of particular significance is the impact of hard-hooved ungulate animals, the introduced sheep, cattle, horses and camels, on the soil in contrast to the much reduced impact of the soft-footed animals, such as the kangaroos and wallabies. According to Heathcote (1987) a sheep treads six times more heavily in relation to its hoof area, and a bullock seventeen times more heavily, than a kangaroo. Hence the softer, less consolidated red soils of Australia's heartland were rapidly disturbed by herds of extensively grazed animals, rendering them susceptible to erosion. Such arid areas are also relatively sparsely vegetated due to low and sporadic rainfall so that in seasons of drought winds of even moderate speed can blow vast clouds of red soil from their place of origin to bank against fences and farm buildings. Heathcote (1987) states:

> By 1888 some inland pastures consisted of 'cane swamps' – level stretches of hard, white clay thinly covered with coarse grass – with only tiny islands of the original surface soil still standing in the midst. To enable the land to carry more stock, pastoralists had rainwater tanks dug at low spots on their runs and at the inlet they usually put in a smaller tank to act as a silt trap and filter. Yet so severe were the effects of soil erosion that, even with this protection, tanks metres deep silted up within five years.

Even in non-arid areas where grazing is widespread, soil erosion is also a problem (Conacher 1986; Carnahan 1986) due chiefly to the removal of vegetation cover and overstocking. In the more humid regions, sheet erosion is a frequent occurrence as the soil is exposed to enhanced overland flow and in semi-arid areas wind erosion is a major problem. In all these examples, not only is the soil cover diminished but biogeochemical cycles are impaired as the nutrient stores are depleted. Conacher (1986) states that of 130 million ha of land used for non-arid grazing in Australia, some 37 per cent was considered by Australia's Department of the Environment in 1975 to require treatment. The state most affected is Queensland, with 17.2 million ha of eroded land, followed by New South Wales where 10.5 million ha have been subject to erosion.

Areas in which arable farming is practised have also been subject to land degradation. Heathcote (1987), referring to Australia in 1888, indicates that croplands were becoming exhausted because of lack of manuring and constant cropping. Chartres (1987) has also addressed this problem and refers to the abandonment of wheat cultivation within 20 years of its initiation in the 1870s, in the semi-arid northern districts of South Australia. Similarly, in the Mallee woodlands of Victoria, clearance for cultivation in the early 1900s created instability in the light sandy soils so that soil exhaustion and soil erosion had become significant problems by the 1930s. Currently, areas such as the winter croplands of Western and South Australia, are subject to both wind and water erosion due mainly to the practice of bare fallowing. The problems are so widespread that in 1975 68 per cent of the 30 million ha used for extensive cropping were designated to be in need of treatment (Department of Environment 1978). Where intensive cropping predominates, as in the sugar-cane region of coastal Queensland and the irrigated areas of New South Wales, Victoria and South Australia where fruit and vines are produced, waterlogging and salinisation are the major problems. As Oliver (1986) points out, salinisation is a widespread natural hazard in the more arid interior of Australia, but the excessive accumulation of salts at or near the soil surface caused by a rise in the water-table by excessive irrigation is now characteristic of many intensive-cropping areas (section 6.3.3). Not only is it a detrimental consequence of agriculture but it is also affecting water supplies to some of Australia's major cities, notably Adelaide and

Perth. Conacher (1986) points to the surprising lack of interest in this issue
by conservation groups, especially as there is no other area on the earth's
surface that has been so rapidly cleared of its natural vegetation. The 15
million ha that comprise Western Australia's wheat belt have been cleared in
the last 80 years and during that time all of its surface waters have become
unsuitable for human consumption. While the restoration of degraded and
eroded soils is scientifically possible, the cost is enormous. Matheson (1986)
states that at 1975 prices the cost of reclaiming the damaged land of South
Australia is $A59 million.

Additional environmental problems relating to agricultural practices include eutrophication and the often detrimental side-effects of crop-protection
chemicals. Mention must, however, be made of the impact of European settlement on Australia's forests. Today, the extent of native forests is only
about one-third of what it was before European settlement, occupying c. 5.5
per cent of the country. Carnahan (1986) and Williams (1988) have described the character of the forests and woodlands which vary from tropical
rainforests in the coastal regions of the Northern Territory and northern
Queensland to subtropical and warm temperate rainforest in southern Queensland and New South Wales to cool temperate rainforest in southern Victoria
and Tasmania. Conacher (1986) reports that almost everywhere logging,
burning and the invasion of access tracks have detrimentally affected the
forest cover. In addition, the location of many forest types in areas of intensive land-use, often near Australia's major cities, has resulted in land-use
conflicts. The most significant impact on Australia's forests involve clear-
felling for woodchip industries and in many instances, particularly in
Tasmania, such exploited forests have been replaced by plantations of exotic
pines rather than of native species.

In relation to the introduction of fauna and flora, Adamson and Fox
(1982) state that one of the most significant introductions from Europe was
the rabbit, which now occupies the arid zone south of latitude 23°S. In particular, rabbits have influenced the establishment of the western myall (*Acacia papyrocarpa*) which requires a particular sequence of favourable rains to
promote germination. Since the arrival of the rabbit, and despite at least
three periods of appropriate rainfall, there has been no regeneration of this
tree because of browsing and all the existing trees, in a rapidly declining
population, became established prior to European settlement. Adamson and
Fox also point out that about 10 per cent of the Australian flora has been
introduced since European settlement with many species having been accidentally imported. Examples (from Wace 1988) include blackberries
(*Rubus* spp.), pampas grass (*Cortaderia selloana*) and privet (*Ligustrum lu-
cidum*). Like the rabbit, some of these introduced plants also instigated environmental change and in some instances the repercussions are only now
being felt. For example, Lonsdale and Braithwaite (1988) have reported on
the spread of a tall prickly mimosa shrub (*Mimosa pigra*) in the wetlands of
northern Australia where it is producing dense thickets that shade out native
plants on which many native animals depend. When this plant was introduced into Australia is unclear, but Lonsdale and Braithwaite attribute its
arrival to early colonial botanists who were investigating the potential of
new crops and suggest that its success has at least been partly due to another
introduced species, the Asian water-buffalo (*Bubalus bubalis*). Since the
1880s this has escaped from captivity and by the 1970s large herds were
causing considerable ecological damage due to overgrazing, especially on

the flood plains of the Adelaide River. Depleted of native plant species, this habitat rapidly became colonised by *Mimosa pigra* which created extensive shrublands in place of green meadowlands and control measures have so far only been partially successful in halting its spread.

In addition, the advent and development of European settlement and associated farming practices have been responsible for the decline in the numbers and populations of many native plant and animal species. Saunders and Hobbs (1989) report that in Western Australia some 104 species of plant have become extinct, most of which were natives of the wheat belt centred on Perth. Thirteen native mammal species, out of a total of forty-six, have also disappeared from the region and of these nine are now extinct on the Australian mainland.

Of all Australia's environmental problems, land degradation due to erosion and salinisation is the most widespread. Conacher and Conacher (1988) believe that these issues must become the collective concern of state and federal governments as well as the concern of individual landholders who must improve their management practices in order to halt the degradation and to rehabilitate the land. As Mabbutt (1978) has pointed out, the moderate risk of desertification is as high as 69 per cent in the semi-arid zones and since arid and semi-arid lands together comprise some 70 per cent of Australia's land surface there is clearly much cause for concern. This concern must not only relate to environmental issues but also to economic considerations. Woods (1984), for example, has summed up the situation by stating that; 'land degradation . . . has been identified as the most significant single issue on the Australian environment scene today, affecting large areas of Australia and critically limiting the scope for sustainable development'.

4.5 CONCLUSION

In the last 2 kyr human beings have considerably developed their ability to manipulate natural resources which in turn has resulted in large-scale environmental change. The landscape of Europe was transformed by Greek and especially Roman colonists who introduced new crops, new farming systems and new technology to their conquered lands, as well as opening up trade routes. In Britain, for example, the opulence of Roman archaeological sites attests to the significance of that civilisation.

Historical, archaeological and palaeoenvironmental studies have revealed evidence for subsequent changes in the British landscape that occurred between the demise of the Roman Empire in the fifth century and the Industrial Revolution of the eighteenth century. The most significant developments which influenced the landscape in this period relate primarily to agricultural practices, notably systems of land tenure, including field systems and enclosure, and the economic significance of woodlands and their exploitation. It is also evident that social and economic factors were inextricably involved in landscape change in Britain throughout the historic period as social hierarchies developed, taxation systems were instituted and settlement patterns evolved. Until the early eighteenth century the population was mainly rurally based, but as industry came to be concentrated in the towns and developed from cot-

tage industry to large-scale manufacture, there was a general flux of people to the towns. Industrial and mining landscapes subsequently developed as they did elsewhere in Europe.

By the time the Industrial Revolution occurred, many European nations had already become well established in other parts of the world, especially in the Americas, Africa and Australia. Just as the Romans annexed most of Europe nearly 2 kyr earlier, introducing and imposing agricultural systems and exploiting the wealth of their colonies, so too did Britain, France, Spain and Portugal exact their price on New and Old World peoples. Social changes brought about by exploitation of human resources were just as important as resource exploitation in transforming colonial landscapes to generate revenues for European homelands. While mining of precious metals was of some significance in landscape change, especially in South America, the major cause of environmental change was the initiation of new agricultural systems. Many of these involved the introduction of non-indigenous animals and new crops, especially cash crops for export, many of which were unsuited to their new environments and resulted in degradation on a large scale, often with continuing repercussions today.

While this review has attempted to concentrate on the environmental changes that have occurred during the last 2 kyr. It is clear that social changes are just as important as the landscape itself and were frequently the motivating force underpinning environmental change. As society has developed and technology has advanced, society has become increasingly able to control its environment though, as the above sections attest, this is often at great cost. The historic record provides sufficient information to teach a great number of environmental lessons which illustrate the need for better environmental management based on an awareness of environmental processes and systems of which human communities are an integral part.

FURTHER READING

Blaikie P, Brookfield H 1987 *Land degradation and society*. Methuen, London and New York

Dodgshon R A 1987 *The European past*. Macmillan Education, Basingstoke and London

Hoskins W G 1988 *The making of the English landscape*. (ed Taylor C C). Hodder and Stoughton, London

Jeans D N (ed) 1986 *Australia – a geography*. Vol 1. *The natural environment*. Sydney University Press, Sydney

Mitchell R D, Groves P A (eds) 1987 *North America: the historical geography of a changing continent*. Hutchinson, London

Newby E 1988 *The countryside in question*. Hutchinson, London

Rackham O 1986 *The history of the countryside*. Dent, London and Melbourne

Williamson T, Bellamy L 1987 *Property and landscape*. George Philip, London

ENVIRONMENTAL CHANGE DUE TO POST-1700 INDUSTRIALISATION

5.1 INTRODUCTION

In Chapter 1 attention was drawn to fuel-powered urban–industrial systems (section 1.1.3, Table 1.2) which, as described in Chapter 4, have developed during the historic period as an infrastructure for wealth-generating and resource-consuming human communities. A major component of such systems is industry, and industrial development almost everywhere on the earth's surface has become a major agent of environmental change, especially since the Industrial Revolution of the eighteenth century. In the ensuing two hundred years, the atmospheric, aquatic and terrestrial environments have been affected by these developments both directly and indirectly and not least by the high concentration of human populations that characterise such systems.

Although there has been a trend towards environmentally benign high-technology industry involving electronics during the last 20 years in many developed countries, fuel-powered urban–industrial systems have been traditionally centred on the so-called 'heavy' industries based on the processing of minerals and agricultural produce. This chapter addresses those changes in environmental quality that have occurred as a response. Since energy is also essential to industrial activity and the urban concentrations that supply the labour force, the environmental implications of energy provision, especially fossil and nuclear fuels, will be examined. This topic is of especial importance because it is now appreciated that the use and misuse of such resources can create environmental problems of a global nature and are causing climatic change. Both acidification, which is especially significant in the Northern Hemisphere where most industrialisation has taken place, and the enhanced greenhouse effect are products of the post-1700 industrial era. Fuel-powered urban–industrial systems, due to localised concentrations of industry and high housing density, also produce large quantities of waste materials ranging from toxic chemicals to domestic rubbish. These wastes frequently create environmental problems that are as severe as those emanating from mineral extraction and energy provision.

There are, however, numerous examples which illustrate that such environmental changes can be halted or even reversed. The reclamation of mine-damaged land, for instance, can provide productive artificial ecosystems, and controls on sulphurous gas emissions from fossil fuels can retard acidification. Such achievements are only possible where sufficient finance is available and they frequently require international co-operation.

5.2 ENVIRONMENTAL CHANGE DUE TO MINERAL EXTRACTION

Since the evolution some two million years ago of *Homo habilis*, the first tool-using ancestor of *H. sapiens sapiens*, human groups have utilised the earth's mineral resources (sections 1.1.4 and 3.2.1) concentrating initially on stone and later, from *c.* 8 kyr BP, on metals, notably tin, copper and iron (section 3.4). There is also evidence that precious metals like gold and silver were much appreciated in prehistoric times; there are gold ornaments from the tombs of the Pharaohs of Egypt for example, as well as gold hoards recorded from the Bronze Age period in Britain and Ireland dating to *c.* 3.5 kyr BP. Moreover, it is apparent (section 4.4) that one of the major stimuli for European expansion into Africa, America and Australia was the search for mineral wealth. The utilisation of such resources not only helped to fuel the industrial developments that occurred in Europe in the nineteenth and early twentieth centuries (sections 4.3.1 and 4.3.2) but also led to the establishment of processing industries *in situ*. As a consequence, both developed and developing nations have undergone environmental changes in those areas where mineral extraction and processing have occurred. The establishment of extractive and processing plant machinery as well as waste disposal have created localised industrial landscapes that are often aesthetically displeasing and frequently hazardous. Extractive industries are also responsible for changing environmental quality at considerable distance from the points of extraction and processing, leading to air and water pollution that can have far-reaching effects. In the last three decades there have also been attempts to reclaim areas that have been locally contaminated, especially in the developed world, which has led to the creation of artificial ecosystems.

5.2.1 ENVIRONMENTAL CHANGE IN AREAS WHERE MINERALS ARE EXTRACTED AND PROCESSED

In areas where minerals are extracted the landscape changes that occur relate to the type of mining that is practised which in turn depends on the nature of the resource and where it is placed relative to the land surface. According to Blunden (1985) all minerals on which a value is placed by society and which are used by society are stock resources. They include aggregates which are used in road and building construction, non-metallic minerals, metalliferous minerals, fuels and precious and semi-precious stones, the variety of which is illustrated in Table 5.1. This shows that the most important methods of extraction are surface working including quarrying, opencast and strip mining and deep mining or, in the case of oil and natural gas, deep drilling. Each of these methods creates its own type of environmental change which is also dependent on how much waste material is produced.

Of all the methods of surface working, strip mining is the most disruptive because it affects a larger surface area than quarrying or opencast mining. There are three types of strip mining: area strip mining which is employed in flat or gently undulating land, mountain top removal used in hilly terrain to produce plateaux and contour stripping which involves the cutting of benches into mountainsides. All of these techniques are used in the USA to extract coal, especially in the Appalachians where Moran *et al.* (1986) state that more than 1.6 million ha of land have been disturbed by these activities. Toy and Hadley (1987) report that prior to the introduction of block-cutting, which involves the placement of newly extracted overburden into areas from which coal has alredy been removed, contour strip mining had created some 40 000 km of contour benches in Appalachia of which 2700 km are subject to major landslides. In the past, these have destroyed neighbouring farmland, roads, reservoirs and streams. Even the relatively stable slopes produced by contour mining are subject to higher than average erosion rates because they remain unvegetated. There is also evidence that hydrological systems may be severely affected by both vegetation removal and enhanced sedimentation. This reduces the flow capacity of stream and river channels, causing an increase in flooding intensity and frequency.

Opencast or open pit mining can also cause considerable environmental change. For example, the Liberty Copper Mine in Nevada is 300 m deep and more than 1 km wide (Moran *et al.* 1986). Open-pit mining is also used to extract uranium ores in the USA, especially where ore is emplaced within 90 and 150 m of the surface and covered with unconsolidated overburden. According to Toy and Hadley (1987) the ratio of overburden to ore in this industry is high, ranging from 8 : 1 to 35 : 1 and this, together with waste materials from processing, can have a significant environmental impact, as it has at the Anaconda Mine in New Mexico. This is the largest open pit uranium mine in the world and occupies 486 ha of which 445 ha are occupied by twenty-eight dump sites containing nearly 2 million t of overburden and mine wastes (Toy and Hadley 1987). As in the case of Appalachian coal-mining, disturbance at Anaconda has affected geomorphological processes by accelerating erosion rates and has disrupted local drainage networks. The tailings, which consist of sands and slurries produced from on-site ore processing, are particularly susceptible to both wind and water erosion. However, one of the most significant environmental hazards associated with uranium extraction relates to residues that are radioactive, some of which have long half-lives that can cause contamination for thousands of years. Few data are available to enable an assessment of this problem either in relation to groundwater contamination or to the risk to human health.

In Togo, open-pit mining is the chief way in which phosphates are extracted from a coastal sedimentary basin in the southern part of the country. According to Allaglo *et al.* (1987), phosphate is the main source of foreign exchange and extraction is concentrated at two extensive sites at Hahotoé and Kpogamé in the Haho river valley which have working faces of 800 m and 1500 m respectively. Here, mining activities have had both environmental and social repercussions. In relation to the latter, mining was only possible after the relocation of several villages and numerous farmers engaged in shifting cultivation and oil-palm production. Resettlement was effected but to distant areas that were not as productive as those in the Haho River Valley and in consequence the traditional way of life was disrupted with many people turning to marketing of foodstuffs and handicrafts. Despite the need for labour in the phosphate mines, this disruption has led to a migration of people into the towns at the expense of the rural community. Soil degradation has also occurred and the dumping of overburden has created an artificial landscape consisting of earth walls several metres high over several thousand hectares which are susceptible to erosion by overland flow

Table 5.1. Mineral resources: Their variety, distribution, output, waste to ore ratios and environmental problems. (From Blunden 1985.)

Class	Examples	Distribution and location	Ratio of ore/mineral to waste
Common rocks	Limestone, chalk, granite, sandstone, slate	Widespread and abundant	Almost all used
Common rocks	Sand and gravel	do.	do.
Earths and clays	Ball clay, stoneware clay, china clay, fullers' earth	Common	All used except for overburden (e)
Common rock-forming minerals	Feldspar, dolomite, mica, quartz, fluorspar	Common but (b) limited source	1:1 down to 1:50
Precious and semi-precious stones	Diamonds, rubies, sapphires, emeralds, opal, garnet, amethyst, jade	Rare	Stones are a minute percentage of waste rock
Common minerals	Asbestos, vermiculite, pyrites, talc, soapstone, alum, barium, gypsum	Fairly abundant in limited locations	
Less common minerals	Graphite, sillimanite, wollastonite, Cryolite	Infrequently found	
Salts	Salt, rock salt, sodium salts, borax, potash, nitrate, phosphate	Common and fairly abundant in limited locations	
Abrasives	Corundum, emery, pumice, commercial garnet	Rarely located but abundant when found	
Common metal ores (ferrous)	Magnetite, haematite, limonite	Abundant but in limited localities	
Common metal ores (non-ferrous)	Bauxite, galena, nickel ores, tin ores, copper ores, zinc	Limited distribution	
Less-common metals	Manganese, antimony, cadmium, chromium, cobalt, mercury		
Rare metals	Indium, germanium, lithium, caesium, selenium, tellurium, tungsten, thorium, titanium, uranium, vanadium, zirconium	Rare to very rare	1:100 down to 1:5,000,000
'Noble' metals	Gold, silver, platinum, palladium	Very rare	Ore contains about 0.1 per cent metal
Fossil fuels	Coal	Fairly common	2:1 (deep mining) 1:15 (opencast)
	Oil	Abundant but rarely found	All used either crude, refined or in by products
	Peat	Common	All used

and are unsuitable for cultivation. Some of these problems have been overcome by introducing leguminous plants to protect the soil surface and to enhance the organic component and thus the cohesiveness of the soil. Environmental problems also occur in the coastal strip where a treatment plant was established. This has led to the removal of plantation coconut palms which, together with dust and smoke and clay dumping in the sea, means that the area is much less attractive to tourists.

The mining of aggregates for road and building construction can also bring about considerable environmental change which tends to be localised

World output measured in	Usual method of working	Possible environmental impacts	Remarks
Thousands of million tonne	Quarrying on surface of hillside	Scenic scars, loss of habitats but interesting when worked out	except for up to 95% wastage in slate
do.	Wet or dry surface pits	Voids; flooding; lowered surface levels; drainage	sometimes creating new water habitats and recreation areas
Hundreds of million tonne	Surface working	Lowered surface levels; drainage problems; pollution; tips from china clay	except for china clay where high percentage of waste material (1:10)
Million tonne	Surface or hillside quarrying	Scenic scars	need selective quarrying
Thousands of grammes (kilogrammes)	Open pit sands and gravels; underground mining	Voids and scenic scars	or found in working other minerals
Million tonne	Quarrying on surface or hillside	(as rocks): risks of pollution to water	
Hundreds of thousand tonne	Adit mining into veins and dykes	(as rocks): risks of pollution to water	
Million tonne	Deep mining, surface quarries; alluvial mining and solution mining	Waste heaps; subsidence; saline flashes	
Million tonne	Surface working of outcrop and adits into veins	(as rocks)	
Hundreds of million tonne	Deep mining. Pillar and stall longwall; drift mines; outcast	Waste deposits; hill and vale restoration	
Million tonne	Historically by deep mining, now mainly open pit: some alluvial (tin)	Voids; waste heaps; tailing dams and lakes; polluted run-off; toxic wastes	
Hundreds of thousand tonne	Deep mining mainly by adits; some open pit	Toxic wastes	most are only got as a by product
Ore output varies from under a tonne to thousand tonnes, according to scarceness and demand. Metals usually measured in 100 lb. ounces (kilogrammes)	Various	Toxic wastes, radiation and similar risks	
Million troy ounces, (kilogrammes)	Deep mines with shafts and galleries or drift mines or alluvial mining	Voids; waste heaps; scenic scars	or as by products
Hundreds of million tonne	Deep mines, with shafts and galleries or drift mines opencast, strip and auger mines	Subsidence; shale tips; scenic damage; air pollution from burning tips; liquid effluent; pollutants; temp. scenic damage by opencast	
Hundreds of million tonne	Land or sea walls	Oil spillage at sea or from pipelines; spoil heaps from oil shale working	
Million tonne	Surface working	Lowered land levels; drainage problems; may destroy or preserve bog habitats	

at the point of extraction. The problem is widespread in Britain and Bradshaw and Chadwick (1980) estimate that approximately 1000 ha of land are used annually to produce 100 million t of sand and gravel. The main impact of this industry is loss of scenic value, though reclamation schemes can restore the land effectively, providing viable agricultural land and water recreation facilities. In the Maldive Islands in the Indian Ocean, coral is now the main construction material and its use has created a unique set of environmental problems. Brown and Dunne (1988) report that there has been considerable disruption of the biological systems that underpin coral reef maintenance. Biological surveys of mined and unmined sites show that at the former there has been a major reduction in the variety and abundance of coral as well as a reduction in the variety and abundance of coral-reef fish. In the worst cases, living coral has been almost totally depleted and even 10 years after mining has ceased there is little evidence of recovery.

In the case of deep mining, Stein (1987) states that the most significant effect is subsidence which is caused by the collapse of overlying rocks into excavated chambers. In Britain for example, subsidence is a major problem associated with the mining of salt and coal. This is also a problem in the USA, where approximately 25 per cent of the country's 3250 km^2 of underground coal mines have been affected (Coates 1987). Subsidence can occur in working and abandoned mines and Coates (1987), as well as giving numerous examples of building collapse in the USA, indicates that the landscape features created by subsidence over abandoned mines are sinkholes and troughs (or pits and sags). The former occur when overburden collapses into a chamber with steep walls and an increasing diameter with depth whilst troughs are shallow near-circular depressions that develop when the overburden sags downward as underground supporting pillars collapse. Dunrud (1984), for example, has described sinkholes and troughs from Beulah, North Dakota which have been produced by the subsidence of lignite coal mines which were worked between 1918 and 1952.

Coates (1987) has also documented some of the problems associated with salt mining, which include subsidence, the creation of linear hollows or flashes which result from the collapse of brine runs, and surface lowering due to salt dissolution. Ege (1984) has also described several sinkholes which have developed at Grosse Ile in Michigan where solution mining of salt began in 1951 and in 1971 two sinkholes developed extending to 60 m and 135 m in diameter. Other earth disturbances that can occur as a result of deep mining include rockbursts as well as vertical and horizontal rock displacements.

5.2.2 CHANGES IN ENVIRONMENTAL QUALITY IN AREAS DISTANT FROM THE SOURCE OF MINERAL EXTRACTION

While the impact of mineral extraction invariably creates environmental change in the immediate vicinity of the mining, there is frequently a more widespread change in soil, aquatic and atmospheric environmental quality at distance which may be related to both extraction methods and mineral processing. Of particular significance is the use of fossil fuels in mineral processing that are contributing to the enhanced greenhouse effect, but since this relates to environmental change due to energy consumption it will be considered in section 5.3 and this section will concentrate on the changes in environmental quality that occur in response to the extraction and processing of minerals and which may be due to deliberate, incidental or accidental contamination.

One of the major causes of changes in environmental quality is contamination by heavy metals such as lead, cadmium and mercury. Mining activities are not the only source of these metals as they are also released in waste products from chemical and manufacturing industries and a great deal of heavy metal contamination results from the presence of these metals in ores which are being extracted for other minerals. In addition, increasing concern about the effects of such contaminants on human health and wildlife has led to numerous research projects to determine the way in which these substances enter ecosystems and are transported via biogeochemical cycles. Hart and Lake (1987) have summarised several such studies that have been undertaken in Australia. The South Esk River in northeast Tasmania, for example, has been polluted by zinc and cadmium derived from the mining of tin and wolfram (the latter is a tungsten ore). Norris *et al.* (1980, 1981, 1982) have examined the relationship between the concentrations of these metals and the macroinvertebrate fauna and found that, even as far as 80 km downstream from the point at which the pollution entered, the populations and diversity of species were still much lower than in upstream uncontaminated sites that were used as a control. The King River in western Tasmania is also heavily polluted with copper and zinc as well as lesser amounts of lead and cadmium due to acidic drainage from disused mine shafts and waste dumps which has resulted in a depletion of fish and macroinvertebrate populations (Hart and Lake 1987). Similarly, the Finniss River in the Northern Territory is still experiencing pollution by copper, zinc manganese and sulphate due to the receipt of drainage from spoil tips, mine pits etc. despite the cessation of uranium- and copper-mining in 1971.

Mercury is another metal which frequently causes ecosystem contamination and may constitute a threat to wildlife and human health. High concentrations occur because it is used in the extraction of mineral ores, especially gold. This is illustrated in a recent study by Martinelli *et al.* (1988) who have examined the mercury levels in the sediments and biota of the Madeira River in the Amazon basin, Brazil. This river is of especial significance because it flows through Rondonia State that has been subject to development since 1980 as gold mining has intensified. This development has resulted in accelerated deforestation as population has increased (Fearnside 1986), as well as ecosystem contamination. This latter has arisen because mercury is used in two phases of alluvial gold mining. It is used to separate and amalgamate the gold as river sediments are sieved, resulting in an inevitable release of at least some of the mercury that poses a threat, via inhalation, to workers. Martinelli *et al.*'s examination of mercury levels in Madeira River sediments and fish show that the major hazard caused by this development relates to human health, since mercury concentrations in the fish widely harvested for food were much higher than the 0.5 $\mu g\ g^{-1}$ recommended by the World Health Organisation.

Another example of widespread contamination of the environment due to mineral extraction has been documented by Chansang (1988) in the context of tin mining and coastal pollution in Thailand. The industry is centred on alluvial deposits along the Andaman coast where environmental problems have been created by the methods of mining and by mine tailings. The alluvial deposits consist of cassiterite which is mined by gravel pumping on land

and dredging in the shallow coastal waters and swamps. The resulting lighter materials are washed out as mine tailings and are deposited in old mine pits where the solids settle out and the water is either recycled or fed into natural waterways. Areas which have been thus affected suffer from deforestation, a decline in aesthetic value which is detrimental to a growing tourist industry, and similar geomorphological problems to those described in section 5.2.1. Beyond the point source, runoff containing suspended materials that can sediment out in the waterways and the sea creates highly turbid waters, and Chansang reports that arsenic contamination of surface waters has occurred in at least one mining district in southern Thailand. Bucket dredging, which is used to extract cassiterite from shallow coastal waters, can create similar environmental problems especially in relation to tailings which are discharged directly into the water.

Apart from turbidity and the conflict of interest that occurs between the mining and tourism industries, the character of the coastline has changed considerably since the early 1900s when mining began. Chansang (1988) states that this is particularly noticeable in the Phuket Bay area due to both on- and off-shore mining. Accelerated deposition of waste materials has caused coastal accretion which in turn makes navigation difficult for local fishermen and creates unsuitable habitats for shellfish. The impact of these mining activities on biological resources is also considerable. For example, mining in mangrove swamps has altered the structure and composition of the sediments and the resulting reduction in nutrients and organic matter has hindered the process of mangrove recolonisation. Suspended material has detrimentally altered the abundance of plankton and benthic organisms in the Phang-nga Bay region where the cockle-based fishing industry has been adversely affected. Dredging and excessive siltation have altered coral reef function and in extreme cases the reefs have been destroyed. A combination of excessive silt and a decrease in light availability owing to turbidity has curtailed reef growth in many areas, though Chansang states that recovery is possible if sediment is removed.

In the USA, there are also widespread examples of environmental problems in drainage systems that receive runoff from mine waste. Moran *et al.* (1986) state that more than 60 per cent of acid drainage in the USA derives from runoff from coal-mine spoil. This occurs because the wastes are often sulphur-rich and as rainfall percolates through the material sulphuric acid forms which then enters the drainage network. In the Appalachian region, for example, Moran *et al.* (1986) state that some 16 000 km of waterways have been thus polluted. Similar problems occur in Britain and Goudie (1986) reports pH values as low as 2 or 3 in mine drainage waters and discoloration due to the precipitation of iron compounds. Oil extraction is another cause of declining environmental quality, especially in the oceans into which it is often released accidentally. Some examples of this type of pollution are given by C A M King (1987) who quotes the *Torrey Canyon* disaster of 1967 when this oil-tanker ran aground on the Sevenstone Reef, off the coast of Cornwall. The resulting oil slick proved fatal for marine and coastal wildlife, especially birds, and King states that the detergents employed to disperse the oil proved to be more damaging than the oil itself. Jackson *et al.* (1989) have also reported on the ecological effects of a major oil spill that occurred in 1986 close to the Caribbean entrance to the Panama Canal, where intertidal mangrove and subtidal coral reef ecosystems had, in 1968, been affected by an earlier oil spill. Within a year of the 1986 spill, dead red mangroves (*Rhizophora mangle*) were observed along *c.* 27 km of the Panamanian coast and comparisons of pre- and post-oil slick data on the epibiota of the mangroves reflect a massive decline in algae and invertebrates, the populations of which showed only patchy recovery some 15 months after the spill. Similar detrimental effects were observed in the coral reefs, where the oil caused coral mortality, and in sea grass (*Thalassia testudinum*) communities where infaunal communities were badly affected. Apart from accidents such as this, extensive oil pollution of the marine environment is caused by the discharge of contaminated ballast water that is loaded on to empty tankers to ensure stability as they return to base. New methods of draining and the provision of separate ballast tanks should, however, help to alleviate this problem.

5.2.3 THE RECLAMATION OF MINE-DAMAGED LAND

In the last two decades, numerous programmes have been established to rehabilitate land made derelict by mining activity. This in itself constitutes environmental change, and, while it is rare for such contaminated areas to be restored to their former status, artificial ecosystems with considerably enhanced aesthetic and economic values may result. Just as the problems created by the extractive industries vary according to the mineral, so do the reclamation procedures, as is illustrated by the following examples. There is also a growing trend involving comprehensive surveys and impact assessments prior to mineral extraction which, together with legislation relating to aftercare, can help to minimise the effects of mining and make reclamation more feasible and less costly.

In Britain, the problems of reclaiming derelict land have been addressed by Bradshaw and Chadwick (1980), Bradshaw (1983, 1984), Broughton (1985) and Finnecy and Pearce (1986), and include urban and industrial dereliction as well as mine-damaged land, though only the latter will be discussed here. Bradshaw (1984) points out that the chief cause of dereliction is the removal of soil and one way to rapidly improve the environment is to replace topsoil: but unless this has been stored after its extraction from the site in question it is a very expensive undertaking. In consequence, many reclamation schemes involve the direct treatment of site materials which necessitates the identification of the specific problems and deficiencies of the waste in question. In colliery spoil, for example, there are deficiencies of nitrogen and phosphorus which are essential plant nutrients and the abundance of pyrite (iron sulphide), which combines with water to produce sulphuric acid, often results in a soil pH of between 2 and 4. The former problem can be overcome by dressing with nitrate and phosphate fertilisers while the latter is ameliorated by addition of lime. The amounts of these compounds required will depend on how much pyrite is present and on the quantities of iron and aluminium oxides which can bind phosphorus and render it unavailable to plant growth. According to the Department of Environment (1986) there are 11 000 ha of land contaminated with colliery spoil and another 200 ha are taken annually. Since only 300 ha are restored annually this is an enduring problem.

Bradshaw (1984) has also discussed the problems associated with the reclamation of metalliferous wastes in Britain which necessitate chemical analyses of the wastes to identify the major nutrient deficiencies. Where concentrations of metals, such as lead and zinc, are high enough to be toxic to plants, cultivars of species like red fescue (*Festuca rubra*) which are tolerant of such concentrations can be successfully used to establish a vegetation cover. Alternatively, a covering of an inert substance such as colliery spoil can be used to provide a near-surface environment for plant growth that is uncontaminated by the underlying toxic spoil. Examples of successfully reclaimed metalliferous wastes include Pars Mine, Gwynedd and tailing ponds near Eyam in Derbyshire (Department of Environment 1986). At the former site, a disused lead/zinc mine that closed in 1960, metalliferous waste tips presented an environmental hazard both *in situ* and to the neighbouring Conway Valley. A reclamation scheme was instituted by the Welsh Development Agency in 1977 which involved covering the tips with inert gravelly waste from a nearby quarry to provide a barrier against the upward movement of toxic metals. This was seeded with a grass mixture containing a metal-tolerant variety of red fescue, along with dressings of fertiliser and lime to counteract nutrient deficiencies and high acidity. Drainage to the local stream was also controlled by ensuring that runoff from the waste was passed through a limestone filter bed which, together with diversion of the stream, helped to minimise pollution in the drainage network. The scheme was so effective that a grass sward rapidly developed and grazing is now allowed although in financial terms the cost was high: £400 000 was needed to reclaim just 3 ha. A similar success has been achieved by the reclamation of ponds near Eyam, Derbyshire, which have been used to dump waste from lead, zinc and fluorspar extractive industries. Here, the pond or lagoon walls, which are now sited so as to create the least environmental impact, are grassed over. After filling with tailings they were treated with sewage sludge, a good source of nutrients, as well as fertilisers and seeded with a variety of grasses, legumes and shrubs. Plant growth proved to be good and within 10 years trees have become established on the oldest lagoon and grazing is now allowed on a limited basis.

Since coal is a very important source of energy, it is widely extracted and wherever extraction occurs environmental problems ensue. The problems and reclamation schemes that are extant in coal-mining regions of the USA have been referred to in section 5.2.1. Such problems also occur in eastern Europe and Szegi *et al.* (1988) have examined reclamation schemes that are being carried out in relation to the Visonta Thorez Mining Company's activities in the foothills of the Màtra Mountains, Hungary. Here, open-cut mines are used to extract the coal and a land-use plan has assisted in the development of a reclamation scheme. Topsoil is not removed from the area and efforts are made to ensure that the most suitable overburden materials are deposited on the surface of the dumps to promote reclamation. Szegi *et al.* report that the best soil structure was achieved by mixing clay and sand and that soil microbial populations were improved by ploughing in plant residues and adding fertilisers. Within 8 years a natural succession of vegetation had developed, consisting of a closed grassland over a chernozem-like fertile soil, which was then suitable for afforestation. Currently, the main tree species that are cultivated are robinia (*Robinina pseudoacacia*), giant poplar (*Populus euramericana* cv. *robusta*) and Italian poplar (*P. euramericana*) and on some reclaimed spoil wastes wheat is cultivated.

There are numerous examples of mine-waste reclamation schemes in Australia where most of the largest mining operations have developed in the last 20 years and which are mainly situated in Australia's rangelands (Farrell

1986). State legislation ensures that environmental impact assessments are carried out prior to the commencement of mineral extraction and this has resulted in a great deal of research relating to land rehabilitation. Rhodes (1986) has described the methods used to restore land contaminated with waste from opal mining at Lightning Ridge in New South Wales. Although the development of mining began in this area in 1902, activities have expanded in the last two decades and include both shaft and open-cut mining which produce a saline waste that also has a high clay content. The waste dumps have been reshaped into broad-based contour banks to pond water which facilitates the leaching of toxic salts and a loam topsoil is used to provide a medium for plant growth. Rhodes's study shows that vegetation establishment proceeded most rapidly where topsoil had been employed and although this was much slower on untreated wastes because of high salinity, it was expected to improve as salts were leached. Overall, the risks of chemical pollution and erosion were considerably reduced as a result of these restorative measures. A similar approach to the reclamation of gold-mine wastes in the Kalgoorlie–Boulder area of Western Australia has been detailed by Burnside *et al.* (1986). Here, some 500 ha of waste have accumulated since mining began 90 years ago and are particularly susceptible to wind erosion. A combination of contouring, the application of nickel smelter slag as a buffer, fertilising and seeding with saltbush (*Atriplex spp.*) has resulted in a stable vegetation cover that affords protection from wind erosion.

Bauxite mining in Australia has also created extensive contaminated areas as well as land-use conflicts. In southwestern Australia, for example, the Alcoa Company has established mines in the Darling Ranges where conflicts of interest arise because some of the bauxite is located in *Eucalyptus* spp. forest on the Darling Plateau which is an important timber-producing area. Nichols *et al.* (1985) report that continued access to this area, which has sufficient bauxite reserves for several decades, will depend on the success of Alcoa's rehabilitation programme, the primary aim of which is to regenerate a stable forest ecosystem. To achieve this an overall plan is formulated, taking into account the floral and faunal characteristics of those areas which are considered favourable for alumina extraction as well as the potential effect of mining on local hydrological conditions. Where mining is to proceed, topsoil is removed and any commercial timber growing *in situ* is harvested while waste timber is stockpiled. The topsoil is usually transferred to another mine undergoing rehabilitation which allows for more rapid restoration. Sandy overburden is also stockpiled. After bauxite extraction, the pit faces are bulldozed to produce gentler slopes and the compacted pit floor is ripped, and sumps are constructed to facilitate water retention to reduce the risk of discharging sediment-laden water into streams. Overburden and topsoil are replaced and since the latter is freshly derived from a new site it contains a viable seed bank that, according to Tacey and Glossop (1980), gives rise to a vegetation cover similar to that of undisturbed forest. Tree planting and the seeding of understorey species are then carried out to accelerate the recovery of the vegetation. Seeding is particularly important to introduce native species that do not readily germinate from topsoil and to encourage rapid growth of legumes such as *Acacia* spp. which enhance the nitrogen content of the soil. Thereafter, monitoring is carried out to ensure that the scheme is successful and remedial measures are effected where necessary. According to Nichols *et al.* (1985), 2500 ha of the 3500 ha of land that have been cleared for mining in the last 20 years have been rehabilitated.

Langkamp and Plaisted (1987) have reviewed the use of native plant seed in land restoration programmes in Australia and state that the most common species used are *Acacia* spp. and *Eucaluptus* spp. In addition, some 60 per cent of the seed is collected on site rather than being purchased, emphasising the use of local seed varieties. Brooks (1987) has also reviewed the importance of native plant seed in the rehabilitation of land that has been degraded by the mineral sands industry. For example, beach spinifex grass (*Spinifex hirsutus* habill.) has been successfully used to stabilise dunes along 45 km of coastline on North and South Stradbroke Islands in Queensland. Seed, harvested by contract pickers, was sown along with fertiliser, resulting, between 1969 and 1980, in the rehabilitation of 860 ha of land.

These examples indicate that restoration, rehabilitation and reclamation of land rendered derelict by mineral extraction are feasible in a wide range of environments and in relation to a wide range of minerals. Numerous further examples are given in Bradshaw and Chadwick (1980), and Arndt and Luttig (1987), all of which illustrate that given sufficient finance and expertise such activities can be powerful agents of environmental change.

5.3 ENVIRONMENTAL CHANGE DUE TO FOSSIL-FUEL BURNING AND INDUSTRIAL CHEMICALS

In the last few years much concern has been expressed about the long- and short-term environmental changes which have been caused by the use of fossil fuels. As discussed in section 4.3, the widespread use of such fuels began with the Industrial Revolution and while their extraction brings about environmental change on site, there is increasing concern about the changes that are occurring in the atmosphere, especially in the context of carbon dioxide concentrations that are effecting climatic change. In addition, the emission of nitrous and sulphurous gases into the atmosphere and their subsequent deposition is now accepted as one of the major causes of terrestrial and aquatic acidification. In extreme cases, this latter has degraded aquatic ecosystems and rendered water supplies unpotable. Other contaminants, derived from industrial chemicals, are also contributing to environmental change via air pollution and may also be a threat to human health. Examples include chlorofluorocarbons (CFCs), that affect the ozone layer in the stratosphere, and lead emissions from vehicular traffic and industrial processes. These issues have been widely debated in the scientific and popular press and while the consequences of these processes may be severe, it could be argued that the most significant results of such debate have been to bring environmental issues into the public eye and into the political arena. In addition, international collaboration in terms of both scientific endeavour and political liaison have been promoted which can, in the long term, only be beneficial to all nations and their environments.

5.3.1 THE ENVIRONMENTAL IMPACT OF CHANGING ATMOSPHERIC CARBON DIOXIDE AND OTHER GREENHOUSE GAS CONCENTRATIONS

Reference has been made in section 1.2.2 to the long-term changes in atmospheric concentrations of both carbon dioxide and methane that have occurred during the glacial–interglacial cycle. As Fig. 1.3 shows, higher concentrations of carbon dioxide occur during the interglacials than during the glacial periods and as Stauffer *et al.* (1988) demonstrate, methane concentrations exhibit similar trends. These data imply that a relationship exists between climatic change and the global carbon cycle though it has not yet been established precisely how this relationship functions. As discussed in section 1.2.2, there is evidence for enhanced marine productivity during glacial stages which may have helped to deplete the atmospheric pool of carbon dioxide. However, it is not clear whether changing carbon dioxide (and methane) concentrations during this 120 kyr cycle are a cause or a result of climatic change. Lyle (1988), for example, believes that enhanced productivity in the equatorial oceans during the glacial stages is a result of, rather than a cause of, climatic change. Further research on these interrelationships should help to elucidate the cause and effect system and this may assist in

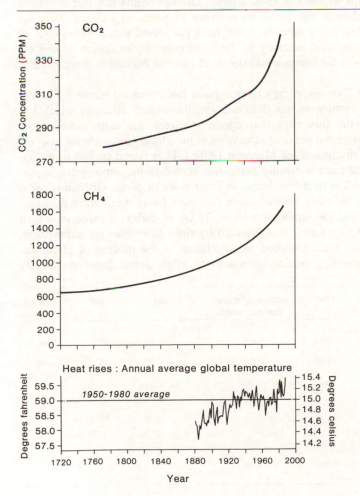

Fig. 5.1. Changes in the concentrations of atmospheric carbon dioxide and methane during the last 200–300 years in relation to changes in average global temperatures. (Based on Neftel *et al.* 1985; Friedli *et al.* 1986; Gribbin 1988a; Khalil and Rasmussen 1987.)

the formulation of models which seek to address the potential effects of currently increasing greenhouse gas concentrations on global temperatures (see Bach 1988 for a discussion).

Indeed, while accurate determinations of atmospheric composition have shown that increases in these gases have occurred over the last 40 years or so, polar ice core data allow this record to be extended back to the pre-industrial period (reviewed in Mannion 1989b). Data for carbon dioxide and methane concentrations for the last 200–300 years are given in Fig. 5.1 and have been discussed by Siegenthaler and Oeschger (1987). They show that prior to the Industrial Revolution the concentration of carbon dioxide was approximately 270 ppm but by 1953 it had increased to *c.* 312 ppm. Measurements of carbon dioxide concentrations in the atmosphere have also been made at Mauna Loa in Hawaii since 1957 (Fig. 5.1) and while they confirm the ice core data they show that carbon dioxide concentrations have continued to rise to the current level of 350 ppm. Moreover, it is inevitable that increases will continue to occur as fossil fuel burning and deforestation increase. Wellburn (1988), for example, indicates that by the year 2000, concentrations will be in excess of 400 ppm. This is endorsed by Gribbin (1988a) who states that between 1850 and 1950 approximately 60 Gt of carbon was burnt, mainly as coal, as industrialisation proceeded (section 4.3). While this in itself is considerable, Gribbin points out that a similar amount of carbon is now being burnt every 12 years. In addition, Detwiler and Hall (1988), using data for 1980, have calculated that *c.* 0.4–1.6 Gt of carbon are contributed annually to the atmosphere by oxidation of soil organic matter and the burning and decay of cleared vegetation from tropical forests alone.

As Table 5.2 shows, energy consumption has increased markedly during the twentieth century, as has deforestation, the overall effect of which has been to alter the flux rates that operate between the main atmospheric, oceanic and terrestrial pools or reservoirs in the global biogeochemical cycle (for a general discussion see Mannion 1986e). Thus stored carbon from biomass and fossil fuels is rapidly being transferred to the atmosphere, a proportion of which is then transferred to other sinks or pools. Gribbin (1988a) reports that by the early 1980s 5 Gt of fuel were being burnt annually, causing an input into the atmosphere of *c.* 18 Gt of carbon dioxide of which approximately 50 per cent is reabsorbed by sinks other than the atmosphere. Some may have been absorbed by vegetation in the process of photosynthesis thus increasing primary productivity, while some dissolves directly

Table 5.2. Trends in the pattern of world energy consumption. (The data, from various sources, are approximate.)

Year	Millions of tonnes coal equivalent	% coal	% gas	% oil
1980	9000	30	19	40
1960	4000	41	15	39
1940	2000			
1920	1500			
1900	1000			
1880	650			
1860	400			

into the oceans and is incorporated into bicarbonates and carbonates. What is of paramount concern is the effect that this has already had, and will continue to have, on global climate via the so-called greenhouse effect. This of course is a natural feature of the earth's climate system and involves counter-radiation of infrared heat by certain tropospheric gases, of which carbon dioxide is one of the most important, back to the earth's surface; without this, surface temperatures would fall markedly. The greenhouse effect is thus essential to the maintenance of atmospheric and life-support systems. The current debate relates to how much more heat is being trapped by these enhanced concentrations of greenhouse gases that may create a positive feedback leading to global warming. In consequence, much effort is being expended to determine if warming has already occurred and what, if any, impact it has had on the earth's surface. Moreover, because atmospheric carbon dioxide concentrations are likely to increase, it is important to determine what future warming trends may occur and what the consequences of these might be.

While carbon dioxide is the most abundant greenhouse gas, it is not the only one. Nitrous oxide, ozone and CFCs also absorb infrared radiation and it is well established that the concentrations of these have also increased due to human activity. Wellburn (1988) indicates that the current concentration of nitrous oxide is 0.30 ppm and predicts that by the year 2050 this will rise to 0.35 ppm due to the extensive use of nitrate fertilisers and the denitrifying effects of bacteria in the soil. Increasing concentrations of ozone in the troposphere, due to emissions of unburnt hydrocarbons that react with oxides of nitrogen, are also occurring (see Fig. 5.5). As discussed by Krupa and Manning (1988), increasing ozone concentrations in the troposphere are not only contributing to the enhanced greenhouse effect but are also known to damage plant health and productivity. As will be discussed in section 5.3.3, increases in CFCs are also occurring and these are more effective trappers of heat than carbon dioxide. Data from observed radiance profiles reported by Evans (1988) lend support to the view that CFC emissions have already modified the long-wave radiation budget by 0.1 per cent, causing enhanced warming.

Attention has already been drawn to the increasing concentration of methane in the atmosphere (Fig. 5.1) which has been reported by numerous workers (Stauffer *et al*. 1985, Rasmussen and Khalil 1984; Khalil and Rasmussen 1985, 1987). As Pearce (1989) has discussed, the sources of this additional methane are varied. They include the bacterial decomposition of material in rubbish dumps (section 5.4.1) and rice fields, as well as gaseous emissions from cattle, due to bacterial breakdown of cellulose in the animals' guts, car exhausts, global wetlands and the regular burning of vegetation. Measurements of the isotopic composition of methane in the air bubbles of polar ice cores suggest that one of the main causes of atmospheric methane enrichment during the last few decades is indeed biomass burning (Craig *et al* 1988), the most obvious source of which is the large-scale deforestation that is occurring in tropical regions (section 7.3.1). Although the present concentration of methane is relatively low at 1.7 ppm, it is in marked contrast to 0.78 ppm recorded in polar ice for 1771 and according to Blake and Rowland (1988) its concentration is increasing by *c*. 1.2 per cent annually. Methane is an effective heat trapper and its importance is reflected in Raynaud *et al*.'s (1988) suggestion that its contribution to global climatic warming at the opening of the last interglacial may have been as much as 25 per cent of that due to carbon dioxide. As these data show, any predictions about global warming must take into account these gases and their effects, over and above that of carbon dioxide. In fact, Ramanathan (1988) has suggested that by the year 2030 their combined impact will be just as significant in global warming as the extra carbon dioxide produced.

In terms of the impact of these increases in greenhouse gas concentrations, there is evidence (e.g. Jones *et al.* 1986) that average annual global temperatures have increased, as shown in Fig. 5.1. Satellite-derived records of sea-surface temperatures for the period 1982–88 also indicate that the global ocean is undergoing a gradual warming of *c.* 0.1 °C per year (Strong 1989). How such data are interpreted, however, is debatable. For example, pre-1980 temperature fluctuations may be interpreted as representing a levelling of temperature increase, possibly reflecting a temporary equilibrium between enhanced greenhouse warming and cooling due to increased dust-loading. This latter has increased as a result of industrial pollution and particulate emissions from forest clearance by burning; because it is likely to scatter incoming solar radiation, it should lead to surface cooling and thus help to counteract the enhanced greenhouse effect. Nevertheless, the slight increase of 0.3 °C in global temperatures between 1970 and 1980 and the continued increase into the 1980s are now considered as convincing evidence for the enhanced greenhouse effect (Gribbin 1988a). Some caution must, however, be exercised since reliable data are only available from the 1850s, which is not a long record against which to establish precise causes. Neither is it unequivocal that the warming is due entirely to enhanced concentrations of greenhouse gases. Although unlikely, the correlation between rising greenhouse gas concentrations and temperature increases may be mere coincidence. There is also the possibility, predicted from evidence which derives from long-term ice core, ocean core and terrestrial palaeoecological data (sections 1.2 and 2.2), that the earth could be entering a further ice age. Is it even conceivable that the 'Little Ice Age' (section 2.5.1) represented the onset of the next glacial stage which was prevented from achieving its full expression by the enhanced greenhouse effect brought about by industrialisation and extensive deforestation?

Obviously there are no precise and unambiguous answers to these questions, nor will there be until it is possible to comprehend the global climatic system and its interplay with biogeochemical cycles. At present, concern about increasing temperatures has resulted in a plethora of models (see Dickinson 1986 for a discussion) geared to formulating predictions for future global temperature changes and their impact on both society and the ecosystems and agroecosystems that sustain it. Many of these predictions suggest that global temperatures will increase dramatically during the next century and while sceptics such as Smil (1987a) warn, quite rightly, that such predictions should be used with caution, it is understandable and indeed necessary that governments should take account of likely future events. The dilemma, it seems, lies between the probability of an ice age and a hothouse!

In order to assist the formulation of predictive models, numerous workers have examined various aspects of the biosphere and their changes during the last 200 years to determine if any trends are obvious that can be related to increasing atmospheric carbon dioxide levels. For example, Woodward (1987) has examined the stomatal density in a wide range of plant species collected as herbarium specimens over the last 200 years. His results show that stomatal density has decreased by *c*. 40 per cent, and controlled experiments on a range of modern species confirm that this is most likely to have been caused by increasing carbon dioxide. This implies that a physiological response has been instigated as decreased concentrations of stomata apparently enhance carbon dioxide uptake with more efficient assimilation of water. This may constitute one mechanism whereby productivity is enhanced and also indicates that the biosphere is already responding to a changing atmosphere. This is also suggested by LaMarche *et al.* (1984) who have noted an increased growth rate in a range of subalpine conifers including the bristlecone pine (*Pinus longaeva*) in the western USA. Another biotic effect considered to be due to global warming is that of the decline in red spruce (*Picea rubens* Sarg.) populations in the eastern USA. Using historical and modern data on the composition of spruce–hardwood stands in central New Hampshire, Hamburg and Cogbill (1988) have identified a declining trend in red spruce populations since 1800. While they acknowledge that clearance and logging by European colonists (section 4.4.2) may have contributed to this decline, they argue that because of warming, which is reflected in yearly and summer temperature reconstructions by Bradley *et al.* (1987b) and with which the coniferous–deciduous boundary is closely correlated, red spruce populations are gradually being reduced. This trend, Hamburg and Cogbill state, may also be being aggravated by pollution such as acidification and/or pathogens. These conclusions are not unequivocal, but if warming trends are significant in the decline of red spruce and its replacement by other species that prefer higher temperatures, the implication is that global vegetation belts and agricultural belts will also shift.

Concerns such as these have led to numerous predictions as to what might occur if the warming trend continues. As Kerr (1989) reports, most climate researchers, while convinced that enhanced greenhouse warming will occur (and is probably already occurring), accept that currently available models are insufficiently precise to be accurate predictors of future trends. Of particular debate is the role that cloud cover plays in regulating the earth's surface temperature. Data presented by Ramanathan *et al.* (1989), based on satellite observations, show that clouds exert a cooling effect on the current climate of the earth. This cooling effect is the net result of reduced heating due to clouds blocking incoming solar radiation and the warming effect which they exert by trapping energy reradiated from the earth's surface. These data also show that this cooling effect is not globally uniform but must be included in models constructed to predict future temperature and precipitation trends. With this new information, existing models may be modified to provide a more accurate picture of likely future events. At present most models indicate that the warming trend will not be globally uniform. There is a suggestion, for example, that high latitudes will warm by three or four times the average (reported in Gribbin 1988a) and that rainfall patterns will also be affected because of changes in circulation patterns. Precisely what future temperature and rainfall patterns will be, however, is a matter of considerable debate as has been discussed by Mitchell and Warrilow (1987): this makes predictions about the ecological impact of global warming equally evasive (see Emanuel *et al.* 1985, Pain 1988, Skiba and Cresser 1988, Woodward 1989 and Roberts 1989 for discussion). Figure 5.2 illustrates what might happen to global vegetation belts in the next 500 years as a result of 'greenhouse' warming. While this is a conjectural representation of a futuristic global scene, it does add weight to the prediction of

Hamburg and Cogbill (1988), referred to above, in relation to changing forest boundaries. Other workers, for example Pastor and Post (1988), have applied the parameters predicted by such models to define the response of forests in the northeast part of the USA to what might be a warmer and drier climate. Using a forest productivity and soil process model in conjunction with climate model predictions involving a doubling of carbon dioxide, they show that the major changes will occur at what is presently the boundary between the boreal and cool temperate forest. For example, where soils retain sufficient moisture for tree growth, productivity and biomass will increase, but will decrease where moisture storage is inadequate. Pastor and Post also predict that changes in vegetation will alter soil nitrogen availability and thus exert a positive feedback that will magnify the vegetation changes.

Fig. 5.2. (A) The present-day distribution of the earth's vegetation zones; (B) The possible distribution of the earth's vegetation zones in the year AD 2040. (From Woodward 1989.)

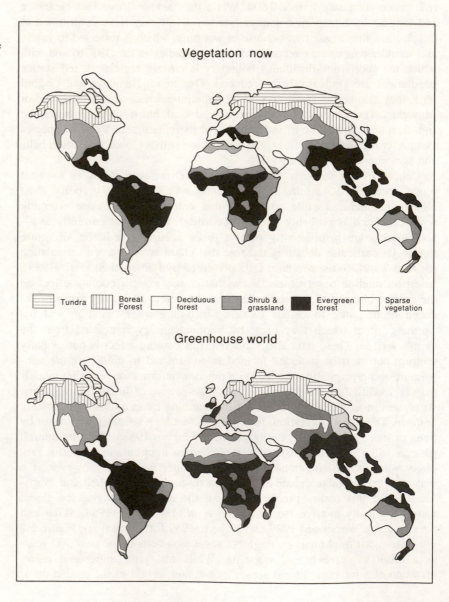

Vegetation now

| Tundra | Boreal Forest | Deciduous forest | Shrub & grassland | Evergreen forest | Sparse vegetation |

Greenhouse world

Examples of possible scenarios based on this approach are given in Fig. 5.3, which shows that if climatic warming alters forest composition in favour of hardwoods, which are richer in nitrogen than conifers, nitrogen is made more available in the soil via litter decomposition, which in turn leads to increased productivity. Conversely, if the climatic warming leads to relative drought, as it may do on well-drained sandy soils, and the development of a vegetation type that is relatively nitrogen-poor or one in which nitrogen is not readily circulated, then productivity may decrease. The overall conclusion that emanates from this study is that interactions between the hydrological cycle, which will also be affected by global warming, and the carbon and nitrogen biogeochemical cycles, can create a positive feedback that in its entirety has a far greater effect than that due to the original perturbation.

If, as Gribbin (1988b) has suggested, there is now general agreement between the available climactic models that polar regions will warm more than the global average, the tundra regions of the globe will be severely affected. While the character of the vegetation will change as boreal forest boundaries reach higher latitudes, there is also the possibility that even more carbon will be released into the atmosphere as the extensive tracts of peat deposits begin to decompose. This prospect has been examined by Billings (1987) who has attempted to determine the carbon budgets of such areas in Alaska during the post-glacial period. His data show that throughout this period the sites investigated have acted as carbon sinks, and while they still are sinks there is reliable evidence to suggest that if carbon dioxide levels double (from the pre-industrial levels of c. 270 ppm) tundra ecosystems will become a further source of carbon as water tables are lowered and organic deposits are oxidised. This may equally apply to organic matter stored in soils, especially in the boreal zone, and since the warming is likely to occur rapidly (in the next 30 years or so) there must exist the possibility that some ecosystems will not be able to achieve equilibrium. If this occurs, then the boreal forests and tundra zones are the most vulnerable.

Global agricultural systems will certainly be affected by global warming

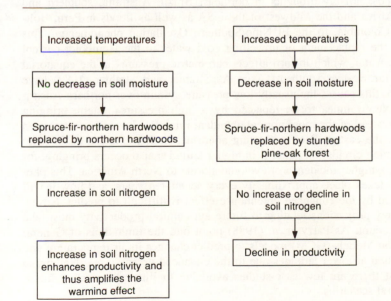

Fig. 5.3. Potential changes in the boreal/cool temperature hardwood forests of the northeast USA that may occur as a response to global warming. (Based on Pastor and Post 1988.)

as has been discussed by Smit *et al.* (1988) and Parry *et al.* (1988). In general, enhanced carbon dioxide concentrations are beneficial to crop productivity, as suggested above in relation to bristlecone pines. The effects of altered temperature and rainfall patterns on agricultural systems are, however, more difficult to predict and are likely to be greater in areas that are currently marginal. Warrick *et al.* (1986) report that in mid- to high-latitude cereal growing regions a rise of 1 °C may cause a displacement towards higher latitudes of several hundred kilometres. They also suggest that in North America and European mid-latitude grain producing regions a 2 °C increase in average temperatures might produce a decline in yield of between 3 and 17 per cent due to increased evapotranspiration, accelerated rates of plant development and a reduction in the period of yield formation. These trends are also suggested by Williams *et al.* (1988). While some mitigation of the warming effects may occur if precipitation increases, they will be accentuated in those areas where precipitation decreases. Conversely, in higher latitudes crop productivity is expected to increase. Bergthorsson *et al.* (1988) opine that in Iceland there will be a *c.* 66 per cent increase in hay yields and a *c.* 50 per cent increase in pasture productivity which will decrease the need for animal feed and increase the carrying capacity of grazing lands. Increases of spring wheat (20 per cent), barley (14 per cent) and oats (13 per cent) are predicted for Finland (Kettunen *et al.* 1988) while, in the region around Leningrad in the USSR, Pitovranov *et al.* (1988) report that climatic conditions up to the onset of the twenty-first century are likely to enhance winter rye production with a subsequent decrease in production as summer precipitation increases. What may happen in semi-arid regions, many of which in the developing world currently experience great difficulty in sustaining food production and are susceptible to short-term annual fluctuations in climate, is even more difficult to predict.

The situation is made more complex by periodic changes in ocean currents, especially in the eastern Pacific Ocean, which influence atmospheric circulation and create abnormal weather patterns. There is evidence, for example, to link some of the extreme climatic events that occurred in the early 1980s, notably droughts in northeast Brazil, Australia, southern and eastern Africa and the Midwest of the USA as well as floods in Peru, Bolivia and Colombia, to the El Niño/Southern Oscillation phenomenon. This involves the replacement of upwelling cold water in the Humboldt current by warm water, which in turn affects barometric pressures in the equatorial zone as far west as southeast Asia. As Strahler and Strahler (1989) have discussed, this causes the usually low pressure system over northern Australia and New Guinea to be replaced by a high pressure system, bringing drought instead of the more normal abundant rainfall. The converse situation occurs in the eastern Pacific, causing abnormal flooding, and a chain reaction affecting circulation patterns in higher latitudes also occurs bringing, for example, a higher incidence of cyclonic storms to North America. This phenomenon takes place approximately every seven–ten years, and how it will be affected by the enhanced greenhouse effect is difficult to predict. Nevertheless, any projections relating to future agricultural productivity must take it into account. As Parry *et al.* (1988) point out, the limitations of General Circulation Models (GCM) models to predict changes in air temperature and precipitation at lower latitudes due to the enhanced greenhouse effect are so great that there are few case-studies available to illustrate possible future agricultural scenarios.

The problems of accurate prediction have also been highlighted by Pittock (1988) in relation to Australia. On the basis of current models, Pittock indicates that in inland northern Australia temperatures are likely to be *c.* 2 °C higher by 2030 than at present and 3–4 °C higher further south. There is also the possibility of reduced rainfall in the southwest of Western Australia and increased rainfall in southeast Australia as well as a higher incidence of tropical cyclones along the northeast coast. However, as Holland *et al.* (1988) point out, the latter may well be influenced by the El Niño/Southern Oscillation regime. Since there are so many uncertainties relating to actual future climatic conditions, predictions about agricultural systems are even more tenuous because there are so many additional factors to consider, such as soil moisture regimes and precipitation/evaporation ratios. J S Russell (1988) has suggested that the major impact of carbon dioxide-induced climatic changes is likely to occur along the drier frontiers of arable cropping in southern and northern Australia, where wheat and sorghum respectively constitute the major crops. On the one hand, increases in rainfall in subtropical northern areas may facilitate the expansion of arable agriculture but, on the other hand, higher temperatures causing increased evaporation rates along the southern inland frontier may result in its retraction.

Just as global warming will influence ecological and agricultural systems, it may have considerable consequences for the global hydrological cycle. Reference has already been made to its impact on precipitation rates and Fig. 5.2 shows one possible global pattern of vegetation communities that may emerge if warming occurs. There is much debate as to the effect of warming on the polar ice caps, though Robin (1986) suggests that changes in the melting and accumulation rates may counterbalance each other. On the other hand, it is likely that many small glaciers and ice caps will melt at a greater rate and will contribute to rising sea-levels. Models based on correlations between past sea-levels and temperature which have been discussed by Robin suggest that a global warming of *c.* 3.5 °C ± 2.0 °C would cause a rise in sea-level of between 20 and 165 cm, brought about not only by melting ice but also thermal expansion of ocean waters and changes in water storage on land. Greater rises in sea-level may occur if parts of the polar ice caps undergo more extensive melting and/or collapse as may be the case for the Greenland and West Antarctic ice sheets. According to Sugden (1988) the latter is particularly sensitive to global warming because it is a marine ice sheet, resting on a bed that is below sea-level. If warming changes the mass balance of this ice mass to such an extent that it collapses, global sea-levels would rise by 5 m, with disastrous implications for ports and low-lying, often highly populated, floodplain and delta regions. Sugden suggests that there is not yet sufficient data to warrant a firm prediction about the West Antarctic ice sheet and believes that collapse is certainly not imminent, but recent work by Dansgaard *et al.* (1989) indicates that the Greenland ice cap may be even more susceptible to rapid melting.

It is clear that global warming could have a dramatic impact on global ecology and agriculture as well as considerable social consequences, so it is imperative that accurate predictive models are developed to facilitate future planning. As Smithson (1988) and Schneider (1989) point out, society will either have to adjust to such changes or instigate measures to curb greenhouse gas emissions. The latter must involve alternative energy policies, more efficient energy production from fossil fuels, a reduction in the rate of deforestation and the initiation of afforestation programmes. All of these measures will require considerable international cooperation

5.3.2 ACIDIFICATION

According to Persson (1987) and McCormick (1985), acidification emerged as a major environmental problem in the late 1960s when Scandinavian ecologists drew attention to declining fish stocks and the European atmospheric chemistry network provided data to show that precipitation was becoming progressively more acidic. The problem is now considered to be acute, especially in industrialised countries and has already prompted the initiation of preventative measures at an international level.

While the term 'acid rain' is often used loosely to describe air pollution that involves the formation of acids in the atmosphere, it is acid deposition that creates environmental problems. As shown in Fig. 5.4, the main gases involved in the production of acid deposition are sulphur and nitrogen oxides, especially sulphur dioxide (SO_2), nitrogen dioxide (NO_2) and nitrous oxide (NO) (together these latter two are known as NO_x). Although small amounts of these gases are produced by natural processes such as volcanic eruptions, the major input into the atmosphere is due to the burning of fossil fuels and industrial processes. As Table 5.2 shows, energy consumption has increased during the last two decades and while this has exacerbated the greenhouse effect (section 5.3.1) it has also resulted in increased emissions of sulphur and nitrogen oxides. Once in the atmosphere, these gases combine with hydroxyl radicals or monatomic oxygen to produce acids, as

Fig. 5.4. The processes involved in the formation and deposition of acid pollution.

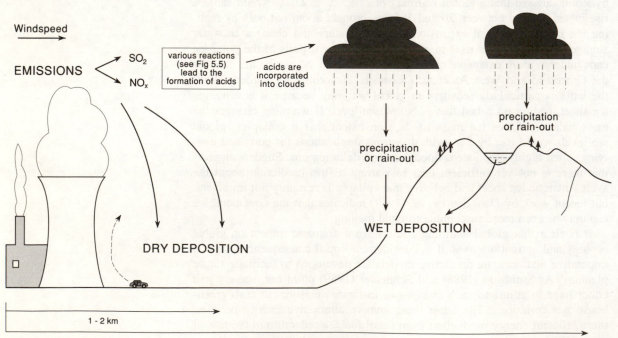

Windspeed

EMISSIONS

SO₂

NOₓ

various reactions
(see Fig 5.5)
lead to the
formation of acids

acids are
incorporated
into clouds

DRY DEPOSITION

precipitation
or rain-out

precipitation
or rain-out

WET DEPOSITION

1 - 2 km

100's or 1000's km

shown schematically in Fig. 5.5, in reactions that are enhanced by sunlight. These processes have been described by Wellburn (1988) and occur in the troposphere where the acids become incorporated into clouds (because they have high water solubility). This can create very low pH values in clouds, and Mohnen (1988) states that water collected near the base of clouds in the eastern USA in the summer typically has a pH of 3.6, though values as low as 2.6 have been recorded. This can have important implications for high-altitude vegetation communities, especially forests, that are directly exposed to the cloud base. Ultimately, as depicted in Fig. 5.4, the acid rain may be deposited hundreds of kilometres from the source of pollution as precipitation occurs, a process that Mohnen describes as '. . . a direct consequence of the atmosphere's self-cleaning nature'. This is the process of wet deposition. Alternatively, dry deposition of sulphur and nitrogen oxides as gases, aerosols or dry particles can occur, usually close to the emission source (Fig. 5.4). Both types of deposition can create environmental problems and it is generally considered that some two-thirds of this acidic pollution are due to sulphurous emissions while one-third is due to nitrous emissions (Clarke 1986).

Where acid rain occurs it will vary spatially and temporally in relation to emission sources and prevailing meteorological conditions, especially wind direction. Park (1987, 1988) has examined the global patterns of acid

Fig. 5.5. The formation (simplified) of the major components of acid rain in the troposphere.

A. Sulphurous and sulphuric acids

SO_2 is emitted from natural and anthropogenic sources and dissolves in cloud water to produce sulphurous acid:

$$SO_2 + H_2O \longrightarrow H_2SO_3 \rightleftharpoons H^+ + HSO_3^-$$

Sulphurous acid can be oxidised in the gas or aqueous phase by various oxidants:

$$SO_2 \xrightarrow{\text{oxidant}} SO_3$$

Aqueous sulphur trioxide forms sulphuric acid:

$$SO_3 + H_2O \longrightarrow H_2SO_4 \rightleftharpoons H^+ + HSO_4^- \rightleftharpoons 2H^+ + SO_4^2$$

B Nitrous and nitric acids

N_2O is emitted by the process of denitrification and although relatively inert it is a greenhouse gas. NO and NO_2 (collectively designated as NO_x) are produced by combustion processes and lightning. They are involved in many chemical processes, some of which damage the ozone layer in the stratosphere:

$$O_3 + NO \longrightarrow NO_2 + O_2$$

Other chemical processes may generate ozone in the troposphere causing photochemical smogs:

$$NO_2 + \xrightarrow{\text{light}} NO + O$$
$$O + O_2 \longrightarrow O_3$$

In addition, nitric and nitrous acids may be produced:

$$2NO_2 + H_2O \longrightarrow HNO_3 + HNO_2$$

These acids are components of acid rain along with sulphurous and sulphuric acids.

deposition and points out that there are several regions which have been severely affected. These include Scandinavia, northern Europe, eastern Canada and the northeast USA (the situation in the latter has been discussed in detail by S E Schwartz 1989), all of which are located in the industrialised region of the temperate zone in the northern hemisphere and which experience relatively high precipitation rates on areas of acid bedrock. Such areas are particularly vulnerable to acid deposition damage not only because they are in receipt of pollution but because acid bedrock, with its attendant poor soils, offers little buffering capacity. While little is known about the consequences of acid deposition in the USSR, which is also heavily industrialised, it is now apparent that environmental problems are occurring in some parts of China (e.g. Zhao and Sun 1986) and there is increasing concern that many parts of the developing world will experience environmental degradation as industrialisation proceeds.

As stated above, the Scandinavians were among the first to recognise the acidification problem and prompted much of the research that has been undertaken in the last two decades. Much of this research has focused on lake ecosystems and although many of the resulting data point to fossil-fuel combustion as the major cause of declining pH it is by no means a universally accepted explanation. Research on Norwegian and Swedish lakes, which has been reviewed by Battarbee and Charles (1987), R B Davis (1987) and Mannion (1986d, 1989a, b) has presented the issue in perspective by examining the temporal trends in lake pH that have developed over the last 200 years. Palaeoenvironmental data, notably diatom biostratigraphy (many species of diatoms are sensitive indicators of pH), chemical analysis of heavy metals and soot particle concentrations, show that in many lakes pH has fallen markedly. In Lake Gårdsjön in southwest Sweden, for example, Renberg and Wallin (1985) record a pH decline from c. 6.0 to 4.5 since 1960, and in a study on twelve lakes in southern and central Finland by Tolonen et al. (1986), six were found to have experienced an accelerated pH decline in the last 20 years. Renberg and Wik (1985a, b) have also shown that soot particle distribution in the sediments of Lake Gårdsjön shows a similar trend to that exhibited by statistics for coal production and fossil-fuel combustion in Europe. In addition, there are many similar studies that show an increase in heavy metal concentrations as diatom-inferred pH declines, and in some cases data for fish catches show a decline that parallels the pH decline.

Studies carried out in Britain, notably in Scotland, have shown that considerable changes in lake pH have occurred since 1850 (reviewed in Battarbee 1984, Battarbee et al. 1988a and Mannion 1987b). Some of the results are summarised in Table 5.3, which shows that pH declines of up to one pH unit have occurred since c. 1840. In some instances, such as Loch Grannoch (Flower and Battarbee 1983, Flower et al 1987), the pH decline has been even greater. While these data do not conclusively show that atmospheric pollution derived from fossil-fuel combustion is the major cause of declining pH, other palaeoenvironmental data, namely heavy metal concentrations and soot particle counts, strengthen the case. In Loch Laidon, for example, which is situated in the Rannoch Moor Nature Reserve in the central Scottish Highlands, Flower et al. (1988) have shown that the decline of c. 0.7 of a pH unit since 1850 has been accompanied by increased lead and zinc concentrations and they attribute increased soot particle concentrations since c. 1930 to the increased national use of oil as a major energy source. Jones *et al.* (1989), investigating the pH history of the Round Loch of Glenhead for the entire post-glacial period, have also shown that the post-1800 acidification is not a product of long-term natural processes such as soil leaching. In particular, they point out that even after peat initiation began in the catchment some 4 kyr BP, there was no parallel increase in lake acidity. While there are suggestions that accelerated acidification may have been caused by afforestation (e.g. Harriman and Morrison 1982), since the most widely employed species are conifers that produce an acid litter, Battarbee *et al.* (1985) have been able to eliminate this possibility for most of the Galloway lakes because their investigations show that pH declines began prior to afforestation and occurred in catchments that have never been afforested. Data from several other lakes, however, indicate that afforestation can contribute to lake acidification. Battarbee *et al.* (1988a) present several examples where acidification has occurred after afforestation. At Llyn Berwen in mid-Wales, afforestation in 1962–3 and the excavation of further deep drainage channels

Table 5.3. Examples of changes in the pH of lake waters that have occurred since *c.* 1840 in the UK, Europe and North America. (Data from references quoted in text.)

Site	Location	pH change	Approx. date of initial pH change
L. Enoch	U.K.	0.9	1840
L. Grannoch	U.K.	1.2	1925
L. Dee	U.K.	0.5	1890
Round L. Glenhead	U.K.	1.0	1950
L. Laidon	U.K.	0.7	1850
Grosser Arbersee	W.Germany	0.8	1965
Kleiner Arbersee	W.Germany	0.8	1950
Gårdsjön	Sweden	1.5	1960
Hovvatn	Norway	0.75	1918
Holmvatn	Norway	0.5	1927
Malålajärvi	Finland	1.0	1950
Hirvilampi	Finland	0.7	1950
Big Moose L.	U.S.A.	1.0	1950 - 1960
Woods L.	U.S.A.	0.4	1930's
Ledge Pond	U.S.A.	0.6	1880's
Beaver Lake	Canada	0.6	1950's
Lake B	Canada	1.6	1955
Lake CS	Canada	1.0	1955

NB This is just a selection of the many lakes that are known to have become acidified since c. 1850 in 1974 are considered to be responsible for declining fish populations and increasing acidity. Similarly, at Loch Fleet in Galloway peat erosion occurred after drainage was carried out for afforestation and Anderson *et al.* (1986) have shown that pH declined from 6.6 in 1961 to 4.4 in 1975.

Apart from establishing the historical perspective on the impact of acid deposition on British lake ecosystems, there have been numerous studies directed at examining the effects on other ecosystems (e.g. Ashmore *et al.* 1988). For example, Lee *et al.* (1988) have discussed the possible consequences for wetlands and, on the basis of field observations and laboratory experiments, have suggested that acid deposition may be responsible for the declining floristic diversity of Pennine peatlands. They point to the particular susceptibility of many *Sphagnum* species to high sulphur dioxide concentrations and draw attention to the relative tolerance of *S. recurvum*, which is the most widespread *Sphagnum* species in the Pennines today. In addition, experiments by Ferguson and Lee (1983) relating to transplanted *Sphagnum* species show that growth remains poor, despite a recent decline in sulphur pollution. This they suggest may be a response to increasing atmospheric nitrogen deposition, although it is not clear how interactions between sulphur and nitrogen pollutants affect *Sphagnum* growth. Skiba *et al.* (1989), using data from 123 sites in Scotland, have also shown that peats with the highest acidity and lowest base saturation are found where acid deposition is greatest which implies that acid deposition can play a significant role in soil acidification. Other studies, as reviewed in Brown and Turnpenny (1988) have been directed at examining the effects of increasing acidity on fish. Such studies show that pH influences calcium and aluminium concentrations. Aluminium is more soluble in acidic conditions and at sufficiently high concentrations it can be toxic to fish, especially in the early stages of their development and especially when calcium is limiting. There is also evidence that high fish mortality occurs when sudden pulses of acid waters develop as may occur after a particularly heavy rainfall or rapid snowmelt.

These examples illustrate the interplay that occurs between acid deposition, either by altering pH or by enhancing sulphurous compounds, and other biogeochemical cycles, especially that of nitrogen. They also reinforce the view expressed in section 5.3.1 that the initiation of positive feedback can have greater repercussions than those caused by the original disturbance. According to Rudd *et al.* (1988), experimental acidification of two small lakes in Ontario, Canada indicates that the nitrogen cycle is particularly sensitive to acidification. Their data show that at pH 5.4–5.7 the activity of nitrifying bacteria, which oxidise ammonia to nitrate, is inhibited resulting in an accumulation of ammonia. While the long-term effect of this on the function of the lake ecosystem is as yet unknown, any blockage of such an important biogeochemical cycle cannot be advantageous. One potential problem suggested by Rudd *et al.* may occur during the winter months when ammonia accumulates under an ice cover and is then utilised by algae in the early spring. This causes hydrogen ion accumulation at a time when pH may be depressed by spring melt, thus exacerbating acidification. In addition, there has been much concern expressed about forest damage and in the early 1980s much of this was considered to be a direct result of acid rain. While a review of this problem by Blank *et al.* (1988) indicates that widespread forest demise in temperate regions is unlikely, their data indicate that significant damage is occurring. Magnesium, potassium and manganese deficiencies, excess nitrogen deposition and localised ammonium concentrations may be involved, but the question remains as to why these problems are occurring and whether or not acidification, in its broadest sense, is responsible. Certainly, Hinrichsen (1988) describes numerous cases where acid rain has caused extensive forest damage in both eastern and western Europe.

Environmental problems due to acidification are not confined to Scandinavia and Britain. There is palaeoecological evidence for accelerated acidification in several lakes in West Germany, the Netherlands and Austria, data for some of which are given in Table 5.3. Arzet *et al.* (1986), for example, have shown that in Grosser and Kleiner Arbersees pH values have declined by *c*. 0.8 pH units. In the former, the pre-1915 pH was *c*. 5.5 and declined gradually until 1965 when an accelerated decline began to pH 4.7. The changes in diatom assemblages on which the pH reconstructions were based were also paralleled by changes in cladoceran microfossils (Cladocera are arthropods which are components of the order Insecta) as well as increases in heavy metals such as lead, aluminium, cadmium, copper, nickel and chromium. There is also palaeoecological research which points to enhanced acidification in North America, especially in the northeastern USA and in the industrialised belt of Canada that adjoins the Great Lakes. Much of this work has been summarised by R B Davis (1987), while Schindler (1988) has discussed the general problem of acidification and its causes and consequences in relation to North American sulphurous emissions. As Table 5.3 shows, lakes in the Adirondack Mountains have been particularly susceptible to enhanced acidification largely because they occur on acid bedrock which offers little buffering capacity and because they are in receipt of acid precipitation from industrialised areas.

Of the Adirondack lakes investigated, declines of 1.0 or more pH units have occurred in Lake Honnedaga (Charles and Whitehead 1986) and Big Moose Lake (Charles 1984; Charles *et al.* 1987). In the latter, the diatom assemblages indicate that during the period 1800–1950, pH was stable at *c*. 5.7 but declined rapidly after 1950 to a pH of *c*. 4.7. A recent study by Davis *et al.* (1988) of Woods, Sagamore and Panther Lakes in the Adirondack Mountains also shows that pH has declined by between 0.3 and 0.5 pH units in recent decades. Even where there is evidence for watershed disturbance, as in the case of Woods Lake during the 1950s, which would tend to increase pH (section 4.4.2), the lake continued to acidify. There is also evidence for accelerated acidification in many Canadian lakes. Dickman and Thode (1985) have reported the inferred diatom pH values of four lakes in Ontario, three of which are located within 20 km of a siderite (iron ore) smelting plant, while a fourth lake some 100 km upwind of the plant was examined as a control site. Beaver Lake, situated near the smelter, has become rapidly acidified in the last 30 years with a decline in pH from 5.8 to 5.2. The other two lakes near the plant have, however, experienced a slight increase in pH which Dickman and Thode attribute to the deposition of alkaline fly ash from the plant itself and from slag heaps and/or to the increased weathering and dissolution of local carbonate-rich greenstones. Despite a slight increase in pH, enhanced concentrations of sulphur and pyrite in the surface sediments of these lakes indicate that they are receiving industrially produced pollutants.

The determination of historical trends in pH are important because they provide a means of assessing rates of change and they may assist in the prediction of future values. For example, Schell (1986) has examined the record of anthropogenically derived elements in the Spruce Flats peat bog in the Laurel Mountains of the Alleghenies, Pennsylvania. His results show that heavy metal deposition has increased since *c.* 1920 and that sulphur, chlorine and bromine concentrations have become enriched. As in the case of carbon dioxide (section 5.3.1) these results imply that peatlands may act as a sink for atmospheric pollutants. Ultimately such sinks may release their pool of accumulated sulphur, as suggested by Nriagu *et al.* (1987) who believe that there is already re-emission of anthropogenically derived sulphur from wetlands as dimethylsulphide, thus exacerbating present sulphurous emissions. A further implication is that acidification will continue at current levels for quite some time even if sulphurous emissions are curtailed (see below). Moreover, reference has already been made to the role of dimethyl-sulphide emissions from the ocean (section 1.2.2) as a potential regulator of global climate, and if that is accepted it must also be acknowledged that wetlands have a significant role to play in climatic change.

To date, most of the research on acidification has focused on the temperate zone of the northern hemisphere. However, there is increasing concern about the potential impact of acidification in tropical regions, especially as developing countries increase their energy consumption as industrialisation proceeds. This problem has been addressed by Rodhe *et al.* (1988) who point out that biomass burning and deforestation in these regions also contribute to acidification by releasing sulphurous and nitrous oxides. While the extent of current acidification has not been identified, there are some parts of the tropics which are already highly industrialised as in southeastern Brazil (Moreira-Nordemann *et al.* 1988), for example, where atmospheric chemistry data show that soluble nitrate and sulphate concentrations have gradually increased since 1976. In addition, Moreira-Nordemann *et al.* have shown that sulphur emissions and deposition rates in this region are similar to those in many parts of Europe and North America. Despite this, and the presence of slightly acidic soils with low cation exchange capacities, pH values monitored along the major rivers lie in the range 6.0–7.5, which suggests that little or no accelerated acidification of either soils or surface water has so far occurred. There is, however, evidence to show that nitrogen dioxide emissions from fossil fuel and biomass burning may produce locally high ozone concentrations. This occurs because photolysis of nitrogen dioxide takes place in the atmosphere and the resulting monatomic oxygen produced can then combine with molecular oxygen, as shown in Fig. 5.5. Both Crutzen *et al.* (1985) and Fishman *et al.* (1986) have shown that seasonally high ozone concentrations occur in Brazil, especially during the burning season. While this is a greenhouse gas, it has also been shown to cause damage to ecosystems in the temperate zone, though there is as yet no data to show if deleterious effects have occurred in the tropics.

Although research on acidification in tropical regions is only just beginning, recent papers indicate that there are many areas where increasing industrialisation, in combination with poorly buffered soils, may give rise to future problems. Sanhueza *et al.* (1988) have discussed the increasing sulphurous and nitrous oxide emissions in Venezuela and the development of the Orinoco heavy oil belt, while Isichei and Akeredolu (1988) have examined the possibilities of enhanced acidification in Nigeria, especially in southern Nigeria and the Kano region. Data for much of Africa and South America are limited in extent but there is clear evidence for acidification in China. According to Zhao *et al.* (1988), coal combustion is the major source of air pollution in China, where energy consumption has increased ten fold in the last 30 years. Data on the acidity and chemical composition of precipitation samples collected since the late 1970s show that some 90 per cent of the sampling sites with a mean pH of less than 5.6 are situated to the south of the Yangtze River. While the data show that acid rain is concentrated in urban regions which are the major sources of both sulphur dioxide and particulate matter, measurements from more remote areas also show that some of these are in receipt of acid rain. Zhao and Xiong (1988) have examined the impact of acid rain on soils, forests and crops and report that there are some instances of damage. Dieback of Masson pine (*Pinus massoniana*) plantations south of the city of Chongqing that began in 1982 has been attributed to acid rain and there is evidence for damage to stone and concrete structures in both Chongqing and Guiyang.

These examples illustrate the widespread occurrence of acid rain and its role in environmental change, and because it is now acknowledged as one of the most significant pollution problems of the 1980s some inroads have been made into developing ameliorative strategies. Some of these have resulted in further environmental change. Short-term solutions have been sought to alleviate immediate problems and in some lake ecosystems liming has been successfully employed to restore productivity. In Lake Gårdsjön in Sweden, for example, the increased availability of phosphorus after liming due to complex interactions between the lime, dissolved oxygen concentrations, organic carbon and nitrogen, have led to enhanced phytoplankton productivity (Broberg 1988). Results from this study also suggest that liming reduces the amount of aluminium in solution which is advantageous to fish populations; its reduction may also contribute to enhanced primary productivity because aluminium is thought to depress the rate of carbon dioxide uptake in aquatic photosynthesis. Liming has also been carried out at Loch Fleet, a small upland acid lake in southwest Scotland and Howells (1987) reports that pH improved rapidly, even within 5 days in some parts of the lake, with simultaneous declines in aluminium concentrations. Activities such as liming do not, however, provide a long-term solution to acidification since they do not address its causes. As Mohnen (1988) and Schindler (1988) discuss, the most significant measures that can be taken relate to curbing the sources of the pollutants. This is an obvious solution and its efficacy is borne out by the recent work of Wright *et al.* (1988) who have monitored the effects of shielding the acid-sensitive Lake Risdalsheia in southern Norway from acid precipitation. After construction of a roof and the application of 'clean precipitation', Wright *et al.*'s data show that changes caused by acidification can be reversed. In particular, the flux of strong-acid anions, mainly sulphate and nitrate, in runoff decreased as acid deposition decreased. Wright *et al.* report that nitrate concentrations decreased by 60 per cent within 2 weeks after the commencement of the experiment and that sulphate concentrations began to decline within 4 months.

How much of a reduction in pollutant emissions is necessary appears to vary inter- and intra-regionally and Schindler (1988) has suggested that annual sulphate deposition must be limited to between 9 and 14 kg ha^{-1} in order to protect the most sensitive aquatic ecosystems. Since annual values of between 20 and 50 kg ha^{-1} are currently recorded in eastern North America, significant reductions must occur before the problem is eliminated. Although it is unlikely that such a goal will be achieved, it is already apparent that attempts to curb emissions in Europe that began in the early 1980s have had an effect. The Geneva Convention which was signed in 1979 and came into effect in 1983, as well as the so-called '30 per cent club', a protocol to this convention signed in 1985 by many acid-producing countries, constitute examples of international collaboration aimed at solving environmental problems. As Haigh (1988) describes, the latter protocol has been signed by twenty European countries including the USSR (notable exceptions are the USA, Britain and Poland) and its aim is to reduce sulphur dioxide emissions by some 30 per cent of 1980 levels by 1992. There are many ways such reductions can be achieved including desulphurisation, which is currently being employed in West German power stations and is being introduced into British ones, the use of less sulphur-rich fossil fuels, the development of alternative energy sources and more efficient technologies for energy provision from fossil fuels. Some of these possibilities have been discussed by the Institute of Chemical Engineers (1988). What the overall result will be in terms of environmental change over the next decade or so remains to be seen, and it may well be that a 30 per cent reduction in sulphurous emissions will prove to be insufficient to combat the problem. Moreover, it will be necessary to address the problem of nitrogen oxide emissions as well as those of sulphur dioxide.

There are already numerous examples of lake ecosystem recovery which have occurred where pollutant emissions have been reduced. Battarbee *et al.* (1988b) have reported that diatom communities in the most recent sediments of several Scottish lochs are responding to pH declines due to post-1970 reductions in British acid emissions. Similarly, Henriksen *et al.* (1988) have suggested that lower sulphate loadings in lakes in southern and eastern Norway, while still being elevated, may be due to the general decrease in the consumption of heavy fuel oils in Western Europe that has occurred since 1979. There are further examples of lake recovery in eastern Canada, where smelter closures and controls on sulphur dioxide emissions in the last 15 years have reduced emissions to about one-third of their early 1970s values. As Schindler (1987) indicates, many of these lakes now have lower concentrations of aluminium and toxic metals as well as lower sulphate concentrations and increased pHs, and in some cases trout have become re-established. Thus, the future is not entirely bleak and it is encouraging to note that, in many cases, acidification is reversible. Moreover, it is to be hoped that developing countries will take note of the lessons to be learned from the developed nations and avoid, as far as possible, the ecological consequences of acid deposition. However, there is also the possibility that reducing sulphurous emissions will remove one of the factors that may be holding in check enhanced greenhouse warming (section 5.3.1). This has recently been discussed by Wigley (1989), who points out that sulphur dioxide emissions produce sulphate aerosols in the atmosphere which can act as cloud condensation nuclei. These in turn influence climate by their effects on cloud formation and albedo, producing an overall cooling, as more solar radiation is reflected from cloud surfaces. Consequently, this cooling trend could be counteracting, at least in part, enhanced greenhouse warming. While this is speculative, there remains the possibility that mitigating one environmental problem by reducing sulphur dioxide emissions may actually accelerate the rate at which another environmental problem, enhanced greenhouse warming, becomes manifest.

5.3.3 THE OZONE AND LEAD PROBLEMS

In addition to increases in the concentrations of greenhouse gases and acidification which have initiated mechanisms of environmental change, human activities have caused changes in the ozone layer in the stratosphere and increasing concentrations of atmospheric lead. Both of these perturbations to the environment have significant implications for human health as well as for the earth's ecosystems.

The issue of the stratospheric ozone layer is quite separate from the increasing concentrations of tropospheric ozone which are contributing to the enhanced greenhouse warming, as discussed in section 5.3.1, and relates to its disturbance by long-lived pollutants. Figure 5.6 shows the position in the stratosphere of the ozone layer which is particularly important because it filters out incoming ultraviolet (UV) radiation and thus acts as a screen against UV–B radiation that can increase the occurrence of some forms of skin cancer and cataracts. Concern was first expressed about the possibility of stratospheric ozone depletion in the early 1970s due to the advent of supersonic aircraft which fly in the lower stratosphere and which emit nitrogen oxides. While these gases are potential catalysts for the destruction of ozone, it is now acknowledged that this is a very minor factor in comparison to the effect of another group of pollutants known collectively as Freons or chlorofluorocarbons (CFCs). These compounds are non-toxic, non-flammable and chemically inert liquids or gases. These properties make them useful for a wide range of applications including aerosol propellants, refrigerants, cleansers for electronic components and in the production of foamed plastics. According to Clarke (1986) global production of the two

Fig. 5.6. Depletion of the ozone layer and its relationship with UV–B radiation inputs to the troposphere. (Data on graph are generalised from Farman *et al.* 1985.)

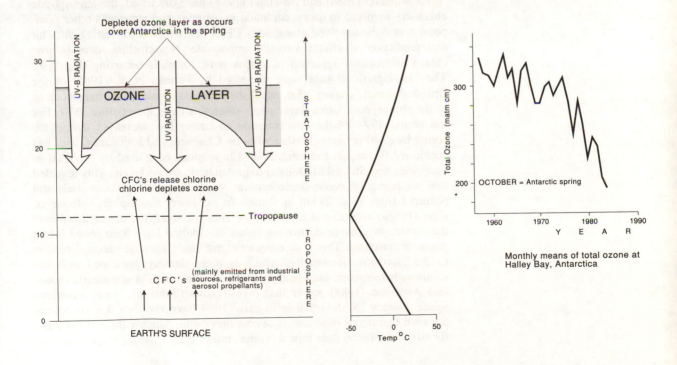

Monthly means of total ozone at Halley Bay, Antarctica

most common CFC gases, Freon 11 ($CFCl_3$) and Freon 12 (CF_2Cl_2) rose rapidly from less than 50 000 t per annum in 1950 to 725 000 t per annum in 1976, of which some 90 per cent is released directly into the atmosphere. The remaining 10 per cent, mostly used for refrigerants, is eventually released when the equipment in which it is used is discarded. Although these gases are released into the troposphere which underlies the stratosphere (Fig. 5.6) and wherein they act as greenhouse gases (section 5.3.1), these gases do not rapidly degrade and eventually enter the stratosphere where they are subject to intense UV radiation: the same radiation as is absorbed by ozone. This can lead to photodissociation so that chlorine atoms are released (Fig. 5.6). As Rowland (1988) has discussed, laboratory experiments have clearly demonstrated that chlorine destroys ozone and it is likely that other halogens, especially bromine, have a similar effect.

Even before there was clear evidence for destruction of the ozone shield, theoretical work suggested that increasing emissions of CFCs would lead to a build-up of chlorine of sufficient magnitude to impair its protective function. In addition, the inert nature of the CFCs means that they have long residence times in the atmosphere which would ensure that, even if no further emissions were to occur, the destructive process would continue for some considerable time. Such arguments have led to some nations adopting regulations to control CFC emissions from aerosol sprays. According to Dotto and Schiff (1978), the USA, Canada and several Scandinavian countries instigated measures between 1976 and 1978 but little was done to control CFC emissions from other sources. That these and further measures are necessary is underlined by the research of Cunnold *et al.* (1986) who have shown that Freon 11 has a lifetime of *c.* 75 years, while that of Freon 12 is *c.* 110 years. This means for example, that some 36 per cent of Freon 12, in the atmosphere of 1988 will still be present in the year 2100, declining to 6 per cent by the year 2300.

As Stolarski (1988) and Rowland (1988) have discussed, the atmospheric chemistry involved in ozone depletion is complex and numerous other compounds may be involved along with CFCs. This makes modelling difficult and prediction of effects virtually impossible. Nevertheless there is now clear evidence that depletion of stratospheric ozone is occurring (Fig. 5.6). The first significant data were presented by Farman *et al.* (1985) of the British Antarctic Survey who established that an ozone 'hole' has occurred in the stratospheric ozone layer over Antarctica each spring since 1977. For the period 1977–84 the concentration of ozone has decreased during the spring by *c.* 40 per cent. Further work by Chubachi and Kajiwara (1986) has confirmed this report and satellite data have since been used by Stolarski *et al.* (1986) and Stolarski (1988) to map Antarctic ozone levels. This revealed that the region of ozone depletion was wider than the continent itself and occurred from 12 to 24 km in altitude in the lower stratosphere. Moreover, Kerr (1988a) reports that there is now concern about the ozone layer over the Arctic since ozone-destroying forms of chlorine have been found in the Arctic atmosphere. This is of especial significance because ozone depletion in the Northern Hemisphere, which is more densely populated than the southern hemisphere, may lead to a major increase in skin cancers. Pearce and Anderson (1989) report that investigative flights by North American Space Agency (NASA) planes in early 1989 have revealed that conditions are such that ozone depletion is almost inevitable. Already there is evidence for ozone depletion (this time a 'crater' rather than a 'hole') but it is not yet clear whether this is due to normal atmospheric dynamics or to a real ozone loss. McElroy and Salawitch (1989) also believe that ozone depletion will be a persistent rather than a short-lived phenomenon and thus requires prompt mitigating action.

While there is still much debate as to the actual causes of such ozone holes (see Gribbin 1988c and Kerr 1988b for a discussion) there does not appear to be much doubt that CFCs are at least partly contributory (e.g. Rowland 1986). This is because CFCs release chlorine that combines with oxygen to produce chlorine monoxide, which Barrett *et al.* (1988) have shown is of primary importance in ozone destruction (Fig. 5.6). Even before Farman *et al.*'s (1985) Antarctic data were available, an international Convention for the Protection of the Ozone Layer was established in 1985 and a first protocol was agreed in September 1987. This is the Montreal Protocol which agrees to limit both the production and emissions of CFCs. It aims for a freeze in consumption of CFCs at 1986 levels by mid-1990, with a 20 per cent reduction in mid-1994 and a further 30 per cent reduction by mid-1999 (Tolba 1987; Everest 1988). Similar declines in production are also planned. In the meantime, many large chemical companies such as du Pont (Glas 1988) and ICI are already developing alternative ozone-benign chemicals. Such measures should at least curtail the rate of ozone depletion but may not, as Wigley (1988) points out, be sufficient to curtail the greenhouse effect of these gases.

While it is not yet clear what the effects of stratospheric ozone depletion are or will be in the future, there is concern about possible increases in skin cancer due to the enhanced receipt by the earth's surface of UV–B radiation. In addition, C Woods (1988) has discussed the difficulties of predicting the effects of enhanced UV–B radiation on ecosystems and agroecosystems, since what little research there has been to date has concentrated on bacteria. There may be even more serious consequences for global climate since ozone effectively warms the stratosphere and creates a temperature inversion at the tropopause. As there is a decrease in temperature with height in the troposphere, as shown in Fig. 5.6, the warmer stratosphere acts as a containment to vertical motion in the troposphere which includes the convective processes that generate clouds and precipitation. If this inversion is weakened due to ozone depletion there will be repercussions for convective processes which will affect atmospheric circulation and thus global climate. Additionally, as depletion of the ozone layer enhances the amount of radiation received in the troposphere, it promotes warming of both the lower atmosphere and the earth's surface. How this warming trend would be counteracted by cooling due to reduced thermal radiation from a cooler stratosphere is debatable though, as discussed in section 5.3.1, there is available evidence, albeit limited (Evans 1988), which indicates that an overall warming would occur.

The enhanced greenhouse effect, acidification and ozone depletion are all examples of atmospheric pollution that have occurred in tandem with industrialisation and deforestation. There is also concern about increasing concentrations of heavy metals that derive from similar anthropogenic emissions and perturbations to biogeochemical cycles. Such metals include lead, mercury, zinc, cadmium and arsenic, all of which may be harmful to human health. Attention here will focus on lead, since elevated levels of this are thought to present the greatest risk to human health.

Evidence for enhanced lead levels in the environment has been reviewed by Livett (1988) and Mannion (1989b) and derives from palaeoenvironmental records preserved in ice cores, peats and lake sediments (see examples given in sections 4.2.3 and 4.4.2) as well as from measurements of atmospheric lead concentrations which have been collected in some areas over the last two decades. For example, many of the lake sediments discussed in section 5.3.2 which contain biological evidence for acidification also contain a record of increasing lead concentrations. In addition, data from Arctic and Antarctic ice cores (e.g. Boutron and Patterson 1986, 1987) allows the reconstruction of pre-industrial atmospheric lead concentrations which can be used as base-line data against which to examine the magnitude of post-industrial changes. Such studies indicate that up to 99 per cent of the lead in recent Arctic ice is derived from anthropogenic rather than natural sources like dust and volcanic activity. Shen and Boyle (1987) have shown that trends in lead concentrations and lead isotopic distributions in the annual growth layers of certain corals mirror those of the ice cores and that they can be used to reconstruct temporal changes in surface-water lead concentrations. For example, Shen and Boyle's data show that lead concentrations in the Sargasso Sea were c. 15–20 pM (pico Molar) prior to the American industrial revolution, increasing to c. 90 pM by 1923 as rates of fossil-fuel consumption and metal smelting increased. A further enhancement occurred in the 1940s when leaded petrol was introduced, reaching a peak of 240 pM in 1971. By 1984, however, lead concentrations had declined to 128 pM in response to the US government's decision to gradually eliminate lead in petrol.

Monitoring of ambient lead concentrations in the atmosphere has also revealed changes in lead levels. Cawse (1987) has reported that the concentration of lead in air at near ground level at four sites in rural Britain has declined during the 1972–81 period. This Cawse attributes to the reduction of lead emissions from petrol-driven vehicles and a decline in lead from industrial sources as a result of either the economic recession and/or improvements in emission controls. In addition, a survey of lead concentrations in 5235 house dusts and 4650 garden soils derived from 53 locations in the Britain reported by Culbard *et al*. (1988) has revealed that there are considerable spatial variations. The results indicate that the major factors determining lead concentrations in house dust are (i) lead concentrations in soils and the extent of soil exposure adjacent to the house, (ii) whether or not paints with a high lead content were used for decoration, and (iii) the age of the house, with higher lead concentrations being generally found in older dwellings.

As O'Neill (1985) points out, these enhanced lead levels are due to the fact that lead is used as a main and subsidiary substance in many industrial processes such as paper-making, is added to petrol as an anti-knock agent and is often emitted in the process of ore-smelting for the production of ferrous and non-ferrous metals. According to Jaworski (1987), using data from 1979–80, the major sources of anthropogenic lead emissions to the atmosphere are from petrol and waste oil combustion. This combined with emissions from metal smelting and relatively minor inputs from wood combustion, phosphate fertilisers and natural emissions means that most of the lead output finds it way directly into the atmosphere. From there, as shown in Fig. 5.7, lead reaches vegetation, soils and humans as well as aquatic ecosystems. If lead concentrations were uniformly distributed on a global basis, as a result of atmospheric and other earth system dispersion mechanisms, it is likely that no general environmental impact would be manifest.

This, however, is not the case and there are a substantial number of case studies that illustrate the localised impact of elevated lead levels on both ecosystems and humans.

In relation to the latter, Nriagu (1988) and Hutton (1987) have discussed numerous problems that may occur if people come into sustained contact with elevated concentrations of lead. Impaired blood synthesis, hypertension, hyperactivity and brain damage may result because lead is a neurotoxin and acts as a cumulative poison. It can combine with a large number of biomolecules, including amino acids, haemoglobin, a variety of enzymes, DNA and RNA and thus interfere with many metabolic pathways. Children are also considered to be more susceptible to lead poisoning than adults because they absorb a higher proportion of ingested metal. They can suffer from acute poisoning if they consume dirt, dust or lead paint. There is particular concern about the exposure of children to high lead levels in urban atmospheres which, as S Smith (1986) points out, may be implicated in the impairment of intelligence, behaviour and performance. A survey reported by Needleman *et al.* (1979) involving schoolchildren in Boston, USA, examined the relationship between lead concentrations in shed deciduous teeth and performance in intelligence tests. The results indicated that children with lower lead dentine concentrations performed better than those with higher levels of lead. Earickson and Billick (1988) have also shown that in the late 1970s in the

Fig. 5.7. The biogeochemical cycle of lead and its pathway to humans.

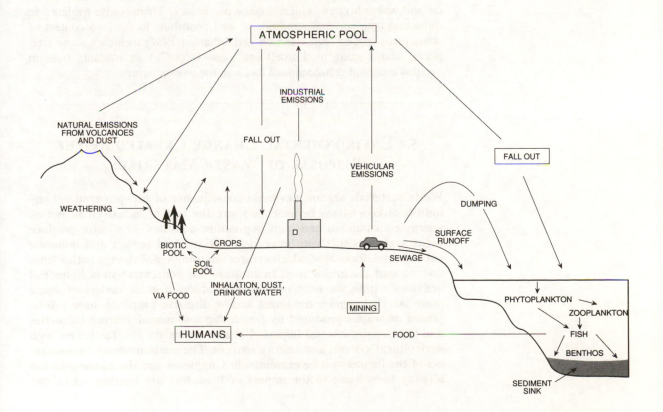

cities of Louisville, Kentucky, and Detroit, Michigan, higher blood lead levels in children were prevalent in inner-city areas and in some cases exceeded concentrations that are considered hazardous. Other investigations, in West Germany (Winneke 1983) and Britain (Yule and Landsdown 1983), have revealed similar relationships. As a result of these health concerns, some countries have instituted measures to reduce the amount of lead in the environment. The USA's decision to phase out lead in petrol is one such example and Elsom (1987) reports that for the period 1975–84 average lead levels at six urban US sites has decreased by 70 per cent. Similarly, Page *et al*. (1988) have reported a 52–61 per cent decline in airborne lead at several sites in Wales, which they suggest is due to a European Community directive in early 1986 to reduce the amount of lead in petrol.

Elevated lead concentrations can also have ecological consequences. Wong (1987) states that carp raised in Hong Kong ponds, which are fertilised by chicken and pig manure, often show gill damage. The flesh of these animals also contains higher lead concentrations than fish treated with a commercial diet of hibifex worm. This is because sewage generally contains elevated lead levels. When used as a fertiliser it can, along with atmospheric lead, cause enhanced concentrations in soil, with implications for crops. McGrath (1987) has documented data from the Market Garden Experiment at Woburn, Britain, which was established in 1942 to compare the impact on the soil of various types of fertiliser, including sewage sludge and sludge–straw compost. Both treatments markedly increased the concentrations of various heavy metals including lead until 1961 when the sludge treatment was replaced with inorganic fertilisers. The data also show little evidence of leaching or movement of the metals below the depth to which the soil was cultivated, which indicate persistence. There is also evidence to show that both soil and atmospheric lead contribute to the lead content of many plant species (e.g. Harrison and Johnston 1987) including some crop plants, and a study by Kardell and Larsson (1978) on roadside trees in Sweden indicated enhanced lead levels in the woody tissue.

5.4 ENVIRONMENTAL CHANGE CREATED BY THE DISPOSAL OF WASTE MATERIALS

Waste materials are an inevitable consequence of fuel-powered urban–industrial ecosystems because they are the foci of industrial activities, energy consumption and high population densities. The latter produce waste materials that can be crudely divided into sewage and domestic rubbish, the disposal of which creates environmental change both within and without the urban area. In addition, the concentration of industrial activities within the urban complex produces a great variety of waste materials that require treatment and/or disposal. Emphasis here will be placed on wastes produced by processing and manufacturing industries and their environmental impact. Urban systems are also fuelled by both agricultural systems and energy sources. The environmental consequences of the former will be examined in Chapter 6 and since reference has already been made to the impact of fossil-fuel use (section 5.3.1), this

section will consider the problems associated with the use of nuclear power, an alternative energy source which has been promoted in the developed world since the 1950s.

5.4.1 DOMESTIC WASTE

High population densities in urban areas give rise to large amounts of waste water and sewage as well as domestic rubbish. The removal of sewage from urban areas only began in the 1840s; previously it frequently contaminated water supplies causing epidemics of diseases like typhoid and cholera. Such problems still occur in many developing countries but even in developed countries, where sewage-treatment processes are widely employed, contamination of fresh waters and the nearshore marine environment frequently result from sewage disposal. Sewage, although it mainly consists of water, is rich in nitrate and phosphate, of which no more than 50 per cent is removed by treatment. The remainder is released into drainage systems and is a major contributory factor to cultural eutrophication which can profoundly alter the characteristics of aquatic ecosystems. Since agricultural runoff also contributes to this process it will be examined in Chapter 6. Sewage can also cause pollution by promoting bacterial growth in coastal waters as Hungspreugs (1988) has reported for Indonesia, Malaysia and the Philippines, all of which eject untreated sewage into coastal waters.

The disposal of domestic rubbish presents a different set of problems. In Britain (Geofile 1987) most municipal waste, which includes industrial/commercial and domestic rubbish, is dispatched to some 4000 landfill sites. In 1985, London alone produced 13.1 million t of waste of which 41 per cent was disposed of in London itself, mostly in disused gravel pits. Much of the remaining waste was transported to landfill sites in neighbouring counties. Such sites can give rise to environmental problems which depend on the nature of the waste. Noxious odours may constitute a local nuisance, especially during the active life of the landfill. Gases such as hydrogen sulphide can be produced by the action of sulphate-reducing bacteria if the landfill contains sulphate waste and rotting vegetable material. Methane is also generated where rotting organic matter ferments under anaerobic conditions. This can continue for a considerable time after the landfill site has been closed, which can be particularly hazardous because at sufficient concentrations methane can form an explosive mixture with air. Parker (1983a) documents several problems that have occurred in Britain as a result of building over a landfill site in which methane had accumulated to dangerous levels. In some cases explosions damaged buildings and in one case landfill gas diffused into a school playground. Walsh *et al.* (1988) have also documented an example of a landfill site at Port Washington, New York, where emissions of methane and other volatile organic compounds (VOC) caused concern among the residents of nearby housing. The risks of explosion and to human health were sufficient to warrant the construction of a gas extraction system as well as a high-temperature incinerator to destroy the VOC emissions. Walsh *et al.* report that monitoring since 1984 has shown that these measures have been successful in treating these problems. As well as problems associated with methane, landfill sites are subject to subsidence that can cause structural damage to buildings. Moreover, ground-water may become contaminated by leachate from the landfill and this can only be prevented by using heavy-duty impermeable lining which must be in place before the landfill site is used (Parker 1983b).

Rubbish disposal in the USA has been examined by Neal and Schubel (1987) who state that some 150 million t of solid waste are produced annually from municipal and industrial sources. According to O'Leary et al. (1988), c. 75 per cent of this waste is dumped in some 6000 municipal landfill sites which are subject to the same problems common to British sites. They also point out that, as in Britain, more stringent regulations governing the use of landfill sites and the reduction in new site availability means that alternative disposal methods must be developed rapidly. This is a difficult task in view of the diversity of waste materials. O'Leary et al. call for both resource conservation and resource recycling. The former, which is not yet widely practised, could include the minimisation of packaging and the production of more durable goods. Alternatively, recycling requires the collection, separation and reuse of waste materials, especially paper, glass, metals, plastics and organic wastes.

In Europe, glass recycling is fairly commonplace. In Switzerland, 21.7 kg per head were recycled in 1984, with 13.9 kg in the Netherlands but only 2.2 kg in Britain (Geofile 1987), although this is increasing with the provision of more bottle banks. The recycling of glass, metals and other materials not only limits the problems of waste disposal but also conserves raw materials and reduces energy consumption. Most successful recycling programmes rely on the participation of individual residents, as O'Leary et al. (1988) describe for Marin County, California, where a voluntary programme results in the recycling of 22 per cent of its municipal waste, reducing the overall cost of waste disposal by c. $50 000. Many wastes can also be used to provide a viable energy source. According to Geofile (1987) combustible domestic waste in the UK has the potential to provide c. 1.5 million t of coal equivalent energy annually. This can be obtained in several ways including the use of the heat energy which is produced from incinerators that are currently employed to reduce the volume of waste. Although only eight of the forty-seven existing incinerators in Britain are presently being used in this way, the potential is illustrated by the Edmonton incinerator in east London. This burns 400 000 t of waste annually and, via recovery boilers, produces electricity to the value of £4 million (Geofile 1987). At Tronville-en-Barrois in northeast France, Daget and Leroy (1988) report that between 5000 and 7000 t of burnable industrial waste and 30 000 t of household refuse are combusted annually and the steam produced is sold to the Rhovyl factory, a member of the Rhône-Poulenc group. Other ways of producing energy from waste include extracting the combustible component which is itself a fuel, heating waste in the absence of oxygen to produce hydrocarbon oils and harnessing the potentially dangerous methane that is characteristic of many landfill sites, as is occurring at several sites in Britain.

Similar technology is available in the USA, though O'Leary et al. (1988) point out that there are drawbacks. For example, incinerators may cause air pollution by emitting particulate matter and noxious gases. The ash must also be disposed of and may even be designated as hazardous waste if it contains high concentrations of lead and cadmium, which makes disposal more expensive and necessitates the maintenance of at least some landfill sites. Nevertheless, there is considerable scope to refine existing technology which can minimise these hazards and result in more efficient resouce and energy use.

5.4.2 INDUSTRIAL WASTE

All of the problems associated with the disposal of domestic waste apply equally to the disposal of solid industrial waste. However, some industries produce very different types of waste, which have a varied range of environmental impacts. Aquatic and soil environments are most at risk from industrial wastes, especially those which contain heavy metals and synthetic chemical compounds and can have serious repercussions for human health.

Detergents can also cause considerable water pollution as has been discussed by Ramade (1987). These are synthetic compounds, whose residues enter drainage systems from sewage and industrial waste water. Many are not biodegradable, especially tetrapropylene benzene sulphonate (TBS), although there is now legislation in many countries which requires that detergents are formulated with a considerable proportion of biodegradable substances. These compounds can reach relatively high concentrations in near- and offshore waters where untreated sewage is emitted into the sea, as in the case of Marseille. In addition, and also discussed in detail by Ramade, the use of such detergents to disperse oil slicks can have more severe ecological effects than the oil itself.

Heavy metal pollution may occur in aquatic ecosystems as a result of industrial emissions and in extreme cases may be a threat to human health. Hutton (1987) has discussed the effects of methyl mercury poisoning on the central nervous system and reports that it can impair sensory, visual and auditory functions especially in unborn foetuses. There are several examples of methyl mercury poisoning that have proved fatal on a relatively large scale. One of the best known examples is that which occurred in Japan in the 1953–75 period around Minamata Bay and the Agaro River (Smith and Smith 1975). The discharge of methyl mercury, from a local chemical plant engaged in the production of acetaldehyde, entered marine food chains and mercury-rich residues became concentrated in higher trophic levels comprised of shellfish and fish. These were harvested and consumed by local fishermen, resulting in approximately 100 deaths and disablement for up to 1000 people. As Hutton (1987) reports, there are many other populations reliant on fish which are suspected of suffering from methyl mercury poisoning though not as severe as the Minamata example. The discharge of cadmium-rich industrial effluent can also create health problems and Friberg *et al.* (1974) have reported that in several localities in Japan there is a higher than average incidence of renal dysfunction. This is attributed to the sustained consumption of locally-grown rice exposed on a long-term basis to elevated cadmium levels that originated in discharges from non-ferrous metal smelters (and mines) and which contaminated the water of paddy-fields.

Ground-water and soils may also be contaminated by heavy metals. The former has been addressed by Lühr (1986) who points out that contamination can have serious consequences for domestic water supplies and is not easily remedied. He states that in Baden-Wurttemburg, Federal Republic of Germany, there have been 150 cases of ground-water pollution with chlorinated hydrocarbons. These substances include polychlorinated biphenyls (PCBs), which are used in electrical transformers and condensers as well as in the production of plastics, and polyvinyl chlorides (PVCs) which are widely used plastics. Luhr states that most of the contamination by these chemicals is due to mishandling during production, storage and transport. Finnecy (1988) reports several accidents which have resulted in soil contamination by PCBs, including one incident near Kingston, Tennessee, USA, where a truck driver, having been warned of leakage, dumped the entire load by the roadside. The leaking PCB was then spread by heavy rainfall, resulting in the contamination of 52 km^2 of soil. In an effort to repair the damage, some 2300 m^2 of contaminated soil had to be removed to Texas for safe disposal at a total cost of $1 million.

Polychlorinated biphenyls can also have detrimental effects on aquatic environments. Like mercury and cadmium, PCBs can enter food chains and undergo the process of bioaccumulation or biological magnification. This means that they become more concentrated as they pass from one trophic level to the next and eventually the concentrations become so high that fish are considered unsafe for human consumption. As Moran *et al.* (1986) point out, most of the predator fish in Lake Michigan have concentrations of PCBs of up to 15 ppm which is considerably in excess of the 2 ppm limit recommended as safe for human consumption by the US Food and Drug Administration. As a result, the US Environmental Protection Agency has banned the commercial sale of Lake Michigan's salmon and trout. Since 1977, however, the manufacture of PCBs in the USA has been discontinued and this, together with more careful disposal of these chemicals, has led to gradually declining PCB concentrations. In terms of human health, elevated levels of PCBs are thought to cause chloracne, which is a skin disorder similar to acne, impaired liver function, nausea and headaches. While there is evidence for declining PCB concentrations in Lake Michigan, Tanabe (1988) believes that there will be no immediate decline from a global point of view because of the large amounts of PCBs that are still present in electrical equipment and in landfills. He also reviews the evidence which suggests that the organisms most at risk from PCB toxicity are marine mammals which constitute the highest trophic levels in marine ecosystems and which, therefore, are especially vulnerable to bioaccumulation.

Dioxins are another group of organic compounds that can have serious ecological repercussions, especially in relation to vertebrates including humans. The most toxic dioxin is 2,3,7,8-tetrachloro-dibenzo-paradioxin (TCDD) which may occur as an impurity in the manufacture of the herbicide 2,4,5-T. Its release into the environment can occur as a result of the application of this herbicide, as happened during the Vietnam War when 'Agent Orange' was used as a defoliant. This resulted in considerable ecosystem and agroecosystem impairment as well as detrimental effects on US troops and Vietnamese. As a waste product from pesticide production, TCDD must be treated with great care because decontamination processes are both difficult and expensive. This is illustrated by the problems experienced after the Seveso disaster which occurred in Italy in 1976 when there was an explosion from a chemical plant that released substantial amounts of trichlorophenol containing dioxins including TCDD (Reggiani 1983). Chloracne and other dermatological disorders occurred in the local population, along with more serious liver and kidney complaints. Moreover, soil decontamination has posed severe problems because there is no generally accepted way for disposing of dioxin-contaminated material, although incineration is probably the safest. Skinner and Bassin (1988), for example, have reported on the development by the US Environmental Protection Agency of a mobile incinerator which was used to burn nearly 1 million kg of dioxin-containing solid wastes from a contaminated site in Missouri. Subsequent monitoring of waste residues and waters showed that the method was almost 100 per cent efficient at removing dioxin constituents.

5.4.3 NUCLEAR WASTE

In 1984, approximately 3 per cent of the world's energy requirements were supplied by nuclear power, having increased by a factor of five since 1973 (Earth Report 1988). How much this will increase in the next few decades is debatable because of increasing concern about the safety of reactors and the problems posed by the disposal of radioactive wastes. This concern has heightened since 1986 in the wake of the Chernobyl reactor accident in the USSR which caused the deaths of at least 31 people, acute radiation sickness in at least 200 others and will contribute in the longer term to the deaths of many more.

There are many nuclear reactors currently in operation, mostly in the developed world. There are, for example, 37 reactors of various types in Britain and 34 in France, out of a world-wide total of 380 (Bunyard, 1988). All of these produce waste materials which are radioactive to a greater or lesser degree as shown in Table 5.4. There are also low-level radioactive wastes produced by industry and medicine, the disposal of which has been reviewed by Boustead (1985) and includes incineration, landfill tipping and discharge of liquid waste into the sewage system. Since the radioactive content of these materials is so low it is generally considered that they pose no serious environmental threat, or threats to human health, provided that the appropriate regulations are observed. Such disposal methods are, however, unsatisfactory for intermediate and high-level radioactive wastes and there is no generally acceptable method of disposal, although plans are afoot to develop geological sites for long-term storage and dumping as has been discussed by Lau (1987).

Problems arise from the disposal of nuclear waste because many of the waste materials contain radioactive isotopes that generate large quantities of heat and will remain active for many hundreds of thousands of years. Rox-

Table 5.4. Types of nuclear waste.

Designation	Examples	Disposal
1. Low-level wastes	Discarded working clothes Floor sweepings & refuse Laboratory equipment Milling wastes	Sealed landfill repositories
2. Intermediate-level wastes	Chemical sludge Metal fragments	Sealed landfill repositories? Underground geological sites?
3. High-level wastes	Reprocessing solvents Spent fuel-rods	Land-based geological sites? Deep-sea geological Sites? Burial in ice caps?
4. Transuranic wastes	Americum - 243 Curium - 242 Plutonium - 239	

burgh (1987), for example, states that such high-level waste will require isolation from the biosphere for between 10^4 and 10^5 years to comply with 'acceptable risk' guidelines. Disposal in geological formations would, therefore, appear to be a reasonable solution but, as Chapman and McKinley (1987) discuss, the choice of site must take into account stability and the potential impact of such wastes on ground-water (hydrogeology). Moreover, in order to avoid any contamination it will also be necessary to develop containment canisters that are sufficiently durable to prevent leakage. There is therefore a great deal of research to be undertaken before such disposal is possible, and although there have been suggestions that disused salt-mines and stable igneous formations will provide suitable repositories, there is always the uncertainty associated with such long time-scales.

Alternative disposal methods have been suggested, the most likely of which is the use of the marine environment especially at depth beneath the sea-bed. International political pressure (Van Dyke 1988) has so far resisted this approach largely because of fears generated by deliberate and accidental release of low-level radioactive waste into coastal waters which have had serious ecological repercussions. Nations such as Japan and Britain still consider that ocean disposal is a viable and relatively safe option. In fact, several European nations, including Britain, offloaded low-level wastes in the northeast Atlantic until 1983 when pressure from the London Dumping Convention, set up in 1972, called a halt to this activity (Blowers and Lowry 1987) while further research was conducted into the potential environmental impact of such wastes. Recently, several land-based sites in Britain have been designated as potential repositories to alleviate the problem of low- and intermediate-level waste (Strange 1988), all of which have generated considerable opposition both locally and nationally.

This issue is far from being resolved either in Britain or elsewhere and events of the past few decades have done little to gain popular support for waste disposal programmes. Releases of waste have created ecological problems and there have been suggestions that increased incidences of childhood leukaemias occur in populations close to nuclear reactors. This latter has been discussed by Craft and Openshaw (1987) and is a controversial topic. In relation to the former, there are several examples which illustrate the potential environmental impact of accidental leakages of radioactive waste. These, and the general impact of such waste on aquatic environments and biota, have been discussed by Ramade (1987), who points out that the processes of bioaccumulation, similar to those described in section 5.4.2 for heavy metals, may create a hazard to human health. For example, the nuclear fuel reprocessing plant at Windscale (now Sellafield) in Cumbria, Britain, discharged into the Irish Sea in 1983 liquid wastes with substantially higher radioactivity than regulations permitted. The spill was highly publicised by Greenpeace and certainly did nothing for the reputation of British Nuclear Fuels Limited, though the repercussions in terms of human health and marine ecology are as yet unknown. Similar leakages have occurred from the Cap de la Hague reprocessing plant in France (Boyle and Robinson 1987). Ramade (1987) has also reported higher than average radioactivity in the water, benthic silts and algal biomass of the Meuse River in France which receives effluent from the Chooz nuclear reactor established in 1967.

The long-term effects on ecosystems and human health, if any, of these releases are a matter of much speculation and it is speculation rather than fact that besets the nuclear industry. This is an unsatisfactory basis for planning for future energy provision on a national or global scale. As Table 5.2 shows, most of the current energy requirements are satisfied by fossil fuels but these, too, as discussed in sections 5.3.1 and 5.3.2, pose considerable environmental threats. What problems might ensue from future fusion rather than fission reactors also remain to be seen and there is certainly no immediate prospect for reactors of this kind. In addition, very little research on a global level has been devoted to renewable energy sources such as wave, wind, water and solar power. In view of the rapidly encroaching greenhouse environment and increasing world energy demands, civilisation is rapidly entering a period of radical rethinking of energy policies. Proverbially it is 'betwixt the devil and the deep-blue sea'!

5.5 CONCLUSION

There is no doubt that industrialisation, especially during the last 200 years, has exacted a heavy toll on global environments. The exploitation of mineral resources has scarred, and will continue to scar, those landscapes which have developed over mineral-bearing rocks. As the examples presented above illustrate, the technology and expertise are available to limit and ameliorate the environmental change that such activities create *in situ*. Stricter controls and effective reclamation schemes, facilitated by legislation, could also go a long way towards curtailing the wider detrimental consequences of mineral extraction. At least the impact of such activities is immediately apparent, which is in contrast to the atmospheric pollution and its subsequent effects on terrestrial and aquatic environments. The enhanced greenhouse effect, accelerated acidification, high heavy metal concentrations and stratospheric ozone depletion are all products of the industrial age but have only come to light in the last two decades. They are all contributing, insidiously, to environmental change which occurs sufficiently slowly that ecological thresholds are only now being recognised. All are related to the interplay between the various earth/atmosphere processes that involve global atmospheric, geological, geomorphological, hydrological, pedological and biological systems. These are united by energy transfers and by biogeochemical fluxes and it is these that have been so perturbed by human activities. In many cases, drastic measures are needed to counteract their potentially major impact on civilisation. Such threats to human well-being will necessitate international political co-operation and much forethought for future energy policies in particular. These will need to consider the advantages and disadvantages of nuclear energy in tandem with those of fossil fuels. Industrial development and its impact is not the only agent of environmental change and in the Chapters 6 and 7 the influence of agriculture on the developed and developing world will be explored.

FURTHER READING

Arndt P, Luttig G W (eds) 1987 *Mineral resources' extraction, environmental protection and land-use planning in the industrial and developing countries*. E Schweizerbart'sche Verlagsbuchhandlung, Stuttgart

Blowers A, Pepper D (eds) 1987 *Nuclear power in crisis*. Nichols, New York, and Croom Helm, London and Sydney

Bolin B, Döös B R, Jäger J, Warrick R A (eds) 1986 *The greenhouse effect, climatic change and ecosystems*. John Wiley; Chichester, New York, Brisbane, Toronto and Singapore

Neal H A, Schubel J R, 1987 *Solid waste management and the environment: the mounting garbage and trash crisis*. Prentice-Hall, New York

Parry M L, Carter T R, Konijn N T (eds) 1988 *The impact of climatic variations and agriculture. Vol I Assessments in cool temperate and cold regions, vol II Assessments in semi-arid regions*. Kluwer Academic Publishers, Dordrecht

Ramade F, 1987 *Ecotoxicology* (trans by L J M Hodgson). John Wiley, Chichester, New York, Brisbane, Toronto and Singapore

Rowland F S, Isaksen I S A (eds) 1988 *The changing atmosphere*. John Wiley, Chichester, New York, Brisbane, Toronto and Singapore

Toy T J, Hadley R, 1987 *Geomorphology and reclamation of disturbed lands*. Academic Press, New York and London

6

THE ENVIRONMENTAL IMPACT OF AGRICULTURE IN THE DEVELOPED WORLD

6.1 INTRODUCTION

As discussed in Chapters 3 and 4, the development and spread of agricultural systems since the initial domestication of plants and animals 10 kyr BP has had profound effects on global environments. Not only have landscapes changed in appearance as ecosystems have been transposed into agroecosystems to support fuel-powered urban systems but there have been considerable environmental changes brought about by the application of science to agricultural problems. Many of these changes are a direct result of manipulating biogeochemical cycles and energy flows, and relate especially to the use of artificial fertilisers and crop protection chemicals. The former augment naturally occurring nitrate and phosphate compounds which are essential to growth, while the latter are chiefly aimed at simplifying trophic interrelationships by eliminating so-called pests that utilise energy in competition with the intended crop. While landscape change is often rapid and observable, many of the changes that have occurred, and are continuing to occur, because of the application of agricultural chemicals, are less easy to pinpoint and, as in the case of many industrial processes (Ch. 5), significant environmental impacts have ensued as inadvertent consequences of such high-technology agriculture. Cultural eutrophication, which is due in large part to fertiliser use, is one such example. Soil erosion, a problem frequently associated with developing areas (Ch. 7), is now a significant problem in developed nations as a result of agricultural methods; and salinisation is fast becoming a problem in arid and semi-arid regions. Agricultural methods in the last two decades, aimed at more intensive food production, have also caused the destruction of natural habitats at a hitherto unprecedented rate, a process that has generated considerable acrimony between agriculturalists and conservationists. Moreover, the use of crop-protection chemicals has had widespread ecological repercussions though there is a growing trend towards the use of environmentally benign compounds. While many of these environmental changes are now occurring in the developing world as agriculture is becoming more technologically- rather than traditionally-based, they are particularly apparent in the developed world on which this chapter will concentrate.

6.2 LANDSCAPE CHANGE

As examined in section 4.3.2, the increasing sophistication of agricultural techniques in the post-1750 period has resulted in extensive landscape changes in Britain. Widespread changes also occurred in Europe as well as in North America, Africa and Australia as European colonisation proceeded (sections 4.4.2 and 4.4.3). As agriculture in the developed nations has intensified since the Second World War to achieve self-sufficiency in food production, older agricultural landscapes have been destroyed and replaced by those that characterise the 1980s. Much of this intensification has been achieved by political manipulation and in many developed nations agriculture is no longer a free-market enterprise but is controlled by interventionist policies. While these were established, for example, in Britain in the 1940s (section 4.3.2), political control of agriculture has become even more significant in Europe consequent upon the formation of the European Economic Community (EEC) in 1957 and which Britain joined in 1973. The operation of a Common Agricultural Policy (CAP) has provided protectionism for agriculture and stimulated the development of agribusiness especially via intervention price agencies. In effect, subsidies are provided, the amount depending on the product, to guarantee target prices for agricultural commodities. The CAP also provides grants for various forms of farm improvements such as drainage and modernisation.

These policies have transformed agricultural practices and in so doing have created widespread landscape change by directly and indirectly promoting more intensive food production, to such an extent that surpluses of nearly all staple animal and plant products necessitate expensive storage within the EEC or cheap disposal to external countries. In particular hedges, wetlands and woodlands have been much reduced and concern by environmentalists has highlighted the conflict of interest between agriculture and conservation. Additionally, more insidious environmental problems have been exacerbated by intensive crop production, the most significant of which are soil erosion and cultural eutrophication.

6.2.1 THE DEMISE OF HABITATS

One of the most important consequences of intensive post-war farming practices on the British landscape is the destruction of habitats. Hedgerows, woodlands, wetlands, moorlands, heathlands and downland have all diminished in extent as farmers have sought to increase agricultural productivity. This subject was brought to public attention by Shoard in her book *The theft of the countryside* which was published in 1980 and which fired the agriculture versus conservation debate that will be discussed in section 6.3.2.

Hedgerow destruction in Britain has become a particularly emotive issue because it represents a huge loss of wildlife habitats. Body (1987) states that *c*. 200 000 km of hedgerows have been removed since the Second World War which, taking account of replacement hedges, amounts to a net loss of 170 000 km or 22 per cent of the extent of pre-1940 hedges in England and Wales. In Norfolk alone there was a 45 per cent loss of hedgerows between 1946 and 1970 (Munton 1983), increasing to 80 per cent by 1984 (Blunden and Turner 1985). Barr *et al.* (1986), based on results of a survey by the Institute of Terrestrial Ecology (ITE), have indicated that between 1978 and 1984 hedges were being lost at annual rate of just under 4800 km, with most of this (*c*. 3200 km) occurring in England. These changes have taken place for several reasons. Firstly, the increasing use of farm machinery has encouraged the amalgamation of smaller fields. Blunden and Turner (1985) state that a square field of about 20 ha facilitates the most efficient use of machinery and it is therefore not surprising that most hedgerows have been removed to consolidate fields in those regions where cereal-growing is predominant, especially in East Anglia. Secondly, the removal of hedgerows makes more land available for crop production, which makes economic sense if prices are guaranteed via protectionist policies. For example, 1 ha of land is gained by the removal of 0.88 km of a 2 m wide hedge (Blunden and Turner 1985) and has been made even more economically viable by the provision of grants from the Ministry of Agriculture Fisheries and Food (MAFF) for the replacement of hedges by barbed-wire fences. These latter are cheaper to maintain than hedges and have also replaced some 1400 km of stone-walling between 1978 and 1984 (Barr *et al.* 1986). Such fences, however, do not provide an appropriate alternative wildlife habitat to hedgerows, the significance of which has been discussed in Way and Greig-Smith (1987). For example, Southerton and Rands (1987) have pointed out that up to 90 per cent of Britain's partridge population uses hedgerows as breeding grounds and the loss of this habitat is considered to be mainly responsible for the significant decline in numbers of both grey (*Perdix perdix*) and red-legged (*Alectoris rufa*) partridges. It is not just the loss of this habitat that is significant in terms of Britain's flora and fauna but the fact that hedgerows (because they act as field boundaries) are often affected by crop-protection chemicals. The use of both insecticides and herbicides has tended to reduce the overall floristic and faunistic diversity of surviving hedges.

Many woodlands have suffered a fate similar to that of hedgerows and for similar reasons. Unlike the situation in pre-industrial Britain (sections 4.2.2 and 4.2.3) when woodland was very much an integral part of agricultural enterprises, it is no longer particularly economic because it occupies land that can produce a much more rapid and significant financial return if a crop is produced. Barr *et al.* (1986) indicate that some 24 700 ha of broad-leaved woodland were removed from Britain during the period 1977–84, much of which constitutes what Rackham (1986) describes as ancient woods that originated in the pre-1700 period, and Peterkin (1983) has suggested that, nationwide, there has been a post-war decline of between 30 and 50 per cent of ancient woodland. This represents a huge loss to the British countryside of a much-valued habitat for wildlife. In addition, Essex (1987) has pointed out that much of the remaining broad-leaved woodland that exists as small plots of *c*. 10 ha or less on farms has been neglected because of lack of financial incentive; there is, apparently no longer a ready market for woodland produce that was so important in the pre-industrial period. Metal and plastic products have superseded wood and market forces have thus led to a decline in woodland management expertise. Fragmentation of woodland lots, which began with the early agriculturalists some 5 kyr BP (section 3.3) and which has become accentuated as more and more land has been taken for agriculture throughout the historic period, has also resulted in economic non-viability. As will be discussed in section 8.2, many woodland areas have been converted to coniferous plantations by the Forestry Commission, resulting in a net loss from the British landscape of broad-leaved mixed woodland. Again, both the removal of woodland and the conversion of broad-leaved woodland to coniferous plantation have been stimulated by the economic incentives of more rapid returns for less initial outlay, the provision of grants via CAP policies for land improvement and tax advantages.

Moorland areas of upland Britain which, prior to 1950, were mainly used for rough grazing have also been transformed by more intensive agricultural practices as well as by the large-scale planting of coniferous forests (section 8.2). Among the most severely affected areas are the uplands of Mid-Wales and the North York Moors where between 1950 and 1980 there have been net losses of 28 and 25 per cent respectively, which amounts to 28 400 ha in the former and 17 100 ha in the latter (Barr *et al.* 1986). In both cases much of this loss is due to agricultural improvement to support more intensive grazing. Wathern *et al.* (1988), for example, have examined the pattern of land-use change in Clwyd, North Wales, in relation to incentive payments under the EEC Less Favoured Areas directive (LFA). This latter was established in 1975 to promote development and to assist farmers with low incomes which, in many upland regions, is implemented via direct payments in the form of annual grants per animal under the Hill Livestock Compensatory Allowances (HLCAs). In Clwyd, Wathern *et al.*'s data show that between 1977 and 1983 the number of sheep attracting HLCAs increased from 363 115 to 416 029 and the grant encouraged an increase in high-rate sheep (special hill breeds) which attracted a higher HLCA payment. Since increasing sheep numbers to such high proportions increases grazing pressure on moorland that is of low carrying capacity, many farmers have obtained further EEC payments as grants for improvements, including land drainage, the ploughing-up of moorland and its replacement with more nutritious seed mixtures as well as for fertiliser applications. This led to a significant decline in rough grazing from *c.* 5000 ha in 1971 to *c.* 2000 ha in 1981. Wathern *et al.* have also shown that the average farm size increased as amalgamation of farm units occurred, which is considered in general terms by MacEwen and Sinclair (1983) to be due to the ability of farmers with larger holdings to more readily provide capital to support grant applications. Thus EEC subsidies are fuelling social as well as land-use changes and promoting fragmentation of natural habitats. This latter, as Webb (1986) has discussed, is also a problem in lowland heaths such as those in East Anglia, Dorset and Surrey where expansion of urban areas is as significant a factor in this decline as agricultural intensification and afforestation. It is of interest to note that urbanisation is one of the main reasons why land has been lost from agriculture in the post-war period in EEC states in general (Briggs and Wyatt 1988).

Wetlands too have suffered as a consequence of land reclamation for agriculture. According to Body (1987) an area of wetland equivalent to the size of the Isle of Wight is lost every 4 years at current rates of drainage of *c.* 10 000 ha annually. While drainage schemes on a grandiose scale have been implemented in wetland areas such as the Somerset Levels and have epi-tomised the agriculture v. conservation debate that will be discussed in sec-tion 6.2.3, there are large numbers of smaller bog, marsh and wet meadow sites that have disappeared. As Newbold (1988) has pointed out, land drain-age is brought about by river or arterial drainage and field drainage, result-ing in an overall reduction in the level of the water-table. This enables ploughing to take place with subsequent crop seeding. Not only is there a loss of habitat, which is vital to flora and fauna adapted to wetland environ-ments, but there may also be other deleterious effects involving water quality. For example, deep drainage may penetrate saline water-tables that may then release salt water which is disadvantageous to both crops and wildlife. There have been cases where pyrite-rich and sulphide-rich peats have been exposed to drainage water which has then adversely affected wildlife and which require expensive remedial measures (Newbold 1988). In addition, wetlands are particularly susceptible to cultural eutrophication due to intensive fertiliser use, as will be discussed in section 6.3.1

The overall effects of such land-use changes are numerous, one of the most significant of which has been to fragment natural and semi-natural habitats to such an extent that many plant and animal species are threatened with extinction. Landscapes have become less diverse, both in terms of habi-tat and land-use type, and much more open as fields have been amalgamated into larger units. However, as pointed out in section 4.3.2, there are changes afoot in the CAP of the EEC as a response to agricultural overproduction and the 1990s should be a period of agricultural extensification. Already the possibility of set-aside, which involves taking land out of agriculture, is being considered as an agricultural policy along with numerous other possi-bilities for land-use (Harvey *et al.* 1986) and alternative employment strategies (e.g. Agriculture Economic Development Committee 1987). The views of many interested parties have been advanced in Baldock and Conder (1987) and a contribution by Green and Potter (1987) in the same volume has proposed a strategy which attempts to reconcile the interests of agricul-turalists and conservationists. This will be examined in section 6.2.3. How the anatomy of the British, and indeed the European, countryside will de-velop in the next 20 years or so as a result of changes in the CAP remains to be seen.

6.2.2 SOIL EROSION AND SOIL PROTECTION

While the demise and fragmentation of natural and semi-natural habitats rep-resents an obvious change to the environment, there has been increasing concern about environmental change due to soil erosion. This is a problem which is not confined to Europe; it is a major problem in many developing countries, as will be discussed in section 7.2.3, and of significance in de-veloped nations such as Australia (section 4.4.3) and North America.

The factors which influence soil erosion are presented in Fig. 6.1 and involve all the components of earth surface systems, type of land-use and whether or not any conservation measures are undertaken. In simple terms, soils tend to be removed from upland regions and deposited in lowland areas or in the oceans. The rate of this natural process of terrain deflation has been altered by the initiation and spread of agricultural systems during the last 10 kyr (section 3.3). Not only is land from which soil is removed affected, but areas in which it is deposited may be adversely affected as ditches and irrigation systems become infilled. As shown in Table 6.1 the major agents of erosion are water and wind, the significance of which depends on the overall climatic regime and the density of the vegetation or land-use cover which affords protection. In virtually all parts of the world, clearance of land for agriculture has enhanced rates of erosion and thus erosion constitutes one of the major agents of landscape change.

As Morgan (1987) has pointed out, soil degradation in the EEC has only been recognised as a significant problem since 1980 and much of it is considered to be a result of changing agricultural practices in the last 30 years. The areas of the EEC which are severely affected are concentrated in the sandy and loam belt of northern Europe and in the Mediterranean region. De Ploey (1986) has examined the soil erosion problem in the loess loamy areas of western and central Europe from where annual erosion rates of between 3 and $100\,t\,ha^{-1}$ have been recorded, the highest being in areas of steeper slopes. This is attributed to the demise of the more traditional intercropping methods and the increased size of fields encouraged by mechanisation. Similar reasons are advanced by Morgan (1986b) for enhanced soil erosion in the sandy and loamy soil areas of northern Europe, where soil structure has been detrimentally affected by a reduction in organic content as the extent of

Fig. 6.1. Factors affecting soil erosion. (From Morgan 1986a.)

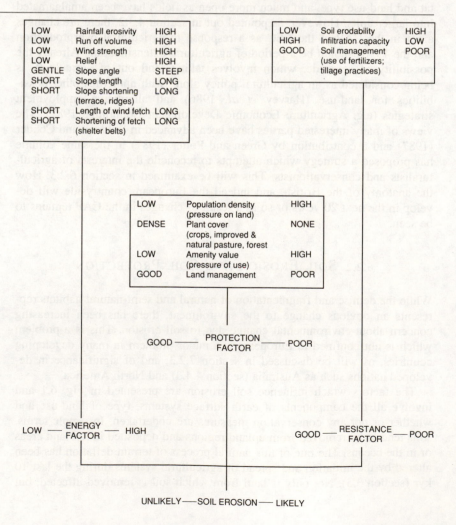

LOW	Rainfall erosivity	HIGH
LOW	Run off volume	HIGH
LOW	Wind strength	HIGH
LOW	Relief	HIGH
GENTLE	Slope angle	STEEP
SHORT	Slope length	LONG
SHORT	Slope shortening (terrace, ridges)	LONG
SHORT	Length of wind fetch	LONG
SHORT	Shortening of fetch (shelter belts)	LONG

LOW	Soil erodability	HIGH
HIGH	Infiltration capacity	LOW
GOOD	Soil management (use of fertilizers; tillage practices)	POOR

LOW	Population density (pressure on land)	HIGH
DENSE	Plant cover (crops, improved & natural pasture, forest	NONE
LOW	Amenity value (pressure of use)	HIGH
GOOD	Land management	POOR

GOOD —— PROTECTION FACTOR —— POOR

LOW —— ENERGY FACTOR —— HIGH

GOOD —— RESISTANCE FACTOR —— POOR

UNLIKELY —— SOIL EROSION —— LIKELY

grass leys has been reduced and by mechanisation which has caused soil compaction. As has been suggested by Steenvoorden and Bouma (1987), remedial measures to halt and reverse such degradation necessitate the regular inclusion of manure in the cropping cycle as well as a reduction in the amount of tillage. If the latter is replaced by grass leys to encourage soil biotic activity, infiltration rates will be increased, thus reducing the potential for soil erosion by water.

According to Yassoglou (1987), the high erosivity of rainfall and the high incidence of steep slopes, coupled with the long history of exploitation which has reduced the vegetation cover, have rendered many Mediterranean regions susceptible to erosion and reduced the productivity potential. A study by Chisci (1986) in the Apennine hill region of Italy, for example, shows that land degradation due to landslides and water erosion has accelerated in the last 40 years. As in the case of northern Europe, Chisci attributes much of this to changing agricultural practices. Using data from sites in the Apennines, he has shown that vineyards and orchards have increased at the expense of forage crops, pastures and forest between 1954 and 1976 and that the intercropping of herbaceous crops with trees has gradually ceased, while the incidence of landslides during the same period has increased. He also

---

A. Erosion by water

1. Rainsplash :	May consolidate the soil surface by encouraging the formation of a crust that reduces the infiltration capacity and thus promotes greater surface runoff - another erosive agent. May disperse the soil by detaching particles which may then move downslope.	
2. Overland flow :	Occurs when storm water or prolonged rainfall results in a saturated soil causing sheet flow or a series of braiding channels in which soil particles are carried downslope.	
3. Subsurface flow :	May occur in subsurface layers of the soil or in pipes transporting fine and colloidal particles downslope.	
4. Rill erosion :	Occurs where overland flow becomes concentrated in channels and, although ephemeral, rills are very significant in the downslope movement of soil particles.	
5. Gully erosion :	These are permanent features which enhance erosion by headwall and bank corrosion.	
6. Mass movements :	Slides, rockfalls and mudflows can cause large amounts of material to be moved downslope.	

Table 6.1. The processes involved in soil erosion. (Based on Morgan 1986a.)

B. Erosion by wind

How significant wind is as an agent of erosion depends of the velocity of the moving air and how effective the land-cover is as a protection.

1. Suspension :	Fine partricles of small diameter are transported high in the air and often over long distances.
2. Surface creep :	Coarse grains are rolled along the ground.
3. Saltation :	Grains are moved along the ground surface in a series of jumps.

suggests that remedial measures will necessitate the conversion of arable land on steeper slopes to permanent pasture or forest. Remedial measures of a similar nature have been prescribed in Finkel (1986) for Mediterranean lands in general and pinpoint the necessity for an increase in the organic content of soils to enhance their cohesion and thus reduce their susceptibility to erosion.

In Britain, soil erosion has only been recognised as a significant problem since *c.* 1980 in common with the rest of the EEC (Morgan 1987), despite earlier warnings (e.g. the Agricultural Advisory Council 1970) that the more intensive post-war agricultural practices, and the likelihood of further intensification with Britain's advent into the EEC, could have detrimental effects on the soil resource. As several workers (e.g. Arden-Clarke and Hodges 1987, Morgan 1987) have pointed out, it is impossible to assess the full extent of the problem in the absence of a regular country-wide monitoring programme, but it is clear from the rising number of reported cases that soil erosion is increasing (Boardman 1988). Evans and Cook (1986) have distinguished three major categories of soil erosion in Britain which are given in Table 6.2 along with examples of specific case-studies. These categories primarily reflect the significance of wind and water as erosive agents in upland and lowland situations, though in many uplands and pastures animals are also agents of erosion along with increased recreation pressure. In relation to the overall national situation in Britain, upland erosion is insignificant but, as Evans and Cook (1986) have discussed, it is in many cases of sufficient intensity to warrant rapid remedial action. In the national context, the wind and water erosion of lowland soils is more extensive and more critical. As Table 6.2 shows, there are numerous examples of wind-induced soil erosion episodes, especially in eastern England where dried peaty or sandy soils are particularly susceptible to removal. Such events tend to be localised and, while they cause crop damage by abrasion, in the national context they too are peripheral in importance to erosion by water.

Table 6.2. Categories and examples of soil erosion in the UK.

Categories	Examples	Approximate losses in te ha^{-1} yr^{-1}	Source
Erosion of upland pastures and moors by wind, water and animals	Very few studies on rates of erosion but peat moors are particularly susceptible c. 3750 km^2 throughout Britain.		Evans and Cook, 1986
Wind erosion of arable soils	Vale of York	21 - 44	Morgan, 1985
	Barmby Moor and Market Weighton, Vale of York	c. 21	Wilson and Cook, 1980
Water erosion of arable soils	Hilton, East Shropshire	15 - 17, rising to >40 in adverse seasons of 1976 and 1983	Harrison-Reed, 1986
	Silsoe, Bedfordshire	>10	Morgan, 1986a
	Norfolk	195	Evans and Nortcliffe, 1978
	Albourne, nr. Brighton	241	Boardman, 1983

N.B. Morgan (1980) estimates that tolerable rates of soil erosion are in the order of 2 te ha^{-1} yr^{-1}, Boardman (1986) believes that erosion rates in excess of 0.5 tonnes/ha./year constitute accelerated erosion.

Reference has already been made (section 4.1) to erosional episodes that have occurred in the historic period as a result of water erosion and these have been more fully reviewed by Speirs and Frost (1987). In the last 20 years, the amount of soil erosion via water has apparently increased in Britain due especially to the practice of winter cereal cultivation that leaves soil bare and unprotected in autumn and winter months (Boardman and Robinson 1985). The lack of crop residues in soils (Hodges and Arden-Clarke 1986) and field enlargement (Evans and Cook 1986) are also contributory factors. In terms of rates of erosion it is difficult to generalise because much of the published data relate to extreme events. Morgan (1980) has estimated that the annual rate of soil formation is $c.$ 0.2 t ha^{-1} and that annual losses of soil of up to 2.0 t ha^{-1} are acceptable, though Boardman (1986) believes that the latter figure should not be in excess of 0.5 t ha^{-1}. As Table 6.2 shows, many of the soil erosion incidents that have been reported in the last 10 years reflect annual erosion rates considerably above 0.5 t ha^{-1} and most are in excess of 2.0 t ha^{-1}. Britain is, therefore witnessing a diminution of one of its most valuable resources, but despite this there is as yet no national soil conservation policy, the case for which has been examined by Boardman (1988).

In other developed countries, soil erosion is also a major problem. Moran *et al.* (1986) state that in the USA 85 per cent of all soil erosion originates from cropland and according to the *Gaia atlas of planet management* (Myers 1985) about one-third of US croplands, consisting of more than 50 million ha, are experiencing a decline in productivity because of this degradation. The problem is particularly acute in the Great Plains. It was in this region that the 'Dust Bowl' of the 1930s developed, giving rise to a major soil erosion event. Overgrazing and the rapid expansion of wheat cultivation, which was facilitated by the introduction of tractors during the 1920s, detrimentally affected the soil structure. A series of drought years during the 1930s further depleted the vegetation cover so that huge dust storms developed which, according to Coffey (1978), covered nearly 4 million km^2 and extended from Canada to Mexico. While this is one of the most infamous instances of soil erosion, dust storms, albeit on a much reduced scale, still frequently occur in the Great Plains to such an extent that Cook and Ellis (1987) describe them as '. . . the scourge of the Great Plains . . . [which] develop when soils of low rainfall areas are poorly managed'. They suggest that the most effective measures to reduce soil erosion in this area include the maintenance of rough cloddy surfaces, ensuring that the soil is covered with crops or residues to enhance cohesiveness, including green manure and crop rotations suitable for the particular location and the practice of wind-strip cropping, which involves the planting of crops in alternate strips with meadow at right angles to the direction of prevailing winds. These measures will also help to protect against water erosion, especially after heavy rains.

As pointed out above, soil erosion not only affects the areas from which soil is removed but also affects the environment where it is deposited. In the USA, for example, Moran *et al.* (1986) state that $300 million are spent annually by the United States Army Corps of Engineers to dredge 300 million m^3 of sediment from US waterways. Apart from cost there are often ecological consequences of such deposition; as well as silting due to sediment accumulation, high inputs of nutrients, notably nitrogen and phosphorus, into aquatic ecosystems may also occur causing eutrophication.

Remedial measures are therefore essential not only to combat soil erosion but to safeguard neighbouring ecosystems and agroecosystems. Hudson (1987) has presented two examples from Australia, which has severe soil erosion problems (section 4.4.3), that illustrate what can be achieved by conservation measures. In the Eppalock catchment in Victoria, a project was undertaken between 1960 and 1975 by the Soil Conservation Authority, to reclaim already eroded land and to curtail the erosion from grazing land in order to reduce sedimentation in Eppalock reservoir. The programme involved the provision of gully control structures, tree planting, silt traps and the improvement of pasture management which included the aerial application of fertiliser and so-called 'chisel seeding' involving seeding and fertiliser treatment in narrow furrows. Erosion rates were sufficiently reduced to allow the enlargement of the dam creating Eppalock reservoir and various cost–benefit exercises showed that, overall, agricultural productivity increased. The Australian Soil Conservation Study (1978) concluded that the project was successful both in economic and environmental terms. Another project on the east Darling Downs in southeast Queensland was established in 1972 to repair sheet, rill and gully erosion over several thousand hectares of sloping basaltic soils that caused flooding and salt deposition over neighbouring lowlands. As a result of remedial actions, which involved mainly mechanical protection measures such as the construction of contour banks and waterways, wheat yields rose and the opportunity for extra cropping increased allowing the production, on average, of three crops every 2 years. While the landowners themselves contributed 71 per cent of the costs, the extra revenue from increased productivity rapidly began to compensate for this. In addition, state costs of 29 per cent began to be recouped as the costs for river, drain and road maintenance were reduced. Hudson (1987) does, however, point out that a subsidy to the landowners contribution is required if the latter are to see a fairly rapid return and are thus encouraged to undertake such schemes.

These examples illustrate that soil erosion is now recognised as a significant problem whereas it was virtually ignored until 20 years ago. Its major causes have also been identified as being largely due to post-war agricultural practices and there are remedial measures that can be taken to curtail and even eliminate it, not simply for the benefit of agricultural land itself but also for the benefit of adjacent environments and their human communities. What is more difficult to predict is the effect of scientific developments such as genetic engineering (section 8.4), which may increase yields and thus sustain productivity at the expense of other environmental parameters.

6.2.3 THE AGRICULTURE VERSUS CONSERVATION DEBATE

The issues discussed in sections 6.2.1 and 6.2.3 have, in the past two decades especially, given rise to a polarisation of views relating to agriculture on the one hand and conservation on the other in many developed countries, particularly in Europe. This conflict has been alluded to in section 4.3.3, and in the developed world it is now clear that both issues are significant in political arenas. Such polarisation is unfortunate since it implies that conservation is an anathema to agriculture, and vice versa, and it suggests that there is little room for compromise. This is a serious debate which is particularly relevant in the late 1980s in Europe as the CAP is about to be redefined (section 6.2.1) because of huge food surpluses. Conservationists are lobbying for consideration to be given to habitat and landscape protection to form an integral part of the new CAP. While this is not guaranteed, it does of course provide an excellent opportunity to reconcile conservation with agriculture and perhaps avoid the acrimonious conflicts which have characterised this debate in the last decade. Moreover, external factors, such as the enhanced greenhouse effect (section 5.3.1), may ultimately require reconciliation between conservationists and agriculturalists in order to ensure acceptable landscape development in the future.

Precisely when views on agriculture and conservation began to polarise is difficult to pinpoint, but it is essentially a post-war development that has intensified as agriculture has evolved into agribusiness and as conservation movements have become more intense and politically aware. As Lowe *et al.* (1986) have pointed out, the last 20 years in particular have witnessed a shift of focus in Britain from urban–rural conflicts, which are now beginning to re-emerge in the media as new land is being sought for urban development in the southeast, to countryside conflicts involving not only agriculture and conservation but also forestry. These issues have also become significant in local and national politics (section 4.3.3) which has brought them widespread publicity and transposed them into issues that can win or lose elections. The post-war period has also seen increasing government control in agriculture, especially via the CAP, in conservation which is under the jurisdiction of the Nature Conservancy Council (NCC) and in forestry that is governmentally influenced by tax incentives and the Forestry Commission (section 8.2.2). The latter was established in 1919 in response to Britain's poor woodland reserves and lessons learnt during the First World War which illustrated the nation's reliance on imported timber.

As Shoard (1987) has pointed out, the rapid spread of conifers promoted by the Forestry Commission as well as private landowners in the 1950s and 1960s began to give rise to public concern, especially as the Forestry Commission enjoys a high degree of autonomy and has considerable powers for land purchase. What is perhaps more significant, however, is the fact that until recently the most widely planted trees were conifers, especially the Sitka spruce (*Picea sitchensis*) which is not a native British species but is favoured because it can tolerate relatively poor soils and provides a relatively rapid harvest when compared with broad-leaved deciduous species. While the '. . . march of the conifers' as Shoard describes it, across the countryside raised public concern, the main issues that led to government intervention, via the 1981 Wildlife and Countryside Act (WACA), were related to landscape change brought about by the intensification of agriculture. The inception of this Act and its subsequent implementation appears to have created as many problems as it was intended to solve, and its implications have been discussed by Blunden and Curry (1985), Newby (1988) as well as Shoard (1987) and Lowe *et al.* (1986). The latter in particular expound the view that the WACA '. . . is an Act whose passage did more than anything to highlight the issues and polarise the conflict between agriculture and conservation'.

There is also considerable conflict in relation to financing, since the government, via taxation, provides funds for the NCC to purchase or rent land that is considered to be of especial ecological or geological significance. While this approach is admirable in concept it has to be balanced against the fact that the British government, via their commitment to the EEC and its

CAP, also subsidise agriculture and forestry out of public taxes. Conflict also arises because there may be arguments about what should be protected and what should be designated as a site of special scientific interest (SSSI). Such sites, which are intended as prime examples of specific habitats, numbered 4842 in March 1986 and were first designated in 1951 under the National Parks and Access to the Countryside Act of 1949. Because of their protected status, any planning proposals that may affect them must be referred to the NCC. Despite this, and prior to the WACA, the NCC had drawn attention to the fact that such sites were disappearing or being damaged at a rapid rate. For example, an NCC report (1981a) based on surveys of SSSIs carried out in 1980, showed that some 15 per cent of the sites sampled had been either completely wiped out or badly damaged in 1980 alone, largely because the NCC had little power to enforce protection,   relying instead on voluntary agreement by landowners, and because even then the financial compensation scheme was inadequately funded. The WACA did little to ameliorate this situation and pressure from the National Farmers Union (NFU) and the Country Landowners Association (CLA)   ensured that the new Act did not strengthen the NCC's hand by giving it statutory powers. As Blunden and Curry (1985) state; 'The consultative papers embodied the view that control of farming operations were unnecessary and potentially counter-productive. Conservation objectives should be secured, it argued, through the voluntary co-operation of farmers and landowners, encouraged, where necessary, by conservation agencies.'

In addition, an amendment to the bill which was prompted by the MAFF required that where an improvement grant had been refused to safeguard an SSSI or a national park, there would have to be a compensation payment by the NCC or the National Parks Authority to the farmer. The only really positive aspect of the bill in relation to conservation was the requirement that one year's notice should be given of any intended landscape modification by the farmer. Clearly, the bill was very much on the side of the farming lobby and not pro-conservation. Shoard (1987) and Newby (1988) have discussed numerous examples of how the WACA has been implemented since 1981. In some cases, such as the Somerset Levels, the conflict reached the national media, though in this particular instance the confrontation had begun in the mid-1970s and focused on west Sedgemoor, 11 km east of Taunton, which was the subject of a grant application to the MAFF for financial assistance for drainage. Unresolved in 1981, the proposals were dealt with under the terms of the WACA in 1982 when the NCC proposed the designation of 1000 ha as an SSSI. Objections were raised, with counter-proposals from the CLA and MAFF for considerably reduced areas of 500 and 350 ha respectively. The NCC, however, persisted but at great cost to the ever-tolerant taxpayer. Eventually, in 1983, some thirty agreements were reached with local farmers involving compensation of *c*. £150 000 per annum (1983 prices) for the whole of west Sedgemoor and more than £1 million for the rest of the Somerset Levels.

Moreover, the NCC were required to notify some 40 000 owners of SSSIs and in about one-third of these compensation is now being demanded. Many of these cases have been discussed by Shoard, who describes the compensation provisions in the WACA as 'a protection racket' with farmers (and afforesters) in such a position that whatever they do they cannot lose financially. The taxpayer bears the cost whether it is for agricultural improvement or for SSSI maintenance. Nevertheless, further plans have been formulated to ensure compensation in some parts of Britain which have been designated as Environmentally Sensitive Areas (ESAs) by MAFF under the 1986 Agriculture Act. Under this scheme, farmers would be entitled to compensation payments for not initiating damaging landscape change. As Shoard (1987) points out, only 0.6 per cent of England and Wales has been designated as ESAs, so the impact of this scheme will be minimal, and once again the taxpayer picks up the tab.

All of this is occurring at a time when agricultural productivity is considerably in excess of requirements, which makes the situation even more ridiculous than the examples above suggest. One question that must be asked is whether the forthcoming CAP reorganisation will be able to go any way towards solving this problem. A policy of agricultural extensification has been suggested as one way of reducing food production and the implications of such a policy for landscape change have been discussed in Baldock and Conder (1987). As Potter (1988) reports, this policy is now becoming reality and the extensification scheme, implemented via an amendment to the 1985 EEC Structures Regulations, came into effect on 1 July 1988. Under this scheme, EEC member states are required to construct and implement plans to facilitate the extensification of crop and livestock production. In Britain, such a plan has been devised by MAFF (1987) which requires action for arable production initially, with beef production next in line. Farmers will be eligible for payments if they reduce the area used for cereal production by at least 20 per cent for at least 5 years, provided there is no simultaneous increase in the production of other surplus crops. The land that is thus set aside can be converted into fallow, forestry or other non-agricultural uses. Potentially, such changes could benefit conservation and mark a return to a more diverse landscape in those parts of Britain, such as East Anglia, which have become much more homogeneous as large-scale cereal production has come to dominate the landscape in the last 20 years. However, there is no guarantee that farmers will not simply reduce cereal hectarage by the required 20 per cent and then intensify their production of a 'non surplus' crop on the remaining land that could still lead to habitat destruction. As Potter (1988) points out, the MAFF (1987) proposal is deficient as far as conservation objectives are concerned because it does not require the compilation of an overall farm conservation plan which characterises similar schemes in operation in the USA. These latter have been discussed by Ervin (1987) who draws attention to the US Food Security Act of 1985 that is being implemented via an Acreage Reduction Programme and a Conservation Reserve Programme.

A further shortcoming of the extensification policy, in terms of conservation objectives, is the fact that farmers need join the scheme only on a voluntary basis. Thus the principle of voluntary co-operation of farmers towards conservation that is embodied in the WACA is maintained. Moreover, the success of the scheme will depend entirely on how many farmers participate and this in turn, taking what may perhaps be described as a cynical approach, will depend on the size of incentive payments for set-aside. Potter (1988) has suggested that one way of making the scheme more effective would be to include the targeting of specific areas that would benefit most from set-aside. Such a scheme has also been examined by Green and Potter (1987) who have indicated that target areas could include those which have pollution problems due to nitrate fertilisers (section 6.3) or soil erosion, or which contain land that could be used to develop recreational potential.

They also point out that areas which have already been designated as ESAs could be the precursors of target areas. The MAFF (1987) plans in conjunction with targeting could provide a rural land-use policy that, if formalised, could be extremely beneficial for conservation and more economic to the taxpayer but not necessarily to the farmer. However, as Cloke (1989) has discussed, Department of the Environment (DoE) proposals that were mooted at the same time as the MAFF report add another facet to this debate. The DoE (1987) have changed rural planning objectives, which hitherto had placed the agricultural use of rural land as the major priority, to include land-use practices which will promote rural economic revival and environmental protection. The diminution of protection for agricultural land may present opportunities for developers, especially since there is a land shortage for housing, to exploit these 'relaxed' rules. This, Cloke (1989) suggests, may be preparing the way for a renewed attack on the countryside and a further undermining of the planning process, which is reflected in the increase in the rate of planning permissions that have been granted by government as a result of appeals made in the wake of refusals by local authorities. In 1979, the figure was 29 per cent, rising to 40 per cent in 1985. Moreover, Johnston (1987) has drawn attention to the fact that the DoE's proposals in relation to environmental protection may not be all-embracing but more akin to a two-tier hierarchy, with strict controls on land-use changes in areas that are already designated as special, i.e. the national parks, and very relaxed and flexible rules for the remainder. What the outcome of all these changes will be remains to be seen, but whether conservation interests will receive more than a cursory consideration is doubtful.

6.3 CULTURAL EUTROPHICATION AND SALINISATION

Since the first agricultural systems were established 10 kyr BP (section 3.3), farmers have sought to influence soil fertility because the presence of available nutrients in the soil is essential for crop production. The early agriculturalists in the Middle East, especially in the valleys of the Nile and Tigris, recognised the importance of fertile silt deposited by floods and in many cases instituted measures to control the floods so that silt deposition was ensured in crop-growing areas. Similarly, the use of animal manures and human sewage has been recognised throughout history as a means of increasing soil fertility and of improving soil structure. The most important nutrient elements that are essential to plant growth are nitrogen and phosphorus, and if they are in short supply in the soil plant productivity will be impaired. Until the Industrial Revolution of the 1700s, enhancement of soil nutrients was effected via manuring in traditional farming systems (section 4.2) that involved both crops and livestock; often the latter were allowed to roam on fields left fallow so that organic matter and nutrients were replenished until a further crop was planted. In addition, many crop rotations involved leguminous crops which enhanced the nitrogen content of the soil by the activity of nitrifying bacteria in root nodules, and the ploughing in of plant residues after the crop was harvested.

Today, however, in developed nations these practices have been largely replaced by high-technology agriculture wherein nutrients are replenished by the application of artificial fertilisers. These were first produced in the early 1900s when the Haber process was developed which facilitated the fixation of nitrogen from the atmosphere, a process that was hitherto only possible via the action of bacteria. Since the Second World War nitrate, phosphate and potassic fertilisers have been widely available and applied on a large scale in developed countries. Their application, together with mechanisation, has been responsible for increased food production in these areas; and since the 1960s these substances have been increasingly used in developing countries. Although the increase in food production is a beneficial effect of fertiliser use, research in the last two decades has revealed that there are also detrimental effects. The most significant of these is the cultural eutrophication of freshwater aquatic ecosystems that are in receipt of drainage from agricultural land. Consequently many wetland habitats have suffered a detrimental change in their flora and fauna, which, in many cases, has been exacerbated by sewage inflow that is also nutrient rich. In addition, some ground-water and aquifers are now known to contain nitrate levels that are considered hazardous to human health and which are creating problems for domestic water supply industries. Cultural eutrophication has also occurred and is continuing to occur in estuaries and coastal environments to the detriment of their ecology.

In drier regions, where the chief factor limiting crop productivity is water availability, the long-term and intensive use of irrigation has also created environmental change. In North America, salinisation of both surface waters and soils is now a significant problem and while it is a process, like eutrophication, which can occur naturally, modern agricultural techniques have exacerbated the problem for developed as well as developing nations. Neither is the problem confined to surface waters, as aquifers can develop high salt concentrations, creating further problems for the provision of domestic and agricultural water.

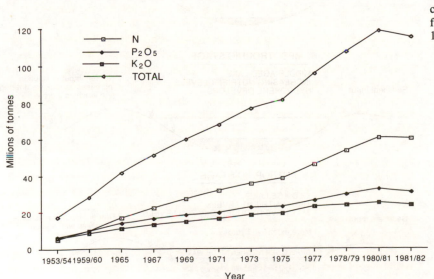

Fig. 6.2. Growth in world consumption of inorganic fertilisers. (Based on FAO 1981a, b.)

6.3.1 THE GROWTH OF FERTILISER USE AND THE CULTURAL EUTROPHICATION OF SURFACE FRESH WATERS AND COASTAL REGIONS

As Fig. 6.2 shows, the growth of fertiliser use has been especially marked since 1960 and the consumption of nitrate fertiliser in particular has outstripped that of both phosphate and potassic (potash) fertilisers. The production of all three is big business for agrochemical companies and has contributed significantly to the development of agriculture into agribusiness. Olson (1987) suggests that such fertilisers account for at least 30 per cent of all agricultural production in the USA, for example, and that they are responsible for the status of the USA as a major exporter of agricultural produce. Undoubtedly, artificial fertilisers have contributed to the pre-eminence of other food-exporting nations such as the EEC states. Statistics for Britain, for example, show that the use of nitrogen fertilisers has increased by a factor of three since 1963 and that some 1.5 million t of phosphate are imported annually from phosphate mines in Senegal, Morocco and Tunisia (Body 1987).

In effect, the artificial production of fertilisers and the mining of phosphates are influencing the biogeochemical cycling of nutrients (these have been discussed by Mannion 1986b), which occurs naturally as nutrients are

Fig. 6.3. The natural process of lake eutrophication.

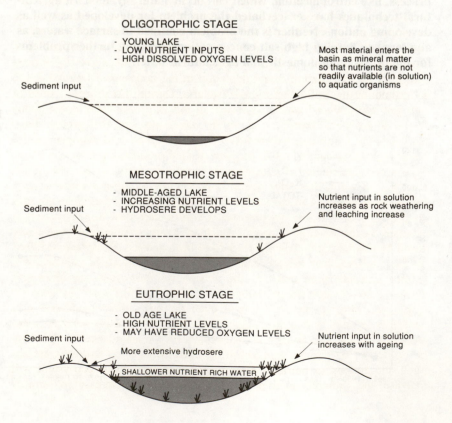

OLIGOTROPHIC STAGE

- YOUNG LAKE
- LOW NUTRIENT INPUTS
- HIGH DISSOLVED OXYGEN LEVELS

Sediment input

Most material enters the basin as mineral matter so that nutrients are not readily available (in solution) to aquatic organisms

MESOTROPHIC STAGE

- MIDDLE-AGED LAKE
- INCREASING NUTRIENT LEVELS
- HYDROSERE DEVELOPS

Sediment input

Nutrient input in solution increases as rock weathering and leaching increase

EUTROPHIC STAGE

- OLD AGE LAKE
- HIGH NUTRIENT LEVELS
- MAY HAVE REDUCED OXYGEN LEVELS

Sediment input

More extensive hydrosere

SHALLOWER NUTRIENT RICH WATER

Nutrient input in solution increases with ageing

absorbed by plants from the soil, itself derived from rock weathering, and returned to the soil by litter decomposition. In the course of the natural bio-geochemical cycles of nitrogen and phosphorus, lakes and other freshwater aquatic ecosystems will become enriched via the process of eutrophication as they act (especially lakes) as a sink for sediments derived from their catchments, as is shown in Fig. 6.3. The ocean basins also act as a nutrient sink since they receive particulate matter from the continental land masses. Ultimately, the sediments which accumulate in the oceans may be uplifted as mountain masses are once again raised to undergo denudation processes. Lake sediments will similarly experience burial and/or erosion so that event-ually the nutrients locked in their sediment store will re-enter circulation. Obviously these temporal processes, which occur on a time-scale of many thousands to many millions of years, will vary spatially according to the bedrock, soil and erosive processes that are controlled by the climatic condi-tions in any given area.

As Moss (1988) has pointed out, natural lake eutrophication as depicted in Fig. 6.3 is an idealised situation and there is evidence that lakes may undergo oligotrophication, or nutrient decline, as they mature. Nevertheless, apart from the uplift of ocean sediments, most of the processes involved in the transfer of sediments and nutrients from one storage pool to another are influenced by human activity. Soil erosion is one such process that accel-erates the transfer of particulate matter from catchments and land masses into lakes and the oceans respectively. Since soil particles contain nutrients, the movement of these are similarly affected. Moreover, nutrients may be transferred from one pool to another via leaching, whereby soluble com-pounds may be dissolved in water and are thus transported in solution into freshwater and salt-water ecosystems. Both of these processes are important in eutrophication; and human activity, via agricultural methods, has accel-erated these transfers to such an extent that major pollution problems have developed as a result. It is also possible that the application of nitrogen fertilisers is exacerbating ozone depletion in the atmosphere (section 5.3.3) by promoting denitrification by soil bacteria. During this process oxides of nitrogen are produced which, as shown in Fig. 5.5, may break down ozone in the stratosphere. Ronen et al. (1988) have suggested that ground-water aquifers may contribute between 0.8 and 1.7 million t of nitrogen oxides annually, or between 10 and 20 per cent of total biospheric production.

The accelerated use of fertilisers in developed nations since the 1950s (Fig. 6.2) is one of the major reasons why the rate of cultural eutrophication has increased, though sewage effluent and runoff from urban areas are also contributory factors. The nutrient that is contributed most from fertilisers is nitrogen in the form of nitrates, which are very soluble and thus easily washed out of the soil to which they have been applied. Phosphate fertiliser, on the other hand, is not so readily soluble and although it contributes to cultural eutrophication much of the phosphorus that causes enrichment is derived from sewage sludge (which is also used as fertiliser). Because ni-trogen and phosphorus are essential plant nutrients, their abundance in a natural ecosystem will limit productivity, along with factors such as water and light availability. Thus, in a lake ecosystem the abundance of algae will be influenced by nutrient input from the catchment. Once fertilisers are ap-plied, the amount of nutrients entering the lake (and river) ecosystem will increase and promote algal population growth. This increase in primary production is initially beneficial, but as eutrophication proceeds the water quality will decline and adversely affect ecosystem function.

As algal productivity increases, algal blooms will occur and use up dissolved oxygen, and if dense algal mats build up they will limit the exchange of oxygen between the atmosphere and the water. Other organisms in the lake will die through lack of oxygen, which is also depleted by the enhanced decomposition of organic matter. Anaerobic conditions will thus develop and anaerobic decomposition along with the reduction of iron compounds to ferrous salts will cause discoloration of the water and produce hydrogen sulphide odour. As well as being aesthetically displeasing, these developments adversely affect water quality. The diversity of aquatic organisms, of both producer and consumer type, declines so that blue-green algae proliferate and only coarse fish species survive. Sediment input from the catchment will also cause the lake basin to silt up so that as eutrophication proceeds the water depth declines and hydroseral succession is accelerated. This latter is the process of vegetation colonisation that occurs as the lake ages: enhanced inputs of nutrients and sediments speed it up so that the lake ages more rapidly until eventually it becomes extinct. Not only are natural habitats like lakes affected in this way but the silting up of reservoirs can be a problem for domestic water supplies and be costly to remedy. The eutrophication of aquifers supplying domestic water may also be a hazard to human health and the amenity use of lakes and reservoirs may be considerably reduced. Nitrate pollution in rivers is also a serious problem. In the USA, for example, Smith *et al.* (1987) report data for the period 1974–81 from some 383 monitoring stations located in the nation's major river basins. In 116 of these, nitrate concentrations have increased, compared with a decrease in only 27. The most significant increases have been in drainage basins, such as the Grand River in Michigan, which are extensively cultivated. As Henderson-Sellers and Markland (1987) have discussed, there have also been instances where toxins have been produced by algae which are hazardous to animals or humans. They quote the example of secretions from the blue-green alga *Microcystis* which may have caused cattle deaths in subtropical areas.

Runoff from agricultural land can also cause cultural eutrophication of coastal regions and is made worse by inputs of sewage effluent and urban runoff. The effects of this nutrient enrichment tend to be most acute in shallow shelf areas and in enclosed estuaries where the nutrients are not rapidly and freely diluted by exchange of water with the open oceans. The Mediterranean Sea is a case in point since it occupies an enclosed basin and receives drainage from many intensively cultivated and densely populated nations. In the Gulf of Lyon, for example, Bellan-Santini and Leveau (1988) state that the River Rhône contributes nitrates and phosphates at concentrations which are eight to ten and three to ten times respectively higher than in deep Mediterranean waters. These inputs promote rapid phytoplankton growth which are similar to the algal blooms that occur in surface fresh waters. Marchetti *et al.* (1988) also report that algal blooms or 'red tides' frequently occur in the Adriatic Sea as a result of nutrient inputs from the River Po and are adversely affecting the tourist and fishing industries. The algal blooms consist of diatoms and dinoflagellates and an extreme case in 1984 involved the coverage of some 200 km of coastal waters from the mouth of the River Po to Ancona. According to Todini and Bizzarri (1988), these blooms are generally extensive enough to create anoxic conditions in the subsurface waters which causes high fish mortality and offensive odours.

Another example of coastal pollution due to cultural eutrophication is that of Chesapeake Bay on the east coast of the USA. As a result of deteriorating water and habitat quality in the area, the US Environmental Protection Agency (EPA) undertook a 5-year study, beginning in 1975, to examine the problem and devise a management strategy. Details of this study have been summarised by Makuch and Woodward (1987) and Bonner (1988). The area of the bay consists of $162\,000\,km^2$ and 50 per cent of the land-derived water enters via the Susquehanna River which contributes 40 per cent of the nitrogen and 21 per cent of the phosphorus. The EPA studies also revealed that the most significant source of these nutrients, 85 per cent of the nitrogen and 60 per cent of the phosphorus, originated from intensively farmed cropland and that livestock production also contributed to nutrient loading. The basis of the remedial programme that is now established is to improve water quality by adapting agricultural practices via an intensive educational programme. Participation in the project is voluntary but payments are available to farmers who institute best management practices. Monitoring programmes in the next few years will reveal how successful or otherwise these, and other measures to control point source pollution such as sewage, have been.

The control of eutrophication is thus a major problem in developing countries and both remedial and preventative measures are necessary to diminish it. The problem is compounded by the fact that even after nutrient inputs are curtailed eutrophication may continue for decades as nutrients are recycled from the deposited sediments and the biomass. Preventative measures may include legislation to limit the quality and quantity of discharge from industry, etc. and/or nutrient removal prior to discharge to reduce nutrient loading. This latter, though costly, can be readily applied to sewage disposal. Björk (1988) has described successful attempts at lake restoration, principally in Sweden, which involve sediment dredging and the construction of modern sewage-treatment plants that can effect the mechanical, biological and chemical removal of phosphorus. In Lake Biwa, Japan, legislation controlling the nutrient content of industrial and agricultural effluents, coupled with a ban on the use of phosphate-containing detergents, has reduced the concentrations of nitrogen and phosphorus entering the lake by 20 per cent since 1980, despite the fact that population and industry have continued to grow (Petts 1988). The problem of control is a much more difficult one where fertiliser runoff is concerned because it comes from a diffuse rather than point source. The only effective long-term solution will be to restrict the use of fertilisers and, as referred to in section 6.2.3, this could be achieved in Britain if those areas of the country suffering most acutely from this problem were targeted for agricultural extensification which is now required under the CAP. Even if this was implemented immediately, it would not instantly remove the problem and other remedial measures, as discussed in section 6.3.2, are necessary.

6.3.2 THE EFFECTS OF CULTURAL EUTROPHICATION ON DOMESTIC WATER SUPPLIES

Apart from accelerating the lake-ageing process, the intensive use of fertilisers in many developed countries is now considered to be responsible for the contamination of aquifers by high nitrate concentrations. In both Europe and the USA this has serious implications for the supply of domestic water since there is evidence that excess nitrates may be hazardous to human health.

Where agricultural land to which fertilisers are applied drains into or is underlain by porous rocks such as chalk, limestone and sandstone, nitrate that is not taken up by the crop will percolate in drainage water to the sub-strata beneath the water table. Addiscott (1988), quoting data collected from the Rothamsted Experimental Station, Harpenden, Britain, indicates that dur-ing a particularly wet spring rain can remove as much as 30 per cent (15 per cent is a more average value) of the nitrogen in fertiliser before it can be absorbed by the crop. However, Addiscott also points out that experiments using radioactive tracers show that a winter wheat crop, for example, to which 190 kg of nitrogen per hectare are applied as fertiliser, leaves only 1–5 kg in the soil after harvest. While this is a relatively small residual amount it appears that in the post-harvest period the soil can release consid-erably more nitrate that finds its way into aquifers. This latter, Addiscott (1988) believes, is derived from organic compounds containing nitrogen which reside in the topsoil and which, remaining unavailable to crops, are broken down by soil bacteria into nitrate. Apparently, autumnal conditions are particularly suitable for this process because the soil still retains warmth and is receiving increased moisture, but in the farming calendar it is a period when either the fields are bare after the summer harvest and/or contain a newly sown crop that is not yet able to make use of the available nitrate. Thus the Nitrate Co-ordination Group's (1986) conclusions suggest that the problem of eutrophication of aquifers is not confined to direct fertiliser use, though it remains a product of agricultural practices (including fertiliser treatment) that indirectly provide the organic residues in soil which promote such bacterial activity.

While the Rothamsted evidence is thought provoking as to causes, there is little doubt that enhanced nitrate levels in, for example, Britain, are rising. As Croll and Hayes (1988) have pointed out, the greatest increases in aquifer nitrate levels have occurred in the south and east of England. Lin-colnshire, Cambridgeshire and East Anglia have been particularly badly af-fected because they are the regions in which agriculture has become most intensified since the 1970s when Britain joined the EEC. As shown in Fig. 6.4, these areas contain some of the major aquifers that are tapped for dom-estic water supplies and as the graphs in Fig 6.4 show, these are the areas in which rivers also have unacceptably high nitrate levels. Similarly high ni-trate levels are characteristic of aquifers which are located in the agricultural areas of many developed nations. The problem in West Germany, for example, has been reviewed by Conrad (1988) where high nitrate concentra-tions have been recorded in ground-water which is used to supply some of the major cities such as Frankfurt, Bremen and Hanover. The problem is also acute in parts of the USA (Fairchild 1987). In Nebraska, for example, aver-age nitrate concentrations in ground-water increased by 25 per cent between the late 1960s and early 1970s (Canter 1987). A survey by Gormly and Spalding (1979) in Nebraska showed that in 183 out of 256 ground-water samples nitrate concentrations exceeded 10 mg l^{-1} and that most of this was derived from artificial fertiliser. Ground-water data from the Big Spring Ground Water Basin in Iowa (Libra *et al.* 1987) show that between 1965 and 1985 nitrate concentrations increased from *c.* 15 mg l^{-1} to *c.* 45 mg l^{-1}, which is attributed to a 250 per cent increase in nitrate fertiliser use on

A

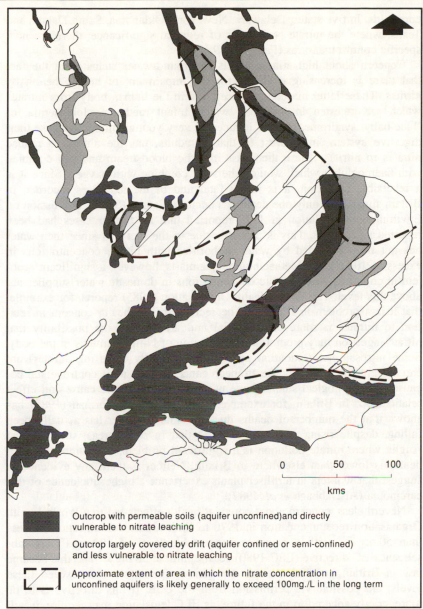

Fig. 6.4. (A) The outcrop of major aquifers in England and their susceptibility to nitrate pollution; (B) Mean annual nitrate concentrations in selected English rivers. (Based on Nitrate Coordination Group 1986.)

▨ Outcrop with permeable soils (aquifer unconfined)and directly vulnerable to nitrate leaching

▨ Outcrop largely covered by drift (aquifer confined or semi-confined) and less vulnerable to nitrate leaching

⬚ Approximate extent of area in which the nitrate concentration in unconfined aquifers is likely generally to exceed 100mg./L in the long term

B

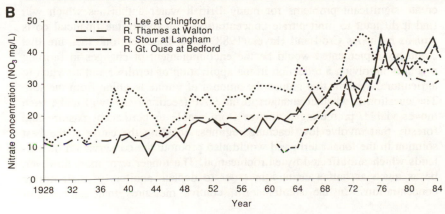

cornfields. In five states, Delaware, New York, Oklahoma, South Dakota and Texas, where the nitrate problem is of regional significance, there are now specific control measures (Fairchild 1987).

Concern about high nitrate levels in ground-water stems from the fact that there is increasing evidence for the impairment of human health by nitrites. These latter may be produced within the human body from nitrates which are ingested in food and water. Infant methaemoglobinaemia, or 'blue-baby' syndrome, may be induced in very young children because their digestive system, in contrast to that of adults, has the ability to reduce nitrates to nitrites. These then pass into the bloodstream and can combine with haemoglobin which would otherwise combine with oxygen. Since it is a reversible condition, it is rarely fatal and of the ten cases recorded in Britain since 1949 only one death has occurred: and a Royal Commission on Environmental Pollution in 1979 reported that no further cases had been reported since 1972. This is probably due to the fact that since then water has not been provided by water authorities with nitrate concentrations in excess of $100 \, \text{mg} \, l^{-1}$. Methaemoglobinaemia is, however, a significant problem in countries where nitrate concentrations in domestic water supplies are above this level. The World Health Organisation (1985) reports, for example, that it is a problem in Hungary. The second area of health concern in relation to nitrates is more controversial and arises from the possibility that nitrate ingestion may promote the production of N-nitrosamines in the body. Some nitrosamines (oxidation products of naturally occurring amines) are carcinogens that may produce stomach cancer. The issue is controversial because epidemiological studies have not revealed a specific cause and effect relationship. In Britain, for example, such a study by Forman (1985) has shown that the number of deaths due to stomach cancer has actually been falling, despite rising nitrate levels, and that in some areas, such as East Anglia where nitrate pollution is a significant problem, the number of such deaths is lower than elsewhere in Britain. Neither is there any evidence to suggest that workers in fertiliser plants experience a higher incidence of this carcinoma (Al-Dabbagh *et al.* 1987).

Nevertheless, concern about potential health effects led to a World Health Organisation recommendation in 1970 to limit nitrate concentrations to less than $50 \, \text{mg} \, l^{-1}$, with a maximum acceptable level of $100 \, \text{mg} \, l^{-1}$. A subsequent EEC directive (EEC 1980) set the limit at $50 \, \text{mg} \, l^{-1}$ and this became law in Britain in 1985, though derogations (permissions to exceed these levels) are possible via permission from the DoE. If this directive is to be more strictly adhered to in the future, as EEC legislation may require, it will create significant problems for many British water authorities which will find it difficult to limit nitrate concentrations. Inevitably the financial costs will be high. As Croll and Hayes (1988) have discussed, one measure that could be implemented would be the encouragement of changes in farming practices involving a reduction in the application of fertiliser and a switch to agricultural systems that reduce the amount of nitrate leaching from the soil. The question is whether changes in the CAP (section 6.2.3) will make such moves viable, promoting a change from arable to permanent pasture and forestry that involve low leaching regimes. Tackling the cause is the best solution in the longer term and would also promote the conservation of wetlands which are affected by eutrophication. The longer term may, however, be as much as half a century in order to deplete aquifers of their nitrate concentrations. In the shorter term, control measures that can be implemented by water authorities are already available and are, in some cases, being used. According to Croll and Hayes (1988) the cheapest and most widely used control option is that of blending high-nitrate and low-nitrate water within a service reservoir or water tower. Other measures include the removal of nitrates by ion exchange, which has been successfully applied by Anglian Water, and removal by microbiological denitrification. Both of these methods are complex and expensive. The Nitrate Co-ordination Group (1986) has estimated that the total cost of complying with the EEC 50 mg l^{-1} standard will be more than £199 million over the next 20 years and will be particularly expensive for those water authorities that operate in regions where there are already high nitrate levels.

6.3.3 SALINISATION

Salinisation is a process whereby the concentration of salts, notably sulphates, chlorides and carbonates, increases in soils, ground-water and surface waters as a result of the exposure of water to the atmosphere. As is evident in many parts of the arid and semi-arid world, these salts concentrate naturally, giving rise to landscape features such as salt flats. In these areas, evaporation rates are high so that saline water is brought to the surface by capillary action; once the water itself has been entrained into the atmosphere, accumulations of salt are left in the soil. Such salt accumulations can deter vegetation growth, leaving the regolith susceptible to wind erosion and to water erosion when storm events occur. Human activity, via agricultural systems which depend on irrigation water, can aggravate these difficulties by accelerating the exposure of water to the atmosphere. In extreme cases, salt concentrations can become so high that land has to be abandoned for agricultural purposes. Moreover, surface waters and ground-waters may develop high salt concentrations where they are in receipt of drainage waters from irrigated areas; the problem is compounded (as is shown in Fig. 6.5) when these waters are used to supply further irrigation systems.

Figure 6.5 illustrates the various ways that irrigation programmes can influence salinity concentrations. From this it is apparent that, regardless of the mechanisms involved, it is the transfer of water from concentrated to diffuse sources that is the major agent of environmental change. Salinisation is a significant problem for irrigated soils in climatic zones where evapotranspiration exceeds precipitation, especially where drainage is inadequate and where rates of water application do not exceed the rates necessary to promote leaching. Goudie (1986) has drawn attention to the fact that salinity problems may also occur in coastal regions, as in Israel and California, where overpumping of fresh water from aquifers that are liable to marine incursion causes the entry of salt water into the aquifer and its rise to the surface. There is also evidence that the removal of natural vegetation can alter local hydrological cycles so that the reduced interception of rainfall and reduced evapotranspiration rates allow more water to penetrate soils and thus promote a rise in ground-water. Subsequent evaporation leads to salt deposition which may then give rise to higher salt concentrations in stream drainage.

According to Earth Report (1988) there are some 2.2 million km^2 of irrigated land on the earth's surface of which between 30 and 80 per cent suffer to some extent from salinisation, alkalinisation and waterlogging.

Alkalinisation occurs where the salts consist of sodium compounds, mainly carbonates and bicarbonates, that lead to loss of soil structure and the development of a hard crust that makes agriculture impossible. Some 900 km^2 of land are thus affected in the USSR, though the problem is most widespread in Australia where some 3000 km^2 of land are so degraded (Earth Report 1988). Similarly, permanent waterlogging may occur in areas where continuous irrigation is practised so that the land is never allowed a fallow period. The outcome is a rise in the water table which promotes salinisation as well as causing waterlogging: the latter is now a problem in 10 per cent of the world's irrigated lands and, as Shanan (1987) has discussed, it impairs crop productivity by reducing the amount of air in the root zone.

While these problems are particularly acute in developing countries (section 7.2.2), they are also a source of concern in developed nations. In the USA, for example, between 25 and 35 per cent of all the irrigated land suffers from excess salinity (Earth Report 1988), and in Australia (section 4.4.3) the problem is epitomised in the Murray River basin where Peck *et al.* (1983) have estimated that irrigation practices contribute between 36 and 52 per cent of net salt inputs. Moreover, there are examples of the spread of

Fig. 6.5. The interrelationships between irrigation systems and salinisation.

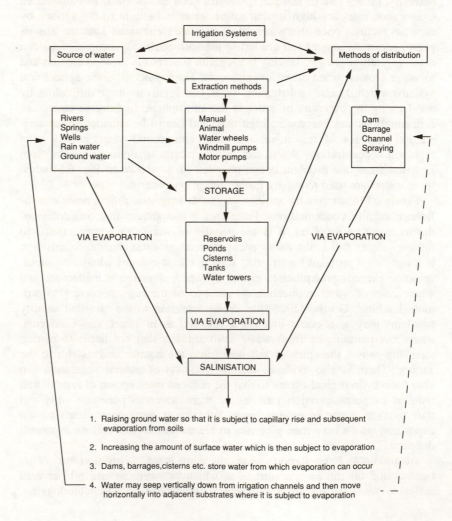

1. Raising ground water so that it is subject to capillary rise and subsequent evaporation from soils

2. Increasing the amount of surface water which is then subject to evaporation

3. Dams, barrages, cisterns etc. store water from which evaporation can occur

4. Water may seep vertically down from irrigation channels and then move horizontally into adjacent substrates where it is subject to evaporation

saline seeps (saline soils that have formed in non-irrigated areas) due to geomorphological and hydrological processes which have been exacerbated by agricultural practices. These have been discussed by Daniels (1987) and Berg *et al.* (1987), citing examples from North America, and are attributed to the movement of water through soil profiles below the rooting zone into salt-rich bedrock which eventually reappears at the surface. Any land-use practices that accelerate the rate of down-profile water movement will exacerbate what are essentially natural processes. In Harper County, Oklahoma, for example, Berg *et al.* (1987) state that the incidence of saline seeps increased between 1975 and 1985, by which date 1300 ha of 65 000 ha of wheatland was known to be affected. This accelerated growth of seeps is attributed to the maintenance of a summer fallow when most (62 per cent) of the annual precipitation occurs. Thus, water freely percolates through the soil into underlying salt-rich Permian redbeds and then reappears in lower landscape positions where saline seeps develop.

Environmental problems associated with irrigation schemes in the USA are exemplified in California where water is transported from the Colorado River via a 714 km aqueduct system (Moran *et al.* 1986). On its journey, through an arid or semi-arid region, more than 10 per cent of the water evaporates, thus increasing salt concentrations which are high enough to warrant mixing with water from sources in northern California in an effort to meet the standards necessary for drinking-water provision. The use of this water to irrigate crops in the Imperial and Coachella Valleys of southern California ensures that the water becomes even more saline, creating water-quality problems in the lower Colorado as it flows through Mexico. To mitigate these problems, an agreement was reached in 1973 between the USA and Mexico, involving the USA in a $350 million desalinisation project at Yuma, Arizona. Water quality is thus being maintained only at considerable cost.

According to El-Ashry and Gibbons (1988), salinity is the most important water-quality problem throughout the arid and semi-arid western states of the USA, and results not only from irrigation practices but inputs into rivers from saline springs and ground-water originating in salt-rich rock formations. The cost is considerable in terms of crop losses, the corrosive effects on piping and domestic and industrial appliances, and increased costs of water treatment. In the San Joaquin Valley of California, for example, crop yields have declined by 10 per cent, amounting to annual financial losses of $31.2 million (El-Ashry and Gibbons 1986). In the Grand Valley of the upper Colorado improvements to irrigation techniques and water-transport systems have been initiated. Howe and Ahrens (1988) have shown that here salinity problems stem from 25 000 ha of land that is irrigated by unlined canals and the receipt of ground-water from the Mancos shale formation, a high salt-bearing shale, into which the valley is incised. Lining part of the Government Highline Canal and its lateral channels has already reduced salt loads entering the river, though the cost of expanding the scheme to other parts of the valley will be considerable (in excess of $1.5 million). Other remedial measures include the use of evaporation ponds to reduce the salt content of water after it has been used for irrigation and before it is returned to the river, as well as the use of crop rotations involving salt-tolerant and salt-sensitive crops. However, as Canter (1986) points out, the recycling of water must be carefully managed to avoid the development of even higher salinity concentrations and subsequent impairment of crop productivity.

Salinisation is also a major problem in Australia and is particularly acute in the Murray–Darling River basin in southeast Australia where naturally high salt levels are augmented by the receipt of drainage from irrigated lands. Pigram (1986) states that; 'Much of the problem stems from the fact that the river and its tributaries form the drainage system as well as the main source of water for irrigation in southeast Australia, and for domestic water for South Australia.' This is Australia's largest river system, draining more than 1 million km^2 and 81 per cent of its annual runoff of 2.3×10^{13} l is used for irrigation. The river basin has also been modified to regulate river flow for various purposes such as improvement in navigation, flood control, hydroelectric power as well as domestic and industrial water supply. The Menindee Lakes Scheme, completed in 1960, is one such example which allows flood waters to be stored in a series of basins in the Darling catchment that were hitherto dry depressions. Evaporation from these water bodies is itself a cause of increased salt concentrations, creating problems for water supplies to Broken Hill and for downstream consumers. In the Murray basin, rising salinity levels in soils and the river itself are adversely affecting irrigated agricultural systems.

Rising salinity levels are not, however, entirely a consequence of human interference in the drainage basin. As Pigram (1986) has pointed out, the bedrock in the region, having been deposited in either a marine environment or derived from lacustrine and floodplain sediments, gives rise to groundwater with naturally high salt concentrations. As well as contributing relatively saline water to the river basin, these sedimentary formations contribute to relatively high salt concentrations in soils. Irrigation merely accentuates the problem by enhancing the amount of surface water which is then subject to evaporation and which encourages the water table to rise via capillary action. In some instances waterlogging occurs in the root zone and salinity problems may be aggravated by seepage which also occurs in non-irrigated soils. Moreover, surface and subsurface drainage from irrigated land in the Murrumbidgee, Shepparton and Kerang regions into the Murray River can adversely affect agricultural productivity downstream in the Sunraysia and Riverland regions. In the upper Murray, Pigram quotes typical salinity levels of 40–50 ppm of total dissolved solids but nearer Adelaide, average salt concentrations are 400–500 ppm. This has repercussions, not only for agriculture in the lower Murray, but also for Adelaide's domestic water supply.

In order to mitigate these problems and to encourage better use of water resources, various measures have been introduced since the late 1970s. Tiled drains and piped water supplies have led in some areas to a considerable reduction in the amount of water needed for irrigation and improved drainage has reduced the amount of waterlogging. Pumping from shallow aquifers can also reduce waterlogging and salt concentrations in the root zone. As well as on-farm measures, some of which carry a subsidy for implementation, there have been extensive public engineering projects to combat the problems of the Murray–Darling basin. These involve pumping water into evaporation basins, some of which are used to harvest salt for industrial use. Improved management, which needs to circumvent the problems of inter-state and inter-agency jurisdiction over land-use and water resources, is clearly essential if such environmental degradation is to be halted.

Another example of salinisation due to irrigation is that of the Aral Sea in the USSR. In this case, unlike the examples given above, salinisation and desiccation are an indirect rather than direct effect of irrigation. Micklin (1988) has pointed out that between 1960 and 1987 the level of the Aral Sea has declined by 13 m and its area decreased by 40 per cent. Located in the desert region of the south-central Soviet Union, the Aral Sea is a large, shallow, saline water body, the water level of which is determined by the balance between inflow from rivers, ground-water and precipitation; and outflow via evaporation. While the lake has a long history of flooding and desiccation associated with the climatic changes of the Quaternary period, its current problems are mainly the result of human activity, though periods of low precipitation in 1974–75 and 1982–86 are also contributory factors. The major reason for creation of a negative water balance has been the removal of water from the Amu Dar'ya and Syr Dar'ya, rivers that normally contribute most of the Aral Sea's water, for irrigation. As Micklin (1988) establishes, this is not a recent innovation in the Aral basin; even in 1900 some 3 million ha of land were irrigated, increasing to 5 million ha by 1960.

By 1985, the irrigated area had increased to nearly 6.5 million ha, and reached 7.6 million ha by 1987 requiring some 104 km^3 of water. This increase in water use has not been counterbalanced by reductions in natural losses and has been aggravated by expansion of the irrigated region into dry steppe (e.g. Golodnaya in Hungary) which has required vast quantities of water to mitigate soil-moisture deficit, and the construction of huge reservoirs which expose water to the atmosphere and thus promote evaporation. The Karakum Canal also diverts at least 14 km^3 of water annually from the Aral Sea. All of these changes have created what various Soviet scientists have described as an ecological disaster, giving rise to dust and salt storms, ground-water depression as well as concerns about water supplies and economic losses in agriculture, fisheries and hunting and trapping. There are also indications that such large-scale desiccation has prompted climatic change involving a trend towards continentality with a decline in relative humidity and a reduction in the length of the growing season. The exposure of some 27 000 km^2 of bottom sediments between 1960 and 1987 has resulted not only in massive salt accumulation that inhibits revegetation but a loose mobile surface that is susceptible to deflation. Micklin (1988) indicates that c. 43 million t of salt are removed from the Aral basin annually and are deposited as aerosols in rain and dew over 1.5×10^5 to 2×10^5 km^2. Although calcium sulphate is the most abundant salt, environmental degradation is created by sodium chloride and sodium sulphate, which are particularly toxic to plants and which have contributed to crop losses on an economically significant scale. Salinisation of the lake itself has adversely affected aquatic productivity: only four of twenty-four native fish now remain and commercial fish catches have virtually disappeared with associated employment consequences. Declining surface water levels have also adversely affected ecologically significant deltaic regions, initiating desertification and habitat destruction so that commercial hunting and trapping have declined. Depressed ground-water levels have caused the desiccation of wells and springs and created problems for the supply of drinking water. Micklin reports that there is not yet a scheme in place to alleviate these problems, although there is considerable local pressure for the resurrection of a plan proposed in the early 1980s to divert waters from the Ob and Irtysh Rivers of Siberia. The environmental consequences of such a scheme may, however, be just as detrimental as the problems it seeks to address.

6.4 THE ENVIRONMENTAL IMPACT OF CROP PROTECTION CHEMICALS

Crop-protection chemicals are compounds that are artificially produced on a large scale to improve the efficiency of crop production by eliminating competition from crops, protecting them from disease and enhancing or controlling growth. The vast majority of crop-protection chemicals are pesticides, the objective of which is to reduce or eliminate plant and animal species which detract from the crop biomass by either, in the case of plants, competing for light and nutrients or, in the case of animals, by consuming part of the biomass. Because such chemicals exterminate organisms they are also referred to as biocides and, as shown in Table 6.3, there are various groups of pesticides that are designated according to target species. Crop-protection chemicals also include substances that have been developed to safeguard crops and livestock from disease (the latter are generally referred to as animal health products) as well as plant growth regulators (PGRs), the objective of which is to influence the manner of crop growth so that harvesting can be made

Table 6.3. Pesticide categories.

	Herbicides	Fungicides	Insecticides	Acaricides	Nematicides	Molluscicides	Rodenticides	Plant Growth Regulators
Target Organisms	Weeds	Fungi	Insects	Mites	Nematode worms	Snails, slugs	Rodents	Crops
Examples of Types of pesticides and typical products	**Phenoxyacids** 2, 4 - D MCPA	**Pyrimidines** Ethirimol Fenarimol	**Organochlorines** DDT Dieldrin	**Organochlorines** Dicofol	**Fumigants** Methylbromide Dibromochloropropane	**Aldehydes** Metaldehyde	**Coumarins** Warfarin Coumatetryl Brodifacoum	**Hormones** Gibberellic acid Ethylene
	Bipyriliums Paraquat Diquat	**Alanines** Furalaxyl Ofurace	**Organophosphates** Terbuphos Dimethoate	**Organotins** Cyhexatin	**Carbamates** Aldicarb Oxamyl	**Carbamates** Methiocarb Thiocarboxime	**Inorganic** Zinc phosphide	**Triazoles** Paclobutrazol
	Phosphonates Glyphosate	**Triazoles** Triadimefon Flutriafol	**Carbamates** Aldicarb Carbofuran	**Tetrazines** Clofentezine	**Organophosphates** Fenamiphos			
	Pyrazoliums Difenzoquat		**Pyrethroids** Permethrin Cypermethrin Fenvalerate Tefluthrin Cyhalothrin					
	Aryloxy - Phenoxyacetic acids Diclofop-methyl Fluazifop-butyl							
	Nitrodiphenylethers Fomesafen							
	Acetanilides Alachlor							

more efficient or crops can be manipulated to maximise their use of
light and nutrients. Such chemicals, in conjunction with plant and animal breeding programmes that began with the initial domestication of
particular wild species *c*. 10 kyr BP (section 3.3.1), underpin modern agricultural systems in both the developing and developed nations. As will
be discussed in section 8.4, the methods of both the crop-protection industry and plant and animal breeding are beginning to break new
ground via genetic engineering.

Crop protection is not entirely an adjunct of twentieth-century agriculture. Historically, crop rotation (sections 4.2 and 4.3) was used as a
means of promoting the biological control of so-called 'pests', though
rather ineffectually in relation to modern chemically based procedures.
Hand weeding to remove competition from undesired plants has also
been practised since antiquity. Crop-protection chemicals are, however,
a relatively recent development, emanating from the post-Second World
War ethos of politically stimulated agricultural production. By this time,
artificial fertilisers were being widely used (section 6.3.1) and consequent increases in crop productivity no doubt stimulated the development of other artificially produced chemicals that could magnify plant
and animal productivity with little concomitant increase in labour.
Moreover, wartime research into nerve gases and deforestation agents
provided an embryonic chemical data base from which many modern
crop protection chemicals have been derived. These developments occurred against a backdrop of growing world hunger and rampant diseases like malaria that were (and still are) transmitted via insect vectors.

Inevitably crop-protection chemicals promote environmental change
because their primary objective is the deflection of energy flows, which
are the basis of ecosystem function, from unwanted components of the
trophic structure to the harvest. Crop-protection chemicals have their
protagonists and their antagonists because there have been both successes and failures ecologically and environmentally; because their
misuse can present a threat to human health and because they constitute
'big business' for agricultural concerns that are almost exclusively based
in the developed nations of Europe, North America and Japan.

According to the *UK pesticide guide* (Ivens 1988) there are some 475
MAFF-approved products that are currently available to agriculturalists
in Britain for the management of pests, weeds and diseases or for crop
growth regulation. There are numerous others which, although still used
in many developing countries, are no longer sanctioned in Europe and
the USA; add to that those new compounds which are in the development stages and those which are currently receiving approval from registration bodies (such as MAFF in the UK and the EPA in the USA), and
the sum total represents a powerful array of chemical tools developed
by humans to manipulate what are essentially natural processes of energy transfer. Here the successes and failures of some of the earlier organochlorine and organophosphate insecticides will be examined as well
as the trend towards the use of environmentally benign products which
began in the 1970s with the pyrethroids in response to the institution of
more rigorous registration requirements. The final section will consider
the impact of a range of herbicides.

6.4.1 ORGANOCHLORINE AND ORGANOPHOSPHATE COMPOUNDS: SUCCESSES AND FAILURES

As Brader (1987) has discussed, the history of widely available crop-protection chemicals emanates from the 1940s, prior to which the elimination of pests was mainly undertaken by the use of crop rotations and weeding. Such practices are, however, not in keeping with the philosophy of modern agricultural systems wherein monoculture and the use of minimum labour are the norms. As the latter have developed (sections 4.3 and 6.2), increasing reliance has been placed on synthetic compounds designed to control pests chemically and has replaced biological control which is intrinsic to crop rotation systems. Among the earliest synthetic insecticides were the thiocyanates produced in the 1930s which, because of the presence of the chemically reactive thiocyanate group acting as a toxophore (i.e. toxin-carrying group), behaved as a broad-spectrum insecticide. Its use as the commercial product Lethane was limited owing to its toxic effect on non-target organisms and the development in 1939 of DDT. The latter, an organochlorine compound, is probably one of the most publicised pesticides because, along with related compounds, it has proved to be a very significant environmental contaminant. Similar publicity has been achieved by organophosphate insecticides which owe their origins to research during the Second World War into potential nerve gases.

When it was first discoved to have insecticidal properties, DDT was heralded as a major breakthrough in pest control, not just for crop pest control but also for public health purposes. According to Horn (1988), DDT was first used as a crop-protection chemical in 1941 to control an outbreak of Colorado potato beetle in Switzerland. It was also used on a large scale during the Second World War to prevent disease outbreaks among civilians and army personnel; an epidemic of typhus, for example, in Italy in 1943 was arrested by DDT sprays to control body lice. For several years after it was a major adjunct of the World Health Organisation's (WHO) malarial control programme. For several reasons which have been discussed in detail by M B Green *et al.* (1987), DDT was considered to be a major step forward in pest control. Firstly, it was thought to have a low acute toxicity to mammals which gave it a big advantage over the thiocyanates; nor did it cause skin irritation so that handling was relatively safe. Secondly, it is a stable compound that does not readily degrade, which provides advantages for storage and transport. Thirdly, it was found to be active against a wide variety of insect pests, requiring only cuticle contact and not ingestion via the stomach. Finally, its manufacture is relatively easy and can be undertaken in rapidly constructed plant. The second point in particular is now known to be environmentally disadvantageous: not only is DDT chemically stable to the conditions (e.g sunlight, water) it meets after spraying, but it largely withstands metabolic processes non-target organisms use to detoxify exogenous chemicals. Nevertheless, its success as a combatant against widespread disease is unquestionable, especially in view of the crisis period in which it was developed.

In terms of environmental impact the use of DDT has had some disastrous consequences. Although it is not very soluble in water, a characteristic that was originally thought to be advantageous, DDT and its metabolites

DDD and DDE are readily transferred through the trophic structure of eco-systems, i.e. the food chains and food webs. This occurs because these sub-stances are stored in oils and fats that constitute part of the body tissues of animals and are passed on from one trophic level to the next, often under-going a process known as biological magnification. This means that the higher up in the trophic structure an organism is, the more DDT and residues it will contain. For example, Woodell *et al.* (1967) have examined such residues in the components of an estuarine ecosystem on the east coast of the USA and found that while the concentration of such compounds in the water is only 0.000 05 ppm the concentration increases to between 23 and 26 ppm in fish-eating birds which are at the head of the food chain. High concentrations of these compounds are now generally considered to be one of the main reasons why populations of predatory birds have declined, either by causing death directly or by impairing reproductive ability. Potts (1986), for example, cites eggshell thinning due to such residues as a major reason why there has been a decline in populations of the peregrine falcon and sparrow-hawk. In addition, broad-spectrum insecticides like DDT can have adverse effects on insect pest populations over a longer term because they alter the natural relationship between pests and their predators, which are often other insects. Thus they can adversely influence natural biological con-trol. Horn (1988) cites the example of the European red spider mite, which did not become a pest of apple crops until after the use of DDT and organo-phosphorus compounds which effectively eliminated the mite's natural pre-dators. A similar case of disruption of biological control has been described by Dempster (1967, 1968a, b, c) who has examined the impact of DDT on cabbage white butterfly (*Pieris rapae*) populations in a crop of Brussels sprouts. The initial impact of spraying brought about a significant reduction in the pest, but because of the chemical's non-target-specific activity the natural predators of the pest were also eliminated. Ultimately, the cabbage white resumed its significance as a pest because of this and because the persistence of DDT in the soil prevented ground-living predators from re-gaining pre-application population levels.

However, DDT is not the only organochlorine insecticide to promote un-expected and unwanted ecological consequences. Aldrin, dieldrin and endrin (cyclodienes) all derive from the same chemical family and dieldrin, in par-ticular, has had a considerable environmental impact. Its use and effects have been reviewed by Moore (1983) and Sheail (1985), both of whom de-scribe its effects on birds of prey. The use of dieldrin as both a sheep-dip and seed dressing, and the fact that it is more toxic to mammals than DDT (Green *et al.* 1987), has caused declines in populations of birds of prey and, according to Earth Report (1988), to declines in otter populations in Britain. Earth Report (1988) also cites the example of declines in sandwich tern populations in the Wadden Sea of the Netherlands where the number of breeding pairs fell from more than 40 000 in the 1940s to only 1500 in 1964. As in the case of DDT, biological magnification occurs as concentra-tions of fat-soluble residues of these compounds increase with trophic pre-eminence.

The tale is, unfortunately, similar as far as organophosphorus compounds are concerned; not because they are ineffective as pesticides but because some have had long-term effects that were not envisaged at the time they were conceived. In these compounds the toxophore is a phosphorus-contain-ing group attached to a variety of organic molecules designed overall to attack insect nervous systems. Examples of the very large number of organo-phosphorus compounds that have been used as insecticides are given in Table 6.3. Closely related to this category, with the same mode of action, are the carbamates such as aldicarb and carbofuran. The environmental impact of both groups has been discussed by Dempster (1987) who points out that the organophosphates replaced organochlorine compounds for the treatment of cereal seeds to control wheat bulb fly. The use of carbophenothion in particular resulted in several cases of geese poisoning; in 1971 500 greylag geese died after feeding on recently sown fields and in 1974–75 deaths of both greylag and pinkfooted geese occurred. Moreover, spraying of oilseed rape with another organophosphate, triazophos, has caused the death of honey-bees.

Fig. 6.6. Toxicity tests required for the registration of a new pesticide by the US Environmental Protection Agency. (Based on Cardona 1987.)

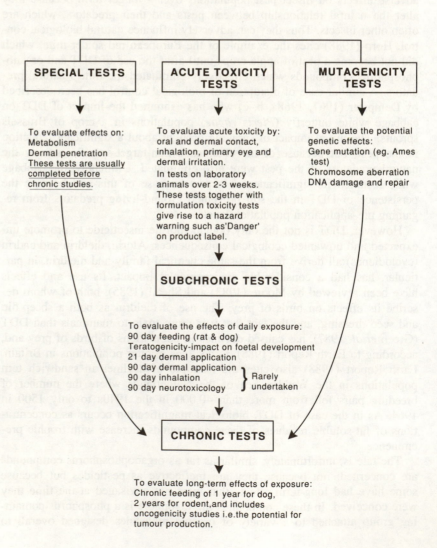

6.4.2 MIMICKING NATURAL INSECTICIDES; THE PYRETHROIDS

The controversy surrounding the environmental impact of many of the earlier pesticides has resulted in much more stringent registration requirements in developed nations. Registration includes legislative measures that are designed to protect the environment and to promote human safety, and are based on risk assessment and risk management. As stated above, the registration authority in Britain is the MAFF and in the USA it is the EPA. The toxicology requirements of the latter for registration of a new pesticide are given in Fig. 6.6. Details of the environmental tests that are necessary are given in Table 6.4. Because of these measures, it can take up to 10 years from the time that a new compound is synthesised in the laboratory to when it is available for marketing. Moreover, the cost is considerable and while it varies from product to product, Thomas (1987) believes that the total cost of research and development, including manufacturing plant, may well be in excess of £15 million. For example, in the case of the pyrethroids (see below), laboratory tests on fish established the need for a more in-depth study involving the full life cycle costing up to £250 000 just for this small part of the registration requirements. Field studies on non-target organisms may cost in excess of £1 million, as do the mandatory 2-year feeding studies.

Economic considerations, coupled with the fact that insects may rapidly become immune to pesticides (the phenomenon of *resistance*) and the increasing concern of environmentalists, stimulated the post-war chemical industry to seek new compounds derived from natural products. Attention was

Table 6.4. Environmental tests required for the registration of a new pesticide by the US EPA. (B D Cavell pers. comm.)

---

1. Metabolism studies in crops and animals

A. Identification of crop metabolites

B. Identification of rotated crop metabolites

T C. Feeding radiolabelled pesticide and/or plant metabolites to ruminant (eg. goat) and hen, followed by identification of metabolites in tissues, milk and eggs.

T D. Determination of pesticide accumulation in fish and identification of metabolites

3. Residue Studies

A. Analysis of pesticide and metabolite residues in:
  i.   Crops and processed crops
  ii. Rotated crops
  T iii. Animal tissues, milk, eggs.
  iv. Soil
  T v. Water (for aquatic pesticides)

T B. Run-off studies (for pesticides toxic to fish)

T C. Groundwater studies and analysis for pesticides which leach

2. Environmental studies in the laboratory

A. Identification of products of hydrolysis and photolysis in water, soil and air.

B. Identification of metabolites formed in soil under aerobic and anaerobic conditions

C. Soil leaching studies on the pesticide and its soil metabolites.

4. Ecology tests

A. Laboratory tests on non-target organisms:
  i.   Fish toxicity (acute and partial life cycle
  T ii. Fish full lifecycle
  iii. Toxicity to *Daphnia* (acute)
  T iv. Toxicity to *Daphnia* (lifecycle)
  v.   Toxicity to birds
  vi. Effects on bird reproduction
  vii. Effects on bees

T B. Mesocosm studies involving the identification of pesticide effects on aquatic organisms and fish in synthetic ponds

T C. Other field studies determined by laboratory tests eg. monitoring pesticide residue levels in avian diet if pesticide is toxic to birds

T : Denotes studies that have been triggered by laboratory studies which suggest adverse effects.

turned to the so-called *insect powder* which was used as an insecticide in the nineteenth century. This is derived from the dried flower heads of pyrethrum (*Chrysanthemum cinerariaefolium*), a plant native to the Caucasus–Iran region of Asia and to the Adriatic coast of Yugoslavia (Davies 1985). Subsequently, pyrethrum was grown commercially in East Africa as a source of pyrethrins which are the active insecticidal compounds. This was the basis from which a new range of insecticides, the pyrethroids, have been developed. As Davies indicates, the pyrethrins, once their chemical structures were ascertained, provided a template for the development of the pyrethroids which are synthetic analogues.

As shown in Table 6.3, there are now a range of pyrethroids available that represent the culmination of some 60 years of research, much of which was undertaken at Rothamsted Experimental Station in Britain and subsequently continued by several chemical companies such as Sumitomo, Shell, Roussel Uclaf and ICI. The latter, for example, marketed permethrin in 1977. This, together with cypermethrin, deltamethrin and fenvalerate are broad-spectrum contact insecticides which are active against lepidopterous larvae and are thus suitable for use in cotton crops where the most significant pests are the cotton bollworm and tobacco budworm. The advantages of pyrethroid insecticides relate to their non-susceptibility to biological magnification. As Hill (1985) has pointed out, there is no evidence to show that this occurs in food chains as it does with DDT. Moreover, the toxicological effects of the pyrethroids on mammals, as deduced from tests required by the EPA (see Fig. 6.6) appear to be relatively slight (Litchfield 1985) and then only at higher dosages than would be normally applied in crop spraying. This latter is another advantage of the pyrethroids: they are so potent as insecticides that only low dosages are required to bring about a substantial decrease in insect populations. Green *et al.* (1987) advise that an application rate of only *c*. 50 g ha^{-1} is necessary and that new products may have an application rate of as little as 5 g ha^{-1} in some crops. Thus, while such compounds are difficult and expensive to produce they are still cost-effective for the farmer to use.

Leahy (1985) has also reviewed existing data on the fate of pyrethroids in the environment. The use of radiolabelled pyrethroids (i.e. molecules containing radioactive carbon) in field experiments has shown that they are easily degraded, especially under aerobic soil conditions. This is due to their chemical structure which still retains some of the biodegradable features of the pyrethrins. Even under anaerobic conditions, breakdown occurs via similar pathways to produce carbon dioxide. The rate of degradation varies; cypermethrin, for example, has a half-life ranging from 1 to 10 weeks and permethrin has a half-life of 5–55 days. Moreover, leaching experiments in soils suggest that once in the soil pyrethroids are virtually immobile, largely because they are hydrophobic which means that they do not readily dissolve in soil water and bind instead with the organic component of the soil. Thus, because of rapid degradation and immobility, there is less chance that pyrethroids will contaminate the environment beyond the site of application and to date there have been no deleterious effects noted on soil microflora and microfauna. There is, however, evidence to show that pyrethroids are toxic to fish. Hill (1985) reports that fish are five times more sensitive to pyrethroids than mammals and that pyrethroids can deplete populations of aquatic arthropods, though in the case of the latter, recovery can be rapid. Fish toxicity is a disadvantage for treating rice crops, because fish are often present in paddy fields and may be harvested for human consumption. As a result, one of the goals of the pesticide industry is to develop pyrethroids that are less toxic to fish than those currently available. This is an important market because rice is grown on a widespread basis as a staple crop.

Among the pyrethroids to reach the market recently is tefluthrin. This is the first pyrethroid designed specifically as a soil insecticide for the treatment of soil pests mainly in corn (maize) crops. Such insects, like rootworm and cutworm, are usually treated by carbamates and organophosphates, the disadvantages of which include their toxicity to non-target organisms and their susceptibility to leaching into ground water. Tefluthrin is more potent than these older insecticides while retaining acceptable toxicity levels on non-target species including mammals. The trials which were conducted on tefluthrin as a prerequisite to registration in the USA further indicate that it is not toxic to seeds and will not give rise to contamination of ground-water via leaching (ICI promotional literature).

Clearly, the pyrethroids represent an effective group of insecticides that have been shown, after over 10 years of extensive use, to present minimal environmental risks. Whether this remains the case as their use increases and more monitoring programmes are instituted remains to be seen.

6.4.3 HERBICIDES

Discussion here will be limited to the environmental effects of the phenoxy-acids, the bipyridyliums, glyphosate and some of the more recently developed selective herbicides. These have been chosen because they not only reflect the chronological development of herbicides since the Second World War but also because their use has both solved and stimulated agronomic problems relating to weed control.

The phenoxyacid herbicides, which include 2,4-D (2,4-dichlorophenoxyacetic acid) and MCPA (4-chloro-2-methylphenoxyacetic acid), were developed as a result of chemical research during the Second World War and are among the first of the so-called hormone herbicides. They have the capability of eliminating broad-leaved weeds and have been widely used in the management of cereal crops since they have only very limited effects on monocotyledons. According to Green *et al.* (1987) these herbicides were modelled on the plant hormone, auxin, which controls cell elongation and root development and their mode of action involves the causation of excessive growth in certain plant tissues that ultimately causes death. They were cheap to produce and showed low toxicity to humans and other mammals. In terms of the environment, one of the most significant effects of these chemicals has been a massive reduction in broad-leaved species in both cultivated fields and neighbouring field margins and hedgerows which have also been affected by imprecisely directed foliar spraying. Moore (1983), for example, reports that the use of MCPA in England has depleted poppy (*Papaver* spp.) populations but has also led to an increase in populations of wild oats (*Avena fatua*). This latter, since it is a monocotyledon, has flourished because, like the cereal crop that the herbicides were designed to optimise, it is not greatly affected by phenoxy acids. In addition, Potts (1986) has reviewed the evidence that relates the decline in partridges in Britain and Europe at least in part to the use of herbicides, including the use of phenoxy acids. Herbicides have contributed to this because they eliminate weeds on which insects feed; these insects and their larvae are essential for the survival of partridge chicks. This is another example of the disruption of food chains by pesticide and herbicide use that has had unforeseen repercussions. The proliferation of wild oats has created another agronomic problem since it is just as much an unwanted 'pest' of cereal crops as the broad-leaved species it has replaced. This has resulted in the development of a range of new herbicides such as difenzoquat to eliminate wild oats and prompted the search for much more species-specific herbicides.

In the 1950s, a new group of broad-spectrum herbicides were produced which were designed to eliminate all plant species. This may seem an unlikely target for the farmer, but the objective was to remove any competition from arable fields prior to seeding and thus facilitate 'no tillage' agricultural practices which eliminate ploughing and render the soil less susceptible to erosion. The best-known of these chemicals are paraquat and diquat, the bipyridylium herbicides. Their mode of action involves inhibition of photosynthesis. Their use eliminated the need for pre-seeding preparation, especially as these substances are rapidly immobilised and inactivated when they enter the soil system. As Kirkwood (1987) has pointed out, both of these products have proved successful, not only because they are very effective herbicides but also because they facilitated the development of direct drilling. This is another aspect of 'no tillage' practices and allows the almost simultaneous application of herbicide, crop seed and fertiliser, once again reducing the time and labour required for crop setting and facilitating the maintenance of crop residues as soil-cohesives. There is, however, some concern about the longer-term environmental efficacy of these compounds; de Haan (1987), for example, has suggested that their use on sandy soils should be excluded because of the inadequacy of cation exchange capacity to completely bind these herbicides. The inference from this is that soil water may contaminate aquatic ecosystems where these active ingredients are very toxic to fish. Paraquat in particular is also toxic to humans and mammals, and because of this it has attracted publicity in cases where it has been swallowed accidentally, or deliberately in suicide attempts. These are operator-use problems which can occur with any toxic chemical (just as drug misuse occurs) and must be weighed against the benefits of the chemical in question.

Glyphosate is another broad-spectrum herbicide that has similar properties to the bipyridylium herbicides. It is an organophosphorus compound (unrelated to the organophosphorus insecticides discussed in section 6.4.1) that is applied to the foliage and is rapidly translocated to the roots. It is, according to Green et al. (1987), more toxic to perennials than paraquat but is like the bipyridylium herbicides in so far as it kills off residual vegetation after harvest. In contrast to the rapid-kill action of paraquat, glyphosate is slow-acting and does not immediately impair the translocation system; it is thus more effective at eradicating weeds by attacking their roots and in consequence it has a longer-lasting effect. According to Bowmer (1987), glyphosate has no effect on submerged aquatic plants and once in the soil system it is inactivated so that its residues do not affect future crops. It has also been effectively used in sprinkler irrigation systems with apparently no adverse effects (Comes et al. 1976).

As stated above, the use of the phenoxyacid herbicides to control broad-leaved weeds in cereal crops gave rise to further problems, notably the proliferation of wild oats (Avena fatua). This and similar problems prompted the search for new herbicides that were more selective. Hutson and Roberts (1987) have discussed seven herbicides that have been developed to deal specifically with the problem of wild oats in cereal crops, of which difenzoquat and diclofop-methyl are widely used. The former was first marketed in 1973 and can be applied at the post-emergent stage of crop growth. It is most effective as a controller of wild oats in barley crops and works by causing the death of meristematic tissue. Diclofop-methyl can also be used as a post-emergence herbicide to control wild oats by inhibiting shoot and root growth. It has a short half-life of less than 24 hours, degrading to diclofop acid which has a half-life of 14–49 days and complete degradation to carbon dioxide occurs between 100 and 150 days. Other herbicides that can control grass weeds in grass crops include propanil, a chloroanilide that is effective for the post-emergent control of grass weeds in rice. Herbicides that can control broad-leaved weeds in broad-leaved crops have also been developed. One example is fomesafen, which is designed to eliminate broad-leaved weeds in soya bean crops and is applied as an early post-emergent spray (*The pesticide manual* Worthing and Walker 1987). Because most of these compounds are inactivated rapidly on contact with the soil there is little danger of widespread environmental contamination.

6.5 CONCLUSION

Undoubtedly, agricultural practices have transformed the landscape of developed nations and have affected environmental quality. The loss of wildlife habitats has changed the character of the countryside and, while this issue has been discussed here in relation to the British countryside where hedges, wetlands and woodlands have disappeared at an alarming rate since the Second World War, habitat fragmentation is a serious threat to conservation in most developed nations today. Moreover, surplus food production, especially in the EEC and well exemplified in Britain, has given rise to an acrimonious debate wherein polarised views of conservationists on the one hand and agriculturalists on the other seem very far from reconciliation, despite the opportunity for this that is currently being presented by CAP reorganisation. High-technology agriculture has also resulted in depletion of the soil resource, so that soil erosion is now recognised as a significant problem in Britain and Europe as well as Australia and North America and derives from the replacement of more traditional crop rotations by monoculture and the consequent loss of organic residues that are so important for promoting soil cohesivenesss. In semi-arid regions, notably in the USA and Australia, the intensive use of irrigation has also caused degradation of the soil resource by excessive salinisation.

Since the Second World War there has been an escalation of chemical usage in agriculture. Increased applications of artificial fertilisers, while improving harvests, have had deleterious effects on freshwater and coastal ecosystems. The enhanced nutrient inputs into these ecosystems have promoted cultural eutrophication that has altered trophic structures and, in the most severe instances, adversely affected commercial fisheries and tourism. In terms of environmental quality, there are few developed nations that do not have problems with ground-water quality. In some cases high nitrate levels in ground-water used for domestic water supplies are potential health hazards which require expensive long-term mitigation measures. The use of crop-protection chemicals has also caused environmental change; in particular the use of organo-chlorine compounds such as DDT have had profound effects on wildlife. Herbicides to control broad-leaved weeds have altered the balance of weed populations so that, in solving one problem, others are created which require a further battery of chemical tools. At least the development, in the wake of tighter legislative controls, of more environmentally benign compounds like the pyrethroids signifies a more responsible attitude on the part of agrochemical concerns. The relatively short history of these compounds may, however, mean that there will be unforeseen long-term effects; clearly the rapid increase in fertiliser use after the Second World War was never intended to give rise to the deteriorated quality of domestic water supplies that is now manifest. Obviously it is essential to promote efficient food production and ridiculous to expect to return to pre-war traditions, but whatever new developments science brings to agriculture, there is no room for complacency. Science must also bring its considerable powers to bear on solving some of the problems it has already created and utilise its potential with vision, while politics could wield its rhetoric more effectively by ensuring a better balance between agricultural and conservation interests.

FURTHER READING

Barcelona M, Wehrmann A, Keely J F, Pettyjohn W A 1988 *Handbook of groundwater protection*. Taylor and Francis, London

Body R 1987 *Red or green for farmers (and the rest of us)?* Broad Leys Publishing, Saffron Walden

Hallsworth E G 1987 *Anatomy, physiology and psychology of erosion*. John Wiley, New York, Chichester, Brisbane, Toronto and Singapore

Henderson-Sellers B, Markland H R 1987 *Decaying lakes: the origins and control of cultural eutrophication*. John Wiley, New York, Chichester, Brisbane, Toronto and Singapore

Leahey J P (ed) 1985 *The pyrethroid insecticides*. Taylor and Francis, London

Morgan R P C 1986 *Soil erosion and conservation*. Longman, London

Shoard M 1987 *This land is our land*. Paladin Grafton Books, London

Wolman M G, Fournier F G A (eds) 1987 *Land transformation in agriculture*. John Wiley, New York, Chichester, Brisbane, Toronto and Singapore

7

THE ENVIRONMENTAL IMPACT OF AGRICULTURE IN THE DEVELOPING WORLD

7.1 INTRODUCTION

Population growth, the need for foreign currency earnings, and foreign aid have, in the past three or four decades, stimulated agricultural development in developing nations and have thus prompted environmental change. While there are many success stories in terms of increased food supply (China for example can feed its entire population of 1060 million) such developments have also brought about environmental degradation. For the purpose of discussion the impact of agriculture on environment will initially be examined in relation to three distinct regions that exemplify developing world environments, namely arid and semi-arid regions, humid rainforest regions and mountain areas. In the former, which regularly reach media headlines because of famine, the major environmental changes that have occurred are soil erosion, desertification and salinisation. All three are inherent components of the natural earth surface processes that occur in arid and semi-arid regions but have been exacerbated by human activity. These processes are often interlinked and although they will be discussed separately here it is often the case that measures to combat one problem may lead directly to another, or that desertification results from soil erosion and/or salinisation. In rainforest regions, deforestation is the major agent of environmental change and while it has obvious localised effects, especially in relation to soil erosion and soil degradation, there is growing concern that such large-scale destruction of biomass may have implications for climatic change (section 5.3.1). Deforestation is also a significant problem in mountainous regions, notably in the Andes and the Himalayas, and has caused accelerated soil erosion as well as water management problems for downslope piedmont and deltaic regions. Finally, attention will focus on the specific problems of island nations in the developing world where agricultural impacts have been particularly severe.

7.2 Arid and Semi-arid Regions

Arid and semi-arid lands occupy one-third of the earth's surface and support a population of 700 million people. Much of this land area and many of the people are in developing countries, especially in Africa South America and central Asia. The availability of water is the main constraint on food production and while traditional shifting cultivation and nomadic practices are inherently conservation-oriented, the trend towards permanent cultivation and settled herding over the last 50 years has led to widespread environmental change. In some cases land has become so degraded that it is agriculturally worthless. Removal of the natural vegetation, overgrazing and overcropping have resulted in nutrient depletion, widespread soil erosion and desertification (section 7.2.1 for a definition). In order to overcome the problem of an inadequate water supply, many parts of the arid and semi-arid regions have been irrigated. While the construction of dams, reservoirs and drainage channels has changed the character of the landscape, many irrigation schemes, through mismanagement, have created problems of salinisation and waterlogging that counteract the beneficial effects. In extreme cases, irrigation systems have been abandoned, contributing further to land that is annually lost to agriculture. These problems also occur in developed countries (section 6.3.3), but here there is sufficient finance and expertise to initiate reclamation programmes. This, however, is not the case in many developing countries, especially in Africa and thus it is likely that the rate of land degradation will increase indefinitely as populations continue to grow.

7.2.1 Desertification

This issue will be discussed first in this section because it is controversial and because it is also related to the issues of salinisation and soil erosion which will be examined below. There is considerable dissension in the literature as to what precisely constitutes desertification; Kovda (1980), for example, uses the term to describe land aridisation which involves all the processes that culminate in a reduction of the effective moisture content of soils and thus cause a decrease in biological productivity. He makes no distinction between natural processes, such as climatic change, that may promote the spread of arid conditions, and those which are due to human activity. Other sources distinguish between these two groups of factors, referring to natural processes as desertisation and to anthropogenically related ones as desertification. This epitomises the current debate that exists relating to causal factors: while the issue remains unresolved, most of the available evidence points to human activity as the more important catalyst. In consequence, the terms are frequently used to describe what is essentially the spread of desert-like conditions and decreasing biological productivity. Goudie (1986), for example, uses the word 'desertisation' while Botkin and

Keller (1987) and Rapp (1987) use the term 'desertification'. The latter's definition is adopted here:

> . . . . the spread of desert-like conditions of low biological productivity to drylands outside the previous desert boundaries. Desertification is the long-term degradation of drylands, resulting either from over-use by man [sic] and his animals, or from natural causes such as climatic fluctuations. It leads to loss of vegetation cover, loss of topsoil by wind or water erosion, or loss of useful plant production as a result of salinization or excessive sedimentation associated with sand dunes, sand sheets or torrents.

Apart from the Sahel–Saharan zone, desertification is a significant problem in China, Southern Africa and Pakistan as well as in many developed nations such as Australia, North America and the USSR (Fig. 7.1). Estimates of the extent of desertification vary; the *Gaia atlas of planet management* (Myers 1985), for example, suggests that *c.* 10 per cent of the 700 million people that inhabit the arid and semi-arid zones are living in areas that are becoming impoverished and that *c.* 12 million ha of land are degraded annually to such an extent that they are agriculturally unproductive. These data contrast with those of the Independent Commission on International Humanitarian Issues (1986) which opines that some 230 million people are directly threatened by desertification and that annually 21 million ha are rendered almost or completely unproductive. This variation is due to inadequate and imperfect monitoring, but nevertheless indicates that the problem is immense. As Fig. 7.1 illustrates, the greatest risk of desertification is in

Fig. 7.1. The global extent and risk of desertification. (Based on the *Gaia atlas of planet management* Myers 1985.)

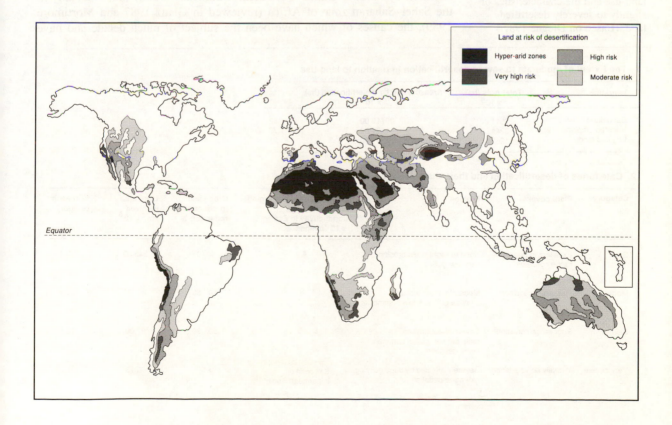

Land at risk of desertification

| | Hyper-arid zones | | High risk |
| | Very high risk | | Moderate risk |

Equator

areas adjacent to the world's hot hyper-arid zones, and include rain-fed crop-lands, irrigated lands and rangelands. Not all desertification is severe or irre-versible, but as shown in Table 7.1, even slightly desertified land experiences a 10 per cent decline in productivity. Moreover, the largest areas that are affected (Table 7.1) are rangelands where overgrazing is the major culprit though, as Cloudsley-Thompson (1988) has discussed, this is often brought about by the encroachment on grazing lands by cash-crop farmers. North (1986), for example, has suggested that widespread cash-cropping of groundnuts in the Sahelian zone has obliquely contributed to desertification because farmers cannot afford either to purchase fertilisers to maintain soil-nutrient status or to use a long fallow period. They are thus forced to extend the area of cultivation on to land hitherto used by pastoralists for seasonal grazing. In consequence, the latter are impelled to maintain their livestock in dry savanna lands all year round. In their natural state, such lands are characterised by large herds of herbivores that seasonally migrate in tune with biomass availability, so it is not surprising that overgrazing and land degradation ensue.

Apart from the problems of precisely delimiting areas that are experiencing desertification, it is equally difficult to determine whether or not rates of desertification are increasing. This is because remedial measures have been effective in some regions (mostly in developed nations) while in others the rate of degradation has increased. Clearly, each region with its attendant physical and socio-economic characteristics must be considered as a separate case.

As stated above, the problem of desertification has been brought to public attention by famines that have resulted in immense loss of life, especially in the Sahel–Saharan zone of Africa (reviewed in Glanz 1987 and Mortimore 1989), the causes of which have been the subject of much debate and have

Table 7.1. The extent of desertification in relation to land-use and the characteristics of slightly to severely desertified land. (Based on Dregne 1987.)

1. The Extent of moderate to severe desertification in relation to land-use

Land-use	Total Area (ha) x 10^5	Area affected by desertification (ha) x 10^5	%
Rangeland	37511.00	30716.00	82
Rain-fed cropland	2244.00	1731.00	77
Irrigated lands	1263.00	271.00	21

2. Categories of desertification and their characteristics

Category	Plant cover	Erosion	Salination or waterlogging of irrigated land. Conductivity in Ece x 10^3 mmhos	Crop yield (productivity) reduction %	Land area involved km^2 x 10^5	% in each category
Slight	Excellent to good range condition	None to slight sheet erosion, very few gullies	< 4	< 10	245.20	52.1
Moderate	Fair range condition	Moderate sheet erosion, shalllow gullies & few hummocks	4 - 8	10 - 50	137.70	29.1
Severe	Poor range condition	Severe sheet erosion, deep erosion gullies common, some deflation	8 - 15	50 - 90	87.00	18.5
Very severe	Virtually no vegetation	Severely affected by deep gullying, extensive deflation	Salt crust on impermeable soils	> 90	00.73	0.1

recently been reviewed by Hulme (1989). Here, drought is the crux of the
matter and whether it is caused by or causes land degradation. If the former
is the case, then a reduced vegetation cover due to mismanagement may
lead, by affecting albedo and soil moisture, to reduced convective processes
and therefore less rainfall; thus self-perpetuating drought becomes the norm.
In this case, land-cover becomes a key factor in determining the internal
climate mechanisms in the Sahel and, by implication, land-use becomes the
most significant way of combating the problem. As Hulme has pointed out,
this hypothesis takes no account of the possibility of influence from external
factors such as global climatic change and the imperfectly understood
ocean–atmosphere interrelationships which, as has been discussed in section
1.2.2, have played a major role in the longer-term glacial–interglacial cycle.
For example, Bradley *et al.* (1987a) have suggested that for the last 30–40
years there has been a general decrease in precipitation in low-latitudes of
the northern hemisphere which are in accord with General Circulation
Model (GCM) predictions based on doubled carbon dioxide levels. Thus the
reduced rainfall trends experienced in the Sahel may reflect the enhanced
greenhouse effect. The question then arises as to whether human activity has
exacerbated and is continuing to exacerbate the drought process and whether
it can be mitigated by better land management. Whatever the answer is there
is little doubt that improving the vegetation cover can only enhance productivity and improve the soil structure so that it is less susceptible to erosion
and degradation.

Notwithstanding this debate, what precisely has happened in terms of environmental change in the Sahel in the last two to three decades? There have
been a plethora of studies at varying scales, which is a reflection of the
Sahel zone's extension some 6000 km from the Atlantic to the Red Sea (Fig.
7.1) as a transition zone between the Sahara Desert and the *Acacia*-domi-
nated savanna lands to the south. As Mensching (1988) has discussed, erratic
rainfall means that the boundary of rainfed cultivation varies from year to
year and, as has been mentioned above, land-use pressures have intensified,
including cash-crop production. In the pre-1965 period a long run of higher
than average precipitation allowed the spread northward of rain-fed cultivation, dominated by millet, and at the same time the increased populations
placed more pressure on the vegetation for fuelwood. After droughts first
began in 1969, the Sahel zone, already one of high risk, became a famine
zone as crop yields declined and the remaining vegetation was depleted by
overgrazing as carrying capacity was exceeded. In consequence, the unprotected soil, depleted of binding organic matter, was rapidly eroded by wind
especially and desert dunes encroached. According to Berry (1988), sand
dune encroachment, deterioration of rangelands and rain-fed croplands have
been severe or very severe in Sahelian West Africa and the Sudan. In
Burkina Faso, for example, observations between 1955 and 1974 have
shown that degraded land and active sand have increased from 181 to 390 ha
and from 56 to 150 ha respectively in the Menegon-Bidi area, which represents only a small proportion of the total 3000 ha of lost arable land in the
Burkina Sahel and which is equivalent to the loss of 800 t of millet or 4500 t
of straw (Mainguet 1986). In the Sudan, apart from the increased extent of
sand dunes along the Nile, El-Karouri (1986) reports a decline in sorghum
production, a staple food, from $1.02 \, t \, ha^{-1}$ in 1961 to $0.46 \, t \, ha^{-1}$ in 1973 in
the Kardofan region as well as similar declines in maize and millet produc-

tivity and a reduction in gum arabic production due to the exploitation of *Acacia senegal* for fuel and clearance.

Outside Africa, desertification is occurring in many other arid and semi-arid regions. In Kuwait, Al-Nakshabandi and El-Robee (1988) have shown that aeolian deposition has resulted in decreased productivity or complete failure of many agricultural enterprises. In contrast to the Sahel zone which is classified as semi-arid, Kuwait is arid (*Desertification Map of the World*, FAO/Unesco 1977) so it is to be expected that desertification is a prominent problem and a major agent of environmental change. In the Abdaly region of northern Kuwait there are some 156 farms which are separated by desert and thus exposed to sandstorms, where metal wind-breaks and shelter-belts have not prevented sand encroachment, largely as Al-Nakshabandi and El-Robee have suggested, due to poor management. Similar problems have occurred in the Al-Wafra region in the south of Kuwait, where desert encroachment has led to the abandonment of farms. Here the annual rate of sand encroachment is $15.5 \, m^3 \, m^{-1}$ which is in excess of the average annual rate of sand encroachment of $14 \, m^3 \, m^{-1}$ (Khalaf 1989). Desertification is also occurring in South America and is most extensive in Argentina where the severest cases are recorded. According to Dregne (1986), wind erosion is particularly acute in the central area of Argentina where dry-farming has resulted in the formation of mobile dunes to such an extent that more than 16 million ha have been affected. Overall in South America, some 22 per cent of the arid regions are severely or very severely affected by desertification and there are few remedial programmes in hand.

The problem is also significant in China where there are *c.* $170 \, 000 \, km^2$ of desertified land, approximately 30 per cent of which has been created since 1920 (Zhu Zhenda 1982, quoted in Kebin and Kaiguo 1989). Most of this is in the northwest where there has been a long history of land-use, involving both degradation and successful reclamation. Songqiao (1988) describes the Mu–Us sandy region on the southeastern margin of the Ordos plateau and the Kolshin sandy region of the west Liao River basin as the worst cases of desertification in Chinese history. In the former, shifting sand dunes have become more extensive due to overgrazing and injudicious cultivation causing the southern margin of the Mu–Us sandy region to extend beyond the northern boundary of the Loess plateau and the northern margin to extend into the Nobq Desert. In northeastern China, Leeming (1985) reports that in the vicinity of the Great Wall in Shaanxi Province the desert margin has advanced markedly in the last 150 years so that sand now extends 70 km south of the Great Wall, and in the nearby Yulin area grazing land and arable fields have been engulfed. Leeming also suggests that the increased incidence of sandstorms in Beijing are another result of poor land management that is creating desertification in northwestern Hebei and the adjacent areas of Inner Mongolia by the clearance of woodland and pasture-land for arable crops.

There are a number of instances in China, however, where oases have been created out of the desert and where desertification has been halted. Songqiao (1988) describes that of the Hexi corridor which is situated between the Mongolian and Tibetan plateaux and which has a long history of cultivation based on irrigation. Moreover, Kebin and Kaiguo (1989) describe the measures suggested by the Project of Protective Forest System which was approved by the government in 1978 to improve conditions in northern China. Between 1978 and 1985 some 5.3×10^6 ha were planted with trees, shrubs and herbs, including a sand-fixation forest belt of 700 000 ha, another 700 000 ha of shelter-belts for arable land and 170 000 ha of shelter-belts for pasture. Eventually some 8×106 ha will be planted to constitute the 'Green Great Wall'. Kebin and Kaiguo also report that grazing and wood removal for firewood are prohibited near oases and villages and that these measures, plus tree planting and irrigation, have been effective in reclaiming parts of Gansu Province. Here, the measures were instituted in 1982 and by 1984 *c*. 26 000 ha of desert had been restored and the shifting dunes fixed. Successes such as this suggest that remedial actions are feasible and can bring beneficial effects in a relatively short time.

7.2.2 SALINISATION AND WATERLOGGING

As discussed in section 6.3.3, salinisation and waterlogging are processes of environmental degradation associated with irrigation. Some 12 per cent of the world's cultivated land is irrigated, of which more than half is affected to some extent by these problems which inevitably lead to a reduction in crop productivity, the very factor that such schemes were established to increase salinisation and waterlogging are particularly significant in arid and semi-arid regions where irrigation is necessary for agriculture, and while they are important in developed nations, they are fast becoming major environmental problems in many developing nations. Earth Report (1988), for example, states that in Pakistan more than 65 per cent of the country's 150 000 km^2 of irrigated land are thus affected; in Egypt 35 per cent of farmland has salinity and waterlogging problems and in Iraq and India the situation is similarly acute. The reasons why salinisation occurs and the mechanisms involved have already been discussed in section 6.3.3 and illustrated in Fig. 5.6.

In Pakistan, salinisation and waterlogging are particularly acute in the Indus Valley where irrigation has been practised since 5 kyr BP; currently some 15×10^6 ha are irrigated by a system that includes the Indus River and its tributaries, 3 storage reservoirs, 19 barrages, 43 canals and 90 000 water-course systems (Shanan 1987). This irrigation system supports large-scale grain production as well as a dense rurally based population. Ground-water is also extensively used to supplement surface-water irrigation: in the Punjab alone there are some 164 500 wells (Sabadell 1988). Waterlogging and sa-linisation have, however, resulted in declining crop productivity to such an extent that crop yields in the region are now among the lowest in the world. According to Shanan (1987), irrigation efficiencies are so low that between 35 and 45 per cent of the water entering the canal system never actually reaches the fields; losses are due to evaporation and unlined drainage ditches. The latter combined with poor drainage in an area with an average slope of only 1 : 5000 has resulted in raised water-tables and extensive waterlogging. Shanan, referring to a 1978 survey of 14.6×106 ha, asserts that in 13 per cent of the area the water-table was less than 1.8 m below the surface and in a further 41 per cent of the area it was between 1.8 and 3 m depth. Moreover, rates of water-table rise are rapid, at between 30 and 40 cm per year, and already large areas of the Indus basin have been transposed into saline waterlogged swamps, though remedial measures involving gov-ernment-controlled drainage schemes have helped to mitigate this problem.

Salinisation in the region is extensive because of inadequate natural drainage and the fact that much of the ground-water in the underlying aquifer is also saline. More than 1 million ha are currently classified as severely saline and are mostly unsuitable for crop production because of either highly saline water in the root zone or the presence of salt crusts on the soil. As Sabadell (1988) has discussed, remedial measures have been initiated, beginning in 1958 with the Salinity Control Reclamation Project I (SCARP). Currently SCARP V is in operation, the aim of which is to encourage pumping from non-saline groundwater areas in order to ameliorate waterlogging problems. Plans are also afoot to ensure the discharge of highly saline drainage water, via large outfall drains, into the lower reaches of the Indus whence it can be flushed into the sea in the flooding season; and to divert some of the saline water to evaporation lakes in nearby desert areas so that salt can be removed. Such measures inevitably incur substantial costs which in turn increases the cost of crop production.

Egypt is another example of a country which, like Pakistan and China, has a long history of irrigation, in this case in the Nile Valley (section 3.4.2) beginning some 5 kyr BP. In the last 200 years the irrigation system has been extended to increase the number of crops grown annually and especially to increase the cultivation of cotton which is a major export crop. Stanhill (1986) suggests that the ensuing rise of the water table was initially beneficial, but by 1947 waterlogging and salinisation had reduced the cotton crop to half of its potential. The opening of the Aswan Dam in 1970 was also initially considered to be beneficial to Egypt's agricultural productivity, as its capacity to control the Nile's sometimes erratic flow facilitated the conversion of all arable land to perennial cropping. Each cultivated hectare of land in Egypt now produces, on average, five crops every 3 years. This represents a large increase in productivity compared with pre-1970 levels but it has been achieved at great cost in terms of environmental degradation and human health. In relation to the latter, the increased amount of year-round open water has caused the spread of several water-borne diseases into the rural population. The most significant of these is schistosomiasis (bilharzia), a debilitating disease that can cause liver fibrosis and bladder cancer, which is transmitted to humans by a parasitic worm that requires water-snails as an intermediate host. According to Earth Report (1988) the incidence of this disease increased significantly in the immediate post-1970 period in villages adjacent to Lake Nasser, the lake dammed by the Aswan Dam, though subsequent public health measures have brought the disease under control.

In terms of environmental change, the same problems that characterise the Indus basin of Pakistan have ensued in the Nile Valley. Firstly, the salinity of irrigation water has increased due, as Stanhill (1986) explains, to the high rates of water loss from Lake Nasser which is situated in an arid region where evaporation is particularly rapid. Using data for the period 1954–74, Khalil and Hanna (1984) have demonstrated that since the scheme was initiated the dissolved salt content of the Nile at the head of the delta has increased by 29 per cent. Secondly, since half of the water that is emitted from the reservoir for agriculture is transported, via evaporation and transpiration, to the atmosphere much more salt is deposited in the soil. This amounts to 6 million annually and because of elevated ground-water levels its removal by leaching is impaired. Exchanges between surface water and ground-water also mean that the latter is becoming more saline. Incidental, but significant for environmental change, is the effect that the Aswan Dam has had on the fertility of the land situated in the lower reaches of the Nile.

According to Earth Report (1988), some 100 million t of nutrient-rich silt were deposited anually in the pre-Aswan period but is now reduced to just a few tonnes per year, necessitating extensive fertiliser use at considerable cost and, presumably, inviting long-term eutrophication problems that characterise many developing countries (section 6.3.1). Rapid siltation at Aswan is also a major ongoing problem.

Irrigation programmes in the Sudan since 1955, where cotton is a major export crop as it is in Egypt, have again created considerable environmental change. Environmental degradation in this region is not confined to pre-independence times (before 1955) as post-independence practices and policies have not fared much better despite considerable financial assistance from the World Bank (Wallach 1988). Apart from changing the landscape of Sudan, especially in the Gezira region to the south of Khartoum by canal construction, the irrigation projects have not resulted in the increased production of cash crops that was initially envisaged. This Wallach attributes to the overall control of government and aid agencies that assigns to the farmers a passive role in land management. Salinisation and waterlogging are also creating environmental degradation in Iraq where some 50 per cent of the country's 36 000 km^2 of irrigated land is affected. Much of this occurs as a result of the Greater Mussayib Irrigation Project. This was established in the 1953–56 period and is located c. 60 km south of Baghdad in the alluvial plains between the Tigris and Euphrates, using water from the latter. As Clark (1986) points out, the project was considered to be a failure in both technical and economic terms within 10 years of its inception, not least because of resulting poor drainage, increasing soil salinity and excessive silting.

In China, as discussed by Smil (1984) and Songqiao (1986), salinisation and waterlogging have occurred extensively in irrigated regions, chiefly in the north China plain and the eastern provinces. According to Songqiao (1986), about 20 per cent of China's 1×10^8 ha of cropland are affected by salinisation. In the Tarim River basin in the northwest province of Xinjiang, between 15 000 and 60 000 m^3 of water per hectare are used annually for irrigation, but inadequate drainage means that the system is inefficient resulting in considerable water loss and salinisation. Similarly, in the Huimin prefecture of Shandong Province (northeast China) irrigation works constructed between 1957 and 1960 led to a rapid rise in the water-table and increasing salt levels of such magnitude that many irrigation systems have been abandoned. Irrigation schemes in other parts of Shandong as well as the neighbouring provinces of Heenan and Hebei have also proved to be less efficient than originally envisaged (Leeming 1985). This is partly due to the fact that reservoir construction is incomplete, many are unsafe and the water-distribution systems are often incomplete or inadequate so that water cannot reach the fields. As a result, water loss is high due to evaporation and seepage which promote waterlogging and salinisation. Concern is also being expressed about the proposed construction of a large dam at the north of the Three Gorges on the Yangtze River. As Jhaveri (1988) reports, this project, which has the support of the World Bank, is being undertaken to reduce the threat of flooding, to provide hydroelectric power and to improve navigation. There is, however, a great deal of opposition to the project as there is no guarantee that these objectives will be achieved, because large-scale relocation of displaced farmers will be necessary and because there are likely to be profound and detrimental ecological consequences. In relation to the latter, the reduced flow of fresh water into the estuary will allow the intrusion of salt water and thus affect biological productivity that will rebound on fisheries and the supply of water for industrial, agricultural and domestic use. Increased salinisation is thus a real prospect for the lower Yangtze if this project proceeds. Here, the cause will be a very different one to that associated with irrigation but may have significant repercussions for the exacerbated salinisation of one of China's most productive agricultural regions.

7.2.3 SOIL EROSION

On a global basis, soil erosion is particularly serious in dry tropical regions and is, therefore, a major problem in many developing countries. According to the *Gaia atlas of planet management* (Myers 1985), approximately 75 000 million t of soil are lost annually from the land surface and the areas that are most severely affected are shown in Fig. 7.2. Comparing this with Fig. 7.1, which illustrates the global distribution of desertification, it is clear that the two processes are often interrelated. While soil erosion is an integral part of natural denudation processes, human activity, especially injudicious agricultural practices, has greatly accelerated natural rates of soil erosion affecting

Fig. 7.2. The global extent of soil erosion (based on the *Gaia atlas of planet management* Myers 1985.)

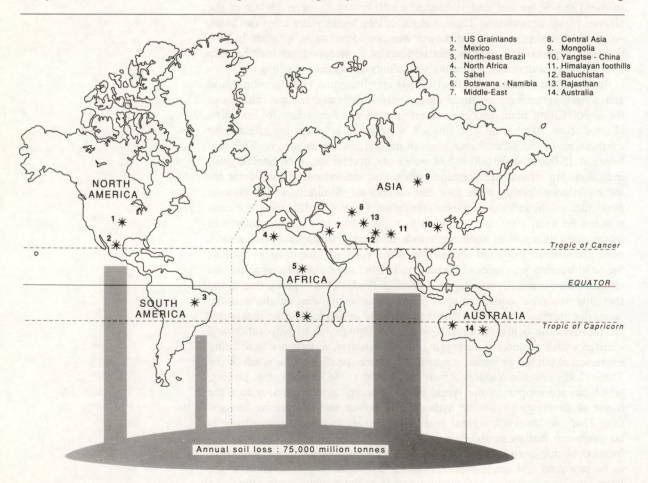

1. US Grainlands	8. Central Asia
2. Mexico	9. Mongolia
3. North-east Brazil	10. Yangtse – China
4. North Africa	11. Himalayan foothills
5. Sahel	12. Baluchistan
6. Botswana – Namibia	13. Rajasthan
7. Middle-East	14. Australia

Tropic of Cancer

EQUATOR

Tropic of Capricorn

Annual soil loss : 75,000 million tonnes

not only areas from which soil is removed but areas in which it is deposited. The problem is likely to increase because, as Pimentel *et al.* (1987) point out, most of the world's fertile land is already being cultivated – which means that most newly cultivated areas will be on marginal land, often on steep slopes. For agriculture, the most significant result of accelerated soil erosion is a reduction in productivity. As in the case of developed countries (section 6.2.2), the major agents of soil erosion are wind and water, the efficiency of which depends on many other factors such as angle of slope, land-use and vegetation cover (see Fig. 6.1). According to Kovda (1983) soil erosion has increased by a factor of five since the beginning of settled agriculture and has resulted in the destruction of $c.\ 4.3 \times 10^7$ ha of productive land. Buringh (1981) has estimated that annually the global loss of agricultural land due to soil erosion is 3×10^6 ha. These data reinforce Lal's (1988) view that accelerated soil erosion is a major global problem. Among the developing nations that are worst affected by soil erosion are Mexico, Ethiopia and many more African states, as well as India, Pakistan and China (see review in Brown and Wolf 1984). In India, for example, 6000 million t of topsoil are lost annually, while in the highlands of Ethiopia the annual figure is 1600 million t (Earth Report 1988). Not all of this is due to soil losses from agricultural systems since deforestation also increases soil erosion rates (sections 7.3 and 7.4), and in contrast there are numerous examples where remedial measures have actually reduced soil erosion.

It has long been recognised that the human factor is just as significant an influence on rates of erosion as physical features, as has been highlighted by a study of potential versus actual erosion in Zimbabwe by Whitlow (1988). Since rural development here is a major aim of government policy, such research is an essential prerequisite to the formulation of efficient management programmes: clearly, long-term development of this kind is only sustainable if the soil resource is adequate, especially in a country that already has a widespread soil erosion problem. Whitlow's comparison (Fig. 7.3) between the occurrence of actual erosion, as deduced from aerial photographs, with a survey of potential erosion hazards based on environmental factors such as rainfall erosivity, soil erodibility and slope, indicates that there is poor agreement between the two. According to a potential erosion hazard map produced by Stocking (1975), a modified version of which is given in Fig. 7.3, the areas with the highest erosion potential are located mainly in the northern part of the country especially in the Zambesi Valley and the Mutoko District. In contrast, Whitlow's (1988) map of actual erosion indicates that the most severely eroded lands are in the region to the east and south of Masvingo, including the Save River basin. There is some correspondence between the two maps in the Mutoko District but the main correlation is between actual erosion and land tenure systems. As Fig. 7.3 shows, the Communal Lands are more heavily eroded than the General Lands. The latter is a term used to refer to former 'white' areas of pre-independence Zimbabwe and are commercial farmlands, while the Communal Lands are peasant farming areas, of which nearly 27 per cent are subject to extensive or very extensive erosion, which compares with only 1.6 per cent of the General Lands. Whitlow's survey also shows that non-agricultural land in Zimbabwe is not seriously affected by erosion, since 95.2 per cent of these areas are in the lowest erosion classes (Fig. 7.3), and that in Zimbabwe there are 1.83×10^6 ha of eroded land overall, of which 83 per cent occurs in the Communal Lands. Here population levels are highest, with 25.5 people km^{-2}

as compared with 7.6 people km^{-2} in the General Lands, indicating that population densities and erosion rates are directly related. As Zinyama and Whitlow (1986) have pointed out, erosion problems are likely to increase in the Communal Lands, where a population growth of 3.6 per cent per year means that the population will double in less than 20 years. In the absence of soil conservation, the productivity of these lands will inevitably decline rapidly; Elwell and Stocking (1984) have suggested that the soils of the Save Valley, for example, will only be able to support maize cropping for another

Fig. 7.3. Potential erosion hazards in relation to actual erosion and land tenure in Zimbabwe. (Based on Whitlow 1988.)

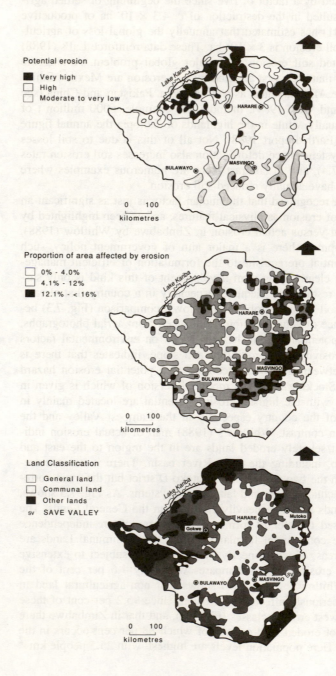

Potential erosion

- ■ Very high
- □ High
- □ Moderate to very low

0   100
kilometres

Proportion of area affected by erosion

- □ 0% - 4.0%
- □ 4.1% - 12%
- ■ 12.1% - < 16%

0   100
kilometres

Land Classification

- □ General land
- □ Communal land
- ■ Other lands
- sv SAVE VALLEY

0   100
kilometres

10 years. Moreover, enhanced soil erosion is creating other problems. Of 130 dams constructed in the last 50 years in the Masvingo District, more than half are badly silted (Elwell 1985). These data not only confirm the severity of erosion in parts of Zimbabwe but reinforce Blaikie and Brookfield's (1987) view (section 4.4.1) that social factors are a significant component of soil erosion problems and must, therefore, be accorded sufficient consideration in soil conservation programmes.

Soil erosion, exacerbated by land-use practices, is a widespread problem in Africa despite and because of many colonial (section 4.4.1) and post-colonial soil conservation schemes. In Tanzania, for example, the Dodoma section of the semi-arid central region has a long history of both accelerated soil erosion and attempts at conservation. As Christiansson (1988) describes, rotational bush-fallowing and permanent agriculture are gradually replacing shifting cultivation in an area that experiences a long dry season and a short intense wet season. Clearance of semi-arid savanna, coupled with overgrazing and friable soils, has resulted in annual degradation rates of between 1 and 10 mm per year, the higher rates occurring on overgrazed slopes. As well as contributing to declining soil fertility, such high sediment removal rates are causing problems with water supply by increasing reservoir siltation rates. Colonial soil conservation measures during the 1930–50 period, which involved hedge planting, contour ridging of cultivated land and gully control, proved to be ineffective because of the unpopularity of controls on stock movement and resettlement. This, combined with a 47 per cent increase in the livestock population, and an increase in human populations, led to even greater degradation between 1957 and 1964 and prompted local prohibition of clearance and cultivation. In addition, the post-independence government inaugurated a resettlement programme, involving villagisation of the scattered rural population, to improve service availability and promote rural development. This in turn led to increased degradation that has been exacerbated by the subsequent use of marginal lands for cultivation. Currently, a new programme is in operation to develop arable cultivation, but incorporating soil and water conservation measures which include the planting of wind-breaks and forests as well as contour farming to minimise erosion. Christiansson (1988) reports that between 1973 and 1983, 11 400 ha of land were reclaimed under the auspices of this project which includes educational projects and a policy of livestock destocking. Remedial measures to curb soil erosion, involving the use of grass hedges, have also been successful in several southern Indian states. Sattaur (1989) reports that planting of vetiver grass (*Vetiveria ziganiodes*) has helped to counteract soil erosion on slopes as steep as 50 per cent. If planted along contours, the grass, which is unpalatable to livestock except in its early growth stages and thrives even in arid areas, will rapidly form easily managed hedges that act as a wind-break as well as a trap for eroded soil particles.

China is another developing country where soil erosion is a serious problem, with an average annual rate of erosion of 43 t ha^{-1} (Pimentel *et al.* 1987). It is acute in the Loess Plateau which occupies 530 000 km^2 of north and central China where fine-grained silts derived by wind erosion from the deserts of Mongolia and northwest China were deposited during the Tertiary and Quaternary periods. The depth of these deposits varies from less than 10 m to more than 200 m and the major drainage system is that of the Huanghe River, which is also known as the Yellow River since it carries a huge volume of yellow silt from the Loess plateau into the Yellow Sea. Songqiao

(1986) states that the silt amounts to some 1.6×10^9 t per year and that the rate of erosion from the middle reaches of the Huanghe River basin is 100 t ha^{-1} per year. The region has a long history of human activity (section 3.2.1), and although erosion has always been a problem it has intensified considerably in the last 100 years as deforestation has accelerated and grasslands have been degraded. According to Smil (1984), severe erosion is now symptomatic of c. 80 per cent of the region, of which more than half is very seriously affected. The major agent of erosion is water, especially during the summer months when two-thirds of the annual rainfall occurs in heavy thunderstorms and thus has high erosivity which is enhanced by a much diminished vegetation cover. As Zachar (1982) has described, the poor cohesiveness of loess soils, due to the paucity of binding colloids, means that they are characterised by high erodibility which is made worse by leaching that rapidly removes cations like calcium and magnesium. In consequence, the Loess plateau has extensive rill and gully systems and even ravines which, in addition to the more gradual loss of topsoil, have resulted in decreased crop and livestock productivity. The magnitude of erosion is reflected in the silt content of the Huanghe River: before it enters the Loess lands it has an average silt content of 2 kg m^{-3} of water, but when it leaves the region after its confluence with the Weihe the average silt content is 35 kg m^{-3} which can rise to several hundreds of kilograms after storms (Smil 1984). The amount of silt that the Huanghe brings to the China Sea (1.6×10^9 t per year) represents a 25 per cent increase over the last 30 years and is due mainly to the conversion of grasslands to arable fields (Smil 1987b).

These data, plus those given in section 6.2.2 in relation to soil erosion in the developing world, provide a range of examples that indicate the magnitude of the global soil erosion problem. The resulting loss in crop productivity is grave cause for immediate concern, even if it can be partially offset by more intensive use of fertilisers.

7.3 TROPICAL FOREST REGIONS

On the earth's surface, environmental change is a continuous process and much of this change is attributable to agriculture. In Europe, for example, the removal of temperate forest began more than 5 kyr BP when permanent agricultural systems replaced the hunting and gathering strategies of the mesolithic period (sections 3.3.2 and 3.3.3); and has continued ever since, though post-war afforestation policies have redressed the balance to some extent (section 8.2). In the tropics, however, environmental change is occurring at an unprecedented rate where deforestation is creating local and, in all probability, global environmental problems since the demise of tropical rainforests in particular may well be contributing to the enhanced greenhouse effect (section 5.3.1). The reasons for such large-scale deforestation are complex. Almost all of the world's tropical forests are in developing countries where rapid population growth means that the pressure on land for food production is high. Undoubtedly, indigenous populations have accelerated rates of deforestation in their search for more extensive arable and grazing lands, and as populations increase so too will the pressure on land. External factors have also stimulated deforestation: these include the increasing import-ance of cash crops which are exported to earn foreign currency, in-creased logging activities and the establishment of extensive ranches to satisfy the wood and meat requirements respectively of the developed world. Many of these enterprises are controlled by external corporations or by a landed élite that comprises only a small proportion of the popu-lation, and while they are responsible for a great deal of environmental degradation they provide little benefit to the majority of the indigenous people. The removal of the protective forest cover leads to accelerated soil erosion, which in turn affects local hydrological regimes and causes accelerated silting of water-bodies. Apart from the problems associated with complete deforestation, extensive areas of primary forest have been degraded so that they are no longer as productive in terms of biomass, and sufficiently fragile that they too face extinction in the coming de-cades.

7.3.1 DEFORESTATION IN TROPICAL RAINFOREST REGIONS

As shown in Fig. 7.4, tropical forests occupy a considerable area of the earth's surface, comprising 2×10^7 km^2, which amounts to nearly half of the world's forested lands (Furtado and Ruddle 1986). Of the major forest re-gions in South and Southeast Asia, Central Africa and Central and South America, Amazonia is the largest, occupying nearly 1000 million ha. These forests vary in character from closed forests to open woodlands and include mangrove forests that occur in coastal regions. In their natural state, tropical forests, especially tropical rainforests, are among the most productive of the earth's ecosystems producing two or three times as much organic matter per unit area (e.g. 400–600 t ha^{-1}) than temperate or boreal forests (typically 200 t ha^{-1}) and as numerous writers have pointed out they are also the most diverse ecosystems in terms of numbers of plant and animal species (P W Richards 1986, Walker 1986). The reasons for this diversity have been sub-ject to much debate (section 2.4.2) and while it is not yet resolved, the fact

Fig. 7.4. The distribution of tropical rainforests and the extent of present and potential future deforestation. (Based on Girling and Jackman 1989 and Earth Report 1988.)

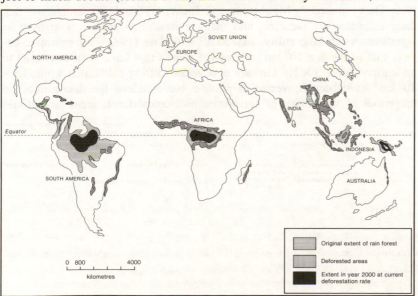

remains that such forests house a huge genetic resource that has only been fractionally realised to yield what have ultimately become significant commercial products such as rubber. The loss of this resource has been discussed by Lovejoy (1989) and it is almost as significant as the local and global environmental repercussions, in view, for example, of the search by agrochemical and drug companies for effective natural compounds. The most rapid rates of deforestation are occurring in the tropical rainforest regions, but deforestation is also significant in the savanna woodlands that occupy the drier tropical and subtropical regions. This will be discussed in section 7.4.3 and the current section will focus specifically on the tropical rainforest.

There are varying estimates of the amount of the world's tropical forests that have already been removed and at what rate deforestation is proceeding. Nevertheless the data given in Table 7.2 are the most widely quoted, and illustrate that the area already affected is immense and that average rates of deforestation in these regions are sufficiently high that there is a real danger that forests will disappear altogether in the next 200 years, especially as reforestation is replacing only *c.* 10 per cent of the cleared forest (Lanly 1982). The data show that the largest deforested area is in Central and South America where some of the highest rates of loss are occurring. According to *World resources 1988–1989* (World Resources Institute 1988), 0.6 per cent of the world's tropical moist forests are cleared annually on average, with similar values for all three of the major tropical rainforest regions. This generalisation, however, masks the fact that there are considerable variations from country to country in each of these regions. Some of the highest annual rates are occurring in the Ivory Coast and Nigeria where annual losses are currently reaching 5.2 per cent; in Costa Rica, Sri Lanka and El Salvador the annual rates are between 3.6 and 3.2 per cent.

The most significant reasons for deforestation are the spread of shifting cultivation, increasing plantation agriculture and large-scale ranching, logging, mineral extraction and road and dam construction. Only the impact of agricultural practices will be discussed here. According to Arnold (1987), shifting cultivation is the main cause of deforestation, causing 70, 50 and 35 per cent of the deforestation in Africa, Asia and tropical America respectively. Data reported by Malingreau and Tucker (1988), however, suggest that these estimates are incorrect and that conversion to pasture is at least as significant as shifting cultivation. Salati and Vose (1983), for example, believe that of the $8 \times 10^6 \, km^2$ of tropical forests that have been converted to agriculture, some $3 \times 10^6 \, km^2$ are now under shifting cultivation while $3.5 \times 10^6 \, km^2$ have been converted to pasture. Nevertheless, the data reflect the magnitude of the impact of agriculture on tropical forest areas. Sometimes

Table 7.2. Estimates of the extent and rates of tropical deforestation,

	Extent (millions of hectares)			Rates of deforestation (millions of hectares per annum)					
				Closed forests				Open Woodlands[2]	
	Land Area[1]	Area of forest & woodland[2]	Area of forest and woodland as a % of total Land area[2]	All Tropical[2]		Moist Tropical[3]			
				Area	% of total	Area	% of total	Area	% of total
Africa	2190	896	40	1.33	0.61	1.20	0.59	2.34	0.48
Asia & Pacific	945	410	43	1.82	0.59	1.61	0.61	0.19	0.61
Latin America	1680	1067	64	4.12	0.61	3.30	0.54	1.27	0.59

Sources : 1. FAO (1984).   2. Lanly, 1982.   3. Grainger, 1984.

the movement of farmers into these regions is actively encouraged by government policies; elsewhere it is an indirect result of policies that have forced peasants off their lands in order to develop cash cropping and ranching, a process that began with colonial settlement (section 4.4). In South America, for example, landownership especially in the developed coastal zones is concentrated in a small proportion of the population who are engaged in plantation agriculture or ranching. As a consequence, there is a growing population of landless farmers whose only alternative to migrating to the ghettos of the major cities is to invade the forests. Shifting agriculture is not in itself environmentally harmful, as is evidenced by the long and generally successful history that this type of agriculture has enjoyed in tropical regions. The clearance of small areas of forest, followed by burning to release the nutrients stored in the biomass, ensures a sufficiently fertile soil to provide an adequate crop for 2–3 years. Problems arise, however, when it becomes impossible to allow a long enough fallow period between cropping for the forest to redevelop and thus restore the nutrient content of the ecosystem. This occurs because most tropical rainforest biogeochemical cycles involve a tight intra-system relationship between the living biomass and the litter which contains the major reservoirs of nutrients; this is in contrast to the biogeochemical cycles of temperate and boreal forests wherein the soil plays a much more significant role in nutrient recycling (see Mannion 1986e for a more complete discussion of these relationships).

More intensive use of tropical forests is occurring where pressure on land is so acute that fallow periods of insufficient duration are creating environmental degradation. Scott (1987), for example, has examined the impact of more frequent clearance that is now being practised by the Campa Indians in the Gran Pajonal area of central Peru, where primary and secondary forest is interspersed with savanna and grassland. The Campa Indians have been forced into the more remote regions of Gran Pajonal due to the migration of Peruvian settlers from the coastal and Andean cities. Traditional Campa agriculture is based on garden or chacra plots which are used mainly for the cultivation of manioc, although plantains, bananas, sweet potatoes and beans are also grown on a smaller scale. Initially, garden plots of *c.* 1 ha are created by felling (slashing) and the felled trees are burnt after a period of drying. While any one group may cultivate two or three different gardens of varying ages at any one time, the nutrient stocks are rapidly depleted and within 3 years the plot is abandoned and secondary forest begins to re-establish. Scott (1987), on the basis of biomass and nutrient data, believes that a 15-year fallow period is adequate to allow the replenishment of nutrients stocks to support a 2–3-year cycle of cultivation. However, new colonists in Gran Pajonal are employing a fallow period of only 7 years, which is likely to cause long-term nutrient depletion so that maintenance of crop productivity will only be possible with the addition of artifical fertilisers. Similar problems are occurring in Rondonia in the southwest of Brazil, where the Polonoroesti road-building project is attracting some 70 000–80 000 settlers per year as the forest is opened up. The area has already lost 30 per cent of its forest cover (Earth Report 1988). Many of the new colonists are, as Fearnside (1985) has commented, using a fallow period that is much too short for sustained agriculture. In many cases the annual crops planted in the first few years are rapidly being replaced by pasture which itself is frequently proving to be uneconomic and environmentally detrimental.

Further large-scale deforestation is occurring in response to government-sanctioned development projects, many of which involve cash cropping and ranching. In Indonesia, for example, there is a government policy to encourage the migration of people from the densely populated islands of Java, Madura and Bali to the more sparsely populated outer islands of the archipelago. This programme, titled Repelita, has been discussed by Ross (1986) who indicates that it operates via a series of 5-year plans. That for 1983–88 involves the resettlement of 1.2 million families, most of whom will be engaged in agriculture, bringing the total number of resettled people to 3.6 million (Earth Report 1988). Each family is provided with 3.5 ha of land of which 1 ha is used for rain-fed arable crops. By 1982, some 180 000 ha of land had been cleared, with a further 1 million ha likely to be cleared by the completion of Repelita IV in 1988, involving c. 300 000 ha per year in mostly primary forest areas that are cleared by burning after initial felling. In the earlier 5-year plans many environmentally destructive problems arose; the relocated Indonesians found that on arrival, despite a policy of grass planting on a contour basis, soil erosion had already occurred resulting in nutrient depletion. As a result, there have been changes to land-clearance contracts, including the replacement of grasses by leguminous species that provide a better protective cover and enhance the nitrogen content of the soil. Also, the responsibility for ensuring that such planting is actually carried out is now a binding part of the clearance contract, as is the application of initial fertiliser to ensure the success of newly sown legumes. Nevertheless, as Suwardjo (1986) has discussed, these programmes have not only caused accelerated soil erosion, which in Sumatra may amount to as much as $500\, t\, ha^{-1}$ per year, but also a loss of soil fertility, especially in areas cleared mechanically rather than by hand. The former brings subsoil with a high aluminium content to the surface and this, in tandem with soil compaction and inadequate fertiliser use, has often resulted in poor harvests. What remains unclear is whether this redistribution of Indonesian people has actually reduced the environmental problems associated with high populations in Java, Madura and Bali where deforestation and soil erosion are acute. Or does it mean that the problems of environmental degradation are being magnified and transferred to hitherto uncompromised regions? Once again, the interplay between politics and environment is apparent.

Schemes of a similar nature are underway in Amazonia where, as Johns (1988) has discussed, the rainforest is also threatened by logging and mining enterprises and road construction. The development of Amazonia began in 1960 after the completion of the Belém–Brasilia highway that opened up the eastern part, and in the mid-1960s the government adopted numerous policies that, via tax incentives, were designed to encourage private sector development (Browder 1988). One outcome of these policies has been the establishment of large-scale North American-style cattle ranching. As *World resources 1988–1989* (World Resources Institute 1988) points out, development of this type was initially considered to be more advantageous than other types of agriculture because it required relatively little new infrastructure, it could utilise abundant available labour and there was an expanding North American market for cheap pasture-reared beef. The ultimate goal was the creation of an industry, originally funded by foreign investment, that would be self-sustaining and a major earner of foreign currency. In the period 1965–83, encouraged by tax incentives, 470 cattle ranches with an average size of 23 000 ha were established in Amazonia which, according to Repetto (1988a), accounted for c. 30 per cent of the total deforestation apparent from remotely sensed data collected between 1973 and 1983. The schemes have proved to be both financially and environmentally unsatisfactory. On the one hand, the high rate of government subsidies has benefited individual investors but resulted in considerable losses to the national economy that have done nothing to help Brazil repay its huge international loans. On the other hand, loss of soil fertility after forest clearance and the invasion of weeds can result in a rapid decline in the carrying capacity of these ranches.

As Repetto (1988a) has discussed, the continued availability of subsidies for conversion of forest to pasture makes it more economic for the investor to clear further forest than to purchase fertiliser or control weeds in existing pasture. Indeed, Malingreau and Tucker (1988) report that there is evidence from remotely sensed data for the recolonisation by forest vegetation of some ranches in the Matto Grosso following the abandonment of farms that were never economically or ecologically viable (see Fearnside 1984). In spite of this, similar schemes are still being undertaken: in the Grande Carajás region, centred on Belém, 30 000 km^2 of forest will be cleared for ranching as part of a large-scale development plan involving mining, the establishment of heavy industry, road and rail construction, and a further 15 000 km^2 of forest will be removed to provide charcoal for pig-iron smelting (Fearnside 1989). Large-scale cattle ranching is also one of the main reasons for forest decline in Central America. Problems similar to those in Amazonia have been experienced in Costa Rica, but concern about forest demise stimulated in part by lumber companies' realisation that a resource vital to their enterprise is rapidly diminishing, has resulted in the establishment of a series of national parks within which local industry (such as small-scale farming and logging) is encouraged (Simons 1988).

7.3.2 THE CONSEQUENCES OF TROPICAL RAINFOREST DEMISE

There is little doubt that the rapid deforestation of tropical regions is contributing to the enhanced greenhouse effect. For example, Goreau and de Mello (1988) have shown that deforestation in Amazonia has appreciably altered the fluxes of carbon dioxide, nitrous oxide and methane from denuded soils to such an extent that they are likely to exacerbate the greenhouse effect, and thus mitigating measures should be undertaken which involve rainforest conservation as well as controls on combustion sources. As this has been discussed in section 5.3.1, it will not be examined again in this section, which will concentrate on the local, though widespread, environmental change that occurs as a result of tropical deforestation and its often adverse economic consequences.

Of particular importance is the effect that deforestation has on tropical soils. This varies according to land-use and from region to region depending on soil nutrient status, and is linked to the biogeochemical cycling of nutrients between the atmosphere, soil and biomass. Interference with or removal of the latter will inevitably lead to changes in the reservoirs of nutrients and their inter-reservoir fluxes. The tight intra-system cycling of nutrients that occurs in tropical rainforests between the biomass and the litter means that soils are rapidly depleted of nutrients once the vegetation is removed, as illustrated in Fig. 7.5. In addition, removal of the protective vegetation cover and its replacement with a crop or pasture often results in accelerated soil erosion that exacerbates nutrient deficits. Rapid oxidation of soil organic matter is also promoted. As a result, many tropical agroecosystems exhibit soil erosion and rapidly declining soil fertility, which in turn affect crop productivity, often with serious economic consequences. Even within a relatively short time (5–10 years) a situation may develop wherein the economic gain is sufficiently diminished that the enterprise becomes self-destructive as the environmental costs increase. Careful management is thus essential if agricultural enterprises are to survive.

Sioli (1985) has examined the effects of deforestation in relation to the Amazonian environment and points out that the disruption of biogeochemical cycles by burning renders nutrients susceptible to leaching. While ash may temporarily increase soil nutrient content, it is readily leached so that nutrients are removed into ground-water or into surface runoff. Further losses from the ecosystem occur as crops and/or animals are harvested and exported; and such cumulative losses, unless they are compensated for with artificial fertilisers, often lead to farm abandonment. Sioli warns that 'dust bowl' conditions may develop as the protective vegetation cover is removed causing soils to dry out, and in some parts of Amazonia where seasonality is more pronounced there is already evidence of blown dust on newly constructed roads. Soil erosion by water also increases and there is the possi-

Fig. 7.5. The characteristics of tropical rainforest biogeochemical cycles under different management practices.

1. Undisturbed

ATMOSPHERE

B = Biomass

L = Litter

S

E

Species diversity is maintained

2. Swidden or Slash/burn shifting agriculture (2 - 3 year crop production)

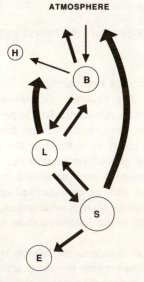

Species diversity is reduced but nutrient cycles can be restored to those similar to 1 if sufficient fallow periods are allowed .

3. Permanent cultivation

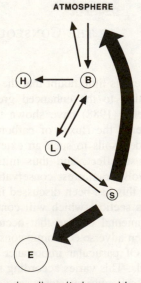

Species diversity is considerably reduced. (H) will diminish with time as (L) and (S) stores of nutrients diminish.

B = Biomass,　S = Soil,　L = Litter,　H = Harvest,　E = Soil erosion

N.B: Arrows and circles are drawn proportionately : Larger circles and thicker arrows indicate larger reservoirs and larger fluxes of nutrients.

bility of what Sioli describes as sandification. This may occur at the exposed soil surface as raindrops selectively erode fine clay particles, leaving heavier sand particles: with time this process can affect deeper parts of the soil profile, impairing its water-retaining capacity to such an extent that even after agriculture has been abandoned the forest may be unable to recolonise. As Buschbacher *et al.* (1987) have pointed out, it is doubtful if many of the pastures that were created in the eastern Amazon basin in the 1970s (section 7.3.1), and have since been abandoned, will ever return to forest: they may be permanently covered in heathlike vegetation. Based on a study of fifteen abandoned sites in the Paragominas region south of Belém, each of which experienced varying degrees of land-use intensity, Buschbacher *et al.* have shown that only those sites where low- and medium-intensity use were prac- tised are likely to return to a forest cover. Their data are summarised in Table 7.3, which shows that pasture with a low intensity land-use exhibits characteristics that most closely resemble those of undisturbed forest, i.e. a high above-ground biomass in which most of the nutrient stocks are located and a diverse flora which includes many species found in mature forest. This is in contrast to high intensity areas where mechanical removal of vegetation

Land Use	Low intensity	Medium intensity	High intensity	
	After cutting and burning pasture grasses are seeded. Grass success is poor, no weeding and few animals are grazed. <1 animal per ha.	After cutting and burning pasture grasses are seeded. Grass success is good. Periodic burning and weeding are practised, intermediate grazing pressure: 1 animal per ha.	After cutting and burning pasture grasses are seeded. Grass success is good. Weeding and burning are practised regularly, and areas are cleared with heavy machinery. Mowing occurs annually. High grazing pressure > 2 animals per ha.	Table 7.3. The characteristics of pastures in the Paragominas region of Amazonia 8 years after abandonment. (Based on Buschbacher *et al.* 1987.)
Above ground biomass	88.9	37.0	4.7	t/ha.
Below ground biomass	6.3	8.9	1.2	t/ha.
Total biomass	95.2	45.9	5.9	t/ha.
Current biomass as a % of potential forest biomass	25	12.05	1.54	
Vegetation type	mostly trees	79% trees 16% vines 5% shrubs, herbs, grasses	4% trees 96% shrubs, herbs, grasses	
Diversity	High, with a high proportion of species characteristic of mature forest	High - medium	Low	
Nutrient characteristics				
In Biomass In soil	Highest Lowest	Intermediate Intermediate	Lowest Highest	

coupled with intensive weeding and mowing have altered the environment to such a degree that forest recolonisation is unlikely.

Methods of deforestation and subsequent management practices not only influence the potential for forest regeneration but also influence the impact of deforestation on runoff and soil erosion. For example, Maass *et al.* (1988) have examined the soil erosion losses that have occurred as agroecosystems have replaced tropical deciduous forest on the Pacific coast of Jalisco, Mexico. Using data collected over a 2-year period from plots under a variety of management techniques, ranging from maize cultivation to a range of pasture grasses, they report that soil erosion and nutrient losses were greatest from maize (*Zea mays*) and guinea grass (*Panicum maximum* Jacq.) plots. Up to 130 t ha^{-1} of soil per year were lost from these plots, which compares with less than 0.2 t ha^{-1} per year from undisturbed forest. However, tests on the effects of a variety of conservation measures, including the incorporation of grass strips in cultivated maize fields and mulching with leaf litter from undisturbed forest, showed that the latter was particularly effective and reduced erosion by more than 90 per cent while, due to the nutrient input, productivity was increased by *c*. 30 per cent.

The effects of deforestation and management on tropical soils has also been discussed by Lal (1986), who cites examples in the humid tropics where deforestation has resulted in accelerated soil erosion. This is reflected in the increased sediment load of many rivers, especially in Southeast Asia where, as Fig. 7.4 shows, deforestation is occurring rapidly. Suspended sediment load data, however, provide only a crude measure of overall erosion and do not reveal the proportions of that load which are due to agriculture, logging, urban development, etc. Conversely, individual site studies do not reveal the overall magnitude of erosion but nevertheless illustrate some of the trends which occur when the forest cover is removed. Lal (1981) has examined the effects of deforestation on runoff and erosion in several small watersheds in the Ibadan region of Nigeria. His data show that between 1978 and 1981 there was virtually no storm runoff or soil wash where forest was undisturbed; similar results were obtained for the catchment in which traditional farming was practised. Where mechanical clearance was undertaken, 200 mm of runoff and 15 t ha^{-1} of soil were lost annually as compared to 48 mm of runoff and 5 t ha^{-1} of soil wash where manual clearing, followed by mechanised tillage, were practised. Lal concludes that in this region the best methods of clearance and cultivation to conserve soil are manual clearing followed by no-tillage planting.

Similar experiments have been reported from the Ivory Coast by Roose (1986) who has compared runoff and erosion from several plots, one of which was deforested and maintained as a bare soil by ploughing, and others in which a variety of perennial, annual and tree crops were grown. His data confirm many of the conclusions of Lal (1981). Firstly, the method of land clearance is significant as a determinant of erosion which is least after manual clearing – and where mixed cropping is practised which maintains a protective vegetation cover all year round. Secondly, land-use practices that involve tree crops in combination with legumes are also less likely to lead to soil degradation, while mechanised clearance for arable cropping is least beneficial, often leading to abandonment within 2 or 3 years. The maintenance of at least a partial tree cover is particularly advantageous because it guarantees a supply of nutrients via litter fall, as well as affording protection against soil erosion. The significance of tree crown or canopy cover as a control on soil erosion has also been investigated by Ruangpanit (1985) in the mountainous region of northern Thailand where shifting cultivation is extensive. His data show that runoff and soil erosion are considerably increased when the crown cover is low. With a crown cover of 20–30 per cent, average erosion was 15.9 kg ha^{-1} but with an 80–90 per cent crown cover it was reduced to 7.0 kg ha^{-1}. Moreover, the data show that once the crown cover is reduced below *c*. 70 per cent, runoff and erosion increased rapidly but that there was little difference when crown cover was between 70 and 90 per cent. Thus, Ruangpanit concludes that in such regions, especially where it is necessary to ensure watershed protection so that downstream regions are not affected by flooding or excessive silting, crown cover should be maintained at *c*. 70 per cent with as little bare soil as possible.

Inevitably, where soil erosion and declines in soil nutrients occur, there will be a decline in crop productivity, as has been discussed by Lal (1985, 1986) in relation to Amazonian pastures. This will vary according to the crops being grown and management practices; it can be minimised if soil conservation measures, fertilisers and suitable crop rotations are utilised, including intercropping with legumes. Nevertheless, ill-suited land-use and poor management can lead to environmental degradation with implications for present and future national economies. The examples of Brazilian and Central American ranching, as discussed above, are cases in point. Different problems but with similar consequences are occurring in the Philippines and have been described by Myers (1988), who points out that the mainstay of the country's economy is based on its natural resources, especially its forests. There are also pressures to raise agricultural productivity to accommodate population increases, though most of the land that can be thus exploited is in the uplands and is consequently susceptible to erosion. These are the areas in which the remaining forest lands are located; now only 22 per cent of the country is forested in comparison to nearly 100 per cent in 1900 and 66 per cent in 1945 (Myers 1988), which in itself constitutes a loss of revenue as timber exports (a major source of foreign currency) have declined in the last 20 years.

There is already evidence that, in the absence of suitable management plans, the uplands of the Philippines will rapidly undergo environmental degradation. Myers points out that by 1986 the population in the uplands was in excess of 18 million, representing one-third of the total, mainly rurally based, population. Many of these people are migrants from the lowlands, where most of the country's agriculture is located, who have little money to invest to ensure success in the longer term and who lack security of tenure to make farming the heritage enterprise that it is in many nations. These facts, coupled with population growth, suggest that by the year 2000 most of the remaining forests will have disappeared and been replaced with subsistence farming with a little surplus income derived from cash crops.

Myers believes that soil erosion is already a problem and that at least 90 000 km^2 of land are so badly affected that they can no longer sustain crop production. Open grasslands, for example, currently experience an annual loss of 84 t ha^{-1} of soil, with overgrazed areas losing 250 t ha^{-1}, which compares with 12 and 3 t ha^{-1} annually from soils under secondary and primary forest respectively. While there are no data from the Philippines that indicate what effect these soil losses will have on productivity, information from other tropical regions (e.g. Pimentel *et al*. 1987) suggests that productivity will drop by between 15 and 70 per cent depending on the rate of soil formation in relation to the rate of soil loss. In addition, there will be off-site repercusssions, especially on watersheds which supply not only domestic water but also hydroelectric power and irrigation projects. Excessive siltation will reduce the operational life span of dams and reservoirs and downstream areas are likely to witness an increase in flooding. These problems are being made worse by logging practices which, unless carefully managed, will continue to contribute to excessive soil erosion. Deforestation in the Philippines, especially that for agricultural development, is likely to be a major handicap to its economic development unless appropriate land-use strategies are implemented. As Myers mentions, there are already some programmes in operation which suggest that the national resource base can be manipulated to accommodate the growing needs of the population without serious impairment of soil fertility. These include social forestry, in which most land is used for tree growing and the harvest is balanced against a planting programme; and agroforestry in which the production of food crops is the primary objective but includes a large number of tree crops. Such enterprises will, however, need to be expanded if the environment and the population are to be protected in the longer term.

7.3.3 SAVANNA REGIONS

Savanna regions occupy *c.* 20 per cent of the earth's land surface, comprising some $23 \times 10^6 \, \mathrm{km}^2$ located between the equatorial rainforests and the mid-latitude arid and semi-arid deserts. Savannas are most extensive in Africa, where they occupy 65 per cent of the land area. Savannas also occupy 60 per cent of Australia, 45 per cent of South America and 10 per cent of India and Southeast Asia (M M Cole 1986). Floristically such regions are complex (Johnson and Tothill 1985), the common feature being a continuous grass layer with varying amounts of trees and/or shrubs. All are influenced by a strongly seasonal climate with abundant rainfall during the summer months and a dry period of between 4 and 8 months. All of the world's savannas have been affected by human activity and, as Table 7.2 shows, deforestation is occurring at a rapid rate due to agricultural development and fuelwood collection. The problems are most acute in Africa where population pressures are also greatest, though modification of South American savannas is increasing; desertification is occurring in some areas as a result of overgrazing.

The various land-uses that are practised in African savannas have been described by Okigbo (1985) and include nomadic herding, shifting cultivation on a 2–3 year basis, semi-permanent cultivation or rotational bush-fallow, intensive dryland agriculture involving rotations and intercropping, and more intensive flood-land cultivation where small-scale irrigation is practised. The most successful agricultural systems in terms of sustained productivity and the least environmentally degrading are those which involve crop rotations and an adequate fallow period. Traditionally, as Okigbo points out, a production unit of this kind will consist of a number of fields centred around garden plots that are permanently cultivated; each field has a specific inter-cropping and fallowing pattern and the system as a whole relies on manual labour rather than mechanisation, with limited inputs of fertilisers and pesticides. This semi-permanent cultivation is now more widespread than slash-and-burn shifting cultivation and has increased as nomadic groups have become more sedentary and integration of crops and livestock has occurred. In areas with high population densities (c. 100 people km^{-2}), intensive dryland agriculture is becoming increasingly important and in many cases there is no fallow period although intercropping is common. Where there is seasonal flooding or irrigation, as in West Africa, rice is cultivated – and specialised cash cropping is increasing in the savanna zone as a whole. Despite these changes, some of which have proved to be environmentally degrading, there is still a food crisis because population growth is rapid (2–3 per cent per annum) and farming systems are failing to provide the necessary increase in productivity of c. 4 per cent per annum (Okigbo 1985). For example, Tarrant (1987) has shown that while world cereal yields are increasing, those for Africa are actually declining and exhibit increased annual variability especially in semi-arid regions like the savanna. Hadley (1985) also documents the poor success rates of many development projects in African savannas where, overall, crop and arable production have grown by only 2 per cent, necessitating a massive increase in food imports. It is also significant that the small improvements in productivity are due not to better production methods, but to increases in animal populations and the amount of land under cultivation. Dyson-Hudson (1984) has also commented that since c. 1970 the equivalent of $US600 million has been given as development funds to Africa's rangelands but has brought few rewards as far as more efficient and productive pastoralism is concerned.

There is also evidence that land degradation is accelerating, often as a result of incautious schemes to improve productivity, and as a consequence of overgrazing and firing. Billé (1985), for example, has described the encroachment of bush at three sites in southern Ethiopia in relation to grazing pressure. Tree and shrub numbers greatly increase as grazing pressure increases but there is a decline in the productivity of grasses which also become more inaccessible to livestock as the canopy closes; with moderate tree densities, grass productivity is enhanced. This can be promoted by burning which removes woody tissue and locally enriches the soil. It must, however, be carefully controlled because it is essential that a cover of perennial rather than annual grasses is maintained as the latter are more susceptible to drought. The maintenance of a partial tree cover is also to be encouraged in order to provide extra forage and a protective soil cover which helps combat desertification. This is a major problem in the Sahel zone where cash cropping has been mooted by Earth Report (1988) as one of the major causes of environmental degradation, and while the case presented may be oversimplified it is worth reiterating since cash cropping in general is not (if past performance is taken as a measure) the answer to Africa's development problems. Earth Report states that the introduction of peanuts as a cash crop in the 1950s and 1960s led farmers to become dependent on peanut harvests as their main source of income; as prices declined by 22 per cent between 1967 and 1969, so did soil fertility as less money was available for fertilisers. In order to maintain living standards, marginal land was brought into cultivation causing disruption of the traditional interplay between cultivators and nomadic herders; the former provided millet and sorghum as staple crops which they exchanged for animal products and the benefits of having their lands fertilised by animal herds. Fallow lands brought into cultivation reduced the range for grazing and restricted the distribution of much needed animal dung as fertiliser. The onset of drought in the 1970s simply compounded and brought to a head a situation that was almost inevitable from its inception, the root of which was fuelled by European interests to counter-act competition from soya bean imports from the USA. There are, of course, other arguments that pertain to the Sahel disaster (section 7.2.1).

Savanna regions outside Africa have also experienced development problems that have resulted in environmental change. In South America where savannas occupy some 2×10^8 ha, there have been many modifications of the natural vegetation for a variety of agricultural purposes ranging from large-scale ranching to intensive cropping based on irrigation. According to Cochrane *et al.* (1985), the land-use practised depends mainly on how well or badly the savannas are drained. In poorly drained areas extensive cattle ranching is predominant while in better-drained areas annual cropping is expanding and in some cases, especially in Venezuela, irrigation is making a major contribution to agricultural development. Cochrane *et al.* state that *c.* 80 per cent of tropical America's savannas are mostly well drained, with the largest single expanse in central Brazil. Here, in common with the Llanos area of the Orinoco basin in Venezuela, the vegetation comprises *cerrados* which M M Cole (1986) defines as savanna woodland. Cochrane *et al.* (1985) describe these two regions as; 'undoubtedly the most rapidly expanding agricultural frontiers in the Americas'. As communication networks have improved in the last three decades, there has been a shift away from cattle ranching to grain production. After clearance, rice is cultivated, followed by soya beans and maize and eventually semi-permanent pastures are established. Cassava, sugar cane, fruit crops, coffee and cotton are also grown and irrigation in the Venezuelan region is widely used for grain production. In Brazil, for example, the total area of crops has increased from *c.* 5×10^6 ha to 8.8×10^6 ha (excluding cultivated pastures), with noteworthy increases in dryland rice, maize, wheat and soya-bean production between 1970 and 1980. Moreover, Cochrane *et al.* believe that there is considerable potential for increased productivity as new cultivars are developed that are better suited to the relatively poor soils and if irrigation is extended, especially in Brazil. Such developments in South America are not without adverse environmental consequences, though they are more limited than those of African savannas where population levels are much higher. For example, Pla *et al.* (1985) report that in the northern central plains of Venezuela rain-fed production of sorghum and maize have resulted in accelerated erosion and an increase in flood frequency. The former is due to soil exposure before sowing, inadequate soil protection by seedlings in the early stages of crop growth and the absence of crop residues, while the latter relates to erratic rainfall and the removal of the natural vegetation cover.

In terms of large-scale ranching and beef production in the savannas of South America, the nutritional value of the pasture grasses is, according to Vera *et al.* (1986), relatively low and thus the carrying capacity is limited. Ranches are usually large (1500–3000 ha) and average herd size is *c.* 600. Vera *et al.* believe that there is potential for improving productivity, including the introduction of legume-rich swards, though as yet the developments in cropping have far exceeded efforts to improve pasture lands. Grazing pressures have also altered the savanna environment of India, as has been discussed by Gadgil and Meher-Homji (1985) in relation to the Deccan plateau which is the most degraded of India's savanna lands. This is due to competition for land between grazing and cropping as well as a reduction in the vegetation cover for fuelwood. As a consequence land has become unproductive as unpalatable weeds have replaced nutritious fodder. Similarly in the Western Ghats, much of the region is deforested and overgrazed and rates of soil erosion have increased, a situation which is not being improved by the replacement of buffalo and cattle by goats.

Overall, the world's savanna lands (those in Australia have been omitted from this discussion as this chapter deals specifically with developing countries) present both considerable potential and considerable environmental degradation. As in many of the cases of environmental change discussed in this text, social or historical factors underlie many of these changes.

7.4 MOUNTAINOUS REGIONS AND ISLANDS

World population is increasing at a rate of between 1.5 and 2.0 per cent per annum (section 9.3.3) and most of the projected growth that will occur by the year 2000 will be in the developing world, mirroring a well-established trend. As the foregoing sections have illustrated, population pressures, often stimulated by other factors such as economics and land ownership, are frequently the underpinning cause of environmental change, especially as agriculture has spread into areas that are only marginally productive or where injudicious land-use practices have been established. This section will concentrate on those parts of the earth's surface where rapid environmental change is taking place with considerable repercussions for neighbouring regions. Thus, attention will focus on the Himalayan region of Asia and the Andean region of Central and

Fig. 7.6. The location of sites discussed in section 7.4.

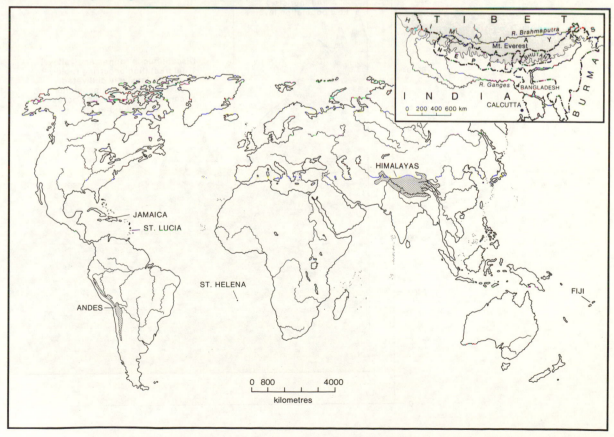

South America where development is occurring rapidly and which, because they constitute watershed areas, are affecting downstream areas. Finally, attention will focus on island communities in the developing world where land-use has created specific environmental problems that are frequently related to watershed abuse.

7.4.1 THE HIMALAYAS

The Himalaya mountain range, as shown in Fig. 7.6, extends for almost 3000 km from the southern edge of the USSR, through northern Pakistan, India and Bangladesh, to the borders of Burma and southern China. According to Karan (1987), the population of the region is in excess of 33 million and is increasing at more than 2 per cent per annum. In consequence, hitherto untouched lands are now being exploited; and more intense land-use pressures coupled with an increased demand for fuelwood are bringing about environmental change at an unprecedented rate. As Ives (1987) has discussed, it is widely believed that the situation in the Himalaya will reach crisis proportions by the turn of the century, affecting not only that region

Fig. 7.7. Schematic representation of the zones of the Himalaya and their characteristics. (Based on Karan and Iijima 1985.)

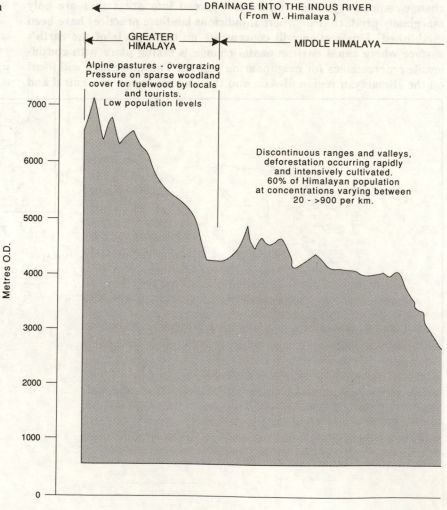

but also downstream and deltaic areas that are in receipt of drainage from the Ganges and Brahmaputra Rivers. In 1988, media reports of a massive flooding episode that occurred in Bangladesh singled out deforestation in the Himalaya as the most important cause. This is, however, disputed (Cohen in *The Independent*, 17 Sept 1988) and highlights the complexity of the Himalayan socio-economic and ecological balances. To examine these problems examples will be presented against a backdrop of the region's natural divisions, in order to highlight the significance of environmental change. The sites referred to are given in Fig. 7.6.

To divide the Himalaya into natural regions is itself difficult because the ecology is complex, as Schweinfurth (1984) has discussed. However, Karan and Iijima (1985) have suggested a tripartite subdivision of the region which is depicted in Fig. 7.7. Each zone is currently experiencing a range of pressures which are listed in Table 7.4. As Ives (1987) has pointed out, the issue of environmental degradation in the Himalaya is extremely complex and has been extensively debated during the 1980s, giving rise to what he describes as the Himalaya Environmental Degradation Theory (HEDT). This invokes the operation of vicious circles, involving deforestation for arable cultivation

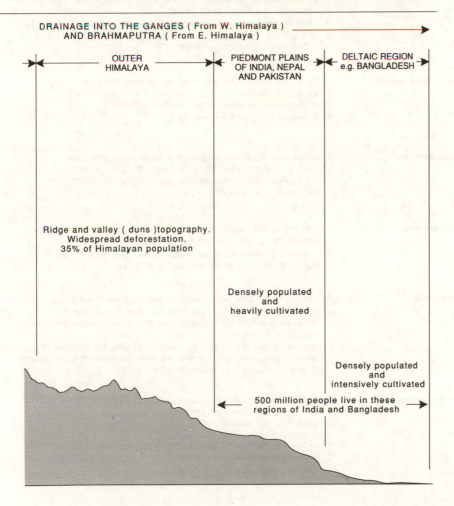

DRAINAGE INTO THE GANGES (From W. Himalaya)
AND BRAHMAPUTRA (From E. Himalaya)

OUTER HIMALAYA

PIEDMONT PLAINS OF INDIA, NEPAL AND PAKISTAN

DELTAIC REGION e.g. BANGLADESH

Ridge and valley (duns)topography.
Widespread deforestation.
35% of Himalayan population

Densely populated and heavily cultivated

Densely populated and intensively cultivated

500 million people live in these regions of India and Bangladesh

and fuelwood underpinned by rapidly increasing population pressure; as land is degraded by accelerated erosion, even steeper slopes are cultivated and more forest is cleared. This view is espoused by Myers (1986), who believes that deforestation in the Himalaya has been responsible for flood disasters in the lower reaches of the Ganges and Brahmaputra and the higher incidence of flooding that has occurred since 1940; apparently flooding now affects some 18×10^6 ha of land as compared with 6×10^6 ha in the early 1950s. Such a theory is, according to Ives (1987), too simplistic not least because much of the data on deforestation and fuelwood consumption on which it is based are unsound. For example, M Thompson *et al.* (1986) have highlighted the fact that estimates of the latter vary by a factor of 67! That such discrepancies arise is due to compilation of data at a local scale and its subsequent incautious use to derive estimates at a regional scale. The comments made in Fig. 7.7, concerning land-use pressures in the Himalayan

Table 7.4. Factors contributing to environmental degradation in the Himalaya. (Based on Ives 1987.)

1. Population Increases	A. Population growth is estimated at 2.6% p.a. on an average with some local increases in excess of 3.0% to 3.5%p.a. The population will double in 27 years.
	B. The increases are exacerbated by illegal immigration from India
	C. In excess of 3 million refugees from Afghanistan are now settled in Pakistan's Hindukush- Himalaya[1]
2. Population needs	A. Increased demand for fuelwood and construction timber
	B. Increased demand for grazing land as animal herds have multiplied in line with human population growth
	C. Increased demand for arable land.
3. Deforestation	A. Worst-case scenarios suggest that massive deforestation has occured in the last 30 years. Ives (1987), suggests that the available data are unsatisfactory and often conflicting.
	B. Decline in forest quality
4. Soil erosion.	A. Has intensified locally and is considered to be due to deforestation and terrace construction on steep slopes for cultivation.
	B. Is affecting downstream areas and deltaic regions as the sediment load of the Ganges and Brahmaputra increase
5. Fuel-needs	A. Increasing demand for fuelwood is depleting the forest cover
	B. As the forest cover is depleted the time and energy needed to collect fuelwood increases so that alternative sources are used, especially animal dung.
	C. Increasing use of animal dung means that soils are deprived of fertilizer and productivity is reduced. More land may then be cleared in order to maintain an adequate food supply
6. Other factors	A. The size of land holdings is diminishing. An average family of seven has only 1 hectare of land.
	B. Decline in the amount and quality of animal fodder result in reduced secondary productivity
	C. Increasing tourism causes added pressure on fuel resources
	D. Poor road and dam construction
	E. Political infighting and instability

[1] Allan, (1987)

zones, thus represent a generalised overview which may be grossly inaccurate at the local scale. Similarly, management and development plans may not be generally appropriate and should be tailored to alleviate local pressures within an integrated regional framework.

Deforestation still remains a crucial issue in the Himalaya but the temporal and spatial pattern of its occurrence is, in the light of more recent research, very different from that hitherto envisaged. For example, Myers (1986) states that between 1947 and 1980 Nepal's forest cover declined from 57 per cent to 23 per cent, but Mahat *et al.'s* (1986a, b, 1987a, b) work in the Middle Hills of Nepal (Sindhu Palchok and Kabhri Palanchok districts) suggests a different spatial and temporal pattern. Their data indicate that serious deforestation was occurring more than 200 years ago and was most severe between 1890 and 1930. More recently, reforestation has occurred naturally on abandoned farm terraces where grazing pressures have been low. Mahat *et al.* also show that the area of forested land has not changed very much since 1950, although forest quality has declined as grazing pressure has increased. Using records of oral history from these two districts, Gilmour (1988) has shown that tree cover has actually increased on private farmland over the last 20 years and while there is still an overall loss of forest it is not as acute as the HEDT suggests. Similarly, Byers's (1987) work in the Mount Everest National Park indicates that there has been less forest removal than envisaged and that shrubs/grassland and forested slopes below 4000 m OD are stable. Nevertheless, soil erosion is an appreciable problem in some Alpine pastures of the park due to overgrazing in a transhumance system, fuelwood collection and periglacial processes. There are also variations in the temporal and spatial patterns of deforestation in the Indian Himalaya; in Uttar Pradesh, for example, Tejwani (1987a) reports that forest losses have been extensive and that much of what remains is degraded. In the Dehra Dun Valley some 16 per cent of the forest cover has disappeared during the last 100 years (J F Richards 1987). Moreover, Tucker (1987) has pointed out that the first period of large-scale deforestation in northern India occurred in the 1850s and 1860s as the British colonisation of India gained momentum and railways were constructed to gain access to the upper Ganges and Indus plains.

Not only is the extent of deforestation variable but the reasons why it is occurring also vary from region to region. Mahat *et al.* (1986a, b, 1987a, b) believe that in the Middle Mountain region of Nepal the loss of forest is due mainly to the increased requirements for arable land rather than to the need for fuelwood. As Ives (1987) comments, findings such as these have important implications for the formulation of mitigating plans; the introduction of more efficient wood-burning stoves, for example, while reducing the need for fuelwood does not provide a substitute for arable land. In fact, Hrabovszky and Miyan (1987) advocate land-use intensification rather than clearance of new land as the most effective way to increase food production in the Nepal Himalaya. This, they argue, could be achieved, at least partially, by increasing the area of irrigated land especially in the Terai plains of southern Nepal. There is also much uncertainty about the contribution of injudicious agricultural practices to soil erosion. Traditionally, rain-fed terraces are constructed on steeper slopes in the Middle Mountains for the production of maize, millet and buckwheat. Undoubtedly landslips occur, exacerbating soil erosion as the protective vegetation cover is impaired, but the extent of slope failure is due to climatic conditions, especially rainfall intensity, and the degree of terrace maintenance. The problem is worse in some areas than it is in others but, as Karan and Iijima (1985) point out, soil erosion is particularly acute where steep slopes are cultivated without terracing. In the Sikkim Himalaya, for example, forest clearance of steep slopes for maize and rice cultivation have accelerated erosion rates as is evidenced by dry gullies and an increased sediment load of rivers. Such erosion is also contributing to accelerated sedimentation in reservoirs but it is not the only cause, as Tejwani (1987b) has discussed in relation to reservoirs in the Indian Himalaya. Road and reservoir construction and mining all contribute to increased sediment yields, as well as deforestation and over-grazing, leading to losses in reservoir capacity of up to 60 per cent. Tejwani believes that the small size of agricultural landholdings and their fragmentation is a major obstacle to the implementation of soil conservation measures in the Indian Himalaya. Once again this highlights the significance of social and administrative factors in environmental management.

Thus the causes and effects of land-use practices vary considerably from region to region in the Himalaya, so that a general theory such as the HEDT becomes untenable. This is stressed by Ives *et al.* (1987), who argue the case for more research to obviate the problems associated with the extrapolation of data, often erroneously, from the micro- to the macro-scale within the Himalaya region. Then there is the question of the relationship between activities in the Himalaya and events downstream. Again the link between the two is more complex than is suggested by the HEDT. Hamilton (1987) refutes the HEDT suggestion that widespread deforestation in the Himalaya is the prime cause of flooding in the lower reaches of the Ganges and the Brahmaputra and argues that large-scale flooding, such as that of 1985 in India when 237 people were killed (and presumably that in Bangladesh in 1988), could not be prevented even if the entire Himalaya were forested. Such catastrophic events, he believes, are more likely to be due to the receipt of a considerable volume of rainfall in a short space of time on to soils which are already saturated, as occurs during the monsoon season. Hamilton also points out that the replacement of forest by well-maintained agricultural terraces may actually reduce the amount of soil erosion, and Ives (1987) provides a timely reminder that the Himalaya are undergoing tectonic uplift which itself may be of sufficient magnitude to account for much of the increased sediment load of the major drainage systems. Undoubtedly land-use practices influence flooding and erosion, but ignoring the impact of natural processes in the search for a human scapegoat is not going to pre-empt the potential land crisis of the Himalaya in the twenty-first century. In view of the diversity of the environment, the variations in cultural, social and political organisation as well as rapid population growth, there is an overwhelming need for development and management plans that are practicable at a local level, are politically acceptable to all Himalayan nations and are equally beneficial to those extra-Himalayan regions that are affected by intra-Himalayan policies. The task is formidable and impossible to achieve without international co-operation.

7.4.2 THE ANDES

The Andes also have a long history of human occupation which has transformed the landscape. As discussed in section 3.2.1, there is much debate as to when people first colonised the Americas but it occurred at least 12 kyr BP and there is evidence (section 3.3.1) that some early plant and animal domestications occurred in Central and South America. The Andes of Peru, for example, provided animals like the llama and alpaca which were domesticated approximately 7 kyr BP, and in the Tehuacán Valley of Mexico the first permanent agricultural systems of the Americas were developed *c*. 8 or 9 kyr BP. It was here that maize (*Zea mays*) was first domesticated. The major civilisations of the Americas, notably the Olmecs and Mayas which thrived between 3 kyr and 1 kyr, dominated the lowland regions adjacent to the Gulf of Mexico but by *c*. 600 AD (The Times, *The World*, 1986) the major centres of early American peoples had become established in the high Andean basins. Ultimately, the great civilisations of the Aztecs and Incas developed. The former established themselves on the margins of Lake Texcoco in the fourteenth century. By 1428 they had established a city state, nurtured by food production on the lake margins, but in 1521 the state fell to Cortés and Mexico was annexed by Spain. The Incas, on the other hand, were a short-lived civilisation of the fifteenth century which created an empire that extended some 3200 km along the Andes from what is now Ecuador to northern Chile. They undertook numerous engineering feats, including the construction of roads, bridges and tunnels as well as extensive terracing and irrigation systems to improve crop production. This empire was also destroyed by the Spanish colonists who eventually captured the capital, Cuzco, in 1533.

The vestiges of these empires, as well as those of the Olmecs and Mayas, are represented in the landscape by the remains of vast temples, road networks and terracing. The latter were constructed to both conserve moisture and to reduce soil erosion and occur on slopes as steep as 25°. Gischler and Jauregui (1984) have demonstrated that in Peru much of this pre-Hispanic terracing is abandoned but could be renovated to enhance food production more economically than by developing new lands. Moreover, the success of these pre-Hispanic cultures implies that their food-producing systems were effective. Millones (1982) believes that the value of the soil as a resource was fully acknowledged by the Incas and is reflected in the many thousands of hectares that were contour terraced and irrigated by water stored in artificial lakes (*chochas*). He argues that the arrival and conquests of the Spanish not only brought about the destruction of a sophisticated culture but also had a ruinous effect on the environment. The aim of such colonial imposition (section 4.4.2) was mainly to exploit the natural resources for the benefit of Spain. Precious metals were the chief resources sought by the invaders and the silver-mines of Potosí in Peru are a case in point (section 4.4.2). The indiscriminate exploitation of Andean forests to provide wood for mines and as fuel, in tandem with burning for the creation of pastures and subsequent overgrazing, are, according to Millones, mainly responsible for the demise of these high forests and their fauna.

Further serious environmental consequences have arisen from the introduction of grazing herbivores (such as cattle, sheep, goats, horses, donkeys and mules) to which the Andean environment is not naturally adapted but which are the mainstay of modern Andean populations. Parallels can be drawn with Australia (section 4.4.3) and the island of St Helena (section 7.4.3). As Millones points out, erosion is now a crucial problem in most Andean environments. Generalisations are, however, difficult to make for a region which is so diverse due to altitudinal changes and considerable climatic variation. As a guideline, the major zones are summarised in Table 7.5. Overall, the potential for agriculture is limited by topography, especially slope angles and water availability. As a result those areas, notably the paramos plains and intermontane valleys, which are suitable for herding and crop-growing are experiencing environmental problems due not simply to over-exploitation, but to poor management such as the lack of rotational grazing and the replacement of traditional crops with cash crops. Land-use and the vulnerability of sloping terrain to erosion are, however, not the only causes of environmental degradation.

Land-tenure systems, leading to decreasing farm size and fragmentation, and high levels of population growth are among the social factors contributing to environmental change. Stadel (1986), for example, has discussed the significance of these factors in relation to agricultural development in the Cordillera region of Ecuador. Here, the rural population density is 208 km^{-2} and the annual increase in population is *c*. 3.1 per cent, but the amount of agricultural land per head of population is only 0.52 ha. Moreover, in the Pelileo–Patate region (eastern Cordillera of Ecuador), Stadel states that nearly 60 per cent of the farms (*minifundia*) are less than 1 ha and some 94.3 per cent are less than 5 ha. The haciendas, in contrast, are not only larger ( )5 ha to 10 000 ha) but occupy nearly 63 per cent of the agricultural area including a much higher proportion of the best agricultural land. Thus, many *minifundia* have restricted or no access to irrigation water and are often too small to support a family so that employment is sought elsewhere.

In terms of rates of erosion that are actually occurring within the Andean region, a study by Harden (1988) is illustrative of the impact of various land-use practices in the Rio Ambato catchment in the central Ecuadorian

Table 7.5 A summary of the major zones in the central Andes and the present and potential land-uses. (Based on Millones 1982.)

Zone	Current Land Use	Potential Land Use
Super-arid desert. Semi-arid desert and dry low mountains.	Permanent agriculture is possible only with irrigation. Seasonal herding. Lumbering.	Potential could improve overall with permanent irrigation.
Thorn bush, thorn steppe and dry forest.	Limited agriculture with irrigation. Seasonal herding. Dry season cultivation	Good potential with irrigation except in areas where topography and water deficiencies are limiting
Humid forests	Subsistence agriculture. Diversified agriculture. Cattle herding. Dryland agriculture eg. tubers, legumes and cereals	Good agriculture and herding on fertile soils. Favourable for forest plantations
Humid paramo (grasslands)	Extensive sheep and llama herding	Good potential for herding but is very degraded, needs good management
Humid tundra	Nomadic herding	Low potential for herding
Very humid forest (tropical and sub-tropical)	Limited and localised agriculture and herding	Low agricultural potential; good for forest reserves and wood extractors
Very humid paramos	Extensive sheep herding on natural and cultivated pastures	Good potential for herding
Very humid tundra	Sheep and auchenid herding (for wool)	Moderate potential for cattle herding
Rainforest	Mostly unused	Topography limiting
Rainy paramos	Limited herding	Low potential for herding
Rainy tundra	Herding of sheep	Low potential and overgrazed
Nival zones	Unused	Potential for tourism

Andes. Here, elevations range from 2200 m in the valley to 6310 m which is the summit height of Mount Chimborazo. Of the total area of 1300 km^2, 31 per cent is cultivated, 65 per cent is used mainly for sheep grazing, 3 per cent is ice-covered or bare rock and the remaining 1 per cent is urban. The average size of holding is between 3 and 6 ha, and below 3000 m irrigation is practised. There is very little flat land and cultivation is common on unterraced land with slopes of 20–35 per cent. Harden's data indicate an annual range of soil losses varying from 0 to 836 t ha^{-1}, with the highest rates of erosion occurring where soils are exposed to drought, overgrazing or tillage. Of the various land-uses in the region, soil erosion is most severe at intermediate altitudes where barley, corn, tubers, etc. are cultivated. Harden estimates that under current conditions productivity can only be maintained for between 10 and 75 years. Inevitably there are underlying social complexities, such as land tenure and population growth, which are contributing to the problem but there is also evidence, from locations within the drainage basin where conservation measures are being introduced, that terracing and contour farming can not only reduce the risk of erosion but also increase productivity.

While there is no way of knowing whether these rates of erosion are typical or atypical of Andean regions in general, the data nevertheless give cause for concern and emphasise the role of soil erosion as a major agent of environmental change. What is perhaps more disturbing is Harden's statement that, apart from a few recently introduced measures, efforts to conserve the soil resource are not being undertaken, implying that soil conservation is not an intrinsic component of local agricultural practices.

7.4.3 SMALL ISLANDS

By virtue of their isolation and limited land area, many small islands have undergone considerable environmental change much of which is a consequence of agricultural developments. To illustrate such changes, attention will focus on two Caribbean islands, Jamaica and St Lucia, plus St Helena and Fiji.

In Jamaica there is a long history of environmental change due to land-use practices. As Eyre (1987) reports, there is considerable variation of opinion relating to rates of deforestation; FAO (1985), for example, quote a figure of 3.0 per cent per year which is assumed to be due to commercial logging. Eyre (1987), on the other hand, believes that the figure is more like 3.3 per cent. This is based on a detailed survey of 687 km^2, which is *c.* 6 per cent of Jamaica's total land area. In all of the forested areas sampled by Eyre, commercial lumber production was responsible for only a proportion of the deforestation. The remainder was due to clearance for cultivation and pasture. Of the 500 sites sampled, most of the deforestation was manifest as small parcels of land between 20 and 25 ha in size. This, Eyre opines, is occurring because of social factors similar to those discussed in section 7.2.1 in relation to desertification; i.e. the need to generate foreign exchange, declining employment opportunity in urban centres and fragmentation of landholdings. While the forest losses are themselves helping to transform the landscape, they are also contributing to accelerating rates of soil erosion because the sites are frequently on steeply sloping land. The land itself rapidly becomes degraded and land in receipt of drainage from these slopes is also adversely affected. Moreover, 2.7 per cent of the deforested land is used for the cultivation, in small isolated tracts, of *Cannabis sativa* (marijuana) which is considerably lucrative although illegal.

At a more local level, Barker and McGregor (1988) have examined the landscape changes that have occurred in the Yallahs basin, a drainage basin of 180 km^2 situated in the Blue Mountains northeast of Kingston, Jamaica's capital. Here, land degradation due to natural and cultural factors is widespread. The landscape, as part of a geologically young mountain region with steep slopes, is naturally predisposed to mass movement. As Barker and McGregor point out, however, land-use practices have also played a significant role in landscape change since colonial times when deforestation began. In the eighteenth century, for example, coffee plantations were established. Coffee was cultivated on the steep slopes while housing and processing plants were located on flatter ridges. Fire was used for forest clearance and because slopes were steep soil erosion was rapid; its effects were often so serious that productivity rapidly declined and new areas were cleared. By the mid-nineteenth century, coffee plantations had largely been abandoned. The next major phase of land degradation came after the abolition of slavery in 1838 and the rise of peasant agriculture. Farmers tended small plots in a bush-fallowing system and employed fire for clearance. The agriculture was essentially subsistent, with any available surplus being marketed in Kingston.

During the later nineteenth and early twentieth centuries cash cropping gradually increased, including the resumption of coffee cultivation but on a much more limited basis than hitherto. In addition, an expanding Kingston required increasing amounts of fruit and market garden produce which are currently the main products. Apart from the impact of agriculture on steep slopes, there are additional pressures on the landscape of which deforestation is the most significant. As in Eyre's (1987) study, clearance is for agriculture as well as lumber, and coffee growing is increasing to produce an export crop and bring in foreign exchange. McGregor (1986), for example, reports that in the upper Yallahs basin there is extensive sheetwash erosion, slope failures and extensive gullying. Much of this is due to a combination of deforestation and the use of fire for clearance, which leave the soil susceptible to erosion, especially during periods of heavy rainfall which are relatively common. Barker and Spence (1988) propose that the most effectve way of combating these problems is to encourage the development of so-called food forests which involve the intercropping of food-producing trees and shrubs. Such systems are effective as conservation strategies and are economically successful elsewhere in Jamaica. Diverse cropping such as this is ecologically sound because it is much more akin to the rainforest that it replaces, in contrast to monoculture, and provides a year-round protective cover for the soil.

The problems of land degradation which characterise the Jamaican landscape are commonplace in many other Caribbean islands. Rojas *et al.* (1988) have reviewed the situation in St Lucia where less than 5 per cent of the island's 617 km^2 can be cultivated without incurring environmental problems. Since large plantations occupy the best agricultural land, most of the rural population cultivate small plots of less than 0.4 ha on the steep slopes of the mountainous central region where there are thin volcanic soils. Some 25 per cent of the cultivated land is being used in a way that is not sustainable. The practice of slash and burn shifting cultivation, along with intensive mixed cropping, is causing accelerated soil erosion and, as the moisture-retaining capacity of the soil is impaired, the incidence of flooding is increasing. The outcome is thus similar to that of Jamaica. The social factors are also similar, including high rural populations, small landholdings and limited opportunities for alternative occupations. Unsuitable large-scale farming is also being practised in some areas such as the Praslin watershed where bananas are grown for export. When demand is high or prices increase there is a tendency to cultivate marginal areas, but when the economic situation reverses the opposite trend occurs and cultivation focuses on the most productive land. As Rojas *et al.* point out, injudicious land-use practices on the steeper slopes have adverse effects on downstream agricultural lands, including silting and flooding. Thus conservation programmes must involve integration between upland and lowland agricultural systems. The problem is further compounded in St Lucia because the amount of land under cultivation is sufficient to support only 40 per cent of the rural population and, since there are few opportunities in urban centres to provide alternative livelihoods, pressures on land will continue to occur. Nevertheless, as Rojas *et al.* indicate, there are some mitigating actions that can be taken. For the small farmer on steep watershed slopes the food forest, as suggested for the Yallahs Basin of Jamaica, would be a more ecologically sound food-producing system. Hence sustainable agriculture could replace unsustainable agriculture, reducing the impact of erosion and flooding on downstream agricultural areas.

St Helena, in the South Atlantic Ocean, is another example of an island that has been transformed by human activity. Cronk (1989) has examined the course of vegetation development since the sixteenth century, and the subsequent demise of virtually all the natural flora and its replacement by introduced species. Much of the destruction of the native vegetation is attributed to the introduction of grazing animals, notably goats, pigs and cattle. These were first brought to St Helena in the sixteenth century by the Portuguese, and later, sheep were introduced. Today, although sheep and goats roam on ranges set aside specifically for that purpose, escapees still damage the vegetation but to a much lesser extent. During the 300 years following their introduction, Cronk indicates that these herbivores prevented regeneration of the natural vegetation by consuming seedlings and removing the bark of saplings. The resulting openings, devoid of protective vegetation cover, were then subject to erosion which in turn precluded regeneration. To replace the depleted vegetation a range of species were planted on the island in the nineteenth century, including the maritime pine (*Pinus pinaster*) and blackwood (*Acacia melanoxylon*), as well as a variety of herbs and shrubs which have now established specific vegetation zones. These have replaced the indigenous species, some of which, for example gumwood (*Commidendrum robustum*), scrubwood (*C. rotundifolium*) and ebony (*Trochetiopsis melanoxylon* alt. f. Marais) have been successfully established in trial plantings.

Land-use practices have also altered the Fijian landscape, as has been discussed by Clarke and Morrison (1987) who point out that this is the result of sugar-cane cultivation which has been the mainstay of Fiji's economy since the 1880s. In 1973 the industry came under national control and since then it has expanded from nearly 44 000 ha to more than 70 000 ha and employs more than 22 per cent of the island's labour force. Much of this development has involved sugar-cane cultivation on sloping terrain in contrast to its confinement to flat alluvial areas prior to 1960. It is this which has resulted in accelerated erosion. At Seaqaqa on the island of Vanua Levu, one such scheme was initiated in the mid-1970s with financial support from the World Bank. Clarke and Morrison report data on soil erosion, collected between 1978 and 1983 from a 5–8° slope at Seaqaqa, which show that between 15 and 20 cm of soil were lost over the site as a whole, which is equivalent to an annual overall loss of $34 \, t \, ha^{-1}$, and that the soil became more compacted with a loss of organic matter. Exchangeable bases also declined markedly, reflecting a considerable decline in fertility, as the topsoil was lost. At another site near Nadi on Vanua Levu, on an 18–22° slope annual soil losses were even higher at $90 \, t \, ha^{-1}$ and exchangeable aluminium levels increased to such an extent that the metal reached toxic levels.

As Clarke and Morrison discuss, their data are comparable with other studies in Fiji: such losses were known to be occurring more than 20 years ago but went unheeded in the wake of development. However, the main underpinning causes of this erosion appear to be methods of management and land tenure rather than erosivity and erodibility (section 6.2.2), especially as sugar-cane provides a protective cover for most of the year. While the problem was recognised as early as the 1930s, when institutions and regulations were created to combat it, these have been either ignored altogether or simply not enforced. This, Clarke and Morrison believe, is a response to the need to increase employment and to maintain standards of living. Moreover, the system of land tenure, wherein the land belongs to the indigenous Fijians and can only be leased to Indo-Fijians (the descendants of indentured cane workers who were drafted in from India in the early colonial period) militates against conservation measures because it ensures the political dominance of the former; and the encouragement of production ensures that such land is seen to be in use, an artefact to maintain internal stability. These factors plus preferential marketing arrangements and external financial support for development projects have all contributed to land degradation.

Once again, these examples illustrate the significance of social, economic and political factors in land-use policies (or their absence) that fail to consider conservation measures as a necessary prerequisite for long-term sustainable productivity and development.

7.5 CONCLUSION

There is no doubt that agriculture has transformed the environments of all developing countries. While it is essential, not only for the support through food supply for indigenous populations but also to provide a sound base on which economic progress can be made, it is unfortunate that in so many cases injudicious land-use practices have negated the very factor, increased productivity, that they sought to improve. The reasons for this are manifold and often rooted in the historic past though, as discussed in section 4.4, colonialism cannot be used perpetually to excuse failure. This is especially true in the light of the many more recent and post-independence projects that have failed, despite the often sizeable investments in the form of aid. This of course is not to exonerate outside influences *in toto* because even the most altruistic of

such schemes have regularly failed to take into account the specific requirements of local groups and their inherent land-management skills.
Moreover, the fundamental social structures and traditional land-management practices of many indigenous populations have often been dismissed as more or less irrelevant to modern-day needs.

The very inception of agriculture (section 3.3) was based on the manipulation of natural biotic resources, emphasising the close relationship
between environment and agriculture in all its forms. In the developed
world, the harnessing of fossil fuel energy as well as other scientific developments, and their application to agricultural systems, has opened up
a new range of agricultural possibilities: but all this has happened over
a relatively long time period and is not without its environmental implications. Such expertise is not easily extrapolated to regions where the
environment is markedly different. All agricultural systems are underpinned by the processes of energy flows and biogeochemical cycles
which, when disrupted, bring about environmental degradation. In the
developing nations, which are mostly located in the tropical and subtropical regions, an understanding of how these fundamental environmental processes work is only now being achieved. In many instances
this is too late to obviate desertification and soil erosion. But equally, in
many cases such degradation can be halted by more careful consideration of environmental processes and social requirements, as this chapter has shown.

Land-use has to be balanced to achieve sustainable use. Land, productivity and conservation should not be inimical or mutually exclusive.
That they have frequently become so, not solely in developing countries,
is a fundamental error which will exact an even greater toll in the
longer term.

FURTHER READING

El-Swaify S A, Moldenhauer W C, Lo A (eds) 1985 *Soil erosion and
conservation*. Soil Conservation Society of America. Ankeny, Iowa, USA

Glanz M H (ed) 1987 *Drought and hunger in Africa*. Cambridge University Press

Ives J D, Messerli B 1989 *The Himalayan dilemma: reconciling development and conservation*. Routledge and Kegan Paul, London

Joss P J, Lynch P W, Williams O B (eds) 1986 *Rangelands: a resource
under seige*. Cambridge University Press

Lal R, Sanchez P A, Cummings Jr R W (eds) 1986 *Land clearing and
development in the tropics*. A A Balkema, Rotterdam and Boston

Mortimore M 1989 *Adapting to drought: farmers, famines and desertification in West Africa*. Cambridge University Press

Repetto R, Gillis M (eds) 1988 *Public policies and the misuse of forest
resources*. Cambridge University Press

Whitehead E E, Hutchinson C F, Timmerman B N, Varady R G (eds) 1988 *Arid lands today and tomorrow*. Westview Press, Boulder, Colorado, and Belhaven Press, London

ADDITIONAL AGENTS OF ENVIRONMENTAL CHANGE: FORESTRY, RECREATION, TOURISM, SPORT AND BIOTECHNOLOGY

8.1 INTRODUCTION

Not all of the environmental changes that have occurred in the recent past are due to the impact of industry and agriculture. Throughout history, both have involved either the manipulation and/or the destruction of the world's forests. This continues today as the natural forest resource is managed to provide wood and wood-based products in both the developed and developing world. In addition, afforestation programmes are under way in many nations to augment the rapidly diminishing natural forest resource and in some cases to halt environmental degradation. Both forest management and afforestation are responsible for direct and indirect environmental change. Moreover, in the last four decades increasing automation and the rise in living standards in the developed world have resulted in increased leisure time which in turn has brought increased pressures on the environment via recreation, tourism and sport. The development of such 'industries' has also been facilitated by improved communications and transport as well as the need to generate income in areas that have been adversely affected by the economic recession of the early 1980s or which are unsuitable for other kinds of economic activity such as agriculture. Similarly, the need to generate foreign currency has stimulated tourism in regions that would have been virtually inaccessible 15 years ago. Such activities, however, especially where wildlife habitats and wildscapes are concerned, often have adverse and environmentally degrading consequences which, in some instances, are leading to the destruction of the very resource that attracts the visitors. At the very least, the growth of tourism has affected the environment by prompting the construction of hotel and resort complexes, nature trails and safari parks etc.

Another recent innovation is that of biotechnology, which involves the use of organisms (especially bacteria) in industrial and technological processes and which is being applied to a variety of environmental management problems such as waste treatment. Associated with this is the even more recent development, in the 1980s, of genetic engineering.

While this has its origins in the manipulation of plant and animal species that began *c.* 10 kyr BP (section 3.3) it has been confined to plant and animal breeding programmes. Now, however, science has provided the means to manipulate the basic genetic material that all plants and animals are made of, namely DNA (deoxyribonucleic acid) and already this has resulted in exciting progress in forensic science, pharmacology and disease control. Genetic engineering is also being applied to the production of new crop strains and agents, such as viruses, that can protect existing crops from pests and frost. Currently there is much international debate relating to the circumstances in which bioengineered species should be released into the environment and whether or not their impact will be entirely beneficial. Genetic engineering thus constitutes an important potential agent of environmental change.

8.2 FORESTRY

There are few forested areas of the world that remain untouched by human activity and those that do remain are unlikely to survive intact in the future. As Chapters 3 and 4 illustrate, forests have featured significantly in the historic development of the world's industrialised countries, especially in the temperate zone. This is illustrated by the fact that there is little natural forest left in western Europe as a whole and that forest resources were much prized by colonial powers in the eighteenth and nineteenth centuries (see section 4.4.2 in relation to North America). Indeed, many industrialised nations today, as well as importing wood and wood products from other developed nations, rely to an extent on timber which is imported from the developing world. Because of such ready markets, tropical and semi-tropical forests are increasingly being exploited by lumber industries, some of which are well-managed enterprises while others are major causes of forest degradation. Thus the management of forests on a global basis constitutes an agent of environmental change in both the developed and developing world.

In addition, and in response to rapidly dwindling forest resources, there are in many nations afforestation programmes on both small and large scales. In some cases, as in the UK, afforestation is widespread and like agriculture in the UK (section 6.2.3), the rationale behind it is economically- rather than ecologically-based. Afforestation programmes are also being initiated in many tropical regions in an effort to mitigate the effects of deforestation and to ensure the availability of forest resources for future generations. Deforestation is, however, occurring at a much more rapid rate than afforestation. Afforestation on a localised scale is also occurring in many developing countries to provide a protective cover for the soil in agricultural systems that are threatened by excessive soil erosion and desertification (section 7.2), the provision of fuelwood and, in many cases, a crop. This type of afforestation is generally known as agroforestry. Like forest manipulation, afforestation also modifies the environment and must thus be regarded as a significant agent of environmental change.

8.2.1 FOREST MANIPULATION IN THE DEVELOPED WORLD

As an example of forest manipulation in the developed world, emphasis here will be on forestry in North America. Here, after a rather shaky start in the colonial period (section 4.4.2), forestry is now practised on a sustainable basis involving a wide range of silvicultural techniques. The transition from unsustainable to sustainable resource use involves a change from exploitation to careful management. This is essential if renewable resources like

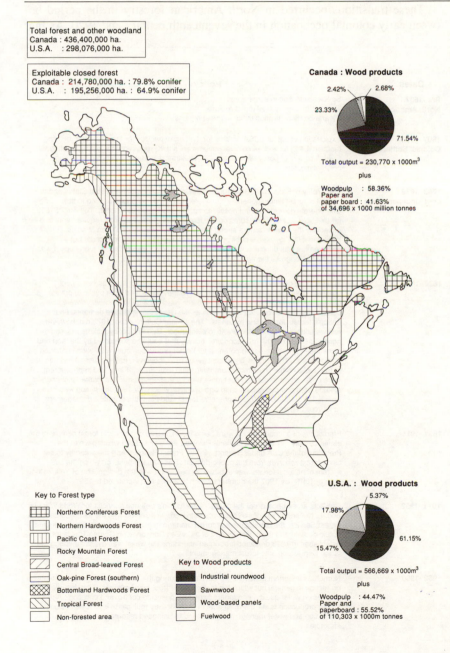

Total forest and other woodland
Canada : 436,400,000 ha.
U.S.A. : 298,076,000 ha.

Exploitable closed forest
Canada : 214,780,000 ha. : 79.8% conifer
U.S.A. : 195,256,000 ha. : 64.9% conifer

Fig. 8.1. The forest regions of North America and the output of wood-based products in 1985. (Data are from E G Richards 1987.)

Canada : Wood products

2.42%   2.68%
23.33%
71.54%

Total output = 230,770 x 1000m³

plus

Woodpulp   : 58.36%
Paper and
paper board : 41.63%
of 34,696 x 1000 million tonnes

U.S.A. : Wood products

5.37%
17.98%
61.15%
15.47%

Total output = 566,669 x 1000m³

plus

Woodpulp   : 44.47%
Paper and
paperboard : 55.52%
of 110,303 x 1000m tonnes

Key to Forest type

Northern Coniferous Forest
Northern Hardwoods Forest
Pacific Coast Forest
Rocky Mountain Forest
Central Broad-leaved Forest
Oak-pine Forest (southern)
Bottomland Hardwoods Forest
Tropical Forest
Non-forested area

Key to Wood products

Industrial roundwood
Sawnwood
Wood-based panels
Fuelwood

forests are to be maintained in a state that is conducive to future use. While both exploitation and management are agents of environmental change, the latter is overtly conservational in nature because the objective is optimum return on a long-term basis. In contrast, exploitation tends to involve the rapid diminution of resources, often to such an extent that the capacity for renewal is destroyed and optimum returns are short-lived. (Such concepts are relevant to the use of all renewable resources and not just forests.) The transition from exploitation to management is, however, underpinned by a change in economic attitudes, from those that are based on short-term high returns to those that recognise the need for sustainability in order to achieve long-term ongoing returns.

These transitions occurred in North American forestry in the period between early colonial occupation in the seventeenth century and 1920. As Fig.

Table 8.1 The development of forest policy in the USA. (Based on Bonnicksen 1982.)

Dates	Policy
Pre -1607 North Americans	Species selection in some areas. Hunting, gathering in all forest regions. Clearance for cultivation in some forest regions
1607 -1783 Colonial Settlers	Exploitation of eastern USA forests for timber, especially for local fuel and building (section 4 4 2) as well as colonial government's (UK) requirements for shipbuilding. Overall control of policy lay with local administrators and the dictats received from colonial masters.
1783 -1830 post - Independence	The Treaty of Paris in 1783 recognised the independence of the United States and the control of forest lands, generally considered to be inexhaustible, passed to the Confederate government but hostilities against the British continued. The war of 1812, for example, put new pressures on the forest resource due to army requirements and especially the need to form a strong navy. By 1817, due to depletion of ships, congress instituted a law to reserve public-domain lands supporting oak and cedar but enforcement was difficult and illegal cutting continued. Nevertheless a precedent was set giving Congress the right to control the use of public lands.
1830 -1891	The peopling of the continent continued and the demand for land, as settlement proceeded westward, resulted in the massive transfer of land from public to private ownership. Pressures on the forest resource reached a peak as railways were constructed and unforested areas such as the Great Plains placed demands on the nation's forests for building materials. The Timber Culture Act of 1873 did, however, require settlers in unforested areas to plant trees. By 1878 policy makers realised that agriculture was not the only economic activity that could be supported by the land and turned their attentions to the potential for timber production but exploitation continued on a large scale. The Timber Trespass Law of 1831, however, halted much of this mis-use of the public domain by lumber companies and individuals. Fines and imprisonment were imposed on those who cut timber without authorisation. This marked a change in attitude from one of exploitation to one of conservation. By 1867 legislation was being enacted in numerous states to preserve forest lands and the scientific management of resources began.
1891 -1911	Predictions of a timber famine were being made, based on the rapid forest demise of the earlier century. In 1891 the General Revision Act was passed which gave to the President of the USA under Section 24 (The Forest Reserve Act) the authority to set aside forest reserves from the public domain. This was the basis on which the U.S. system of national forests was established beginning with the designation of Yellowstone Park in 1891. By 1907 the number of such reserves had increased to 159
1911 -1952	Conflicts arose because of the needs of the nation's defence services for World Wars I and II. Nevertheless conservation interests were well served with the establishment of a Forest Service, the development of forest management policies in both the private and public domain and the establishment of a Civilian Conservation Corps. This latter, established in 1933 deflected labour, an abundance of which was available during the Great Depression, into forest management.
1952 -1980	Numerous important policies were developed during this period relating to environmental protection in general but which led to improved forest management. They include policies on water quality, endangered species, pesticide control and pollution. Although timber production is still the main goal of USA forestry multiple use policies (including recreation and water management) have led to balanced resource management strategies.

8.1 shows, the forest regions of North America are both extensive and diverse, which makes it difficult to offer a generalised historical perspective. What is clear, however, is that the early European colonists entered a land in which native Americans had already influenced forest character (section 4.4.2). In addition, the temporal basis of North American forest use has varied in relation to the extension of early colonial settlers across the continent, but as Table 8.1 illustrates, the turning-point in US forest history came in 1891 with the General Revision Act. At this time, fears of a timber famine were being expounded as earlier laws had failed to redress the impact of lumber companies and agricultural development and it was becoming increasingly apparent that public lands were being sacked of their natural timber resources. This Act, however, allowed the establishment of forest reserves and marked a change in attitude to the nation's forests which had hitherto been considered as inexhaustible. This change in attitude from exploitation to conservation was undoubtedly influenced by growing industrialisation and urbanisation and by the recognition of the need to manage catchments, water supplies, etc. Nevertheless, the prime objective of forest management remains that of timber production.

As Mather (1987) observes, the forest area of the USA has remained roughly the same since c. 1920 but annual growth rate has increased by 350 per cent more than in 1920. This is a response to sustainable management policies which encourage growth and entail the maintenance of forests, not at optimum timber volume but at optimum growth rates. The adoption of such policies at a critical time in forest resource use averted what politicians like President Theodore Roosevelt described as a potential timber famine. Forest policies, securely ensconced in an effective and enforceable legislative infrastructure, which were inaugurated in 1891 and subsequently reinforced by later statutes (Table 8.1), were essential controls on the transposition of natural forests into managed forests. As in any stable, mature ecosystem, losses via the death of organisms, in this case trees, will be balanced by new growth. Tree removal in such a system, as occurred in the 1607–1900 period of US history, will inevitably lead to forest demise, but if the ecological system is carefully managed there are large-scale opportunities to reap a timber harvest without jeopardising sustainability. The basis of this depends on the relationship between annual growth and annual harvest: maximum tree growth is attained before old age. Thus, if a forest is managed to achieve maximum growth rather than maximum timber volume, a characteristic of mature climax forest, it can both thrive and produce a substantial harvest in the long term (provided no exogenous effects such as climatic change occur and as long as soil nutrient status is maintained).

Today, the US national forest system comprises 95 million ha of forest land, which is approximately 25 per cent of the national total; the remaining area is privately owned. This is in contrast to Canada, where 94 per cent of the forest area is publicly owned. As Repetto (1988b) has pointed out, much of the US national forest consists of old-growth timber and is often in less accessible areas which contrasts with many privately owned forests where productivity is higher and which are more accessible. This is partly a result of private acquisition of forest lands prior to the General Revision Act of 1891, when it made more economic sense to annex high quality, easily accessible forests. Nevertheless, because of the wilderness value of the national forests and the adoption of multiple use policies by the US national forest system, there remain conflicts of interest which arise because actual timber production is often uneconomic and many conservationists have argued against the commercial production of timber, proposing instead that such areas should be maintained as wilderness for recreation and conservation. Most of the nationally owned forest is in the western USA and is dominated by softwood, while almost 90 per cent of private commercial forests are in the east where hardwoods are more important (Fig. 8.1). According to Sedjo (1987), the USA is the world's largest producer of industrial wood, accounting for nearly one-quarter of global production. Of this, 76 per cent is softwood and the remaining 24 per cent is hardwood. Production is centred in the Pacific northwest and the south and the various products are given in Fig. 8.1. Despite high productivity, however, the USA remains a net wood importer, most notably from Canada.

Table 8.2. Silvicultural techniques. (Based on Lorimer 1982 and D M Smith 1986.)

1. Intermediate Techniques

These are undertaken between the establishment of seedlings and harvest
A. The regulation of species composition and growth rates
  (i) Release cuttings: The removal of larger trees of competing, undesirable species in stands of saplings or seedlings. This may involve the use of herbicides.
  (ii) Improvement cuts: The removal of diseased or poor-performing species at the post-sapling stage to improve quality
  (iii) Thinning: The density of a stand may be reduced in order to promote growth of the remaining trees. This can be executed by low, high or mechanical thinning which involves the cutting of lower or higher canopy species or the clearance of strips respectively. Thinning may be undertaken periodically eg. every 10 years
  (iv) Fertilising: This is important to promote productivity where some nutrients, eg. nitrogen are deficient

2. Prediction of forest growth

This is important in order to determine the volume of the annual cut. Currently, forest-growth models are widely used and are based on observable relationships between growth, age, site quality and competition.

3. Regeneration

A. Natural regeneration
  This occurs in a variety of ways including advance regeneration. This includes seedlings and saplings that were established prior to harvesting, sprouting from stumps and regeneration from the seed bank. How effective this is and how rapidly it occurs depends on a variety of factors including the quantity and regularity of seed production, germination success, local microclimate, competition and predation by insects and mammals.
B. Artificial regeneration.
  This is more manageable and predictable than reliance on natural regeneration and ensures the regeneration of desired species in the desired mix.
  (i) Direct seeding by hand or mechanically: This is especially appropriate where it is necessary to seed large areas rapidly and is most successful where logging debris is thin or absent.
  (ii) Planting: This is more effective than direct seeding but is more expensive because of the extra costs involved in the nursery production of seedlings.

4. Harvesting methods

These will depend on the nature of the stands
A. Even-aged stands
  (i) Clear-cutting: All trees are removed from a given area in a relatively short time but it is no longer a favoured technique because of adverse aesthetic and environmental impacts such as the acceleration of soil erosion
  (ii) Seed-tree methods: These involve the maintenance of scattered mature trees to act as a seed source
  (iii) Shelterwood: Trees are maintained to provide seed and shelter for new seedlings. Once these are established the older trees can be removed.
  (iv) Coppicing: This involves the removal of the upper portions of mature trees so that subsequent sprouts from the old bole can be harvested; is not widely used.
  Using these methods in even-aged stands it is only possible to approach sustained yield by cutting a small proportion of a forest annually so that over a fifty or hundred year period the entire forest is periodically cut
B. Uneven-aged stands
  These are managed by selective cutting involving the harvesting of scattered trees or groups of trees. Such an approach ensures that uneven-aged stands are maintained and that disturbance to the ecosystem is minimal.

Timber production is maintained by a variety of practices which, since colonial times, have transformed the character of North American forests. While extensive tracts of virgin forest remain from which sawnwood and plywood are derived, there has been a growing trend since the Second World War towards fibre-based products from plantations and second- and third-growth forests. Silvicultural practices vary enormously and have been described by D M Smith (1986) and Lorimer (1982). The aim of such practices is to achieve sustained yield involving optimum growth and regeneration; ideally it involves the maintenance of equal numbers of trees in each age class, but as D M Smith (1986) discusses, this is rarely achieved *in toto* especially in old-growth or second-growth forests where age-class distribution is naturally disposed to older trees. Redressing the balance through thinning can thus take several decades without any significant financial return. As a result, most management techniques in North American forests approach, rather than achieve, a situation of sustained yield. In general, silvicultural techniques include the regulation of regeneration, species composition and growth and may be designed to enhance aspects of forestry, such as improvement of habitats for wildlife, that are not related to timber production. Effective management requires accurate timber inventories, data on productivity and predictions of future growth; determination of the rotation age, which is the age of a stand at harvest, is also crucial and depends on the species and the time period required for optimum growth.

As Table 8.2 shows, there are many silvicultural techniques that can improve productivity; all influence the structure of forests and are thus agents of environmental change. There are also indirect impacts of silviculture which relate not only to forest management but to the construction of roads and the effect of forest removal on watershed management. The removal of trees constitutes the removal of both biomass and nutrients so it is important for sustainable yield that logging rotations are sufficiently long to allow replenishment. Table 8.2 also shows that herbicides and fertilisers are frequently used in silvicultural practices and, as discussed in sections 6.3.1 and 6.4.3, these can have detrimental environmental impacts. In forestry, these chemicals can lead to a decline in water quality and to declines in aquatic fauna and flora. Road construction can also lead to soil erosion which can be exacerbated by the dragging or skidding of logs from the place of cutting to areas where they are loaded on to vehicles for transport. With careful management, however, these problems can be kept to a minimum. In relation to silviculture itself D M Smith (1986), based mainly on the North American experience, states that: 'It is entirely within the realm of possibility to conduct forestry permanently without the degradation that is almost inevitable in agriculture . . . However, realization of this potentiality is not automatic.'

8.2.2 FOREST MANIPULATION IN THE DEVELOPING WORLD

Forestry practices in the developing world are diverse and complex and in many cases the absence of overall institutional control of forests coupled with other pressures, such as expanding agriculture, has resulted in indiscriminate exploitation. Even where there are national forest-management policies they are often difficult to enforce, especially where other interests, notably the potential of forest products to earn foreign currency, are involved. The absence of the concept of sustained yield, which underpins much of forestry practice in the developed world, is of particular concern for the long-term prospects of forest survival. There are many factors involved in the exploitation of forests in the developing world, many of which have been discussed in section 7.3 in relation to soil erosion and desertification, not least of which is rapid population growth. Multinational logging companies must also take their share of the blame for poor forest-management strategies in many developing countries, especially in Southeast Asia, where little heed is paid to conserving the remaining forest or to the effect of logging and heavy machinery on the soils. Moreover, there is often, as Wyatt-Smith (1987) has discussed in relation to the exploitation of tropical moist forests, inadequate information about terrain conditions, species composition, growth rates and tree life cycles which compound the problems of resource management.

Many of these problems are exemplified by the current state of forestry in Nigeria which has been reviewed by Adegbehin (1988). Here, forest reserves occupy some 9.7 per cent of the nation's land area and are most abundant in the lowland rainforest belt in the southern part of the country. These reserves produce most of Nigeria's industrial roundwood which provides the raw material for various wood-based industries, notably plywood, particle board and match production as well as pulp and paper. This industrial wood accounts for 20 per cent of Nigeria's wood consumption while the other 80 per cent is consumed as fuelwood which is mainly derived from the more northerly savanna zones. Wood shortages for both uses are now widespread, not least because many rainforest areas outside the reserves, which in the pre-1960 period supplied about 50 per cent of the country's timber output, are now exhausted. Deforestation and agricultural encroachment are among the reasons for this but forest-management policies have also been inadequate. As Adegbehin points out, assessment of the resource base itself has been poor and existing inventory data are both incomplete and out of date. In addition, the volume of timber removed in logging operations is either not recorded or is inaccurate. Thus there is no closely managed relationship between potential supply and its exploitation. Indeed, what data are available suggest that the current rate of roundwood removal, $c.$ 6.75 million m^3 per year, will result in depletion within 10 years despite the initiation of plantation forestry since the 1960s.

Much of this overexploitation is due to poor institutional control. For example, the government, via State Forestry Services and the Federal Department of Forestry, controls and implements regeneration and afforestation schemes but logging is transacted via the private sector with few enforceable controls. This latter is illustrated by the fact that until recently operating licences were issued more or less indiscriminately to any company that wanted to set up a sawmill. Such an *ad hoc* approach is not conducive to efficient use of present resources nor is it appropriate for long-term planning. Already there are sawmills that cannot operate at full capacity because of wood shortages. Improvements in the overall forestry infrastructure, involving inventory acquisition through to logging, would at least go some way towards achieving better resource use. Other mitigating measures could involve the encouragement of private concerns to develop their own plantations, as is already occurring on a small scale, not only in the rainforest regions but also in savanna regions where *Eucalyptus* is being successfully cultivated to provide fuelwood and poles. The fuelwood shortage in these

areas could also be alleviated to a degree by the introduction of more efficient wood-burning stoves, and industrial use of wood could be improved by
minimising waste.

Poor infrastructure in the forestry industry of Nigeria is not, however, the
only factor that has transformed the forest landscape. Silvicultural management has been practised since the 1920s, beginning first with regulation of
the felling cycle and then the stimulation of natural regeneration by cutting
climbers, removing uneconomic species and canopy thinning in the 1930s,
as has been described by Kio and Ekwebelam (1987). None of these techniques proved particularly successful and in 1944 the tropical shelterwood
system (TSS) was introduced, based on management techniques that had
already proved successful in parts of the tropical forests of Malaysia. The
TSS involved similar techniques to those described above but they were
more aggressively applied with specific time periods between each operation. Nevertheless there was insufficient regeneration of desired species,
largely because of the different life cycles, fruiting cycles and density of
desired Nigerian species in comparison with the Malaysian forest species on
which the methodology was based. (This is another example of the inappro-
priateness of transposing management and land-use practices from one discrete ecological system to another.) Other problems were also experienced,
including the damage of saplings during the logging phase of TSS, which
opened the habitat to colonisation by secondary species, and the availability
of light as the canopy was opened up encouraged the growth of unwanted
climbers and weeds. Thus the lack of fundamental ecological knowledge has
played a significant role in the shaping of these forests and lack of foresight
has led to the demise, by deliberate poisoning and girdling, of many species
which are now considered to be commercially viable. Eventually TSS was
abandoned and subsequent schemes to encourage restocking by enrichment
planting of desired species also proved unsuccessful, not only in Nigeria but
also in Ghana (Asabere 1987) and West Africa (Nwoboshi 1987). In all of
these cases the authors recommend that the best way of ensuring future
timber resources is to organise forestry on a plantation basis; this will
necessitate massive afforestation schemes to combat the losses of natural
forest and appropriate infrastructures to ensure survival. As is shown in Fig.
7.4, Nigeria stands to lose, at current rates of deforestation, all of its rainforest by the year 2000 and with a rapidly growing population solutions are
needed immediately.

As in the African countries discussed above, forest industries also provide
a major source of foreign income in Malaysia. According to Tang (1987) the
forest sector contributed 14.1 per cent of the total export earnings in 1983
which is equivalent to 6.8 per cent of the gross national product (GNP).
Extensive logging, together with the expansion of agricultural land, will deplete Malaysia's forest resources by the turn of the century unless effective
management programmes are instigated. To this end, Tang reports that some
13.8 million ha of Malaysia's forests have been designated as permanent
forest estate (PFE), of which 9.1×10^6 ha are productive forests that are
intended to be managed on a sustained yield basis (see section 8.2.1 for a
definition). Whether this can be achieved is debatable because management
schemes implemented to date have not been uniformly successful due to the
tremendous variation in ecology and terrain. Unless effective schemes can
be designed, Malaysia's timber industry may depend on the establishment of
plantations, as has been suggested as the saviour of African forestry (see

above). While the efficient exploitation of Malaysia's forests is beset by problems similar to those discussed above for Nigeria, there have been attempts to implement governmental control. This has been discussed by Douglas (1983) and includes government allocation of lands for agricultural development as well as controls on wood harvest volumes. These, however, are not always strictly implemented and in some cases logging operations have been sanctioned which are in direct conflict with the needs of indigenous groups. This has recently been highlighted by the imprisonment, in January 1989, of groups of forest dwellers who have obstructed the construction of forest roads (Cross 1989). There are also studies from Malaysia, which are illustrative of the effects of logging practices in tropical regions in general, which show that the destructive effect is far greater than just the removal of trees. Johns (1985), for example, has examined the impact of logging in part of west Malaysia where the harvest consisted of 3.3 per cent of the trees per ha but which, by damaging saplings and soils, caused an overall loss of nearly 51 per cent of the trees. Other indirect effects include the opening up by forest roads of hitherto inaccessible forests to cultivators, resulting in even more and often indiscriminate forest destruction.

More covert reasons may also underlie the inability (or reticence) of government forest agencies in developing countries to enforce regulations. These include the need for foreign currency and the attraction of foreign companies and their interests in developing economies. Such pressures may be offset by the newly established International Tropical Timber Organisation (ITTO), the remit of which is to administer the International Tropical Timber Agreement. As Cross (1988) reports, there are thirty-six countries producing tropical timber and thirty-three market countries which are party to this agreement that not only aims to regulate the tropical timber trade but to promote substainable use and conservation of tropical forests. How the latter will be achieved remains to be seen, but it has been mooted that a surcharge should be levied on tropical timber, to be paid by the market, which could be used to undertake research into ways of achieving and ensuring tropical forest survival. This, and similar organisations, may well become agents of environmental change in the not too distant future.

There is also the corollary that the economic significance of tropical timber will ensure its survival (Cross 1988). The economic significance of British woodlands throughout history (sections 4.1 and 4.2) did not, however, ensure their survival to any great extent, nor is there any guarantee that tropical forest plantations will succeed, though as Mather (1987) points out, their prospects are promising. Other factors may also contribute to the survival or demise of tropical forests. For example, will developing nations be able to reduce their reliance on forest resources as other aspects of their industrial economy begin to achieve importance? Mather draws some interesting parallels between the development of agricultural systems and that of forestry. He believes that the direct exploitation of natural forest, as is occurring in many tropical regions, is equivalent to 'hunting-gathering' while the managed natural forests of North America, for example, have reached the 'farming' stage. He states that: 'if a similar stage can be quickly reached in tropical LDCs (Least Developed Countries), and if plantation forests can be established without serious problems of ecological sustainability or pest outbreaks, then prospects for future timber availability are brighter than the currently rapid rates of deforestation in many tropical countries would at first suggest'. Is there also the possibility that the environmental movement will reduce the demand for such forest products in the developed nations by educating the public in the undesirable environmental consequences (e.g. the enhanced greenhouse effect and the loss of genetic resources) of over-exploitation?

8.2.3. THE ENVIRONMENTAL IMPACT OF AFFORESTATION AND REFORESTATION

Afforestation and reforestation are both characteristic of modern forestry (the former is the planting of forests on land previously unoccupied by trees while the latter involves the re-establishment of trees on formerly forested land that has been cleared). Much of it occurs as plantation forestry, the prime objective of which is to produce wood and wood products. There is also an increasing trend towards agroforestry which involves a combination of tree and agricultural crops; the silvicultural component may be used to provide a crop and to ensure environmental protection. Both afforestation and reforestation are agents of environmental change, affecting not only the floral elements of the environment but also the faunal elements and earth surface systems of water, sediment and nutrient transfer.

According to Sedjo and Clawson (1984) plantation forests on a global basis occupy some 9×10^7 ha which is equivalent to about 3 per cent of the extent of the world's closed forests. Approximately 40 per cent of plantation forest is in the developed world, a further 50 per cent is in the Communist Bloc especially in China (section 7.2.1) while the remainder is in the developing world, though the rate of planting is not sufficient to compensate for the rates of deforestation. In all cases, plantation forestry involves both af-forestation and reforestation as is exemplified by the situation in the UK. Here, such programmes have until recently been largely undertaken by the Forestry Commission (FC) which was established in 1919 as a result of the Forestry Act. As discussed in section 6.2.3, FC policies are not without their critics (e.g. Shoard 1987); many conservationists believe that the widespread use of alien conifers is neither environmentally nor aesthetically beneficial to the British landscape. In addition, many of the debates which relate to the conservation versus agriculture conflict (section 6.2.3) are equally relevant to forestry which, like agriculture, is not a free-market enterprise. There are, for example, subsidies in the form of grants and, until 1988, tax advantages available to individuals willing to invest in forestry and which are often seen as the major impetus to afforestation and reforestation with little regard to the environmental consequences. There is also much criticism of the FC because of the high degree of autonomy that it enjoys and its legally-enforceable powers that allow for the compulsory purchase of land.

In order to understand fully the role of forestry as an agent of environmental change in Britain, it is necessary to examine the historical perspective which has been discussed by Stewart (1987). The major developments in forestry and forestry policies are summarised in Table 8.3 which shows that more than 2×10^6 ha of land, mainly in the uplands, have been af-forested or reforested. According to Campbell (1988) the British wood-processing industry is now highly efficient by international standards and has increased self-sufficiency to 16 per cent, reducing the cost of imports. While the expansion of forestry in Britain (Table 8.3) has had environmental

Table 8.3. The major developments and policies in UK forestry (Based on Stewart 1987.)

Period Pre – 1914

Tree planting on private estates; small scale commercial growing of European larch (*Larix decidua*) and Norway spruce (*Picea abies*); no overall institutional control but the establishment of colonial forest organisations (notably Dehra Dun in India) led to the introduction of forestry courses at Oxford University. The early twentieth century recommendations, relating to plantation forestry, by these new foresters were largely ignored by the government.

1919 – 1939

The First World War highlighted the dearth of U.K. forest resources as the need for timber escalted. Government intervention of felling practices on private estates ensued and a policy of afforestation began with the establishment of the Forestry Commission in 1919. Financial constraints limited the FC to the purchase of marginal land, mainly in the uplands where there was opposition from hill farmers. Grants were also made available, covering 25 per cent of costs, for planting by individuals though such concessions were not taken advantage of on any large scale. In 1922 the Geddes Committee on National expenditure reported that the FC's policies were uneconomic and it narrowly escaped abolition.

1939 – 1957

At the start of the Second World War, the UK's forest resources were still in a parlous state and once again necessitated government intervention in the running of private estates, introducing felling licences to restrict harvesting for non-strategic purposes. New policies were instituted in 1943 and adopted by the post-war government. The area to be afforested was increased to 1.2 million ha and a further 0.8 million ha were to be created by re-stocking existing woodlands but little consideration was given to environmental factors or to criteria for the selection of existing woods for 'improvement'. The private sector also become more involved in afforestation as high income tax rates in post-war Britain made the already available tax incentives far more attractive. Moreover 1940's legislation relating to conservation (Section 4.3.3) excluded both forestry and agriculture from rigid controls. The 1947 Agriculture Act, which guaranteed prices via deficiency payments, also ensured that afforestation was relegated to the poorest areas which were inevitably in the uplands.

1957 – 1979

Afforestation for strategic purposes thus became incidental to a forestry industry, the case for which was rationalised by the Zuckerman Committee of 1957. This emphasised the role of forestry in maintaining the rural economy through employment opportunities in depressed areas though integration between forestry and agriculture remained elusive due to separate ownership. Various administrative reorganisations in the FC occurred in the 1960's but it continued to operate on revenue principles rather than on profit maximisation and benefitted from Government funding. Despite the fact that forestry, as a nationalised industry did not meet Government criteria in terms of rates of financial return; it was considered to provide a better social benefit than hill farming, despite fluctuations in labour demands relating to the planting-culting rotation cycle. The 1960's also witnessed increasing opposition to forestry schemes by conservationists which led, for the first time, to official recognition that landscaping advice, albeit subsidiary to timber production, was needed, prompted also by increasing concern about the effect of afforestation on water quality. Although a Government cost-benefit study in 1972 highlighted poor social and economic returns forestry policies remained intact. The replacement of Estate Duty with Capital Transfer Tax provided even more attractive fiscal conditions for the transfer of wealth from one generation to the next. Declining rates of private afforestation in the mid-1970's at least partially due to more rigorous, though still legally unenforceable, consultation procedures required by the FC. This decline was halted in 1977 as grants were raised and forest land was granted the same privileges as farmland in relation to Capital Transfer Tax. By this time the 1943 target of c.2 million ha had been achieved and justification for a further 1 to 1.8 million ha was couched in terms of import-saving by a Royal Commission report in 1977.

1980 – 1987

Forestry policies continued intact; rates of afforestation were to be maintained on the basis of import savings but were to be encouraged by the private rather than the nationalised sector. FC approval was no longer necessary and some FC forests were sold to private enterprises. As a result planting rates in the private sector doubled. Of the 25,000 ha afforested in 1983/84, two thirds were due to private investors, who by this had become heavily involved in the afforestation of bare ground rather than the re-stocking of existing woodlands. High-rate tax payers thus continued to benefit enormously despite various mid-1980's reports that the exchequer was losing vast sums as a result and that returns for the sale of FC forests was not as high as might be expected. No policy changes followed. The Wildlife and Countryside Act of 1981 did little to improve the relationship between forestry and coservation; compensation payments were made available by the NCC to prevent the afforestation of SSSI's and to promote the designation of new SSSI's. By this time attention was being drawn to the fact that UK forestry policies had already resulted in a considerable loss of upland habitats. The forestry versus conservation debate became just as vehement as the agriculture versus conservation debate (Section 6.2.3). In 1985 the FC modified it's policies as a result, too late of course to retrieve lost sites of ancient woodland. These new moves involved higher grants for the planting regeneration of broad-leaved species and the removal of grants for the replacement of broadleaved woods by conifers. An amendment act in 1985 to the Wildlife and Countryside Act also charges the FC with conservation duties; its effects are yet to be seen. Moreover, the role of the private sector in forestry, as discussed by the Commons Public Accounts Committee in 1927, is no longer seen as socially or economically beneficial to the nation in general.

Post 1987

In the wake of CAP reorganisation (Section 6.2.3) as a result of agricultural surpluses, forestry it could be argued, has gained a new impetus. The extensification of agriculture may result in increased afforestation of land that is marginal for agriculture. On the other hand, fiscal changes in the 1988 budget mean that forestry is no longer as financially advantageous to individual high-rate tax payers. Environmental concerns about the role of afforestation in the acidification of lakes and streams continue.

repercussions, as are discussed below, increasing self-sufficiency should at least partially reduce the pressures for the exploitation of tropical forests.

Forestry policy has wrought considerable changes in the character of British upland landscapes. For example, 52 per cent of the trees planted by the FC in Scotland and Wales are Sitka spruce (*Picea sitchensis*) which is not a native British species. Neither are Norway spruce (*P. abies*) and lodge-pole pine (*Pinus contorta*) which are also widely used in forestry pro-grammes because they grow relatively quickly and can tolerate the poor soils that are characteristic of British uplands. Apart from such aesthetic changes, involving the blanketing of large areas with uniform tree stands planted in regular rows, there is evidence to show that afforestation pro-grammes have led to the alteration of other floral and faunal elements of these ecosystems. For example, the density and diversity of ground flora will vary according to the rotation cycle and the tree species which comprise the canopy. Hill (1987) reports that under unthinned Sitka spruce older than 15 years there is very little ground flora; only bilberry (*Vaccinium myrtillus*) will persist. This means that silviculture of spruce on a 55-year rotation is less conducive to vegetation diversity, which attains its maximum only in the early years when light conditions are favourable.

Not all silvicultural practices are as extreme and the character of the ground flora will also depend on the land-use prior to afforestation. In a study of six sites in southern Britain, which were previously occupied by ancient woodland, Kirby (1988) has shown that considerable variations in ground flora occur in relation to the rotation cycle, the canopy species and its density. His data show that immediately after felling, the ground flora increases rapidly in density and diversity but declines as the canopy begins to close (the thicket stage) and increases again with tree thinning. The data also show that at the thicket stage in coniferous plantations the ground flora is much less diverse and dense than in control sites of similar age which consist of semi-natural mixed oak (*Quercus* spp.) stands. Beech (*Fagus* spp.) had a similar dampening effect while plantations of oak and conifers together, provided that the blocks or strips of oak are sufficiently large, had a better developed ground flora than that under conifers alone. Afforestation also affects bird populations. Where it occurs on open land, bird species characteristic of open country are replaced by those which prefer the limited cover afforded by young trees and are in turn replaced, as the forest matures, by those species which are forest dwellers (Bibby 1987). Overall, however, afforestation in Britain has had an adverse impact on bird populations (Ratcliffe and Oswald 1987). In Galloway, for example, the reduced breed-ing performance of golden eagles is considered to be directly related to afforestation due to loss of open moorland which is their main feeding area.

Apart from the effects of afforestation and reforestation on flora and fauna, there are other environmental implications. For example, the change of land-use from moorland to coniferous plantations in British uplands has affected soils and soil processes as well as the quality and quantity of water yield. The effects of afforestation on soils varies considerably and relates to soil type, species composition of the forest and management, including soil-preparation techniques. Ploughing, which is commonly used to prepare up-land sites for afforestation, results not only in the drying out of soils and peats, but also in nutrient losses which are in excess of those occurring in undisturbed habitats. Such losses reduce as the plantation matures but rarely return to pre-disturbance levels because subsoil is exposed and weathering is promoted. The construction of drains, as Hornung *et al.* (1987) have discussed, tends to reduce the residence time of water in the soil or peat. In addition, aeration is promoted by preparation techniques which increase the rate of decomposition of soil organic matter and the release of nutrients. Drainage, via ditch and channel provision, in preparation for planting also increases the drainage network within a catchment. Francis (1988) quotes the example of Llanbrynmair Moors, Mid-Wales, where drainage density was increased from *c.* 3 km to over 200 km of stream length per 100 ha. There is also evidence that drainage schemes increase flooding frequency and the total amount of runoff (Robinson 1986). Accelerated runoff and nutrient losses also occur as a result of thinning and especially clear felling. Under mature coniferous forest further changes in soil properties occur. Soil drying is promoted both by tree roots, which create large pores that are not characteristic of soils under grassland and moorlands, and the reduction of throughflow that occurs due to greater interception of precipitation by a tree canopy. The latter is also more effective than grassland or moorland at capturing particulates and aerosols from the atmosphere. Nutrient availability is thus enhanced but such scavenging also results in the trapping of pollutants, which can retard growth. Enhanced inputs of sulphur dioxide and nitrogen oxides due to this process are thought to be contributing to acidification (Blackie and Newson 1986).

The production of conifer litter, which is base-poor, also contributes to increased acidity. This has been reviewed by Hornung (1985) and Hornung *et al.* (1987) who report the replacement of mull or moder by mor humus on brown earth or brown podzolic soils. This causes an increase in the amount of fulvic acid, the acidification of near-surface horizons and a decline in exchangeable bases. All of these trends promote and/or accelerate podzolisation which in turn promotes leaching of iron and aluminium and the more acidic a soil profile becomes, the more decomposition of organic material is inhibited. All of these processes affect soil and soil water chemistry which subsequently influences the quality of runoff. Numerous studies (e.g. Stoner and Gee 1985, Bull and Hall 1986) have compared the water chemistry of streams draining afforested areas with that of streams draining nearby moorland. Overall solute concentrations, notably chloride, sulphate and aluminium, are higher in the former which are also more acidic. As Hornung *et al.* (1987) point out, most concern has been voiced about increasing acidity and aluminium concentrations, which mainly occur where afforestation has been undertaken on areas underlain by acidic bedrock, because of their impact on invertebrate and fish populations. Egglishaw *et al.* (1987), for example, have shown that salmon catches have declined in many Scottish streams and rivers which drain afforested catchments, and Ormerod *et al.* (1987) have discussed the reduction in diversity that occurs in the invertebrate faunas of streams in Wales after afforestation. The latter are particularly restricted by pH, while fish catches are sensitive to both low pH and aluminium concentrations as well as increased sedimentation rates which occur in the establishment phase of afforestation (Francis 1988).

Water yield as well as water quality is affected by afforestation and reforestation. While the amount of runoff increases in the establishment phase it declines as the plantation matures. Research on the Plynlimon catchment in upland Wales, for example, indicates that streamflow from the afforested area is *c.* 15 per cent less than from nearby grassland (Blackie and Newson 1986). This occurs because forest vegetation intercepts a greater percentage of rainfall than grassland (or moorland) and returns more water to the atmosphere via evapotranspiration. Changes such as these affect the rate of aquifer recharge and thus indirectly affect streamflow. Although data relating to the seasonal distribution of runoff are limited, there are indications that post-drought recharge rates of forest soils are reduced and that more rapid flood response is characteristic of all stages of the rotation cycle when compared with non-afforested catchments (Binns 1986).

In the developing world, plantation forestry is also increasing, though there are few data available which facilitate an assessment of environmental impact. Obviously, the introduction of exotic taxa and the establishment of trees where few or none existed previously will alter the landscape. A distinction must also be made between agroforestry and plantation forestry; the former involves the integration of silviculture with agricultural systems while the latter is entirely given over to timber production. Agroforestry, as K F S King (1987) discusses, has been a component of agricultural systems since the latter began to develop (section 3.3). It remains a component of many, more traditionally based, agroecosystems and as discussed in section 4.4.1, a return to such practices is now considered to be one answer to Africa's poor record as a provider of sufficient food for its population. However, King also believes that traditional agroforestry led to the establishment of plantation forestry because of colonial timber requirements in the nineteenth and early twentieth centuries that culminated in the separation of agricultural and forestry interests. This process began in Burma in 1806 with the establishment of teak plantations (the forerunner of the Dehra Dun forest organisation in India referred to in Table 8.3). Although agroforestry practices continued to be significant in tropical agricultural systems, in the ensuing period they achieved increasing importance in development policies from the 1970s as a means of optimising tropical land-use (Bene *et al*. 1977). As a consequence, the International Centre for Research in Agroforestry (ICRAF) was established in 1977. In the words of King (1987) the potential of agroforestry is ' . . . fast becoming recognised as a system which is capable of yielding both wood and food and at the same time of conserving and rehabilitating ecosystems'.

Reference has already been made to the intercropping of trees with cereals, legumes, etc. in many African agricultural systems (section 4.4.1) to increase food production and as a means of soil conservation, and to the planting of trees (section 7.2.3) to combat erosion and desertification. Swaminathan (1987) has also advanced the view that agroforestry is one of the keys to achieving what he describes as ecological and nutritional security. The latter, he argues, can only be accomplished if an adequate food supply is produced within an ecologically sustainable system. The maintenance (or planting) of a partial tree cover will help to conserve the soil resource by maintaining the organic components via litter supply; soil cohesiveness will thus be improved which, together with the wind- and water-break effect of trees, will reduce soil erosion. The litter component will also help to maintain nutrient status which can also be manipulated if careful thought is given to the mixture of species (both tree and crop) to be grown in juxtaposition. Such control will promote tight intra-system nutrient cycling and obviate to a degree the need for artificial fertilisers.

As Nair (1985) has pointed out, there are many different types of agroforestry systems ranging from shifting cultivation to agrisilvicultural practices. These are briefly described in Table 8.4, and there are numerous examples which indicate that, overall, carefully managed agroforestry enterprises can be successful in so far as they provide a sustainable food supply and are environmentally conservational. In relation to shifting cultivation Unruh (1988), for example, has examined the factors underpinning successful fallow management in the Iquitos region of the Peruvian Amazon. The first stage in cultivation involves forest clearance (though particular tree species which are valuable for timber are usually spared) and as annual crop plants such as manioc (*Manihot esculenta*) and maize (*Zea mays*) are cultivated, perennial species such as pineapple (*Ananas comosus*) and banana (*Musa* spp.) are planted along with numerous other fruit trees, palms and shrubs that can be used for a variety of purposes from thatching to dyes and medicines. These are slower-growing species than the annuals and will not be productive until the swidden stage is complete and in many cases not until the subsequent fallow is well established; the different ages at which the perennials mature also facilitates a phased harvest so that the fallow stage is not unproductive. This system, in tandem with additional planting of species like peanuts (*Arachis hypogaea*) at the end of the cropping cycle and the protection of useful species by controlling forest regrowth (by limited slashing) in the later stages of the fallow cycle, creates a diverse ecosystem which contains patches of useful species as well as natural forest regrowth.

Competition from weeds, notably the grass *Imperata* which can inhibit forest regeneration, is also discouraged by these practices because of the fragmented pattern of bare ground and the shade effects of perennials which also contribute to the renewal of soil nutrient pools. Nutrient renewal also occurs more rapidly under a managed fallow system than it does under unmanaged fallow for a number of reasons. Firstly, it influences the quality and spatial distribution of litter. Regular slashing to protect useful species results in a litter richer in new leaves which are more nutrient-rich, espe-

Table 8.4. A classification of agroforestry systems and their characteristics. (From Nair 1985.)

Categorization of systems (Based on their structure and function)				Grouping of systems (According to their spread and management)	
Structure (Nature and arrangement of components, especially woody ones)		Function (Role and/or output of components, especially woody ones)	Agro-ecological/ environmental adaptability	Socio-economic and management level	
Nature of components	Arrangement of components				
Agrisilviculture (crops and trees incl. shrubs/trees and trees)	*In space* (Spatial) Mixed dense (e.g. Home garden)	*Productive function* Food Fodder	Systems in/for Lowland humid tropics Highland humid tropics	*Based on level of technology input* Low input (Marginal)	
Silvopastoral (pasture/animals and trees)	Mixed sparce (e.g. most systems of trees in pastures)	Fuelwood Other woods	(above 1,200 m a.s.l. e.g. Andes India, Malaysia)	Medium input High input	
Agrosilvopastoral (crops, pasture/animals and trees)	Strip (width of strip to be more than one tree)	Other products	Lowland subhumid tropics (e.g. savanna zone of Africa, Cerrado of South America)	*Based on cost/benefit relations* Commercial	
Others (multipurpose tree lots, apiculture with trees, aquaculture with trees, etc.)	Boundary (trees on edges of plots/fields)	*Protective function* Windbreak Shelterbelt Soil conservation	Highland subhumid tropics (Tropical highlands) (e.g. in Kenya, Ethiopia)	Intermediate Subsistence	
	In time (Temporal) Coincident Concomitant Overlapping Sequential (separate) Interpolated	Moisture conservation Soil improvement Shade (for crop, animal, and man *sic*.)			

cially in relation to nitrogen and phosphorus, than older leaves and slashing usually occurs only after the re-establishment of a root mat which helps to bind nutrients that would otherwise be lost via leaching. Secondly, the persistence of a canopy enhances the interception of nutrients from precipitation. For the longer term, Unruh also suggests that the persistence of useful species will be enhanced because their seed banks in the soil are increased; thus in the subsequent swidden–fallow cycle the abundance of such species will increase spontaneously. These ecological considerations, together with the economic advantages that are apparent, must commend the system as one that has successfully modified a traditional subsistence system into a more economic one without major detrimental effects. Environmental change is here registered as a modification of forest composition rather than as weed-infested secondary rainforest. Once again the maintenance of diversity is a key to success.

Diversity is also a characteristic of the agroforestry system known as homegarden which is typical of many traditionally based food-producing systems in Southeast Asia (Soemarwoto 1987). Tree crops, annual crops and animals are intermixed to provide a sustainable production base. As in the case of the Peruvian Amazon, crops for a variety of purposes are produced. In Java, homegardens have increased in extent in the last 50 years and now account for c. 18.5 per cent of agricultural land. Soemarwoto has also compared data on soil erosion from homegardens, which are family-run plots of c. 1–2 ha, with those from plantation forests and cultivated fields in Java and Thailand. In the homegardens erosion rates are virtually nil while cultivated fields suffer soil erosion to varying degrees of slight, moderate or severe. Such facts speak for themselves and clearly emphasise Richards's (1985)

Fig. 8.2. Alley-cropping as an agroforestry technique and its advantages. (Adapted from Kang and Wilson 1987.)

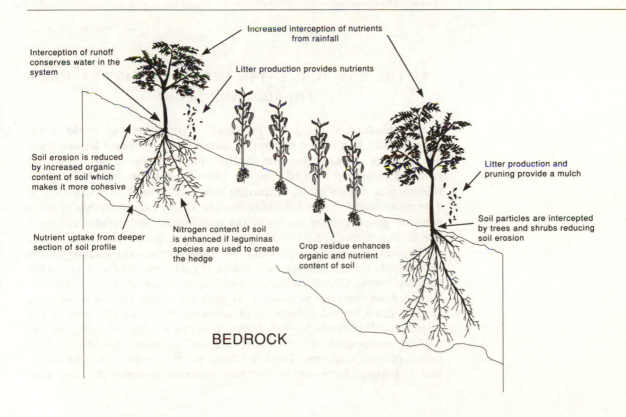

Increased interception of nutrients from rainfall

Interception of runoff conserves water in the system

Litter production provides nutrients

Soil erosion is reduced by increased organic content of soil which makes it more cohesive

Litter production and pruning provide a mulch

Nutrient uptake from deeper section of soil profile

Nitrogen content of soil is enhanced if leguminas species are used to create the hedge

Crop residue enhances organic and nutrient content of soil

Soil particles are intercepted by trees and shrubs reducing soil erosion

BEDROCK

view (section 4.4.1) that there is much to be gleaned from traditional agri-cultural/agroforestry methods if sustainable development is to be achieved in the light of current and projected population growth.

New agroforestry techniques have also been developed to increase pro-ductivity without disrupting the basic symbiosis which exists between tree crop and annual crop. In Nigeria, for example, alley-cropping has been de-veloped since the 1970s. It involves the cultivation of arable crops between hedgerows of planted shrubs and trees (Kang and Wilson 1987). The latter are usually leguminous species which enhance the nitrogen content of the soil to the benefit of the arable crop and regular pruning to prevent shading of the crop provides a further source of nutrients as a mulch. The advantages of the system are illustrated in Fig. 8.2 and, like the Peruvian example dis-cussed above, the fallow stage is contributing to crop productivity as well as providing protection against soil erosion. Moreover, if animals are integrated into the system, the prunings from the hedges can be used to supplement their fodder. According to Kang and Wilson, the best results are achieved if leguminous species are used to create the hedge, and trials carried out in Nigeria have shown that the most promising species are *Leucaena leucoce-phala* and *Gliricidia sepium* which will grow successfully even on degraded land. Trials have also shown that crops like maize (*Zea mays*) and cassava (*Manihot esculenta*) provide higher yields when alley-cropped with legumin-ous bushes and trees because of the increased availability of nitrogen which also results in a considerably reduced fertiliser requirement.

As these examples illustrate, both plantation forestry and agroforestry are significant agents of environmental change. Not only do they alter the physiognomy of the landscape but also the geomorphic, pedologic and hy-drological processes.

8.3 THE ENVIRONMENTAL IMPACT OF RECREATION, TOURISM AND SPORT

As the standard of living has increased in the developed world it has brought with it a higher disposable income and increased leisure time. The average working week in the UK, for example, is now about 37 hours as compared with 60 hours in 1900. In addition, paid holiday en-titlements are more generous, having increased from 2 weeks in 1963 to 4 or more weeks in 1985 (Geofile No 118 1988), car ownership is more common giving greater access to the countryside and greater affluence means that finance is available for enjoyment purposes. These trends are typical of westernised society. In these nations, the countryside is increasingly being exploited as a source of recreation and as a venue for sporting events. Greater affluence and improved air travel have also en-couraged an increase in tourism to such an extent that it is now the world's third largest industry and accounts for *c*. 12 per cent of the world's GNP (Geofile No 118 1988). Tourism is also becoming an im-portant component of developing nations' economy because it is a source of foreign income. Trips to China, South America, the Caribbean and Indonesia, for example, are now common features of many tour operators' brochures. Although they are discussed here as separate issues, tourism, recreation and sport are not mutually exclusive. The latter two may be the attractions prompting the former, but where the countryside or environmental features are the foci of interest, large influxes of people and the attendant services that they require can bring about environmental change. The very landscape that creates the market for tourism and/or recreation may itself be put at risk in the absence of careful management. The examples which follow illustrate a range of landscape changes created by recreation, tourism and sport.

8.3.1 RECREATION

Recreation in its broadest sense involves any pleasurable occupation of leisure time. Thus, many recreational activities do not impinge on the physical environment or landscape with which this section is concerned. Here, the definition of recreation follows that of Goldsmith (1983) who states that it is ' . . . the pursuit of informal leisure in the countryside; its effects are to damage the vegetation by trampling, to accelerate the loss of soil and to disturb animals'. Activities which create such damage include a variety of sports, such as skiing and boating, as well as camping, walking, riding and picnicking.

Trampling of vegetation is one of the most widespread environmentally degrading repercussions of recreation and can also lead to excessive soil erosion. Numerous studies have been undertaken in US national parks which illustrate the ecological impact of visitors on camp and picnic sites, nature trails and footpaths. In the Grand Canyon National Park, Arizona, D.N. Cole (1986) has investigated twelve high-use and twelve low-use campsites located away from the main tourist access routes in three desert vegetation types consisting of desert scrub, catclaw (*Acacia greggi*) and piñon–juniper (*Pinus edulie–Juniperus osteosperma*) communities. In all cases, soil compaction, changes in infiltration rates, soil organic matter, litter and soil moisture content as well as vegetation cover were recorded. The data revealed that human impact was greatest with initial use; further increases in use levels exhibited a non-linear relationship, illustrating that once a campsite had been established, higher-use levels could be sustained without incurring disproportionate damage. In relation to the vegetation communities in which the campsites were located, the major difference in impact related to campsite core size which tended to be larger in piñon–juniper areas due to the more open nature of the vegetation and the less rugged nature of the areas on which it is dominant. Recommended measures to combat this expansion include the planting of cacti in the core periphery and the on-site education of the public via publicity material emphasising the need for core confinement.

This and other studies (e.g. Cole and Fichtler 1983, Stohlgren and Parsons 1986) have led to the conclusion that the most appropriate management strategy for such wilderness areas is to restrict camping to a few designated sites, where activity can be sustained without excessive damage. Cole and Marion (1988) have also examined visitor impact in three areas of east coast national parks to determine if the same conclusions apply to a different, more moist area than that of the arid west. All three sites investigated, in the Delaware River catchment, are accessible only by boat with camping occurring in a variety of campsites including camp-grounds, designated primitive sites and undeveloped user-selected sites. In each area Cole and Marion recorded a range of soil and vegetation characteristics from both recreational and undisturbed control sites. Although variations were apparent from site to site in relation to pre-existing environmental characteristics and intensity of use, the study highlighted some general trends with implications for management strategies. Most significant is the fact that the soil and vegetation characteristics on low-use campsites were more similar to those of high-use sites than to control sites, with significant tree damage, reduced tree regeneration, changes in and disappearance of ground flora and compacted soils. Although the damage on user-selected sites was not as heavy as that on outfitter sites, which were almost completely devegetated, discarded rubbish was more abundant indicating that the provision of disposal facilities in the latter were effective. The overall conclusion from the study was similar to that from west coast parks and Cole and Marion recommend that the provision of designated sites is the most appropriate strategy for minimising the effects of recreation in these wilderness areas.

Jim (1987a) has also addressed the problem of recreational impact in the Shing Mun Country Park in Hong Kong. This is one of twenty-one country parks established between 1977 and 1980 in which there are more than 440 recreational sites where facilities such as barbecues and children's play apparatus are provided. In view of the high population of Hong Kong (*c*. 5.5 million) and their proximity to urban areas, these sites are popular for informal leisure-time activities; already there is evidence that serious degradation has occurred due to heavy use (Jim 1987b). Jim (1987a) states that in the 1985–86 period Shing Mung received some 600 000 visitors, mainly for picnics and barbecues in sixty designated sites. For each of these sites Jim recorded data on a number of variables indicative of soil erosion and site attractiveness which allowed the compilation of three index sites relating to high, medium and low levels of use. He found, for example, that cover values for vegetation, litter and bare ground were distinct between sites that had been moderately and severely affected with a less distinct gradation occurring between slightly and moderately disturbed sites, and that noticeable exposure of mineral soil occurred only after the vegetation cover was reduced by *c*. 40 per cent. Once this had happened, however, the soil was subject to compaction and crusting as well as erosion by sheetwash. At the most disturbed sites shrub and herb species were considerably reduced in density and diversity as the amount of bare ground, up to 45 per cent at some sites, increased. Since there is little potential for the development of new recreation sites in the Shing Mun Country Park, Jim suggests that a management strategy designed to make the distribution of visitors between sites more equable would be appropriate to minimise damage and especially to protect those sites which are currently undergoing excessive damage. Such a strategy would involve the provision of more facilities at, and better access to, under-used sites and the removal of some facilities from heavily used areas to reduce recreational pressure and to promote recovery.

Footpath erosion is also a common feature of landscapes that are widely used by walkers. In the Peak District National Park, for example, a recent report (Clouston in *The Guardian*, 2nd May 1989) states that in this, the oldest of the UK's national parks, there are more than 4000 serious faults in the park's 4000 footpaths. This is mainly the result of heavy visitor use; in 1987 the park received 18.5 million visits. Footpath erosion is a significant problem in all the UK's national parks and, as Edington and Edington (1986) have pointed out, there are several strategies that can be employed to mitigate walking pressures. Visitors may be diverted from sensitive areas by reorganising car parking, picnicking facilities and footpaths. Alternatively, artificial footpath surfaces, which are not as susceptible to erosion, may be provided. Edington and Edington quote the examples of asphalt-surfaced paths in the Rocky Mountain National Park of the USA, the use of limestone chippings on a bed of plastic sheeting to protect erosion-susceptible peat in the North York Moors National Park in the UK and the use of wood chips on paths along the shores of Derwent Water in the Lake District National Park.

Apart from damage caused by trampling and erosion, more widespread and long-lasting degradation can occur as a result of recreation activities. Accidentally created fires can have devastating affects on a landscape. In the Fynbos heathlands of South Africa, for example, *c.* 13 per cent of fires are caused by camp-fires or smokers, while in southern France more than half the fires are a result of recreationists, notably accidents from discarded cigarettes and children playing with fire (from data quoted in Goudie 1986). Fire, especially when high temperatures are obtained, will destroy the above-ground woody biomass and litter and may impair the reproductive potential of plants by reducing the seed bank in the soil. Such accidentally created fires are usually most devastating after a long dry period when the organic content of the litter and soil is experiencing moisture deficiency and the presence of dry kindling provides a good fuel supply. In such circumstances seed banks are impaired and even below-ground roots may be damaged. Thus recovery of the ecosystem is slow.

Additional recreational impacts on countryside areas occur because of formal and informal sporting activities which will be discussed in section 8.3.3.

8.3.2 TOURISM

Tourism is a distinctive type of recreation which involves the movement of people, on a temporary basis, to destinations beyond their usual residence and the activities which they then pursue. It is one of the world's fastest-growing industries which has burgeoned since the Second World War, and especially since the 1960s. World Travel Organisation data (quoted in Pearce 1987) reflect a trebling of international tourist arrivals in the last 20 years, reaching 284 million in 1984 as compared with 93 million in 1963. Domestic tourism has also increased within this period. The reasons for this demand, mainly confined to developed nations where there is a large disposable income and significant holiday entitlements, have been discussed in detail by Boniface and Cooper (1987) and Pearce (1987) and are related to improvements in transport as well as financial considerations. Although Pearce has demonstrated that the major generating and receiving nations are developed nations, especially in Europe and North America, there has been a marked increase in tourism to developing countries which is actively encouraged to generate foreign currency. This latter has been discussed by Cater (1987) who states that ' . . . the development of tourism has been regarded as a panacea for the economic malaise of many of the least developed countries (LDCs) faced with a narrow resource base and serious balance of payment difficulties'. In Nepal, for example, receipts from tourism constitute some 46.4 per cent of export earnings and while there are adverse environmental effects of this development, as will be discussed below, tourism is an important source of employment, as it is in many developing countries.

While much international tourism is undertaken to enjoy cultural attributes, much of it is also prompted by scenic, wildlife and marine features. Thus, tourism and conservation are closely interlinked and, as Farrell and McLellan (1987) point out, it is essential that tourism and its policy-makers should take account of the sustainability concept which, while being particularly relevant to agricultural development and forestry practices, is equally important in the context of tourism. On the one hand, heavy visitor pressures to a particular landscape feature may cause degradation to such an extent that it is no longer an attraction; tourism thus becomes self-defeating. On the other hand, closure of a feature to tourism for conservation purposes is undesirable, because it defeats the purpose of conservation which is its preservation for future generations. Some degree of accommodation between conservation and tourism is essential, involving the management of both place and people, possibly in a similar way to that employed in the US national parks (section 8.3.1). Successful management policies have been employed in the centre of Australia, for example, where the major attractions

Fig. 8.3.The organisation of tourism facilities in Australia's Uluru National Park

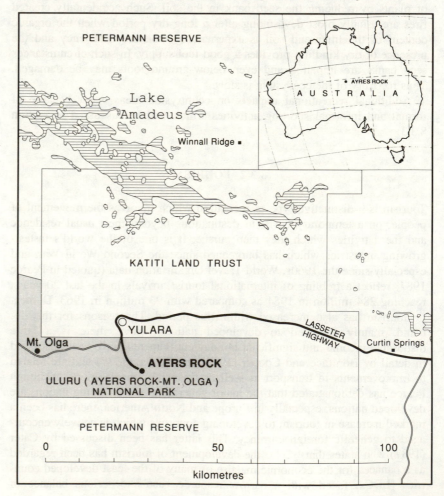

are Ayres Rock and the Olgas. Until a decade ago, there was little control on campsites and motels were constructed at the base of Ayres Rock giving free access to climbers and walkers. This began to promote excessive erosion and Aboriginal concerns relating to infringements of their sacred sites which abound in the region. As a result, a new resort, Yulara, was constructed which as Fig. 8.3 shows is 19 km from the rock itself and 37 km from the Olgas. This resort has a large range of facilities, including two luxury hotels, shops, restaurants, camp-grounds, an information centre and an airstrip. Visitors to the area are encouraged to confine their living requirements to the resort and are bussed out to the various landmarks where rangers of the Uluru National Park provide guided tours and prevent entry to certain Aboriginal sites. In this way, footpaths can be opened or closed according to erosional pressures and Aboriginal wishes are respected. This is one example where conservation and tourism enjoy a sustainable symbiotic relationship.

Elsewhere, however, management strategies have not been as successful. In the Galápagos Islands, for example, the attractions of natural beauty and a unique wildlife are leading to serious environmental problems. This island archipelago is situated in the Pacific Ocean *c.* 1000 km west of Ecuador and is famous as the source of inspiration for Charles Darwin's evolutionary theory. The islands have never been joined to South America and because of their isolation they contain large numbers of endemic organisms. As de Groot (1983) reports, 90 per cent of the land area was declared a national park in 1959 and the Charles Darwin Research Station was established in 1960 on Santa Cruz Island, the aim of which was to undertake scientific research and to begin a programme of goat eradication. These animals, introduced by pirates and whalers between the sixteenth and nineteenth centuries, denude the vegetation and compete with the giant tortoise (*Geochelone elephantopus*). This programme, which is being undertaken in conjunction with the Ecuadorean National Park Service established in 1968, has successfully eradicated goats and a number of other introduced species on many of the islands. Such conservation work is, however, being hindered by the huge growth in tourism that has occurred since 1970, and although there is in theory a master plan which in the mid-1970s allowed for a maximum of 12 000 visitors per year, de Groot states that since 1979 this number has been increasingly exceeded. More cruise ships have been registered, aircraft capacity has grown and traffic in small locally operated tourist boats and private yachts has increased. As a result, trails are being eroded and unofficial ones created by parties without an official guide. Rubbish is discarded; that from boats is washed ashore and there is greater disturbance of the animal life.

Even before organised tourism on a large scale occurred, there was evidence that animal behaviour was being disrupted. Harris (1972–73) reported that territorial breakdown among the islands' iguanas (*Conolophus subcristatus*) was occurring because the animals were deserting their territories to assemble in visitor-frequented areas to be fed. This impaired breeding activity and led to a complete ban on artificial feeding. There are also fears that the increased tourist traffic will bring introduced plant and animal species which may bring about the extinction of endemic species. Although Adsersen (1989) believes that the major threat to conservation is not from tourism but from land-use via agriculture and sand and gravel extraction, there is still much cause for concern, especially if hotels and tourist resorts are developed. Moreover, de Groot's fears, expressed in 1983, have been reiterated by Emory in 1988 who states that in 1986 some 26 023 tourists visited the islands and that the problems of environmental protection are being exacerbated by the influx of mainland Ecuadoreans seeking wealth in the tourist trade. In 1987, following an exceptionally high influx of tourists in August 1986, tighter regulations were introduced for tourist agencies, more guides were being trained and the waters surrounding the islands were declared a marine resources reserve. Further protection, involving better supervised tour groups, should also ensue, following the decision in 1989 to offset a proportion of Ecuador's national debt in a debt-for-nature deal which requires Galápagos protection.

Tourism has also had a significant impact on many national parks in Africa which attract visitors for safari holidays, the forerunners of which were the big-game safaris of the late nineteenth century. Today, hunting is no longer allowed and tourists visit these national parks to view and photograph the wildlife in their natural habitats. In many of these parks, which are mostly located in savanna regions, tourists regularly drive off the existing game-viewing tracks into the dry terrain and there is concern that increased tourist traffic will detrimentally alter the environment. This has been discussed by Onyeanusi (1986) in relation to the Masai Mara National Reserve in Kenya, where there are more than 40 000 visitors annually, involving a considerable amount of off-road driving in order to obtain close-up views of large carnivores like the cheetah (*Acinonyx jubatus*), leopard (*Panthera pardus*) and lion (*P. leo*).

Such activity is necessitated by the provision of only 420 km of game-viewing in a reserve of 1673 km^2 and the fact that there are relatively low populations of the carnivores, individuals of which do not always locate themselves in convenient spots! Onyeanusi's study involved an assessment of the impact of vehicle tyres on off-road tracks in a specific area of what is predominantly grassland savanna. As would be expected, the amount of damage increased as the number of vehicles using the tracks increased but the greatest reduction in vegetation cover was caused by initial vehicle runs. The study also shows that grasslands with a high above-ground biomass lose their standing crop more rapidly than those with a lower biomass. Extrapolating his results to the entire Nature Reserve, Onyeanusi estimated that the actual loss of biomass was low. Thus, while the visual impact of the extra trackways implied that significant damage was taking place, the actual ecological impact was relatively small. Nevertheless there is clearly a negative impact on the environment, in terms of aesthetic qualities, which could be minimised by the provision of more primary, designated trackways. There is also the possibility that increased tourist traffic could exacerbate this problem further and the formulation of a management plan in the near future could be beneficially prescriptive.

Another area where a policy of sustainable tourism is to be welcomed is the Himalaya. In Nepal in particular, tourist attractions include eight of the world's highest mountain peaks, notably Everest and Annapurna. Since the late 1950s especially, when Nepal opened its borders to outsiders, trekking and mountain-climbing groups have increased markedly and, as is the case in many developing countries, have been encouraged as a source of foreign income. As Kohl (1988) has reported with a dazzling photographic portrait (by William Thompson and Galen Rowell) the fuelwood crisis, which is endemic to the region, is being aggravated by the fuelwood requirements of tourists. Inefficient stoves are kept burning day and night to provide heat and food for the tourist lodges in Sagarmatha, the Mount Everest National Park. This situation may well be aggravated by the construction of an air-strip above the Sherpa village of Namche Bazar and the renovation of a Japanese-run hotel. This village, which is situated along the trail from Lukla to Everest Base Camp, has undergone tremendous changes as the number of tourists to Nepal has risen from less than 10 000 per year in 1960 to almost 250 000 in 1988; there are also plans to increase that number to *c*. 1 million by the year 2000. Approximately 20 per cent of these tourists will visit Sagarmatha and, while this is welcomed as a source of employment, there are drawbacks.

Apart from the increased pressures on fuelwood, rubbish disposal is disfiguring the landscape, especially along the trail from Lukla, through Namche Bazar, to the Everest Base Camp. Climbing expeditions into the peaks themselves have also left behind piles of rubbish, and Cullen (1986) points out that the problem is compounded by the fact that in such a high Alpine environment decomposition rates are very slow so that discarded materials may persist for several years if not decades. Moreover, expeditions tend to congregate in a few favoured areas which provide rapid access to peaks as well as adequate water supplies and shelter from natural hazards like avalanches. Add to this the rapid growth in the numbers of expeditions, climbers and trekkers which has occurred in recent years and it is not surprising that the problem has reached massive proportions despite the availability of new access sites from Tibet which was opened to climbers in 1980. Obviously, the harsh terrain and the inhospitable weather conditions mean that rubbish disposal is a subordinate concern, in relation to climbing goals and survival, of climbers in the mountain peaks, the major problem areas are the base camps. Apart from transporting rubbish out of the area, which is costly, Cullen has discussed the advantages and disadvantages of four methods of on- or near-site disposal. Incineration, for example, can effectively reduce the volume of rubbish but still leaves the problem of non-combustible material; covering with rocks is not an ideal solution because the rubbish may be uncovered by scavenging yaks, herders and climbers; incarceration in glacier crevasses is not recommended because it is likely that the rubbish will ultimately reappear. Interring the rubbish in pits where there is suitable ground is probably the best solution but sites must be carefully selected to avoid contamination of water supplies and may require mechanical diggers in view of the huge volume of rubbish. This is more costly and is not ideal but it is nevertheless feasible. Moreover, expedition companies, individuals and host countries must play a more significant role in combating this problem. Nepal's climbing permits, for example, require an undertaking that rubbish will be adequately disposed but it is rarely enforced. Cullen suggests that peak fees, which are currently paid for the right to climb specific peaks, could include a refundable charge for environmental protection and that this should be sufficient to cover the costs of a clean-up operation if the expedition party fails to comply.

These examples illustrate the close interrelationships that exist between environment and tourism. Neither is viable without the other and both require careful management to ensure that their viability is perpetuated.

8.3.3 SPORT

Sporting activities which utilise the landscape are many and varied and may be elements of both recreation and tourism. In the broadest sense they are what Edington and Edington (1986) describe as 'active physical pursuits' such as skiing, climbing and sailing. Some of these sports necessitate the use of motor-powered vehicles which can be the major agents of environmental change and in some cases, such as trail-bike racing, the environmental damage can be substantial. Large-scale sporting events, such as the Winter Olympics, can also bring about environmental change which is not just a consequence of the sporting events themselves but is also due to the infra-structure necessary to provide facilities for a large number of competitors and spectators.

Edington and Edington have described the environmental impact of the 'Hare and Hounds' trail-bike race which takes place between Barstow and Las Vegas across the California Desert of the USA. This is an arid, fragile environment that is easily damaged by the mechanical impact of motor-cycle tyres and according to Luckenbach (1975, quoted in Edington and Edington 1986) the 'Hare and Hounds' race has resulted in the destruction of some 140 000 creosote bushes (*Larrea divaricata*), 64 000 burro-bushes (*Franseria dumosa*) and 15 000 Mojave yuccas (*Yucca schidigera*) due to mechanical impact and the exposure of plant roots by subsequent soil erosion. Other desert flora and fauna have also been adversely affected by this type of activity as well as the use of dune-buggies and jeeps. Soil compaction by vehicle tyres in recreation areas of the Californian Desert has caused a reduction in the population of annual ephemerals by reducing water penetration that is essential to remove germination inhibitors from the soil seed bank (Webb 1982). Changes in plant cover can subsequently influence faunal populations by altering food supplies and habitats.

Sailing, boating and water-skiing can also have adverse effects on aquatic ecosystems both directly and indirectly. In the Norfolk Broads, Britain, for example, aquatic plants have been damaged by the mechanical action of propellers and boat hulls which have also accelerated bank erosion. The discharge of sewage from boats has also contributed to eutrophication problems in the region (which is mainly due to runoff of fertilisers from adjacent arable land). The popularity of the area, which attracts some 2000 hired boats and 3000 private craft in the summer months (Crawford 1985), is gradually causing the impoverishment of what is generally considered to be one of Britain's most attractive wetland areas. There are also numerous reports that sailing and other water-based recreational sports can have adverse affects on water-birds that abound on many of Britain's artificially created reservoirs (e.g. Tuite 1982). This is a particular problem when sailing is extended into the winter period and can result in a reduction of overwintering species.

Skiing can also have a significant environmental impact, since provisions for it extend over relatively large areas. This has been discussed by Mosimann (1985) in relation to ski *piste* construction in the Swiss Alps. His study of more than 200 sites in the cantons of Grison and Valais involved the collection of data on a range of variables relating to relief, the degree of site modification in *piste* construction such as the amount of levelling, soil characteristics, vegetation cover and its disturbance as well as impact assessment, notably sheet, rill and gully erosion, sediment deposition and landslipping. The relationships between site factors and soil erosion which emerged from this study are given in Table 8.5. This shows that slope form and soil moisture status are particularly influential in determining erosion rates. These factors are also important, along with altitude, in the establishment of new vegetation communities once *piste* construction has been completed. Revegetation is particularly limited where intensive erosion has occurred at altitudes above 2200 m above sea-level where harsh climatic factors, as well as disturbance by erosion, restrict revegetation. Between 2000 m and 1600 m above sea-level, vegetation recovery is more rapid but only where erosion is at a minimum and even then it may take between 5 and 8 years after seeding. Below 1600 m above sea-level, revegetation is much more rapid except on poorly drained slopes. Mosimann has also noted that on some revegetated *pistes* there are sharp boundaries separating well-vegetated and poorly vegetated areas. This occurs because of local variations in soil properties; on the upper part of the slope the soil may be truncated but on the lower slopes the soils are mixed with layers of various depths. Such variations affect nutrient and water transfers within the soil profile which in turn influence the vegetation communities and the degree of success achieved by reseeding. Mosimann suggests that some of these problems could be overcome if particularly sensitive areas are avoided, especially those above 2000 m above sea-level, and if the topsoil is restored after levelling, etc.

A further study on the environmental impact of sport is that of Rodriguez (1987) who has examined the effects on the water quality and biota in the Rio Hondo watershed of New Mexico, USA, where a ski industry was established in the 1960s. In terms of water quality, one of the most significant effects of this industry relates to the discharge of treated sewage into the Rio Hondo as the ski resort rapidly grew beyond the capacity of the treatment plant that was constructed in 1967. A monitoring programme established in 1974 revealed that there was considerable deterioration in water quality in

---

A. The most significant factors

      (i)   Slope form
      (ii) Soil moisture status
      (iii) Runoff frequency
      (iv) Size of catchment
    Overall, the greatest erosion occurs where there are long, concave linear
    hollows which have no moisture deficit whilst least erosion occurs on ridges

B. Intermediate factors

      (i)   Shallow soils with low water-retention capacity
      (ii) Length of piste - between 150m and 180m erosion rates rise steadily;
           at lengths greater than 180m erosion rates increase more rapidly
      (iii) Stone content of soils - the higher this is the less compaction occurs
           during piste construction

C. The least significant factors

      (i)   Angle of slope - the effect of this is most marked during periods
          of heavy snowmelt or heavy rainfall

D. Variable factors

      (i)   Rock type - overall this has a limited influence on rates of erosion.
          The most readily eroded rock type, as evidenced by rill and gully
          development, is gneiss. Schists may be more susceptible to
          landslides whilst marls are also subject to relatively high rates of
          erosion but other rock types show little variation

Table 8.5. The relationships between site factors and soil erosion on ski *pistes* in the cantons of Grison and Valais, Switzerland. (Based on Mosimann 1985.)

the stretch of river between the sewage-treatment plant and the mouth of the canyon, including high phosphorus concentrations and high populations of faecal coliform bacteria which presented a health hazard. A survey of the biota of the river between 1979 and 1981 revealed that the macroinvertebrate fauna had been adversely affected, involving loss of diversity and the proliferation of a few species which are tolerant of high levels of pollution. However, the construction of a new sewage-treatment plant in 1983–84 resulted, in subsequent years, in a marked improvement of both water quality and biota illustrating that problems such as this are not irreversible but avoidable. Kariel and Kariel (1988) have also examined the impact of new facilities constructed in Alberta's (Canada) Kananaskis Valley to accommodate the 1988 Winter Olympic Games. Already a highly developed multipurpose recreation area, plans for further development have generated concerns about wildlife protection, especially in relation to a herd of bighorn sheep whose range includes Mount Allan that houses one of the main Olympic *pistes*. Mitigating measures proposed to minimise the impact of large numbers of visitors include the cordoning off, by erection of a barrier, of the ski area to prevent people climbing the ridge and the provision of forage in specific locations to attract the sheep into areas that are least disturbed.

More passive sports, such as angling, can also have an environmental impact. Discarded lead shot, lead weights and fishing lines can all adversely affect wildlife. The latter can entrap adult birds and if it is incorporated into nests it can cause chick mortality. Discarded lead shot-gun pellets and lead fishing weights are also considered to be a significant cause of game-bird mortality in both North America and Britain. Game-birds are not the only species to be so affected and much concern has recently been voiced in the British media about the adverse affects of lead accoutrements on swans. According to a Nature Conservancy Council Report (1981b) significant declines in swan populations in many parts of Britain are due to the ingestion of lead shot and weights which find their way on to lake and stream beds from where they are consumed as grit. Hardman and Cooper (1980), for example, report that the swan herd on the River Avon at Stratford declined from a population of eighty in 1963 to just four in 1978, much of which is attributed to lead ingestion.

As Edington and Edington (1986) report, there are also numerous examples where wildlife populations have been adversely affected by recreational hunting as well as the particularly obnoxious practice of over-hunting of particular species to provide wildlife souvenirs. The over-hunting of African elephants as a source of ivory for ornaments and jewellery is a case in point in this latter context. However, in relation to recreational hunting, a classic example of overexploitation is that of the Arabian oryx (*Oryx leucoryx*) in the Middle East. Prior to the Second World War this species was hunted, as part of a traditional subsistence economy, by Bedouin tribes but with the development of the oil industry and the introduction of modern vehicles and weapons, hunting parties organised on a large scale rapidly reduced oryx populations to such an extent that they were virtually eliminated. The only herds of the animals which now inhabit the area are derived from animals that have been successfully reintroduced since the late 1930s.

Sporting activities, like recreation and tourism, can, as these examples illustrate, have a considerable environmental impact. Careful management can, however, mitigate such effects so that sporting activities do not have to be incompatible with conservation interests.

8.4 A NEW AGENT OF ENVIRONMENTAL CHANGE: BIOTECHNOLOGY

Biotechnology is a general term that embraces aspects of biochemistry, microbiology and chemical engineering which, in combination, have harnessed the capacities of living organisms, mainly microbes and cultured tissue cells, to undertake specific processes with industrial, agricultural and medical applications. Many of these applications have been used to tackle environmental problems such as pollution control, especially in the treatment of sewage, industrial and agricultural effluents as well as rubbish disposal. These are examples of environmental biotechnology which are relatively recent innovations in comparison with the long-standing use of such techniques in industrial processes like brewing and fermentation. Increasingly, environmental biotechnology is being heralded as a means of controlling and improving environmental quality and it is also being applied to mineral extraction and resource recycling. The latter, as will be discussed below, is particularly important in a world where the resource base is diminishing rapidly.

What is of more environmental significance, however, is the subdiscipline of biotechnology that is known as genetic engineering. Since its inception in the early 1970s, genetic engineering has been welcomed as a major scientific breakthrough because of the potential that it provides to manipulate organisms from the most simple life-forms, such as bacteria, to the most complex, including *Homo sapiens sapiens*. At the same time misgivings have been expressed, mainly in relation to two aspects of the science. Firstly, much of the research focuses on human embryos which raises ethical considerations hitherto unprecedented, and while such research is still in its early stages it is clear that the ability to manipulate human life itself requires well-defined and enforceable legislation. Secondly, there is a need to determine how genetically engineered organisms will react when released into the environment. This remains an unanswered question until such organisms are released and monitored but it does require a cautious and controlled approach if lessons are to be learnt from the often detrimental effects that have accrued from the introduction of organisms into non-indigenous environments as biological controls or as inadvertent introductions. (Examples of both of these have been discussed in section 4.4.3 in relation to Australia.)

Such a cautious approach to the potential of genetic engineering is also to be applauded in the wake of the dilemmas that have been created by the harnessing of nuclear power, the science for which was developed in the 1940s in response to weaponry requirements in the Second World War. Promoted thereafter as a source of cheap and clean energy, neither of which has actually been realised some 40 years on, nuclear power is a source of considerable debate in the late 1980s because of its annihilation potential in the case of warfare and the problems that characterise waste disposal from nuclear power plants (section 5.4.3). While nuclear power and genetic engineering may appear on the surface to be unconnected they have much in common; the term nuclear, for example, relates to nucleus which is a characteristic of both inorganic atoms and organic cells that comprise the fundamental components of living organisms. In the former, nuclear power can be harnessed by splitting the nuclei of atoms that comprise the basis of all matter; in the latter the onus is on changing the nature of DNA which is the component of all living cell nuclei that have the capability of transferring characteristics from one generation to the next. The manipulation of such traits is not new because a form of genetic engineering has been in operation since humans, *c.* 10 kyr BP (section 3.3.1), first began to select plants and animals for agricultural purposes. Such selection has been continued throughout history, and is continuing today in plant and animal breeding programmes. Whatever the drawbacks of genetically engineered organisms ultimately prove to be, and as yet there is very little evidence available, there are a number of possibilities that, at least in theory, could prove to be environmentally beneficial. Some of these potentialities will be discussed below.

8.4.1. ENVIRONMENTAL BIOTECHNOLOGY I: AGRICULTURAL APPLICATIONS

Biotechnology has an extremely wide range of applications in agriculture, among which are crop improvement, biological control of pests and the enhancement of nitrogen fixation, all of which influence environmental quality.

In the context of crop improvement, plant breeding programmes utilise several biotechnological techniques to produce stocks of plants with particularly advantageous characteristics such as disease resistance. For example, it is possible to exploit the capacity that many plants have for asexual or vegetative reproduction to produce stocks from cuttings. Stocks of potatoes, apples, strawberries as well as an array of garden plants are produced in this way. Plants can also be produced using tissue culture techniques, as has been discussed in detail by Tudge (1988) and Cocking (1989), wherein complete plants can be produced from tissue cells, even single cells, grown *in vitro*. The chief applications of tissue culture are given in Table 8.6 and range from the relatively simple production of large numbers of plants by cloning to the more sophisticated production of new species and useful chemicals, as well as facilitating genetic engineering which will be discussed in section 8.4.3.

As Tudge (1988) discusses, the facility of plants to regenerate from a few cells is related to the characteristic known as totipotency. This means that each individual cell has the ability to develop into any kind of cell that the organism will require for survival. It is characteristic of both plant and animal cells; in the latter totipotency is lost at an early stage in embryonic development but in plants all cells maintain this ability throughout the life span of the individual. In theory, therefore, it is possible to produce new plants from any group of cells as long as they are provided with an appropriate growth medium. In practice, most plant production using tissue culture utilises cells that are known as *callus*, a mass of undifferentiated cells which are produced to repair damage, or cells from leaves, roots or stems (see discussion in M G K Jones 1986), although it is not yet possible to regenerate all plants in this way and in the context of agriculture, the cereals are the most notable exceptions.

Tissue culture has facilitated the production of several disease-resistant crops by side-stepping the tendency of plants to pass infections between generations via seeds, tillers or tubers. For example, it is now possible to produce cassava seedlings, the parental line of which is usually affected by a mosaic virus, by culturing unaffected cells that can be propagated in sterile conditions (Tudge 1988). This would be impossible using simple cuttings and such disease resistant strains would be an obvious advantage to many farming systems in Africa, where cassava is a major crop, especially if disease resistance can be combined with high productivity. The cloning of plants using tissue culture is also being used to produce improved crop strains and, as Tudge points out, it has considerable potential for the improvement of oil palms, coconuts and tea, all of which are important economic crops in many developing countries.

As Table 8.6 shows, two further plant attributes are being exploited to produce new crop plants. The first is somaclonal variation, a characteristic recognised in cloned species which exhibit variation in genetic structure. As Skinner (1985) points out, plants or clones derived from the parent plant are not always genetically identical and those that differ from the parent plant are known as somatic variants or 'sports'. The ability of plants to give rise to such variation has both advantages and disadvantages. On the one hand, clones produced with the object of reproducing desired attributes may be disappointing because the genetic deviation from the parent may mean that the attributes are lost. On the other hand, somaclonal variation provides a new range of material by expanding the gene pool of a particular species, with which plant breeders can experiment. This property has been recognised in many plant species. For example, Kunakh and Savchenko (1988) have reported somaclonal variation in two related stocks of maize, of which one displayed a greater variety of morphological features and adaptability. Similarly, Larkin *et al.* (1988) have reported somaclonal variation in cultivars of wheat which produced a range of traits in mature individuals, including variation in resistance to the herbicide glyphosate. As Cocking (1989) points out, many of these traits would ultimately be revealed in conventional plant breeding programmes but tissue culture provides a much more rapid means of assay. The recognition of desirable attributes in many cloned

Table 8.6. The applications of tissue-culture techniques for crop production and improvement. (Based on Tudge 1988 and Cocking 1989.)

1. The production of new lines of crops that, in contrast to the parent line, are disease free

2. The generation of large numbers of clones of useful plants which are identical to the parent

3. The creation, via somaclonal variation and somatic hybridisation, of new varieties and species of plants. (see text for explanation of terms)

4. The maintenance and storage of germplasm which is a form of genetic conservation that ensures the survival of genetic pools for possible future use

5. The production of plant chemicals which are commercially useful as pharmaceuticals, agrochemicals, dyes and oils.

6. The facilitation of plant genetic engineering

species has already resulted in the improvement of crop plants like the potato, tomato, lettuce and sugar-cane. Somatic hybridisation, which involves the fusion of protoplasts (the basic plant cell minus its cell wall) from either the same or different species to produce a new cell with two sets of chromosomes, is also being developed to produce new crop plants. To date, successful experiments have been carried out on rice and tomato to produce hybrids, but no such crops are available on a commercial basis. The potential of the method is, however, illustrated by experiments undertaken on a mutant variety of tobacco (*Nicotiana tabacum*), which has an inbred resistance to the antibiotic streptomycin, and petunia (*Petunia hybrida*). The resulting hybrids were resistant to streptomycin, a characteristic inherited from tobacco, and capable of growing on nitrate, an ability conferred by petunia genes (Cocking 1989).

Crop improvement is only one aspect of the application of biotechnology to agriculture. Attention has also been focused on the enhancement of soil nitrogen by the use of nitrogen-fixing bacteria which, if successful on a large scale, could go some way towards reducing environmental problems associated with the widespread use of nitrogen fertilisers (section 6.3.1). As discussed in section 8.4.3, the bacterium *Rhizobium* spp. is one of the main bacteria involved in nitrogen fixation via its symbiotic relationship with leguminous plant species, and much work has been undertaken on the beneficial effects on crop productivity which may ensue if seeding with this bacterium is undertaken. Johnston (1989) and Day and Lisansky (1987) point out that there are a range of *Rhizobium* spp. which individually are host-species specific, which fix nitrogen from the atmosphere only when present in root nodules and which vary considerably in their ability to fix nitrogen. These characteristics suggest that a number of preconditions are necessary before the addition of *Rhizobium* to either plant or soil will be effective in promoting nitrogen enhancement. Firstly, the crop has to be a legume; secondly, the *Rhizobium* species selected will need to be one that has the capability of forming a symbiotic relationship with the host (though there is the possibility as discussed in section 8.4.3, that genetic engineering could simplify this aspect of the procedure); and thirdly, it is important that the bacterial strain should be efficient at nitrogen fixation. Moreover, Day and Lisansky point out that other environmental factors, such as soil type, are also determinants of nitrogen-fixing efficiency as is competition between naturally occurring *Rhizobium* spp. and inoculated species.

It is also important to realise that the efficiency of nitrogen fixation by *Rhizobium* spp. is determined to a large extent by the amount of nitrogen salts in the soil, so the application of nitrate fertiliser will actually inhibit bacterial nitrogen fixation. The options thus include the development of *Rhizobium* spp., which are active even when nitrates are abundant, or to reduce fertiliser application. The latter is preferable from an environmental viewpoint in order to minimise the potential affects of eutrophication. *Rhizobium* seeding, either by direct inoculation into soil or by inoculating legume seeds, has been successful in North America where soya beans are widely grown in soils where there are no naturally occurring rhizobial bacteria. This is chiefly because the soya bean and its naturally occurring symbiotic bacteria are natives of the Far East (Johnston 1989). The implication of this is that the introduction of leguminous crops to non-indigenous areas might well benefit, in terms of productivity enhancement, by the associated introduction of rhizobial strains.

One of the more obvious applications of biotechnology in agriculture is that of biological control. As Waage and Greathead (1988) have discussed, this is not a new approach to pest control but one that has been used throughout the centuries, reaching commercial proportions by the 1900s. Some examples of biological control have been referred to in section 4.4.3 in relation to Australia and in many instances it is clear that the introduction of alien species has proved ecologically disastrous. Currently, however, biological control of plant, animal and viral pests is gaining new status as one component of integrated pest management strategies. Pickett (1988), for example, has discussed the role of biological agents as components of crop-protection strategies which involve the use of pyrethroid insecticides (section 6.2.3). The use of such organisms, Pickett believes, will help to overcome problems of pesticide resistance in target species and to reduce the hazards of chemical use to beneficial organisms and the environment. Among the possibilities is the use of semiochemicals (behaviour-controlling chemicals), such as insect pheromones, to encourage the efficacy of biological control agents like fungal pathogens by ensuring closer contact between the target insect and the latter. There are also a range of organisms, notably bacteria, fungi and viruses, which produce fatal infections in many insect species, and which have a restricted range of host species. Many strains of *Bacillus thuringiensis*, for example, are insect pathogens because they produce insecticidal chemicals and, as Payne (1988) has discussed, there are now a number of commercially available strains which are used to control a variety of insects. For example, it is used in West Africa to control blackfly which is a carrier of the disease onchocerciasis and which has developed resistance to many pesticides. It is also widely used to control mosquito populations. Similarly there are two commercially available fungi, *Verticillium lecanii* and *Metarhizium anisopliae*, which are used to control aphids and whitefly in glasshouse crops, and spittle bugs which are a pest of sugar-cane in Brazil.

These are just a few examples of the use of modern biological control agents, though as Jutsum (1988) points out, the commercial value of these is currently less than 1 per cent of the global market value of crop-protection and public health agents (mainly chemicals) which currently amounts to $16 000 million annually. Nevertheless, many agrochemical companies are undertaking extensive research programmes on biological control. Little work has so far focused on plant pathogens, but it is likely that this will ultimately develop as another component of integrated pest-management strategies. There is also considerable potential for the development of novel biological control agents by genetic engineering. How successful such efforts will prove to be will not only depend on commercial sales potential but also on the costs which will be incurred in laboratory and field testing procedures, similar to those discussed in relation to crop protection chemicals in section 6.4, which are necessary for registration.

While there are many further applications of biotechnology in agriculture, such as in the treatment of agricultural waste, the examples given above testify to its potency as a future agent of environmental change, a potency which is likely to increase exponentially as genetic engineering develops (section 8.4.3).

8.4.2 ENVIRONMENTAL BIOTECHNOLOGY II: OTHER APPLICATIONS

There is no specific title to this section because there are so many applications of biotechnology with implications for environmental quality. Biotechnology is widely applied in the treatment of industrial effluents and sewage and reference has already been made, in section 6.3.2, to the potential that it provides for the denitrification of water intended for domestic consumption. Obviously, any such processes that can enhance environmental quality are to be welcomed, provided that they themselves do not lead to inadvertent environmental deterioration. Other applications of biotechnology which are relevant to environmental management include resource recycling, such as the use of organisms to scavenge useful materials from waste products, mineral extraction or biomining which involves the bacterial leaching of mineral ores, and energy production. This latter involves the production of food energy and fuel energy which can supplement animal feedstocks and fossil fuels respectively. In some cases, it is possible to combine several objectives such as the treatment of sewage to produce fuel or food energy.

The process of anaerobic digestion, which involves the use of mixed populations of microorganisms to produce methane and carbon dioxide from organic wastes, is used to treat industrial, agricultural and domestic wastes and has been discussed by Barnes and Fitzgerald (1987) and Hawkes and Hawkes (1987). The processes involved are complex, involving a variety of bacteria that can break down organic molecules such as proteins, lipids and polysaccharides (cellulose and starch are included in the latter) in the absence of oxygen. These reactions take place in a variety of digesters that are designed to deal with specific types of waste products. Municipal sewage works have used such methods to treat sewage since the early 1900s and the biogas produced, which consists on average of 70 per cent methane and 30 per cent carbon dioxide (Hawkes and Hawkes 1987), can be used to power the digestion plant itself. In addition, the resultant sludge can be used as fertiliser. Biogas produced in this way is not widely used as an alternative energy source in the developed world, but is now widely used in China where several million small-scale digesters have been constructed to produce fuel for cooking and lighting at a local level. There are also analogies between this type of energy production and that produced by the decomposition of organic rubbish in landfill sites where anaerobic conditions promote the often hazardous production of methane (section 5.4.1). As Richards (1989) discusses, there are currently 26 out of 300 possible landfill sites in Britain which are producing energy on a commercial basis, and there is considerable scope for increased biogas production as there is in West Germany and the USA. Moreover, Richards also points out that burning of methane in this way is globally beneficial because it is a much more potent trapper of heat in the atmosphere than the equivalent carbon dioxide produced by its combustion (section 5.3.1).

The aerobic treatment of sewage and wastes from food, chemical and pulp and paper industries is also a well-established practice and involves the microbial decomposition of dissolved organic compounds. The chief aim is to reduce the solid volume of waste, offensive odours and to effect pathogen removal. Like anaerobic digestion, the aerobic processing of waste material produces methane which can be used as a biogas fuel. The processes and technologies involved in aerobic waste treatment have been discussed by Best *et al.* (1985) and Forster and Johnston (1987) who point out that treatment plant must be designed according to the waste in question. However, Litchfield (1989) has also described examples of how aerobic sewage treatment can be manipulated to produce single-cell proteins. These latter are the agglomerated, and subsequently dried, cells of single-celled microorganisms like algae, yeasts, fungi and certain bacteria which can be cultivated on a large industrial-scale basis for the production of protein that can be used for either human or animal consumption. This can be produced in two ways: by harnessing organisms that photosynthesise and by using biotechnological methods that involve the provision of non-photosynthetic organisms with oxygen, nutrients such as carbon, nitrogen and phosphorus, and energy. Bacteria and algae are the most commonly used photosynthesising organisms in single-cell protein production and are best cultivated in shallow ponds where temperatures are high and an adequate nutrient supply is present. For example, the blue-green alga *Spirulina maxima* has been produced on a commercial basis from Lake Texcoco in Mexico and, in common with similar projects in Hawaii, Taiwan, Israel and Thailand, the dried algal products are sold as health foods. In Israel, sewage treatment has been successfully combined with single-cell protein production; the sewage provides the nutrients while the year-round high light intensities promote rapid algal growth. The resulting biomass is thermally dried to remove pathogens and the final product is used as an animal feed.

Single-cell protein production from non-photosynthetic organisms has also reached the stage of commercial availability, mainly as animal feed. Pruteen®, for example, is one such product which was developed by ICI plc in the 1960s and early 1970s mainly as an alternative to soya-bean meal. The process involves the bacterium *Methylophilus methylotrophus*, which utilises methanol as its energy source, and the provision of nutrients such as ammonia (to provide nitrogen), phosphorus, calcium and potassium. According to Litchfield (1989), the dried product consists of 72 per cent protein but, although it is an acceptable animal feed supplement, the drop in world soya-bean meal prices mean that it is now no longer produced on a commercial basis. Technology such as this, however, is used in the production of a wide variety of other food products for both animal and human consumption, as has been discussed by Beech *et al.* (1985), such as yeasts, flavouring, gums and vitamins. Of the products currently available for human consumption, Mycoprotein® is perhaps the best-known single-cell protein. It consists of fungal mycelia, from the fungus *Fusarium graminearum*, which is produced by fermentation using glucose as the energy source and ammonia as the nitrogen source. The end product resembles meat in so far as it is fibrous and can be flavoured and/or coloured accordingly. Beech *et al.* (1985) have compared its dietary characteristics with those of lean raw beefsteak, and although it has a protein content of *c.* 47 per cent, which is nearly 20 per cent less than the beefsteak, it contains half the fat and is rich in fibre.

Mineral extraction using organisms is another aspect of biotechnology that is relevant to environmental quality and its increasing use as a mechanism for extracting minerals from ores or from mined materials simply harnesses the natural ability of many organisms to break down mineral-containing rock. As Pooley (1987) discusses, bacterial leaching is relevant to the recovery of metals that occur as sulphide ores and it involves the oxidation of sulphides to sulphates that are more soluble, providing solutions from which the metals can be more easily extracted. The bacteria involved in this process are known as chemolithotrophs because they have the ability to produce energy for growth from the oxidation of inorganic sulphurous compounds. According to Woods and Rawlings (1989) the most important organisms are *Thiobacillus ferrooxidans, T. thiooxidans, Leptospirillum ferrooxidans* and several *Sulfolobus* spp. which can not only utilise inorganic substances as their energy source but also survive in highly acidic conditions and work at high temperatures. The chief metals that are being recovered using bioleaching are copper and uranium, though it is also possible to obtain cobalt, nickel, zinc, lead and gold.

The advantages of bioleaching over the conventional recovery of minerals are many. Firstly, where near-surface ores have been depleted deep-seated ores may be extracted by *in situ* leaching, obviating the need to undertake extensive and environmentally damaging excavation (section 5.2.1). Secondly, low-grade sources of minerals and waste dumps can be efficiently exploited. Leachate must, however, be carefully controlled to avoid contamination of surface and below-ground drainage, though further economies can be made by recycling the leaching solution; if such a process was applied on a large scale the widespread contamination of land and water by natural mine-leaching processes could be considerably reduced. One example of dump leaching is that used at the Kennecott Chino Mine in New Mexico, USA, from which there is a daily yield of cement copper of 45–50 t (Pooley 1987). The cement copper, which is produced from the leachate by the addition of scrap-iron, can then be further refined by smelting.

These processes may also be used to remove impurities such as arsenides which detract from the value of mineral concentrates. There is also the possibility that such processes may be useful in the desulphurisation of coal; this could be a useful adjunct in combating the acidification of ecosystems (section 5.3.2) due to fossil-fuel combustion. Woods and Rawlings (1989) also point out that genetic engineering has considerable application in this field by developing improved strains of the relevant bacteria which are more efficient, can operate on a wider variety of substrates and in a wider variety of environmental conditions.

Such advances could also have considerable applications in the field of resource recycling, one aspect of which involving the use of sewage to produce single-cell protein has already been discussed above. As yet, however, there are no well-established treatments than can effect the removal of, for example, metals and phosphates from waste water. The contamination of land and water by such substances constitutes a pollution hazard that could be reduced by scavenging mechanisms which could provide a means of recycling these substances for industrial and agricultural use. In consequence the pressure on primary sources would be reduced. The prospects for such developments, along with others to assist in the reclamation of contaminated land and oil spills, have been discussed by Forster and Wase (1987). Clearly, biotechnology will have an increasing role to play in environmental quality during the next few centuries, especially if existing methodologies can be improved by genetic engineering (see below).

8.4.3 GENETIC ENGINEERING

Genetic engineering involves the manipulation of DNA, the basic chromosomal unit that exists in all cells and which contains genetic information that is passed on to future generations. Plant and animal breeding programmes have utilised a crude form of genetic engineering by crossing or interbreeding related species in the anticipation that the offspring will contain preferred characteristics. In the case of plants, for example, the end product may be a species that is relatively drought resistant, a high carbohydrate yielder or one that is easy to harvest. In the case of animals the objective may be high meat, wool or milk production. Virtually all of the plants and animals that comprise the earth's agricultural systems have been manipulated in this way. Such breeding programmes, in conjunction with the use of fertilisers and crop-protection chemicals, have given rise to what is commonly known as the 'Green Revolution' of the twentieth century. Now, however, it is possible to identify specific gene components that contain the relevant hereditary information. Moreover, the technology is available to transpose that part of the chromosome into a related species which will then produce offspring bearing the particular characteristic. As Marx (1989) has discussed, the science of genetic engineering has been developed only since the 1940s and especially since the 1970s, but its origins really began with the efforts of Charles Darwin and Gregor Mendel who, in the mid-nineteenth century, established the principles of heredity. Subsequent developments, including the isolation of cell components, the recognition of DNA in the cell nucleus as the purveyor of hereditary information and the determination of its structure in the 1950s by Watson and Crick, have all paved the way for the genetic engineering of the 1980s.

The basis of genetic engineering is recombinant DNA technology which is also variously known as gene cloning and *in vitro* genetic manipulation. Recombinant DNA is produced by combining DNAs from different sources, the process of which has been discussed in detail by Gingold (1988). In essence it consists of inserting foreign DNA – which contains the genetic information necessary to confer the target characteristic – into a vector. The latter, which may be a plasmid (extrachromosomal molecules of DNA that exist in many bacteria) or a phage (normally a bacterial virus), must be capable of being recognised by the host in order for replication to occur. This was first undertaken by Paul Berg and his research group at Stanford University in California who joined genes from the bacterium *Escherichia coli* with DNA from simian virus 40 (SV40). Using similar procedures it is now possible to engineer organisms that can produce relatively large quantities of useful substances. For example, Gage (1989) has discussed some of the medical applications that have resulted from this type of work, notably the production of interferon which is a potential anti-viral and anti-cancer agent that until recently was only available in very small quantities by extracting it directly from human cells. It is also now possible to manufacture human insulin, which is essential for diabetics who have become immune to animal-derived insulin, and growth hormones to treat children with growth-deficiency complaints.

How then are such developments likely to affect the environment? Firstly, there are concerns that genetic engineering may, inadvertently, produce new pathogens that are detrimental to the environment by interacting with naturally occurring species or which adversely affect human health. Secondly, the techniques, although not widely developed to date, may culminate in the creation of more productive plant and animal crops that could help alleviate food scarcity problems in developing countries by increasing the viability of traditionally based agroecosystems, thus obviating the need for the cultivation of new lands. Indirectly, this could lead to less environmental degradation by reducing land-use pressure in areas that are already heavily cultivated and subject to degradation via soil erosion and desertification, and by reducing the impetus for deforestation (Ch. 7). Similarly the engineering of plants to produce their own crop-protection chemicals and nutrients, especially nitrogen, could go some way towards offsetting the often detrimental side-effects that artificially produced pesticides and fertilisers can exert on the environment (sections 6.3 and 6.4).

The potential of genetically engineered organisms to wreak environmental havoc have been discussed by Bains (1987) and Barkay *et al.* (1989). The former makes the point that genetically engineered bacteria tend to be much less viable than their naturally occurring counterparts and thus tend to die off rapidly. He also allays fears that such organisms might find applications in biological warfare since they tend to be target specific and would probably be more harmful to their producers than to their recipients in the light of the necessary sophisticated transmission technology that would be economically unfeasible. Such fears, however, should not be dismissed lightly in so far as genetic engineering is still in its infancy. Barkay *et al.* (1989) also draw attention to the fact that genetically engineered bacteria may affect global biogeochemical cycles by usurping the role that naturally occurring bacteria currently play in helping to control flux rates of nutrients from one pool to another. Bacteria, along with fungi, are well established as agents of decomposition in soils wherein they break down organic matter to release carbon dioxide and nitrogenous compounds. Any organisms that might lead to increased release of carbon dioxide, or methane, are clearly not to be welcomed in a world that is currently experiencing warming due to the enhanced greenhouse effect. There is also the possibility that genetically released organisms might, while being beneficial to some plants and animals, prove to be harmful to others, including humans. Because of such concerns there has been considerable opposition to the testing of genetically engineered organisms in the field, as is exemplified by the furore surrounding the release of the so-called 'ice minus' bacterium. This was developed by recombinant DNA techniques from the bacterium *Pseudomonas syringae* which commonly occurs on the surface of many plant species and contains a specific protein in its cell membrane that promotes ice damage to plants by nucleating ice formation at temperatures in the range 0 to –2 °C. Using genetic engineering it is now possible to remove the gene that produces this protein and to produce large volumes of the new bacterium which, if sprayed on to newly planted crops, will considerably reduce frost damage. As Lindow (1985), the creator of this virus, discusses, it has the potential to save millions of dollars which are regularly lost in the USA as a result of frost damage to crops. Objections to field trials in the USA have, however, resulted in considerable litigation and, more importantly, brought to public attention the potential dangers of released engineered organisms.

In this case the misgivings appear to be unfounded, but it does highlight the need for adequate controls on such experiments, both from a national and international perspective, since it is always possible that genetic engineering firms, which are now proliferating in the USA, Japan and northwest Europe, will turn to those, usually developing countries, where regulations are not as strict as those of, for example, the Environmental Protection Agency (EPA) in the USA. In fact, regulations governing genetic engineering in the laboratory and the field are not yet well established in many countries and there are no internationally accepted guidelines. Essentially, this relates to risk assessment but it is made especially difficult because genetic engineering affects so many regulatory bodies, including those concerned with public health as well as the environment. The current state of regulation in the USA is discussed by Perpich (1989) who highlights the roles of the EPA, the Food and Drug Administration (FDA), the US Department of Agriculture (USDA) and the National Institute of Health (NIH) as well as the Biotechnology Science Coordinating Committee (BSCC) which was established in 1985 to formulate policies and coordinate the interests of the existing monitoring bodies in terms of public health and environmental implications. A M Russell (1988) has also discussed the roles of these organisations as well as those in Britain and the necessity for international agreements.

Having discussed the potential drawbacks of genetically engineered organisms in the environment, it is important to remember that recombinant DNA techniques have presented possibilities that, in theory at least, may provide considerable environmental benefits. There is, for example, the potential to manipulate crop yield by influencing the genes which control photosynthesis and respiration, the main plant metabolic processes which involve carbon fixation and its release. As has been discussed by Jones and Lindsey (1988), it is now possible to clone the maize chloroplast genome and to synthesise the protein ribulose bisphosphate carboxylase-oxygenase ('Rubisco') which is crucial to carbon dioxide fixation. If, eventually, it becomes possible to increase productivity in this way, and such crop plants are developed on a large scale and for use in a wide variety of environments, it may help to reduce the impact of the enhanced greenhouse effect as well as increasing global food supplies. Moreover, it may also be possible to engineer plants that scavenge other greenhouse gases, such as methane, from the atmosphere. Although this is a futuristic outlook it is clearly a long-term possibility now that science has revealed the nature of genetic composition. The potential will, however, depend on the identification of 'useful' genes in both cultivated and wild plants. This, as Tudge (1988) discusses, is a major reason why it is necessary to prevent plant extinction, as is currently occurring in tropical rainforest regions where deforestation is proceeding at a rapid rate (section 7.3.1), and preserve as large a gene pool as possible. The earth's flora and fauna contain in their genetic make-up a huge, virtually untapped, resource and it is in the interest of future generations to keep it intact.

As well as the possibility of engineering plants to increase productivity, advances have already been made in the engineering of plants that are pest-, herbicide- or disease-resistant and in the development of nitrogen-fixing non-leguminous species (Jones and Lindsey 1988). Genetic engineering has opened up possibilities for the introduction of genes which confer the ability to produce either insecticidal toxins or semiochemicals which alter insect behaviour. For example, the bacterium *Bacillus thuringiensis* has the ability to produce crystalline spores which act as natural insecticides. They contain the so-called 'Bt' toxins which are effective against a variety of insects including the budworm (*Heliothis virescens*). It is now possible to clone the gene that controls Bt production and experiments have proved successful in introducing the gene into tobacco (*Nicotiana tabacum*) plants which subsequently develop resistance to the pest. Moreover, Schell *et al*. (1989) point out that it is now possible to engineer plants, by introducing *B. thuringiensis* genes encoded for toxin production, that develop resistance to tobacco hornworm (*Manduca sexta*) and the large white butterfly (*Pieris brassicae*). Apparently, different strains of the bacterium produce different toxins which are active against a wide range of insects. This, Schell *et al*. believe, may one day facilitate the production of crop plants that have an inbuilt resistance to the specific insects that feed on them. Similar advances have been made in producing plants that have engineered resistance to viruses and fungi. For example, it is now possible to engineer tobacco and tomato (*Lycopersicum esculentum* or *Solanum lycopersicum*) plants that are resistant to the tobacco mosaic virus. The possibility that crop plants could be engineered to exhibit herbicide resistance is also significant because it may eliminate the need to produce target-specific herbicides such as those discussed in section 6.4.3. While the crop itself will be resistant to herbicides the weed competition will not and can thus be considerably reduced by a broad-spectrum herbicide. Although no such crops are as yet commercially available, agrochemical companies are actively pursuing this line of research and a number of potential developments have been discussed by Chaleff (1986) and Buck (1989).

Much attention is also being focused on the possibility of engineering non-leguminous crop plants that can fix nitrogen by developing a symbiotic relationship with nitrogen-fixing bacteria. There are few naturally occurring organisms which have the ability to fix nitrogen from the atmosphere and those that can are prokaryotes (organisms with no membrane separating the DNA-containing organelles from the rest of the cell). They include a range of bacteria, e.g. *Azotobacter klebsiella* and *Rhodospirillium* as well as several blue-green algae. Some higher plants, notably the legumes like clover (*Trifolium* spp.) and lucerne (*Medicago sativa*), can establish a symbiotic relationship with the bacterium *Rhizobium* spp. which is also a nitrogen-fixer and which forms root nodules on the host plant. If such an association could be encouraged in crop plants like the cereals, the additional nitrogen made available by the bacteria would reduce, or possibly even eliminate, the need for artificial nitrate fertilisers and thus halt the eutrophication process in aquatic habitats and aquifers. In addition, the ability to promote nitrogen fixation would be a great advantage in the reclamation of derelict land (section 5.2.3) where nitrogen is almost always a limiting factor to growth. According to Jones and Lindsey (1988) the promotion of nitrogen fixation can be achieved in several ways, some of which involve genetic engineering. For example, it is possible to produce strains of bacteria which will promote root nodulation by transferring plasmids (see p.299 for definition) from nodulating species to non-nodulating bacteria. There is also the possibility that gene transfer could increase the efficiency of nitrogen fixation in symbiotic bacteria and promote fixation under nitrogen-rich soil atmosphere conditions.

However, the greatest potential lies in the possibility of promoting nodulation in non-symbiotic plants, as has been discussed by Johnston (1989) and Long and Ehrhardt (1989). The important factors that need to be identified to achieve this relate not only to the genetic components that promote nitrogen fixation in *Rhizobium* spp. but also the nature of the host–bacterium interaction. In nature, bacteria enter the host plant through root hairs via an infection thread and their presence promotes cell division to create root nodules. The infection thread continues to grow through and between the host plant's root cells so that the bacteria in the infection thread are isolated and eventually released into the nodule cells. Known as bacteroids, they then begin the process of nitrogen fixation and the resulting ammonia is absorbed by the host plant which combines it with glutamic acid to produce glutamine. This latter then circulates the fixed nitrogen to the rest of the plant. Thus the process is extremely complex and will require a great deal of scientific endeavour, though a recent breakthrough (Díaz *et al*. 1989) regarding the role of root lectins, which are carbohydrate-binding proteins, in determining host specificity suggests that science is making considerable progress on this problem.

8.5 CONCLUSION

Although the topics discussed in this chapter are diverse, none can be lightly dismissed as a significant agent of environmental change. In a temporal context, the state of modern forestry represents the culmination of woodland resource use that probably began with the earliest hominids. Recreation, tourism and sport are products of the industrial era, and especially the result of increasing leisure time since the Second World War. Biotechnology, in the form of plant and animal breeding, also has a long history, beginning with the first agriculturalists *c*. 10 kyr BP, but developments in genetic engineering in the 1970s and 1980s are opening up possibilities that have no historical parallels and thus there are no base-line data against which it is possible to predict future environmental changes that genetically engineered organisms may promote. For all of these agents of environmental change, economic and political considerations are primary factors in their operation and future development. Unfortunately, environmental considerations often play a subservient role to economic and political expediency and the concept of long-term sustainability is rarely attributed more than cosmetic attention.

In relation to forestry in the developed world there are a number of dichotomies. Firstly, in North America foresight and management have promoted a vigorous sustainable wood industry, despite the early pillages of European settlers in the colonial era. This is in contrast to Britain where woodland exploitation throughout prehistory and history has left a landscape largely bereft of natural woodland and where a mantle of alien conifers dominates many upland areas. Secondly, there is the increasing demand in the developed world for wood and wood products which is placing more pressure on indigenous forests, while in many developing countries land and fuelwood scarcity as well as the need to earn foreign currency are prompting wood harvesting at a hitherto unprecedented rate and often under inadequate management. Forest survival is thus threatened on a large scale. The irony of this is reflected in forest destruction on the one hand and the apparent success of agroforestry (social forestry) as a means of sustainable agricultural development on the other hand. Dilemmas such as these have no obvious readily implemented solutions, nor are they conducive to gene pool conservation or to the amelioration of the enhanced greenhouse effect.

The environmental impacts of recreation, tourism and sport are insignificant in relation to those posed by forest demise. Nevertheless, all three activities can adversely affect the environment and if uncontrolled they can result in the destruction of landforms, fauna and flora that first motivated the activity. Planning and management, if the political and economic will is there to implement them, can effect sustainable recreation and tourism which is essential if such industries are to continue as a source of income in developed and developing countries. Furthermore, all three activities could and should work to the advantage of environmental conservation by encouraging people into new landscapes and thus heightening their environmental awareness so that they themselves become part of the environmental protection movement. Education is probably the best form of conservation because public opinion influences politicians, as is exemplified by the environmental debates of the late 1980s that figure so prominently in the media.

Finally, biotechnology has played a significant role in improving productivity via traditional plant and animal breeding programmes and in controlling environmental quality via waste-water treatment, and it is now beginning to feature prominently in mineral extraction. Biotechnology has, however, brought civilisation to the verge of another environmental experiment in the context of the release of genetically engineered organisms. The questions that must be asked relate to the promises that it presents, especially in the context of world food supplies and the alleviation of environmental pollution, and the caution that it necessitates in relation to the potential ecological havoc it may wreak. Both proponents and protesters are right to present their views and it is incumbent on politicians to ensure that adequate regulatory controls provide as large a degree of environmental protection as is possible when dealing with the relatively unknown.

FURTHER READING

Britton S, Clark W C (eds) 1987 *Ambiguous alternatives: tourism in small developing countries*. University of the South Pacific

Edington J M, Edington M A 1986 *Ecology, recreation and tourism*. Cambridge University Press

Forster C F, Wase D A J (eds) 1987 *Environmental biotechnology*. Ellis Horwood, Chichester

Marx J L (ed) 1989 *A revolution in biotechnology*. Cambridge University Press

Mergen F, Vincent J R (ed) 1987 *Natural management of tropical moist forests*. Yale University, School of Forestry and Environmental Studies, New Haven, Connecticut

Richards E G (ed) 1987 *Forestry and the forest industries*. Martinus Nijhoff, Dordrecht, Boston and Lancaster

Steppler H A, Nair P K R (eds) 1987 *Agroforestry: a decade of development*. International Council for Research in Agroforestry, Nairobi

Williams M 1989 *North Americans and their forests*. Cambridge University Press

CONCLUSION AND PROSPECT

9.1 PREAMBLE

During the last 2–3 Myr the earth has experienced large-scale environmental changes which relate to the alternation of cold and warm stages, or glacial and interglacial periods. The evidence from terrestrial deposits, ocean cores and ice cores indicates that there have been at least seventeen such cycles, each lasting approximately 120 kyr, with the warm part of the cycle occupying between 10 kyr and 20 kyr. Thus, climatic change in itself has been very significant in promoting environmental change by influencing energy flows and biogeochemical cycling which both affect and are affected by biota. Against this continuum of environmental change, human evolution and dispersion have occurred, culminating in the evolution of *Homo sapiens sapiens* and the subsequent spread of the species to all but the most inhospitable parts of the globe. As the current interglacial became established, early neolithic civilisations began to develop techniques that subsequently changed the face of the earth. The domestication of plants and animals and the initiation of permanent agriculture provided the basis for organised, planned food production, supplementing and often replacing the uncertainty of hunting and gathering food-procurement strategies and providing the opportunity for permanent settlement. From these beginnings modern agricultural systems have developed, leading to the modification and replacement of interglacial ecosystems and the alteration of earth-surface processes. Small-scale industrial activities, often associated with agriculture and metal production, also developed as a wider range of natural resources were exploited, culminating in the Industrial Revolution of the eighteenth century. Primarily based in Europe, industrialisation rapidly spread to what are now the developed nations, introducing another potent agent of environmental change. Currently, industrialisation is spreading to developing nations where it is seen as a prerequisite to achieving the relatively high standards of living that characterise developed countries.

There are two agents of environmental change which are shaping the earth's surface in the current interglacial period. The first is climate and in view of palaeoenvironmental evidence (Ch. 1) there is every reason to believe that another ice age/cold period will ensue in the next four to five millennia. The second agent of change is *H. sapiens sapiens,* a relatively recent development in terms of the evolution of the earth's biota but one that has already altered the earth's surface to such an extent that in many areas it is no longer possible to identify the natural components of the interglacial environment. The tools of *H. sapiens sapiens* are chiefly agriculture and industry, both of which are primarily influenced by science and technology and controlled by energy inputs and economic and political expediency.

While it is difficult to present an adequate summary of all the topics discussed in this book, other than to state the obvious in relation to the parlous condition of planet earth, it is even more difficult to provide a prognosis as to the fate of the environment and the fate of the human race. Although humans are often perceived as the ultimate controllers of their environment, it is clear that science has not yet progressed to the stage where a more complete or more effective control is possible. For example, science has not yet solved the world's energy problems, which include the provision of an adequate supply of food energy as well as fuel energy. There have also been many intentional, often environmentally detrimental, modifications of earth-surface processes, which have occurred as a result of past and present resource use and which society is either unable or unwilling to combat. Although science has begun to make inroads into the uses of biotechnology, especially genetic engineering, to improve environmental quality and agricultural productivity it is unlikely that progress will be sufficiently rapid to help in combating the enhanced greenhouse effect or its impact. (Fig. 5.1) There is also the question of population increases, on both a global and national basis. There is no doubt that the global family is increasing rapidly and any population increases mean that there is more pressure on a diminishing resource base.

What prognoses can be offered, then, in the light of these facts, bearing in mind that predictions can only be, and even then hesitantly, based on past experience coupled with realistic projections relating to technological potential? On the one hand, there is the pessimistic stance which espouses the attitude that people are self-destructive and by modifying or destroying the life-support systems on which they rely they are condemning *H. sapiens sapiens* to extinction. On the other hand, there is the optimistic view, the protagonists of which believe that scientific and technological developments will open up new opportunities to expand the existing resource base and thus accommodate the increasing pressures that are exerted by an expanding global population. Difficulties in interpreting the fossil record mean that it is virtually impossible to state with certainty that there are grounds for adopting the first approach. The fossil record is unequivocal in documenting that extinctions have happened in the past but it is rarely possible to determine precisely why they have occurred. What is significant, however, is that life on earth has evolved in tandem with changes in the composition of the atmosphere, each influencing the other in a complex interrelationship.

The second approach is much easier to justify in so far as there are numerous precedents throughout history which testify to the efficiency of *H. sapiens sapiens* as an inventor of artefacts that can expand the resource base. Increased food production during the last 10 kyr is a case in point. The production of food surpluses, especially in what are now the developed nations, has led to a situation wherein the vast majority of the population are no longer engaged in food production but which nevertheless enjoy a high degree of food security. Nineteenth- and twentieth-century developments in the discovery and exploitation of new fossil-fuel resources and their application to food production have also facilitated the support of much larger populations than those of the preceding historic period. The recent developments in biotechnology also illustrate that innovation is continuing. The real questions are whether or not such innovations can proceed at the same pace as changes in the environment occur and hence counteract potential threats to survival, and whether or not these innovations are themselves instigators of positive feedback.

In relation to the first question, it should be of some concern that knowledge has not yet progressed to the stage where the two basic mechanisms that sustain life on earth, photosynthesis and climate dynamics, are fully understood. Both control the underpinning functions of all earth-surface and atmospheric processes, as well as human activities, by virtue of energy transfers. Despite the sophistication of civilisation it is still almost entirely dependent on photosynthesising organisms, mainly green plants, for food energy, the production of which is still largely determined by climate. Understanding the complex process of photosynthesis, possibly improving it and even finding a way to mimic it may be one key to ensuring the future of society. The subject of climate dynamics is another more expedient matter if even the most conservative predictions about the impact of the enhanced greenhouse effect are to be heeded. The world is already experiencing global warming (Fig 5.1) but it is still not clear what the precise relationship is between atmospheric carbon dioxide concentrations and climatic change. Palaeoenvironmental research has much to offer in the elucidation of this problem, illustrating that once again it is necessary to turn to the past, in addition to understanding current atmospheric processes, to provide answers for the future.

That technological innovations instigate positive feedback in earth–atmosphere interrelationships and thus cause environmental change is also a matter of fact. Fossil-fuel burning associated with industrialisation, and biomass burning associated with forest clearance for agriculture, are the main causes of the enhanced greenhouse effect; acidification is a consequence of fossil-fuel burning, and cultural eutrophication, salinisation and excessive soil erosion are all consequences of agricultural innovations. It is with just caution that present and future innovations must be treated. What impact genetically engineered organisms will have on the environment and on natural flora and fauna remains to be seen. In many ways this is an even bigger unknown factor than the enhanced greenhouse effect since there are, locked in the geological record, some precedents for the impact of changing carbon dioxide levels that provide at least a limited basis for prediction. There are no such precedents for the impact of genetically engineered organisms. Genetic manipulation holds much promise for the future, but it is unlikely that it will be free of hazards, and the ability to control evolution in this way is indeed a powerful tool that must be treated with the respect it deserves, including a soundly based international legislative infrastructure.

Environmental history records that civilisation has already created a wide range of potent instruments of environmental change. The effects of these will have to be confronted in the ensuing decades, a formidable task requiring a wide range of both social and technological strategies. It is not enough to identify local, national and global impacts or the agents and rates of change. This is just the first stage in understanding the problems; the next stage is to take concerted action. There are both shades of despair and glimmers of hope that colour the inexorable transition to the twenty-first century. Political instability due to loss of food security as the enhanced greenhouse effect exacts its toll on food-producing systems, may undermine all that is good about planet earth by initiating even more wars than there are at present; nuclear war could eliminate civilisation completely. Conversely, the late 1980s have witnessed widespread concern with environmental issues which have pervaded all levels and colours of political activity. Is this, then, likely to lead to a situation, unprecedented in history, of international cooperation, usurping the role of the unidentified extraterrestrial threat that has hitherto been the only common, probably imagined, threat to civilisation? If so, then perhaps the environmental changes that have so far occurred to the detriment of the earth's life-support systems have not occurred in vain, provided, that is, that positive feedback has not passed the point of no return, promoting changes in the earth's atmosphere that are inevitable and unsuitable for the continuance of the human race.

9.2 CONCLUSION

Most of the evidence presented in this text indicates that the state of the earth is somewhat precarious. In the context of the Quaternary time-scale this is obvious, since palaeoenvironmental evidence confirms that the last 2–3 Myr have witnessed tremendous environmental changes centred on the oscillation of glacial/interglacial periods. Indeed, the latter appear to be exceptions to the norm in so far as each occupies only 20 per cent of the time that glacial periods occupy. The earth has already experienced some 10–12 kyr of the current interglacial which poses the question as to how much more time need elapse before another ice age will ensue. There is also the question of whether or not human activity, via the enhanced greenhouse effect (Fig. 5.1), is actually postponing or even eliminating the possibility of another ice age.

In relation to the immediate state of the earth, the opening statement of this section may be presenting a somewhat false view since the literature collated for this text concentrates, by and large, on the detrimental impact of human activities on the earth and its atmosphere. This is a function of the overall available literature rather than the specific selection of data to highlight adverse effects. It may be that researchers have a propensity to publicise environmental deterioration, whereas successful environmentally benign activities are not so much ignored but diluted by the mass of data on the former. Be that as it may, there is a general consensus that climatic change is about to occur at rates unparalleled in the history of the current interglacial period. It is also a matter of fact that soil erosion and desertification, to name but two examples of environmental degradation, are increasing. All of these environmental changes impact on society's potential for survival and are a result of civilisation's past and present use of resources.

To separate people from environment is impossible; all resources derive from the environment and all society exists as a result of resource manipulation. Such manipulation varies both temporally and spatially and depends on a variety of factors, not least of which is climate because it plays a major role in agriculture which is the main manifestation of biotic resource use. Without sustained food production, mineral exploitation and industrialisation would be impossible. Food availability is fundamental to the maintenance and development of human communities and food security is the basis on which developed countries have attained high standards of living and a situation to which all developing countries aspire. Food security in developed countries has, however, been achieved at great environmental cost, not least of which relates to the production of fertilisers and crop-protection chemicals. Attempts in developing countries to achieve food security have also resulted in a considerable environmental toll. Emulations of westernised agriculture in developing countries have so far failed to provide food security and have, in fact often exacerbated environmental problems like soil erosion which may well inhibit future improvements.

Energy consumption from fossil fuels is also an underpinning cause of many environmental changes that have occurred as a result of industrialisation. This began on a large scale in Europe in the mid-eighteenth century with the onset of the Industrial Revolution. Apart from the enhanced greenhouse effect (section 5.3.1), the other environmental impacts of industry such as acidification are mainly confined to the Northern Hemisphere but are not necessarily confined by national boundaries. This explains why environmental issues have become so important in national and international politics. Such awareness is at least a good omen for the future.

9.2.1 THE QUATERNARY PERIOD IN PERSPECTIVE

That the Quaternary period was characterised by the oscillation of glacial/interglacial periods is well established, though there are still problems to be solved before a complete reconstruction of Quaternary environments can be achieved. During the glacial periods there were major expansions of ice sheets and glaciers in mid and high latitudes where ice covered large parts of both hemispheres which now enjoy a boreal or temperate climate. Even where ice was absent, periglacial conditions prevailed. In low latitudes which were unaffected directly by ice cover, the extent of desert, savanna and tropical forest changed as ecotonal boundaries responded to climatic change. During the interglacial periods, conditions similar to those of the present prevailed, with ice sheets retreating towards the poles causing a rise in sea-levels. In high latitudes, tundra and boreal forest formation succeeded the ice, mixed- and broad-leaf-temperate forests and steppe developed in mid latitudes while in the low-latitude tropics deserts, savannas and tropical forests assumed positions similar to those that they currently occupy (Fig. 5.2). Palaeoenvironmental data also indicate that the glacial/interglacial stages were not uniform; during the last glacial stage, for example, there were at least two warmer periods when interstadial conditions prevailed. These are relatively short-lived periods when temperatures ameliorated but were not sufficiently high, or the period too short, to promote vegetational development similar to that of an interglacial period. Similarly, there is evidence to suggest that interglacial conditions have varied; the 'Little Ice Age' which occurred from the mid-fifteenth century to the mid-nineteenth century represents a cold period during the Holocene.

A comparison of stratigraphic records and their fossils also reveals that, while the overall trends are similar, each individual glacial and interglacial stage varied in relation to its predecessor and successor. For example, the oxygen isotope record of ocean cores indicates that ice volume was probably greater during the penultimate glacial stage than during the last glacial stage (Fig. 1.2). There is also fossil evidence which shows that even within a restricted area, each interglacial was characterised by different plant and animal assemblages. The present interglacial period in Britain, for example, contrasts with the two earlier interglacial periods in so far as spruce (*Picea*) and fir (*Abies*) are both absent from the native flora, although they have been subsequently introduced by humans. There is an even bigger variation in faunal assemblages; during the last interglacial (the Ipswichian), species such as hippopotamus (*Hippopotamus amphibius*), narrow-nosed rhinoceros (*Dicerorhinus hemitoechus*) and straight-tusked elephant (*Palaeoloxodon antiquus*) were important components of the British fauna. This contrasts with the late Devensian/Holocene fauna that is characterised by more familiar animals like red fox (*Vulpes vulpes*), badger (*Meles meles*) and red deer (*Cervus elaphus*), though there is evidence to show that as the last ice sheet waned numerous large herbivores became extinct. Such an extinction phase is also recorded in other parts of the world and is the subject of much debate. Currently two causes, which are not necessarily mutually exclusive, are being proposed, involving rapid environmental change and the possibility of overkill by human communities.

The palaeoenvironmental record has also revealed a number of other important factors which relate to the transitional periods between warm and cold stages and vice versa. Firstly, the termination of a cold stage is characterised by relatively rapid temperature changes and relatively rapid deglaciation (as is illustrated in Figs 1.2 and 1.3), probably taking no more than two or three millennia. Secondly, there is evidence that interglacial periods may end abruptly with rapid ice-sheet accumulation and temperature declines occurring in the space of only a few centuries!

As well as establishing the events of the Quaternary period, ocean-core and ice-core data have contributed to the controversial question of why climate changes. The cyclical nature of the stratigraphic record and the high degree of correlation which exists between cores from different parts of the globe has led to the reinstatement of the so-called 'astronomical theory' that was refined in the 1920s by Milankovitch. This theory involves the external control of the earth's climate by periodic changes in the earth's orbit around the sun, changes in the angle of the earth's axis and the precession of the equinoxes which results from the wobble of the earth's axis of rotation. It is, however, likely that other factors, notably volcanic eruptions, sunspot cycles and orogenic uplift, have also influenced climate, possibly to a lesser degree than orbital forcing but nevertheless of significance for a comprehensive understanding of climate mechanisms.

That other factors are important in climatic change has also been emphasised by the discovery that the carbon dioxide content of the atmosphere has varied in a cyclic pattern which mirrors the glacial/interglacial cycle. The atmosphere of the last glacial stage was characterised by comparatively low concentrations of carbon dioxide, while the atmosphere of the last and current interglacial periods contained, on average, 60 ppm more carbon dioxide. Why this is so is again a matter for debate and it is unclear whether changes in carbon dioxide concentrations are a consequence of or a cause of climatic change. Unravelling this relationship should go some way towards the development of predictive models for evaluating the future impact of the enhanced greenhouse effect. Clearly, the mechanisms influencing atmospheric carbon dioxide concentrations must involve considerable changes in the flux rates (and the agents of fluxes) that effect the transfer of carbon dioxide from its atmospheric, biotic and oceanic stores. During glacial stages, the atmospheric pool of carbon dioxide was depleted and it is likely, given the depression of global temperatures, that the terrestrial biotic and soil carbon pools were also depleted. This leaves the oceans as the major repository of carbon dioxide either by direct solution or by increased primary productivity. If this is the case, does it mean that the oceans are acting as a buffer to the enhanced greenhouse effect by absorbing industrially produced carbon dioxide? Or does it mean that the recent, albeit relatively small, increases in global temperature are due to the reduced ability of the oceans to absorb ever increasing volumes of carbon dioxide?

Increasing carbon dioxide concentrations in the atmosphere are but one consequence of human activity. The last two centuries have witnessed an escalation in the intensity of resource use by human communities, but this is a mere morsel in relation to the time that hominids have been present on the earth's surface. As Fig. 1.1 shows, the evolution of hominids from ape-like ancestors began some 4 Myr BP. By 2.5 Myr BP *Homo habilis* had developed the ability to make stone tools, though it is likely that earlier hominids may have been using wooden tools. The evidence, much of which derives from East Africa which is generally reckoned to be the cradle of civilisation, indicates that hunting and gathering on an organised basis and the use of fire characterised these early palaeolithic groups by 1.5 Myr BP as they radiated into Asia. Biomolecular evidence also suggests that the immediate ancestors (*H. sapiens*) of modern humans (*H. sapiens sapiens*) originated in Africa and subsequently radiated into Europe and Asia, and eventually to the Americas and Australasia. This occurred against the backdrop of the last interglacial/glacial cycle, but there is little evidence to suggest that these groups had any significant impact, or at least long-lasting irreversible impact, on the environment. As hunter-gatherers and subsistent food-procuring strategists they appear not to have been significant agents of environmental change though there is some speculation as to the role of later palaeolithic groups in the demise of many large herbivores as the last ice sheet waned.

However, by this time in the Near East human communities were beginning to harness biotic resources on a basis hitherto unprecedented. Centred on some of the earliest permanent settlements, the domestication of plants and animals was under way, marking a significant departure in the human manipulation of biotic resources, from relatively opportunistic exploitation to the planned, highly organised agroecosystems that were the forerunners of modern agricultural systems. Thus the onset of the current interglacial witnessed the emergence of a new and potent agent of environmental change, notably agricultural *H. sapiens sapiens*, representing a very important threshold in environmental development. The emergence of human communities as controllers of the components and energy flows in ecosystems is particularly significant because it is the main feature which contrasts the current interglacial with its earlier counterparts. From these beginnings agricultural systems developed, supporting permanent settlements, population increases and ultimately industrial development.

9.2.2 THE ENVIRONMENTAL IMPACT OF INDUSTRIALISATION: A PERSPECTIVE

The emergence of fuel-powered urban–industrialised systems, which developed as a result of the Industrial Revolution of the mid-eighteenth century, brought with them a range of new agents of environmental change. These relate to the underpinning factors that sustain industrialisation. The first is resource use, which involves the extraction and processing of minerals as well as food processing; these support all manufacturing industry. The second is the dependence of industrial processes on energy. The third is the high concentration of population in fuel-powered urban–industrial systems that is essential for their function and which generates large amounts of industrial and domestic waste.

Mineral extraction has been going on for centuries and today industry relies on an immense range of minerals for a variety of purposes. There are also large-scale extractive industries involved with energy provision, notably the mining of coal, oil, natural gas and uranium, as well as those supplying fertilisers, notably phosphate mining. Extractive industries create environmental change by disfiguring landscapes at the point of extraction and polluting drainage networks that can result in the contamination of distant areas. The science and technology required to combat such problems are already available and will no doubt improve. What is often lacking, however, is the legal infrastructure to ensure that post-operational reclamation measures are implemented. The responsibility clearly lies with the exploiting companies who could either reduce their profit margins or pass on the cost of such schemes to the consumer.

Industrialisation has only been made possible by the exploitation of energy sources, especially fossil fuels. The environmental impact of this is considerable, affecting both the earth's surface and its atmosphere. The most important aspects of this impact are acidification and the enhanced greenhouse effect. Fossil-fuel consumption is not entirely to blame for the enhanced greenhouse effect since increasing methane production from certain types of agricultural systems, the release of carbon dioxide as the world's forests are cleared by burning and the industrial use of chlorofluorocarbons (CFCs) are also contributing to the atmosphere's store of heat-trapping compounds. Chlorofluorocarbons are also causing the depletion of ozone in the stratosphere which may, because of an increase in the amount of ultraviolet radiation, lead to increases in some forms of skin cancer and cataracts.

The enhanced greenhouse effect has already been discussed at some length (sections 5.3.1 and 9.1) and since it relates to the immediate future rather than the present, further discussion will be reserved until section 9.3.1. This is not intended to suggest that global warming is insignificant but simply to acknowledge that its effects remain a matter for speculation and are thus more relevant to a discussion of the earth's future prospects than to an examination of perspective. The acidification of ecosystems, particularly in the northern hemisphere where most industrialisation has occurred, has arisen because of emissions of sulphurous and nitrous oxides that combine with water to produce acids which, when deposited, have detrimental effects on plants and animal communities by reducing biotic diversity. The impact of acidification can be both gradual and catastrophic; the latter events tend to occur where large volumes of acids are stored in winter snowfall which can melt quickly in the spring months causing rapid pH changes in melt-water-receiving rivers in which fish mortality can be considerable. Such events are short-lived and comparatively rare in comparison with the more gradual acidification that has occurred in many ecosystems in the last 200 years.

This was first brought to public attention in the early 1970s by Scandinavian scientists who were becoming increasingly alarmed at declining fish stocks in lakes and rivers and the discovery that in some localities well water was of such low pH that it could no longer be used for human consumption. The reluctance of pollution-producing nations, including Britain, to acknowledge this problem (the 'it's alright as long as it's not in my back yard' syndrome) resulted in considerable irritation at a political level, as it has between the USA and Canada where a similar problem exists. Subsequently, the problem was discovered to be much more widespread and acidification has since been pinpointed as one of the reasons for European forest decay. In addition, palaeoenvironmental investigations of numerous lakes in poorly buffered areas has convincingly revealed the close correlation between industrial development, pH declines and diminishing fish stocks.

Once this link was established, it did, however, instigate political initiatives intended to develop mitigating policies. In West Germany, for example, there has been a move to introduce scrubbers into power stations to remove sulphur dioxide and thus curtail acid-producing pollutants at source. There is now a general agreement among many European countries to gradually reduce sulphurous emissions by at least 30 per cent by 1992. While this is unlikely to completely solve the problem of acidification, it is at least a move in the right direction and tackles the problem at source, which is much more effective than short-term solutions such as lake liming. There is also evidence that the reduction of pollution can have an ameliorative effect fairly rapidly, which implies that if international co-operation can be achieved acidification is one problem that can be solved. The irony of this, however, is that recent research has suggested that reducing sulphur dioxide pollution may reduce cloud cover in the northern hemisphere by diminishing the supply of cloud condensation nuclei and thus exacerbate the enhanced greenhouse effect! A partial solution to both problems necessitates a reduction in fossil-fuel use, which in turn means a switch to alternative energy sources (section 9.3.3). Such measures, together with the elimination of lead in petrol, would also result in a decline in atmospheric lead, a metal associated with impaired health in children, and another agent of declining environmental quality.

Fuel-powered urban–industrial systems are not only major energy consumers but also significant generators of vast amounts of waste products which include sewage and rubbish as well as industrial and nuclear waste. The disposal and treatment of these waste materials also promotes environmental change, though the developing field of biotechnology is providing improved methods of treatment and resource recycling. Landfill sites that are used for domestic rubbish disposal are aesthetically displeasing and occasionally dangerous if methane is produced by rotting organic materials; sewage disposal, even in the developed world where sewage treatment is common, is a major contributor to the cultural eutrophication of lakes, rivers and coastal regions. Nevertheless, there are mitigating measures that can be taken to reduce the environmental impact of what are essentially valuable resources. Methane production from landfill sites, for example, can be harnessed to provide a source of energy and the general public of many nations are becoming increasingly aware that substances such as glass, paper, tins and organic refuse can be effectively recycled. The technology is also available to ensure better use of sewage; already there are schemes for the production of single-cell protein that can be used for animal feed.

Industrial waste is also difficult to dispose of because much of it is classified as hazardous; high concentrations of mercury and polychlorinated biphenyls (PCBs), for example, can accrue in aquatic ecosystems so that fish become unsuitable for human consumption. Even more hazardous to human health are dioxins. Substances as potentially harmful as these are best destroyed by high-temperature incineration, but although the technology is available it must be used with great care in order to minimise risk. While most waste-treatment procedures have been developed in the industrialised nations and are expensive, there is a growing trend to export such wastes to developing countries where regulations relating to disposal are less restricting and not always easily enforced. This is no answer to the problem and simply reflects the irresponsible attitude of richer nations towards developing nations, an attitude which must be curbed by international, strictly enforceable legislation. This is something of a dichotomy in the light of public resistance in developed nations to the land-based disposal of nuclear waste. This is a major problem, especially in relation to the disposal of medium- and high-level nuclear waste, and none of the solutions so far advanced, which include ocean burial and confinement in specific geological strata, have met with approval. This is because of the very long time spans, hundreds of thousands of years, which are required for the isolation of these wastes before they can be considered safe. Such wastes are being stockpiled until acceptable solutions have been found; they are thus gradually becoming a problem for future generations by default.

The development and maintenance of fuel-powered urban–industrial systems is thus exacting a considerable toll on the environment. The greatest legacies are the enhanced greenhouse effect, acidification, stratospheric ozone depletion, eutrophication and heavy metal pollution; it is yet to be determined what impact the disposal of nuclear waste will have. These problems have arisen mainly as a result of fossil-fuel energy consumption and the ability that this confers on human communities to support high population levels in manufacturing and service industries. As will be discussed in section 9.3.3, growing industrialisation in developing nations is likely to exacerbate these problems on a global basis. On a more optimistic note, however, growing recognition of these problems and their increasing political status does at least mean that ignorance cannot be used as an excuse for allowing environmental deterioration to continue.

9.2.3 THE ENVIRONMENTAL IMPACT OF AGRICULTURE: A PERSPECTIVE

In order to sustain ever-increasing human populations, agriculture has expanded and developed since its inception some 10 kyr BP. The range of domesticated plants and animals has increased and the processes of domestication have become more sophisticated, with new possibilities on the immediate horizon as a result of developments in genetic engineering. Agricultural systems are similar to ecosystems in so far as they function via energy flows and biogeochemical cycles. Human communities have manipulated these processes by selecting plant and animal species which provide a particularly good source of carbohydrate, protein or fibre and eliminating the populations of other organisms which are either competitors for primary productivity or reduce primary productivity by deflecting nutrients and solar energy away from the crop. Until recently, this manipulation was achieved by traditional practices including rotations, hand weeding and manuring, with the only energy inputs, other than solar energy, being human and sometimes animal labour. Indeed, in many parts of the world this is still the most important way that management is effected. In the last two centuries, and especially since the Second World War, there has been a growing trend for agriculture to become more energy intensive. Labour is no longer the major energy input into the agricultural systems of the developed world; it has been replaced by large-scale mechanisation and the widespread of artificial fertilisers and crop-protection chemicals.

Both types of agriculture have had and are continuing to have a very significant impact on the environment, though the underpinning reasons are often quite different. In developing nations, population pressures constitute the main impetus for agricultural development, though financial considerations involving the need to generate funds for development projects may be just as significant. In developed nations, guaranteed food security is a necessary prerequisite for political superiority and as a means of supporting the large proportion of the population that is engaged in industrial and service occupations. Both high- and low-energy input agriculture occur in developed and developing nations, but in general the latter are characterised by low-energy input systems because of the high costs involved in what is essentially the translation of fuel energy into food energy. The converse obtains in developed nations, where high-energy input agriculture is the norm and forms the basis for agribusinesses that support extensive food-preparation industries. While all agricultural systems are influenced by environmental parameters such as water availability, soil type and climate, the economic and political factors are, therefore, just as significant as agents of environmental change as the systems themselves.

Whatever form they take agricultural systems replace natural ecosystems and usually involve a reduction in biotic diversity. The reduction in the extent of natural habitats and their fragmentation are among the underlying reasons for a historically unparalleled rate of extinction. What is perhaps most worrying, however, is the loss of a significant gene pool just at the time that science is beginning to learn how to manipulate the very basis of life. This is one of the major objections being raised to the demise of the tropical forests which not only contain a huge genetic store but numerous plants and animals which may be important sources of pharmaceuticals, dyes and agrochemicals. That there should be some destruction of natural habitats for the sustenance of human communities is inevitable, and indeed developed nations, especially European nations, have not provided environmentally conserving precedents for developing countries to emulate. It is thus hardly surprising that countries like Brazil are beginning to resent the pressures being brought to bear by many rich nations in relation to the development of Amazonia.

In the developed world, the environmental impacts of agriculture are many and varied. The temperate zone of Europe, which throughout history has been one of the most densely populated parts of the earth's surface, has little remaining natural vegetation. In Britain, for example, the landscape is almost entirely a cultural rather than a natural one. There is of course no turning back, but what is most disturbing is the seemingly unnecessary destruction of wetlands, hedges and woodlands in the post-war period in response to agricultural protectionism. The artificial price control of agricultural produce, first by successive post-Second World War governments and then under the auspices of the European Economic Community's (EEC) Common Agricultural Policy (CAP), has resulted in habitat demise and landscape change by promoting more intensive food production. While self-sufficiency in food production is important, the politically controlled system has, for 10 years or so, resulted in food surpluses that are almost as expensive to store as they are to produce; despite this, habitat demise and fragmentation are still occurring, some of which is also due to afforestation policies.

Agricultural expansion in Europe, Australia and North America has resulted in the depletion of the soil resource. The reasons for this vary but all relate to injudicious agricultural practices, notably farming systems which no longer include a fallow period or which eliminate the organic component of the soil so that it loses its cohesiveness. In Australia, the underlying reason for widespread soil erosion is the introduction of hard-hoofed animals into an environment that evolved in association with soft-footed animals. The recognition of soil erosion as a major problem in Europe is a development of the 1980s, but even in 1989 there are few national soil conservation programmes. The fact that soil erosion has only recently been recognised as a significant problem is largely a consequence of its effects being masked by increased crop productivity due to applications of fertiliser and crop-protection chemicals.

There is no doubt that these latter have dramatically improved crop productivity but both have also brought about environmental change. The intensive application of nitrate fertilisers, for example, is a contributory factor to the cultural eutrophication of lakes, rivers aquifers and coastal regions; the other factors involved are sewage effluent and runoff from urban areas. Fertiliser application in combination with farming practices that promote the bacterial release of nitrate from soil organic residues are giving rise to such high nitrate concentrations in some aquifers that the water is not considered suitable, either by EEC or World-Health Organisation (WHO) standards, for human consumption. Similar problems are also common in the USA. The widespread use of crop-protection chemicals, notably insecticides and herbicides to eliminate plant and animal pests, have also had widespread ecological repercussions. In 1939 DDT, probably the most widely publicised pesticide, was developed and its subsequent use in crop protection and malaria control was heralded as a significant breakthrough in pest control. However, DDT, together with related compounds like dieldrin, have also had disastrous unforeseen consequences. The propensity of such substances to undergo biological magnification as they and their derivatives are transferred from one trophic level to the next is now known to be responsible for the decline in populations of birds of prey. The use of herbicides has resulted in a large-scale decline of wild plants in hedgerows and meadows. It is, however, encouraging to see that some of these lessons have not gone unheeded; most agrochemical companies are now attempting to develop crop-protection chemicals such as the pyrethroids that have fewer undesirable effects on the environment. It is also gratifying that procedures for the registration of new crop-protection chemicals are much more rigorous than they were a decade ago and include a battery of environmental tests to ensure, as far as possible, environmental and human safety.

The environmental changes that have occurred in developed nations as a result of agricultural practices are, however, relatively minor when compared with those of many developing countries. This is because food production in developed nations is sufficient to sustain their populations, which are either falling slightly or maintaining equilibrium, and unless there is a very substantial decline in productivity, the environmental degradation is unlikely to lead to large-scale loss of life. In addition there is available the scientific means of mitigating many of these problems and, in theory at least, the financial ability to instigate conservation programmes. It is also encouraging to witness the emergence of environmental problems as key issues at all political levels and the growing awareness of the general public in relation to environmental protection. This is highlighted by the growing influence of European Green political parties which, in the 1989 European elections to the EEC Parliament, won 34 seats out of a possible 518, representing a 70 per cent increase on the 1984 elections. In Britain, the Greens did not actually win any seats but did capture some 15 per cent of the vote. Such concern for the environment, it may be argued, is only possible where food security has been achieved and indeed, where food security is taken for granted. This is not the case in most developing nations where the impact of agriculture has had, and is continuing to have, a large-scale detrimental impact that threatens the lives of millions of people. In many cases the degradation is so severe that only draconian conservation measures (if such were economically feasible) could bring land back into agricultural use on a sustainable basis.

The most significant impacts of agriculture in the developing world are deforestation, desertification, salinisation and soil erosion, all of which are due to two main factors: high population growth rates and inappropriate agricultural practices. The former may require that new, often marginal, lands should be brought into cultivation, while the latter can rapidly deplete soil nutrient stores so that productivity declines and soils become more susceptible to erosion. In many arid and semi-arid areas environmental degradation, notably desertification, has ensued as traditional shifting cultivation and nomadic herding have been replaced by permanent cultivation and settled herding. Although remedial measures can combat this problem many developing nations do not have the technological or financial ability to institute such measures, and even where foreign aid is available reclamation schemes have not always been successful. Neither do mitigating schemes help to solve the underlying problems of high population pressures and the often competing land-uses which relate to cash cropping, subsistence cultivation and animal herding.

Irrigation schemes in many developing countries have also enjoyed varying degrees of success and failure. In the worst cases, salinisation and waterlogging have led to farm abandonment. In the Indus Valley of Pakistan, for example, where extensive irrigation is practised, crop yields are now among the lowest in the world while population levels are increasing at considerably more than the global average. Soil erosion is also a major cause of declines in crop productivity and is due to both deforestation and unsuitable farming practices. Once again it tends to be highest where population pressures are greatest, rather than where soil types and rainfall regimes present the greatest potential erosivity and erodibility. Successful measures to curb this, notably social forestry and agroforestry, are being developed and although they provide good prospects for the future they have so far been inaugurated only on a relatively small scale.

Rapid rates of deforestation are also a significant cause for concern, not least because of the impact on the enhanced greenhouse effect. At a local scale, methods of tree removal can accelerate soil erosion and often the soils, impoverished by loss of nutrients from the biomass, are rapidly depleted of nutrients so that crop productivity declines markedly within 2–3 years. Deforestation can also be significant in increasing the frequency and magnitude of flooding in downstream catchment areas. Resulting soil erosion can also increase sedimentation in lakes, streams and reservoirs, threatening croplands well beyond the area in which deforestation is occurring. Not all deforestation is, however, the result of agricultural expansion; other factors include the ready markets for wood and wood products in the developed world, the scarcity of fuelwood in semi-arid areas and the production of charcoal for smelting.

There is no doubt that the impact of agriculture on the earth's surface has been immense. In developed nations the problems are not as acute as they are in many developing nations where food security is still in doubt. The development of agricultural systems in Europe, North America, etc. and their high rates of productivity have in the past provided the means for industrialisation and higher standards of living. Achieving similar goals is the aim of developing nations but whether or not high population levels and continued high levels of population growth, coupled with vast areas of degraded and poorly productive land, will hinder or prevent this occurring is a major issue which cannot be ignored by developed nations.

9.3 PROSPECT

Just as the physical and biological characteristics of, and processes on, the earth's surface have combined with social and economic factors to determine environmental change in the past, they will continue to do so in the future. Because of the complex nature of environmental change, predictions about future trends are notoriously difficult and often imprecise. The myriad of established and potential stimuli also make it

difficult to select those factors which are likely to have the greatest environmental impact. Nevertheless, the main categories of agents of environmental change used throughout this text, namely climate, industry and agriculture, remain appropriate to any discussion of the future since the experience of the past implicates these as the underlying causes of both deliberate and inadvertent environmental change.

It is perhaps easiest to examine climatic change in relative isolation because there are predictions which can be made on the basis of the palaeoenvironmental record. What is more problematic, however, is an assessment of how the enhanced greenhouse effect will deflect the predicted course of natural climatic change. There is also the question of whether or not international agreements will be established to curb the emissions of greenhouse gases and thus halt or reduce global warming. Another factor in this equation is how rapidly industrialisation will proceed in developing nations using conventional fossil-fuel energy resources, which may exacerbate the enhanced greenhouse effect and give rise to pollution problems which are currently confined to developed nations. The use of fossil-fuel energy also underpins to a degree future developments that may occur in agriculture; adequate food production is likely to remain a challenge in many developing nations and if current technology is employed to help solve this problem there is likely to be a large increase in the use of artificial fertilisers and crop-protection chemicals. Energy production may itself change in the ensuing decades as alternative sources are developed, though some of these, notably nuclear power, may institute environmental changes of equal or greater magnitude than fossil-fuel energy.

Both industrial and agricultural development in future decades will be influenced by population growth and scientific advances such as genetic engineering. The impact of population growth is inevitably going to be greatest in developing nations. More pressure will thus be exerted on existing agricultural systems and on remaining natural vegetation communities, notably tropical forest regions, as more land is required for cultivation. This also makes the need for industrialisation more imperative in these nations to offset land shortages, to provide alternative employment to rural activities and to produce goods that can be exchanged for foreign currency in place of cash crops. How scientific developments like genetic engineering will affect the environment remains to be seen. Existing work indicates that there is considerable potential for improving environmental quality and food production by engineering crops that can produce their own pesticides, for example, or produce higher yields of carbohydrates, proteins, etc. Genetically engineered organisms will undoubtedly be among future agents of environmental change but they may not all be environmentally benign. Taking a more futuristic approach, there is always the possibility that science will eventually be able to mimic the basic process of photosynthesis. In theory, this would be a master stroke: despite all scientific and technological achievements, civilisation is still dependent on autotrophic green plants for the basic sustenance of life.

9.3.1 THE CLIMATIC FUTURE

Palaeoenvironmental data indicate that the Quaternary period has witnessed what in geological terms can be described as extremely rapid environmental change. Since the last glacial stage ended *c*. 10 kyr BP the earth should now be beginning to cool with the approach of the next ice age. This, however, is not the case since meteorological records reveal that global warming is occurring due to the enhanced greenhouse effect, although there is some disagreement as to the precise rate.

As Gribbin (1989) has pointed out, there is the real possibility that the enhanced greenhouse effect is preventing the onset of the next ice age. It is also pertinent to examine the possibility that may have already done so. There is widespread evidence for cooling during what is generally recognised as the 'Little Ice Age' of the fourteenth to the early nineteenth century. By this time, large-scale deforestation had already occurred in Europe, releasing carbon dioxide hitherto locked in biomass stores into the atmosphere, and industrialisation based on fossil-fuel consumption was under way. This may be considered as an outrageous statement but it is, nevertheless, a point worth making. While it is unequivocal that interglacial environments were characterised by climatic variation, a point discussed by Roberts (1989) in relation to the Holocene, there is no precedent for cold periods similar to the 'Little Ice Age' in earlier interglacial periods. This could be due to paucity of evidence and/or the difficulties involved in establishing the high-resolution time-scales which are necessary to identify such relatively short-lived events. Whatever else the promotion of such a possibility implies, it highlights an increasing need to investigate pre-Holocene interglacial deposits as repositories of information on the response of ecosystems to natural agents of environmental change which are unaffected by human activity.

It is now widely accepted that the major instigators of climatic change during the Quaternary period are periodic changes that occur in the earth's orbital characteristics. Recent research has also revealed that climatic change is linked to changes in the concentration of carbon dioxide in the atmosphere. While it is not yet clear how this interrelationship functions, it highlights the significance of the greenhouse effect in regulating the earth's climate, as is shown schematically in Fig. 9.1. During the last ice age, for example, there was considerably less carbon dioxide in the atmosphere than in the previous interglacial or in the pre-industrial period of the present interglacial. This means that the greenhouse effect (as distinct from the enhanced greenhouse effect) of carbon dioxide in the atmosphere was reduced, causing or exaggerating the cooling due to astronomical forcing, and leading to the build up of ice sheets. The converse situation obtained as an ice age terminated. Since the major agents of fluxes between the atmospheric, terrestrial and oceanic pools of carbon dioxide are living organisms, the astronomical forcing factors must somehow promote or demote organic productivity. The implication is that during ice ages organic productivity was higher than during interglacials, which seems somewhat enigmatic in view of the much greater extent of ice cover during the former and generally lower global temperatures. Does it mean that biological productivity was significantly increased in areas of middle and low latitudes and those exposed by lower sea-levels or does it mean that marine productivity increased? Moreover, how much more organic productivity, terrestrial or marine, is required to account for a decline of between 40 and 60 ppm of carbon dioxide in the ice-age atmosphere? These are all pertinent questions in relation to the impact of post-industrial increases in atmospheric carbon dioxide.

It is equally important to determine how quickly these changes occurred and which parts of the earth's surface reacted more rapidly. Evidence from the Greenland ice cap (Dansgaard *et al.* 1989) indicates that the final cold stage of the last glacial period (the Younger Dryas, see Table 2.2) was very rapid, with a rise in temperature of 7 °C in just 50 years. Analyses of dust in the ice core also suggest that in only 20 years climate changed from being dry and stormy to wetter and calmer conditions. These data imply that the change from one stable climatic regime to another may occur very rapidly indeed and that future climatic changes in response to the enhanced greenhouse effect may be equally rapid rather than gradual. This study also highlights the sensitivity of the Greenland ice cap to climatic change and reinforces the view derived from General Circulation Models (GCMs) that

Fig. 9.1. Climatic change: The interplay between astronomical forcing factors and atmospheric carbon dioxide concentrations.

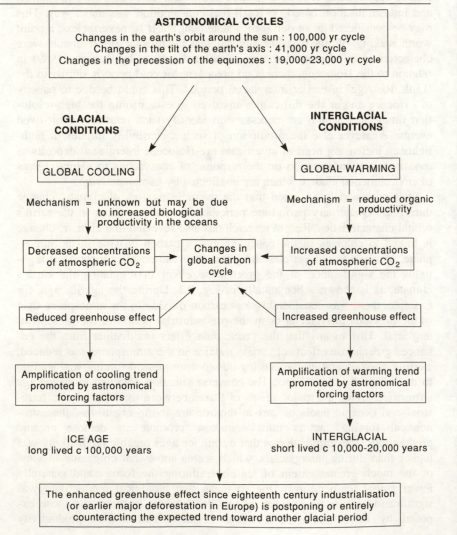

higher latitudes will warm more rapidly than lower latitudes. The latest GCMs (reported by Peel 1989) indicate that a 5 °C increase in temperature will occur over the next 30 years but that high latitudes will experience temperature increases of as much as 12 °C. The implications of this are enormous in relation to agricultural production, ecosystem survival and settlement patterns. For some nations the advantages of extended growing seasons will be considerable, for others the rapid loss of agricultural and silvicultural interests will be economically disadvantageous and there are already fears that many Pacific islanders will need to be evacuated as rising sea-levels engulf their atolls. It is also likely, even if international agreements are instituted in the next few years to curb carbon dioxide emissions, that the mechanisms for climatic change are already entrained. There is clear evidence, for example, that emissions of carbon dioxide are increasing. New Scientist No. 1671 (1989) reports that emissions have increased by 10 per cent since 1983, with a 1.6 per cent increase between 1986 and 1987, bringing total emissions to 5.6 billion t per year.

The climatic future is indeed uncertain; neither to fry nor to freeze is particularly acceptable, but what is perhaps more important is the possibility that some degree of political turmoil could ensue as nations lose or gain resource bases at such a rate that the face of global politics changes to an even more precarious state than presently.

9.3.2 INDUSTRIALISATION: ITS PROSPECTIVE IMPACT ON ENVIRONMENT

Although there are many aspects of industrialisation which will continue to have a considerable impact on the environment, it is likely that the increased use of energy resources will play the most significant role in future environmental change. This is especially true if civilisation continues to rely on fossil-fuel energy and if that reliance is coupled with inadequate controls on carbon dioxide emissions. There are a number of factors which are relevant to any debate on the future course of global energy consumption. The first is the growing industrialisation of many developing nations and the nature of the energy sources that this involves. The second relates to energy policies that will be adopted in the light of predictions about the impact of the enhanced greenhouse effect.

As populations have increased in developing countries, details of which will be discussed in section 9.3.3, there has been a growing trend towards industrialisation. The energy base on which this depends is fossil fuel and, as Flavin and Durning (1988) have pointed out, many developing nations are experiencing the early stages of industrialisation which are energy-intensive, a situation that is analogous to that of the pre-1900s in the developed world. This reliance on fossil fuels is inevitably going to exacerbate the enhanced greenhouse effect well into the twenty-first century unless there are major changes in energy policies involving a move towards alternative energy sources and the more efficient use of fossil fuels. The implementation of such policies would also have two further consequences. Firstly, the environmental impact of acidification, which is not yet a serious problem in most developing countries, would be reduced. Developing nations would thus avoid many of the problems associated with acidification that are currently occurring in the developed world. Secondly, the reliance of many developing countries on imported oil would be reduced, as would the necessity for subsidies on energy prices. As a result, more finance would be available for other development projects and the cost of manufactured goods would decline so that trading would become more competitive.

These suggestions have obvious advantages, not only for developing countries but also for developed nations. What is more problematic, however, is the establishment of policies for alternative energy sources and for promoting the more efficient use of fossil fuels. The latter problem is more easily tackled than the first, since there are already technologies available to enhance the efficiency of fossil fuels as energy sources and there is plenty of scope for further improvement. According to Flavin and Durning (1988), most industrial economies have improved energy efficiency by between 20 and 30 per cent since 1973. For example, in Japan, the USA and Britain, energy intensities between 1973 and 1985 declined by 31, 23 and 20 per cent respectively, prompted initially by rapid increases in oil prices in 1973. Nevertheless economic growth has continued, which indicates that once a certain level of development has been reached economic growth can be sustained without increasing energy demand. There is also an array of measures that can be taken to improve energy efficiency, ranging from the small-scale domestic level to the large-scale industrial level, and on all counts the reduced energy bills can rapidly compensate for the initial outlay involved in the installation of energy-saving devices. On a global basis, therefore, there is vast scope for energy conservation.

It will also be necessary to develop alternative energy sources and while this is widely recognised as warranting immediate action, there is much debate as to which avenues to follow. The publicity achieved in the media about the potential impact of the enhanced greenhouse effect has, for example, led to a resurgence of campaigns for increased production of nuclear-generated electricty. Winteringham (1988), for example, has presented data on the comparative detriments of coal- and nuclear-based electricity from which it is clear that emissions of greenhouse gases would be considerably reduced if nuclear-based energy replaced coal-based energy. Nevertheless, nuclear-based energy is unpopular in the wake of the Chernobyl accident of 1986 and the costs of constructing and maintaining nuclear power stations are so high, notwithstanding the problems involved in the disposal of nuclear waste, that this option is not particularly viable. Nor is it appropriate for developing countries because of the enormous capital investment, an investment that would provide better dividends if it was applied to the development of alternative energy sources.

What viable alternative energy sources are there then to fossil fuels and nuclear-based electricity? In the last decade, environmental organisations have been extolling the virtues of renewable energy. In terms of world-wide energy consumption renewable energy sources contribute c. 21 per cent of which 15 per cent derives from biomass and c. 6 per cent derives from hydroelectric power (Shea 1988). There are also possibilities involving the harnessing of wind and solar power. The use of biomass as a fuel has some controversial aspects, especially where it contributes to woodland depletion as it does in many developing countries which are now experiencing a fuelwood crisis. In the USA, however, wood-burning power plants using waste materials from wood-based industries successfully provide electricity to several million homes as well as to industrial plants. Brazil has also developed biomass fuel, and ethanol derived from sugar-cane now provides about 50 per cent of the national automotive fuel (Shea 1988). Where, however, wood shortages are so acute that animal dung is used as an energy source it constitutes an inappropriate use of biomass because it deprives agricultural systems of a primary source of nutrients. Moreover, the use of biomass as an energy source still generates carbon dioxide and thus contributes to the enhanced greenhouse effect.

The development of hydroelectric power also has its advantages and disadvantages. The harnessing of hydroelectric power has been particularly successful in Scandinavia, France and North America and has occurred without significant environmental detriment. However, the growing trend to harness hydroelectric power in many developing countries has resulted in gigantic projects involving the flooding of large areas, loss of agricultural land and the relocation of thousands of people. These factors, coupled with poor watershed management that shortens the working life of reservoirs by accelerating siltation, frequently represent losses that are too high a price to pay for relatively short-term gains. This, however, is more a manifestation of poor management than it is of any inherent disadvantages in hydroelectric power.

The harnessing of solar, wind and wave energy has not yet been achieved on a widespread basis largely because they are only viable under certain environmental circumstances. Solar energy is mainly used for heating domestic water in countries which receive a high proportion of solar energy for a large part of the year. Similarly, windmills and wind turbines are effective only in areas that regularly receive adequate wind strength as in Denmark and the Netherlands. Objections have, however, been raised about the displeasing aesthetic effect of large numbers of windmills concentrated in specific areas. Little effort has been invested in the development of wave energy. At the current state of technological development, solar, wind and wave energy can thus play only a limited role in solving the world's energy problems. Biomass fuels and hydroelectric power, if managed wisely, will be able to contribute a great deal of the world's energy in the ensuing decades but the most effective way forward, at least in the short term, is to increase the efficiency of energy production from fossil fuels and possibly to devise some means of trapping and using the resulting greenhouse gases. Reducing greenhouse gas emissions will also require curbs on their production from sources other than fossil fuels. The development and instigation of energy policies will require appropriate national and international co-operation with developed nations providing the lead and the finance for research and development programmes. Ultimately the harnessing of nuclear fusion as a major source of 'clean' energy may solve the world's energy problems though there is no sign at present that science is at all close to developing the appropriate technology.

9.3.3 Agriculture: its Prospective Impact on Environment

Speculations as to how agriculture on a global basis will affect the environment in the ensuing decades is made doubly difficult in view of the problems involved in predicting the impact of the enhanced greenhouse effect on agricultural systems. That aside, the fact remains that as global populations continue to grow there will be an ongoing need to increase food production.

Currently, world production of food is just about adequate to feed the earth's population, but the situation is made more complex by the fact that neither food production nor rates of population growth are evenly distributed on a spatial basis. Political and economic factors also conspire to preclude the even distribution of food so that in some parts of the world there is a food surplus while in many developing nations there is a food shortage. To a certain extent this is a reflection of the physical constraints, such as water availability and soil type, that the environment imposes on agricultural systems, but it also results from variations in agricultural techniques, notably variations in energy inputs, as well as differentials in rates of population growth.

According to *World resources 1988–1989* (World Resources Institute 1989), the population of the earth is currently about 5000 million, but what is more significant in relation to future food production is the rate of population growth that has characterised the post-1950 period and which forms the basis for the extrapolation of global and inter-regional population growth rates into the twenty-first century. These have been discussed by Merrick *et al.* (1986) and El-Hinnawi and Hashmi (1987) and are presented in Fig. 9.2. This shows that population growth rates have increased dramatically since *c.* 1950, doubling in just 37 years which is in contrast to the previous doubling of population from 1250 million to 2500 million that occurred over more than a century. These trends are startling, and while they reflect increased life expectancy and improved health care, they also reflect the rapid increase in pressure that has been brought to bear on earth resources and on food-producing systems. The trends illustrated in Fig. 9.2 also indicate that the most significant population increases have been in developing nations where some 75 per cent of the world's population is now concentrated. Although global population growth rates are gradually declining and many nations, especially in the developed world, have undergone a demographic transition from a state of growth to one of population equilibrium, there are still thirty-seven developing nations where population growth rates are in excess of 3 per cent per annum. Most of these are in Africa where populations are expected to double in less than 23 years. Elsewhere in the developing world population growth rates are declining; in South America the declines have

Fig. 9.2. Rates of global population increase. (A) Population growth 1950–2010; (From United Nations 1986.) (B) Average annual rate of population growth since 1950. (From Merrick *et al.* 1986.)

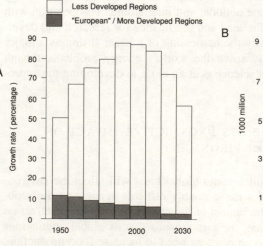

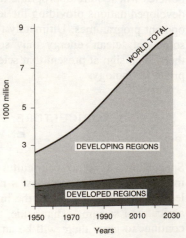

been small while in China the population growth rate has been halved in the last 10 years. Equally important, however, is the difference in the composition of populations between developed and developing nations. In the former only 22 per cent of the population is in the under-15 age-group and 11 per cent is in the 65+ age-group, while in the latter 37 per cent of the population is under the age of 15 and only 4 per cent is aged 65+; in Africa 45 per cent is in the under-15 age-group and 3 per cent is aged 65+ (World Resources Institute 1989). Thus, improving health care coupled with high fertility rates and a large proportion of people entering their reproductive years provides an inbuilt momentum for future high population growth even if fertility rates decline. This means that the annual addition to the global population, currently 85 million people, will continue to increase and the figure is projected to peak at 89 million by the year 2000 (IUCN 1987).

These population trends have considerable implications for agricultural systems, especially those in areas which are already under pressure and where the soil and forest resources are exhibiting signs of depletion due to unsustainable exploitation. There are two major trends occurring in global agricultural systems which relate to economic status and population growth rates. In the developed world there is a trend towards extensification, which is especially apparent in Europe and North America, due to the production of surplus foodstuffs, while in the developing world the trend is towards agricultural intensification as the demand for food increases. As Alexandratos (1988) has discussed, the extrapolation of future trends in world agriculture on the basis of past trends is unsatisfactory since it is underpinned by the assumption that those factors which shaped the past will continue, unchanged, to influence the future. Such factors include trade patterns, changes in demands for cash crops, the development and implementation of new technologies and whether or not increases in food production, which have characterised many developing nations in the past decade, can be sustained. Clearly, these factors, along with population growth rates, will vary considerably from nation to nation. Overall, it is unlikely that pressures on the land in developing nations will diminish in the ensuing decades; even if demands from indigenous populations remain static or decline, the need to generate finance for industrialisation etc. via the export of cash crops is likely to increase. According to the Population Reference Bureau (1987) most of the projected population increase, which will occur by the year 2025 and which will amount to some 3000 million people, will be in parts of Africa where there are already severe environmental problems.

An increase in food output in the developing world can be achieved by either bringing new lands into cultivation or by increasing the productivity of existing agricultural systems. If, as Pimentel et al. (1987) believe, the best land is already being cultivated, the gains to be made by cultivating marginal areas are likely to be relatively low and would probably not accommodate the demands made by increasing populations. Moreover, the resulting depletion of the natural vegetation cover, especially tropical forests, may well result in accelerated soil erosion, difficult watershed management and a decline in biological diversity. In relation to increasing the productivity of land which is already cultivated, World Resources Institute (1989) has shown that in the last decade food production per capita has risen despite a decline in the amount of land available per capita. This has been made possible by improved technological inputs, notably irrigation, pesticide and fertiliser applications, and the use of improved plant varieties. Not all such innovations have, however, been entirely successful; poorly managed irrigation schemes, for example, have caused a decline in crop productivity and even the abandonment of hitherto productive land. Such mismanagement is avoidable and if agricultural systems are to continue to increase their productivity, soil and water conservation measures must be fully implemented.

It is also encumbent on developed nations to ensure that the potential of genetic engineering is brought to bear on the problems facing agriculture in the developing world. Undoubtedly there are considerable benefits to be gained from the propagation of new and improved crops in the developed world, but the most generally beneficial role that genetic engineering could play in safeguarding the environment and enhancing the quality of life would be to devote its considerable potential to improving food production in those parts of the world where the need is greatest. The transference of such technology from the richer to the poorer nations is more a matter for politics than it is for science, but it is in the global interest to ensure that lives and the environment are not sacrificed out of ignorance.

Political policies can also influence attitudes towards fertility control. This is particularly important for those nations where a large proportion of the population are entering their child-bearing years. As Jacobson (1988) discusses, reducing fertility, especially to the level of replacement rather than increment, is an essential prerequisite for economic development and improvements in standards of living, as well as being necessary to relieve pressure on resources and the environment. Effective policies on fertility control are not easy to implement because underpinning social values often inhibit their acceptance, despite the obvious advantages of smaller families in terms of improved health care, education and employment. Holden (1988) reports that there are also difficulties associated with the dissemination of information and with the provision of trained advisers. In view of the fact that some 50 per cent of the world's population is currently below marriage age, it is even more imperative that adequate provision is made for education in fertility control in the ensuing decades. Nevertheless, there are some encouraging trends which illustrate that fertility control policies can be effective. In Taiwan and South Korea, for example, populations have reached equilibrium and these nations are now emerging as major economic forces. There is still much progress to be made before these trends are emulated elsewhere but this will only be possible if education, the status of women and contraceptive methods are improved.

In developed nations the post-Second World War increases in energy inputs into agricultural systems have ensured high levels of food production. These inputs have taken their environmental toll, but it is also apparent that adequate controls can halt or reverse environmental degradation. Once again this is dependent on political will and in view of increasing environmental awareness it is to be hoped that improvements rather than deterioration in environmental quality will characterise the twenty-first century. There may well be another 'green revolution' in the making as genetic engineering opens up the possibility of developing disease- and pest-resistant crops and animals as well as crops with an inbuilt ability to provide for their own nitrogen requirements. In addition, food surpluses in North America and Europe have led to policy decisions to reduce food production via programmes of extensification. This is not the case in Eastern Bloc countries which still import large volumes of foodstuffs, but in EEC nations and the USA the move towards extensification is to be welcomed. There are, however, fears that some extensification policies, notably those formulated in the EEC which are now being adopted in Britain, for example, will lead to a different but equally damaging form of rural exploitation such as relaxed controls on urban expansion and forestry. Extensification provides an opportunity to effect a degree of reconciliation between agriculture and conservation by encouraging the preservation of wildlife habitats and by reducing the rates at which habitats are being destroyed. It also affords an opportunity to reduce fertiliser applications and thus curtail the spread of cultural eutrophication. It remains to be seen whether a more satisfactory balance between economic and conservational interests can be achieved by this recent change in the EEC's CAP.

9.4 ENDPIECE

There are grounds for both pessimism and optimism in relation to the global future and there are also a great number of unknown factors, not least of which is the climatic future. Whether the earth becomes warmer, due to the enhanced greenhouse effect, or cooler, as another ice age approaches, is particularly significant in so far as the resulting temperature and precipitation regimes will alter the pattern of world agriculture. It now seems likely that global warming will ensue and the general consensus of climate modellers indicates that warming will not be globally uniform. Lower latitudes will experience a lesser degree of warming than higher latitudes, but beyond that predictions about the impact of the enhanced greenhouse effect vary, especially in relation to the reaction of the Greenland and West Antarctic ice sheets. If large-scale melting occurs, global sea-levels will rise and flood low-lying coastal zones with enormous implications for nations like Bangladesh, and many of the world's largest cities. What is certain, however, is that the configuration of the earth's ecosystems and agricultural systems will change. Since political and economic stability is underpinned to a large extent by food security, it is unlikely that the impact of global warming will be entirely without political repercussions, especially if it occurs in rapid surges rather than gradually. This highlights the interrelationships between political, social and economic factors and agricultural systems. If the latter change then feedback mechanisms inevitably mean that there will be adjustments in the former; the magnitude of these adjustments will depend on the inherent buffering capacity of the overall infrastructure. Perhaps the impact of the enhanced greenhouse effect in developing countries will provide part of the solution to the problems associated with feeding their growing populations in much the same way that the Industrial Revolution of the eighteenth century provided the wherewithal to support Europe's growing population. Micawberism such as this may well become reality though it is equally possible that quite the reverse could occur.

Aside from the potential impact of the enhanced greenhouse effect, which is unlikely to be entirely detrimental since it will open up new possibilities as well as causing disruption, there are other pessimistic augurs for the global future. Rapidly increasing populations in many developing countries are likely to exacerbate existing fuelwood and food shortages. Rates of deforestation and soil erosion are set to increase as more agricultural land is needed in the developing world in general. Both reflect losses of two vital resources, not least of which is the unprecedented rate of plant and animal extinctions which represent a reduction in the largely untapped global gene pool. What is equally disturbing, however, is the fact that some of these problems could be solved if there was greater transference of appropriate technologies from the richer to the poorer nations. This does not set an encouraging precedent for the effective transfer of current and future scientific innovations, notably those afforded by genetic engineering. This latter, since its potential environmental impact is as yet untested, may not provide a panacea for much of what besets the world's food supply problems (indeed it is difficult, in the light of historical fact, to envisage a situation where any such innovations are entirely free of direct and indirect detrimental environmental consequences) but it does offer considerable scope for improvement provided that adequate controls are imposed. Such controls require political as well as scientific endeavour and international co-operation.

On a more positive note, there are some encouraging signs which imply that civilisation is at least recognising the necessity of achieving a symbiotic relationship with environment. This is manifest in the technological expertise that is available to halt and reverse many of the adverse effects of human activities. Examples include the reclamation of derelict land, pollution abatement and measures to combat acidification and salinisation. The late twentieth century has witnessed an important new beginning in this respect but the challenge remains gargantuan. The challenges are not all within the remit of environmental scientists; slowing the rate of world population growth is all important. Achieving population equilibrium in those nations where population is still increasing rapidly will require changing attitudes towards the family unit as well as towards the status and education of women. It is a somewhat telling fact that almost all of the available fertility control methods are directed at only half the world's population. Statements relating to fertility control are easy to write but changing deep-rooted beliefs is a complicated long-term task which requires a sensitive approach and a good education system. It is nevertheless a fact that without population control, pressures on the earth's resources will increase and a sustainable future will remain elusive.

Equally important in terms of the future prospect for the earth and its life-support systems is the growing awareness of the general public about environmental issues. Large-scale tragic events, such as the Sahel famines and the Bangladesh floods of the 1970s and 1980s, along with local issues like waste disposal and loss of wildlife habitats have heightened public concern. Media coverage of environmental degradation and public statements by scientists and environmental organisations have resulted in the growing importance of so-called 'green' issues as components of local, national and international politics. The 1980s have witnessed the signing of international agreements on combating acidification and protecting the ozone layer. Such agreements are the first of their kind and represent the formal recognition that environmental problems are not just the remit of national governments and that collective measures are essential for their mitigation. Both of these agreements have been signed by only a small number of nations but they nevertheless represent the opening of a new era of co-operation. The next such development may involve some level of international agreement to curb carbon dioxide emissions in order to reduce the impact of the enhanced greenhouse effect. Perhaps environmental issues will ultimately lead to some semblance of global unity as issues such as the arms race pale into insignificance.

The information presented in this text highlights three major areas that merit further investigation and research investment. The first relates to the substantial role of palaeoenvironmental studies in determining the causes, rates and impact of climatic change; without such base-line data any simulations of future environmental change will remain even more speculative than they are at present. Associated with this, and underlined by the somewhat vague statements that have been made in relation to the potential impact of the enhanced greenhouse effect, is the inadequacy of predictive models. This implies a relatively low level of understanding as to how the basic life-support systems of the earth operate and interrelate with the biota. Investment in this aspect of environmental research would easily be repaid by facilitating the formulation of sustainable land-use policies. The third area worthy of increased research involves the roles of science and technology as agents that can cause and reverse the direct and indirect environmental impacts of both agriculture and industry. Whether better planning and more forethought could have obviated some of the detrimental impacts of past scientific innovations is a matter for speculation, but it is with this hindsight that the environmental applications of biotechnology and genetic engineering should be approached. Finally, it is abundantly clear that earth-surface processes cannot be considered in isolation from the human factor because the latter is one of the most important instigators of positive feedback as well as being a significant instigator of measures to combat positive feedback. Acknowledging this on an individual, national and globally collective basis is the first step to achieving a symbiotic and sustainable, as opposed to a combative unsustainable and mutually destructive relationship between civilisation and environment. This is the challenge and the responsibility that confronts each and every global citizen. As Pearl S Buck said in her novel 'The Good Earth', which was published in 1931, 'It was true that all their lives depended upon the earth'.

FURTHER READING

Botkin D B, Caswell M F, Estes J E, Orio A A (1989) *Changing the global environment.* Academic Press, Boston, Massachusetts

El-Hinnawi E, Hashmi M H, (1987) *The state of the environment.* Butterworths, London

Milne A (1988) *Our drowning world: population, pollution and future weather.* Prism Press, Bridport, UK

Moore J W (1986) *The changing environment.* Springer-Verlag, New York

Roberts N (1989) *The Holocene; an environmental history.* Blackwell, Oxford

Rosswall T, Woodmansee R G, Risser P G (eds) (1988) *Scales and global change.* John Wiley, Chichester

Simmons I G (1989) *Changing the face of the earth.* Blackwell, Oxford

State of the World 1988. Worldwatch Institute and W W Norton, New York

REFERENCES

Adamson D A, Fox M D (1982) Change in Australian vegetation since European settlement. In Smith J M B (ed) *A history of Australasian vegetation*. McGraw-Hill, Boston, Massachusetts pp 109–46

Addiscott T (1988) Farmers, fertilisers and the nitrate flood. *New Scientist* **120** (1633): 50–4

Adegbehin J O (1988) Meeting the increasing wood demand from the Nigerian forests. *Journal of World Forest Resource Management* **3**: 31–46

Adsersen H (1989) The rare plants of the Galápagos Islands and their conservation. *Biological Conservation* **47**: 49–77.

Agricultural Advisory Council (1970) *Modern farming and the soil*. HMSO, London

Agriculture Economic Development Committee (1987) *Directions for change: land use in the 1990s*. Television South and AEDC, London

Al-Dabbagh S, Forman D, Bryson D, Stratton I, Doll, R (1987) Mortality of nitrate fertiliser workers. *British Journal of Industrial Medicine* **43**: 507

Alexandratos N (ed) (1988) *World agriculture: Toward 2000*. Food and Agriculture Organisation, Rome and Belhaven Press, London

Allaglo L K, Areba A, D'Almeida N C, Gu-Konu E Y, Kounetsron K, Seddoh K F (1987) Togo, its geopotential and attempts for land-use planning – a case study. In Arndt P, Lüttig G W (eds) *Mineral resources' extraction, environmental protection and land-use planning in the industrial and developing countries*. E Schweizerbart'sche Verlagsbuchhandlung, Stuttgart, pp 243–70

Allan N J R (1987) Impact of Afghan refugees on the vegetation resources of Pakistan's Hindukush–Himalaya. *Mountain Research and Development* **7**: 200–4

Allison T D, Moeller R E, Davis, M B (1986) Pollen in laminated sediments provides evidence for a mid-Holocene forest pathogen outbreak. *Ecology* **67**: 1101–5

Al-Nakshabandi G A, El-Robee F T (1988) Aeolian deposits in relation to climatic conditions, soil characteristics and vegetation cover in the Kuwait desert. *Journal of Arid Environments* **15**: 229–43

Amman B, Chaix L, Eicher U, Elias S A, Gaillard M-J, Hofmann W, Siegenthaler U, Tobolski K, Wilkinson B (1984) Flora, fauna and stable isotopes in Late-Würm deposits at Lobigensee (Swiss Plateau). In Mörner N-A, Karlén W (eds) *Climatic changes on a yearly to millennial basis*. D Reidel, Dordrecht, pp 67–73

Andersen S Th (1966) Interglacial vegetation succession and lake development in Denmark. *Palaeobotanist* **15**: 117–27

Andersen S Th (1978) Local and regional vegetational development in eastern Denmark in the Holocene. *Danmarks Geologiske Undersøgelse Årbog 1976*: 5–27

Anderson D (1987) Managing the forest: The conservation history of Lembus, Kenya, 1904–63. In Anderson D, Grove R (eds) *Conservation in Africa: People, politics and practice*. Cambridge University Press, Cambridge, pp 249–68

Anderson D M (1984) Depression, dust bowl, demography and drought: The colonial state and soil conservation in East Africa during the 1930's. *African Affairs* **83**: 321–43

Anderson N J, Battarbee R W, Appleby P G, Stevenson A C, Oldfield F, Darley J, Glover G (1986) *Palaeolimnological evidence for the acidification of Loch Fleet*. Palaeoecology Research Unit, Department of Geography, University College, London, Working Paper No. 17

Aniol R W, Eckstein D (1984) Dendroclimatological studies at the northern timberline. In Mörner N-A, Karlén W (eds) *Climatic changes on a yearly to millennial basis*. D Reidel, Dordrecht, pp 273–9

Arakawa H 1956 Climatic change as revealed by the blooming dates of the cherry blossoms at Kyoto. *Journal of Meteorology* **13**: 599–600

Arden-Clark C, Hodges R D (1987) The environmental effects of conventional and organic/biological farming systems. 1. Soil erosion, with special reference to Britain. *Biological Agriculture and Horticulture* **4**: 309–57

Arkhipov S A, Bespaly V G, Faustova M A, Glushkova O Yu, Isayeva L L, Velichko, A A (1986a) Ice-sheet reconstructions. *Quaternary Science Reviews* **5**: 475–88

Arkhipov S A, Isayeva L L, Bespaly, V G, Glushkova O Yu (1986b) Glaciation of Siberia and North-east USSR. *Quaternary Science Reviews* **5**: 463–74

Armstrong W A (1981) The flight from the land. In Mingay G E (ed) *The Victorian countryside* (2 vols). Routledge and Kegan Paul, London, vol 1 pp 118–35

Arndt P, Lüttig G W (eds) (1987) *Mineral resources' extraction, environmental protection and land-use planning in the industrial and developing countries*. E Schweizerbart'sche Verlagsbuchhandlung, Stuttgart

Arnold C J (1988) *An archaeology of the early Anglo-Saxon kingdoms*. Routledge and Kegan Paul, London

Arnold J E M (1987) Deforestation. In McLaren D J, Skinner B J (eds) *Resources and world development*. John Wiley, Chichester, pp 711–25

Arzet K, Krause-Dellin D, Steinberg C (1986) Acidification of four lakes in the Federal Republic of Germany as reflected by diatom assemblages, cladoceran remains and sediment chemistry. In Smol J P, Battarbee R W, Davis R B, Meriläinen J (eds) *Diatoms and lake acidity*. Dr W Junk, Dordrecht, pp 227–50

Asabere P K (1987) Attempts at sustained yield management in the tropical high forests of Ghana. In Mergen F, Vincent J R (eds) *Natural management of tropical moist forests*. Yale University, School of Forestry and Environmental Studies, New Haven, Connecticut, USA, pp 47–70

Ashmore, M R , Bell J N B, Garretty C (eds) (1988) *Acid rain and Britain's natural ecosystems*. Centre for Environmental Technology, Imperial College, London

Ashworth A C, Hoganson J W (1984) Testing the Late Quaternary climatic record of southern Chile with evidence from fossil coleoptera. In Vogel J C (ed) *Late Cainozoic palaeoclimates of the southern hemisphere*. A A Balkema, Rotterdam, pp 85–102

Assadourian C S (1987) The spatial organisation of the colonial economy. In Archetti E P, Cammack P, Roberts B (eds) *Sociology of developing societies: Latin America*. Macmillan Education, Basingstoke, pp 21–6

Astill G (1988) Fields. In Astill G, Grant A (eds) *The countryside of medieval England*. Blackwell, Oxford, pp 62–85

Atkinson T C, Briffa K R, Coope G R (1987) Seasonal temperatures in Britain during the past 22,000 years, reconstructed using beetle remains. *Nature* **325**: 587–92

Australian Department of Resources and Energy (1983) *Water 2000: A perspective on Australia's water resources to the year 2000*. Australian Government Publishing Service, Canberra

Australian Soil Conservation Study (1978) *Economic evaluation of the Eppalock catchment soil conservation project*. Commonwealth and State Government Collaborative Soil Conservation Study 1975–1977, Report No. 9. Australian Government Publishing Service, Canberra

Bach W (1988) Modelling the climatic response to greenhouse gases. In Gregory S (ed) *Recent climatic change: A regional approach*. Belhaven Press, London, pp 7–19

Bainbridge D A (1985) The rise of agriculture: a new perspective. *Ambio* **14**: 148–51

Bains W (1987) *Genetic engineering for almost everybody*. Penguin Books, London

Baker R G (1984) Holocene vegetational history of the western United States. In Wright Jr H E (ed) *Late-Quaternary environments of the United States* (2 vols). University of Minnesota Press, Minneapolis and Longman, London, vol 2 *The Holocene*, pp 109–27

Bakewell P (1987) Mining. In Bethell L (ed) *Colonial Spanish America*. Cambridge University Press, Cambridge, pp 203–49

Baldock D, Conder D (eds) (1987) *Removing land from agriculture*. Council for the Protection of Rural England and Institute for European Environmental Policy, London

Bankoff H A, Winter F A, Greenfield H J (1980) Archaeological survey in the lower Moravia valley, Yugoslavia. *Current Anthropology* **21**: 268–9

Barkay T, Chatterjee D, Cuskey S, Walter R, Genthren F, Bourquin A W (1989) Bacteria and the environment. In Marx J L (ed) *A revolution in biotechnology*. Cambridge University Press, Cambridge, pp 94–102

Barker D, McGregor D F M (1988) Land degradation in the Yallahs Basin, Jamaica: historical notes and contemporary observations. *Geography* **73**: 116–24

Barker D, Spence B (1988) Afro-Caribbean agriculture: a Jamaican maroon community in transition. *Geographical Journal* **154**: 198–208

Barker G (1985) *Prehistoric farming in Europe.* Cambridge University Press, Cambridge

Barkov N I, Korotkevich E S, Gordiyenko F G, Kotlyakov V M (1977) The isotope analysis of ice cores from Vostok station (Antarctica) to the depth of 950 m. In *Isotopes and impurities in snow and ice.* International Association of Scientific Hydrology, Washington DC, Publication No. 118, pp 382–7

Barnes D, Fitzgerald P A, (1987) Anaerobic wastewater treatment. In Forster C F, Wase D A J (eds) *Environmental biotechnology.* Ellis Horwood, Chichester, pp 57–113

Barnola J M, Raynaud D, Korotkevich Y S, Lorius C (1987) Vostok ice core provides 160,000-year record of atmospheric CO_2. *Nature* **329**: 408–14

Baron J, Norton S A, Beeson D R, Herrman R (1986) Sediment, diatom and metal stratigraphy from Rocky Mountain lakes with special reference to atmospheric deposition. *Canadian Journal of Fisheries and Aquatic Science* **43**: 1350–62

Barr C J, Benefield C B, Bunce R G H, Ridsdale H, Whittaker M (1986) *Landscape changes in Britain.* Institute of Terrestrial Ecology, Monkswood, UK

Barrett J W, Solomon P M, de Zafra R L, Jaramillo M, Emmons L, Parrish A (1988) Formation of the Antarctic ozone hole by the ClO dimer mechanism. *Nature* **336**: 455–8

Bassett M G (1985) Towards a 'common language' in stratigraphy. *Episodes* **8**: 87–92

Battarbee R W (1984) Diatom analysis and the acidification of lakes. *Philosophical Transactions of the Royal Society of London* **B305**: 451–77

Battarbee R W, Charles D F (1987) The use of diatom assemblages in lake sediments as a means of assessing the timing, trends, and causes of lake acidification. *Progress in Physical Geography* **11**: 552–80

Battarbee R W, Flower R J, Stevenson A C, Rippey B (1985) Lake acidification in Galloway: a palaeoecological test of competing hypotheses. *Nature* **314**: 350–2

Battarbee R W, Flower R J, Stevenson A C, Jones V J, Harriman R, Appleby P G (1988) Diatom and chemical evidence for reversibility of acidification of Scottish lochs. *Nature* **332**: 530–2

Battarbee R W plus fifteen others (1988) *Lake acidification in the United Kingdom 1800–1986: evidence from analysis of lake sediments.* Ensis, London, prepared for the Department of the Environment/Palaeoecology Research Unit, Department of Geography, University College, London

Bednarik R G (1989) On the Pleistocene settlement of South America. *Antiquity* **63**: 101–11

Beech G A, Melvin M A, Taggart J (1985) Food, drink and biotechnology. In Higgins I J, Best D J, Jones J (eds) *Biotechnology: principles and applications.* Blackwell, Oxford, pp 73–110

Bell M (1983) Valley sediments as evidence of prehistoric land-use on the South Downs. *Proceedings of the Prehistoric Society* **49**: 119–50

Bellan-Santini D, Leveau M (1988) Case study: eutrophication in the Golfe du Lyon. In *Eutrophication in the Mediterranean Sea: receiving capacity and monitoring of long term effects.* Unesco Reports in Marine Science No. 49, pp 107–21

Bene J G, Beall H W, Côte A (1977) *Trees, food and people.* International Development Research Centre, Ottawa

Bennett K D (1988) Holocene pollen stratigraphy of central East Anglia, England, and comparison of pollen zones across the British Isles. *New Phytologist* **109**: 237–53

Beresford M W, Hirst J G (1971) *Deserted medieval villages: studies.* Lutterworth Press, London

Berg M (1985) *The age of manufactures, 1700–1820.* Fontana Press, London

Berg W A, Cail C R, Hungerford D M, Naney J W, Semple G A (1987) Saline seep on wheatland in Northwest Oklahoma. In Fairchild D M (ed) *Ground water quality and agricultural practices.* Lewis Publishers, Chelsea, Michigan, pp 265–72

Berger W H, Killingley J S, Vincent E (1987) Time scale of the Wisconsin/Holocene transition: oxygen isotope record in the western equatorial Pacific. *Quaternary Research* **28**: 295–306

Berglund B E (1983) Palaeoclimatic changes in Scandinavia and on Greenland – a tentative correlation based on lake and bog stratigraphical studies. *Quaternary Studies in Poland* **4**: 27–44

Berglund B E (ed) (1986) *Handbook of Holocene palaeohydrology and palaeoecology.* John Wiley, Chichester

Berglund B E, Lemdahl G, Liedberg-Jönsson B (1984) Biotic response to climatic changes during the time span 13000–10000 BP – a case study from SW Sweden. In Mörner N-A, Karlén W (eds) *Climatic changes on a yearly to a millennial basis.* D Reidel, Dordrecht, pp 25–36

Bergthorsson P, Bjornsson H, Dyrmundsson O, Gudmundsson B, Helgadottir A, Jonmundsson J V (1988) The effects of climate variations on agriculture in Iceland. In Parry M L, Carter T R, Konijn N J (eds) *The impact of climatic variations on agriculture* (2 vols). Kluwer Academic Publishers; Dordrecht, vol 1 *Assessment in cool temperate and cold regions,* pp 381–509

Berry L (1988) Desertification in the Sudan–Sahelian zone: The first ten years since the 1977 desertification conference. In Whitehead E E, Hutchinson C F, Timmermann B N, Varady R G (eds) *Arid lands: today and tomorrow.* Westview Press, Boulder, Colorado, and Belhaven Press, London, pp 577–82

Best D J, Jones J, Stafford D (1985) The environment and biotechnology. In Higgins I J, Best D J, Jones J (eds) *Biotechnology: principles and applications.* Blackwell, Oxford, pp 213–56

Bibby C J (1987) Effects of management of commercial conifer plantations on birds. In Good J E G (ed) *Environmental aspects of plantation forestry in Wales.* Institute of Terrestrial Ecology, Monkswood, UK, pp 70–5

Billé J C (1985) Some aspects of bush encroachment in the African rangelands. In Tothill J C, Mott J J (eds) *Ecology and management of the world's savannas.* Commonwealth Agricultural Bureau, Slough, pp 213–16

Billings W D (1987) Carbon balance of Alaskan tundra and taiga ecosystems: past, present and future. *Quaternary Science Reviews* **6**: 165–77

Binns W O (1986) Forestry and fresh waters: problems and remedies. In Solbé J

F de L G (ed) *Effects of land use on fresh waters*. Published for the Water Research Centre by Ellis Horwood, Chichester, pp 364–77

Birchfield G E, Weertman J (1983) Topography, albedo-temperature feedback, and climate sensitivity. *Science* **219**: 284–5

Birks H H 1975 Studies in the vegetational history of Scotland. IV. Pine stumps in Scottish blanket peats. *Philosophical Transactions of the Royal Society of London* **B270**: 181–226

Birks H J B (1986) Late-Quaternary biotic changes in terrestrial and lacustrine environments, with particular reference to north-west Europe. In Berglund B E (ed) *Handbook of Holocene palaeoecology and palaeohydrology*. John Wiley, Chichester, pp 3–65

Birks H J B, Peglar S M (1979) Interglacial pollen spectra from Sel Ayre, Shetland. *New Phytologist* **83**: 559–75

Björk S (1988) Redevelopment of lake ecosystems – a case study approach. *Ambio* **17**: 90–8

Blackie J R, Newson M D (1986) The effects of forestry on the quantity and quality of runoff in upland Britain. In Solbé J F de L G (ed) *Effects of land use on fresh waters*. Published for the Water Research Centre by Ellis Horwood, Chichester, pp 389–412

Blaikie P (1985) *The political economy of soil erosion in developing countries*. Longman, London

Blaikie P (1986) Natural resource use in developing countries. In Johnston R J, Taylor P J (eds) *A world in crisis?* Blackwell, Oxford, pp 107-26

Blaikie P, Brookfield H (1987) *Land degradation and society*. Methuen, London

Blake D R, Rowland F S (1988) Continuing worldwide increase in tropospheric methane, 1978 to 1987. *Science* **239**: 1129–31

Blank L W, Roberts T M, Skeffington R A (1988) New perspectives on forest decline. *Nature* **336**: 27–30

Blowers A, Lowry D (1987) Out of sight: out of mind: the politics of nuclear waste in the United Kingdom. In Blowers A, Pepper D (eds) *Nuclear power in crisis*. Nichols, New York, and Croom Helm, London, pp 129–63

Blunden J (1985) *Mineral resources and their management*. Longman, London

Blunden J, Curry N (eds) (1985) *The changing countryside*. Croom Helm, London

Blunden J, Turner G (1985) *Critical countryside*. BBC Publications, London

Blytt A (1876) *Essay on the immigration of the Norwegian flora during alternating rainy and dry periods*. Cammermeye, Christiana

Boardman J (1976) The olive in the Mediterranean: its culture and uses. *Philosophical Transactions of the Royal Society of London* **B275**: 187–96

Boardman J (1983) Soil erosion at Albourne, West Sussex, England. *Applied Geography* **3**: 317–29

Boardman J (1986) The context of soil erosion. *Journal of the South East Soils*

Discussion Group **3**: 2–13

Boardman J (1988) Public policy and soil erosion in Britain. In Hooke J M (ed) *Geomorphology in environmental planning.* John Wiley, Chichester, pp 33–50

Boardman J, Robinson D A (1985) Soil erosion, climatic vagary and agricultural change on the Downs around Lewes and Brighton 1982. *Applied Geography* **5**: 243–58

Body R (1987) *Red or green for farmers (and the rest of us)?* Broad Leys Publishing, Saffron Walden

Boniface B G, Cooper C P (1987) *The geography of travel and tourism.* Heinemann, London

Bonner P A (1988) The evolution of the Chesapeake Bay program. *The Environmental Professional* **10**: 110–20

Bonnicksen T M (1982) The development of forest policy in the United States. In Young R A (ed) *Introduction to forest science.* John Wiley, New York, pp 7–36

Botkin D B, Keller E A (1987) *Environmental studies: Earth as a living planet* 2nd edn. Merrill, Columbus

Bottema S (1975) The interpretation of pollen spectra from prehistoric settlements (with special attention to Liguliflorae). *Palaeohistoria* **17**: 17–35

Boustead I (1985) Radioactive waste disposal. In Porteous A (ed) *Hazardous waste management handbook.* Butterworths, London, pp 281–97

Boutron C F, Patterson C C (1986) Lead concentration changes in Antarctic ice during the Wisconsin/Holocene transition. *Nature* **323**: 222–5

Boutron C F, Patterson C C (1987) Relative levels of natural and anthropogenic lead in recent Antarctic ice. *Journal of Geophysical Research* **92**: 8454–64

Bowen D Q, Richmond G M, Fullerton D S, Šibrava V, Fulton R J, Velichko A A (1986a) Correlation of Quaternary glaciations in the northern hemisphere. *Quaternary Science Reviews* **5**: 509–10

Bowen D Q, Rose J, McCabe A M, Sutherland D G (1986b) Correlation of Quaternary glaciations in England, Ireland, Scotland and Wales. *Quaternary Science Reviews* **5**: 299–340

Bowler J M (1976) Aridity in Australia: origins and expression in aeolian landforms and sediments. *Earth Science Reviews* **12**: 279–310

Bowmer K H (1987) Herbicides in surface water. In Hutson D H, Roberts T R (eds) *Herbicides.* John Wiley, Chichester, vol 6 pp 271–355

Boyden S (1987) *Western civilisation in biological perspective.* Clarendon Press, Oxford

Boyle M, Robinson M (1987) Nuclear energy in France: a foretaste of the future. In Blowers A, Pepper D (eds) *Nuclear power in crisis.* Nichols, New York, and Croom Helm, London, pp 55–84

Brader L (1987) Plant protection and land transformation. In Wolman M G, Fournier F G A (eds) *Land transformation in agriculture.* John Wiley, Chichester, pp 227–48

Bradbury J P (1975) *Diatom stratigraphy and human settlement in Minnesota.* Geological Society of America Special Paper No. 171

Bradley R S (1985) *Quaternary paleoclimatology.* George Allen and Unwin, Boston, Massachusetts

Bradley R S, Diaz H F, Eischeid J K, Jones P D, Kelly P M, Goodness C M (1987a) Precipitation fluctuations over northern hemisphere land areas since the mid-19th century. *Science* **237**: 171–5

Bradley R S, Ives P T, Eischeid J (1987b) *The climate of Amherst.* University of Massachusetts Press, Amherst

Bradshaw A D (1983) The restoration of mined land. In Warren A, Goldsmith F B (eds) *Conservation in perspective.* John Wiley, Chichester, pp 177–99

Bradshaw A D (1984) Land restoration: now and in the future. *Proceedings of the Royal Society of London* **B223**: 1–23

Bradshaw, A D, Chadwick M J (1980) *The restoration of land.* Blackwell, Oxford

Brain C K, Sillen A (1988) Evidence from the Swartkrans cave for the earliest use of fire. *Nature* **336**: 464–6

Brassell S C, Eglinton G, Marlowe I T, Pflaumann U, Sarnthein M (1986) Molecular stratigraphy: a new tool for climatic assessment. *Nature* **320**: 129–33

Bray W (1988) The palaeoindian debate. *Nature* **332**: 107

Briggs D, Wyatt B (1988) Rural land-use change in Europe. In Whitby M, Ollerenshaw J (eds) *Land-use and the European environment.* Belhaven Press, London

Brimblecombe P (1977) London air pollution 1500–1900. *Atmospheric Environment* **11**: 1157–62

Brimblecombe P (1987) *The big smoke: a history of air pollution in London since medieval times.* Methuen, London

Broberg O (1988) Delayed nutrient responses to the liming of Lake Gårdsjön, Sweden. *Ambio* **17**: 22–7

Broecker W S, Andree M, Klas M, Bonani G, Wolfli W, Oeschger H (1988) New evidence from the South China Sea for an abrupt termination of the last glacial period. *Nature* **333**: 156–8

Broecker W S, van Donk J (1970) Insolation changes, ice volumes and the ^{18}O record in deep-sea cores. *Reviews of Geophysics and Space Physics* **8**: 169–97

Brooks D (1987) Case study 1: the use of native seed by the mineral sands industry. In Langcamp P (ed) *Germination of Australian native plant seed.* Inkata Press, Melbourne, pp 115–20

Broughton F (1985) The reclamation of derelict land for agriculture: technical, economic and land-use planning issues. *Landscape Planning* **12**: 49–74

Browder J O (1988) Public policy and deforestation in the Brazilian Amazon. In Repetto R, Gillis M (eds) *Public policies and the misuse of forest resources.* Cambridge University Press, Cambridge, pp 247–97

Brown A G, Barber K E (1985) Late Holocene palaeoecology and sedimentary history of a small lowland catchment in Central England. *Quaternary Research* **24**: 87–102

Brown B E, Dunne R P (1988) The environmental impact of coral mining on coral reefs in the Maldives. *Environmental Conservation* **15**: 159–66

Brown D J A, Turnpenny A W H (1988) Effects on fish. In Ashmore M R, Bell J N B, Garretty C (eds) *Acid rain and Britain's natural ecosystems*. Centre for Environmental Technology, Imperial College, London, pp 87–96

Brown L R, Wolf E C (1984) *Soil erosion: quiet crisis in the world economy*. Worldwatch Paper No. 60

Brugam R B (1978) Pollen indicators of land-use change in southern Connecticut. *Quaternary Research* **9**: 349–62

Buck K (1989) Brave new botany. *New Scientist* **122** (1667): 50–5

Bull K R, Hall J R (1986) Aluminium in the Rivers Esk and Duddon, Cumbria, and their tributaries. *Environmental Pollution* **B12**: 165–94

Bunn H T, Kroll E M (1986) Systematic butchery by Plio/Pleistocene hominids at Olduvai Gorge, Tanzania. *Current Anthropology* **27**: 431–42

Bunyard P (1988) Nuclear energy after Chernobyl. In Goldsmith E, Hildyard N (gen eds) *The Earth report: monitoring the battle for our environment*. Mitchell Beazley, London, pp 33–50

Burgess R L, Sharpe D M (1981) Introduction. In Burgess R L, Sharpe D M (eds) *Forest island dynamics in man-dominated landscapes*. Springer-Verlag, New York, pp 1–5

Buringh P (1981) *An assessment of losses and degradation by productive agricultural land in the world*. Working group on soils policy, Food and Agriculture Organisation, Rome

Burnside D G, Riches J R H, Addison J S (1986) The use of *Atriplex* spp. under rain-fed conditions to stabilise mine waste dumps. In Joss P J, Lynch P W, Williams O B (eds) *Rangelands: a resource under siege*. Cambridge University Press, Cambridge, pp 175–6

Buschbacher R J, Uhl C, Serrao E A S (1987) Large scale development in eastern Amazonia. In Jordan C F (ed) *Amazonian rain forests*. Springer-Verlag, Berlin, pp 90–9

Bush M B (1988) Early mesolithic disturbance: a force on the landscape. *Journal of Archaeological Science* **15**: 453–62

Bush M B, Flenley J R (1987) The age of British chalk grasslands. *Nature* **329**: 434–6

Bush M B, Hall A R (1987) Flandrian *Alnus*: expansion or immigration? *Journal of Biogeography* **14**: 479–81

Butlin R A (1982) *The transformation of rural England c. 1580–1800*. Oxford University Press, Oxford

Butzer K W (1976) *Early hydraulic civilisation in Egypt: a study in cultural ecology*. University of Chicago Press, Chicago

Butzer K W (1984) Late Quaternary environments in South Africa. In Vogel J C (ed) *Late Cainozoic palaeoclimates of the southern hemisphere*. A A Balkema, Rotterdam, pp 253–64

Byers A (1987) Landscape change and man-accelerated soil loss: the case of Sagarmatha (Mt Everest) National Park, Khumbu, Nepal. *Mountain Research and Development* **7**: 209–16

Byers D S, MacNeish R S (eds) (1967–76) *The prehistory of the Tehuacán valley* (5 vols). University of Texas Press, Austin

Campbell J (1988) British forestry – an international perspective. *Commonwealth Forestry Review* **67**: 115–28

Canter L W (1986) *Environmental impacts of agricultural production activities*. Lewis Publishers, Chelsea, Michigan

Canter L W (1987) Nitrates and pesticides in ground water: an analysis of a computer-based literature search. In Fairchild D M (ed) *Ground water quality and agricultural practices*. Lewis Publishers, Chelsea, Michigan, pp 153–74

Cantor L (1982) Forests, chases, parks and warrens. In Cantor L (ed) *The English medieval landscape*. Croom Helm, London, pp 56–85

Cantor L (1987) *The changing English countryside 1400–1700*. Routledge and Kegan Paul, London

Cardona R A (1987) Current toxicological requirements for registration. In Ragsdale N N, Kuhr R J (eds) *Pesticides: minimising the risks*. American Chemical Society, Washington DC, pp 14–19

Carnahan J A (1986) Vegetation. In Jeans D N (ed) *Australia – a geography* (2 vols). Sydney University Press, Sydney, vol 1 *The natural environment*, pp 260–82

Carney H J (1982) Algal dynamics and trophic interactions in the recent history of Frains Lake, Michigan. *Ecology* **63**: 1814–26

Cater E A (1987) Tourism in the least developed countries. *Annals of Tourism Research* **14**: 202–26

Cawse P A (1987) Trace and major elements in the atmosphere at rural locations in Great Britain 1972–81. In Coughtrey P J, Martin M H, Unsworth M H (eds) *Pollutant transport and fate in ecosystems*. Blackwell, Oxford, pp 89–112

Chaleff R S (1986) Herbicide resistance. In Day P R (ed) *Biotechnology and crop improvement technology*. British Crop Protection Council Monograph No. 34, pp 111–21

Champion T, Gamble C, Shennan S, Whittle A (1984) *Prehistoric Europe*. Academic Press, London

Chansang H (1988) Coastal tin mining and marine pollution in Thailand. *Ambio* **17**: 223–8

Chapman N A, McKinley I G (1987) *The geological disposal of nuclear waste*. John Wiley, Chichester

Chappell J, Shackleton N J (1986) Oxygen isotopes and sea level. *Nature* **324**: 137–40

Charles D F (1984) Recent pH history of Big Moose Lake (Adirondack Mountains, New York, USA) inferred from sediment diatom assemblages. *Verhandlingen Internationalem Vereinigung für Theoretische Angewanate Limnologie* **22**: 559–66

Charles D F plus twelve others (1987) Paleolimnological evidence for recent acidification of Big Moose Lake, Adirondack Mountains, NY (USA) *Biogeochemistry* **3**: 267–96

Charles D F, Whitehead D R (1986) The PIRLA project: paleoecological investigations of recent lake acidification. *Hydrobiologia* **143**: 13–20

Charlson R J, Lovelock J E, Andreae M O, Warren S G (1987) Oceanic phytoplankton, atmospheric sulphur, cloud albedo and climate. *Nature* **326**: 655–61

Chartres C (1987) Australia's land resources at risk. In Chisholm A, Dumsday R (eds) *Land degradation: problems and policies.* Cambridge University Press, Cambridge, pp 7–26

Chisci G (1986) Influence of change in land use and management on the acceleration of land degradation phenomena in Apennine hilly areas. In Chisci G, Morgan R P C (eds) *Soil erosion in the European Community.* A A Balkema, Rotterdam, pp 3–16

Chorley R J, Kennedy B A (1971) *Physical geography: a systems approach.* Prentice-Hall, New Jersey

Christiansson C (1988) Degradation and rehabilitation of agropastoral land – perspectives on environmental change in semiarid Tanzania. *Ambio* **17**: 144–52

Chubachi S, Kajiwara R (1986) Total ozone variations at Syowa, Antarctica. *Geophysical Research Letters* **13**: 1197–8

Clapperton C (1979) Glaciation in Bolivia before 3.27 Myr. *Nature* **277**: 375–7

Clark G A, Straus L G (1983) Late Pleistocene hunter-gatherer adaptations in Cantabrian Spain. In Bailey G (ed) *Hunter-gatherer economy in prehistory.* Cambridge University Press, Cambridge, pp 131–48

Clark J G D (1954) *Excavations at Star Carr.* Cambridge University Press, Cambridge

Clark J G D (1972) *Star Carr: a case study in bioarchaeology.* McCaleb Module in Anthropology No. 10, published by Addison-Wesley, Reading, Massachusetts

Clark W M (1986) Irrigation practices: peasant-farming settlement schemes and traditional cultures. *Philosophical Transactions of the Royal Society of London* **A316**: 229–44

Clarke A G (1986) The air. In Hester R E (ed) *Understanding our environment.* Royal Society of Chemistry, London, pp 71–118

Clarke W, Morrison J (1987) Land mismanagement and the development imperative in Fiji. In Blaikie P, Brookfield H *Land degradation and society.* Methuen, London, pp 176–85

Clay C G A (1984a) *Economic expansion and social change: England 1500–1700.* Cambridge University Press, Cambridge vol 1 *People land and towns*

Clay C G A (1984b) *Economic expansion and social change: England 1500–1700.* Cambridge University Press, Cambridge vol II *Industry, trade and government*

Cleere H (1976) Some operating parameters for Roman ironworks. *Bulletin of the Institute of Archaeology, London* **13**: 233–46

Clements F E (1916) *Plant succession: an analysis of the development of vegetation.* Carnegie Institute Publication No. 242, pp 3–4, Washington

Cloke P J (1989) Land-use planning in rural Britain. In Cloke P (ed) *Rural land-use planning in developed nations.* Unwin Hyman, London, pp 18–46

Cloudsley-Thompson J L (1988) Desertification or sustainable yields from arid environments. *Environmental Conservation* **15**: 197–204

Clouston E (1989) Park pays for peak of popularity. *The Guardian* 2 May 1989, p 4

Coates D R (1987) Subsurface impacts. In Gregory K J, Walling D E (eds) *Human activity and environmental processes.* John Wiley, Chichester, pp 271–304

Cochrane T T, de Azeredo L G, Thomas D, Netto J M, Adamoli J, Verdesio J J (1985) Land use and productive potential of American savannas. In Tothill J C, Mott J J (eds) *Ecology and management of the world's savannas.* Commonwealth Agricultural Bureau, Slough, pp 114–24

Cocking E C (1989) Plant cell and tissue culture. In Marx J L (ed) *A revolution in biotechnology.* Cambridge University Press, Cambridge, pp 119–29

Coffey M (1978) The dust storms. *Natural History* **87**: 72–83

Cohen N (1988) Doomsday view of floods nonsense, scientists say. *The Independent* 17 Sept 1988, p 4

Cole D N (1986) Recreational impacts on back country campsites in Grand Canyon National Park, Arizona, USA. *Journal of Environmental Management* **10**: 651–9

Cole D N, Fichtler R K (1983) Campsite impact on three western wilderness areas. *Journal of Environmental Management* **7**: 275–88

Cole D N, Marion J L (1988) Recreation impacts in some riparian forests of the eastern United States. *Journal of Environmental Management* **12**: 99–107

Cole M M (1986) *The savannas: biogeography and geobotany.* Academic Press, London

Colinvaux P (1987) Amazon diversity in the light of the paleoecological record. *Quaternary Science Reviews* **6**: 93–114

Colinvaux P (1989) The past and future Amazon. *Scientific American* **260**: 68–74

Collier J (1964) *Indians of the Americas: the long hope.* New American Library, New York

Collis J (1984) *The European Iron age.* Batsford, London

Coltori M plus eleven others (1982) Reversed magnetic polarity at an early lower palaeolithic site in central Italy. *Nature* **300**: 173–6

Comes R D, Bruns V F, Kelley A D (1976) Residues and persistence of glyphosate in irrigation water. *Weed Science* **24**: 47–50

Conacher A J (1986) Environmental conservation. In Jeans D N (ed) *Australia – a geography* (2 vols). Sydney University Press, Sydney, vol 1 *The natural environment*, pp 315–39

Conacher A, Conacher J (1988) The exploitation of the soils. In Heathcote R L (ed) *The Australian experience*. Longman Cheshire, Melbourne, pp 127–38

Conrad J (1988) Nitrate debate and nitrate policy in FR Germany. *Land Use Policy* **5**: 207–18

Cook R L, Ellis B G (1987) *Soil management: a world view of conservation and production*. John Wiley, New York

Coope G R (1977) Fossil coleopteran assemblages as sensitive indicators of climatic changes during the Devensian (last) cold stage. *Philosophical Transactions of the Royal Society of London* **B280**: 313–40

Coope G R (1986) Coleoptera analysis. In Berglund B E (ed) *Handbook of Holocene palaeoecology and palaeohydrology*. John Wiley, Chichester, pp 703–13

Coope G R, Lister A M (1987) Late-glacial mammoth skeletons from Condover, Shropshire, England. *Nature* **330**: 472–4

Craft A, Openshaw S (1987) Children, radiation, cancer and the Sellafield nuclear reprocessing plant. In Blowers A, Pepper D (eds) *Nuclear power in crisis*. Nichols, New York, pp 244–71

Craig H, Chou C C, Welhan J A, Stevens C M, Engelkemeir A (1988) The isotopic composition of methane in polar ice cores. *Science* **242**: 1535–9

Crawford P (1985) *The living isles*. BBC Publications, London

Crawford R D (1984) Turkey. In Mason I L (ed) *Evolution of domesticated animals*. Longman, London, pp 325–34

Croll B T, Hayes C R (1988) Nitrate and water supplies in the United Kingdom. *Environmental Pollution* **50**: 163–87

Croll J (1864) On the physical cause of the change of climate during geological epochs. *Philosophical Magazine* **28**: 121–37

Croll J (1875) *Climate and time*. Appleton, New York

Cronk Q C B (1989) The past and present vegetation of St Helena. *Journal of Biogeography* **16**: 47–64

Cronon W (1983) *Changes in the land: Indians, colonists and the ecology of New England*. Hill and Wang, New York

Cross M (1988) Spare the tree and spoil the forest. *New Scientist* **120** (1640): 24–5

Cross M (1989) Dispute grows over Malaysia's forest. *New Scientist* **121** (1650): 27

Crowder M (1982) *West Africa under colonial rule*. Hutchinson, London

Crutzen P J plus nine others (1985) Tropospheric chemical composition measurements in Brazil during the dry season. *Journal of Atmospheric Chemistry* **2**: 233–56

Culbard E B, Thornton I, Watt J, Wheatley M, Moorcroft S, Thompson M

(1988) Metal contamination in British urban dusts and soils. *Journal of Environmental Quality* **17**: 226–34

Cullen R (1986) Himalayan mountaineering expedition garbage. *Environmental Conservation* **13**: 293–7

Cunliffe B W (1984) *Danebury: an Iron Age hillfort in Hampshire. The excavations of 1969–1978* (2 vols). British Archaeological Research Reports (British Series), Oxford, No. 52

Cunliffe B W (1985) Man and the landscape in Britain 6000 BC – AD 400. In Woodell S R J (ed) *The English landscape: past, present and future*. Oxford University Press, Oxford, pp 48–67

Cunnold D M plus eight others (1986) Atmospheric lifetime and annual release estimates for CFCP$_3$ and CF$_2$CP$_2$ from 5 years of ALE data. *Journal of Geophysical Research* **91**: 10797–817

Currant A P (1986) Man and the Quaternary interglacial faunas of Britain. In Collcut S N (ed) *The palaeolithic of Britain and its nearest neighbours*. Department of Archaeology and Prehistory, University of Sheffield, pp 50–2

Currie R G, Fairbridge R W (1985) Periodic 18.6–year and cyclic 11–year induced drought and flood in north-eastern China and some global implications: *Quarternary Science Reviews* **4**: 109–34

Daget G, Leroy J B (1988) Waste-derived heat in Tronville (France). *Waste Management and Research* **6**: 79–80

Daniels R B (1987) Saline seeps in the northern Great Plains of the USA and the southern prairies of Canada. In Wolman M G, Fournier F G A (eds) *Land transformation in agriculture*. John Wiley, Chichester, pp 381–406

Dansgaard W (1987) Ice core evidence of abrupt climatic change. In Berger W H, Labeyrie L D (eds) *Abrupt climatic change*. D Reidel; Dordrecht, pp 223–33

Dansgaard W, Johnsen S J, Clausen H B, Dahl-Jensen D, Grundestrup H, Hammer C U, Oeschger H (1984) North Atlantic climatic oscillations revealed by deep Greenland ice cores. In Hansen J E, Takahashi T (eds) *Climate processes and climate sensitivity*. American Geophysical Union Monograph No. 29, pp 288–98

Dansgaard W, White J W C, Johnsen S J (1989) The abrupt termination of the Younger Dryas climate event. *Nature* **339**: 532–3

Davies J H (1985) The pyrethroids: an historical introduction. In Leahey J P (ed) *The pyrethroid insecticides*. Taylor and Francis, London, pp 1–41

Davis M B (1976) Erosion rates and land-use history in southern Michigan. *Environmental Conservation* **3**: 139–48

Davis M B (1981) Outbreaks of forest pathogens in forest history. *Proceedings of the IV International Palynological Conference (1976–1977)* **3**: 216–27

Davis M B (1984) Holocene vegetational history of the eastern United States. In Wright Jr H E (ed) *Late-Quaternary environments of the United States* (2 vols). University of Minnesota Press, Minneapolis, and Longman, London, vol 2 *The Holocene*, pp 166–81

Davis O K, Sellers W D (1987) Contrasting climatic histories for western North America during the early Holocene. *Current Research in the Pleistocene* **4**: 87–9

Davis R B (1987) Paleolimnological diatom studies of acidification of lakes by acid rain: an application of Quaternary science. *Quaternary Science Reviews* **6**: 147–63

Davis R B, Anderson D S, Charles D F, Galloway J N (1988) Two-hundred-year pH history of Woods, Sagamore and Panther Lakes in the Adirondack mountains, New York State. In Adams W J, Chapman G A, Landis W G (eds) *Aquatic toxicology and hazard assessment*. American Society for Testing and Materials, Philadelphia, pp 89–111

Davis S J M (1987) *The archaeology of animals*. Batsford, London

Davis W M (1909) The geographical cycle. In Johnson D W (ed) *Geographical essays*. Ginn, New York, pp 254–6

Day C A, Lisansky S G (1987) Agricultural alternatives. In Forster C F, Wase D A J (eds) *Environmental biotechnology*. Ellis Horwood, Chichester, pp 234–94

De Angelis M, Barkov N I, Petrov V N (1987) Aerosol concentrations over the last climatic cycle (160 kyr) from an Antarctic ice core. *Nature* **325**: 318–21

De Ploey J (1986) Soil erosion and possible conservation measures in loess loamy areas. In Chisci G, Morgan R P C (eds) *Soil erosion in the European Community*. A A Balkema, Rotterdam, pp 157–63

De Vorsey L (1987) The new land: the discovery and exploration of eastern North America. In Mitchell R D, Groves P A (eds) *North America: the historical geography of a changing continent*. Hutchinson, London, pp 25–47

Deagan K (1988) The archaeology of the Spanish contact period in the Caribbean. *Journal of World Prehistory* **2**: 187–233

Dean W (1987) *Brazil and the struggle for rubber*. Cambridge University Press, Cambridge

Delcourt H R (1987) The impact of prehistoric agriculture and land occupation on natural vegetation. *Trends in Ecology and Evolution* **2**: 39–44

Delcourt H R, Harris W F (1980) Carbon budget of the southeastern US biota: analysis of historical change in trend from source to sink. *Science* **210**: 321–3

Delcourt P A, Delcourt H R (1987) Late Quaternary dynamics of temperate forests: applications of palaeoecology to issues of global environmental change. *Quaternary Science Reviews* **6**: 129–46

Delcourt P A, Delcourt H R, Cridlebaugh P A, Chapman J (1986) Holocene ethnobotanical and paleoecological record of human impact on vegetation in the Little Tennessee River valley, Tennessee. *Quaternary Research* **25**: 330–49

Dempster J P (1967) The control of *Pieris rapae* with DDT I: the natural mortality of the young stages of *Pieris*. *Journal of Applied Ecology* **4**: 485–500

Dempster J P (1968a) The control of *Pieris rapae* with DDT II: survival of the young stages of *Pieris* after spraying. *Journal of Applied Ecology* **5**: 451–62

Dempster J P (1968b) The control of *Pieris rapae* with DDT III: some changes in the crop fauna. *Journal of Applied Ecology* **5**: 463–75

Dempster J P (1968c) The sublethal effect of DDT on the rate of feeding by the ground-beetle *Harpalus rufipes*. *Entomologia Experimentalis Applicata* **11**: 51–4

Dempster J P (1987) Effects of pesticides on wildlife and priorities for the future. In Brent K J, Atkin R K (eds) *Rational pesticide use*. Cambridge University Press, Cambridge, pp 17–25

Dennell R W (1983) *European economic prehistory*. Academic Press, New York

Department of Environment (1987) *Development involving agricultural land* (draft circular). DoE, London

Department of Environment, Housing and Community Development (1978) *A basis for soil conservation policy in Australia, Report No 1*. Australian Government Printing Service, Canberra

Department of Environment and the University of Liverpool Environmental Advisory Unit (1986) *Transforming our waste land: the way forward*. HMSO, London

Detwiler R P, Hall C A S (1988) Tropical forests and the global carbon cycle. *Science* **239**: 42–7

Díaz C L, Melchers L S, Hooykaas P J J, Lugtenberg B J J, Kijne J W (1989) Root lectin as a determinant of host–plant specificity in the *Rhizobium*-legume symbiosis. *Nature* **338**: 579–81

Dickinson R E (1986) How will climate change? In Bolin B, Döös B R, Jäger J, Warrick R A (eds) *The greenhouse effect, climate change, and ecosystems*. John Wiley, Chichester, pp 207–70

Dickman M D, Thode H G (1985) The rate of lake acidification in four lakes north of Lake Superior and its relationship to downcore sulphur isotope ratios. *Water, Air, Soil Pollution* **26**: 233–53

Diester-Haas L (1976) Late Quaternary climatic variations in northwest Africa deduced from east Atlantic sediment cores. *Quaternary Research* **6**: 299–314

Dillehay T D, Collins M B (1988) Early cultural evidence from Monte Verde in Chile. *Nature* **332**: 150–2

Dimbleby G W (1962) The development of British heathlands and their soils. *Oxford Forestry Memoir* No. 23

Dimbleby G W (1984) Anthropogenic changes from neolithic through medieval times. *New Phytologist* **98**: 57–72

Dodson J R, Greenwood P W, Jones R L (1986) Holocene forest and wetland vegetation dynamics at Barrington Tops, New South Wales. *Journal of Biogeography* **13**: 561–85

Dotto L, Schiff H (1978) *The ozone war*. Doubleday, New York

Douglas J J (1983) *A reappraisal of forestry development in developing countries*. Martinus Nijhoff, Dr W Junk, The Hague

Dregne H E (1986) Desertification of arid lands. In El-Baz F, Hassan M H A (eds) *Physics of desertification*. Martinus Nijhoff, Dordrecht, pp 4–34

Dregne H E (1987) Desertification. In McLaren D J, Skinner B J (eds) *Resources and world development*. John Wiley, Chichester, pp 697–710

Dunrud C R (1984) Coal mine subsidence – western United States. *Reviews in Engineering Geology* **6**: 151–94

Duplessy J C, Delibrias G, Turon J L, Pujol C, Duprat J (1981) Deglacial warming of the northeastern Atlantic ocean: correlation with the paleoclimatic evolution of the European continent. *Palaeogeography Palaeoclimatology Palaeoecology* **35**: 121–44

Dyson-Hudson N (1984) Adaptive resource use strategies of African pastoralists. In di Castri F, Baker F W G, Hadley M (eds) *Ecology in practice*. Tycooly Press, Dublin, and Unesco, Paris, vol I *Ecosystem management*, pp 262–73

Earickson R J, Billick I H (1988) The areal association of urban air pollutants and residential characteristics: Louisville and Detroit. *Applied Geography* **8**: 5–23

Earth Report, The (1988) Goldsmith E, Hildyard N (gen eds) *The Earth report: monitoring the battle for our environment*. Mitchell Beazley, London

Eddy J A (1976) The Maunder minimum. *Science* **192**: 1189–1202

Edgington D N, Robbins J A (1976) Records of lead deposition in Lake Michigan sediments since 1800. *Environmental Science and Technology* **10**: 266–74

Edington J M, Edington M A (1986) *Ecology, recreation and tourism*. Cambridge University Press, Cambridge

Edwards K J, Hirons K R (1984) Cereal pollen grains in pre-elm decline deposits: implications for the earliest agriculture in Britain and Ireland. *Journal of Archaeological Science* **11**: 71–80

Ege J R (1984) Mechanisms of surface subsidence resulting from solution extraction of salt. *Reviews in Engineering Geology* **6**: 203–21

Egglishaw H, Gardiner R, Foster J (1987) Salmon catch decline and forestry in Scotland. *Scottish Geographical Magazine* **102**: 57–61

El-Ashry M T, Gibbons D C (1986) *Troubled waters: new policies for managing water in the American West*. World Resources Institute, Washington DC

El-Ashry M T, Gibbons D C (1988) The West in profile. In El-Ashry M T, Gibbons D C (eds) *Water and arid lands of the western United States*. Cambridge University Press, Cambridge, pp 1–19

El-Hinnawi E, Hashmi M H (1987) *The state of the environment*. Butterworths, London

El-Karouri M O H (1986) The impact of desertification on land productivity in Sudan. In El-Baz F, Hassan M H A (eds) *Physics of desertification*. Martinus Nijhoff, Dordrecht, pp 52–8

Elsom D (1987) *Atmospheric pollution*. Blackwell, Oxford

Elwell H A (1985) An assessment of soil erosion in Zimbabwe. *Zimbabwe Science News* **19**: 27–31

Elwell H A, Stocking M A (1984) Estimating soil life-span for conservation planning. *Tropical Agriculture* **61**: 148–50

Emanuel W R, Shugart H H, Stevenson M P (1985) Climatic change and the broad-scale distribution of terrestrial ecosystem complexes. *Climatic Change* **7**: 29–43

Emory J (1988) Managing another Galápagos species – man. *National Geographic Magazine* **173**: 146–54

Engstrom D R, Swain E B (1986) The chemistry of lake sediments in time and space. *Hydrobiologia* **143**: 37–44

Engstrom D R, Swain E B, Kingston J C (1985) A palaeolimnological record of human disturbance from Harvey's Lake, Vermont: geochemistry, pigments and diatoms. *Freshwater Biology* **15**: 261–88

Ervin D E (1987) Cropland diversion in the US: are there lessons for the EEC set-aside diversion? In Baldock D, Conder D (eds) *Removing land from agriculture.* Council for the Protection of Rural England and Institute for European Environmental Policy, London, pp 53–63

Essex S J (1987) Pressures on farm woodland: present and future trends. In Lockhart D, Ilbery B (eds) *The future of the British rural landscape.* Geo Books, Norwich

European Economic Community (1980) *EEC directive relating to the quality of water intended for human consumption, 80/778.* EEC, Brussels

Evans R, Cook S (1986) Soil erosion in Britain. *Journal of the South East Soils Discussion Group* **3**: 28–58

Evans R, Nortcliff S (1978) Soil erosion in north Norfolk. *Journal of Agricultural Science, Cambridge* **90**: 185–92

Evans W F J (1988) A measurement of the altitudinal variation of greenhouse radiation from CFC-12. *Nature* **333**: 750–2

Everest D (1988) *The greenhouse effect: issues for policy makers.* The Royal Institute of International Affairs and The Policy Studies Institute, London

Eyre L A (1987) Jamaica: test case for tropical deforestation. *Ambio* **16**: 338–43

Fage J D (1978) *A history of Africa.* Hutchinson, London

Fairchild D M (1987) A national assessment of groundwater contamination from pesticides and fertilisers. In Fairchild D M (ed) *Ground water quality and agricultural practices.* Lewis Publishers, Chelsea, Michigan, pp 273–94

Farman J L, Gardiner B G, Shanklin J D (1985) Large losses of total ozone reveal seasonal ClOx/NOx interaction. *Nature* **315**: 207–10

Farrell B H, McLellan R W (1987) Tourism and physical environmental research. *Annals of Tourism Research* **14**: 1–16

Farrell T P (1986) Mining and rangelands: conflicting or compatible? In Joss P J, Lynch P W, Williams O B (eds) *Rangelands: a resource under siege.* Cambridge University Press, Cambridge, pp 147–51

Fearnside P M (1984) Roads in Rondonia: highway construction and the farce of unprotected reserves in Brazil's Amazonian forest. *Environmental Conservation* **11**: 358–60

Fearnside P M (1985) Agriculture in Amazonia. In Prance G T, Lovejoy T E (eds) *Amazonia.* Pergamon Press, Oxford, pp 393–418

Fearnside P M (1986) Spatial concentration of deforestation in the Brazilian Amazon. *Ambio* **15**: 74–81

Fearnside P M (1989) The charcoal of Carajás: a threat to the forests of Brazil's eastern Amazon region. *Ambio* **18**: 141–3

Ferguson P, Lee J A (1983) The growth of *Sphagnum* species in the southern Pennines. *Journal of Bryology* **12**: 579–86

Fiedel S J (1987) *Prehistory of the Americas*. Cambridge University Press, Cambridge

Finkel H J (1986) *Semi-arid soil and water conservation*. CRC Press, Boca Raton, Florida

Finnecy E E (1988) Impacts on soils related to industrial activities: Part II – Incidental and accidental soil pollution. In Barth H, L'Hermite P (eds) *Scientific basis for soil protection in the European Community*. Elsevier, London, pp 259–80

Finnecy E E, Pearce K W (1986) Land contamination and reclamation. In Hester R E (ed) *Understanding our environment*. The Royal Society of Chemistry, London, pp 172–225

Fishman J, Minnis P, Reichle Jr H G (1986) Use of satellite data to study tropospheric ozone in the tropics. *Journal of Geophysical Research* **91**: 14451–65

Flavin C, Durning A (1988) Raising energy efficiency. In *State of the World 1988: a Worldwatch Institute report on progress towards a sustainable society*. W W Norton, New York, pp 41–61

Flenley J R (1988) Palynological evidence for land use changes in South-East Asia. *Journal of Biogeography* **15**: 185–97

Flower R J, Battarbee R W (1983) Diatom evidence for recent acidification of two Scottish lochs. *Nature* **305**: 130–2

Flower R J, Battarbee R W, Appleby P G (1987) The recent palaeolimnology of acid lakes in Galloway, Southwest Scotland: diatom analysis, pH trends and the role of afforestation. *Journal of Ecology* **75**: 797–824

Flower R J, Battarbee R W, Natkanski J, Rippey B, Appleby P G (1988) The recent acidification of a large Scottish loch located partly within a National Nature Reserve and Site of Special Scientific Interest. *Journal of Applied Ecology* **25**: 715–24

Foley R (1987) *Another unique species: patterns in human evolutionary ecology*. Longman, London

Food and Agriculture Organisation (1981a) *Production Yearbook*. FAO, Rome

Food and Agriculture Organisation (1981b) *Fertiliser Yearbook*. FAO, Rome

Food and Agriculture Organisation (1984) *Production Yearbook*. FAO, Rome

Food and Agriculture Organisation (1985) *Production Yearbook* FAO, Rome

Food and Agriculture Organisation, Unesco (1977) *Desertification map of the world*. FAO, Rome

Forester R M, Delorme L D, Bradbury J P (1987) Mid-Holocene climate in northern Minnesota. *Quaternary Research* **28**: 263–73

Forman D (1985) Nitrates, nitrites and gastric cancer in Britain. *Nature* **313**: 620–5

Forster C F, Johnston D W M (1987) Aerobic processes. In Forster C F, Wase D A J (eds) *Environmental biotechnology*. Ellis Horwood, Chichester, pp 15–56

Forster C F, Wase D A J (1987) Biopossibilities: the next few years. In Forster C F, Wase D A J (eds) *Environmental biotechnology*. Ellis Horwood, Chichester, pp 439–48

Fowler P J (1983) *The farming of prehistoric Britain*. Cambridge University Press, Cambridge

Francis I (1988) Afforestation: what really goes down the drain. *Ecos* **9**: 23–7

Friberg L, Piscator M, Nordberg G F, Kjellström T (1974) *Cadmium in the environment* 2nd edn. CRC Press, Cleveland, Ohio

Fridriksson S (1987) Plant colonisation of a volcanic island, Surtsey, Iceland. *Arctic and Alpine Research* **19**: 425–31

Friedli H, Lötscher H, Oeschger H, Siegenthaler U (1986) Ice core record of the $^{13}C/^{12}C$ ratio of atmospheric CO_2 in the past two centuries. *Nature* **324**: 237–8

Fritts M C (1976) *Tree rings and climate*. Academic Press, London

Furtado J I, Ruddle K (1986) The future of tropical forests. In Polunin N (ed) *Ecosystem theory and application*. John Wiley, Chichester, pp 145–71

Gadgil M, Meher-Homji V M (1985) Land use and productive potential of Indian savannas. In Tothill J C, Mott J J (eds) *Ecology and management of the world's savannas*. Commonwealth Agricultural Bureau, Slough, pp 107–13

Gage L P (1989) Gene cloning opens up a new frontier in health. In Marx J L (ed) *A revolution in biotechnology*. Cambridge University Press, Cambridge, pp 42–55

Gajewski K (1988) Late Holocene climate changes in eastern North America estimated from pollen data. *Quaternary Research* **29**: 255–62

Gajewski K, Winkler M G, Swain A M (1985) Vegetation and fire history from three lakes with varved sediments in northwestern Wisconsin (USA). *Review of Palaeobotany and Palynology* **44**: 277–92

Gamble C (1984) Regional variation in hunter-gatherer strategy in the Upper Pleistocene of Europe. In Foley R (ed) *Hominid evolution and community ecology*. Academic Press, London, pp 237–60

Gamble C (1986) *The palaeolithic settlement of Europe*. Cambridge University Press, Cambridge

Geikie A (1863) On the phenomena of the glacial drift of Scotland. *Transactions of the Geological Society of Glasgow* **1**: 1–190

Geikie J (1874) *The great ice age*. W Ibister, London

Geofile No 96, (1987) *Recycling rubbish*

Geofile No 118, (1988) *Theme parks and the leisure industry*

Gilbert G K (1890) Lake Bonneville. *US Geological Society Monograph* **1**: 1–438

Gilmour D A (1988) Not seeing the trees for the forest: a re-appraisal of the deforestation crisis in two hill districts of Nepal. *Mountain Research and Development* **8**: 343–50

Gingold E B (1988) An introduction to genetic engineering. In Walker J M,

Gingold E B (eds) *Molecular biology and biotechnology*. Royal Society of Chemistry, London, pp 25–46

Girling M A, Greig J (1985) A first fossil record for *Scolytus scolytus* (F.)(elm bark beetle): its occurrence in elm decline deposits from London and the implications for neolithic elm disease. *Journal of Archaeological Science* **12**: 347–51

Girling R, Jackman B (1989) Nothing to do with you? *The Sunday Times Colour Supplement* 26 Feb 1989

Gischler C, Jauregui C F (1984) Low-cost techniques for water conservation and management in Latin America. *Nature and Resources* **20**: 11–18

Glanz M H (1987) *Drought and hunger in Africa*. Cambridge University Press, Cambridge

Glas J P (1988) The CFC–ozone issue: alternative products and the Montreal Protocol. *Environmental Conservation* **15**: 178–9

Godwin H (1975) *History of the British flora* 2nd edn. Cambridge University Press, Cambridge

Goldsmith F B (1983) Ecological effects of visitors and the restoration of damaged areas. In Warren A, Goldsmith F B (eds) *Conservation in perspective*. John Wiley, Chichester, pp 201–14

Golson J (1977) No room at the top: agricultural intensification in the New Guinea Highlands. In Allen J, Golson J, Jones R (eds) *Sunda and Sahul: prehistoric studies in Southeast Asia, Melanesia and Australia*. Academic Press, London, pp 601–38

Goreau T J, de Mello W Z (1988) Tropical deforestation: some effects on atmospheric chemistry. *Ambio* **17**: 275–81

Gormly J R, Spalding R F (1979) Sources and concentrations of nitrate–nitrogen in ground water of the Central Platte region, Nebraska. *Ground Water* **17**: 291–301

Goudie A (1983) *Environmental Change* 2nd edn. Clarendon Press, Oxford

Goudie A (1986) *The human impact on the natural environment*. Blackwell, Oxford

Gowlett J A J (1988) A case of developed oldowan in the acheulean? *World Archaeology* **20**: 13–26

Grainger A (1984) Quantifying changes in forest cover in the humid tropics: overcoming current limitations. *Journal of World Forest Resource Management* **1**: 3–63

Grant A (1988) Animal resources. In Astill G, Grant A (eds) *The countryside of medieval England*. Blackwell, Oxford, pp 149–87

Green B H, Potter C A (1987) Environmental opportunities offered by surplus production. In Baldock D, Conder D (eds) *Removing land from agriculture*. Council for the Protection of Rural England, Institute for European Environmental Policy, London, pp 64–71

Green C P plus eight others (1984) Evidence of two temperate episodes in Late Pleistocene deposits at Marsworth, UK. *Nature* **309**: 778–81

Green M B, Hartley G S, West T F (1987) *Chemicals for crop improvement and pest management* 3rd edn. Pergamon Press, Oxford

Greig J (1988) Plant resources. In Astill G, Grant A (eds) *The countryside of medieval England*. Blackwell, Oxford, pp 108–27

Gribbin J (1988a) The greenhouse effect. *New Scientist* **120** (1635), Inside Science No. 13, pp 1–4

Gribbin J (1988b) Modelling the greenhouse world. *New Scientist* **120** (1638): 42

Gribbin J (1988c) *The hole in the sky*. Corgi Books, London

Gribbin J (1989) The end of the ice ages. *New Scientist* **122** (1669): 48–52

Grigg D (1980) *Population growth and agrarian change*. Cambridge University Press, Cambridge

Grigg D (1987) The industrial revolution and land transformation. In Wolman M G, Fournier F G A (eds) *Land transformation in agriculture*. John Wiley, Chichester, pp 79–109

Groenman-van Waateringe W, Pals J P (1982) Newgrange, Co. Meath: pollen and seed analysis. In O'Kelly M J (ed) *Newgrange*. Thames and Hudson, London, pp 219–23

de Groot R S (1983) Tourism and conservation in the Galápagos islands. *Biological Conservation* **26**: 291–300

Groube L, Chappell J, Muke J, Price D (1986) A 40,000-year-old human occupation site at Huon Peninsula, Papua New Guinea. *Nature* **324**: 453–5

Grove J M (1988) *The Little Ice Age*. Methuen, London

Grove R (1987) Early themes in African conservation: the Cape in the nineteenth century. In Anderson D, Grove R (eds) *Conservation in Africa*. Cambridge University Press, Cambridge, pp 21–39

Gruhn R, Bryan A L (1984) The record of Pleistocene megafaunal extinctions at Taima-taima, northern Venezuela. In Martin P S, Klein R G (eds) *Quaternary extinctions, a prehistoric revolution*. University of Arizona Press, Tucson, pp 128–37

de Haan F A M (1987) Effects of agricultural practices on the physical, chemical and biological properties: Part III – Chemical degradation of soil as the result of the use of mineral fertilisers and pesticides: aspects of soil quality evaluation. In Barth H, L'Hermite P (eds) *Scientific basis for soil protection in the European Community*. Elsevier, London, pp 211–36

Hadley M (1985) Comparative aspects of landuse and resource management in savanna environments. In Tothill J C, Mott J J (eds) *Ecology and management of the world's savannas*. Commonwealth Agricultural Bureau, Slough, pp 142–58

Haigh N (1988) Legislative aspects of acid emissions: EEC and UK. In *The problem of acid emissions*. The Institute of Chemical Engineers, London, pp 1–10

Hall D (1988) The late Saxon countryside: villages and their fields. In Hooke D (ed) *Anglo-Saxon settlements*. Blackwell, Oxford, pp 99–122

Hallam J S, Edwards B J N, Barnes B, Stuart A J (1973) The remains of a Late Glacial elk with associated barbed points from High Furlong, near Blackpool, Lancashire. *Proceedings of the Prehistoric Society* **39**: 100–28

Hamburg S P, Cogbill C V (1988) Historical decline of red spruce populations and climatic warming. *Nature* **331**: 428–31

Hamilton A C (1982) *Environmental history of East Africa.* Academic Press, London

Hamilton A C, Taylor D, Vogel J C (1986) Early forest clearance and environmental degradation in south-west Uganda. *Nature* **320**: 164-7

Hamilton L S, (1987) What are the impacts of Himalayan deforestation on the Ganges-Brahmaputra lowlands and delta? Assumptions and facts. *Mountain Research and Development* **7**: 256–63

van der Hammen T, Wijmstra T A, Zagwijn W H (1971) The floral record of the Late Cenozoic of Europe. In Turekian K K (ed) *The Late Cenozoic glacial ages.* Yale University Press, New Haven, Connecticut

Hammer C U, Clausen H B, Langway Jr C C (1985) The Byrd ice core: continuous acidity measurements and solid electrical conductivity measurements. *Annals of Glaciology* **7**: 214

Hansen J, Renfrew J (1978) Palaeolithic–neolithic seed remains at Franchthi Cave, Greece. *Nature* **271**: 349–52

Harden C (1988) Mesoscale estimation of soil erosion in the Rio Ambato drainage, Ecuadoran sierra. *Mountain Research and Development* **8**: 331–41

Hardman J A, Cooper D R (1980) Mute swans on the Warwickshire Avon – a study of a decline. *Wildfowl* **31**: 29–36

Hare R (1954) *Pomp and pestilence: infectious disease, its origins and conquest.* Victor Gollancz, London

Harlan J R (1986) Plant domestication: diffuse origins and diffusion. In Barigozzi C (ed) *The origin and domestication of cultivated plants.* Elsevier, Amsterdam, pp 21–34

Harmon R S plus eight others (1983) U series and amino-acid racemization geochronology of Bermuda: implications for eustatic sea-level fluctuation over the past 250,000 years. *Palaeogeography Palaeoclimatology Palaeoecology* **44**: 41–70

Harriman R, Morrison B R S (1982) Ecology of streams draining forested and non-forested catchments in an area of central Scotland subject to acid precipitation. *Hydrobiologia* **251**: 251–63

Harris C (1987) France in North America. In Mitchell R D, Groves P A (eds) *North America: the historical geography of a changing continent.* Hutchinson, London, pp 65–92

Harris J M, Brown F H, Leakey M G, Walker A C, Leakey R E (1988) Pliocene and Pleistocene hominid-bearing sites from west of Lake Turkana, Kenya. *Science* **239**: 27–33

Harris M P (1972–73) Evaluation of tourist impact and management in the Galápagos. In *World Wildlife Fund Yearbook 1972–73.* World Wildlife Fund, Morges, Switzerland, pp 178–9

Harrison R M, Johnston W R (1987) Experimental investigations on the relative contribution of atmosphere and soils to the lead content of crops. In Coughtrey P J, Martin M H, Unsworth M H (eds) *Pollutant transport and fate in ecosystems.* Blackwell, Oxford, pp 277–87

Harrison-Reed A (1986) Accelerated erosion in arable soils. *Span* **39**: 1–3

Hart B T, Lake P S (1987) Studies of heavy metal pollution in Australia with particular emphasis on aquatic systems. In Hutchinson T C, Meena K M (eds) *Lead, mercury, cadmium and arsenic in the environment.* John Wiley, Chichester, pp 187–216

Hartz N, Milthers V (1901) Det senglaciale ler i Alleørd Teglvaerksgrav. *Meddelelser Dansk Geologisk Forening* **8**: 31–59

Harvey D R plus nine others (1986) *Countryside implications for England and Wales of possible changes in the Common Agricultural Policy.* Centre for Agricultural Strategy, University of Reading.

Harvey L D D (1988) Climate impact of ice-age aerosols. *Nature* **334**: 333–5

Hassan F A (1981) Historical Nile floods and their implications for climatic change. *Science* **212**: 1142–5

Hassan F A, Stucki B R (1987) Nile floods and climatic change. In Rampino M R, Sanders J E, Newman W S, Königsson L K (eds) *Climate: history, periodicity and predictability.* Van Nostrand Reinhold, New York, pp 37–46

Hawkes J G (1969) The ecological background of plant domestication. In Ucko P J, Dimbleby G W (eds) *The domestication and exploitation of plants and animals.* Duckworth and Co. Ltd., London, pp 17–29

Hawkes F R, Hawkes D L (1987) Anaerobic digestion. In Bu'lock J, Kristiansson B (eds) *Basic biotechnology.* Academic Press, London, pp 337–58

Haworth E Y (1985) The highly nervous system of the English lakes: aquatic ecosystem sensitivity to external changes, as demonstrated by diatoms. In *Annual Report of the Freshwater Biological Association* **53**: 60–79

Hays J D, Imbrie J, Shackleton N J (1976) Variations in the earth's orbit: pacemaker of the ice ages. *Science* **194**: 1121–32

Heathcote R L (1983) *The arid lands: their use and abuse.* Longman, London

Heathcote R L (1987) Land. In Davison G, McCarty J W, McLeary A (eds) *Australians in 1888.* Fairfax, Syme and Weldon Associates, Sydney, pp 49–67

Henderson-Sellers B, Markland H R (1987) *Decaying lakes: the origins and control of cultural eutrophication.* John Wiley, Chichester.

Henriksen A, Lien L, Tracaen T S, Sevaldrud I S, Brakke D F (1988) Lake acidification in Norway – present and predicted chemical status. *Ambio* **17**: 259–66

Heusser C J (1984) Late Quaternary climates of Chile. In Vogel J C (ed) *Late Cainozoic palaeoclimates of the southern hemisphere.* A A Balkema, Rotterdam, pp 59–83

Higham N (1987) *The northern counties to AD 1000.* Longman, London

Hill I R (1985) Effects on non-target organisms in terrestrial and aquatic organisms. In Leahey J P (ed) *The pyrethroid insecticides*. Taylor and Francis, London, pp 151–262

Hill M O (1987) Opportunities for vegetation management in plantation forests. In Good J E G (ed) *Environmental aspects of plantation forestry in Wales*. Institute of Terrestrial Ecology, Bangor, pp 64–9

Hinriksen D (1988) Acid rain and forest damage. In Goldsmith E, Hildyard N (gen eds) *The Earth report: monitoring the battle for our environment*. Mitchell Beazley, London, pp 65–78

Ho C-K, Li Z-W (1987) Paleolithic subsistence strategies in North China. *Current Research in the Pleistocene* **4**: 7–9

Hodges R D, Arden-Clarke C (1986) *Soil erosion in Britain: levels of soil damage and their relationship to farming practice*. The Soil Association, Bristol

Holden C (1988) Family planning: a growing gap. *Science* **242**: 370–1

Holderness B A (1981) Agriculture and industrialization in the Victorian economy. In Mingay G E (ed) *The Victorian countryside*. Routledge and Kegan Paul, London, Vol 1, pp 179–99

Holland G J, McBride J L, Nicholls N (1988) Australian region tropical cyclones and the greenhouse effect. In Pearman G I (ed) *Greenhouse: planning for climatic change*. CSIRO Division of Atmospheric Research, East Melbourne, Australia, pp 438–55

Hooghiemstra H (1984) *Vegetation and climatic history of the High Plain of Bogota, Colombia: a continuous record of the last 3.5 million years*. Cramer, Vaduz

Hooghiemstra H (1988) The orbital-tuned marine oxygen isotope record applied to the Middle and Late Pleistocene pollen record of Funza (Colombian Andes). *Palaeogeography Palaeoclimatology Palaeoecology* **66**: 9–17

Hopf M (1986) Archaeological evidence of the spread and use of some members of the Leguminosae family. In Barigozzi C (ed) *The origin and domestication of cultivated plants*. Elsevier, Amsterdam, pp 35–60

Horn D R (1988) *Ecological approach to pest management*. Elsevier, London

Hornung M (1985) Acidification of soils by trees and forests. *Soil Use Management* **1**: 24–7

Hornung M, Stevens P A, Reynolds B (1987) The effects of forestry on soils, soil water and surface water chemistry. In Good J E G (ed) *Environmental aspects of plantation forestry in Wales*. Institute of Terrestrial Ecology, Bangor, pp 25–36

Horton D R (1984) Red kangaroos: last of the Australian megafauna. In Martin P S, Klein R G (eds) *Quaternary extinctions, a prehistoric revolution*. University of Arizona Press; Tucson, pp 639–80

Howe C W, Ahrens W A (1988) Water resources of the Upper Colorado River Basin: problems and policy alternatives. In El-Ashry M T, Gibbons D C (eds) *Water and arid lands of the western United States*. Cambridge University Press, Cambridge, pp 169–232

Howe S, Webb III T (1983) Calibrating pollen data in climatic terms: improving the methods. *Quaternary Science Reviews* **2**: 17-51

Howells G (1987) Acidity mitigation in a small upland lake. In Barth H (ed) *Reversibility of acidification*. Elsevier, London, pp 104–11

Hrabovszky J P, Miyan K (1987) Population growth and land use in Nepal: 'The Great Turnabout'. *Mountain Research and Development* 7: 264–70

Hudson N W (1987) Limiting degradation caused by soil erosion. In Wolman M G, Fournier F G A (eds) *Land transformation in agriculture*. John Wiley, Chichester, pp 153–69

Hulme M (1989) Is environmental degradation causing drought in the Sahel? An assessment from recent empirical research. *Geography* 74: 38–46

Hungspreugs M (1988) Heavy metals and other non-oil pollutants in Southeast Asia. *Ambio* 17: 178–82

Huntley B, Birks H J B (1983) *An atlas of past and present pollen maps for Europe: 0–13,000 years ago*. Cambridge University Press, Cambridge

Hutson D H, Roberts T R (1987) Wild oat herbicides. In Hutson D H, Roberts T R (eds) *Herbicides* (vol 6). John Wiley, Chichester, pp 169–97

Hutton J (1795) *Theory of the Earth*. William Creech, Edinburgh

Hutton M (1987) Human health concerns of lead, mercury, cadmium and arsenic. In Hutchinson T C, Meema K M (eds) *Lead, mercury, cadmium and arsenic in the environment*. John Wiley, Chichester, pp 53–68

Imbrie J, Imbrie K P (1979) *Ice Ages: solving the mystery*. Macmillan Press, London

Independent Commission on International Humanitarian Issues (1986) *The encroaching desert*. Zed Books, London

Institute of Chemical Engineers (1988) *The problem of acid emissions*. Institute of Chemical Engineers, London

International Union for Conservation of Nature and Natural Resources (IUCN) (1987) *Population and sustainable development*. IUCN, Gland, Switzerland

Isaac G L (1977) *Olorgesailie: archaeological studies of a Middle Pleistocene lake basin in Kenya*. University of Chicago Press, Chicago, USA

Isichei A O, Akeredolu F (1988) Acidification potential in the Nigerian environment. In Rodhe H, Herrera R (eds) *Acidification in tropical countries*. John Wiley, Chichester, pp 297–316

Ivens G W (ed) (1988) *The UK pesticide guide*. Commonwealth Agricultural Bureau and the British Crop Protection Council

Iversen J (1941) Landnam i Danmarks stenalder. *Danmarks Geologiske Undersøgelse* Series IV, 66: 20–68

Iversen J (1944) *Viscum, Hedera* and *Ilex* as climate indicators. *Geologiske Förenigens Stockholm Förhandlingar* 66: 463–83

Iversen J (1954) The lateglacial flora of Denmark and its relation to climate and soil. *Danmarks Geologiske Undersøgelse*, Series II, 80: 87–119

Iversen J (1956) Forest clearance in the stone age. *Scientific American* 194: 36–41

Iversen J (1958) The bearing of glacial and interglacial epochs on the formation and extinction of plant taxa. *Uppsala Universiteit Årssk* **6**: 210–15

Ives J D (1987) The theory of Himalayan environmental degradation: its validity and application challenged by recent research. *Mountain Research and Development* **7**: 189–99

Ives J D, Messerli B, Thompson M (1987) Research strategy for the Himalayan region: conference conclusions and overview. *Mountain Research and Development* **7**: 332–44

Jackson J B C plus seventeen others (1989) Ecological effects of a major oil spill on Panamanian coastal marine communities. *Science* **243**: 37–44

Jacobson J (1988) Planning the global family. In *State of the world 1988: a Worldwatch Institute report on progress towards a sustainable society*. W W Norton, New York, pp 151–69

Jamieson T F (1865) On the history of the last geological changes in Scotland. *Quarterly Journal of the Geological Society of London* **21**: 161–95

Jaworski J (1987) Lead. In Hutchinson T C, Meema K M (eds) *Lead, mercury, cadmium and arsenic in the environment*. John Wiley, Chichester, pp 3–16

Jenkins D G (1987) Was the Pliocene–Pleistocene boundary placed at the wrong stratigraphic level? *Quaternary Science Reviews* **6**: 41–2

Jessen K, Milthers V (1928) Stratigraphical and palaeontological studies of inter-glacial fresh water deposits in Jutland and northwest Germany. *Danmarks Geologiske Undersøgelse*, Series II, **48**: 1–379

Jhaveri N (1988) The Three Gorges debacle. *The Ecologist* **18**: 56–63

Jim C Y (1987a) Trampling impacts of recreationists on picnic sites in a Hong Kong country park. *Environmental Conservation* **14**: 117–27

Jim C Y (1987b) Country park usage and visitor impacts in Hong Kong. *Parks* **12**: 3–8

Johns A D (1985) Selective logging and wildlife conservation in tropical rain-forest: problems and recommendations. *Biological Conservation* **3**: 355–75

Johns A D (1988) Economic development and wildlife conservation in Brazilian Amazonia. *Ambio* **17**: 302–6

Johnson H B (1987) Portuguese settlement, 1500–1580. In Bethell L (ed) *Colonial Brazil*. Cambridge University Press, Cambridge, pp 1–38

Johnson R W, Tothill J C (1985) Definition and broad geographic outline of savanna lands. In Tothill J C, Mott J J (eds) *Ecology and management of the world's savannas*. Commonwealth Agricultural Bureau, Slough, pp 1–13

Johnston A W B (1989) Biological nitrogen fixation. In Marx J L (ed) *A revolution in biotechnology*. Cambridge University Press, Cambridge, pp 103–18

Johnston B (1987) Countryside protected for its own sake. *Planning* **719**: 8–9

Jones G A, Keigwin L D (1988) Evidence from Fram Strait (78°N) for early deglaciaton. *Nature* **336**: 56–9

Jones M (1981) Introduction. In Jones M, Dimbleby G (eds) *The environment of* *man: the Iron Age to the Anglo-Saxon period.* British Archaeological Research Reports (British Series), Oxford, No.87, pp 1–5

Jones M (1986) *England before Domesday.* Batsford, London

Jones M G K (1986) Developments in the culture of plant protoplasts and cells and their regeneration to plants. In Day P R (ed) *Biotechnology and crop improvement and protection.* British Crop Protection Council, London, Monograph No.34, pp 3–11

Jones M G K, Lindsey K (1988) Plant biotechnology. In Walker J M, Gingold E B (eds) *Molecular biology and biotechnology.* Royal Society of Chemistry, London, pp 117–47

Jones P D, Wigley T M L, Wright P B (1986) Global temperature variations between 1861 and 1984. *Nature* **322**: 430–4

Jones V J, Stevenson A C, Battarbee R W (1989) Acidification of lakes in Galloway, south-west Scotland: a diatom and pollen study of the post-glacial history of the Round Loch of Glenhead. *Journal of Ecology* **77**: 1–23

Jouzel J, Lorius C, Merlivat L, Petit J-R (1987a) Abrupt climatic changes: the Antarctic ice record during the Late Pleistocene. In Berger W H, Labeyrie L D (eds) *Abrupt climatic change.* D Reidel, Dordrecht, pp 235–45

Jouzel J, Lorius C, Petit J-R, Genthon C, Barkov N I, Kotlyakov V M, Petrov V M (1987) Vostok ice core: a continuous isotope temperature record over the last climatic cycle (160,000 years). *Nature* **329**: 403–8

Jutsum A R (1988) Commercial application of biological control: status and prospects. *Philosophical Transactions of the Royal Society of London* **B318**: 357–73

Kang B T, Wilson G F (1987) The development of alley cropping as a promising agroforestry technology. In Steppler H A, Nair P K R (eds) *Agroforestry: a decade of development.* International Council for Research in Agroforestry, Nairobi, pp 227–43

Karan P P (1987) Population characteristics of the Himalaya region. *Mountain Research and Development* **7**: 271–4

Karan P P, Iijima S (1985) Environmental stress in the Himalaya. *Geographical Review* **75**: 71–92

Kardell L, Larsson J (1978) Lead and cadmium in oak tree rings *Quercus robur* L. *Ambio* **7**: 117–21

Kariel H G, Kariel P E (1988) Tourist developments in the Kananaskis Valley area, Alberta, Canada, and the impact of the 1988 Winter Olympic Games. *Mountain Research and Development* **8**: 1–10

Kebin Z, Kaiguo Z (1989) Afforestation for sand fixation in China. *Journal of Arid Environments* **16**: 3–10

Kerr R (1988a) Evidence of arctic ozone destruction. *Science* **240**: 1144–5

Kerr R (1988b) Ozone hole bodes ill for the globe. *Science* **241**: 785–6

Kerr R (1989) How to fix the clouds in greenhouse models. *Science* **243**: 28–9

Kershaw A P (1978) Record of last interglacial–glacial cycle from northeastern Queensland. *Nature* **272**: 159–61

Kershaw A P (1986) Climatic change and Aboriginal burning in north-east Australia during the last two glacial/interglacial cycles. *Nature* **322**: 47–9

Kettunen L, Mukula J, Pohjonen V, Rantanen O, Varjo U (1988) The effects of climate variations on agriculture in Finland. In Parry M L, Carter T R, Konijn N J (eds) *The impact of climatic variations on agriculture* (2 vols). Kluwer Academic Publishers; Dordrecht, vol 1 *Assessment in cool temperate and cold regions*, pp 511–614

Khalaf F I (1989) Desertification and aeolian processes in the Kuwait desert. *Journal of Arid Environments* **16**: 125–45

Khalil J B, Hanna F S (1984) Changes in the quality of Nile water in Egypt during the twenty-five years, 1954–1979. *Irrigation Science* **5**: 1–13

Khalil M A K, Rasmussen R A (1985) Causes of increasing atmospheric methane: decline of hydroxyl radicals and the rise of emissions. *Atmospheric Environment* **19**: 397–407

Khalil M A K, Rasmussen R A (1987) Atmospheric methane: trends over the last 10,000 years. *Atmospheric Environment* **21** (11): 2445–52

Khotinsky N A (1984) Holocene vegetation history. In Velichko A A (ed) *Late Quaternary environments of the Soviet Union*. University of Minnesota Press, Minneapolis, pp 179–200

King C A M (1987) Ocean processes. In Gregory K J, Walling D E (eds) *Human activity and environmental processes*. John Wiley, Chichester, pp 117–43

King K F S (1987) The history of agroforestry. In Steppler H A, Nair P K R (eds) *Agroforestry: a decade of development*. International Council for Research In Agroforestry, Nairobi, pp 1–11

Kio P R O, Ekwebelam S A (1987) Plantations versus natural forests for meeting Nigeria's wood needs. In Mergen F, Vincent J R (eds) *Natural management of tropical moist forests*. Yale University, School of Forestry and Environmental Studies, New Haven, Connecticut, pp 149–76

Kirby K J (1988) Changes in the ground flora under plantations on ancient woodland sites. *Forestry* (Oxford) **61**: 317–38

Kirkwood R C (1987) Herbicides and plant growth regulators. In Hutson D H, Roberts T R (eds) *Herbicides*. John Wiley, Chichester, vol 6 pp 1–55

Kjekshus H (1977) *Ecology control and economic development in East African history*. Heinemann, London

Klein R G (1979) Stone age exploitation of animals in southern Africa. *American Scientist* **67**: 151–160

Kohl L (1988) Heavy hands on the land. *National Geographic Magazine* **174**: 633–52

Kovda V A (1980) *Land aridization and drought control*. Westview Press, Boulder, Colorado

Kovda V A (1983) Loss of productive land due to salinization. *Ambio* **12**: 91–3

Kristjansson L (1986) The ice drifts back to iceland. In Gribbin J (ed) *The breathing planet*. Blackwell, Oxford, pp 90–3

Krupa S V, Manning W J (1988) Atmospheric ozone: formation and effects on vegetation. *Environmental Pollution* **50**: 101–37

Kukla G (1987) Loess stratigraphy in Central China and correlation with an extended oxygen isotope stage scale. *Quaternary Science Reviews* **6**: 191–219

Kullman L (1988) Holocene history of the forest–alpine tundra ecotone in the Scandes Mountains (central Sweden). *New Phytologist* **108**: 101–10

Kunakh V A, Savchenko E K (1988) Chromosomal behaviour peculiarities in two related stocks of maize *in vitro*. In International Rice Research Institute and Academia Sinica *Genetic manipulation in crops*. Cassell Tycooly, London, p 338

Kutzbach J E, Guetter P J (1986) The influence of changing orbital parameters and surface boundary conditions on climate simulations for the past 18,000 years. *Journal of Atmospheric Sciences* **43**: 1726–59

Kurtén B, Anderson E (1980) *Pleistocene mammals of North America*. University of Columbia Press, New York

Kvasov D D, Blazhchishin A I (1978) The key to sources of the Pliocene and Pleistocene glaciation is at the bottom of the Barents Sea. *Nature* **273**: 138–40

Labitzke K (1987) Sunspots, the QBO, and the stratospheric temperature in the north polar region. *Geophysical Research Letters* **14**: 535–7

Lal R (1981) Deforestation of tropical rainforest and hydrological problems. In Lal R, Russell E W (eds) *Tropical agricultural hydrology*. John Wiley, Chichester, pp 131–40

Lal R (1985) Soil erosion and productivity in tropical soils. In El-Swaify S A, Moldenhauer W C, Lo A (eds) *Soil erosion and conservation*. Soil Conservation Society of America, Ankeny, Iowa, pp 237–47

Lal R (1986) Deforestation and soil erosion. In Lal R, Sanchez P A, Cummings R W (eds) *Land clearing and development in the tropics*. A A Balkema, Rotterdam, pp 299–315

Lal R (1988) Soil erosion by wind and water: problems and prospects. In Lal R (ed) *Soil erosion research methods*. Soil and Water Conservation Society, Ankeny, Iowa, pp 1–6

LaMarche V C, Graybill D A, Fritts H C, Rose M R (1984) Increasing atmospheric carbon dioxide: tree ring evidence for growth enhancement in natural vegetation. *Science* **225**: 1019–21

Lamb H H (1981) Climate from 1000 BC to 1000 AD. In Jones M, Dimbleby G W (eds) *The environment of man: the Iron Age to the Anglo-Saxon period*. British Archaeological Research Reports (British series), Oxford, No.87 pp 53–65

Lamb H H (1982) *Climate, history and the modern world*. Methuen, London

Lamb H H (1984) Climate and history in northern Europe and elsewhere. In Mörner N-A, Karlén W (eds) *Climatic changes on a yearly to millennial basis*. D Reidel, Dordrecht, pp 225–40

Lamb H H (1986) The changing climate. In Gribbin J (ed) *The breathing planet*. Blackwell, Oxford, pp 83–9

Lambert D (1987) *The Cambridge guide to prehistoric man*. Cambridge University Press, Cambridge

Langkamp P, Plaisted M (1987) Perspectives on the use of native plant seed in the Australian mining industry. In Langkamp P (ed) *Germination of Australian native plant seed*. Inkata Press, Melbourne, pp 107–14

Lanly J P (1982) *Tropical forestry resources*. Food and Agriculture Organisation, Forestry Paper No.30. FAO, Rome

Lanpo J (1985) China's earliest palaeolithic assemblages. In Rukang W, Olsen J W (eds) *Palaeoanthropology and palaeolithic archaeology in the People's Republic of China*. Academic Press, London, pp 135–45

Lanpo J, Weiwen H (1985) The late palaeolithic of China. In Rukang W, Olsen J W (eds) *Palaeoanthropology and palaeolithic archaeology in the People's Republic of China*. Academic Press, London, pp 211–23

Larkin P, Ryan S, Brettell R, Scowcroft W (1988) Somaclonal variation and wheat improvement. In International Rice Research Institute and Academia Sinica *Genetic manipulation in crops*. Cassell Tycooly, London, pp 113–15

Larichev V, Khol'ushkin U, Laricheva I (1987) Lower and middle palaeolithic of northern Asia: achievements, problems and perspectives. *Journal of World Prehistory* **1**: 415–64

Lau F-S (1987) *Radioactivity and nuclear waste disposal*. John Wiley, New York

Leahy J P (1985) Metabolism and environmental degradation. In Leahy J P (ed) *The pyrethroid insecticides*. Taylor and Francis, London, pp 263–342

Leakey M D (1979)*Olduvai Gorge: my search for early man*. Collins, London

Leakey R E (1981) *The making of mankind*. Michael Joseph, London

Leakey R E (1982) *Human origins*. Hamish Hamilton, London

Lee J A, Press M C, Studholme C, Woodin S J (1988) Effects of acid deposition on wetlands. In Ashmore M R, Bell J N B, Garretty C (eds) *Acid rain and Britain's natural ecosystems*. Centre for Environmental Technology, Imperial College, London, pp 27–37

Lee J A, Tallis J H (1973) Regional and historical aspects of lead pollution in Britain. *Nature* **245**: 216–8

Leeming F (1985) *Rural China today*. Longman, London

Legge A J, Rowley-Conwy P A (1989) Some preliminary results of a re-examination of the Star Carr fauna. In Bonsall C (ed) *The mesolithic in Europe (Proceedings of the IIIrd International Symposium, Edinburgh, 1985)*. John Donald Publishers Ltd, Edinburgh, pp 225–30

Leggett J (1989) Don't put a reactor in the greenhouse. *The Guardian* 4th July 1989, p 38

Legrand M R, Delmas R J, Charlson R J (1988a) Climate forcing implications from Vostok ice-core sulphate data. *Nature* **334**: 418–20

Legrand M R, Lorius C, Barkov N I, Petrov V N (1988b) Vostok (Antarctica) ice core: atmospheric chemistry changes over the last climatic cycle (160,000 years). *Atmospheric Environment* **22**: 317–31

Lewin R (1987) Africa: cradle of modern humans. *Science* **237**: 1292–5

Libra R D, Hallberg G R, Hoyer B E (1987) Impacts of agricultural chemicals on ground water quality in Iowa. In Fairchild D M (ed) *Ground water quality and agricultural practices*. Lewis Publishers, Chelsea, Michigan, pp 185–215

Lindow S E (1985) Ecology of *Pseudomonas syringae* relevant to the field use of ice-deletion mutants constructed *in vitro* for plant frost control. In Halvorson H O, Pramer D, Rogul M (eds) *Engineered organisms in the environment: scientific issues*. American Society for Microbiology, Washington DC, pp 23–35

Litchfield J H (1989) Single-cell proteins. In Marx J L (ed) *A revolution in biotechnology*. Cambridge University Press, Cambridge, pp 71–81

Litchfield M H (1985) Toxicity to mammals. In Leahy J P (ed) *The pyrethroid insecticides*. Taylor and Francis, London, pp 99–150

Liu D, Menglin D (1984) The characteristics and evolution of the palaeoenvironment of China since the Late Tertiary. In Whyte R O, Leung C-K, So C-K (eds) *The evolution of the East Asian environment*. University of Hong Kong Centre for Asian Studies, Hong Kong, pp 11–40

Livett E A (1988) Geochemical monitoring of atmospheric heavy metal pollution: theory and application. *Advances in Ecological Research* **18**: 65–177

Livett E A, Lee J A, Tallis J H (1979) Lead, zinc and copper analyses of British blanket peats. *Journal of Ecology* **67**: 865–91

Livingstone D A (1982) Quaternary geography of Africa and the refuge theory. In Prance G (ed) *Biological diversification in the tropics*. Columbia Press, New York, pp 523–36

Long S R, Ehrhardt D W (1989) New route to a sticky subject. *Nature* **338**: 545–6

Lonsdale M, Braithwaite R (1988) The shrub that conquered the bush. *New Scientist* **120** (1634): 52–5

van Loon H, Labitzke K (1988) When the wind blows. *New Scientist* **119** (1629): 58–60

Lorimer C G (1982) Silviculture. In Young R A (ed) *Introduction to forest science*. John Wiley, New York, pp 209–34

Lorius C, Jouzel J, Ritz C, Merlivat L, Barkov N I, Korotkevich Y S, Kotlyakov V M (1985) A 150,000 year climatic record from Antarctic ice. *Nature* **316**: 591–6

Loubere P (1988) Gradual Late Pliocene onset of glaciation: a deep-sea record from the northeast Atlantic. *Palaeogeography Palaeoclimatology Palaeoecology* **63**: 327–34

Lovejoy T E (1989) Deforestation and the extinction of species. In Botkin D B, Caswell M F, Estes J E, Orio A A (eds) *Changing the global environment*. Academic Press, Boston, pp 91–8

Lowe J J, Gray J M (1980) The stragigraphic subdivision of the Lateglacial of NW Europe: a discussion. In Lowe J J, Gray J M, Robinson J E (eds) *Studies in the Lateglacial of North-West Europe*. Pergamon Press, Oxford, pp 157–75

Lowe P D (1983) Values and institutions in the history of British nature conservation. In Warren A, Goldsmith F B (eds) *Conservation in perspective*. John Wiley, Chichester, pp 329–52

Lowe P D, Cox G, MacEwen M, O'Riordan T, Winter M (1986) *Countryside conflicts*. Gower/Maurice Temple Smith, Aldershot

Lowe P D, Goyder J (1983) *Environmental groups in politics*. George Allen and Unwin, Boston, Massachusetts

Lühr H-P (1986) Water–a natural resource in danger. In Bender F (ed) *Georesources and environment*. E Schweizerbart'sche Verlagsbuchhandlung (Nägele u Obermiller), Stuttgart, pp 41–6

Lundquist J (1986) Stratigraphy of the central area of the Scandinavian glaciation. *Quaternary Science Reviews* **5**: 251–68

Lyell C (1833) *Principles of geology* . John Murray, London, vol 3

Lyle M (1988) Climatically forced organic carbon burial in equatorial Atlantic and Pacific oceans. *Nature* **335**: 529–32

Maass J M, Jordan C F, Satukhan J (1988) Soil erosion and nutrient losses in seasonal tropical agroecosystems under various management techniques. *Journal of Applied Ecology* **25**: 595–607

Mabbutt J A (1978) Desertification of Australia in its global context. *Search* **9**: 252–6

McCormick J (1985) *Acid earth*. Earthscan, London

McElroy M B, Salawitch R J (1989) Changing composition of the global stratosphere. *Science* **243**: 763–70

MacEwen M, Sinclair G (1983) *New life for the hills*. Council for National Parks, London

McGrath S P (1987) Long-term studies of metal transfers following application of sewage-sludge. In Coughtrey P J, Martin M H, Unsworth M H (eds) *Pollutant transport and fate in ecosystems*. Blackwell, Oxford, pp 301–17

McGregor D F M (1986) Upper Yallahs Valley, Jamaica: an assessment of soil erosion hazard. *Caribbean Geography* **2**: 138–43

McIntosh S K, McIntosh R J (1988) From stone to metal: new perspectives on the later prehistory of West Africa. *Journal of World Prehistory* **2**: 89–133

MacNeish R S (1978) *The science of archaeology?* Duxbury Press, Scituate, Massachusetts

MacNeish R S (1985) The archaeological record of the problem of the domestication of corn. *Maydica* **30**: 171–8

Mahat T B S, Griffin D M, Shepherd K R (1986a) Human impact on some forests of the Middle Hills of Nepal. 1. Forestry in the context of the traditional resources of the state. *Mountain Research and Development* **6**: 223–32

Mahat T B S, Griffin D M, Shepherd K R (1986b) Human impact on some forests of the Middle Hills of Nepal. 2. Some major human impacts before 1950 on the forests of Sindhu Palchok and Kabhre Palanchok. *Mountain Research and Development* **6**: 325–34

Mahat T B S, Griffin D M, Shepherd K R (1987a) Human impact on some forests of the Middle Hills of Nepal. 3. Forests in the subsistence economy of Sindhu Palchok and Kabhre Palanchok. *Mountain Research and Development* **7**: 53–70

Mahat T B S, Griffin D M, Shepherd K R (1987b) Human impact on some forests of the Middle Hills of Nepal. 4. A detailed survey of southeast Sindhu Palchok and northeast Kabhre Palanchok. *Mountain Research and Development* **7**: 111–34

Mainguet M (1986) The wind and desertification processes in the Sahara-Sahelian regions. In El-Baz F, Hassan M H A (eds) *Physics of desertification*. Martinus Nijhoff, Dordrecht, pp 210–40

Makuch J R, Woodward M D (1987) Ground water and agriculture: addressing the information needs of Pennsylvania's Chesapeake Bay program. In Fairchild D M (ed) *Ground water quality and agricultural practices*. Lewis Publishers, Chelsea, Michigan, pp 375–88

Malingreau J-P, Tucker C J (1988) Large-scale deforestation in the southeastern Amazon basin of Brazil. *Ambio* **17**: 49–55

Mangelsdorf P C (1986) The origin of corn. *Scientific American* **255**: 72–8

Manley G (1974) Central England temperatures: monthly means 1659–1793. *Quarterly Journal of the Royal Meteorological Society* **1060**: 389–405

Mannion A M (1986a) Plant macrofossils and their significance in Quaternary palaeoecology. Part I. Introduction. *Progress in Physical Geography* **10**: 194–214

Mannion A M (1986b) Plant macrofossils and their significance in Quaternary palaeoecology. Part II. Applications: preglacial, interglacial and interstadial deposits. *Progress in Physical Geography* **10**: 364–82

Mannion A M (1986c) Vegetation succession and climax. In Thompson R D, Mannion A M, Mitchell C W, Parry M, Townshend J R G *Processes in physical geography*. Longman, London, pp 302–15

Mannion A M (1986d) *Diatoms: algal indicators of environmental change. II. Applications*. Department of Geography, University of Reading, Geographical Papers No. 92

Mannion A M (1986e) The flow of materials within ecosystems: biogeochemical cycles 1. In Thompson R D, Mannion A M, Mitchell C W, Parry M, Townshend J R G *Processes in physical geography*. Longman, London, pp 276–86

Mannion A M (1987a) Fossil diatoms and their significance in archaeological research. *Oxford Journal of Archaeology* **6**: 131–47

Mannion A M (1987b) Aquatic ecosystem development in Scotland: a review based on evidence from diatom assemblages. *Scottish Geographical Magazine* **103**: 13–20

Mannion A M (1989a) Palaeoecological evidence for environmental change during the last 200 years. I. Biological data. *Progress in Physical Geography* **13**: 23–46

Mannion A M (1989b) Palaeoecological evidence for environmental change during the last 200 years. II. Chemical data. *Progress in Physical Geography* **13**: 192–215

Mannion A M, Moseley S P (1990) Pollen diagrams from the Outer Hebrides. In Barber J W A (ed) *The archaeology of the Western Isles*. Central Excavation Unit, Scottish Development Department, Edinburgh, in press

Marchetti R, Gaggino G F, Provini A (1988) Case study: red tides in the Northwest Adriatic. *In Eutrophication in the Mediterranean Sea: receiving capacity and monitoring of long-term effects*. Unesco Reports in Marine Science No. 49, pp 133–42

Marcus L F, Berger R (1984) The significance of radiocarbon dates for Rancho La Brea. In Martin P S, Klein R G (eds) *Quaternary extinctions, a prehistoric revolution*. University of Arizona Press, Tucson, pp 159–83

Markgraf V, Bradbury J P, Busby J R (1986) Paleoclimates in southwestern Tasmania during the last 130,000 years. *Palaios* **1**: 368–80

Marshall L G (1984) Who killed cock robin? An investigation of the extinction controversy. In Martin P S, Klein R G *Quaternary extinctions, a prehistoric revolution*. University of Arizona Press, Tucson, pp 785–806

Martin A R H (1986) Late glacial and Holocene alpine pollen diagrams from the Kosciusko National Park, New South Wales, Australia. *Review of Palaeobotany and Palynology* **47**: 367–409

Martin J H, Fitzwater S E (1988) Iron defiency limits phytoplankton growth in the north-east Pacific subarctic. *Nature* **331**: 341–3

Martin P S (1973) The discovery of America. *Science* **179**: 969–74

Martin P S (1984) Prehistoric overkill: the global model. In Martin P S, Klein R G (eds) *Quaternary extinctions, a prehistoric revolution*. University of Arizona Press, Tucson, pp 354–403

Martin P S, Klein R G (eds) (1984) *Quaternary extinctions, a prehistoric revolution*. University of Arizona Press, Tucson

Martinelli L A, Ferreira J R, Forsberg B R, Victoria R L (1988) Mercury contamination in the Amazon: a gold rush consequence. *Ambio* **17**: 252–4

Marx J L (1989) Heredity, genes and DNA. In Marx J L (ed) *A revolution in biotechnology*. Cambridge University Press, Cambridge, pp 1–14

Mather A S (1987) Global trends in forest resources. *Geography* **72**: 1–15

Matheson W E (1986) Soils. In Nance C, Speight D L (eds) *A land transformed: environmental change in South Australia*. Longman Cheshire, Melbourne, pp 126–47

Meinig D W (1986) *The shaping of America: a geographical perspective on 500 years of history*. Yale University Press, New Haven, Connecticut, vol 1 *Atlantic America, 1492–1800*

Mellaart J (1967) *Çatal Hüyük: a neolithic town in Anatolia*. Thames and Hudson, London

Mellars P A (1976) Fire ecology, animal populations and man: a study of some ecological relationships in prehistory. *Proceedings of the Prehistoric Society* **42**: 15–45

Mellars P A (1987) *Excavations on Oronsay: prehistoric ecology on a small island*. Edinburgh University Press, Edinburgh.

Mensching H G (1988) Land degradation and desertification in the Sahelian zone. In Whitehead E E, Hutchinson C F, Timmermann B N, Varady R G (eds) *Arid lands: today and tomorrow*. Westview Press, Boulder, Colorado, and Belhaven Press, London, pp 605–13

Mercer D, Puttnam D (1988) *Rural England: our countryside at the crossroads*. MacDonald Queen Anne Press, London

Merrick T W, PRB staff (1986) World population in transition. *Population Bulletin* **41**: 1–51

Messer J (1987) The sociology and politics of land degradation in Australia. In Blaikie P, Brookfield H *Land degradation and society*. Methuen, London, pp 232–8

Micklin P P (1988) Desiccation of the Aral Sea: a water management disaster in the Soviet Union. *Science* **241**: 1170–6

Milankovitch M (1941*) Kanon der Erdbestrahlung und seine Anwendung auf das Eiszeitenproblem*. Royal Serbian Academy Special Publication **133**: 1–633

Millones J (1982) Patterns of land use and associated environmental problems of the Central Andes: an integrated summary. *Mountain Research and Development* **2**: 49–61

Mingay G E (1981) Introduction: rural England in the industrial age. In Mingay G E (ed) *The Victorian countryside* (2 vols). Routledge and Kegan Paul, London, vol 1 pp 3–16

Ministry of Agriculture, Fisheries and Food (1987) *Farm extensification scheme: a consultative document*. MAFF, London

Misra V N (1987) Middle Pleistocene adaptations in India. In Soffer O (ed) *The Pleistocene old world: regional perspectives*. Plenum Press, New York, pp 99–117

Mitchell G F (1976) *The Irish landscape*. Collins, London

Mitchell G F, Penny L F, Shotton F W, West R G (1973) *A correlation of Quaternary deposits in the British Isles*. Geological Society of London, Special Report No 4

Mitchell J F B, Warrilow D A (1987) Summer dryness in northern mid-latitudes due to increased CO_2. *Nature* **330**: 238–40

Mitchell R D (1987) The colonial origins of Anglo-America. In Mitchell R D, Groves P A (eds) *North America: the historical geography of a changing continent*. Hutchinson, London, pp 93–120

Mohnen V A (1988) The challenge of acid rain. *Scientific American* **259**: 14–22

Molloy K, O'Connell M (1987) The nature of the vegetational changes at about 5000 BP with particular reference to the elm decline: fresh evidence from Connemara, western Ireland. *New Phytologist* **106**: 203–20

Moore A M T (1985) The development of neolithic societies in the Near East. *Advances in World Archaeology* **4**: 1–69

Moore P D (1975) Origin of blanket mires. *Nature* **256**: 267–9

Moore N W (1983) Ecological effects of pesticides. In Warren A, Goldsmith F B (eds) *Conservation in practice*. John Wiley, Chichester, pp 159–175

Moran J M, Morgan M D, Wiersma J H (1986) *Introduction to environmental science* 2nd edn. W H Freeman, New York

Moreira-Nordemann L M, Forti M C, DiLascio V L, do Espírito Santo C M, Danelon O M (1988) Acidification in southeastern Brazil. In Rodhe H, Herrera R (eds) *Acidification in tropical countries*. John Wiley, Chichester, pp 257–96

Morgan R P C (1980) Soil erosion and conservation in Britain. *Progress in Physical Geography* **4**: 24–47

Morgan R P C (1985) Soil erosion measurement and soil conservation research in cultivated areas in the UK. *Geographical Journal* **151**: 11–20

Morgan R P C (1986a) *Soil erosion and conservation*. Longman, London

Morgan R P C (1986b) Soil degradation and soil erosion in the loamy belt of northern Europe. In Chisci G, Morgan R P C (eds) *Soil erosion in the European Community*. A A Balkema, Rotterdam, pp 165–72

Morgan R P C (1987) Sensitivity of European soils to ultimate physical degradation. In Barth H, L'Hermite P (eds) *Scientific basis for soil protection in the European Community*. Elsevier, London, pp 147–57

Mörner M (1987) Rural economy and society in Spanish South America. In Bethell L (ed) *Colonial Spanish America*. Cambridge University Press, Cambridge, pp 286–314

Morse R M (1987) Urban development. In Bethell L (ed) *Colonial Spanish America*. Cambridge University Press, Cambridge, pp 165–202

Mortimore M (1989) *Adapting to drought: farmers, famines and desertification in West Africa*. Cambridge University Press, Cambridge

Mosimann T (1985) Geo-ecological impacts of ski piste construction in the Swiss Alps. *Applied Geography* **5**: 29–37

Moss B (1988) *Ecology of freshwaters: man and medium* (2nd edn). Blackwell, Oxford

Mott R J, Grant D R, Stea R, Occhietti S (1986) Late-glacial climatic oscillation in Atlantic Canada equivalent to the Allerød/Younger Dryas event. *Nature* **328**: 247–50

Mumford L (1966) *The city in history*. Penguin, Harmondsworth

Munro J F (1975) *Colonial rule and Kamba social change in Kenya highlands*. Clarendon Press, Oxford

Munton R (1983) Agriculture and conservation: what room for compromise? In Warren A, Goldsmith F B (eds) *Conservation in perspective*. John Wiley, Chichester, pp 353–73

Myers N (ed) (1985) *Gaia atlas of planet management*. Pan Books, London

Myers N (1986) Environmental repercussions of deforestation in the Himalayas. *Journal of World Forest Resource Management* **2**: 63–72

Myers N (1988) Environmental degradation and some economic consequences in the Philippines. *Environmental Conservation* **15**: 205–14

Nadler C F, Korobitsina K V, Hoffmann R S, Vorontsov N N (1973) Cytogenetic differentiation, geographic distribution, and domestication in Palearctic sheep (*Ovis*). *Zeitschrift für Saugetierkunde* **38**: 109–25

Nair P K R (1985) Classification of agroforestry systems. *Agroforestry Systems* **3**: 97–128

Nature Conservancy Council (1981a) *Loss and damage in SSSIs in (1980).* Nature Conservancy Council, Peterborough

Nature Conservancy Council (1981b) *Lead poisoning in swans.* Nature Conservancy Council, Peterborough

Neal H A, Schubel J R (1987) *Solid waste management and the environment: the mounting garbage and trash crisis.* Prentice-Hall, New York

Needleman H L, Gunnoe C, Leviton A, Reed R, Peresie H, Maher C, Barrett P (1979) Deficits in psychologic and classroom performance of children with elevated dentine lead levels. *New England Journal of Medicine* **300**: 689–95

Neftel A, Moor E, Oeschger H, Stauffer B (1985) Evidence from polar ice cores for the increase in atmospheric CO_2 in the past two centuries. *Nature* **315**: 45–47

Newbold C (1988) Wetland management, agricultural management and nature conservation. In Park J R (ed) *Environmental management in agriculture.* Belhaven Press, London, pp 235–43

Newby H (1988) *The countryside in question.* Hutchinson, London

Newson L (1987) The Latin American colonial experience. In Preston D (ed) *Latin American development.* Longman, London, pp 7–33

New Scientist (no author) (1989) China leads new surge in output of greenhouse gas. *New Scientist* **123** (1671): 38

Nichols O G, Carbon B A, Colquhoun I J, Croton J T, Murray N J (1985) Rehabilitation after bauxite mining in south-western Australia. *Landscape Planning* **12**: 75–92

Nitrate Co-ordination Group (1986) *Nitrate in water.* Pollution Paper No 26, HMSO, London

Norris R H, Lake P S, Swain R (1980) Ecological effects of mine effluents on the South Esk River, north-eastern Tasmania. I. Study area and basic water characteristics. *Australian Journal of Marine and Freshwater Research* **31**: 817–27

Norris R H, Lake P S, Swain R (1981) Ecological effects of mine effluents on the South Esk River, north-eastern Tasmania. II. Heavy metals. *Australian Journal of Marine and Freshwater Research* **32**: 165–73

Norris R H, Lake P S, Swain R (1982) Ecological effects of mine effluents on the South Esk River, north-eastern Tasmania. III. Benthic macroinvertebrates. *Australian Journal of Marine and Freshwater Research* **33**: 789–809

North R (1986) *The real cost.* Chatto and Windus, London

Nostrand R L (1987) The Spanish borderlands. In Mitchell R D, Groves P A (eds) *North America: the historical geography of a changing continent.* Hutchinson, London, pp 48–64

Novoa C, Wheeler J C (1984) Llama and alpaca. In Mason 1L (ed) *Evolution of domesticated animals.* Longman, London, pp 116–28

Nriagu J O (1988) A silent epidemic of environmental metal poisoning. *Environmental Pollution* **50**: 139–61

Nriagu J O, Coker R D (1983) Sulphur chronicles past changes in lake acidification. *Nature* **303**: 692–4

Nriagu J O, Holdaway D A, Coker R D (1987) Biogenic sulfur and the acidity of rainfall in remote areas of Canada. *Science* **237**: 1189–92

Nwoboshi L C (1987) Regeneration success of natural management, enrichment planting, and plantations of native species in West Africa. In Mergen F, Vincent (eds) *Natural management of tropical moist forests*. Yale University, School of Forestry and Environmental Studies, New Haven, Connecticut, pp 71–91

Oakley K, Andrews P, Keeley L H, Clark J D G (1977) A reappraisal of the Clacton spear point. *Proceedings of the Prehistoric Society* **43**: 13–30

Odum E P (1975) *Ecology*. Holt, Rinehart and Winston, New York

Oka H I (1988) *Origin of cultivated rice*. Japan Scientific Press, Tokyo, and Elsevier, Amsterdam

O'Kelly M J (ed) (1982) *Newgrange*. Thames and Hudson, London

Okigbo B N (1985) Land use and production potentials of African savannas. In Tothill J C, Mott J J (eds) *Ecology and management of the world's savannas*. Commonwealth Agricultural Bureau, Slough, pp 95–106

O'Leary P R, Walsh P W, Ham R K (1988) Managing solid waste. *Scientific American* **259**: 18–24

Oliver J (1986) Natural hazards. In Jeans D N (ed) *Australia–a geography* (2 vols). Sydney University Press, Sydney, vol 1 *The natural environment* pp 283–314

Olson R A (1987) The use of fertilisers and soil amendments. In Wolman M G, Fournier F G A (eds) *Land transformation in agriculture*. John Wiley, Chichester, pp 203–26

O'Neill P (1985) *Environmental chemistry*. George Allen and Unwin, London

Onyeanusi A E (1986) Measurements of impact of tourist off-road driving on grasslands in Masai Mara National Reserve, Kenya: a simulation approach. *Environmental Conservation* **13**: 325–9

Opdyke N D, Glass B, Hays J D, Foster J (1966) Paleomagnetic study of Antarctic deep-sea cores. *Science* **154**: 349–57

Ormerod S J, Mawle G W, Edwards R W (1987) The influence of forest on aquatic fauna. In Good J E G (ed) *Environmental aspects of plantation forestry in Wales*. Institute of Terrestrial Ecology, Bangor, pp 37–49

Otieno A, Rowntree K (1987) A comparative study of land degradation in Machakos and Baringo Districts, Kenya. In Millington A C, Mutiso S K, Binns J A (eds) *African resources* (2 vols). Department of Geography, University of Reading, Geographical Paper No. 97, vol 2 *Management* pp 30–47

Overpeck J T, Petersen L C, Kipp N, Imbrie J, Rhind D (1989) Climate change in the circum-North Atlantic region during the last deglaciation. *Nature* **338**: 553–7

Page R A, Cawse P A, Baker S J (1988) The effect of reducing lead emissions on airborne lead in Wales, UK. *Science of the Total Environment* **68**: 71–7

Pain S (1988) No escape from the global greenhouse. *New Scientist* **120** (1638): 38–43

Palmer R (1977) The agricultural history of Rhodesia. In Palmer R, Parsons N (eds) *The roots of rural poverty in central and southern Africa.* Heinemann, London, pp 221–55

Park C C (1987) *Acid rain: rhetoric and reality.* Methuen, London

Park C C (1988) Acid rain: trans-frontier air pollution. *Geography Review* **2**: 20–4

Parker A (1983a) Behaviour of wastes in landfill–methane generation. In Holmes J R (ed) *Practical waste management.* John Wiley, Chichester, pp 223–34

Parker A (1983b) Behaviour of wastes in landfill–leachate. In Holmes J R (ed) *Practical waste management.* John Wiley, Chichester, pp 209–22

Parry M L (1978) *Climatic change and agricultural settlement.* Archon Books, Folkestone, UK

Parry M L, Carter T R (1988) The assessment of effects of climatic variations on agriculture: a summary of results from studies in semi-arid regions. In Parry M L, Carter T R, Konijn N T (eds) *The impact of climatic variations on agriculture* (2 vols). Kluwer Academic Publishers, Dordrecht, vol 2 *Assessments in semi-arid regions* pp 9–60

Parry M L, Carter T R, Konijn N J (eds) (1988) *The impact of climatic variations on agriculture.* vol 1 *Assessments in cool temperate and cold regions*, vol 2 *Assessments in semi-arid regions.* Kluwer Academic Publishers, Dordrecht

Pastor J, Post W M (1988) Response of northern forests to CO_2-induced climate change. *Nature* **334**: 55–8

Paterson W S B, Hammer C U (1987) Ice core and other glaciological data. In Ruddiman W F, Wright Jr H E (eds) *North America and adjacent oceans during the last deglaciation.* Geological Society of America, Boulder, Colorado, pp 91–109

Payne C C (1988) Pathogens for the control of insects: where next? *Philosophical Transactions of the Royal Society of London* **B318**: 225–48

Pearce D (1987) *Tourism today.* Longman, London

Pearce F (1989) Methane: the hidden greenhouse gas. *New Scientist* **122** (1663): 37–41

Pearce F, Anderson I (1989) Is there an ozone hole over the North Pole? *New Scientist* **121** (1653): 32–3

Pearce R H, Barbetti M (1981) A 38,000 year old archaeological site at Upper Swan, Western Australia. *Archaeology in Oceania* **15**: 173–8

Peck A, Thomas J, Williamson D (1983) *Salinity issues, Water 2000.* Consultants Report No.8 Australian Government Publishing Service, Canberra

Peel D A (1989) Ice-age clues for a warmer world. *Nature* **339**: 508–9

Penck A, Brückner E (1909) *Die Alpen im Eiszeitalter.* Tauchnitz, Leipzig

Pennington W (1977) The Late Devensian flora and vegetation of Britain. *Philosophical Transactions of the Royal Society of London* **B280**: 247–71

Perpich J G (1989) Biotechnology, international competition and regulatory strategies. In Marx J L (ed) *A revolution in biotechnology*. Cambridge University Press, Cambridge, pp 197–209

Perry I, Moore P D (1987) Dutch elm disease as an analogue of neolithic elm decline. *Nature* **326**: 72–3

Persson G A (1987) Acid deposition. In McLaren D J, Skinner B J (eds) *Resources and world development*. John Wiley, Chichester, pp 415–22

Peteet D M (1987a) Paleoenvironmental shift in maritime Canada parallels Europe. *Trends in Ecology and Evolution* **2**: 86–7

Peteet D M (1987b) Younger Dryas in North America – modelling, data analysis, and re-evaluation. In Berger W H, Labeyrie L D (eds) *Abrupt climatic change*. D Reidel, Dordrecht, pp 185–93

Peterkin G F (1983) Woodland conservation in Britain. In Warren A, Goldsmith F B (eds) *Conservation in perspective*. John Wiley, Chichester, pp 83–100

Petts G E (1988) Water management: the case of Lake Biwa, Japan. *Geographical Journal* **154**: 367–76

Pfister C (1978) Fluctuations in the duration of snow-cover in Switzerland since the late seventeenth century. In Frydendahl K (ed) *Proceedings of the Nordic symposium on climatic changes and related problems*. Danish Meteorological Institute Climatological Papers No. 4, Copenhagen, pp 1–6

Pfister C (1984) The potential of documentary data for the reconstruction of past climates. Early 16th to 19th century Switzerland as a case study. In Mörner N-A, Karlén W (eds) *Climatic changes on a yearly to millenial basis*. D Reidel, Dordrecht, pp 331–7

Pickett J A (1988) Integrating use of beneficial organisms with chemical crop protection. *Philosophical Transactions of the Royal Society of London* **B318**: 203–11

Pigram J J (1986) *Issues in the management of Australia's water resources*. Longman Cheshire, Melbourne

Pimentel D plus thirteen others (1987) World agriculture and soil erosion. *Bioscience* **37**: 277–83

Pitovranov S E, Iakimets V, Kiselev V I, Sirotenko O D (1988) The effects of climatic variations on agriculture in the subarctic zone of the USSR. In Parry M L, Carter T R, Konijn N T (eds) *The impact of climatic variations on agriculture* (2 vols). Kluwer Academic Publishers, Dordrecht, vol 1 *Assessments in cool temperate and cold regions* pp 615- 722

Pittock A B (1988) Actual and anticipated changes in Australia's climate. In Pearman G I (ed) *Greenhouse: planning for climatic change*. CSIRO Division of Atmospheric Research, East Melbourne, Australia, pp 35–51

Pla I, Florentino A, Lobo D (1985) Soil and water conservation problems in the central plains of Venezuela. In El-Swaify S A, Moldenhauer W C, Lo A (eds) *Soil erosion and conservation*. Soil Conservation Society of America, Ankeny, Iowa, pp 66–78

Pokras E M, Mix A C (1987) Earth's precession cycle and Quaternary climatic change in tropical Africa. *Nature* **326**: 486–7

Pooley F D (1987) Mineral leaching with bacteria. In Forster C F, Wase D A J (eds) *Environmental biotechnology*. Ellis Horwood, Chichester, pp 114–34

Population Reference Bureau (1987) *Human needs and nature's balance: population, resources and environment*. Population Reference Bureau, Washington DC

von Post L (1916) Om skogsträdspollen i sydsvenska forfmosselagerföljder (föredragsreferat). *Geologiska Föreningens Stockholm Förhandlingar* **38**: 384–94

Potter C (1988) Making waves: farm extensification and conservation. *Ecos* **9**: 32–7

Potter T W (1987) *Roman Italy*. British Museum Publications, London

Potts G R (1986) *The partridge: pesticides, predation and conservation*. Collins, London

Potts R (1984) Hominid hunters? Problems of identifying the earliest hunter/gatherers. In Foley R (ed) *Hominid evolution and community ecology* Academic Press, London, pp 129–92

Powell J M (1976) *Environmental management in Australia 1788–1914*. Oxford University Press, Melbourne

Price T D (1987) The mesolithic of Western Europe. *Journal of World Prehistory* **1**: 225–305

Prince H (1981) Victorian rural landscapes. In Mingay G E (ed) *The Victorian countryside* (2 vols). Routledge and Kegan Paul, London, vol 1 pp 17–29

Protsch R, Berger R (1973) Earliest radiocarbon dates for domesticated animals. *Science* **179**: 235–9

Quivira M P, Dillehay T D (1988) Monte Verde, south-central Chile: stratigraphy, climate change, and human settlement. *Geoarchaeology* **3**: 177–91

Rackham O (1980) *Ancient woodland: its history, vegetation and uses in England*. Edward Arnold, London

Rackham O (1985) Ancient woodland and hedges in England. In Woodell S R J (ed) *The English landscape: past, present and future*. Oxford University Press, Oxford, pp 68–105

Rackham O (1986) *The history of the countryside*. Dent, London

Ramade F (1987) *Ecotoxicology*. John Wiley, Chichester

Ramanathan V (1988) The greenhouse theory of climatic change: a test by an inadvertent global experiment. *Science* **240**: 293–9

Ramanathan V, Cess R D, Harrison E F, Minnis P, Barkstrom B R, Ahmed E, Hartmann D (1989) Cloud-radiative forcing and climate: results from the earth radiation budget experiment. *Science* **243**: 57–63

Ramsay G D (1982) *The English woollen industry 1500–1750*. Macmillan, London

Rapp A (1987) Desertification. In Gregory K J, Walling D E (eds) *Human activity and environmental processes*. John Wiley, Chichester, pp 425–43

Rapport D J, Regier H A, Hutchinson T C (1985) Ecosystem behaviour under stress. *American Naturalist* **125**: 617–40

Rasmussen R A, Khalil M A K (1984) Atmospheric methane in the recent and ancient atmospheres: concentrations, trends and interhemisphere gradient. *Journal of Geophysical Research* **89**: 11599–605

Ratcliffe D A (1984) Post-medieval and recent changes in British vegetation: the culmination of human influence. *New Phytologist* **98**: 73–100

Ratcliffe D A, Oswald P H (eds) (1987) *Birds, bogs and forestry: the peatlands of Caithness and Sutherland*. Nature Conservancy Council, Edinburgh

Raynaud D, Chappellaz J, Barnola J M, Korotkevich Y S, Lorius C (1988) Climate and CH$_4$ change in the Vostok ice core. *Nature* **333**: 655–7

Rees J (1987) Agriculture and horticulture. In Wacher J (ed) *The Roman world* (2 vols). Routledge and Kegan Paul, London, vol II pp 481–503

Reggiani G (1983) Anatomy of a TCDD spill: the Seveso accident. In Saxena J (ed) *Hazard assessment of chemicals*. Academic Press, London, pp 269–311

Renberg I, Wallin J-E (1985) The history of the acidification of Lake Gårdsjön as deduced from diatoms and *Sphagnum* leaves in the sediment. *Ecological Bulletins, Stockholm* **37**: 47–52

Renberg I, Wik M (1985a) Carbonaceous particles in lake sediments–pollutants from fossil fuel combustion. *Ambio* **14**: 161–3

Renberg I, Wik M (1985b) Soot particle counting in recent lake sediments: an indirect dating method. *Ecological Bulletins, Stockholm* **37**: 53–7

Repetto R (1988a) Overview. In Repetto R, Gillis M (eds) *Public policies and the misuse of forest resources*. Cambridge University Press, Cambridge, pp 1–41

Repetto R (1988b) Subsidized timber sales from national forest lands in the United States. In Repetto R, Gillis M (eds) *Public policies and the misuse of forest resources*. Cambridge University Press, Cambridge, pp 353–83

Rhodes D W (1986) Rehabilitation of opal mining areas, Lightning Ridge, New South Wales. In Joss P J, Lynch P W, Williams O B (eds) *Rangelands: a resource under siege*. Cambridge University Press, Cambridge, pp 172–3

Richards E G (ed) (1987) *Forestry and the forest industries*. Martinus Nijhoff Publishers, Dordrecht, for the United Nations

Richards J F (1987) Environmental changes in Dehra Dun Valley, India. *Mountain Research and Development* **7**: 299–304

Richards K (1989) All gas and garbage. *New Scientist* **122** (1667): 38–41

Richards P (1985) *Indigenous agricultural revolution*. Hutchinson, London

Richards P W (1986) The nature of tropical forest ecosystems. In Polunin N (ed) *Ecosystem theory and application*. John Wiley, Chichester, pp 131–44

Rickard J (1988) *Australia: a cultural history*. Longman, London

Rind D, Peteet D, Broecker W, McIntyre A, Ruddiman W (1986) The impact of cold North Atlantic sea surface temperatures on climate: implications for the Younger Dryas cooling (11–10k). *Climate Dynamics* **1**: 3–33

Ritchie J C (1988) *Postglacial vegetation of Canada*. Cambridge University Press, Cambridge

Roberts L (1989) How fast can trees migrate? *Science* **243**: 735–7

Roberts N (1989) *The Holocene: an environmental history*. Blackwell, Oxford

Robin G de Q (1986) Changing the sea level. In Bolin B, Döös B R, Jäger, Warrick R A (eds) *The greenhouse effect, climatic change and ecosystems*. John Wiley, Chichester, pp 323–59

Robinson D A (1978) *Soil erosion and soil conservation in Zambia: a geographical appraisal*. Zambia Geographical Association, Occasional Study No. 9

Robinson M (1986) Changes in catchment runoff following drainage and afforestation. *Journal of Hydrology* **86**: 71–84

Rodhe H, Cowling E, Galbally I E, Galloway J N, Herrera R (1988) Acidification and regional air pollution in the tropics. In Rodhe H, Herrera R (eds) *Acidification in tropical countries*. John Wiley, Chichester, pp 3–39

Rodriguez S (1987) Impact of the ski industry on the Rio Hondo watershed. *Annals of Tourism Research* **14**: 88–103

Rojas E, Wirtshafter R M, Radke J, Hosier R (1988) Land conservation in small developing countries. *Ambio* **17**: 282–8

Ronen D, Magaritz M, Almon E (1988) Contaminated aquifers are a forgotten component of the global N_2O budget. *Nature* **335**: 57–9

Roose E J (1986) Runoff and erosion before and after clearing depending on the type of crop in western Africa. In Lal R, Sanchez P A, Cummings R W (eds) *Land clearing and development in the tropics*. A A Balkema, Rotterdam, pp 317– 29

Ross M S (1986) The development and current status of land clearing for transmigration in Indonesia. In Lal R, Sanchez P A, Cummings R W (eds) *Land clearing and development in the tropics*. A A Balkema, Rotterdam, pp 119–30

Rowland F S (1986) Chlorofluorocarbons and the Antarctic 'ozone hole'. *Environmental Conservation* **13**: 193–4

Rowland F S (1988) Chlorofluorocarbons, stratospheric ozone, and the Antarctic 'ozone hole'. *Environmental Conservation* **15**: 101–15

Rowley-Conwy P (1984) The laziness of the short-distance hunter: the origins of agriculture in western Denmark. *Journal of Anthropological Archaeology* **3**: 300–24

Roxburgh I S (1987) *Geology of high-level nuclear waste disposal: an introduction*. Chapman and Hall, London

Royal Commission on Environmental Pollution (1979) *Agriculture and pollution*. 7th report. HMSO, London

Ruangpanit N (1985) Percent crown cover related to water and soil losses in mountainous forest in Thailand. In El-Swaify S A, Moldenhauer W C, Lo A (eds) *Soil erosion and conservation*. Soil Conservation Society of America, Ankeny, Iowa, pp 462–71

Rudd J W M, Kelly C A, Schindler D W, Turner M A (1988) Disruption of the nitrogen cycle in acidified lakes. *Science* **240**: 1515–17

Ruddiman W F, McIntyre A (1981) The North Atlantic during the last deglaciation. *Palaeogeography Palaeoclimatology Palaeoecology* **35**: 145–214

Ruddiman W F, McIntyre A, Raymo M (1986) Matuyama 41,000-year cycles: North Atlantic ocean and northern hemisphere icesheets. *Earth and Planetary Science Letters* **80**: 117–29

Ruddiman W F, Raymo M E (1988) Northern hemisphere climate régimes during the past 3 Ma: possible tectonic connections. *Philosophical Transactions of the Royal Society of London* **B318**: 411–30

Rukang W, Olsen J W (eds) (1985) *Palaeoanthropology and palaeolithic archaeology in the People's Republic of China* Academic Press, London

Rukang W, Xingren D (1985) *Homo erectus* in China. In Rukang W, Olsen J W (eds) *Palaeoanthropology and palaeolithic archaeology in the People's Republic of China*, Academic Press, London, pp 79–89

Rull V, Salgado-Labouriau M L, Schubert C, Valastro S Jr (1987) Late Holocene temperature depression in the Venezuelan Andes: palynological evidence. *Palaeogeography Palaeoclimatology Palaeoecology* **60**: 109–21

Russell A M (1988) *The biotechnology revolution*. Wheatsheaf Books, Sussex

Russell J S (1988) The effect of climatic change on the productivity of Australian agroecosystems. In Pearman G I (ed) *Greenhouse: planning for climatic change*. CSIRO Division of Atmospheric Research, East Melbourne, Australia, pp 491–505

Russell-Wood A J R (1987) The gold cycle, *c.* 1690–1750. In Bethell L (ed) *Colonial Brazil*. Cambridge University Press, Cambridge, pp 190–243

Sabadell J E (1988) Desertification in the United States and Pakistan: variations on a theme. In Whitehead E E, Hutchinson C F, Timmermann B N, Varady R G (eds) *Arid lands: today and tomorrow*. Westview Press, Boulder, Colorado, and Belhaven Press, London, pp 621–31

Saigne C, Legrand M (1987) Measurements of methanesulphonic acid in Antarctic ice. *Nature* **330**: 240–2

Salati E, Vose P B (1983) Depletion of tropical rain forests. *Ambio* **12**: 67–71

Salinger M J (1976) New Zealand temperatures since 1300 AD. *Nature* **260**: 310–11

Sanhueza E, Cuenca G, Gómez M J, Herrera R, Ishizaki C, Martí J, Paolini J (1988) Characteristics of the Venezuelan environment and its potential for acidification. In Rodhe H, Herrera R (eds) *Acidification in tropical countries*. John Wiley, Chichester, pp 197–255

Sandbach F (1980) *Environment, ideology and policy*. Blackwell, Oxford

Sanderson J B (1974) The National Smoke Abatement Society and the Clean Air Act (1956). In Kimber R, Richardson J J (eds) *Campaigning for the environment*. Routledge and Kegan Paul, London, pp 27–44

Sattaur O (1989) Grass grows into a hedge against erosion. *New Scientist* **122** (1664): 38–9

Saunders D, Hobbs R (1989) Corridors for conservation. *New Scientist* **121** (1649): 63–8

Saunders J J (1987) Britain's newest mammoths. *Nature* **330**: 419

Schell, J, Gronenborn B, Fraley R T (1989) Improving crop plants by the introduction of isolated genes. In Marx J L (ed) *A revolution in biotechnology*. Cambridge University Press, Cambridge, pp 130–44

Schell W R (1986) Deposited atmospheric chemicals. *Environmental Science and Technology* **20**: 847–53

Schindler D W (1987) Recovery of Canadian lakes from acidification. In Barth H (ed) *Reversibility of acidification*. Elsevier, London, pp 2–13

Schindler D W (1988) Effects of acid rain on freshwater ecosystems. *Science* **239**: 149–57

Schneider S H (1989) The greenhouse effect: science and policy. *Science* **243**: 771–81

Schwartz S B (1985) *Sugar plantations in the formation of Brazilian society. Bahia, 1550–1835*. Cambridge University Press, Cambridge

Schwartz S B (1987) Plantation and peripheries, *c*. 1580–1750. In Bethell L (ed) *Colonial Brazil*. Cambridge University Press, Cambridge pp. 67–144

Schwartz S E (1988) Are global cloud albedo and climate controlled by marine phytoplankton? *Nature* **336**: 441–5

Schwartz S E (1989) Acid deposition: unravelling a regional phenomenom. *Science* **243**: 753–62

Schweinfurth U (1984) The Himalaya: complexity of a mountain system manifested by its vegetation. *Mountain Research and Development* **4**: 339–44

Scott G A J (1987) Shifting cultivation where land is limited. In Jordan C F (ed) *Amazonian rain forests*. Springer-Verlag, New York, pp 34–45

Sedjo R A (1987) Forest resources of the world: forests in transition. In Kallio M, Dykstra D P, Binkley C S (eds) *The global forest sector: an analytical perspective*. John Wiley, Chichester, pp 7–31

Sedjo R A, Clawson M (1984) Global forests. In Simon J L, Kahn H (eds) *Resourceful earth*. Blackwell, Oxford, pp 128–70

Senshui Z (1985) The early palaeolithic of China. In Rukang W, Olsen J W (eds) *Palaeoanthropology and palaeolithic archaeology in the People's Republic of China*. Academic Press, London, pp 147–86

Sernander R (1908) On the evidence of postglacial changes of climate furnished by the peatmosses of northern Europe. *Geologiska Föreningens Stockholm Föröhandlingar* **30**: 465–78

Shackleton N J, Imbrie J, Hall M A (1983) Oxygen and carbon isotope record of East Pacific core V19-30: implications for the formation of deep water in the late Pleistocene North Atlantic. *Earth and Planetary Science Letters* **65**: 233–44

Shackleton N J, Opdyke N D (1973) Oxygen-isotope and paleomagnetic stratigraphy of Pacific core V28-239, Late Pliocene to latest Pleistocene. In Cline R M, Hays J D (eds) *Investigation of late Quaternary paleogeography and paleoecology*. Geological Society of America Memoir No. 145, Boulder, Colorado, pp 449–64

Shackleton N J plus sixteen others (1984) Oxygen isotope calibration of the onset of ice-rafting and history of glaciation in the North Atlantic region. *Nature* **307**: 620–3

Shanan L (1987) The impact of irrigation. In Wolman M G, Fournier F G A (eds) *Land transformation in agriculture*. John Wiley, Chichester, pp 115–31

Shea S P (1988) Shifting to renewable energy. In *State of the world (1988): a Worldwatch Institute Report on progress towards a sustainable society*. W W Norton New York, pp 62–82

Sheail J (1985) *Pesticides and nature conservation: the British experience*. Clarendon Press, Oxford

Sheail J (1987) *Seventy-five years in ecology: the British Ecological Society*. Blackwell, Oxford

Shen G T, Boyle E A (1987) Lead in corals: reconstruction of historical fluxes to the surface ocean. *Earth and Planetary Science Letters*. **82**: 289–304

Sherratt A (1981) Plough and pastoralism: aspects of the secondary products revolution. In Hodder I, Isaac G, Hammond N (eds) *Pattern of the past: studies in honour of David Clark*. Cambridge University Press, Cambridge, pp 261–305

Shipman P, Bosler W, Davis K L (1981) Butchering of giant geladas at an acheulian site. *Current Anthropology* **22**: 257–68

Shoard M (1980) *The theft of the countryside*. Temple-Smith, London

Shoard M (1987) *This land is our land*. Paladin Grafton Books, London

Šibrava V (1986) Correlation of European glaciations and their relation to the deep sea record. *Quaternary Science Reviews* **5**: 433–41

Šibrava V, Bowen D Q, Richmond G M (eds) (1986) Quaternary glaciations in the northern hemisphere. *Quaternary Science Reviews* **5**.

Siegenthaler U, Oeschger H (1987) Biospheric CO_2 emissions during the past 200 years reconstructed by deconvolution of ice core data. *Tellus* **39B**: 140–54

Simmons I G (1975) The ecological setting of mesolithic man in the highland zone. In Evans J G, Limbrey S, Cleere H (eds) *The effect of man on the landscape: the highland zone*. Council for British Archaeological Research Reports, Oxford, No. 11 pp 57–63

Simmons I G (1979) *Biogeography: natural and cultural*. Edward Arnold, London

Simmons I G (1983) Mesolithic man and environment in upland Britain: an historiographic approach. In Briggs D G, Waters R S (eds) *Studies in Quaternary geomorphology*. Geobooks, Norwich, pp 215–22

Simmons I G, Dimbleby G W (1974) The possible role of ivy (*Hedera helix L.*) in the mesolithic economy of western Europe. *Journal of Archaeological Science* **1**: 291–6

Simmons I G, Innes J B (1985) Late mesolithic land-use and its impacts in the English uplands. *Biogeographical Monographs* **2**: 7-17

Simmons I G, Innes J B (1987) Mid-Holocene adaptations and later mesolithic forest disturbance in Northern England. *Journal of Archaeological Science* **14**: 385–403

Simons P (1988) Costa Rica's forests are reborn. *New Scientist* **120** (1635): 43–7

Sioli H (1985) The effects of deforestation in Amazonia. *Geographical Journal* **151**: 197–203

Skiba U, Cresser M (1988) The ecological significance of increasing atmospheric carbon dioxide. *Endeavour* **12**: 143–7

Skiba U, Cresser M S, Derwent R G, Fulty D W (1989) Peat acidification in Scotland. *Nature* **337**: 68–9

Skinner F A (1985) Agriculture and biotechnology. In Higgins I J, Best D J, Jones J (eds) *Biotechnology: principles and applications.* Blackwell, Oxford, pp 305–45

Skinner J H, Bassin N J (1988) The Environmental Protection Agency's hazardous waste research and development program. *Ambio* **38**: 377–87

Smil V (1984) *The Bad Earth.* M E Sharpe Inc, Armonk, New York, and Zed Press, London

Smil V (1987a) Fossil-fuelled civilization and the atmosphere. In McLaren D J, Skinner B J (eds) *Resources and world development.* John Wiley, Chichester, pp 363–75

Smil V (1987b) *Energy, food, environment.* Clarendon Press, Oxford

Smit B, Ludlow L, Brklacich M (1988) Implications of a global climatic warming for agriculture: a review and appraisal. *Journal of Environmental Quality* **17**: 519–27

Smith A G (1970) The influence of mesolithic and neolithic man on British vegetation: a discussion. In Walker D, West R G (eds) *Studies in the vegetational history of the British Isles: essays in honour of Harry Godwin.* Cambridge University Press, Cambridge, pp 81–96

Smith A G (1981) The neolithic. In Simmons I G, Tooley M J (eds) *The environment in British prehistory.* Duckworth, London, pp 125–209

Smith A G (1984) Newferry and the boreal–Atlantic transition. *New Phytologist* **98**: 35–55

Smith D M (1986) *The practice of silviculture* 8th edn. John Wiley, New York

Smith G I, Street–Perrott F A (1983) Pluvial lakes of the western United States. In Wright Jr H E (ed) *Late–Quaternary environments of the United States* (2 vols). University of Minnesota Press; Minneapolis and Longman; London, vol 1 *The Late Pleistocene* pp 190–212

Smith R A, Alexander R B, Wolman M G (1987) Water–quality trends in the nation's rivers. *Science* **235**: 1607–15

Smith S (1986) Assessing the ecological and health effects of pollution. In Hester R E (ed) *Understanding our environment.* Royal Society of Chemistry, London, pp 226–94

Smith W E, Smith A M (1975) *Minamata.* Holt, Rinehart and Winston, New York

Smithson P (1988) Carbon dioxide and our environment. *Geography Review* **2**: 30–3

Soemarwoto O (1987) Homegardens: a traditional agroforestry system with a promising future. In Steppler H A, Nair P K R (eds) *Agroforestry: a decade of development*. International Council for Research in Agroforestry, Nairobi, pp 157–70

Songqiao Z (1986) *Physical geography of China*. Science Press, Beijing, and John Wiley, New York

Songqiao Z (1988) Human impacts on China's arid lands: desertification or de–desertification. In Whitehead E E, Hutchinson C F, Timmermann B N, Vardy R G (eds) *Arid lands: today and tomorrow*. Westview Press, Boulder, Colorado and Belhaven Press, London, pp 1127–35

Southerton N W, Rands M R W (1987) The environmental interest of field margins to game and other wildlife: a Game Conservancy view. In Way J M, Greig–Smith P W (eds) *Field Margins*. British Crop Protection Council, Thornton Heath, pp 67–75

Speirs R B, Frost C A (1987) Soil water erosion on arable land in the United Kingdom. *Research and Development in Agriculture* **4**: 1–11

Spencer J E, Thomas W L (1978) *Introducing cultural geography* (2nd edn). John Wiley, New York

Spiegel–Roy P (1986) Domestication of fruit trees. In Barigozzi C (ed) *The origin and domestication of cultivated plants*. Elsevier, Amsterdam, pp 201–11

Stadel C (1986) Del Valle Al Monte: altitudinal patterns of agricultural activities in the Patate–Pelileo area of Ecuador. *Mountain Research and Development* **6**: 53–64

Stanhill G (1986) Irrigation in arid lands. *Philosophical Transactions of the Royal Society of London* **A316**: 261–73

Stauffer B, Fischer G, Neftel A, Oeschger H (1985) Increase of atmospheric methane recorded in Antarctic ice core. *Science* **229**: 1386–88

Stauffer B, Lochbronner E, Oeschger H, Schwander J (1988) Methane concentration in the glacial atmosphere was only half that of the preindustrial Holocene. *Nature* **332**: 812–4

Steenvoorden J H A M, Bouma J (1987) Optimizing the use of soils: new agricultural and water management aspects. In Barth H, L'Hermite P (eds) *Scientific basis for soil protection in the European Community*. Elsevier, London, pp 389–408

Stein V (1987) Terrestrial effects arising from the extraction and processing of solid fuels and non–fuel minerals. In McLaren D J, Skinner B J (eds) *Resources and world development*. John Wiley, Chichester, pp 399–413

Stewart P J (1987) *Growing against the grain: United Kingdom forestry policy 1987*. Council for the Protection of Rural England, London

Stocking M A (1975) Soil erosion potential: the overview. In *Engineering Handbook*. Government Printer, Salisbury, Rhodesia

Stocking M (1985) Soil conservation policy in colonial Africa. In Helms D, Flader S L (eds) *A history of soil and water conservation*. The Agricultural History Society, Washington DC, pp 46–59

Stoermer E F, Kociolek J P, Schelske C L, Conley D J (1985a) Siliceous microfossil succession in the recent history of Lake Superior. *Proceedings of the Academy of Natural Sciences of Philadelphia* **137**: 106–18

Stoermer E F, Wolin J A, Schelske C L, Conley D J (1985b) An assessment of ecological changes during the recent history of Lake Ontario based on siliceous algal microfossils preserved in sediments. *Journal of Phycology* **21**: 257–76

Stohlgren T J, Parsons D J (1986) Vegetation and soil recovery in wilderness campsites closed to visitor use. *Environmental Management* **10**: 375–80

Stolarski R S (1988) The Antarctic ozone hole. *Scientific American* **258**: 20–6

Stolarski R S, Kreuger A J, Schoeberl M R, McPeters R D, Newman P A, Alpert J C (1986) Nimbus-7 satellite measurements of the springtime Antarctic ozone decrease. *Nature* **322**: 808–11

Stoner J H, Gee A S (1985) Effects of forestry on water quality and fish in Welsh rivers and lakes. *Journal of Institute of Water Engineering Science* **39**: 27–45

Strahler A N, Strahler A H (1989) *Elements of physical geography* 4th edn. John Wiley, New York

Strange R C (1988) Radioactive waste disposal. *Radiological Bulletin* **88**: 10–14

Street-Perrott F A, Harrison S P (1985) Lake–levels and climate reconstruction. In Hecht A D (ed) *Paleoclimate analysis and modeling*. John Wiley Inc, International, pp 291–340

Stringer C B (1986) The British fossil hominid record. In Collcut S N (ed) *The palaeolithic of Britain and its nearest neighbours*. Department of Archaeology and Prehistory, University of Sheffield, pp 59–61

Stringer C B, Andrews P (1988) Genetic and fossil evidence for the origin of modern humans. *Science* **239**: 1263–68

Strong A E (1989) Greater global warming revealed by satellite–derived sea–surface–temperature trends. *Nature* **338**: 642–5

Stuart A J (1982) *Pleistocene vertebrates in the British Isles*. Longman, London

Sugden D (1988) Will the West Antarctic ice sheet collapse? *Geography Review* **2**: 26–30

Sutcliffe A J (1985) *On the track of Ice Age mammals*. British Museum (Natural History); London

Suwardjo A (1986) Land development for transmigration areas in Sumatra and Kalimantan. In Lal R, Sanchez P A, Cummings R W (eds) *Land clearing and development in the tropics*. A A Balkema, Rotterdam, pp 131–9

Swaminathan M S (1987) The promise of agroforestry for ecological and nutritional security. In Steppler H A, Nair P K R (eds) *Agroforestry: a decade of development*. International Council for Research in Agroforestry, Nairobi, pp 25–41

Szegi J, Olàh J, Fekete G, Halàsz T, Vàrallyay G, Bartha S (1988) Recultivation of the spoil banks created by open–cut mining activities in Hungary. *Ambio* **17**: 137–43

Tacey W H, Glossop B L (1980) Assessment of topsoil handling techniques for rehabilitation of sites mined for bauxite within the jarrah forest of Western Australia. *Journal of Applied Ecology* **17**: 195–201

Tallis J H (1985) Erosion of blanket peat in the southern Pennines: new light on an old problem. In Johnson R H (ed) *The geomorphology of North-West England*. Manchester University Press, Manchester, pp 313–36

Tallis J H (1987) Fire and flood at Holme Moss: erosion processes in an upland blanket mire. *Journal of Ecology* **75**: 1099–129

Tanabe S (1988) PCB problems in the future: foresight from current knowledge. *Environmental Pollution* **50**: 5–28

Tandeter E (1987) Forced and free labour in late–colonial Potosí. In Archetti E P, Cammack P, Roberts B (eds) *Sociology of 'developing societies' Latin America*. Macmillan Education, Basingstoke, pp 26–33

Tang H T (1987) Problems and strategies for regenerating dipterocarp forests in Malaysia. In Mergen F, Vincent J R (eds) *Natural management of tropical moist forests*. Yale University School of Forestry and Environmental Studies, New Haven, Connecticut, pp 23–45

Tansley A G (1935) The use and abuse of vegetational concepts and terms. *Ecology* **16**: 284–307

Tarrant J R (1987) Variability in world cereal yields. *Transactions of the Institute of British Geographers* New Series **12**: 315–26

Tejwani K G (1987a) Watershed management in the Indian Himalaya. In Khoshoo T N (ed) *Perspectives in environmental management*. Oxford and IBH Publishing PVT, New Delhi, pp 203–27

Tejwani K G (1987b) Sedimentation of reservoirs in the Himalayan region – India. *Mountain Research and Development* **7**: 323–27

Thirsk J (1987) *England's agricultural regions and agrarian history, 1500–1750*. Macmillan, London

Thomas B (1987) Pesticide registration: benefit or bureaucracy? In Brent K J, Atkin R K (eds) *Rational pesticide use*. Cambridge University Press, Cambridge, pp 43–50

Thompson F M L (1985) Towns, industry and the Victorian landscape. In Woodell S R J (ed) *The English landscape; past, present and future*. Oxford University Press, Oxford, pp 168–187

Thompson L G, Mosley-Thompson E (1987) Evidence of abrupt climatic change during the last 1,500 years recorded in ice cores from the tropical Quelccaya ice cap, Peru. In Berger W H, Labeyrie L D (eds) *Abrupt climatic change*. D Reidel, Dordrecht, pp 99–110

Thompson L G, Mosley-Thompson E, Dansgaard W, Grootes P M (1986) The Little Ice Age as recorded in the stratigraphy of the tropical Quelccaya ice cap. *Science* **234**: 361–4

Thompson M, Warburton M, Hatley T (1986) *Uncertainty on a Himalaya scale*. Ethnographica, London

Thompson R D, Mannion A M, Mitchell C W, Parry M, Townshend J R G (1986) *Processes in physical geography*. Longman, London

Times, The (1982) *Concise atlas of world history*. Barraclough G (ed). Times Books, London

Times, The (1986) *The world: an illustrated history*. Parker G (ed). Times Books/Channel Four, London

Todd M (1987) *The South-West to AD 1000*. Longman, London

Todini E, Bizzarri A (1988) Case study: eutrophication in the coastal area of the Regione Emilia Romagna. In *Eutrophication in the Mediterranean Sea: receiving capacity and monitoring of long-term effects*. Unesco Reports in Marine Science No 49, pp 143–152

Tolba M K (1987) Guest comment: the ozone agreement – and beyond. *Environmental Conservation* **14**: 287–90

Tolonen K, Liukkonen M, Harjula R, Pätilä A (1986) Acidification of small lakes in Finland documented by sedimentary diatom and Chrysophycean remains. In Smol J P, Battarbee R W, Davis R B, Meriläinen J (eds) *Diatoms and lake acidity*. Dr W Junk, Dordrecht, pp 169–99

Toy T J, Hadley R F (1987) *Geomorphology and reclamation of disturbed lands*. Academic Press, New York

Troels–Smith J (1956) Neolithic period in Denmark and Switzerland. *Science* **124**: 876–9

Troels–Smith J (1960) Ivy, mistletoe and elm: climatic indicators–fodder plants: a contribution to the interpretation of the pollen zone border VII–VIII. *Danmarks Geologiske Undersøgelse* Series **4**: 1–32

Tucker R P (1987) Dimensions of deforestation in the Himalaya: historical setting. *Mountain Research and Development* **7**: 328–331

Tudge C (1988) *Food crops for the future*. Blackwell, Oxford

Tuite C H (1982) *The impact of water-based recreation on the waterfowl of enclosed inland waters in Britain* (Report). Sports Council, London, and Nature Conservancy Council, Peterborough

Tungsheng L, Shouxin Z, Jiaomao H (1986) Stratigraphy and paleoenvironmental changes in the loess of central China. *Quaternary Science Reviews*. **5**: 489–501

Turner A (1984) Hominids and fellow-travellers: human migration into high latitudes as part of a large mammal community. In Foley R (ed) *Hominid evolution and community ecology*. Academic Press, London, pp 193–217

Turner C (1970) The Middle Pleistocene deposits as Marks Tey, Essex. *Philosophical Transactions of the Royal Society of London* **B257**: 373–440

Turner C, Hannon G E (1988) Vegetational evidence for late Quaternary climatic changes in southwest Europe in relation to the influence of the North Atlantic ocean. *Philosophical Transactions of the Royal Society of London* **B318**: 451–85

Turner J (1981) The vegetation. In Jones M, Dimbleby G W (eds) *The environment of man: the Iron Age to the Anglo-Saxon period*. British Archaeological Research Reports (British Series), Oxford, No 87, pp 67–73

Tyldesley J A, Bahn P G (1983) Use of plants in the European palaeolithic: a review of the evidence. *Quaternary Science Reviews* **2**: 53–81

United Nations (1986) *World population prospects: estimation and projections as assessed in 1984*. United nations, New York

United Nations Environment Programme (1987) *Montreal protocol on substances that deplete the ozone layer*. UNEP, Nairobi

Unruh J D (1988) Ecological aspects of site recovery under swidden–fallow management in the Peruvian Amazon. *Agroforestry Systems* **7**: 161–84

Vail L (1977) Ecology and history: the example of eastern Zambia. *Journal of Southern African Studies* **3**: 129–55

Vail L (1983) The political economy of East-Central Africa. In Birmingham D, Martin P M (eds) *History of Central Africa*. Longman, London, vol 2 pp 200–50

Valladas H, Reyss J L, Joron J L, Valladas G, Bar-Yosef O, Vandermeersch B (1988) Thermoluminescence dating of Mousterian 'Proto–Cro–Magnon' remains from Israel and the origin of modern man. *Nature* **331**: 614

Van Dyke J M (1988) Ocean disposal of nuclear wastes. *Marine Policy* **12**: 82–95

Van Zeist W, Woldring H, Stapert D (1975) Late Quaternary vegetation and climate of south-western Turkey. *Palaeohistoria* **17**: 55–143

Vera R R, Sere C, Tergas L E (1986) Development of improved grazing systems in the savannas of tropical America. In Joss P J, Lynch P W, Williams O B (eds) *Rangelands: a resource under siege*. Cambridge University Press, Cambridge, pp 107–110

Vogal R J (1980) The ecological factors that produce perturbation-dependent ecosystems. In Cairns Jr J (ed) *The recovery process in damaged ecosystems*. Ann Arbor Science, Ann Arbor, Michigan, pp 63–94

Von Richtofen B F (1882) On the mode of origin of the loess. *Geological Magazine* **9**: 293–305

Waage J K, Greathead D J (1988) Biological control: challenges and opportunities. *Philosophical Transactions of the Royal Society of London* **B318**: 111–28

Wace N (1988) Naturalised plants in the Australian landscape. In Heathcote R L (ed) *The Australian experience*. Longman Cheshire, Melbourne, pp 139–50

Wacher J (1987) *The Roman empire*. Dent, London

Wagstaff J M (1985) *The evolution of Middle Eastern landscapes: an outline to AD 1840*. Croom Helm, London

Waldbaum J C (1978) From bronze to iron: the transition from the Bronze Age to the Iron Age in the eastern Mediterranean. *Studies in Mediterranean Archaeology* No 54 (Monograph Series). Paul Aastroems, Göteborg

Walker D (1986) Tropical rainforests. *Science Progress, Oxford* **70**: 461–72

Walker D, Chen Y (1987) Palynological light on tropical rainforest dynamics. *Quaternary Science Reviews* **6**: 77–92

Wallach B (1988) Irrigation in Sudan since independence. *Geographical Review* **78**: 417–34

Walsh J J, Conrad E T, Stubing H D, Vogt W G (1988) Control of volatile organic compound emissions at a landfill site in New York: a community perspective. *Waste Management and Research* **6**: 23–34

Ward D (1987) Population growth, migration and urbanization, 1860–1920. In Mitchell R D, Groves P A (eds) *North America: the historical geography of a changing continent*. Hutchinson; London, pp 299–320

Warrick R A, Gifford R M, Parry M L (1986) CO$_2$, climatic change and agriculture. In Bolin B, Döös B R, Jäger J, Warrick R A (eds) *The greenhouse effect, climatic change and ecosystems*. John Wiley, Chichester, pp 393–473

Wathern P, Young S N, Brown I W, Roberts D A (1988) Recent upland land use change and agricultural policy in Clwyd, North Wales. *Applied Geography* **8**: 147–63

Watts M J (1984) The demise of the moral economy: food and famine in a Sudano–Sahelian region in historical perspective. In Scott E P (ed) *Life before the drought*. George Allen and Unwin, Boston, pp 124–48

Watts W A (1967) Interglacial deposits in Kildromin Townland, near Herbertstown, Co. Limerick. *Proceedings of the Royal Irish Academy* **65B**: 339–48

Watts W A (1971) Postglacial and interglacial vegetation history of southern Georgia and central Florida. *Ecology* **52**: 676–90

Watts W A (1977) The Late Devensian vegetation of Ireland. *Philosophical Transactions of the Royal Society of London* **B280**: 273–93

Watts W A (1980a) The Late Quaternary vegetation history of the southeastern United States. *Annual Review of Ecology and Systematics* **11**: 387–409

Watts W A (1980b) Regional variation in the response of vegetation to Lateglacial climatic events in Europe. In Lowe J J, Gray J M, Robinson J E (eds) *Studies in the Lateglacial of North-west Europe*. Pergamon Press, Oxford, pp 1–21

Way J M, Greig-Smith P W (eds) (1987) *Field margins*. British Crop Protection Council, Thornton Heath

Weaver J E, Clements F E (1929) *Plant ecology*. McGraw-Hill, New York

Weaver P P E, Pujol C (1988) History of the last deglaciation in the Alboran Sea (western Mediterranean) and adjacent North Atlantic as revealed by coccolith floras. *Palaeogeography Palaeoclimatology Palaeoecology* **64**: 35–42

Webb N (1986) *Heathlands*. Collins New Naturalist Series, London

Webb R H (1982) Off-road motorcycle effects on a desert soil. *Environmental Conservation* **9**: 197–208

Webb III T (1985) Holocene palynology and climate. In Hecht A D (ed) *Paleoclimate analysis and modeling*. John Wiley, New York, pp 163–95

Wellburn A (1988) *Air pollution and acid rain: the biological impact*. Longman, London

Wendorf F, Schild R, El Hadidi N, Close A E, Kobusiewicz M, Wieckowska H, Issawi B, Hass H (1979) Use of barley in the Egyptian late palaeolithic. *Science* **205**: 1341–7

Wertime T A (1973) The beginnings of metallurgy: a new look. *Science* **182**: 875–87

West B, Zhou B–X (1988) Did chickens go north? New evidence for domestication. *Journal of Archaeological Science* **15**: 515–33

West R G (1956) The Quaternary deposits at Hoxne, Suffolk. *Philosophical Transactions of the Royal Society of London* **B239**: 265–356

Wheeler J C (1984) On the origin and early development of camelid pastoralism in the Andes. In Clutton-Brock J, Grigson C (eds) Animals and archaeology. British Archaeological Research Reports (International series); Oxford, No 202 vol 3 *Early herders and their flocks* pp 395–410

Whitlow R (1988) Potential versus actual erosion in Zimbabwe. *Applied Geography* **8**: 87–100

Whitney G G (1987) An ecological history of the Great Lakes forest of Michigan. *Journal of Ecology* **75**: 667–84

Wigley T M L (1988) Future CFC concentrations under the Montreal Protocol and their greenhouse–effect implications. *Nature* **335**: 333–5

Wigley T M L (1989) Possible climate change due to SO_2-derived cloud condensation nuclei. *Nature* **339**: 365–7

Wigley T M L, Ingram M J, Farmer G (eds) (1981) *Climate and history: studies in past climates and their impact on man.* Cambridge University Press, Cambridge

de Wilde J C (1967) *Experiences with agricultural development in tropical Africa* (2 vols). Johns Hopkins University Press, Baltimore

Wilkins D A (1984) The Flandrian woods of Lewis (Scotland). *Journal of Ecology* **72**: 251–8

Williams G D V, Fautley R A, Jones K H, Stewart R B, Wheaton E E (1988) Estimating the effects of climatic change on agriculture in Saskatchewan, Canada. In Parry M L, Carter T R, Konijn N J (eds) *The impact of climatic variations on agriculture.* Kluwer Academic Publishers, Dordrecht, vol 1 *Assessment in cool temperate and cold regions* pp 219–379

Williams L D, Wigley T M L (1983) A comparison of evidence for Late Holocene summer temperature variations in the northern hemisphere. *Quaternary Research* **20**: 286–307

Williams M (1982) Marshland and waste. In Cantor L (ed) *The English medieval landscape.* Croom Helm, London, pp 86–125

Williams M (1988) The clearing of the woods. In Heathcote R L (ed) *The Australian experience.* Longman Cheshire, Melbourne, pp 115–26

Williams M A J (1985) Pleistocene aridity in tropical Africa, Australia and Asia. In Douglas I, Spencer T (eds) *Environmental change and tropical geomorphology.* George Allen and Unwin, London, pp 219–33

Williamson T, Bellamy L (1987) *Property and landscape.* George Philip, London

Wilson J P, Ryan C M (1988) Landscape change in the Lake Simcoe–Couchiching Basin, 1800–1983. *The Canadian Geographer* **32**: 206–22

Wilson S J, Cook R U (1980) Wind erosion. In Kirkby M, Morgan R (eds) *Soil erosion*. John Wiley, Chichester, pp 217–51

Wing E (1978) Animal domestication in the Andes. In Browman D L (ed) *Advances in Andean archaeology*. Moulton, The Hague, pp 167–88

Winneke G (1983) Neurobehavioural and neuropsychological effects of lead. In Rutter M, Russell–Jones R (eds) *Lead versus health: sources and effects of low level lead exposure*. John Wiley, Chichester, pp 219–66

Winograd I J, Szabo B J, Coplen T B, Riggs A C, Holesar P T (1985) Two–million year record of deuterium depletion in Great Basin ground waters. *Science* **227**: 519–21

Winteringham F P W (1988) Nuclear power and environment. *Endeavour* **12**: 163–70

Wong M H (1987) A review on lead contamination of Hong Kong's environment. In Hutchinson T C, Meema K M (eds) *Lead, mercury, cadmium and arsenic in the environment*. John Wiley, Chichester, pp 217–33

Woodell G M, Wurster C F, Isaacson P A (1967) DDT residues in an East Coast estuary: a case of biological concentration of a persistent pesticide. *Science* **156**: 821–4

Woods C (1988) Life without a sunscreen. *New Scientist* **120** (1642): 46–9

Woods D, Rawlings D E (1989) Bacterial leaching and biomining. In Marx J L (ed) *A revolution in biotechnology*. Cambridge University Press, Cambridge, pp 82–93

Woods L E (1984) *Land degradation in Australia*. Australian Government Printing Service, Canberra

Woodward F I (1987) Stomatal numbers are sensitive to increases in CO_2 from pre–industrial levels. *Nature* **327**: 617–18

Woodward I (1989) Plants in the greenhouse world. *New Scientist* **122** (1663), Inside Science No 21 pp 1–4

World Health Organisation (1985) *Health hazards from nitrate in drinking water. Environmental Health 1*. WHO, Copenhagen

World Resources Institute (1989) *World resources 1988–1989*. World resources Institute, International Institute for Environment and Development, in collaboration with United Nations Environment Programme

Worthing C R, Walker S B (1987) *The pesticide manual: a world compendium* (8th edn). British Crop Protection Council, Thornton Heath

Wright R F, Lotse E, Semb A (1988) Reversibility of acidification shown by whole–catchment experiments. *Nature* **334**: 670–5

Wyatt-Smith J (1987) Problems and prospects for natural management of tropical moist forests. In Mergen F, Vincent J R (eds) *Natural management of tropical moist forests*. Yale University School of Forestry and Environmental Studies, New Haven, Connecticut, pp 5-22

Wymer J J (1982) *The palaeolithic Age*. Croom Helm, London

Wymer J J (1983) The lower palaeolithic site at Hoxne. *Proceedings of the Suffolk Institute of Archaeology* **35**: 169–89

Wymer J J (1988) Palaeolithic archaeology and the British Quaternary sequence. *Quaternary Science Reviews* **7**: 79–98

Wynn G (1987) Forging a Canadian nation. In Mitchell R D, Groves P A (eds) *North America: the historical geography of a changing continent*. Hutchinson, London, pp 373–409

Xinzhi W, Linghong J W (1985) Chronology in Chinese palaeoanthropology. In Rukang W, Olsen J W (eds) *Palaeoanthropology and palaeolithic archaeology in the People's Republic of China*. Academic Press, London, pp 29–51

Yassoglou N J (1987) The production potential of soils: Part II – Sensitivity of the soil systems in southern Europe to degrading influences. In Barth H, L'Hermite P (eds) *Scientific basis for soil protection in the European Community*. Elsevier, London, pp 87–122

Yule W, Landsdown R (1983) Lead and children's development: recent findings. In *Heavy metals in the environment*. CEP Consultants, Edinburgh, pp 912–16

Zachar D (1982) *Soil erosion*. Elsevier, Amsterdam

Zagwijn W H (1975) Variations in climate as shown by pollen–analysis especially in the Lower Pleistocene of Europe. In Wright A F, Moseley F (eds) *Ice Ages ancient and modern*. Seel House, Liverpool, pp 137–52

Zagwijn W H (1985) An outline of the Quaternary stratigraphy of the Netherlands. *Geologie en Mijnbouw* **64**: 17–24

Zhao D, Sun B (1986) Air pollution and acid rain in China. *Ambio* **15**: 2–5

Zhao D, Xiong J (1988) Acidification in southwestern China. In Rodhe H, Herrera R (eds) *Acidification in tropical countries*. John Wiley, Chichester, pp 317–46

Zhao D, Xiong J, Xu Y, Chan W H (1988) Acid rain in southwestern China. *Atmospheric environment* **22**: 349–58

Zinyama L, Whitlow R (1986) Changing patterns of population distribution in Zimbabwe. *Geojournal* **13**: 365–84

Zohary D (1986) The origin and early spread of agriculture in the Old World. In Barigozzi C (ed) *The origin and domestication of cultivated plants*. Elsevier, Amsterdam, pp 3–20

Zohary D, Hopf M (1988) *Domestication of plants in the Old World*. Oxford University Press, Oxford

Zubakov V A (1988) Climatostratigraphic scheme of the Black Sea Pleistocene and its correlation with the oxygen–isotope scale and glacial events. *Quaternary Research* **29**: 1–24

Zvelbil M (1986) Mesolithic prelude and neolithic revolution. In Zvelbil M (ed) *Hunters in transition*. Cambridge University Press, Cambridge, pp 5–15

INDEX